PERGAMON INTERNATIONAL LIBRARY
of Science, Technology, Engineering and Social Studies

*The 1000-volume original paperback library in aid of education,
industrial training and the enjoyment of leisure*

Publisher: Robert Maxwell, M.C.

IN RESPONSE TO AGGRESSION
(PGPS - 98)

THE PERGAMON TEXTBOOK
INSPECTION COPY SERVICE

An inspection copy of any book published in the Pergamon International Library
will gladly be sent to academic staff without obligation for their consideration for
course adoption or recommendation. Copies may be retained for a period of 60 days
from receipt and returned if not suitable. When a particular title is adopted or
recommended for adoption for class use and the recommendation results in a sale
of 12 or more copies the inspection copy may be retained with our compliments.
The Publishers will be pleased to receive suggestions for revised editions and new
titles to be published in this important international Library.

Pergamon Titles of Related Interest

Alexander/Gleason BEHAVIORAL AND QUANTITATIVE PERSPECTIVES ON
TERRORISM
Cartledge/Milburn TEACHING SOCIAL SKILLS TO CHILDREN:
Innovative Approaches
Goldstein/Segall AGGRESSION AND GLOBAL PERSPECTIVES
Kanfer/Goldstein HELPING PEOPLE CHANGE: A Textbook of Methods,
Second edition
Miron/Goldstein HOSTAGE
Morell PROGRAM EVALUATION IN SOCIAL RESEARCH
Nietzel CRIME AND ITS MODIFICATION: A Social Learning Perspective
Rathjen/Foreyt SOCIAL COMPETENCE: Interventions for Children and Adults

Related Journals*

Addictive Behaviors
Child Abuse and Neglect
International Journal of Law & Psychiatry
Journal of Criminal Justice
Personality and Individual Differences

*Free specimen copies available upon request.

IN RESPONSE TO

Aggression

Methods of Control and Prosocial Alternatives

Arnold P. Goldstein
Syracuse University

Edward G. Carr
State University of New York at Stony Brook

William S. Davidson, II
Michigan State University

Paul Wehr
University of Colorado at Boulder

and their collaborators

Pergamon Press

New York   Oxford   Toronto   Sydney   Paris   Frankfurt

Pergamon Press Offices:

U.S.A.	Pergamon Press Inc., Maxwell House, Fairview Park, Elmsford, New York 10523, U.S.A.
U.K.	Pergamon Press Ltd., Headington Hill Hall, Oxford OX3 0BW, England
CANADA	Pergamon Press Canada Ltd., Suite 104, 150 Consumers Road, Willowdale, Ontario M2J 1P9, Canada
AUSTRALIA	Pergamon Press (Aust.) Pty. Ltd., P.O. Box 544, Potts Point, NSW 2011, Australia
FRANCE	Pergamon Press SARL, 24 rue des Ecoles, 75240 Paris, Cedex 05, France
FEDERAL REPUBLIC OF GERMANY	Pergamon Press GmbH, Hammerweg 6, Postfach 1305, 6242 Kronberg/Taunus, Federal Republic of Germany

Copyright © 1981 Pergamon Press Inc.

Library of Congress Cataloging in Publication Data
Main entry under title:

In response to aggression.

    (Pergamon general psychology series ; v. 98)
      1. Aggressiveness (Psychology) 2. Violence.
3. Control (Psychology) 4. Social control.
I. Goldstein, Arnold P. II. Series. [DNLM: 1. Ag-
gression. 2. Behavior therapy--Methods. BF 575.A3 I35]
RC569.5.V55I5 1981   303.6   81-2385
ISBN 0-08-025580-9   AACR2
ISBN 0-08-025579-5 (pbk.)

Printed in the United States of America

*To those who work to eliminate
violence in all its forms*

Contents

Preface

Aggression and America have long been intimate companions. Born in revolutionary conflict, America has seen 200 years of high levels of collective violence in its Indian, Civil, and international wars, its urban and agricultural riots, its vigilante movements, its racial lynchings, its industrial strikes, its antiwar movement and the reaction thereto, and its long and unremitting insistence on the widespread and generally unregulated private ownership of what now amounts to over 100 million guns. Since 1933, the year in which systematic collection of individual crime statistics began, the resultant FBI Uniform Crime Report has revealed a substantial, if irregular, increase in both crimes against persons and crimes against property. And, even in most recent times (1975–1980) in which there seems to be something of a stabilization in overall crime rates, two of the most violent types of crime—rape and aggravated assault—have still continued to increase rapidly. It is now recognized that domestic violence—both child and spouse abuse—occurs with dismaying frequency in the American home. Thus, both collective and individual aggression in the United States has long been and continues to be high.

This book seeks to describe and evaluate comprehensively what has been done in response to aggression. Its dual focus is aggression controls and aggression alternatives. Controls concern the reduction of aggression, events and techniques that reduce its intensity or frequency, decrease its probability of occurrence, manage or regulate its level, or inhibit its appearance altogether. Alternatives are what to do instead, the substituting of the prosocial for the antisocial, the constructive for the destructive, the progressive for the aggressive.

Our examination of aggression controls and alternatives fully reflects the panorama of psychological and sociological theory and research which has emerged in recent decades bearing on these domains. As will be obvious, the management of and alternatives to aggression, as well as aggression itself, have been the target of particularly widespread and diverse theoretical and investigative attention.

An especially noteworthy feature of this book, central to its purpose, is the multilevel, multidisciplinary nature of its authorship. We are four behavioral scientists, each vitally interested in aggression, yet each with a markedly different perspective on human behavior and its alteration.

Our collaboration in seeking to identify, describe, and elaborate optimally constructive responses to aggression grows directly from our shared belief that the causes of aggression, its acquisition, its instigation, its maintenance are each multiply determined events—events often optimally responded to in a similarly multilevel manner. Concretely, our respective interests and expertise lie in the realms of individual behavior (Edward G. Carr), the small group (Arnold P. Goldstein), at the community level (William S. Davidson), and at the level of the larger society or nation (Paul Wehr). It is our strong conviction that, typically, aggression may be best understood, its control best facilitated, and its alternatives best promoted if approached simultaneously from the individual, small group, community, and societal perspectives. Let us illustrate this viewpoint. An adolescent in an urban secondary school repeatedly behaves in aggressive and disruptive ways; he physically fights with peers, threatens teachers, vandalizes school property. An optimal response to such behaviors might well focus on the youngster himself at first, and consist of efforts at the individual level to extinguish his belligerence and assaultiveness by use of withdrawal of attention, time out, increased response cost, and related contingency management techniques (see Chapter 1) combined with explicit efforts, still at the individual level, to develop his capacity for self-control (see Chapter 3). But if we move beyond this level of intervention to efforts at the small group level, the youngster's aggression may also diminish and suitable alternative behaviors may also emerge to the degree that his peer models can be induced to behave less aggressively (see Chapter 4), if he and his peers are collectively taught and subsequently rewarded for performing an array of prosocial skill behaviors (see Chapter 4), and if moral education, values clarification, or other instruction in ethics and morality are systematically introduced into classroom activities (see Chapter 6). This combination of individually oriented and small group interventions, at times sufficient themselves, are more likely to succeed in both a remedial and a preventive sense if we go further, to the macroorganizational levels of community and societal intervention. Is the youngster's school organized and run in ways that enhance the prosocial and diminish the antisocial (see Chapter 8)? Do his immediate neighborhood and his community at large provide a social support network that facilitates cooperation, caring, and other prosocial behaviors, or is the environment oriented toward enhanced aggression, destructiveness, and fragmentation (see Chapter 9)? Can the youngster's aggressiveness be traced at all to what certain sociological and sociopolitical perspectives hold often lies at the roots of such behavior, namely inadequate housing, high unemployment, insufficient social services, ineffective general economic policy, and other social ills originated at state and federal levels of intervention (see Chapters 10 and 12)? We are, in short, proposing that Johnny vandalized his school last week for individual, small group, community, and societal reasons. If we wish to deter him from further such behavior, and to evoke instead prosocial alternative behaviors, it is crucial that our interventions be similarly multilevel.

Our stance is the same for other forms of individual or collective aggression. The adult criminal may be less likely to engage in recidivistic aggressive behavior if we apply certain aversive techniques (individual level), teach him an array of interpersonal problem-solving skills (small group level), minimize social labeling effects by decisions made in his jurisdiction's criminal justice system (community level), and if the prevailing penological philosophy of his state or country is reintegrative, rather than singularly punitive or retributional (societal level). The gang, the mob, the organized group, the collective engaged in an urban riot are similarly optimally viewed in multilevel interventionist perspective. Can the leader, or individual members construe nonviolent alternatives; can they control their own overt aggression (individual level)? As a group, what is the consensus level of moral development, the group's cohesiveness, its collective capacity for constructive problem solving (small group level)? What neighborhood or local organizations are in place to facilitate nonaggressive solutions to emerging problems, what is their power, their effectiveness, their availability (community level)? What are the traditions and mechanisms available at the larger societal level for the understanding, management, and resolution of collective conflict?

To reflect fully this guiding, multilevel philosophy, we have organized this book into four major parts. Part I is concerned with the individual level of intervention. Its chapters deal with the behavior modification techniques that constitute contingency management, especially in the context of parent-child interactions (Chapter 1); effective use of negotiation and contracting methods, as these might be used in particular to resolve marital conflict (Chapter 2); and an array of procedures, of use in many contexts, for improving one's level of self-control (Chapter 3). Aggression-relevant interventions at the level of the small group are the focus of Part II, particularly a broad array of methods and materials for teaching children and adults interpersonal conflict management and conflict alternative skills (Chapter 4); problem-solving skills (Chapter 5); and enhanced moral and ethical beliefs and behaviors (Chapter 6). Part III turns to the community level of intervention. What can occur at this level to prevent the occurrence of criminal or other aggression (Chapter 7)? How may a community's criminal justice system be structured and operated to facilitate prosocial outcomes (Chapter 8), and what contribution to such outcomes follows from the efforts of a variety of community social support systems (Chapter 9)? Part IV, turning to yet a broader societal level, describes in detail a number of conflict intervention and conflict resolution strategies and operations (Chapter 10); techniques of what has been termed "aggressive nonviolence" (Chapter 11); and the current status in the United States of peace and conflict resolution education and research (Chapter 12).

It is our earnest wish that our multilevel, comprehensive presentation and evaluation of the state of the art and the state of research on aggression controls and alternatives will, in practice, lead to enhanced utilization of what we have described, and thus to more widespread prosocial and constructive behaviors in response to aggression.

I

Individual Controls and Alternatives

Chapter 1
Contingency Management
Edward G. Carr

He that spareth the rod, hateth his son; but he that loveth him, chasteneth him
betimes.
—*Proverbs*, 13:24

I grant that good and evil, reward and punishment, are the only motives to a rational
creature; these are the spur and reins whereby all mankind are set on work and
guided, and therefore they are to be made use of to children too. For I advise their
parents and governors always to carry this in their minds, that children are to be
treated as rational creatures.
—John Locke, *Some Thoughts Concerning Education*.

Throughout history, adults have had strong opinions on how best to
raise happy, productive children and how to discipline children on those
occasions when they have misbehaved. From the *Old Testament* to Dr.
Spock, from Freud to Skinner, sages and experts have put forth their
opinions on this important topic. Why has so much concern been
expressed over this issue? The answer is clear. No society could survive
very long if its younger members were given free rein to take what they
would, to comply only when it was convenient for them, to aggress
whenever there was benefit in doing so, and, in short, to avoid learning
those rules of behavior which produce a balance between the rights of
the individual and the rights of others. In what follows, we shall first
attempt to outline briefly some of the philosophical, religious, psychological, and popular antecedents to current empirical approaches to
child discipline.

PHILOSOPHICAL AND RELIGIOUS ANTECEDENTS

The Bible prescribed harsh measures for bringing the misbehavior of
children under control. This is apparent in the quotation at the beginning
of this chapter and in passages such as these:

Foolishness is bound in the heart of a child; but the rod of correction shall drive it
far from him. *Proverbs*, 22:15.

1

Thou shalt beat him with the rod, and shalt deliver his soul from hell. *Proverbs*, 23:14.

To the extent that a child's misbehavior is seen as the path to eternal damnation, it is perhaps easier for the modern mind to grasp why such severe discipline was condoned and why children's noncompliance was viewed in such an extreme manner:

The eye that mocketh his father, and despiseth the instruction of his mother, let the ravens of the valley pluck it out, and the young eagles eat it. *Luke*, 15:10.

The ancient Greeks, with the exception of the Spartans, tended to deemphasize the role of harsh punishment in bringing children under control. Instead, more emphasis was given to those forms of discipline and restraint that would ensure healthy social development and the production of good citizens who were governed by high moral values. The emphasis was much more on the prevention of undesirable behavior than on its remediation. Thus, in *The Republic*, Plato outlined in considerable detail the curriculum to be used for educating the future rulers of his ideal state. By training both the mind and the body, by exposing the individual to exemplary models, and by preventing intemperance, Plato sought to produce a person who was free of selfish motivation and the lust for destruction. Indeed, Plato argued that without such a well-rounded upbringing, the individual might easily become "like a wild beast, all violence and fierceness" (*The Republic*, p. 120). On the other hand, in a particularly eloquent passage, Plato pointed out the value of exposing youth to moderation and virtue:

then will our youth dwell in a land of health ... and beauty, the effluence of fair works, shall flow into the eye and ear, like a health-giving breeze ... and insensibly draw the soul from earliest years into likeness and sympathy with the beauty of reason. Plato, *The Republic*, p. 105.

Likewise, in *Politics*, Aristotle echoed Plato's sentiments with regard to shielding children from exposure to bad examples in order to prevent later misbehavior.

During the Middle Ages, as the doctrine of original sin gained ascendancy, theologians came to regard the child as inherently evil and depraved. This evil—which could be manifested in many ways including disobedience and aggression—was the target of harsh disciplinary practices that were justified as necessary to save the child's soul.

By the 18th century, philosophers had begun to reject the notion of the "inherently depraved child." Locke, in particular, argued for the view that the infant was a *tabula rasa*, born neither innately good nor innately evil. The child's social development was seen as the result of particular life experiences. In fact, Locke's approach to discipline (the essence of which is summarized in the quotation at the beginning of this chapter) bears a remarkable similarity to modern social learning theory, a theory which will be elaborated upon in considerable detail later in this chapter. Except under unusual circumstances, the child's behavior was to be managed not by harsh punishments or tangible rewards but rather "rationally," through verbal means such as praise and blame:

> If by these means you can come once to shame them out of their faults ... and make them in love with the pleasure of being well thought on, you may turn them as you please and they will be in love with all the ways of virtue. Locke, *Some Thoughts Concerning Education*, p. 85.

Finally, also in the 18th century, Rousseau proposed a theory which was diametrically opposite to that of traditional theological thought, namely that children were born good and if allowed to follow their own instincts would naturally come to do the right thing. Rousseau argued that children developed serious behavior problems as a consequence of being misguided by a corrupt society: "God makes all things good; man meddles with them and they become evil" (*Émile*, p. 5.) Based on this assumption, he proposed an essentially preventive approach to raising children. That is, like Plato and Aristotle before him, he attempted to block the development of misbehavior by removing the child from the influence of bad models and bad institutions:

> This is one reason why I want to bring up Émile in the country, far from those miserable lacqueys, the most degraded of men ... far from the vile morals of the town. *Émile*, p. 59.

The above traditions bear most strongly on broad questions pertaining to salvation, the construction of the ideal state, and the more global aspects of education. As such they have implications for the control of aggressive behavior. But the detailed empirical analysis of this problem had to await the development of psychological science in the late 19th and early 20th centuries. It is to this body of knowledge that we next turn our attention.

PSYCHOLOGICAL ANTECEDENTS

The particular theory that one has about the factors that control aggression in the individual determines, to a great extent, the kinds of management procedures that one employs in order to reduce aggressive behavior. Three such theories have been especially influential within psychology: instinct, drive, and social learning theory. We will outline the instinct and drive theories next while reserving the bulk of this chapter for an exposition of the social learning approach since it is this approach which has had the greatest impact on the direct management of aggressive behavior.

Instinct Theory

The instinct theory of aggression derives mainly from two sources: psychoanalysis and ethology. According to psychoanalytic theory, human behavior is motivated by two sets of opposing instincts: Eros, consisting of all those forces aimed at furthering life, and Thanatos, consisting of all those forces striving for the destruction of life (Freud, 1933). When Thanatos, the death instinct, is discharged outward, the result is aggressive behavior. If this instinctual drive is not expressed, it continues to build up within the individual until it is relieved either by an explosive act of violence or until it is turned inward as self-destructive behavior. Since the aggressive drive is constantly seeking an outlet, the theory is basically a pessimistic one in that aggression is seen as an unavoidable part of human behavior. Indeed, Montague (1968) has argued that instinct theory, in its emphasis on the hostile and destructive nature of humans, relates quite closely to the doctrine of the "innate depravity" of man, a doctrine which we have seen first gained ascendancy in medieval theological thought.

The ethological theory of aggression is based on studies of the behavior of animals in their natural habitat. The results of such studies have been extrapolated to human behavior to produce a theory which is, in many ways, similar to the psychoanalytic account. Again, it is postulated that man has an aggressive or "killer" instinct (Lorenz, 1966). Lorenz, like Freud, suggested that the instinctual system produces an aggressive drive which gradually builds up within the individual. Humans are literally driven from within to commit acts of aggression.

Can anything be done to limit these acts of destruction? The instinct theories generally assume that blocking the expression of aggressive behavior is a very dangerous procedure since the aggressive drive will continue to build up to the point at which explosive acts of violence might occur. Therefore, the treatment should involve a search for safe outlets for aggression; that is, by encouraging individuals to express their aggression in relatively harmless circumstances, the aggressive drive will be drained off and the individual will return to a state of relative calm. This ventilative process is referred to as catharsis and it has had great appeal in both professional and lay circles. But is the approach an effective one? The data suggest it is not. In an early study (Lovaas, 1961), one group of children was encouraged to make abusive remarks to a toy doll; another group was encouraged to make nonabusive remarks. According to the principle of cathartic drainage, the first group would be expected to have become subsequently less aggressive. Instead, this group showed a marked increase in aggressive activity as demonstrated by their greater willingness (compared with the other group) to seek out toys which stressed aggressive modes of play. Apparently, when adults reinforce or encourage aggressive activities in children, the effect is not to produce a catharsis but rather to "whet the child's appetite" for an even greater escalation of aggressive activity.

Other proponents of the catharsis hypothesis have suggested that by "savoring" the aggressive behavior of others, an individual may be able to reduce the level of his aggressive drive. Is this method of vicarious catharsis a viable option for reducing aggression in children? Again, the data are negative. In one study, children who were permitted to watch a series of violent television programs subsequently displayed much more aggressive behavior toward their peers than children who watched nonviolent programs (Steuer, Applefield, and Smith, 1971). A number of studies have shown that children who participate in aggressive activities, either directly or vicariously, do not show a subsequent decrement in their level of aggression (Bandura, Ross & Ross, 1963; Eron, Huesmann, Lefkowitz, & Walder, 1972; Hartmann, 1969; Mallick & McCandless, 1966; Nelsen, 1969). In fact, the level of aggression either remains the same or quite frequently increases. As an approach to treating aggression, then, the instinct theory and its associated catharsis hypothesis have little to recommend them and in fact may be pernicious.

Drive Theory

American psychologists, unlike their European counterparts, have, particularly in this century, rejected the notion that instinct is an important variable in the control of human behavior. In this vein, one important group of psychologists at Yale (Dollard, Doob, Miller, Mowrer, & Sears, 1939) proposed that aggression was best conceptualized not as an *instinct* but rather as a *drive*. Their basic hypothesis was that frustration, conceived of as those stimuli that resulted from the blocking of a goal-directed activity, provided the motivation or drive for aggressive behavior. For example, if a child wanted to play with a toy with which a second child was playing and the latter refused to share the toy, this refusal would constitute a frustrating stimulus for the first child and that child would aggress against the second child.

One important feature of the frustration-aggression hypothesis was that, in contrast to instinct theory, the motivation to aggress was said to be aroused by an external frustration stimulus rather than by an innate force. Thus, aggression was at least tied in some measure to the individual's external environment. The hypothesis had two important effects on people's thinking. First, many people interpreted the hypothesis to mean that frustration *always* produced aggression. Second, each occurrence of aggressive behavior prompted a search for the frustrating stimulus situation which had set off the aggression. A close empirical examination of the above two points reveals some serious flaws. For example, in an early study (Davitz, 1952), one group of children was taught to play in a competitive, aggressive manner while a second group was taught to play constructively. Both groups were then exposed to a frustrating situation. Following this frustration, the group who had been taught to play aggressively showed an increase in aggression in a separate free play situation, whereas the group who had been taught to play constructively showed an increase in constructive play together with a continued low level of aggression. This study demonstrates that the effects of frustration depend on the child's past learning history and, more importantly, that frustration does not always produce aggression. Other studies have shown that when young children are frustrated, a typical response is regression (i.e., displaying immature behaviors) rather than aggression (Barker, Dembo, & Lewin, 1941). Finally, it has also been pointed out that, depending on the individual's learning history, frustration may also produce help-seeking behavior, withdrawal from the frustrating situation, constructive problem-solving efforts, or a number of other nonaggressive behaviors (Bandura, 1973). In short, the notion that frustration always produces aggression is not borne out by the data.

There are some instances, however, when frustration does indeed produce aggression and then the question becomes how to treat the problem. The assumption is made that the build-up of the aggressive drive can be alleviated only through the expression of aggression, that is, by a process of catharsis. But as we saw above, the catharsis hypothesis is refuted by a large body of research and therefore this aspect of the frustration-aggression hypothesis is not helpful in formulating a treatment intervention. A second treatment implication of the hypothesis is that by shielding the individual from all frustrating situations, aggression could be prevented. We do not think that this is a practical treatment goal. Everyday living is simply too full of unpredictability to be able to anticipate and avoid frustrating situations successfully. Further, and perhaps more importantly, we now know that aggression is produced and maintained by many other factors besides frustration. In fact, frustration per se is often one of the less important factors. To sum up, then, neither instinct nor drive theory has led to a conceptualization of aggression that has produced effective treatment interventions. We must therefore look to the third and final approach, social learning theory, for possible answers. Before we do that, however, we will briefly outline what has been referred to as the "popular" approach to child discipline, thereby completing our survey of the historical antecedents to empirically based approaches for dealing with aggression in children.

POPULAR ANTECENDENTS

A common stereotype in our culture is that of the wise grandmother who knows how to control the behavior of her grandchild and who succeeds where the child's mother fails. Grandmother's wisdom derives, in part, from her own longer experience in rearing children and, in part, from the "wisdom of generations," that is, from her having spoken with many people in her lifetime about child-rearing techniques that these people have discovered or that have been taught to them by their mothers and grandmothers. This pool of popular knowledge has, especially in this century, found its way into print. Usually, the disseminators of this knowledge are psychologists and psychiatrists whose frequent contacts with parents have enabled these professionals to understand and describe the most common methods used in child discipline together with some of the principles which, at least in their own opinion, are most important in justifying the use of particular approaches.

In their book, *Better Home Discipline*, Cutts and Moseley (1952), educators by profession, outline a number of ways in which American parents typically attempt to bring the behavior problems of their children under control. Few will be surprised to learn that the most common techniques include scolding, ignoring, explaining why it is bad to behave in a given way, threats, and punishment, usually in the form of depriving the child of privileges, isolating the child in the bedroom, keeping the child in the house with no opportunity to play outside, and, of course, spanking. The large number of techniques discussed in the popular literature are paralleled by the large number of principles and theories advocated in support of particular approaches to child discipline. Ginott (1965), in *Between Parent and Child*, urges parents to adopt the general principle of encouraging their children to express angry feelings but restricting them from performing aggressive acts. Dreikurs (1966), in the *Challenge of Parenthood*, emphasizes the importance of inculcating a mature sense of responsibility in the child so that ultimately the management of behavior problems is based on self-control rather than external control. Finally, Spock (1961), in *Dr. Spock Talks With Mothers*, points to the need for cathartic play activities in order to blow off steam and thus prevent the occurrence of serious destructive acts.

How valuable is this plethora of information and advice? The popular approach does appear to have some merits. Specifically, the techniques and principles offered are apparently effective in controlling behavior problems in some cases. Indeed, if these pragmatic approaches were universally ineffective, society would probably not exist today; it would have been destroyed long ago by the unsocialized aggressive acts of its younger members. Also, as will become apparent later in this chapter, many of the popular approaches have at least a grain of truth in them; they frequently form the basis for approaches that have subsequently been validated within a scientific framework.

Unfortunately, however, the above strengths do not constitute a sufficient basis on which to formulate interventions to deal with serious behavior problems in children. Many weaknesses are apparent. First, the validity of several popular principles has been called into question by recent research. For example, cathartic play is not likely to prevent the development of aggression. In fact, as noted in a previous section, prompting aggressive play may actually cause the child to become more aggressive in a variety of situations. Likewise, encouraging the child to express angry feelings as part of a ventilative process is usually ineffective and sometimes dangerous as a method for reducing aggressive behavior. Secondly, the advice given is often contradictory. On the one hand, parents are told of the need for consistent discipline but, on the other hand, they are warned to ignore minor misbehavior. Part of the problem lies in determining what constitutes "minor" misbehavior. With such abstract advice, it is often difficult to know in a specific case whether to discipline or whether to ignore. The result may be a confused and inconsistent pattern of child rearing. A third point, closely related to the second, is that disciplinary techniques are rarely spelled out in specific enough detail to enable a parent to know what to do in particular instances. When a parent is told to "set limits" or to teach the child "inner rules" for controlling misbehavior, the advice is simply too vague to be useful. The exact methods for achieving such goals are left up to the imagination of each parent. This situation, to be sure, results in different people making different interpretations of a given technique with a corresponding heterogeneity of treatment outcomes. Fourth, and perhaps most important, popular techniques do not rest upon a firm data base. They have not been tested in a systematic fashion in order to evaluate how effective they really are. Instead, most techniques are said to be effective on the basis of testimonials from parents and teachers or expert opinions from a handful of professionals. There are, however, sufficient numbers of failures from such "proven" techniques to suggest that testimonials and expert opinions are no basis on which to advise people on such important matters as how to raise their children. In sum, then, although popular techniques are frequently of use in controlling misbehavior, such techniques are just as often ineffective in individual cases. What is needed are interventions whose efficacy has been demonstrated through systematic evaluation. The detailed discussion of such interventions is the main topic in what follows.

CONTINGENCY MANAGEMENT—SOME DEFINING CHARACTERISTICS

To a large extent, the contingency management approach may be seen as both an outgrowth of and a reaction to the many historical antecedents discussed in previous sections of this chapter. Thus, Locke's emphasis on the role of reward and punishment in child rearing together with the notions held by the ancient Greeks and later by Rousseau concerning the prevention of misbehavior through training socially appropriate behaviors represent strategies which have been incorporated into the contingency management approach. From an historical viewpoint, it is also interesting to note that this approach attributes considerable importance to the influence of the external environment in the maintenance and control of behavior problems. Such a stance is in sharp contrast to that taken by older psychological theories in which the role of inner forces is emphasized. Finally, a key characteristic of the contingency management strategy consists of the detailed specification and empirical validation of treatment procedures. This last feature is a clear reaction to the vague, nonempirical nature of most popular approaches.

In order to understand the rationale of contingency management more fully, it is necessary to view it in perspective, namely as part of a larger *social learning* approach to human behavior. Recall that traditional psychodynamic theories conceptualize human behavior as resulting from the complex interplay of intrapsychic forces. Social learning theory, in contrast, sees human behavior as the result of external environmental influences. Two factors have influenced the shift, still taking place today, from a psychodynamic view of human behavior to a social learning view. The first factor involves the repeated failures of psychodynamically oriented treatment strategies discussed above. The second factor concerns the large number of experimental studies which have demonstrated that many significant human behaviors can be strengthened or eliminated through the manipulation of specific social influences. These demonstrations led many psychologists to look more closely at the relationship between the *external environment* and various aspects of human behavior. Lest the reader be left with the misleading impression that humans are thus conceived of as puppets at the mercy of the environment, two important features of social learning theory must be highlighted. First, the individual is also seen as influencing his own behavior through a number of important cognitive processes. This aspect of the theory will be dealt with in greater detail in Chapter 3. Secondly, behavior change is seen as part of a *reciprocal influence* process; that is, not only does the external environment affect behavior but behavior, in turn, acts back upon the environment to change it. Thus, the individual helps shape the very environment that subsequently affects his behavior.

In this chapter, we deal with one aspect of the broad field of social learning theory, namely contingency management. This term may be defined as "the contingent presentation and withdrawal of rewards and punishments" (Rimm and Masters, 1974, p. 166). We concentrate on those aspects of contingency management which are most relevant to the understanding and control of aggressive behavior. A detailed overview of the broader applications of this approach can be found elsewhere (Bandura, 1969; Becker, 1971; Patterson, 1971; Patterson & Gullion, 1968; Rimm & Masters, 1974; Sulzer & Mayer, 1972).

To begin with, we will use the terms reward and reinforcement interchangeably even though, strictly speaking, they are not exact synonyms. A *reinforcer* is an event that increases the frequency of any behavior which it follows. For example, if by participating in a school play, a child earns the admiration and applause of his peers and parents, the child will be more apt in the future to volunteer to take part in school plays. Praise is said to have functioned as a reinforcing event in this instance because the behavior of acting became more probable after it had been praised. For purposes of definition, we should also note that a reinforcer which is consistently delivered following a specific behavior is said to have been delivered *contingently*. Thus, in the example cited above praise was contingent upon the behavior of acting. One important part of contingency management, then, consists of systematically managing or structuring a social situation so that reinforcers are delivered following specific, desirable behaviors with the result that such behaviors become more frequent.

When the *presentation* of an event following a behavior increases the frequency of the behavior, the event is referred to as a *positive reinforcer*. In the example given above, praise was a positive reinforcer. In contrast, when the *removal* of an event following a behavior increases the frequency of the behavior, the event is referred to as a *negative reinforcer*. For example, if a boy is crying loudly and his mother shouts at him to stop and he does so, the mother's shouting is said to have been negatively reinforced through the removal of an aversive event, namely the child's crying. Negative reinforcers, like positive reinforcers, increase the probability of the behaviors which they follow. In the case given, the mother has learned a new way of terminating an unpleasant event. In the future, she will be more likely to shout at her son when he cries excessively. One can see, then, that negative reinforcement can play an important role in the development of interpersonal problems.

Contingency management also involves the use of procedures which decrease the frequency of a behavior. Specifically, when the *presentation* of an event following a behavior decreases the frequency of that behavior, the event is referred to as a *punisher* or *aversive stimulus*. For example, if a mother spanks her child for running across a busy street and the child becomes less likely in the future to engage in this behavior, then the event of spanking is referred to as an aversive stimulus or punisher because it decreases the future probability that the child will run across the street. Parenthetically, it might be noted that, to the extent that the child's running across the street is aversive to the mother, spanking behavior on the part of the mother will be increased through the process of negative reinforcement described previously.

A second way of decreasing the probability of a given behavior is by *removing positive reinforcers* each time that the behavior occurs. This method stands in contrast to the procedure just outlined, a procedure which entailed the *presentation of aversive stimuli*. To illustrate this new intervention, consider the case of a child who swears at his father with the result that the father takes away television privileges for that night. The child will usually be less likely in the future to swear at his father. It appears that the removal of television, a positive reinforcer, has acted to reduce the future probability of an undesirable behavior, namely swearing.

The above four procedures, that is, positive reinforcement, negative reinforcement, punishment, and the removal of positive reinforcers constitute the basic core of contingency management. These procedures appear deceptively simple but there are a number of complexities, to be reviewed below, which must be attended to if the procedures are to be effective.

At this point, we must digress for a moment to say something concerning the readily apparent emphasis on children throughout this chapter. The reason for this emphasis is that, although contingency management procedures have been used with adults, the greatest application, by far, has been with children. The procedures characteristic of this approach require that the treatment agent have the opportunity to observe the client for a significant portion of each day, if necessary, and that the agent be in a position to control the reinforcers and punishers dispensed to the client. These two preconditions are seldom met with adult populations. It is clear that the situation in which treatment occurs must be a relatively structured one. Fortunately, the home and school environments in which children typically spend most of their waking hours fit all of the constraints outlined above and thus the behavior problems of childhood are often readily amenable to a treatment approach based on contingency management.

In what follows, we first describe some of the more common contingency management procedures. Then, we give a broad summary of the research studies that have helped validate the efficacy of these procedures. Finally, we describe in considerable detail the practical application of these techniques.

CONTINGENCY MANAGEMENT PROCEDURES— AN OVERVIEW

The purpose of this section is to describe very briefly the major contingency management procedures preparatory to presenting the research evidence supporting the use of these methods. There are four important procedures in common use: positive reinforcement, timeout, extinction, and response cost.

Positive reinforcement is the most widely used contingency management procedure. Clinically, it consists of the presentation of a positive reinforcer contingent on the occurrence of a socially appropriate response. Positive reinforcers include so-called unlearned or primary reinforcers (e.g., food) and learned or conditioned reinforcers (e.g., praise, money, gold stars). As we shall see later, many factors influence the effectiveness of a positive reinforcer including the type of reinforcer given, the amount given, the quality of the reinforcer, whether or not the reinforcer is presented immediately after a response, and whether the reinforcer is presented after each instance of a response or only intermittently.

Extinction is a procedure in which a previously reinforced response is no longer reinforced. For example, many problem behaviors of children are maintained because parents attend to these behaviors (i.e., inadvertently positively reinforce them). When the parents are taught to withdraw their attention (i.e., employ extinction), the behaviors eventually decrease in frequency and may disappear altogether.

Timeout consists of removing all sources of reinforcement for a specified period of time whenever the individual displays a particular behavior problem. Unlike extinction, which typically lasts only a brief period of time usually a matter of seconds, timeout is frequently several minutes or more in duration. Further, unlike extinction, timeout involves removing *all* reinforcers and not just one (e.g., not just attention, but also access to food, toys, etc.). The effect of timeout, when used appropriately, is a reduction in the frequency of the problem behavior.

Finally, *response cost* consists of removing certain amounts of reinforcers when a specific problem behavior occurs. This procedure usually takes the form of a fine in which a certain number of tokens or points are lost for a given infraction.

Up to this point, we have been discussing the treatment of aggressive behavior and other behavior problems by means of the presentation or removal of positive reinforcers. The reason for this lengthy discussion is that such methods are by far the most common procedures used in contingency management programs. To give a complete picture of this approach, however, it is necessary to describe some less common procedures that are based on the presentation or removal of *aversive stimuli*. The procedures described next function, in most respects, in a manner which is the inverse of those procedures described above. Thus, the *presentation* of aversive stimuli contingent upon the performance of a given behavior functions in the same way as the *removal* of positive reinforcers in that both procedures act to decrease the frequency of the behavior. Likewise, the *removal* of aversive stimuli contingent upon the performance of a given behavior functions in the same way as the *presentation* of positive reinforcers in that both procedures act to increase the frequency of the behavior.

Punishment

Punishment involves the presentation of an aversive stimulus contingent upon the performance of a given behavior. The result is a decrease in the frequency of that behavior.

There are two kinds of aversive stimuli, primary and conditioned. A *primary* aversive stimulus is an event that is capable of decreasing the frequency of a behavior from the moment of birth. Spanking is an example of such a stimulus. For example, a child plays with matches near some inflammable fluids. The mother sees this dangerous situation and immediately spanks her child. The child will be disinclined to play with matches in the future. It should be clear that spanking is an effective punisher almost from the moment of birth; the child does not have to learn that spanking is a punisher.

In contrast to the above are the events referred to as *conditioned* aversive stimuli such as verbal reprimands. An infant will probably not understand the meaning of such phrases as "No" or "Stop". The punishing value of such phrases is acquired over a period of time. There are two ways to establish an event as a conditioned aversive stimulus. In the first method, the event is *paired with the presentation of a primary aversive stimulus.* Thus, if a mother shouts "No!" on a number of occasions and then spanks her child on each such occasion, the word "No!" will eventually acquire suppressive properties. At that point, merely shouting "No!" will cause the child to discontinue a given behavior. In short, it was the pairing of "No!" with the primary aversive stimulus (i.e., spanking) that resulted in the word "No!" being transformed from a neutral event to a conditioned aversive stimulus.

A second method for establishing conditioned aversive stimuli is to *pair an event with the removal of positive reinforcers.* Thus, if a mother shouts "No!" on a number of occasions and then puts her child in timeout or takes away points (i.e., uses response cost) on each such occasion, then the word "No!" will acquire suppressive properties. We should note at this point that verbal punishment, in the form of reprimands or threats, is the most commonly used kind of conditioned aversive stimulus.

Several factors determine the effectiveness of punishment. First, like all contingency management procedures, punishment must be consistent if it is to be effective. Consider the case in which a mother shouts "No!" at her small child when she sees him pulling out flowers from her garden. If the mother punishes such behavior on only some occasions, it is unlikely that she will eliminate the behavior. Only by reprimanding her child each time that the behavior occurs will she succeed. Secondly, punishment must be immediate. If the child is reprimanded several hours after he has stopped destroying the flowers, the impact of the punishment will be much diminished compared with what it would have been if delivered at the time of the infraction. Thirdly, if the punishment is used too frequently (i.e., on a very large number of behaviors), the child will adapt to it and the aversive stimulus may lose much of its effect. It is important to note that punishment does not teach the child any new ways of behaving. At best, it temporarily suppresses misbehavior. Therefore, like all procedures whose purpose is to decrease the frequency of misbehavior, punishment must be combined with positive reinforcement for alternative, socially desirable behaviors.

Finally, there is the recently developed technique of *overcorrection.* In this procedure, the individual is required to practice a nonaggressive behavior many times on each occasion that he displays an aggressive act. Thus, if a child were to wreck his bedroom during the course of a tantrum, he might be required to practice, over and over again, cleaning up the bedroom and putting everything in its place. Overcorrection is a somewhat complex procedure in that it has two components. One component involves punishment: it is assumed that having to practice a nonaggressive behavior repeatedly constitutes an aversive event for the individual. The second component is an educative one: the individual practices an appropriate behavior to take the place of continued aggressive behavior. Since this procedure does not rely solely on punishment, it has much to recommend it as a potential method of aggression control (Foxx & Azrin, 1972).

Negative Reinforcement

Negative reinforcement involves the removal of an aversive stimulus contingent upon the performance of a given behavior. The result is an increase in the frequency of that behavior.

Although negative reinforcement is rarely used as a treatment procedure, it does figure prominently as a factor in the maintenance of a variety of behavior problems; that is, it is usually seen as contributing to the problem rather than to the solution. For example, consider a situation in which a mother finds her son's noisy play behavior irritating and shouts at the boy to stop. From the child's perspective, the mother's shouting is an aversive stimulus which has the effect of punishing noisy play. The child therefore becomes quiet. More importantly, for our present purposes, let us also consider the situation from the mother's perspective. Her shouting is a behavior which removes an aversive stimulus, namely her son's noisy play behavior. Thus, the mother's shouting is negatively reinforced with the result that the mother will be much more likely to shout at her son in the future whenever he plays noisily. In short, in this example, the mother's shouting is negatively reinforced at the same time as the child's noisy play is punished. Many serious interpersonal problems have their origins in such aversive interactions.

There is at least one instance in which negative reinforcement can, in contrast to the above, contribute to the solution of a problem. Consider a child who has been put in timeout because of loud, disruptive behavior such as screaming and damaging furniture while running about the house. The barren timeout room represents an aversive stimulus to the child. Therefore, any behavior that allows the child to leave such an environment will be negatively reinforced. Many clinicians capitalize on this situation by allowing the child to leave the timeout area only after the child has been quiet and calm for a while. In this manner, more appropriate home behavior will be strengthened through the process of negative reinforcement; that is, the display of such appropriate behaviors leads directly to being let out of the aversive timeout room. Of course, from a treatment standpoint, a more preferable strategy would be a preventative one in which the child's appropriate behavior is strengthened through positive reinforcement, thereby obviating the need for timeout. Nonetheless, it is occasionally necessary to employ timeout and in this situation, the treatment agent can take advantage of the aversive properties of timeout to negatively reinforce and therefore strengthen a variety of desirable behaviors.

We have now reviewed the general contingency management approach and have described, in broad outline, the more commonly used treatment interventions. Our attention now turns to a facet of contingency management largely ignored in more traditional approaches to child discipline, namely the systematic empirical validation of the procedures themselves. In reviewing the research evidence, we not only describe the results of specific procedures but we also attempt to show how such research helps us to understand the factors responsible for the maintenance of aggressive behavior in children.

RESEARCH RELATED TO CONTINGENCY MANAGEMENT

We have stated a number of times that reinforcement plays an important role in the maintenance of aggressive behavior in children. Is there empirical evidence to support this assertion? The answer is affirmative and comes from a number of studies carried out by social learning theorists beginning in the middle 1960s.

In one study (Patterson, Littman, & Bricker, 1967), the aggressive behavior of normal preschool children was studied over a period of several months in a free play situation. The categories of aggressive behaviors recorded included bodily attack and attack with an object. The question of interest was how often did an aggressive act result in positive reinforcement? In this regard, if a child, for example, struck another child and was thereby able to take a toy away from that child, the aggressive act was recorded as being positively reinforced. The results of this study are instructive. Typically, over 80 percent of the aggressive acts resulted in some form of positive reinforcement. To put it another way, the natural environment is a rich source of reinforcement for aggressive behavior, a fact that might help explain why such behavior is so frequently observed in children, even normal children. Related to these findings is an earlier extensive report by Bandura & Walters (1959) concerning the families of delinquent children. These investigators found that, while parents of aggressive boys did not tolerate aggression directed against them, these parents actively encouraged their sons to aggress against peers and other individuals outside of the family. Again, aggressive behaviors were actively supported through a process of social reinforcement.

Aggression is not, of course, limited to peer relationships. Much aggressive behavior is seen in family situations between parent and child. Consider the situation in which a child and his mother are walking along the street and the child decides that he would like to play on the swings which he sees over by the park. The mother tells her child that he cannot play now because they have to go home so that she can make dinner. The child begins to cry but the mother remains resolute. At this point, the child throws himself to the ground and begins to scream and flail at his mother. The mother, seeking to avoid embarrassment as well as to terminate the unpleasant interaction, relents and tells her child that he can play, but only for a short while. What has happened in this instance? The child's aggressive behavior toward his mother has paid off; he has won the opportunity to play. The mother, for her part, has been able to terminate an "ugly scene." The above example, common in cases of severe childhood aggression, has been variously described as a "negative reinforcer trap" (Wahler, 1976) or as "coercive behavior" (Patterson & Reid, 1970). The basic notion here is that the child presents aversive stimuli, in the form of aggression and related behaviors, to an adult. In order to terminate the unpleasant situation, the adult gives in to the demands of the child. By arranging for positive reinforcers to be made available to the child, the adult is negatively reinforced in that the child terminates, for the moment, his aggressive behavior. In this manner, the adult is "trapped" or "coerced" into providing the child with positive reinforcers for aggressive behavior while at the same time, the adult receives in exchange negative reinforcers from the child.

Patterson and his colleagues have examined the problem of coercion in some detail. In one study (Patterson & Reid, 1970), it was found that threats and teasing on the part of one child were successful in producing a great deal of attention from other members of the family. This finding, of course, mirrors that discussed above in that aggressive behavior results in positive reinforcement. But there is another process which helps maintain the aggressive behavior of children. That process involves the strengthening of aggression through negative reinforcement. Patterson & Cobb (1971) have reported that many hyperaggressive children "use" their aggression as a means of terminating aversive situations. Some children become aggressive in response to teasing from their siblings. For example, the sister teases the brother. The brother hits the sister. The sister stops teasing. In this interaction, aggression has resulted in the termination of an aversive stimulus (i.e., teasing) and, therefore, aggression will be strengthened through negative reinforcement. Patterson and Cobb report as well that some children may also become aggressive when confronted with parental demands and/or disciplinary measures. By acting aggressively, the child is not only able to stop his parents from enforcing their demands but he can also terminate any disciplinary measures taken against him as a consequence of his failure to comply with such demands. Again, aggressive behavior functions to terminate aversive stimuli. Finally, we may note that in the Patterson, Littman, & Bricker study cited above, evidence was also presented which demonstrated that many preschool children "use" their aggression to terminate the aggressive behavior of other children. Thus, when a child is attacked, he may counterattack in order to stop the aggressive behavior directed at him. Successful counterattacks are therefore negatively reinforced with the result that aggressive behavior is strengthened.

It appears from the above discussion that the prevalence of aggressive behavior among many problem children can be directly attributed to reinforcement, both positive and negative, delivered contingently upon the display of such behavior. To put it another way, aggression is so frequent simply because it "pays off" so frequently. *The essence of the contingency management approach to aggression control is to change the payoff for aggressive behavior by neutralizing its reinforcement value.* In this regard, extinction presumably works by altering the situation so that the aggressive behavior which was once socially reinforced is now totally ignored. Timeout, in turn, works in two ways. First, it removes the child from the reinforcing situation; that is, aggression now leads to the complete withdrawal of social reinforcement and other privileges. Secondly, the period of isolation imposed during timeout functions as an aversive stimulus; that is, timeout also contains a punishment component. A third method, response cost, works by altering the situation so that aggression now leads to a reduced opportunity for reinforcement. Finally, positive reinforcement of socially desirable, alternative behaviors works, in conjunction with one or more of the above three methods, by making nonaggressive behavior extremely attractive as a new source of social reinforcement to replace the loss of the old source represented by aggressive behavior.

With the above points serving as a treatment rationale, we now focus our attention on the research which demonstrates the efficacy of contingency management procedures. No attempt has been made to describe all the published studies; there are simply too many. Instead, some of the more notable studies validating particular treatment interventions are outlined.

GENERAL FEATURES OF THE RESEARCH STUDIES

The majority of relevant studies deal with physical and verbal aggression. The physical aggression takes many forms including punching, hitting, biting, and choking. The verbal aggression most commonly involves swearing and threats of injury. The severity of these behavior problems becomes all the more ominous in the light of long-term follow-up studies which show that aggressive children tend not to outgrow their aggressive behavior but instead continue to display antisocial behavior as adults (Robins, 1966).

Generally, the types of aggression discussed above are accompanied by a variety of other behavior problems that have an aggressive component. Negativistic, oppositional, and noncompliant behaviors are particularly common among aggressive children much to the anger and disappointment of their parents. Such children are likely to respond to parental requests with outright refusal or by simply ignoring them. Some children make a habit of doing the opposite of what they are told, quite literally standing up when they are told to sit down (Madsen, Becker, Thomas, Koser, & Plager, 1968). Disruptive behaviors including yelling, bossing, purposely distracting others, and destroying property are common in the repertoires of many such children. Severe tantrums may also accompany aggressive outbursts especially in younger children. Finally, in a smaller group of individuals, typically those labeled as retarded or psychotic, but occasionally in young normal children as well, self-directed aggression is sometimes seen. During an aggressive tantrum, in particular, such individuals are likely to bite or scratch themselves or perhaps even hit their heads against solid objects such as a wall or a door.

The types of aggressive behaviors described above have been treated in a wide variety of populations. Normal, retarded, and psychotic children, delinquents, and those with the more global label of "emotionally disturbed," have all benefited from contingency management procedures. These procedures, as mentioned previously, can be implemented most successfully in highly structured environments where adequate opportunities for observing the child and controlling contingencies exist. For this reason, the research studies have centered on the home, school, and institutional environments as preferred treatment settings.

Professionals are rarely involved as treatment agents in carrying out the above procedures. This point deserves some elaboration. The traditional model of service delivery with which the public is familiar is that in which a psychologist or other professional conducts treatment during the "50-minute hour" once a week. However, according to the behavioral viewpoint, effective treatment demands that the social environment of the child be restructured if undesirable behaviors such as aggression are to be eliminated. The social settings in which children live and are therefore most influenced by, are the home, school, and in a few cases, the institutional ward. The time spent in the professional's office represents a small and insignificant portion of the week for the problem child. For these reasons, social learning approaches have stressed the role of nonprofessionals as mediators of treatment. The treatment agent most often employed is typically a parent, teacher, or member of the staff of a ward; almost never is the agent a professional, although the professional does, of course, serve as the consultant in formulating the treatment plan. By training those individuals who interact daily with the child, the professional is able to bring about important therapeutic changes in the social environment. The results of such treatment efforts are discussed next.

Timeout Studies

In one study (Zeilberger, Sampen, & Sloane, 1968), a $4\frac{1}{2}$-year-old child was treated for a variety of severe behavior problems. This child engaged in high rates of fighting, screaming, bossing, and disobeying. He would command other children to play in certain ways and backed up his demands with kicks and punches. He routinely ignored his parents when they asked him to do things. The parents were trained to use timeout. Whenever the child behaved aggressively or disobeyed, a parent would take him to an empty room where he had to remain for two minutes. In addition to timeout, treatment also consisted of social reinforcement (praise) for cooperative play with other children. During the baseline (pretreatment) phase, the child displayed aggressive behaviors between 5 percent to 13 percent of the time and obeyed only 30 percent of parental instructions on the average. During treatment, aggression was eliminated and compliance to parental requests rose to an average of 78 percent. As a check to make sure that these treatment gains were really a function of timeout and social reinforcement rather than some random factor that had nothing to do with the treatment, Zeilberger et al., temporarily discontinued treatment during a reversal phase (so named because the situation is reversed back to what it was during pretreatment). Aggression increased sharply again, and compliance decreased, indicating that the behavioral changes that had occurred during treatment were indeed a function of the timeout and social reinforcement contingencies. Finally, the treatment conditions were reinstated with the result that aggression was again eliminated and compliance increased to a high level. In this manner, Zeilberger et al.

empirically demonstrated the efficacy of the combination of timeout and social reinforcement in the control of aggression.

In another study (Clark, Rowbury, Baer, & Baer, 1973), ward staff at an institution for the retarded were taught to control the aggressive behavior of one 8-year-old child. This child displayed a number of dangerously aggressive behaviors including choking people, other forms of attack such as kicking and hitting, and, finally, destroying classroom materials and furniture. Timeout consisted of a minimum of three minutes of isolation contingent on acts of aggression. When timeout was applied to choking, the frequency of this behavior decreased from an average of 13 instances per hour to less than one per hour. When timeout was subsequently applied to the other types of attack and property damage, these forms of aggression also decreased to a near-zero level. Again, timeout was demonstrated to be an effective aggression control technique.

There are a number of other studies in addition to the above that demonstrate the efficacy of timeout (e.g., Allison & Allison, 1971; Birnbrauer, Wolf, Kidder, & Tague, 1965; Bostow & Bailey, 1969; Calhoun & Matherne, 1975; Drabman & Spitalnik, 1973; Hamilton, Stephens, & Allen, 1967; Hawkins, Peterson, Schweid, & Bijou, 1966; Patterson, Cobb, & Ray, 1973; Patterson & Reid, 1973; Tyler & Brown, 1967; Vukelich & Hake, 1971; White, Nielsen, & Johnson, 1972; Wolf, Risley, & Mees, 1964), especially when the procedure is combined with positive reinforcement for appropriate behaviors.

Extinction Studies

Research on extinction is of particular interest because it bears directly on the question of how social reinforcement for aggression helps maintain that behavior. Pinkston, Reese, LeBlanc, & Baer (1973) worked with one $3\frac{1}{2}$-year-old boy. This child regularly bit and kicked peers, insulted them, and destroyed their toys. Teachers almost invariably attended to such behavior by trying to reason with the child or by gently reprimanding him. Pinkston et al. taught the teachers to discontinue their practice of attending to the child when he was aggressive. The result was a sharp decrease in the amount of aggressive behavior from an average of 28 percent of the time during baseline to negligible levels during treatment. A reversal of treatment (as in the Zeilberger et al. study cited above) showed that extinction was the effective factor in eliminating aggression. Similar findings were obtained by Brown and Elliott (1965) in treating the physical and verbal aggression of a class of nursery school children. Extinction, then, is an empirically validated technique for the treatment of some cases of aggression.

The above findings are of particular interest because they demonstrate that the systematic removal and presentation of social reinforcers for aggressive behavior strongly influences the frequency of performance of that behavior. In this respect, these studies are further support for the hypothesis that reinforcement from the social environment plays a key role in the maintenance of aggression in children.

Several other studies also demonstrate the efficacy of extinction (e.g., Madsen, Becker, & Thomas, 1968; Wahler, Winkel, Peterson, & Morrison, 1965; Ward & Baker, 1968; Williams, 1959), particularly when extinction is combined with positive reinforcement for socially appropriate behavior.

Response Cost Studies

In response cost studies, aggressive behavior is brought under control by placing the child on a token system. This system involves rewarding the child with tokens for appropriate behaviors (i.e., positive reinforcement) and taking away tokens for disruptive or undesirable behaviors (i.e., response cost). In one study (Phillips, 1968), the surrogate parents of several predelinquent boys living in a group home attempted to control the verbal aggression (e.g., "I'll kill you") of their charges by placing the boys on a point system. Points were earned for a variety of desirable behaviors such as keeping one's room neat and doing homework. Points were taken away for aggressive phrases involving threats to others. Points that had been earned could be traded in at a later time for a variety of back-up reinforcers such as television time and the opportunity to stay up late. During the baseline phase, verbal threats averaged between 5 to 20 instances per three-hour period. When fines (response cost) were introduced for this behavior, threats decreased to a near-zero level.

A similar study to that described above was conducted by Christopherson, Arnold, Hill, & Quilitch (1972). These investigators taught the parents of two siblings how to control the bickering and teasing which occurred between the children by the use of a point system. Points were lost for aggressive behaviors and earned for house cleaning activities. Under this regimen, the fighting between the children was reduced to a negligible level.

Some studies (e.g., Burchard & Barrera, 1972; Kaufman & O'Leary, 1972) have employed response cost procedures alone to selected children without also using token reinforcement for appropriate behaviors. In these studies too, aggressive behaviors were sharply decreased compared to what they were prior to treatment.

There are many other studies in the literature that demonstrate the effectiveness of response cost procedures particularly when they are used in conjunction with token reinforcement for appropriate behavior (e.g., O'Leary & Becker, 1967; O'Leary, Becker, Evans, & Saudargas, 1969; O'Leary, O'Leary, & Becker, 1967).

Concluding Comments

These studies represent but a small fraction of a very large research literature demonstrating the usefulness of contingency management procedures for the control of aggressive behavior in children. These studies show, with considerable clarity, that aggressive behavior can be understood and controlled without having to resort to tortuous explanations based on intrapsychic dynamisms or risky interventions based on cathartic drainage. The social environment is seen to be a key determinant of a variety of significant behaviors, including aggression.

Having outlined the major contingency management procedures as well as some of the research evidence pertaining to their efficacy, we will now undertake a detailed explication of the clinical use of such procedures.

APPLYING CONTINGENCY MANAGEMENT PROCEDURES

Training the Treatment Agents

A contingency management program begins with the training of treatment agents, that is, those people who will implement the procedures on a day-to-day basis. These individuals are usually parents, teachers, or ward staff.

There are five skill areas in which treatment agents are trained before they are asked to implement specific treatment procedures:

Skill 1: Understanding basic social learning concepts;
Skill 2: Defining behaviors so that they are measurable;
Skill 3: Counting behaviors;
Skill 4: Monitoring behavior changes;
Skill 5: Selecting a treatment procedure.

These skill areas are important in that contingency management programs have a much higher rate of success when the treatment agent understands the rationale for using a particular procedure as well as the method for determining whether or not the procedure is working. The five skill areas can be broken down as follows:

Skill 1: Understanding Social Learning Concepts

A. The treatment agent should be taught the general concepts of positive and negative reinforcement; types of reinforcement; methods of enhancing reinforcer effectiveness; extinction; timeout; punishment; response cost; and token reinforcement. These concepts were described in broad outline earlier in this chapter. Books are available which teach this material in a programmed learning format with accompanying practice exercises (Becker, 1971; Patterson & Gullion, 1968).

B. In working with the treatment agent, the professional should take every opportunity to direct this individual into conceptualizing behavior problems in social learning terms.

Example. The professional is interviewing the mother of an aggressive child for the first time:

Professional: Tell me about Jim's aggressive behavior.

Mother: Well, uh...I don't know. It's just his nature. He's a mean boy. None of my other kids act like him.

Professional: I see. I wonder though if he's always acting up? Are there any times during the day when he's not fighting?

Mother: Oh yes, most of the time. It's just that when he blows, he really gets mean.

Professional: What you're saying is very interesting. It sounds like he's capable of not being aggressive but that some things really get to him. When is it that he "blows"? When is it that he's at his worst?

Mother: Oh it's mostly with his sister over the TV. When he wants to watch a program, he's got to have his way. When she won't give in, he uses such foul language and he sometimes hits her! I can't believe the way he acts!

Professional: What happens after he hits his sister? Does he get to watch his program?

Mother: Yes. It's the only way we can get them to stop. We can't stand all the shouting and crying.

Professional: Do you think he knows that if he hits his sister, he'll get his way?

Mother: Oh he knows alright. He even says it. He tells her that he's stronger than her and he'll watch any program he likes.

Professional: From what you're saying, his aggression sounds like it really pays off.

Mother: That's for sure.

Professional: Is it possible that Jim keeps hitting his sister because he keeps getting his way every time he does it?

Mother: Oh, I see. I suppose so.

Professional: Maybe it's not his "nature" to be aggressive. After all, he is good most of the time. Maybe he sometimes swears and fights because it pays off so much.

Mother: I hadn't really thought about it that way before.

Discussion. This interaction is a common one at the beginning of training. The parent (or other adult) attributes the child's aggressiveness to some global factor such as bad genes, maliciousness, or emotional conflicts, and ignores the fact that the child's aggression is usually specific to situations in which the aggression produces benefits (i.e., reinforcers) for the child. The professional's role is to guide the parent away from conceptualizing in terms of vague factors and towards seeing aggressive behavior as a function of its reinforcing consequences.

Skill 2: Defining Behaviors So That They Are Measurable

This skill is sometimes referred to as a "pinpointing" or "defining behaviors operationally." The basic task is for the treatment agent to learn to define the behavior problem in very specific terms so that everyone involved in treating the child will know exactly what behaviors are being focused upon.

Example. In interviewing the mother of an aggressive child, the professional tries to get the mother to define the problem behavior in specific terms:

Professional: What is it that bothers you the most about Bob's behavior?

Mother: Well it's his viciousness. He can be really horrible to his younger brother.

Professional: What does he do when he's being vicious?

Mother: Oh, he'll slap him or shove him.

Discussion. The mother initially described the problem in very general terms. Different adults might interpret "viciousness" or "being horrible" in different ways, thereby making it difficult to ensure that everyone would be treating the same problem behaviors. In the example, the professional led the mother into defining the problem in specific, concrete terms. "Slapping" and "shoving" are behaviors that are easy to identify and involve much less interpretation on everyone's part than terms such as "viciousness."

DATA SHEET

Name: Bill W.
Problem behaviors: Hitting sister; shoving sister

Day	Frequency	Time period	Rate
3/1 Sat.	~~HH~~ ~~HH~~	12–5 P.M.	2/hr.
3/2 Sun.	~~HH~~ ~~HH~~ ~~HH~~	12–5 P.M.	3/hr.

Fig. 1.1. Data sheet for recording instances of aggressive behavior.

Skill 3: Counting Behaviors

The treatment agent must be taught to count the behaviors that have been defined operationally. This skill is necessary so that the magnitude of the problem can be systematically measured and assessed. One useful way to count behaviors, especially discrete behaviors such as aggression, is to use a data sheet of the type shown in Figure 1.1. The treatment agent makes a tally mark whenever the child either hits or shoves his sister during a given time period. At the end of the day, the rate of aggressive behavior can be computed by dividing the number of aggressive acts by the duration of the time period in which those acts occurred.

Skill 4: Monitoring Behavior Changes

Once the treatment agent has practiced using the data sheet, the skill of monitoring behavior changes is taught. This skill involves taking baseline (i.e., pretreatment) measures of the rate of aggressive behavior and then, after treatment has been introduced, continuing to take the same rate measures. The best way to teach this skill is to have the treatment agent plot the frequency of aggressive behavior on a graph such as that depicted in figure 1.2.

There are three advantages to teaching the skill of monitoring. First, by plotting the data on a graph, the treatment agent has a simple pictorial representation from which it is easy to see trends in the behavior over time. It is much more difficult to see such trends when one has only an unsummarized series of data sheets to work from. Second, a graph permits the treatment agent to see small changes in the frequency of a behavior which occur slowly, over a long period of time. Consider figure 1.2. During the first five days of treatment, aggressive behavior decreased from a rate of 3 per hour to 1 per hour. This decrease may not be particularly noticeable in the real-life situation and the adult might conclude that the intervention is not worth continuing. In contrast, when

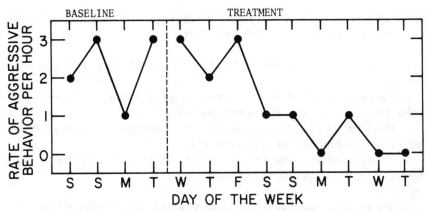

Fig. 1.2. Rate of aggressive behavior per hour for each day of the week.

the data are plotted on a graph, the downward trend is clearly discernible and the treatment agent will more likely be encouraged to continue applying the intervention. Finally, teaching the treatment agent to take a baseline is essential: without a baseline measurement there is no way of knowing whether or not a behavior change represents improvement, in which case the treatment should be continued, or no improvement, in which case the treatment should be changed. For example, suppose that the average rate of aggressive behavior of a child is 1.5 per hour after many days of treatment. This figure would represent an improvement if the average baseline rate were 4.0 per hour but would represent no change if the average baseline rate were 1.1 per hour. If a baseline had not been taken, no such judgement of treatment efficacy would be possible.

Skill 5: Selecting a Treatment Procedure

In advising the treatment agent on the selection of an intervention, two factors should be stressed. First, treatments differ with respect to their degree of aversiveness. Timeout, in which the child is confined in a room for a period of time, is a more aversive procedure than extinction, in which the child is briefly ignored. Second, treatments differ with respect to their degree of artificiality. The use of social reinforcers such as praise and attention is not artificial (i.e., social reinforcers commonly occur in the everyday world of the child) whereas the use of token reinforcers in the form of points or poker chips is quite artificial. The general principle which emerges from considering the above two factors is that the treatment which is selected first should be the one which is the least aversive and least artificial. Based on this principle, the treatment procedures discussed earlier in this chapter can be ranked in descending order of desirability as follows:

1. Positive social reinforcement for appropriate, nonaggressive behavior;
2. Positive social reinforcement for appropriate, nonaggressive behavior plus extinction for aggressive behavior;
3. Positive social reinforcement for appropriate, nonaggressive behavior plus timeout for aggressive behavior;
4. Token reinforcement for appropriate, nonaggressive behavior plus response cost for aggressive behavior.

In each case, we have deliberately listed some form of positive reinforcement first, before mentioning any aversive contingency, in order to stress that good contingency management always has as its primary goal the teaching of socially appropriate behaviors to take the place of aggressive behaviors. We now consider each intervention in turn.

POSITIVE REINFORCEMENT

The essence of positive reinforcement is to strengthen appropriate, nonaggressive behaviors by positively reinforcing them. In so doing, these behaviors will, hopefully, become so frequent and reliable that they will eventually supplant aggressive behaviors. The practical application of positive reinforcement involves the several skill areas described next.

Skill 1: Identifying Positive Reinforcers

A. One should not assume that since an event is a reinforcer for one individual, it must therefore function as a reinforcer for all individuals. One child may be enthusiastic about playing with a certain toy or having an adult read him a story; a different child may be totally apathetic when these same events are presented.

B. One good way of identifying reinforcing events is by observing the effects of a given event on a child's behavior. If the child: (1) asks that the event be repeated; (2) laughs and seems happy when the event is occurring; (3) becomes unhappy when the event is terminated; or (4) will work in order to earn the event, the chances are high that the event is a positive reinforcer and that it can be used to strengthen many appropriate, nonaggressive behaviors.

C. A second method of identifying reinforcers, more particularly, activity reinforcers, is by observing the amount of time that a child chooses to engage in a freely available activity. For example, if a child chooses day after day to play baseball rather than to sing in a choir, there is a good possibility that baseball would function as a powerful reinforcer while singing would not. Likewise, if another child consistently chooses to sing in a choir rather than to play baseball, then it is likely that singing would function as a strong reinforcer and baseball would not. The general rule is that those activities that have a high probability of occurrence in a free choice situation are most likely to function as strong reinforcers.

D. If the above methods do not yield enough information, a third method of identifying reinforcers can be employed. This method involves the use of structured questionnaires. One such instrument is the *Mediation-Reinforcer Incomplete Blank* (MRB) developed by Tharp and Wetzel (1969). The MRB consists of 34 incomplete sentences involving statements such as, "The thing I like to do best with my mother/father is————," or "I will do almost anything to get————." By using a device such as the MRB, an adult can get a better idea of some of the social and material reinforcers likely to be effective for a given child. Importantly, the MRB specifies the *mediator* of the reinforcer as well as the type of reinforcer. This characteristic is noteworthy since some events are reinforcers only when dispensed by certain mediators. Thus, a child may enjoy playing a particular game with his father but not with his mother. Alternatively, praise delivered by the mother may be very powerful but praise delivered by the father may be totally ineffective. The MRB also includes a *reinforcer-rating scale.* Once a reinforcer has been identified, the child rates its potency using a nine-point-scale ranging from "highly reinforcing" (nine) through "moderately effective" (five) to "low or indeterminate power" (one). The rating is carried out by an adult who interviews the child.

A second structured method for identifying reinforcers is the *Reinforcing Event Menu* (REM) (Homme, 1971). This device is especially suited for use with younger children or children whose limited verbal abilities make application of the MRB unfeasible. The REM is a collection of pictures pertaining to a variety of material and activity reinforcers together with a specification of who mediates these reinforcers. The child simply selects from the collection of pictures those which he would most like to work for.

Once the skill of identifying potential reinforcers has been mastered, the treatment agent is ready to learn a variety of other skills pertaining to the effective use of reinforcers.

Skill 2: Using Reinforcers to Strengthen Appropriate Behaviors, *not* to Distract the Child from Engaging in Aggressive or Other Disruptive Behaviors.

Example. A teacher wishes to reduce the aggressive play of one child in a playground situation.

A. The wrong way
   Child: I'm gonna throw sand at you and make you go away. (*Throws sand in the face of another child.*)
   Teacher: (*Walks over to the aggressive child.*) Come on now, you know you shouldn't do that. Why don't you come with me instead and we'll play together on the swings.

B. The right way
   Child: I'm gonna throw sand at you and make you go away. (*Throws sand as above.*)
   Teacher: (*Walks over to the victim.*) You've been playing nicely all morning. I have a special treat for you. Let's go over to the swings and we'll play together. (*After a period of several minutes has elapsed and the aggressor child has played appropriately, the teacher approaches him.*) You've been playing very nicely. Why don't you come with me and we'll all play on the swings.

Discussion. In *A*, the teacher tried to end the aggressive incident by distracting the child. This strategy is a poor one. Although the aggressive behavior may stop temporarily, in the long run it will be strengthened by all the teacher attention made contingent upon it. In *B*, the teacher stopped the aggressive incident by attending to the victim and protecting that child from further abuse. In addition, the teacher attended to the aggressor only after that child had played appropriately for a while. In this manner, play, rather than aggression, was reinforced.

Skill 3: Reinforcing Appropriate Behavior Immediately

Example. A father wishes to reduce the amount of teasing and bickering between his son and daughter.

A. The wrong way
   Son: (*To his sister*) You can borrow my bike to go to the store.
   Daughter: I can? Gee, thanks a lot.
   Father: (*Seven hours later at dinner, while the son and daughter are arguing, the father tries to break up the fight.*) You kids know how to

behave better than this. (*To the son*) Just this morning I saw you lend your bike to your sister.

Son: Yeah, well I'm not gonna do that anymore. She's been on my back all day.

Daughter: (*To her father*) You always take his side. He gave me the bike just so he would look good.

B. The right way

Father: (*Immediately after the son offers his sister the bike*) Son, it's very nice of you to lend your bike to your sister.

Son: (*Smiling*) Oh, that's okay, Dad. She can borrow it whenever she has to go to the store. It's a long walk.

Daughter: (*To her brother*) You're a good sport.

Discussion. In *A*, by waiting too long to reinforce cooperation and by praising his son in the middle of a fight, the father gave the appearance of taking sides and contributed further to the ongoing battle. Even if the siblings had not been fighting, the reinforcer would have been less effective because of the great time delay involved. In *B*, the father used immediate reinforcement. This tactic not only strengthened cooperative behavior in the present but also produced a promise of even more cooperation in the future.

Skill 4: Using Reinforcement Consistently

Positive reinforcement seldom produces an immediate and widespread change in a child's behavior. Instead, it works slowly to strengthen behavior over a period of time. For this reason, it is important, at least initially, to be consistent by reinforcing each instance of a specific, desirable behavior.

Skill 5: Being as Contingent as Possible by Using Descriptive Rather than General Social Reinforcement

Example. A teacher notices that a normally disruptive child is well behaved for the moment. She would like to see more of this behavior.

A. The wrong way

Teacher: You're being a very good boy this morning.

Child: (*Somewhat confused since, an hour before, he had punched the child next to him in the arm.*) I . . . I am? Thank you.

B. The right way

　　Teacher: I like the way you're working on your assignment. It looks like you're getting a lot of the problems done. Keep it up.

　　Child: Thank you. I think I've really got the hang of it now.

Discussion. It is best to clarify, as much as possible, the contingency between the behavior and the reinforcer. One should praise specific, desirable behaviors (as in *B*), not the whole child (as in *A*). By being specific, the teacher communicates the contingency to the child and avoids making the child guess what he is supposed to be doing or, worse, as in *A*, creating the impression that aggression is acceptable if it is followed by good behavior.

Skill 6: Avoiding the Problems Caused by Dispensing Too Much or Too Little Reinforcement

If an adult gives the child too much reinforcement, there is considerable risk of satiating the child on the reinforcer. If too little is given, the quantity of reinforcement received may not be worth the effort to obtain it. In either case, the effectiveness of the reinforcer is compromised. The appropriate amount can only be determined empirically. For example, if a child has been working eagerly to obtain a particular reinforcer but gradually stops working and begins to refuse the reinforcer, satiation might be a factor. In this case, one should reduce the amount of reinforcement given. Similarly, if a child is reputed to value a specific reinforcer but does not appear willing to work for it, a simple test can be employed to determine if too little reinforcement is the problem: give the reinforcer to the child for free. If the child then eagerly consumes the reinforcer and asks for more, it may be possible to use the reinforcer to strengthen appropriate behavior merely by increasing the amount of reinforcement made available for performing such behavior.

Skill 7: Using a Variety of Reinforcers Including Novel Ones When Possible

If a teacher or parent keeps repeating "good boy" each time a child behaves appropriately, the reinforcer may take on a mechanized quality and the child may begin to lose interest in earning praise. The adult appears to be merely "going through the motions" with the result that the praise seems insincere. By varying the reinforcer, the adult can minimize the loss of reinforcer potency. It is better, for example, to mix together a variety of phrases (e.g., "Nice going," "I like it when you behave that way," "I'm proud of you") or to experiment with more exotic, individualized forms of praise (e.g., "You're my favorite, furry little person") than to repeat the same few words over and over.

Skill 8: Using Activity Reinforcers

Appropriate behaviors can be strengthened by making use of the Premack principle. The opportunity to perform a high probability behavior can be used as a reinforcer for a lower probability behavior.

Example 1
Father: (*To his son*) You can watch the football game on TV today but only after you help your brother clean up the recreation room.

Example 2
Mother: (*To her son*) You can go out and play with your friends but first I'd like you to run this errand for me.

Discussion. In each of the above examples, a parent has used a high probability activity (e.g., watching television; playing with friends) as a reinforcer for a lower probability, cooperative behavior. By strengthening cooperative behaviors, one can often reduce the frequency of undesirable behaviors, including aggression. It is important, however, to make the opportunity to engage in the sought after activity contingent upon the performance of the lower probability (cooperative) behavior rather than merely providing the child with free access to the desired activity.

Skill 9: Reinforcing Behaviors which are Incompatible with Aggression

A good strategy for reducing the frequency of aggressive behaviors is to examine the particular circumstances in which aggression occurs and then to try to strengthen those specific behaviors whose performance is incompatible with aggressive displays.

Example 1. Bill is usually disobedient to his parents and occasionally uses foul language when they ask him to do something.

Father: Bill, why don't you go wash up before dinner. (*Bill returns five minutes later all cleaned up.*)
Bill: I'm ready now.
Father: So you are and you did it in record time! After dinner, why don't you pick out the television program you want to see.
Bill: All right!

Discussion. The father took advantage of Bill's rare display of compliance and reinforced the behavior with both social and activity rewards (i.e., praise and television, respectively). By strengthening compliant behavior, the father is strengthening a mode of interaction which is incompatible with aggressive behavior.

Example 2. Tom and John are brothers who are constantly at each other's throats, shouting at each other and sometimes coming to blows. The mother would like to reduce the frequency of their aggressive exchanges.

  Mother: Since it's raining today, you boys will have to stay in the house this afternoon. Why don't you work together on the model airplane kit that Dad bought for you?
  Tom: O.K., I'll get it out of my room.
  John: I wanna build it too.
  Mother: That's O.K., you can both do something. Tom, you get the kit from your room. John, you go downstairs and get some newspapers to spread on the floor so you boys won't make a mess. (*The boys return in a few minutes.*) Well, the way you boys are dividing up the work, it won't take long at all to get that airplane built.
  Both children: Yeah!
  Mother: Let's see if you can both take turns reading the instructions and gluing the pieces together. That way, you can have the airplane built by the time Dad comes home and he can see it.

Discussion. Since the two brothers normally interact by arguing and fighting with each other, the mother deliberately chose an activity which stressed sharing, and taking one's turn as a means of teaching nonaggressive modes of interaction. She praised instances of cooperative behavior. Since the above skills are incompatible with aggressive behaviors, the mother is strengthening behaviors that will eventually replace aggression altogether.

Skill 10: Shaping Appropriate Behaviors in Order to Reduce the Frequency of Aggressive Behavior

Most aggressive children from time to time will exhibit appropriate behaviors which can be reinforced by an adult. The main thrust of this skill area is that of slowly building up these appropriate behaviors so that they occur more often and for longer periods of time.

Example. A teacher wishes to encourage cooperative play between Joe, an aggressive child, and other children in a playground situation.

A. The wrong way

   Teacher: (*Joe has been playing well with the other children for* 20 *minutes. Suddenly, he shoves one of the other children.*) Hey, I told you no fighting on the playground! You promised me you would try to be good.

   Joe: But I was good. (*Pointing to the other child.*) He started it.

B. The right way

   Teacher: (*Joe has been playing well with the other children for* 5 *minutes.*) Well Joe, you look like you're having a good time today. I like the way that you waited your turn and asked Billy to throw the ball to you.

   Joe: Yeah. I like this game.

Discussion. In *A*, the teacher made a very common mistake. She failed to reinforce Joe for behaving appropriately during a period of 20 minutes. Presumably, she was waiting for him to be good for the entire playground period before praising him. In *B*, the teacher reinforced Joe's cooperative behavior after 5 minutes of nonaggressive activity. On the next occasion, she might wait until 10 minutes of cooperative play has occurred before praising him again. By gradually reinforcing longer and longer periods of cooperative play, the teacher would be able to reduce the frequency of aggression by strengthening prosocial behaviors in its place. The most common mistake made is to wait for an aggressive child to exhibit flawless behavior for long periods of time before reinforcing such behavior. A much more effective strategy is to decide what behavior pattern would represent optimal improvement and then to reward the child for making small steps toward that goal. In short, one "shapes" the child's behavior, little by little, until the final goal is reached.

EXTINCTION

The basic component of this procedure is the removal of positive reinforcement for aggressive behaviors which have been either deliberately or inadvertently reinforced in the past.

Skill 1: Knowing When to Use Extinction

A. Extinction is most commonly used with milder forms of aggression in which other individuals are not in any serious danger from the child's aggressive behavior. Disruptive classroom behaviors, verbal aggression in the form of threats and swearing, and low amplitude aggressive behaviors are all potential candidates for extinction especially if the child involved is very young and is not yet able to injure other individuals physically.

B. Extinction is not an appropriate procedure in instances where the aggressive behavior must be stopped immediately because it poses a threat to the safety of either the victim or the aggressor. In such cases, other procedures such as timeout (discussed below) may be used.

C. Extinction is not appropriate if it sets off behaviors that are more dangerous than those the procedure is intended to remediate. One side effect of extinction is that it sometimes produces a transitory burst of aggressive behavior. If one treats swearing by means of extinction and the child suddenly becomes physically aggressive, the procedure should normally be terminated because physical aggression is more serious than swearing, the problem being treated. If, however, physical aggression is the problem being treated, an extinction burst consisting of a transient increase in the level of physical aggression may be tolerated since the ultimate result will be a permanent reduction in the level of physical aggression.

Skill 2: Using Positive Reinforcement for Socially Appropriate, Nonaggressive Behaviors

Extinction is not used by itself to control aggression. Rather, positive reinforcement of socially appropriate, nonaggressive behaviors is used in conjunction with extinction for aggressive behaviors. In fact, extinction is introduced systematically only when it is clear that positive reinforcement of appropriate behaviors alone will not reduce aggression to an acceptable level.

Skill 3: Identifying the Positive Reinforcers Maintaining Aggressive Behaviors

The only way to identify which reinforcers are maintaining aggression is through systematic observation. If the adult suspects that a particular event is maintaining the aggressive behavior, the adult should arrange to have that event withdrawn. If the aggressive behavior then decreases, the reinforcing event has probably been identified and the adult should inform all relevant individuals to withold that event whenever the child subsequently behaves in an aggressive manner.

Example 1. A teacher suspects that a child's use of foul language in class is being maintained by social reinforcement from the child's peers.

Teacher: (*While the problem child is out of class in the principal's office*) Class, I want you to help Fred out from now on by not laughing when he uses bad language. When you laugh, he thinks that it is all right to act that way and then he ends up in the principal's office. If you laugh when he talks that way in the future, I'm going to have to ask those of you who do so to remain after class.

Discussion. The teacher has arranged for all peer reinforcement for foul language to be terminated. If after a few days of extinction, Fred uses less profanity, then peer reinforcement will have been identified as an important factor maintaining the problem behavior. At that point, the teacher will continue the extinction program until the behavior disappears altogether.

Example 2. A father suspects that the angry remarks that his daughter makes whenever her brother teases her are acting as social reinforcers rather than punishers.

Father: (*To his daughter*) You know, I think that when you tell Pete to stop teasing you, he enjoys all the attention he's getting. He seems to know that he's got your goat. I wonder if a better way of handling it is to pretend that his teasing doesn't bother you and to more or less ignore his remarks.

Discussion. Siblings frequently resort to punishing the verbal aggression of other siblings by using threats or reprimands. In some cases, however, such verbal statements function as social reinforcers and strengthen the aggressive behavior. In the example given above, the father helps to arrange for the complete removal of such reinforcers by urging his daughter to discontinue her practice of verbally punishing her brother's teasing. If the frequency of teasing declines after the daughter ceases to make punishing statements, an important factor maintaining aggression will likely have been identified. The extinction procedure can then be maintained until the behavior is eliminated.

Skill 4: Knowing How to Ignore Aggressive Behaviors

Treatment agents who use extinction procedures are faced with the problem of knowing exactly how to ignore aggressive behaviors. The following are some guidelines:

A. Do *not* comment to the child that you are ignoring his behavior.

Example

Mother: (*After her child yells at her for not getting his way*) I've told you before Jimmy that I'm not going to pay any more attention to you when you yell like that. You can yell all day long as far as I'm concerned. I'm just going to ignore it from now on.

Discussion. By making a lengthy, impassioned speech, the mother has subverted her plan of not paying any more attention to her son's yelling. Such speeches often serve as social reinforcers and help maintain the very behaviors they are intended to eliminate.

B. Do *not* look away suddenly when the child behaves in an aggressive manner. Many times an adult will see a child do something aggressive to get attention. At such times, many adults jerk their heads in the opposite direction so as to give the appearance of not noticing the infraction. Any abrupt changes in the behavior of the adult may, however, readily be interpreted by the child as evidence that the obnoxious behavior has been noticed. It is best to ignore the behavior by reacting to it in a matter of fact way by continuing natural ongoing activities such as those described next.

C. *Do* perform activities that are natural for your setting.

Example. A mother notices that her two sons are shouting at one another in a game of one-upmanship. From past experience, she knows that this interaction is a way of getting her attention and that nothing serious will come of it. Since she is sitting on the sofa relaxing anyway, she takes a nearby magazine and begins reading it. The children look at her periodically and seem disappointed. After a while, they stop shouting at each other and begin to play cooperatively. At this point, in keeping with Skill 2, the mother puts down her magazine and comments on how nicely the children are playing with each other. It should be noted that this same episode would be handled differently depending on where in the house the mother was located at the time of the aggressive incident. If she were moving about the house, she could ignore the shouting by engaging in housecleaning activities (especially vacuuming). If she were in the kitchen, she could ignore by starting to cook something. If she were outside, she could ignore by doing some gardening.

D. *Do* protect the victims of aggression. If one child strikes another, the adult must intervene to protect the victim. Even in this case, however, it is possible to ignore the aggression.

Example. Sam has hit Tom while on the playground. The teacher intervenes.

A. The wrong way
   Teacher: Sam! You know you're not supposed to hit other children. I'm surprised at you. Are you all right Tom? Let's walk over to the slide and leave Sam by himself.

B. The right way
   Teacher: Tom, I have an idea. Let's go over to the slide and you can talk to me for a while.

Discussion. In *A*, the teacher is inadvertently reinforcing Sam's aggression by talking to him. In *B*, the teacher not only protects Tom from further aggression but she completely ignores Sam's behavior. By being aggressive, Sam forfeits the teacher's attention for a period of time.

Skill 5: Using Extinction Consistently

The adult must ignore each instance of aggressive behavior. Further, all adults who come in contact with the child must ignore the aggressive behavior.

Example 1. A child has a violent tantrum, screaming and throwing his toys down on the ground, because his mother will not let him go outside to play in the rain.

A. The wrong way
   Mother: (*Ignores the first tantrum. An hour later, however, the child has another tantrum.*) Now look, I can't stand all this noise. You'd better stop it right this minute. I don't care how much you scream, I told you that you can't go outside.

B. The right way. The mother ignores both the first and second tantrums by busying herself with housework and cooking while the child is acting up.

Discussion. In *A*, the mother has used extinction inconsistently. She ignored the first incident but attended to the second. Thus, the aggressive behavior was being intermittently reinforced. Intermittently reinforced behaviors, it will be recalled, show much greater resistance to extinction. The mother has therefore inadvertently made the behavior worse. In *B*, the mother ignored each instance of aggressive behavior. Behaviors subjected to consistent extinction are eliminated more readily.

Example 2. The same incident as was just described but in this case the father is also present.

A. The wrong way
   Mother: (*Ignores the child's tantrum.*)
   Father: (*To his son*) Your mother and I have both told you that you can't go outside so you'd better just stop that noise.

B. The right way. Both parents ignore all tantrums.

Discussion. In *A*, the aggressive behavior was ignored by one parent but attended to by the other. This situation is a variant of intermittent reinforcement. As long as some adults attend to the behavior, the problem will be maintained over time. In *B*, all relevant adults were consistent in their use of extinction. The aggressive behavior will therefore be eliminated more quickly.

Skill 6: Maintaining Extinction for a Long Enough Period of Time for the Procedure to Work.

One common mistake is for an adult to discontinue extinction if the procedure does not work immediately. The following points should be kept in mind when employing extinction:

A. Extinction produces a gradual reduction in the frequency of behavior especially in the case of behaviors that have been intermittently reinforced in the past. As a rule of thumb, the procedure should be applied for at least 4 to 5 days. By that time, a clear decrease in the frequency of aggression should be evident.

B. Recall that, paradoxically, the initial effect of extinction is frequently an *increase* in the rate or intensity of the problem behavior. This increase is invariably short-lived, however, and its presence should not be interpreted as proof that extinction is not working; in fact, quite the opposite. After a short period of time, the extinction procedure will no longer produce this effect.

C. Spontaneous recovery—that is, the reappearance of the problem behavior, for example, on the day after an apparently successful series of extinction episodes—should also not be interpreted as proof that extinction is not working. Typically, the problem behavior will reappear at a much lower level than that exhibited prior to treatment. If extinction is maintained over a period of many days, spontaneous recovery will itself be eliminated.

TIMEOUT

Timeout involves removing all sources of reinforcement for a specified period of time whenever the individual displays aggressive behaviors.

Skill 1: Knowing When to Use Timeout

A. Timeout is used most often in the case of children who display high rates of severely aggressive behaviors that endanger the safety of other individuals. These children are typically in the age range of 2 to 12 years. For older children, different procedures such as token reinforcement and response cost (discussed later in this chapter) and negotiation (discussed in Chapter 2) are commonly used.

B. Timeout is also used for less dangerous forms of aggression in those cases in which the combination of extinction for aggressive behavior and positive reinforcement for appropriate behavior has proven ineffective.

C. Timeout is *not* used when the situation in which the child is aggressive is an aversive one from which he wishes to escape. Such a situation frequently arises in response to parental demands with which the child does not wish to comply. For example, a mother might tell her son that they were going to visit relatives all day. In response to this request, the son throws a violent tantrum, swears at his mother, and makes threatening motions toward her, insisting that he wants to stay at home that day. The mother sends her son to his room believing that she is punishing him with timeout. In fact, however, the son has gotten his way; he has escaped from the aversive situation represented by his having to visit his relatives. The important point here is that for timeout to be effective, it must involve temporary removal of the individual from a positively reinforcing situation, *not* from an aversive situation. In fact, many severely aggressive and disruptive behaviors function as escape responses, allowing the individual to terminate an aversive situation (Carr, 1977; Carr, Newsom, & Binkoff, 1976, 1980). Such behaviors are actually strengthened when they are treated with timeout (Carr, Newsom, & Binkoff, 1980; Plummer, Baer, & LeBlanc, 1977). In such instances, aggression must be treated, not with timeout, but by enforcing compliance with demands, thereby teaching the individual that escape is not possible through acts of aggression.

Skill 2: Using Positive Reinforcement for Socially Appropriate, Nonaggressive Behaviors

As was the case with extinction, timeout is not used by itself. Positive reinforcement of socially appropriate, nonaggressive behaviors is combined with timeout for aggression. All of the skill areas discussed above in the section on positive reinforcement are therefore pertinent and applicable here.

Although one important reason for using positive reinforcement is to strengthen nonaggressive behaviors to the point where they replace aggressive behaviors, there is a second reason for using reinforcement procedures. If extensive use of positive reinforcement is made, then timeout will become all the more aversive since it would involve the temporary termination of a rich diversity of positive reinforcers. In this sense, then, the use of positive reinforcement helps to enhance the effectiveness of the timeout procedure.

Skill 3: Designing a Good Timeout Environment

A. The timeout area should be small and well-ventilated, and have a light and a place to sit.
　B. At home, a bathroom or small bedroom can be modified into an effective timeout area. The key consideration is that the environment must be *boring*; all reinforcers must be removed. There should be no toys, books, television, or people present in the timeout area. If all reinforcers are not removed, the aversiveness of timeout will be attenuated since the child will have an opportunity to entertain himself while in timeout.
　C. In the classroom, a screen can be used to cordon off a corner of the room. The screen should be positioned so that other children are not visible from the timeout area, thereby ensuring that the majority of interesting events will be unavailable to the child while in timeout. The timeout area should be located, if possible, away from any windows that open up onto potentially stimulating parts of the environment such as the playground or street.

Skill 4: Developing Conditioned Aversive Stimuli in Conjunction with Timeout

A. Since the timeout situation is an aversive stimulus, it can be used to help develop conditioned aversive stimuli, that is, conditioned punishers. For example, if the phrase "No, you must not do that" or an equivalent phrase consistently precedes the use of timeout, such phrases will eventually come to function as punishing stimuli by virtue of their being paired with timeout. The advantage of developing such conditioned punishers is that once timeout has brought the problem behavior under control, presenting the conditioned punisher by itself may be enough to suppress the few remaining sporadic instances of misbehavior.
　B. Once these conditioned punishers have been developed, they can also be used to suppress the precursors of those behaviors which normally result in timeout. For example, if a child always swears just before coming to blows, then, rather than waiting for the occurrence of

fighting (a behavior which necessitates the use of timeout), one can deliver a conditioned punisher (e.g., "No, you must not swear") when the precursor behavior (i.e., swearing) occurs. By suppressing the precursor behavior in this manner, the chain of behavior (i.e., "first you swear; then you fight") is broken with the result that fighting is prevented and therefore timeout does not have to be used.

Skill 5: Using Timeout Immediately after an Aggressive Act

A. Timeout, like positive reinforcement and extinction, is most effective when it is used *immediately* after a specific behavior has occurred. Therefore, timeout should be employed as soon as possible after the child has behaved aggressively. To help achieve this goal, the adult should locate the timeout room in a convenient area which does not take a long time to reach.

B. Timeout should not be used for acts of aggression discovered after the fact. For example, a mother finds out that two days ago her son struck another child. The mother should not at this point put her child in timeout; the delay is simply too long and, in any case, the mother would risk putting her child in timeout at a time when he is well behaved. Aggressive behaviors, discovered in retrospect, are best ignored. The mother might, however, wish to tighten her monitoring procedures by checking on her son more frequently when he is playing with other children thereby making it more likely that she will detect any serious acts of aggression at the moment they occur.

Skill 6: Knowing What to Say When Aggression Occurs

A. The adult should make a brief *descriptive* statement to the child about why the child is being put in timeout.

Example. Bill has just hit his sister in the head with a toy shovel.

A. *The wrong way*
   Mother: Bill, you're a bad boy. Go to the timeout room.

B. *The right way*
   Mother: Bill, you cannot stay here if you hit your sister. Go to the timeout room.

Discussion. In *A*, the contingency between aggression and timeout is vague. From Bill's perspective, the timeout might be for hitting, for events preceding the hitting, or for events that happened earlier in the day. Further, the mother has condemned Bill as a person when in fact she only meant to condemn a specific act on his part. In *B*, the contingency between aggression and timeout is clear and direct.

B. The adult should avoid long conversations when putting the child in timeout.

Example. Pete has thrown sand in June's face while on the playground.

A. The wrong way
Teacher: Pete, I told you a thousand times that we do not throw sand at people on the playground. You have to play by the rules here or not at all. How would you like it if June threw sand at you? You wouldn't like it at all. Now I'm going to have to ask you to go to timeout. I don't like to do this but you were bad and I can't let you play like that. You'd better leave now.

B. The right way
Teacher: Pete, you can't stay here if you throw sand at people. Go to the timeout room.

Discussion. In *A*, the teacher's long-winded speech, conducted under the guise of "reasoning with the child" may well function as a social reinforcer. The teacher is showing the child that aggression will result in a great deal of individual attention from her. In this manner, aggressive behavior is likely to be strengthened. In *B*, the teacher pays minimal attention to the aggressive behavior and speaks to the child only long enough to communicate the rule that throwing sand results in timeout.

C. Speak to the child in a matter of fact manner.

Example. Brian has just hit his younger brother.

A. The wrong way
Father: (*Yelling, his face noticeably reddened*) That's the last straw Brian! You'd better get to that timeout room or I'll strap you so hard that you won't be able to sit down for a week. I'm fed up with you.

B. The right way
Father: (*In a calm voice*) Brian, you must not hit. Go to the timeout room.

Discussion. In *A*, the father's cathartic oratory may do much harm and little good. First, he attacked his son verbally without specifying the contingency between aggression and timeout. Secondly, by acting aggressively himself, the father provided a poor model for his son to follow. Thirdly, the aggressive behavior of the father may set off further acts of defiance on the part of his son culminating in a spanking or worse. In *B*, the father realized that timeout, properly applied, is punishment enough in itself. Therefore, no threats or emotional outbursts are necessary.

Skill 7: Using an Effective Duration of Timeout.

A. The standard timeout duration ranges from 1 to 20 minutes with 3 to 5 minutes being the most commonly used duration. Short periods are preferred since there is some tendency for a child to adapt to long duration timeouts with the result that the procedure loses its effectiveness. The adult should begin with a short duration timeout and lengthen the timeout period only if the short duration is ineffective. The adult should not begin with a long duration timeout and then shorten it since such a change may render the procedure ineffective (White, Nielsen, & Johnson, 1972).
   B. A kitchen timer (with a bell) may be used to clock the duration of timeout. The bell provides a cue for both the adult and child that timeout is over.
   C. If a child refuses to go to the timeout room, a twofold contingency may be implemented. First, the child earns one minute extra in timeout for each minute in which he delayed entering the timeout room. This fact should be communicated to him (e.g., "You didn't go into the timeout room until 3 minutes after I asked you to. Because of this, you have to stay in timeout 3 extra minutes"). A second contingency may be added in extreme cases of refusal. Here, not only does the child earn extra time in timeout but, in addition, his refusal results in loss of privileges (e.g., not being allowed to ride his bicycle that day; having to go to bed an hour early).
   D. If the child misbehaves in timeout (e.g., by throwing objects or swearing), the timeout period is extended. For example, if a 5-minute timeout period were being used, the child would be released from timeout 5 minutes after he was put in provided he behaved appropriately for the entire period. If, however, he swore at his parents 2 minutes into the timeout period, the timer would be reset and he would therefore spend a total of 7 minutes in timeout.

Skill 8: Monitoring the Child's Behavior during the Timeout Period

A. If the child appears to be enjoying himself in the timeout room (e.g., he is singing or it sounds as if he is playing games), timeout will probably be ineffective. There are two possible tactics for remedying this problem. First, the timeout room can be modified so that any objects of entertainment, previously overlooked, are removed. If this first strategy fails, a different treatment intervention, such as response cost, may have to be employed.

B. Adults must be aware that the first few times that a child is put in timeout may be quite stormy. The child may act up to such an extent that many extra minutes of timeout are earned. In addition, the child may do property damage. Typically, however, these outbursts will subside after 3 or 4 timeout episodes.

Skill 9: Dealing with Property Damage Produced during Timeout

If the child has thrown a tantrum during timeout and has broken objects or flooded the bathroom floor, two contingencies may be put into effect. First, the child must replace the broken objects out of his allowance. Second, the child must clean up the mess he has created, returning the timeout area to its original state of cleanliness.

Skill 10: Releasing the Child from Timeout

The child should be let out of timeout in a matter of fact manner and allowed to return to his regular activities.

Example. Bill is being let out of the timeout room. His original offense was that he hit his sister.

A. *The wrong way*
   Mother: Well Bill, I hope you've learned your lesson. You know that Dad and I love you very much and feel bad when we have to send you to the timeout room. I understand that your sister bothers you sometime but you have to be nice to her.

B. *The right way*
   Mother: Bill, you've been quiet. You can come out now and go back to your game.

Discussion. In A, the mother offers both apologies and explanations, thereby teaching her son that he can expect a lengthy period of undivided attention from her once he has put in a few minutes in the timeout room. There is the danger that a sequence may develop of the form aggression-timeout-maternal attention. In that case, the long-run product of aggression is social reinforcement with the result that aggression may actually increase. In *B*, the mother provides no such social reinforcement. After the child has been released from the timeout room, the mother should attempt to reinforce some appropriate behavior socially (e.g., play), thereby strengthening a desirable behavior in place of the aggression.

Skill 11: Using Timeout Consistently

As was the case with extinction, timeout must be used consistently or it will not be effective.

A. Each instance of aggression must be followed by timeout. If the aggressive behavior is punished only intermittently with timeout, the procedure will be much less effective (Clark, Rowbury, Baer, & Baer, 1973; Calhoun, & Matherne, 1975).

B. The timeout program must be in effect throughout the day. In addition, each adult who interacts to any significant degree with the child must employ timeout. If only some adults use the procedure, or if the procedure is in effect only during parts of the day, aggressive behavior will not be eliminated.

Skill 12: Using Alternate Forms of Timeout

In some cases, it is easier not to use a timeout room. For example, if the mother is the main source of reinforcement for a child, then she can institute a timeout, of sorts, by leaving the room whenever the child behaves in an aggressive manner (e.g., throws a violent tantrum). In this case, the reinforcing environment (i.e., the mother) is removed from the child in contrast to the typical timeout procedure in which the child is removed from the reinforcing environment.

If all of the above skills are carried out properly, there is typically a noticeable decline in aggressive behavior, at least in the case of normal children, after a period of 3 to 4 days.

RESPONSE COST AND TOKEN REINFORCEMENT

This procedure consists of rewarding the child with tokens or points (we shall use the terms synonymously) for socially appropriate behaviors and taking away tokens or points (i.e., response cost) for misbehaviors. Since tokens are an artificial form of reinforcement, this technique is used only when more natural reinforcers, particularly social reinforcers in the form of attention or praise, are ineffective. Many delinquent and severe conduct problem children do not respond, initially, to adult praise. Further, extinction and timeout sometimes have little effect with these children, especially when their misbehavior is supported by peer reinforcement. In these cases, a combination of token reinforcement and response cost procedures is frequently the treatment of choice.

Token systems have a long and varied history. They have been employed to motivate desirable behavior and reduce undesirable behavior among institutionalized adult schizophrenics. Further, they have been used on classroom behavior problems and in group home settings for predelinquent youths. The scope of such programs is often very large and includes treatment for a variety of problems of which aggression is only one. In what follows, we shall review the highlights of token systems as they are applied to the control of aggressive behavior. The wider applications of token systems are discussed in detail elsewhere (Ayllon & Azrin, 1968; Kazdin, 1977).

For the sake of illustration, we shall describe the application of token systems to the control of aggressive behavior in predelinquent youths living in a group home setting. Such settings have been developed in local communities to treat court-adjudicated youths who would otherwise be sent to large state reformatories (Phillips, 1968).

Skill 1: Defining Target Behaviors

As in all contingency management interventions, the target behaviors involved in the token system must be defined in very specific terms. There are a number of complexities to be considered in defining the behaviors.

A. The adult must develop two lists of target behaviors, one list composed of those behaviors that will earn points and a second list composed of those behaviors that will lose points.

B. With respect to behaviors that will earn points, some specification must be made as to what constitutes an "adequate" performance.

Example. The adult wishes to define "keeping one's room neat" as a behavior that will earn points.

A. *The wrong way*
Definition: "Having a neat room."

B. *The right way*
Definition: "The bed is made. There are no clothes on the floor; they are all hung up in the closet. There are no candy wrappers, crumpled

papers, etc. on the floor; all such items have been placed in the garbage can. The garbage can is emptied before it overflows. All toys and games are on shelves when not in use."

Discussion In *A*, the child must guess as to what constitutes an adequate performance. In *B*, the desired behavior is spelled out in detail and the child knows exactly what to do.

C. The child must be told how to gain access to desired behaviors; that is, the child must know whether a task is assigned or voluntary. In the example just described, the child would be assigned the task of keeping his room neat. In contrast, a task such as washing the windows would be a volunteer job. The definition of each target behavior for which points can be earned must therefore specify whether the task is assigned or done on a volunteer basis.

D. With respect to behaviors which lose points, the definitions must again be very specific. Thus, defining a behavior problem as "acts aggressively" is too vague; defining the problem as "swears, makes threats, and raises voice" is much better. An important additional consideration is that *alternatives* to undesirable behaviors should be clearly specified. To put it another way, merely telling a child that he will lose points for engaging in a variety of aggressive behavior does not tell the child how he *should* behave. The important point to stress is that every effort should be made to specify an alternative behavior to the one being punished with response cost.

Example. The behavior problem is "shouting." Target behaviors: "You will *lose* 100 points for each conversation in which you shout at another person." "You will *earn* 100 points for each conversation in which you talk in a normal tone of voice to another person."

Discussion. Not only has the behavior subject to response cost been clearly specified but an appropriate, alternative behavior which will earn points has also been specified. The child now knows what to do *instead* of shouting.

E. In selecting behaviors that will earn points, it is important to consider which behaviors are likely to be supported by the natural environment after treatment has been terminated. Thus, while it is acceptable to reinforce window washing as an appropriate behavior, it is far better in the long run to strengthen skills such as finding a job, learning to read, and knowing how to converse with a stranger. These latter skills have great survival value in the world at large and there exist many reinforcers in the natural social environment to maintain these behaviors long after the token system has been terminated.

Skill 2: Defining the Currency to Be Used

An important question concerns the form of the event to be used as the unit of exchange in the token system. Sometimes, with retarded individuals, tokens in the form of poker chips are awarded for good behavior and removed for undesirable behavior. With young normal children, popular currencies include gold stars and check marks. With delinquent children, the most popular currency is a point system in which specified numbers of points are earned or lost for particular behaviors.

Skill 3: Selecting the Back-up Reinforcers

A. The back-up reinforcers should be identified using the strategies outlined above in Skill 1 of the section on Positive Reinforcement.

B. Since reinforcer preferences differ from person to person and since a given individual's preferences for specific back-up reinforcers may vary over a period of time, it is essential to include a wide variety of back-up reinforcers in the token system. In this way, there will always be at least a few reinforcers which the individual is motivated to work for.

C. The back-up reinforcers chosen should be strongly valued by the individual. If they are not, not only will the individual fail to be motivated to earn points to purchase the back-up reinforcers but also, and just as importantly, he will not inhibit misbehaviors that lose points. Thus, one could expect, for example, little decrease in the frequency of aggressive behaviors.

D. The cost of the back-up reinforcers should be adjusted so that rare or highly sought after reinforcers cost more than common or less preferred reinforcers.

E. The back-up reinforcers should be described to the child in concrete, detailed terms.

Example. Defining a back-up reinforcer such as "television time."

A. *The wrong way*
   "For 1000 points, you can watch television."

B. *The right way*
   "For 1000 points, you can watch your favorite television program for

one hour beginning at 7:00 P.M. on either Monday, Wednesday, or Friday. You can choose which night."

Discussion. In *A*, the child might believe he had earned unlimited television privileges and become angry when he discovered otherwise. In *B*, the reinforcer is described in enough detail that any possible misinterpretation can be avoided.

Skill 4: Determining How Many Points will be Earned by Specific Behaviors

A. One very important principle here is that behaviors which the child is disinclined to perform should receive larger numbers of points than behaviors which the child performs willingly. For example, a child frequently volunteers to wash the car and rake the leaves but rarely volunteers to do his homework or read the newspaper. An appropriate point assignment might be to award 20 points each for washing the car and raking the leaves and 200 points each (per night) for doing homework and reading the newspaper. Point assignments can thus be adjusted to encourage behaviors of long-term social desirability.

B. Points should not be assigned too liberally and, in any case, should be properly coordinated with the response cost side of the token system (discussed below). The reason for this is simple: If the child earns 10,000 points for raking leaves and loses 100 points for punching his roommate, it follows that points can be earned at such a high rate that there is little reason to inhibit aggressive behaviors. The back-up reinforcers could be earned in spite of considerable misbehavior. To prevent this situation from developing, the system must be designed so that large numbers of points cannot be earned at a high rate.

C. Verbal statements involving praise should be paired with the delivery of points (e.g., "Nice going, you got an *A* in history. Give yourself 2,000 points"). Since the praise is paired repeatedly with points, praise will eventually become a conditioned reinforcer. Once praise is established as a reinforcer, one can begin to fade out token reinforcement and substitute praise in its place, thereby producing a more normalized reinforcement system.

Skill 5: Determining How Many Points Will Be Lost by Specific Behaviors

A. The magnitude of response cost must be carefully controlled. If fines are too large, bankruptcy will ensue and the child will be unable to purchase any back-up reinforcers. Further, if the child develops too large a deficit, he may adopt an attitude of "what do I have to lose?" and engage in considerable misbehavior. On the other hand, if the fines are too small, the child will be able to negate his loss easily by performing any of a variety of appropriate behaviors. In this situation, he may continue to misbehave since response cost does not prevent the child from acquiring the back-up reinforcers. The balancing of response cost and token reinforcement can only be achieved, empirically, by noting the rate at which points are lost and earned and then adjusting the point system to avoid the extremes described above.

B. On some occasions, a child may build up a considerable point deficit through a series of undesirable behaviors. In such situations, one tactic that is frequently used is to increase the number of opportunities available for earning back the points. This strategy serves two purposes. First, it prevents the child from giving up because of the hopelessness of earning back so many points. Secondly, by requiring that the child perform many different appropriate behaviors to cancel the deficit, the strategy strengthens desirable behavior and teaches the child that "a wrong can be righted."

C. Verbal statements involving disapproval should be paired with the removal of points (e.g., "No, Pete, you should not hit. Take off 5,000 points"). Since the disapproval is paired repeatedly with the loss of a positive reinforcer (i.e., points), disapproval will eventually become a conditioned punisher. Once disapproval is established as a punisher, one can begin to fade out response cost and substitute disapproval in its place, thereby producing a more normalized punishment system.

Skill 6: Determining How Often the Token Exchange Should Take Place

A. When the token system is first implemented, it is important that the child experience the direct contingency between earning points and purchasing the back-up reinforcers so that he will come to "value" the points per se. If necessary, the exchange of points should be arranged every hour. Typically, this hourly exchange need only be in effect for a day. Thereafter, the child should be placed on a "daily system" in which points earned on one day buy privileges for the next. Finally, the child should be put on a "weekly system" in which an entire week's earnings are used to purchase privileges for the following week.

B. By delaying the time between which points are earned and points are exchanged, one is teaching the child a new skill: delay of gratification. Since delinquent children are typically deficient in this area, it is worthwhile to build up longer and longer delays between the earning and the exchange of points so as to strengthen their ability to delay gratification, an ability of adaptive significance in the normal social environment.

Skill 7: Advertising and Monitoring the Contingencies

A. The child must be informed, in very specific terms, as to the number of points earned and lost by particular behaviors and the cost of back-up reinforcers. This advertising is accomplished by making a large sign to be posted in a prominent place such as the child's bedroom or the kitchen. Table 1.1 shows one such display.

  B. For purposes of monitoring points, each child should carry with him a small card which lists points earned and lost and the corresponding behaviors involved. Each time that the child performs one of the desired behaviors or one of the undesired behaviors, the adult requests the card, writes down the behavior and the number of points involved, and initials the entry. If the child loses the card or changes any of the entries, large fines are levied to discourage irresponsibility and/or cheating as the case may be.

Table 1.1. Examples of Cost of Privileges Per Week and Number of Points Earned and Lost for Specific Behaviors.

Privileges	Cost in Points
Television	2,000
Ping pong	1,000
Swimming	2,000
Staying up late	2,000
Going to circus	10,000
Behaviors which Earn Points	Points Earned
Doing homework	1,000 per night
Getting an A/B/C/D grade	2,000/1,000/500/250 per grade
Keeping one's room neat	1,000 per day
Dressing neatly	1,000 per day
Greeting people appropriately	100 per instance
Behaviors which Lose Points	Points Lost
Incomplete homework	1,000 per night
F grade	1,000 per grade
Messy room	1,000 per day
Improper dress	1,000 per day
Inappropriate greeting	100 per instance
Swearing	2,000 per instance
Physical aggression	20,000 per instance

*The points listed are arbitrary and for illustrative purposes only. For convenience, the behaviors are listed in abbreviated form; they would usually be described in greater detail.

Skill 8: Fading Out the Token System

An important long-term goal of token systems is to fade out the system itself in favor of a more natural mode of reinforcement. The essentials for accomplishing this goal have been described above as part of the various skill areas. For convenience, we now summarize and elaborate upon the fading procedure.

A. Increase the time between earning the points and redeeming them by proceeding from an hourly to a daily to a weekly system.

B. Establish conditioned reinforcers and punishers by the methods described above (Skills 4 and 5) and then fade out the use of points altogether.

C. Include a feature in the token system whereby an individual can "buy out of" the token system by earning a very large number of points together with committing a very low number of infractions. This is sometimes referred to as a "merit system." Any individual who achieves this level of functioning is permitted all privileges for free provided that he continues to commit few offenses and carries out the tasks required of him adequately. At this level, the evaluation of the child's functioning is made in terms of satisfactory/unsatisfactory ratings rather than by points. If too many unsatisfactory ratings are earned, the child must go back on to the point system; otherwise, he remains off the system.

GENERALIZATION AND MAINTENANCE

There remain two important dimensions of behavior change vis-à-vis aggression control which need to be discussed. The first, *generalization*, refers to the issue of whether the decrease in the frequency of aggressive behavior brought about by treatment in one setting (e.g., the home) will transfer to a variety of other settings (e.g., the school and playground). The second dimension, *maintenance*, pertains to the issue of whether the decrease in aggression produced by treatment in one setting will endure over time, even after the treatment procedure itself has been terminated.

Skill 1: Helping to Bring About the Generalization of Treatment Gains

If the improvements in a child's behavior do not generalize from one setting to another, there are several tactics which an adult can employ to bring about the desired generalization.

A. The most straightforward solution is to *program generalization.* What this means is that the adult takes the treatment that was successful in one setting and applies it in every setting in which the behavior change is desired. For example, a teacher has successfully controlled a child's aggressive behavior at school through the use of timeout. The parents complain, however, that the child is still aggressive at home. The solution would be to introduce the timeout procedure at home as well, thereby producing a generalized suppression in both the home and school settings.

B. A child frequently discriminates between the treatment and non-treatment environments because the two settings are extremely dissimilar. In such cases, the child is observed to be well behaved in the treatment environment and out of control in the nontreatment environment. One way of producing generalization across the two settings is by *making the settings as similar as possible.* For example, if one wants to teach a delinquent to generalize his cooperative behavior from a group home to the school playground, one might set up a situation in the group home which is similar to the playground situation and have the child practice his cooperative behavior there. Once the skill is mastered at home, there is a good chance that the skill will generalize to the school setting because of the great similarity between home and school settings.

C. Sometimes generalization does not occur because the stimulus properties of the treatment setting are too narrow; that is, the child might have been treated by one adult in one specific setting. Consequently, when the child comes into contact with other adults in different settings, his behavior deteriorates. Consider the case of a child whose tantrums are successfully treated at home by his mother who uses an extinction procedure. When the child is outside of the home and/or in the presence of other adults, he resumes the tantrums. One solution to this problem would be to *use many adult treatment agents and employ the treatment in many different settings.* Generally, the result of this procedure is that the child will begin to behave appropriately in all settings and toward all adults, even in situations in which extinction is not explicitly being used.

D. A final strategy for producing generalized behavior change is to *teach general rules of conduct.* For example, if a child is on a token system, the adult might define one desirable behavior pattern as "helping other people." Several examples of this behavior pattern would be described to the child so that he would know how to earn points. Thus, helping another child fix a broken toy, or helping a parent take groceries in from the car, or helping a neighbor mow the lawn would all constitute instances of the desired behavior. Many other helping behaviors, however, not originally specified, should also be reinforced as they arise.

By strengthening a general pattern of behavior rather than a few specific instances of behavior in this manner, the adult teaches the child not only to help others (a behavior that is incompatible with aggression) but, in addition, the adult teaches a general rule of conduct applicable in many settings. The learning of such rules can help promote generalization.

Skill 2: Helping to Bring About the Maintenance of Treatment Gains

Desirable behavior changes are often not maintained over time; that is, the individual's problem behaviors slowly return and the treatment gains vanish. There are a number of strategies for helping to increase the probability that treatment gains will be maintained.

A. One important principle described previously in this chapter is that behaviors which are reinforced intermittently are much more resistant to extinction than behaviors which are reinforced continuously. To put it another way, *intermittently reinforced behavior will be better maintained over time.* Thus, rather than reinforce a rude child for talking politely to his teacher each time that he does so, it would be better, as soon as possible, to reinforce polite talk every other time and, finally, to reinforce only on an occasional, highly intermittent basis. Following this "thinning out" of social reinforcement, the polite behavior will not decrease precipitously if, at some future time, the child is not reinforced for every instance of polite talk.

B. Another valuable tactic is to *teach the child those behaviors that are very likely to be reinforced in the natural environment.* For example, if a delinquent child is taught how to organize a playground game such as baseball or football, this skill is likely to be maintained over time because the natural social environment (i.e., other children) will support and reinforce this type of behavior. On the other hand, teaching the delinquent how to wash windows is much less likely to be supported by the child's natural social environment. Therefore, if a choice exists, the adult should teach behaviors that are likely to be supported by natural contingencies. Organizing games is one such behavior and, fortunately, it is also a behavior which is a viable alternative to delinquent activities.

C. By *creating new kinds of reinforcement for the child's appropriate behaviors,* the adult also helps to make a contribution to the maintenance of those behaviors. For example, if a child is motivated to do his homework only because of the promise of earning points, then it is likely that if the child enters an environment where points cannot be earned, the child will stop doing homework. Such a problem can be prevented by creating social reinforcers, in the manner described above; that is, by pairing praise with points and gradually fading out the points. Since praise is available in the natural environment, the child's homework activities are likely to be maintained there.

D. The final and most obvious strategy is to *reprogram the child's social environment*. If a child's teachers, parents, and relatives all know that when the child strikes another individual, he is always to be put in timeout, then it is likely that any reduction in aggression will be maintained over time simply because all the relevant adults will keep the treatment procedure in effect over time.

CRITIQUE AND SOME FUTURE DIRECTIONS

The contingency management approach is a useful one for the control of childhood aggression. There are, however, a number of unresolved conceptual, ethical, and treatment issues worth noting. Many of these issues will come up again in later chapters of this book. By introducing them now, we hope to produce a greater awareness that even at the level of the individual, aggression control procedures take place within a complex social matrix which influences the direction and eventual success or failure of such procedures. We deal with several of the most salient issues.

Primary Prevention

As we noted at the beginning of this chapter, many influential philosophers, including Plato, Aristotle, and Rousseau, have stressed the importance of exposing the child to nonaggressive models and shielding him from noxious influences so as to prevent the emergence of undesirable behaviors such as aggression. Yet, in our own time, parents, scientists, and governments have shown little inclination to heed the adage that "an ounce of prevention is worth a pound of cure." To a great extent, the procedures detailed in this chapter represent a means for "putting out fires," for dealing with aggressive behavior after it has become a serious problem. Is there any way to prevent the emergence of aggressive behavior or, at least, to minimize the probability of its occurrence? We think so. The answer is likely to be found in the area of parent training and in the development of codes of conduct for the media.

It is often assumed that when an individual becomes a parent, he or she will, by some mysterious process, automatically become knowledgeable about child rearing. The large numbers, however, of parents who seek help from child-guidance clinics and related facilities attest to the fact that such knowledge is often hard to come by. A useful tactic might therefore be to educate parents in simple contingency management procedures before any problems arise. Great stress should be placed on the use of positive reinforcement of socially desirable behaviors coupled with exposing the child to exemplary models of prosocial conduct. Information concerning the use of such procedures could be disseminated to parents through "well-baby" clinics attached to regular hospitals and through the outreach functions of community mental health centers and related social service agencies.

Secondly, there is a strong relationship between televised violence and subsequent aggressive behavior in children (Steuer, Applefield, & Smith, 1971; Eron et al., 1972). One can often guess what was on television the night before by watching the aggressive play of children the next day. Much of the violence, portrayed in minute detail by the media, finds its way into the "innocent" play of children. This author heard one child warn another that he (the first child) was a policeman and could therefore break down the door, smash all the furniture in the house, and beat up anybody that got in the way. Young children clearly do not always interpret media violence in a way that is beneficial to society. The media can help promote the control of aggression by subscribing to a code of conduct that minimizes the level of violence presented, at least during periods of the day when children have easy access to broadcasts. Of course, the evolution of such a code must not impact negatively upon first amendment rights but even given this caveat, it should still be possible to avoid the grisly, detailed, wanton destruction and disrespect for life which characterize a great deal of media programming. Put another way, we must ask ourselves how high a price we are willing to pay just to be entertained. Moderation in the level of media violence should result in fewer aggressive models for children to imitate and a likely diminution in the frequency of serious cases of childhood aggression. This is clearly a form of prevention worth pursuing.

The Child as Contingency Manager

The interventions for aggression control which we have reviewed in this chapter are uniform in one important respect: the child is seen as the passive recipient of treatment. As we noted earlier in this chapter, however, the social learning approach views behavior change as a reciprocal influence process in which the child *influences* his environment (e.g., adults and other children) as well as *being influenced by it*. The thrust of the various techniques we have described has been to minimize the role of the child as an *active* agent in the treatment process. Perhaps the occasional ineffectiveness of contingency management and the problem of maintaining treatment gains stem from the failure of professionals to accord the child a more active role in the behavior change process. In view of this situation, recent work centering on teaching the child to influence adults in socially desirable ways seems to us to represent a healthy shift in the direction of conceiving treatment in terms of reciprocal influence rather than as a unidirectional process with the child in the passive role. With respect to the problem of aggression, there is an increasing awareness that the child who must resort to aggressive behaviors in order to get adult attention might well give up such behaviors if taught more socially appropriate ways of gaining attention. In this sense, the child is viewed as having a social skills deficit and therefore in need of specific training as to which behaviors are most effective in influencing adult behavior in directions that the *child* desires. For example, in one study (Graubard, Rosenberg, & Miller, 1971), children were taught to modify the behavior of their teacher by reinforcing (i.e., praising) her helping and attentive behaviors while ignoring her scolding and negative behaviors. The result was an increase in positive teacher-student contacts and a decrease in negative contacts. Clearly, turning the children into able contingency managers with respect to their teacher's behaviors not only resulted in more desirable interpersonal relationships but also gave the child a new set of skills which were socially acceptable and effective. Such skills are likely both to maintain well over time and to replace less effective behaviors, such as aggression, as a means of influencing adults. This line of research is only in its infancy but a number of studies in addition to the one cited above (e.g., Fedoravicius, 1973; Polirstok & Greer, 1977; Sherman & Cormier, 1974) suggest that this is a fruitful approach to pursue.

Factors Influencing the Labeling of Aggression

The labeling of an act as aggressive is a social judgement process which can be influenced by a variety of factors (Bandura, 1973). Adults may not be able to agree on whether a given behavior is to be considered appropriate or inappropriate. The existence of such discrepancies should serve as a warning to professionals that in some cases of child "problem" behaviors, the client may turn out to be the adult rather than the child; that is, the professional may well have to serve as a child advocate and attempt to convince the adult that the "problem" is one of social misperception on the part of the adult rather than maladaptive behavior on the part of the child.

A variety of subcultural and familial factors may conspire to cause a parent to view minor infractions of rules as serious misbehavior. Thus, if the child arrives five minutes late for dinner, he is showing "defiance," or if the child questions a parental command, however slightly, he is showing extreme "negativism." In such cases, the problem may be that the parent's standards of conduct are excessively strict and the appropriate intervention would be to encourage the parent to adopt more flexible criteria while still maintaining a reasonable level of control. The treatment would *not* be to put the child in timeout or to revoke privileges.

Individual prejudices held by certain adults may occasionally precipitate labeling selected children as aggressive. Thus, while boys may be allowed to play roughly, the same type of behavior in girls may be seen as problematic and requiring treatment. Further, the racial characteristics of some children may predispose certain adults to overreact when these children exhibit even minor misbehaviors. The existence of sexual or racial stereotypes must be frankly recognized by professionals and dealt with either by attempting to change the attitudes of relevant adults or by removing the child from the prejudiced environment altogether.

Finally, some parents, largely through ignorance of normal child development, acquire unrealistic expectations of their children. If a parent complains that his or her child is too rambunctious and that children should be quiet and unobtrusive, the professional must determine whether or not the child's activity level is indeed markedly nonnormative. If it is not, then the professional must attempt to educate the parent as to what constitutes "normal" behavior for a young child. Sometimes the solution is one of simple stimulus control, that is, teaching the parents to control the child's excessive activity at the dinner table or in the living room but allowing the child much more latitude on the playground or in the recreation room. At other times, the solution may involve persuading the adults to adopt standards of conduct which reflect the child's developmental level more realistically.

Problems of Long-Term Maintenance

One common assumption is that the reduction in child behavior problems which occurs after the parent has applied contingency management procedures will function as a reinforcer for the parent's therapeutic activities. The parent, it is predicted, will be so pleased with the reduction in misbehaviors that treatment efforts will be carried out indefinitely with a corresponding long-term reduction in problem behaviors. Such, unfortunately, is not the case. Child behavior change per se frequently does not function to maintain parental therapeutic activities (Mira, 1970; Rickert & Morrey, 1972). How then can long-term maintenance of behavior change be achieved? There are two strategies. One tactic centers on the assumption that parents of extremely difficult children may require periodic professional consultation indefinitely (Patterson, Cobb, & Ray, 1973). That is, it is assumed that the systematic application of treatment intervention may never reach a permanent termination point but, rather, the child (and parents) will have to take part in periodic booster sessions designed to reinstate some or all of the therapeutic strategies whenever the child's behavior problems increase again to an unacceptable level. A second tactic centers on recognizing that for many parents, especially those whose families lack cohesiveness and/or are outside of the social mainstream of their communities, treatment activities are seen as yet another aversive demand in a bleak and pointless existence. Such parents may well require the help of social systems outside the immediate family such as the school, church, or selected neighbors in order to help them better organize their lives and introduce some measure of life satisfaction to them so that they are more willing to undertake the rigors of applying systematic treatment interventions to their child's aggressive behaviors (Wahler, 1976). Frequently, too, marital therapy is called for in order to enhance husband-wife interactions enabling the parents to support each other in carrying out and sharing in the responsibilities of child rearing.

Alternatives to Contingency Management

There are a variety of aggressive behaviors which are not typically amenable to the treatments described in this chapter. Thus, for example, arson, vandalism, and theft are behaviors which normally occur when responsible adults are not present. Since such problems are therefore very difficult to detect, one is usually unable to apply, in any systematic manner, a standard contingency management procedure such as response cost, nor is there any evidence as yet that such a procedure would have any effect on these problems. Quite often these problems are supported by the individual's peers and therefore some of the small group and community level procedures discussed later in this book, are a more appropriate means of intervention.

The majority of older adolescents and adults who exhibit aggressive acts respond best to treatment interventions other than the contingency management procedures described thus far. One simply does not, for example, send a 20-year-old adult to the timeout room. Rather, a variety of interventions, including cognitive and relaxation methods (Chapter 3), and negotiation and contracting (Chapter 2) are typically used with such individuals.

SUMMARY

Contingency management may be seen as both an outgrowth of and a reaction to a variety of traditional philosophical, religious, psychological, and popular viewpoints. The efficacy of techniques such as positive reinforcement, extinction, timeout, and response cost has been validated by an extensive body of research which demonstrates that these procedures can be an effective means for controlling many types of aggression seen in young normal children, delinquents, retardates, and psychotic individuals. Further, these techniques have been applied with success in home, school, and ward settings. It seems likely that this approach will continue to be an important method of aggression control in the forseeable future and that its utility will be enhanced as issues such as prevention, child influences, social judgement biases, and long-term maintenance of treatment gains are more fully addressed.

REFERENCES

Allison, T. S., & Allison, S. L. Time-out from reinforcement: Effect on sibling aggression. *Psychological Record*, 1971, **21**, 81–86.

Ayllon, T., & Azrin, N. H. *The token economy: A motivational system for therapy and rehabilitation.* New York: Appleton, 1968.

Bandura, A. *Principles of behavior modification.* New York: Holt, 1969.

Bandura, A. *Aggression: A social learning analysis.* Englewood Cliffs, NJ: Prentice-Hall, 1973.

Bandura, A., Ross, D., & Ross, S. A. Transmission of aggression through imitation of aggressive models. *Journal of Abnormal and Social Psychology*, 1963, **63**, 575–582.

Bandura, A., & Walters, R. H. *Adolescent aggression.* New York: Ronald Press, 1959.

Barker, R., Dembo, T., & Lewin, K. Frustration and regression: An experiment with young children. *University of Iowa Studies in Child Welfare*, 1941, **18** (Whole No. 386).

Becker, W. C. *Parents are teachers.* Champaign, Ill.: Research Press, 1971.

Birnbrauer, J. S., Wolf, M. M., Kidder, J. D., & Tague, C. Classroom behavior of retarded pupils with token reinforcement. *Journal of Experimental Child Psychology*, 1965, **2**, 219–235.

Bostow, D. E., & Bailey, J. S. Modification of severe disruptive and aggressive behavior using brief timeout and reinforcement procedures. *Journal of Applied Behavior Analysis*, 1969, **2**, 31–37.

Brown, P., & Elliott, R. Control of aggression in a nursery school class. *Journal of Experimental Child Psychology*, 1965, **2**, 103–107.

Burchard, J. D., & Barrera, F. An analysis of timeout and response cost in a programmed environment. *Journal of Applied Behavior Analysis*, 1972, **5**, 271–282.

Calhoun, K. S., & Matherne, P. The effects of varying schedules of time-out on aggressive behavior of a retarded girl. *Journal of Behavior Therapy and Experimental Psychiatry*, 1975, **6**, 139–143.

Carr, E. G. The motivation of self-injurious behavior: A review of some hypotheses. *Psychological Bulletin*, 1977, **84**, 800–816.

Carr, E. G., Newsom, C. D., & Binkoff, J. A. Stimulus control of self-destructive behavior in a psychotic child. *Journal of Abnormal Child Psychology*, 1976, **4**, 139–153.

Carr, E. G., Newsom, C. D., & Binkoff, J. A. Escape as a factor in the aggressive behavior of two retarded children. *Journal of Applied Behavior Analysis*, 1980, **13**, 101–117.

Christopherson, E. R., Arnold, C. M., Hill, D. W., & Quilitch, H. R. The home point system: Token reinforcement procedures for application by parents of children with behavior problems. *Journal of Applied Behavior Analysis*, 1972, **5**, 485–497.

Clark, H. B., Rowbury, T., Baer, A. M., & Baer, D. M. Timeout as a punishing stimulus in continuous and intermittent schedules. *Journal of Applied Behavior Analysis*, 1973, **6**, 443–455.

Cutts, N. E., & Moseley, N. *Better home discipline*. New York: Appleton-Century-Crofts, 1952.

Davitz, J. R. The effects of previous training on post frustration behavior. *Journal of Abnormal and Social Psychology*, 1952, **47**, 309–315.

Dollard, J., Doob, L. W., Miller, N. E., Mowrer, O. H., & Sears, R. R. *Frustration and aggression*. New Haven, Conn.: Yale University Press, 1939.

Drabman, R., & Spitalnik, R. Social isolation as a punishment procedure: A controlled study. *Journal of Experimental Child Psychology*, 1973, **16**, 236–249.

Dreikurs, R. *The challenge of parenthood*. New York: Duell, Sloan, and Pearce, 1966.

Eron, L. D., Huesmann, L. R., Lefkowitz, M. M., & Walder, L. O. Does television violence cause aggression? *American Psychologist*, 1972, **27**, 253–263.

Fedoravicius, A. S. The patient as shaper of required parental behavior: A case study. *Journal of Behavior Therapy and Experimental Psychiatry*, 1973, **4**, 395–396.

Foxx, R. M., & Azrin, N. H. Restitution: A method of eliminating aggressive-disruptive behavior of mentally retarded and brain-damaged patients. *Behavior Research and Therapy*, 1972, **10**, 15–27.

Freud, S. *New introductory lectures on psycho-analysis*. New York: Morton, 1933.

Ginott, H. G. *Between parent and child*. London: Staples Press, 1965.

Graubard, P. S., Rosenberg, H., & Miller, M. B. Student applications of behavior modification to teachers and environments or ecological approaches to social deviancy. In E. A. Ramp and B. L. Hopkins (Eds.), *A new direction for education: Behavior analysis 1971*. Vol. 1, Lawrence, Kansas: University of Kansas, Support and Development Center for Follow Through, 1971.

Hamilton, J., Stephens, L., & Allen, P. Controlling aggressive and destructive behavior in severely retarded institutionalized residents. *American Journal of Mental Deficiency*, 1967, **71**, 852–856.

Hartmann, D. P. Influence of symbolically modeled instrumental aggression and pain cues on aggressive behavior. *Journal of Personality and Social Psychology*, 1969, **11**, 280–288.

Hawkins, R. P., Peterson, R. F., Schweid, E., & Bijou, S. W. Behavior therapy in the home: Amelioration of problem parent-child relations with the parent in therapeutic role. *Journal of Experimental Child Psychology*, 1966, **4**, 99–107.

Homme, L. *How to use contingency contracting in the classroom*. Champaign, Ill.: Research Press, 1971.

Kaufman, K. F., & O'Leary, K. D. Reward, cost, and self-evaluation procedures for disruptive adolescents in a psychiatric hospital school. *Journal of Applied Behavior Analysis*, 1972, **5**, 293–310.

Kazdin, A. E. *The token economy*. New York: Plenum Press, 1977.

Locke, J. *Some thoughts concerning education*. (F. W. Garforth, Ed.) Woodbury, New York: Barron's Educational Series, 1964. (Originally published, 1693).

Lorenz, K. *On aggression*. New York: Harcourt Brace Jovanovich, 1966.

Lovaas, O. I. Effect of exposure to symbolic aggression on aggressive behavior. *Child Development*, 1961, **32**, 37–44.

Madsen, C. H., Becker, W. C., & Thomas, D. R. Rules, praise, and ignoring: Elements of elementary classroom control. *Journal of Applied Behavior Analysis*, 1968, **1**, 139–150.

Madsen, C. H., Becker, W. C., Thomas, D. R., Koser, L., & Plager, E. An analysis of the reinforcing function of "sit down" commands. In R. K. Parker (Ed.), *Readings in educational psychology*. Boston: Allyn and Bacon, 1968.

Mallick, S. K., & McCandless, B. R. A study of catharsis of aggression. *Journal of Personality and Social Psychology*, 1966, **4**, 591–596.

Mira, M. Results of a behavior modification training program for parents and teachers. *Behavior Research and Therapy*, 1970, **8**, 309–311.

Montague, M. F. A. (Ed.), *Man and aggression*. New York: Oxford University Press, 1968.

Nelsen, E. A. Social reinforcement for expression vs. suppression of aggression. *Merrill-Palmer Quarterly*, 1969, **15**, 259–278.

O'Leary, K. D., & Becker, W. C. Behavior modification of an adjustment class: A token reinforcement program. *Exceptional Children*, 1967, **33**, 637–642.

O'Leary, K. D., Becker, W. C., Evans, M. B., & Saudargas, R. A. A token reinforcement program in a public school: A replication and systematic analysis. *Journal of Applied Behavior Analysis*, 1969, **2**, 3–13.

O'Leary, K. D., O'Leary, S., & Becker, W. C. Modification of a deviant sibling interaction pattern in the home. *Behavior Research and Therapy*, 1967, **5**, 113–120.

Patterson, G. R. *Families*. Champaign, Ill.: Research Press, 1971.

Patterson, G. R., & Cobb, J. A. A dyadic analysis of "aggressive" behaviors: An additional step toward a theory of aggression. In J. P. Hill (Ed.), *Minnesota symposia on child psychology* (Vol. 5). Minneapolis: University of Minnesota Press, 1971.

Patterson, G. R., Cobb, J. A., & Ray, R. S. A social engineering technology for retraining the families of aggressive boys. In H. E. Adams and I. P. Unikel (Eds.), *Issues and trends in behavior therapy*. Springfield, Ill.: C. C. Thomas, 1973.

Patterson, G. R., & Gullion, M. E. *Living with children*. Champaign, Ill.: Research Press, 1968.

Patterson, G. R., Littman, R. A., & Bricker, W. Assertive behavior in children: A step toward a theory of aggression. *Monographs of the Society for Research in Child Development*, 1967, **32**, No. 5 (Whole No. 113).

Patterson, G. R., & Reid, J. B. Reciprocity and coercion: Two facets of social systems. In C. Neuringer and J. Michael (Eds.), *Behavior modification in clinical psychology*. New York: Appleton-Century-Crofts, 1970.

Patterson, G. R., & Reid, J. B. Intervention for families of aggressive boys: A replication study. *Behavior Research and Therapy*, 1973, **11**, 383–394.

Phillips, E. L. Achievement place: Token reinforcement procedures in a home-style rehabilitation setting for "pre-delinquent" boys. *Journal of Applied Behavior Analysis*, 1968, **1**, 213–223.

Pinkston, E. M., Reese, N. H., Le Blanc, J. M., & Baer, D. M. Independent control of a preschool child's aggression and peer interaction by contingent teacher attention. *Journal of Applied Behavior Analysis*, 1973, **6**, 115–124.

Plato. *The Republic*. (B. Jowett, Ed. and Trans.) New York: Modern Library, 1935.

Plummer, S., Baer, D. M., & Le Blanc, J. M. Functional considerations in the use of procedural timeout and an effective alternative. *Journal of Applied Behavior Analysis*, 1977, **10**, 689–706.

Polirstok, S. R., & Greer, R. D. Remediation of mutually aversive interaction between a problem student and four teachers by training the student in reinforcement techniques. *Journal of Applied Behavior Analysis*, 1977, **10**, 707–716.

Premack, D. Reinforcement theory. In D. Levine (Ed.), *Nebraska Symposium on Motivation: 1965*. Lincoln: University of Nebraska Press, 1965.

Rickert, D. C., & Morrey, R. S. Parent training in precise behavior management with mentally retarded children. Final report, U. S. Office of Education, Project No. 9-8-016, January 1972.

Rimm, D. C., & Masters, J. C. *Behavior therapy.* New York: Academic Press, 1974.

Robins, L. N. *Deviant children grow up: A sociological and psychiatric study of sociopathic personality.* Baltimore: Williams & Wilkins, 1966.

Rousseau, J. J. *Émile.* (B. Foxley, Ed. and Trans.) London: J. M. Dent, 1911. (Originally published, 1762.)

Sherman, T. M., & Cormier, W. H. An investigation of the influence of student behavior on teacher behavior. *Journal of Applied Behavior Analysis,* 1974, **7**, 11–22.

Spock, B. *Dr. Spock talks with mothers.* Boston: Houghton Mifflin, 1961.

Steuer, F. B., Applefield, J. M., & Smith, R. Televised aggression and the interpersonal aggression of preschool children. *Journal of Experimental Child Psychology,* 1971, **11**, 442–447.

Sulzer, B., & Mayer, G. R. *Behavior modification procedures for school personnel.* Hinsdale, Ill.: Dryden Press, 1972.

Tharp, R. G., & Wetzel, R. J. *Behavior modification in the natural environment.* New York: Academic Press, 1969.

Tyler, V. O., Jr., & Brown, G. D. The use of swift, brief isolation as a group control device for institutionalized delinquents. *Behavior Research and Therapy,* 1967, **5**, 1–9.

Vukelich, R., & Hake, D. F. Reduction of dangerously aggressive behavior in a severely retarded resident through a combination of positive reinforcement procedures. *Journal of Applied Behavior Analysis,* 1971, **4**, 215–225.

Wahler, R. G. Deviant child behavior within the family: Developmental speculations and behavior change strategies. In H. Leitenberg (Ed.), *Handbook of behavior modification and behavior therapy.* Englewood Cliffs, New Jersey: Prentice-Hall, 1976.

Wahler, R. G., Winkel, G. H., Peterson, R. F., & Morrison, D. C. Mothers as behavior therapists for their own children. *Behavior Research and Therapy,* 1965, **3**, 113–124.

Ward, M. H., & Baker, B. L. Reinforcement therapy in the classroom. *Journal of Applied Behavior Analysis,* 1968, **1**, 323–328.

White, G. D., Nielsen, G., & Johnson, S. M. Timeout duration and the suppression of deviant behavior in children. *Journal of Applied Behavior Analysis,* 1972, **5**, 111–120.

Williams, C. D. The elimination of tantrum behavior by extinction procedures. *Journal of Abnormal and Social Psychology,* 1959, **59**, 269.

Wolf, M. M., Risley, T. R., & Mees, H. Application of operant conditioning procedures to the behavior problems of an autistic child. *Behavior Research and Therapy,* 1964, **1**, 305–312.

Zeilberger, J., Sampen, S. E., & Sloane, H. N., Jr. Modification of a child's behavior problems in the home with the mother as therapist. *Journal of Applied Behavior Analysis,* 1968, **1**, 47–53.

Chapter 2
Negotiation and Contracting*
Joan E. Broderick, Jerry M. Friedman, and Edward G. Carr

violence is the last refuge of the incompetent.

—Isaac Asimov, *Foundation*

The terms "negotiation" and "contracting" are usually associated with business deals, management-labor disputes, and government treaties. But the processes of negotiation and contracting are a part of any relationship between people who have to work, play, or live together. The negotiation may not be labeled as such, and the contracts may not be explicit, but they are both nonetheless part of everyone's daily lives.

Training in negotiation skills and contracting has recently become part of the psychotherapy process in working with distressed relationships, particularly among clinicians with a behavioral orientation. The primary purpose of training in these skills is to provide individuals with a means to ease and to resolve conflict between themselves. Problems between married persons and between adolescents and their parents are the most common situations in which negotiation training and contracting are implemented. This chapter will focus primarily on marital therapy as the context for these techniques, since marital distress is one of the three most common reasons that people seek therapy and because the research is well established in this area (Prochaska and Prochaska, 1978).

*The authors wish to acknowledge the thoughtful comments and suggestions offered on this chapter by Dr. Hillary Turkewitz.

The term aggression is not typically associated with marriage. In recent years, however, violence in the family has been attracting increased attention and concern. Estimates of the rate of physical abuse of women by their husbands range from 30 percent (Straus, 1978) up to as high as 50 percent (Walker, 1979). Among the homicides committed annually in the United States, 13 percent involve husbands or wives killing their spouses (Ohrenstein, 1977). Many more spouses suffer nonfatal injury which often results in permanent damage, such as blinding or disfiguration.

Physical violence is the most extreme expression of conflict in marriage. Less dramatic expressions of aggression, however, are evident in almost every marriage at one time or other and characterize most distressed relationships. Aggression has been defined in the literature on assertion training as expressing thoughts, feelings, and beliefs in an inappropriate way which violates the rights of others (Lange and Jakubowski, 1976). The goal of aggression is domination. The aggressor often attempts to achieve this goal by humiliating and threatening others. The aggression observed by marital therapists frequently takes the form of verbal insults, sarcasm, and name calling. These interchanges can be extremely heated and at times stop just short of physical violence. Alternatively, therapists may see "passive" aggressive actions such as ignoring or "forgetfulness." Therefore, although aggression is a term which is not very much a part of marital therapists' vocabulary, the concept is indeed fundamental to marital issues.

In this chapter we describe the conditions in society and the characteristics of marriage which make this relationship susceptible to conflict. We outline the development of marital therapy, negotiation training, and contracting as therapeutic interventions. We present an overview of relevant research in the area and a detailed discussion of negotiation and contracting as they are currently used. The chapter concludes with discussions of clinical considerations which frequently arise when implementing these techniques in a comprehensive treatment program.

BACKGROUND

While there has always been interest in and concern for marriage among clinicians and researchers, it has only been in the last 40 years that a separate specialty has emerged to work with couples in distressed marriages. After World War II, marital therapy began to progress rapidly. This was most likely due to the postwar upsurge in divorce and separation. During this era, psychoanalysis was the dominant approach to therapy in this country and marital therapy was no exception to this trend. Much early marital therapy was actually *concurrent* therapy in which the therapist saw each spouse individually. This form of therapy remained the most widely used form throughout the 1950s. The practice of seeing both spouses together, known as *conjoint* marital therapy, became increasingly popular in the 1960s and 1970s (Haley, 1963; Satir, 1965; Watson, 1963). The use of conjoint marital therapy with a primary focus on the marital relationship, rather than on the individuals, has helped to distinguish marriage therapists as a separate group within the therapeutic community (Olson, 1970). Additional approaches to marital therapy that have been developed include the use of cotherapy teams to work with the couple (Greene & Solomon, 1963; Masters & Johnson, 1970), and group therapy for couples (Cookerly, 1973; Sager, 1976). In the 1960s, with the increasing popularity of behavior therapy, behavioral techniques began to be applied to marital dysfunctions. Behavior therapy, using a social learning model of marital interaction, introduced such concepts as contingency contracting and negotiation training to marital therapy (Stuart, 1969).

From a behavioral point of view, the marital relationship can most simply be conceptualized as a series of reciprocal sequences of behavior and resultant consequences, in which each person's behavior is affected and influenced by the other's behavior. Each spouse provides consequences or reinforcements which may be positive (rewarding) or negative (punitive). A distressed relationship is one in which there are few positive outcomes available for each partner (Stuart, 1969), and/or too many negative outcomes. Since the behavior of each spouse is constantly influencing and controlling the behavior of the other, it is important to view the marital partners as an interdependent system. Behavior of one member of the marital dyad can only be understood in terms of the behavior of the other member. One advantage of a behavioral conceptualization is its simplicity in dealing primarily with objective, observable behavior.

In 1959, Thibaut & Kelley had a dramatic impact on behavioral marital therapy when they published their classic work, *The Social Psychology of Groups*. They presented a model of social interaction that has become known as equity theory. It stipulates that social units (individuals, dyads, etc.) will seek to maximize their rewards or benefits while trying to minimize costs, and that the exchange will follow a pattern of reciprocity such that equilibrium in rewards received by each party is maintained. Upsetting this equilibrium leads to distress, and attempts to bring the exchange back to homeostasis will be initiated (Walster, Walster, & Berscheid, 1978).

Coercion is one of the most commonly observed forms of inducing a return to equilibrium in a disrupted marital system (Patterson & Reid,

1970). When one spouse perceives his or her own input into the relationship to be greater than the partner's input, distress can occur and compensatory outputs are often demanded by the "short-changed" spouse. The need to demand rewards is viewed as a breakdown in the functioning of the system because it implies the partner's reluctance to provide the rewards freely. The partner is likely to resist extraction of rewards by coercive means and may attempt to punish the "demander" for trying to do so. Rewards are often obtained when the partner finally gives in and provides the reward in order to terminate the salient aversive stimuli generated by the "demanding" spouse.

A simple example of the coercive process is as follows: The wife expects her husband to clean out the flower-bed for her, but notices that two weekends have gone by without anything being done. She reflects on the fact that she cleans the house, does the laundry, and cooks on a daily basis, yet her husband will not even spend a few hours doing the flower-bed for her. She feels exploited and unrewarded for her contributions to the relationship. This perceived inequity is stressful and incites the wife to begin demanding that her husband work on the flower-bed immediately. He knows that unless he complies, he will be subject to her anger and nagging for the rest of the afternoon. He is also aware that unless her demands are met, there will be no possibility of sexual interaction between them that evening because she will be in a bad mood. Therefore, he finally goes out and works on the flower-bed feeling angry toward his wife for turning the issue into a sour affair. Furthermore, his motivation stems from avoidance of negative consequences, rather than from a desire to exchange positive behavior for his wife's inputs.

It should be noted that equity theory implies the maintenance of homeostasis of both positive and negative inputs. In the above example, though the wife now feels that she has produced equity by finally getting her husband to do the flower-bed, her husband perceives her as having been demanding and bitchy. His system has been thrown out of equilibrium by the introduction of these negative behaviors by his wife, and he is likely to reciprocate with other demands and critical comments.

The appeal of equity theory to behaviorally oriented marriage theorists is that it provides a framework for conceptualizing the whole spectrum of marital functioning and is suggestive of the process which produces distress from happy or adjusted relationships. A good relationship is produced when each spouse is willing to provide his or her partner with rewards that are equal in value to the rewards received. The introduction of negative behaviors by a spouse will cause the partner to resort to coercive means of obtaining rewards and to reciprocate the negative behaviors.

Since the integration of operant and equity theories, described most notably by Stuart (1969), a growing literature has developed which attests to the utility of this model of marital relations. Stuart outlined what he labeled an "operant interpersonal" treatment for couples, which was a set of techniques based upon the integration of operant and equity theories as well as training in communication. Stuart assumes that at any given time, the marriage relationship represents the best of available alternatives for the couple, the best balance between mutual rewards and costs. In well-functioning relationships, partners willingly exchange positive behavior. In distressed marriages, a change is made in the reinforcement system. Each spouse tries to coerce positive reinforcement from his or her partner while at the same time minimizing the cost to him or herself. Behavioral interventions attempt to reverse this pattern by helping the couple to negotiate more constructive styles of relating and to resolve conflict. The goal is to help the marriage partners regain positive reinforcement value for each other and to eliminate coercive strategies for procuring the reinforcement.

Behavior therapy for couples is based on the assumption that positive strategies should be used to promote change if conflict and distress are to be minimized. Although behavior therapy employs techniques such as negotiation training and contracting, the therapy is much more than a mere collection of techniques. A thorough assessment that examines the idiosyncratic learning history of each couple, dictates individualized interventions.

REVIEW OF RESEARCH

The majority of research on behavioral contracting involves two major types of formal contracting. The *Quid Pro Quo* (tit for tat) contract provides for each person's behavior change to be contingent on a particular change in their partner's behavior. In the *Good Faith* contract, behavior change is rewarded usually by something other than the partner's behavior. These two forms will be described in detail in the following sections.

The efficacy of behavioral contracting in marital therapy has been demonstrated in a number of studies in the past decade (see Jacobson & Martin, 1976; Jacobson, 1978a). Some of the earlier reports were based upon clinical trials without the use of control groups. Stuart (1969) instituted *quid pro quo* contracting with four distressed couples. He had each of his couples record the frequencies of the two targeted behaviors throughout therapy and found that the contracting resulted in satisfactory increases in both which were maintained at follow-ups obtained 12 and 24 months after therapy ended.

Weiss, Hops, & Patterson (1973) conducted a study with ten distressed couples which examined the effects of a "Good Faith" contracting program which also included communication training in the form of negotiation training and problem solving. Though contracting was not the only procedure and a control group was not used, significant pre- to posttreatment changes were observed in both communication and targeted behaviors.

A "reciprocity counseling" program was designed and evaluated by Azrin, Naster, and Jones (1973) with 12 distressed couples. They assumed that discord was the result of nonreciprocated reinforcement. They therefore focused on teaching the couples operant reinforcement principles first in theory and then more specifically as it related to their marriages. Gradually, requests for change in each spouse's behavior were introduced and eventually evolved into the negotiation of *quid pro quo* contracts. The reciprocity counseling intervention was quite brief, lasting only four weeks, but produced significantly more improvement in overall marital satisfaction and in specific areas of the relationship than the four weeks of "catharsis-type" counseling which preceded it. The investigators reported significant improvements on their outcome measures for 11 of the 12 couples involved in this study.

In one of the first well-controlled studies of behavioral marital therapy, Jacobson (1977) treated five distressed couples with a combination of communication training and behavior contracting, while another group of five distressed couples served as an untreated control group. Comparisons of treated and untreated couples on global satisfaction and specific areas of marital satisfaction documented the effectiveness of the interventions. A follow-up 12 months later found that the improvements in the treated group had been maintained. Jacobson (1978b) followed this up in a second study using a larger number of couples and a nonspecific treatment group in addition to a no-treatment control group. He found that the 16 couples in the two behavioral communication and contracting groups improved significantly more than those in the nonspecific treatment group on two measures, and that all three treatment groups improved more than the no-treatment group on a third measure. The comparison between the two behavioral groups, involving the two forms of contracting, resulted in the finding of no discernible difference in effectiveness between the two procedures.

Finally, Turkewitz (1977) examined the effects of communication training alone versus communication training plus behavioral contingency management using informal, written contracts. The results indicated that the two treated groups improved equally, and this improvement was greater than that observed in an untreated control group on most of the self-report indices of marital satisfaction. No differences, however, were detected at posttreatment among the three groups in their communication as measured on a problem-solving task. Quite interestingly, Turkewitz found that younger couples improved more when they were in the group that had both behavioral and communication components, whereas older couples improved more when they were assigned to the communication only group. This interaction of age with treatment strategy is one of the first instances of a guideline for differential application of behavioral interventions.

There is also some evidence of the efficacy of negotiation and behavioral contracting in improving the relationships between parents and their young or adolescent children. By using a combination of negotiation skills training, contingency management, and behavioral contracting approaches, Alexander and Parsons (1973) treated delinquent adolescents (ages 13–16) and their families. They compared the behavioral therapy package with client-centered family therapy, psychodynamic family therapy, and a no-treatment control. The behavioral treatment was found to produce more communication among family members, as well as a lower recidivism rate than any of the comparison groups. Follow-up showed that only 30 percent of the siblings of children in the behavioral group were referred to the juvenile court system compared with from 40–63 percent in the other groups, indicating a significant preventative effect.

Martin (1977) used a treatment that involved contingency management, communication, and negotiation of problem issues for persistent parent-child interaction problems of first- through fifth-grade children. A control group received reading materials on the same topics with no direct therapeutic contact. The treatment group showed significant improvement relative to this control group, with six-month follow-up data indicating sustained effects.

Kifer, Lewis, Green, and Phillips (1974) taught negotiation skills to three parent-child dyads and found that the families showed substantial increments in negotiation behaviors and in the number of agreements reached. Robin, O'Leary, Kent, Foster, and Prinz (1977) investigated the effect of training in problem-solving skills on the communication patterns of mother-young adolescent (ages 10–14) dyads, and showed impressive changes in the use of these problem-solving behaviors as a result of the intervention.

There have also been several studies examining the use of contingency contracting interventions with adolescents. Stuart and Tripodi (1973) compared a group of delinquent and predelinquent teenagers and their families using a contingency contracting intervention with a control group composed of families who refused treatment. The experimental group demonstrated significantly greater improvement in school attendance and grades than the control group. Methodological problems associated with the use of this type of control group, however, make it difficult to interpret the results. In contrast, Weathers and Lieberman (1975) worked with an older adolescent population (ages 14–17) and their parents using an intervention consisting of a session of contract negotiation and two sessions of training in negotiation and communication skills. The authors reported an extraordinarily high drop-out rate and demonstrated virtually no change in the behavior observed at home or in recidivism. They concluded that contracting may not be a viable approach for this population. The extremely short intervention, however, rather than the method itself, could be responsible for their lack of success. Blechman and Olson (1976) used a game format to help families arrive at a negotiated contract. They used single-subject ABA designs with four single-parent families and showed that during the game playing, there were significantly more on-task and fewer off-task verbalizations in discussing a problem than during negotiations without the game. In addition, ratings of unstructured discussions of problems revealed significant gains in on-task behavior from pre- to posttherapy testing, while no decrease in off-task behavior was found.

This brief review of research provides support for the utility of therapy interventions which use systematic negotiation training and contracting with couples and other family groups. With few exceptions, studies have combined both interventions into one treatment package. Consequently, it is difficult to determine the unique effects of each component. The natural sequence of negotiation training to contracting makes it unlikely that contracting would occur without negotiation preceding it. There certainly are, however, instances in clinical work in which formal contracting is not indicated, but where communication and negotiation training are definitely called for. Given the predominant use of informal, rather than formal contracts, research should evaluate this form of the intervention. Moreover, research endeavors in the future could be fruitfully focused upon examining the specific effects of the various skills taught in communication and negotiation training.

The remainder of this chapter focuses on the issues and circumstances that make marriage prone to conflict, as well as therapeutic interventions with a particular emphasis on negotiation and contracting.

MARRIAGE IS PRONE TO CONFLICT

While marriage may be one of the most important relationships that people enter into in their lifetime, it is also one of the more risky and, for some, one of the least satisfying. The estimated United States nationwide divorce rate ranges from 33 to 50 percent (Glick & Norton,

1973). Lederer and Jackson (1968) found that 80 percent of the couples they interviewed in a study of marriage reported having considered divorce at some time in their relationship. For many couples, marriage turns out to be much more of a struggle than they ever expected. In this section, we discuss some of the reasons for the development of this struggle.

The first phase of a relationship usually finds both partners trying to please each other, engaging in many enjoyable activities together, and being able to provide pleasure for each other by their presence alone. This is a period of sexual and other kinds of novelty and discovery. Compared with later years, there are few financial decisions or child-rearing responsibilities. Under these circumstances, the need for negotiation skills is minimal. An unfortunate expectation often develops that the future will continue to be as mutually rewarding with comparably little effort.

The honeymoon, however, does eventually come to an end for some couples quite early in the relationship, and spouses are forced to confront one another on a wide variety of issues. As novelty wears off and as differences in philosophy, goals, priorities, and interactional styles become more salient, the "other side" of each person comes into view. Spouses discover imperfections in each other and annoying habits and attitudes. As these displeasures mount, satisfaction decreases and conflict increases.

Different needs for intimacy, independence, affection, conversation, shared activities, and social contacts emerge and contribute to marital conflict and stress. As the length of their relationship increases, couples often find that interactions and activities that had once been pleasing have become boring or stale. Rather than recognizing this as somewhat inevitable and working to expand interactions into new areas that can provide novelty, many couples tend to see differences as catastrophic, as an indication that they are not right for each other, and that their relationship is doomed. If they are not skilled in dealing with issues constructively, and if they do not attempt to resolve emerging conflict, then there may be a tendency to store up resentment, making it increasingly difficult to resolve *any* issue as time goes by.

The romantic vision of marriage has been grossly overemphasized in the mass media. The idealized view of families with free-flowing warmth, open exchanges of affection, and happy endings to all conflicts invites dissatisfaction with one's own family situation. Individuals are socialized to expect that their own family will resemble this ideal. This, coupled with the tendency to make comparisons with the early days of their own relationship when it may have seemed closer to this ideal, often promotes a sense of despair. Sometimes it is expressed as no longer "being in love," as "losing the magic," or as vague discontent.

In addition to the inevitable disillusionment that many couples experience as the marriage grows older, the very structure of contemporary marriage helps foster conflict. Clearly defined roles of "husband" and "wife," though not necessarily resulting in happiness, help to promote stability. It is not unusual to find couples who have been married for a long period of time, but who interact in a very limited manner and never really get to know one another. They go their separate ways and interact, not as unique individuals, but in terms of their respective roles. These couples often do not show overt signs of distress and may describe themselves as bored rather than unhappy. It is when people begin to question their marital roles and the rights and responsibilities associated with them, or are faced with a change in the family system, that marital distress can become overt. The emergence of the women's movement and parallel changes in men's roles in society have encouraged women to be equal in the marriage partnership. To achieve this equity requires that the standard rules of marital relationships change or become less clearly and less simply defined. Within an equal power structure, rights and responsibilities are open to discussion, compromise is necessary, and consensus is required for decision making. As couples' relationships continue over time and become more complex, rules are inevitably established. These rules may be explicit or implicit, but they cannot be avoided. Whenever the couple completes an interaction, a precedent is established for how a similar situation should be handled in the future. As the list of rules grows, conflict can develop over who makes the rules, exactly what the rules are, and how to enforce the rules. This process requires flexibility and skills which couples may not have available to them.

As roles within the marriage change to incorporate more independence, jealousy can also become a problem. Many people enter marriage expecting it to fulfill their dependency needs and to give them security, while at the same time they seek personal growth and independence in their nonmarital relationships. With greater personal independence, there are more opportunities for the actions of the spouse to be viewed as disloyal. Career opportunities, friendships outside the marriage, and any other environmental factor which may compete with the spouse for the partner's attention may be a source of conflict and distress. As more rewards are present in the outside environment, more are required within the relationship to maintain it as a competitive alternative.

Changing needs and goals across the family life cycle also require an ability to adjust and to compromise. The birth of children (particularly the first), problems associated with middle age, children leaving the home, and retirement all require major changes in the way people structure their lives and their relationships.

We see that the complex, changing demands over time of the marital relationship are a challenge often inadequately met by couples. The media, particularly television and men's and women's magazines, tend to present marriage and family relations in an extremely unrealistic manner. Marital conflict is rarely seen in any form that is comparable to the personal experience of couples in the audience. And even when conflict is portrayed, the method of resolution that is modeled is so often superficial and it can rarely be applied successfully to the couple's own situation. Disillusionment, disappointment, and unhappiness are natural when couples encounter problems for whose effective resolution they do not have the necessary skills.

For other couples, actual disagreements do not have to be present in order for conflict to be experienced. We frequently see how poor communication can produce conflict by itself. Misinterpretation of explanations and failure to explain can lead couples to believe that differences exist when, instead, the problem lies in their communication. Unsuccessful attempts to be assertive can escalate into aggressive behavior which is met with resentment, anger, and retaliation. Aggression is often the last resort in an attempt to have an impact on the spouse who seems to be insensitive or not responsive.

Individuals' unique perceptions of the actions of their spouse, the attributions they make concerning these actions, and their attitude regarding accommodation and compromise all help to determine the level of conflict in a relationship. A distorted view of the spouse, which usually involves generalizing a small number of negative behaviors of the partner to all aspects of the "personality" of the partner, is one of the most common problems. Under these circumstances, when the partner does behave in a desirable way, the behavior is conceptualized by the spouse as an exception to the rule. For example, if a husband clears the desk in the study, his wife may view this as a response to some external pressure such as the expectation of guests and will continue to think of him as a "slob." Likewise, occasional sexual responsiveness by the wife may be accounted for by the husband as due to his wife's having had a drink earlier, and he may continue to think of her in general, as a "cold fish." Thus, broad, trait-like generalizations based primarily on the negative actions of the spouse stand in the way of accurate perceptions of the complex behavioral repertoire of the spouse which includes both positive and negative behavior.

It is clear that the diverse skills required for continued satisfaction as relationships mature and become more complex are not explicitly taught in our society. Couples need skills to maintain good sexual relationships, and to interact effectively in household, financial, and child-management areas. Spouses also need to be able to express happy and angry feelings toward each other, to provide understanding and support, and to be able to solve problems and negotiate change. When faced with the inevitable differences which occur as marriages progress, couples are usually forced to generate their own methods of resolving these differences; clarifying miscommunications is often unsuccessful and can induce hurt to build up over time, which leaves long-lasting scars. Therapy can provide the training required to learn to increase positive behaviors and to negotiate and arrive at acceptable contracts.

INCREASED POSITIVE BEHAVIORS

Before negotiation and contracting can be used effectively as therapeutic interventions, a number of requirements must be satisfied. Most importantly, both partners must be motivated and trusting enough to enter into this activity. Negotiation training requires that each individual be able to reveal how they feel, what their needs are, and how their partner's actions affect them. People may sometimes be afraid to reveal such information to their spouse because they fear criticism or ridicule. They may also be afraid that revealing such information is a sign of weakness and that the information may be used against them at a later time. To the therapist, such lack of trust is an indicator of a poor prognosis for negotiation training in particular.

Another difficulty that may arise in attempting to do negotiation and contracting is that some individuals may believe that any efforts they make toward trying to communicate their needs and desires will fall upon deaf ears. This belief is based on what they consider to be past evidence that their requests or demands were not heeded or even attended to. The therapist must overcome this form of resistance so that the couple can begin to have a dialogue that will lead to effective negotiation and contracting. A third problem encountered is that the very subjects about which the couple needs to negotiate can also be the subjects which trigger enormous amounts of anger, hostility, and fear based on past experience with discussions of these topics. What frequently happens when these topics are brought up for discussion is that the emotional responses are so strong that meaningful dialogue becomes impossible. Even though behavioral contracting ensures that each person receives repayment for behaviors contributed to the relationship, there is an emotional risk in becoming reinvolved in the relationship and deciding to work to make it better. Thus, emotions run very high with both spouses being quite sensitive.

It is important to recognize that the marriage relationship itself carries with it a whole set of implicit contracts that form the bond holding husband and wife together. When almost any marital disagreement is examined closely, it becomes apparent that beneath the anger, the hurt, and the hostility, one or both people feel taken for granted, uncared for, and unsupported. These are violations of the basic implicit contract with which most people enter the marital relationship. Most people enter marriage with the expectation that they will receive, among other things, love, companionship, support, and a sense of importance. For distressed couples, this basic implicit contract has been breached.

All of these negative feelings that have accumulated during the development of distress may require more than a normal amount of positive behavior to counteract. Before negotiation and contracting are begun, we often introduce as a first step an intervention which does not require as much skill training and as much trust, but which serves to increase positive behavior in general. We do this by introducing our adaptation of what Weiss et al. (1973) have labeled "love days" and Stuart (1976) has called "caring days." Since we believe that this is a fundamental technique of great value in marital therapy, we will explain it in detail.

The first step in the procedure is to work with the couple, helping them to generate a list of behaviors which indicate caring. We give them several guidelines to work with in choosing items for the list. First, we encourage them to generate items that are easily performed, are natural, and do not take a great deal of time. Second, items are to be phrased positively rather than negatively. For example, an item such as, "I want her to stop nagging me!" is not acceptable. "Compliment me on completed jobs" would be a positive rephrasing. A third guideline is that each of the items be completely unambiguous; that is, if the therapist were sitting in the client's living room at the time the behavior occurred, it would be clear to him or her that the behavior had transpired. For example, an item such as, "I want him to be nice to me" is unacceptable since "nice" may mean different things to husband and wife. Instead, the therapist would encourage an itemization of particular things that represent "nice" to the requesting spouse. For example:

Therapist: Can you give me another item that would indicate that you feel cared for?

Wife: I would like him to be nice to me more often.

Therapist: What do you mean by nice?

Wife: Well, you know, he's always so nasty to me, I just want him to be nicer than he is.

Therapist: What particular things could he do so that you would think that he was being nice?

Wife: Well, if he would help me clear the table after supper without me having to ask him, that's what I mean by being nice. Or, if he didn't stick his nose in the newspaper as soon as he came home, that would be nice.

Therapist: So one thing we can add to your list that would make you feel cared for would be your husband helping to clear the table after dinner without being asked. Why don't we put that one down? The second item you mentioned was for him to stop burying his nose in the newspaper after dinner. Is there some way you can phrase that in terms of something he could do rather than shouldn't do?

Wife: Well, it wouldn't hurt if he talked to me a little bit after supper.

Therapist: How long is a little bit? How much time would you like him to spend talking to you so that you would feel cared for?

Wife: Well . . . I do have to get the dishes done. So, I don't have too much time myself. . . . I guess about ten minutes.

Therapist: Okay. So another item we can put down on your list that would help you feel cared for is for your husband to spend ten minutes talking to you after supper, before picking up the newspaper. Right?

Wife: Yeah, that would be good.

Therapist: How about if we put it down as just—talk to spouse for ten minutes? In that way, he could feel free to do that at other times as well.

A fourth guideline is to exclude from the list items that are particularly troublesome to the couple at that particular time. For example, if one of the areas of strife or disagreement involves frequency of sexual interaction, unacceptable items would involve having more sex. It should be clear that the purpose of caring days is not to solve the couple's problems, but to help create an environment that will enable them to work constructively on these problems. Consequently, it is important not to endanger this first step by introducing items which are at the core of the couple's conflict. An additional guideline is that items should primarily be behavior directed from spouse to spouse. Frequently, a wife may say, "He can show me he cares by moving the lawn," or a husband may say, "She can show me she cares by taking the car in for servicing." Such items should be kept to a minimum because, while they may represent caring in an indirect manner, they do not involve each spouse having a directly positive impact on the other.

A final guideline is to be sure that those items listed can be performed on a regular basis. For example, "Send me a card on my birthday" is an unacceptable item because it can only be performed once a year. The majority of items should be able to be performed on a daily basis, and no item should included which cannot occur at least once a week.

People frequently have difficulty conceptualizing being cared for in terms of these small everyday behaviors, and frequently it takes considerable skill on the part of the therapist to help them generate such a list. Themes which seem to recur from couple to couple in generating their list include items that involve touching, such as holding hands, hugging, kissing; items that involve help and consideration such as helping with the dishes and putting the children to bed; items that involve shared interests such as watching television together, taking a walk, or going to a basketball game; and items that indicate personal attention such as complimenting appearance, clothing, and accomplishments. A typical list of items can be found in Figure 2.1.

There are several problems involved in generating a list that is acceptable to both parties. These need to be closely attended to by the therapist. First, it is important that both partners contribute to the list approximately equally. This may be particularly difficult when one spouse is prolific in the generation of items while the other is reticent. This may be an indication that one of the spouses is either not ready for or feels reluctant to perform caring behaviors, or one spouse feels so threatened by the other that he or she has difficulty asking for caring behaviors. It is important for the therapist to make clear to both spouses that the appearance of an item on the list does not require that it be

1. Kiss spouse
2. Hold hands
3. Call just to say hello
4. Use pet name
5. Give compliment to spouse about appearance
6. Compliment spouse about something they've done
7. Compliment spouse in front of other people
8. Ask about how day went
9. Take a walk together
10. Ask spouse to go out for a drink
11. Bring spouse breakfast in bed
12. Talk together in bed
13. Go to bed at same time
14. Switch to other person's T.V. program
15. Make arrangements for babysitter
16. Prepare special dinner
17. Give a body massage
18. Sit next to spouse watching T.V.
19. Go shopping with spouse
20. Say, "I love you."
21. Shave beard on weekends
22. Make arrangements for a "date"
23. Talk pleasantly to in-laws
24. Help put kids to bed
25. Talk about fun times in past
26. Discuss future plans together
27. Bring little gift or card for no particular occasion
28. Prepare snack, coffee
29. Take a shower together
30. Talk about something important to you
31. Wink at spouse
32. Play *Scrabble* together
33. Look nice at dinner (makeup, wear shoes)
34. Help with business papers
35. Take complete phone messages
36. Ask what's bothering spouse
37. Keep kids away when practicing piano
38. Help with dinner clean up
39. Stay awake through 11 o' clock news
40. Watch spouse bowl in league

Fig. 2.1. Illustration of "caring days" list.

performed. This encourages both spouses to feel perfectly free to list items even if they feel their spouse will not do them or will not like them. The couple is told to view the list as a menu from which they can then select particular things to do.

It is our practice to keep working with the couple until a list of approximately 40 items has been generated. Lists with fewer items tend to be exhausted quickly and do not provide a sufficiently broad range of items for selection. The items are always listed in a manner so that they can apply to either spouse. For example, if the wife says, "I would like my husband to help me clear the table after dinner," the item would be listed as "Help clear table." It is also important for the therapist to guide the couple into including some more romantic items on their list. These might include items such as taking a shower together, having a candle-light dinner, or simply saying, "I love you."

One of the reasons for generating a single list for both spouses is that we have found, much to the surprise of the couple, that they have many items in common. We use a legal-size pad and have the clients cut out the center of the entire pad, except the last sheet, leaving strips of paper on each side of the center sheet. The items generated are written on this last sheet, the "tabs" remaining from the cut-out sheets are used for check marks, one side for the husband, the other side for the wife, one sheet per day (see Figure 2.2).

Once the list has been generated, the spouses are instructed to perform anywhere from five to ten items a day (an exact number should be stipulated by the therapist). At first, each spouse is responsible for keeping a record of which he or she did by checking them off on the list. There is no restriction against doing the same item more than once in a given day, as long as the total number of checks for the day equals the amount specified by the therapist. The spouses are instructed to leave the chart in a mutually convenient place (such as a bedroom dresser) and to make sure they check off items each day. They are instructed not to discuss their spouse's check marks even when they do not recall receiving what their partner checked. Each partner is responsible only to the therapist for completing the specified number of behaviors. In contrast to both types of contracts which will be discussed later, there are no contingencies involved for completion of the caring items.

After two or three weeks of performing and self-recording caring behaviors, the therapist instructs the husband and wife to record what the spouse did rather than what each did him or herself. It is possible for spouses to remind each other of particular behaviors they performed, but if the partner doesn't recall it, it does not get checked. Only those behaviors each spouse is aware of having received are checked. This

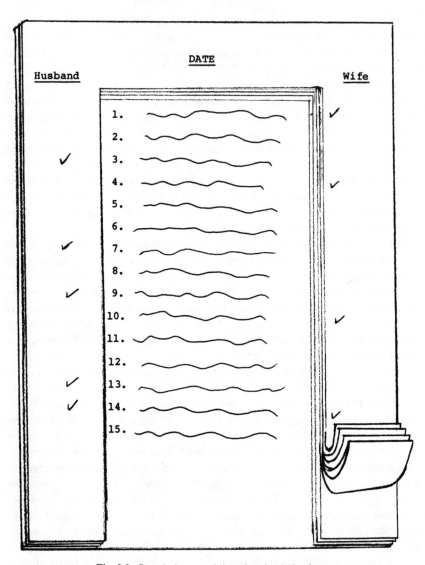

Fig. 2.2. Sample layout of list of caring behaviors.

procedure heightens each spouse's awareness of the positive expressions by their partner.

After a week, we add one more feature. At bedtime, both spouses leave a note on the partner's nightstand expressing thanks for the caring item they enjoyed the most that day. After several weeks, we usually tell the couples that they may stop keeping records, but that the activities should continue just the same. The goal is to terminate the formal aspects of this technique before they become boring.

With many couples, caring days is an extremely effective intervention. When a husband and wife follow explicit instructions to behave in a very positive, caring, concerned way toward one another, then it is difficult for them to continue feeling negatively toward and rejected by their mate. In other words, *cognitive dissonance* is created. They are behaving in a positive way, while presumably feeling negatively. These conflicting behaviors and feelings, according to dissonance theory, need to be reconciled. Because the positive behaviors are mandated by the therapist and therefore cannot be eliminated, one way to reduce the dissonance is for the couple to reduce their negative feelings toward each other.

Often when people come to therapy expressing a great deal of anger, this anger is actually an "umbrella" feeling, covering other feelings such as fear, frustration, or hurt. By using caring days, some of the anger dissipates and there is the opportunity to bring to the surface some of these other feelings which have had little opportunity to emerge.

Caring days also serves as a solid foundation for negotiation and contracting. From the outset, when the couple has to list at least 40 caring behaviors, they begin to make explicit to one another the types of behaviors which will meet their individual needs. This may be the first time that a couple actually articulates these needs to one another in such detail. As caring days are used by the couple over the course of a few weeks, they begin to understand very clearly how they can be most effective in displaying their care to one another and to understand what things they can do to meet the needs of the other person. They now have at their disposal very explicit behavioral methods of showing care. To the extent that caring days helps diffuse anger and resentment, the couple can begin to develop the skills necessary for effective negotiation.

NEGOTIATION TRAINING

Negotiation is a process by which both spouses generate constructive alternatives to past distressful behavior in an attempt to compromise and reach a consensus. It is a form of conjoint problem solving with each partner learning both to express his or her own requirements and to listen to his or her partner's; to decide which points are open for compromise and which are not; and to arrive at mutually acceptable agreements. Clearly this process can only take place effectively if the couple has good communication skills available and, therefore, the teaching of such skills is a primary element of negotiation training.

A prerequisite to negotiation is the ability to state and communicate one's desires clearly. It is not surprising for a therapist to encounter spouses who are unable to respond to their partner's needs simply because they are unaware of them, or because they cannot understand the reasons underlying the demands being made. A first step in negotiation training is teaching people to reveal *what* they want and *why* they want it. Couples are encouraged to phrase their requests in terms of positive changes as opposed to demanding that negative behavior be stopped. That is, as mentioned above, to suggest what their partners *can* do rather than what they shouldn't do. This form of communication is much more palatable and is therefore more likely to be complied with, and least likely to be met by a defensive response. Spouses are encouraged to be specific so that it is completely clear to their partner exactly what it is they are asking for.

Other strategies of effective communication include responding directly to criticism or complaints, rather than with criticisms of their own, and not interrupting but allowing their spouse to complete a thought before reacting. Keeping the conversation focused on the present or future rather than dwelling on past occurrences and keeping comments focused on observable behavior rather than on inferred motives or character assassinations are valuable rules. Once these rules are explained to the couple, they can practice them in sessions through behavior rehearsal and role playing. By using guided practice, the therapist can provide feedback on how well the skills are being applied in the session, and couples can be instructed to have similar practice sessions at home.

More specifically, a training session would begin with a topic chosen in conjunction with the therapist. The couple is encouraged to interact and discuss this topic using their developing skills. The therapist should interrupt this interaction and help the spouses to pinpoint the destructive statements that contribute to anger and frustration, and to help them generate more productive alternative responses. It is usually best to start with a topic of some concern and of some emotional value for the couple, but not with one that is so emotionally charged as to make it impossible for the participants to concentrate on their newly developing skills. Only when they become more proficient in these communication and problem-solving skills should they proceed to some of the more volatile issues in their relationship.

An obvious prerequisite for effective negotiation is the ability for the couple to understand what each is saying to the other. Therefore, skills they need to develop early are to be able to ask for clarification and elaboration of what their partner is saying and to verify with their partner that they heard the message correctly. One spouse speaks and limits his or her statement to a few sentences, and this is followed by the other spouse summarizing what he or she heard. This summary is a necessary step before the second spouse is allowed to initiate a response of his or her own. The spouses continue to speak to each other alternating speaker and listener roles with the listener reflecting the content of the message. The speaker is always given an opportunity to comment on the accuracy of the reflection and to make corrections when needed before proceeding.

Couples are also taught to express their feelings, particularly negative ones, in a way least likely to promote a defensive response. One of the best ways to do this is to train clients to phrase their statements in a way that describes the impact of their partner's behavior on them, rather than criticizing the behavior itself. Telling their spouse how their behavior makes them feel leaves less room for a defensive response. For example, "I feel hurt when you read the paper at breakfast because it makes me think you don't want to talk to me" is more desirable than "you're always reading the paper and I want you to stop it right now." Often, people need a lot of help expressing feelings and have difficulty differentiating feelings from thoughts. Also important is helping people see the distinction between expressions of feeling and insults. Changing the statement "You are a disgusting slob," to "I feel that you are a disgusting slob" does not change the nature of the statement. But "I feel angry when I find clothing strewn all over the house" conveys the message and is less likely to produce negative feelings in response.

It is not unusual for distressed spouses to feel that it is a futile effort to try to satisfy their partner. The pattern of bitter complaining to one another about their dissatisfactions with rare mention of what they are satisfied with results in the feeling that the partner will always find something wrong and never focus on the positive; for example: "Last week I *did* help by giving the baby a bath before bed, but all you did was complain that I didn't put away the shampoo and powder when I was done. Nothing is ever good enough for you!"

Early in therapy, spouses in a distressed relationship wish to spend a considerable amount of time telling the therapist all the things that are wrong with their mate. This has the dual purpose of venting some of their anger and hostility, as well as trying to enlist the therapist as an ally. Such complaining sessions, however, are usually just replays of what has transpired at home. They rarely provide new information for either spouse. Consequently, they are not a productive use of therapy time since they do not lead to change or growth. In addition, some couples take licence in the therapy session and use the presence of the third party as an opportunity to say particularly spiteful, hurtful things that they would not ordinarily say at home. Some clients may feel that it is part of the therapeutic process to vent their feelings fully. Our goal as therapists is to avoid getting caught up in the couple's negative system of complaining and to help them identify the underlying issues. To do this, we insist early in therapy that couples verbalize those qualities of their partners that they consider positive and explain why they have decided to participate in the difficult process of psychotherapy instead of dissolving their relationship. For those whose initial reaction is that they cannot think of anything positive about their mate, the therapist helps them generate at least three things even if those things are out of their past, rather than their present, relationship together. This exchange of positive statements is something that may not have happened in the relationship for quite a while and has the immediate effect of breaking a long-standing pattern of complaining and counter-complaining. Each person is now faced with the possibility that perhaps the spouse does indeed care.

Once communication training is underway, negotiation training can begin. Negotiation training allows couples to deal with areas of conflict while learning the skills that will then be available for use with future issues. The following is an example of a couple's dialogue in one of the early sessions of communication and negotiation training:

Bob: The thing that really gets me is that she's always running around and spending all this time with the kids and never has two minutes to sit down and talk to me.

Therapist: Tell that to her, not me.

Bob: Okay, I'm just tired of having to spend all of my evenings alone, with you always so busy and always having a million other things to do and not having any time to spend with me.

Alice: How can I sit in front of the television all night with all the things I'm stuck doing and the work I have to do? If you would lift a finger and help out a little bit around the house, maybe I wouldn't be so busy.

Bob: You're just like your mother, you make work for yourself around the house. And another thing, you're always on the kids. You drive them crazy with all your picking and nagging.

Therapist: Let's stop for a moment now and take a look at what's happening. Alice, can you summarize so far what you've heard Bob saying?

Alice: He expects me to just be able to drop whatever I'm doing whenever he wants and spend the whole evening with him. He doesn't appreciate all the time that it takes to take care of the children and just do the normal chores around the house, which he doesn't help out with. (*She turns to Bob*) And you, you just ignore the kids. You know it wouldn't be such a bad idea if once in a while . . .

Therapist: Let's stop here. Notice that the discussion has shifted to the topic of the children and you are no longer talking about what you were originally concerned with. Alice, can you go back and summarize what Bob's original point was?

Alice: He expects me to just be able to drop whatever I'm doing whenever he wants and spend the whole evening with him. He doesn't appreciate all the time that it takes to take care of the children and do all of the normal chores around the house, which he never helps out with.

Therapist: I heard you saying two things just now. The first part of what you said is your summary of what you heard Bob saying. In the second part, you seem to be adding on your reaction to what Bob's saying. Can we hold off with that for a while and just have you summarize what you heard him say?

Alice: Okay. What I said is he expects me to be able to drop whatever I'm doing and spend all my time with him.

Therapist: Is that what you meant to communicate to Alice?

Bob: No, not at all. I don't really expect her to spend all her time with me. I just don't want to be ignored.

Therapist: Well you can see by this short exchange so far that what you are trying to say hasn't gotten across to Alice. One of the reasons that partners sometimes don't hear one another is because they are saying things in a way which makes the other one defensive. And, as a matter of fact, we just saw Alice trying to defend herself a few moments ago. Bob, can you make your point again, but try to phrase it in a way that you think might make Alice more likely to listen. To do that, you might want to remember to try not to be accusatory and to talk about your own feelings and needs.

Bob: I would like it if, in the evenings, you would spend more time with me. I know you have lots of work with the kids and the house, but I count also.

Therapist: Good. Can you explain how you feel when Alice doesn't spend as much time with you as you would like?

Bob: I feel as if everything else counts more than me.

Therapist: But how does that make you feel?

Bob: ... I guess I feel bad because it makes me feel she doesn't care for me.

Therapist: Now Alice, can you just try to summarize what you heard Bob say so far?

Alice: He is saying...

Therapist: Tell him.

Alice: You were saying that you want me to spend more time with you.

Therapist: Did you also hear him say something about how he felt?

Alice: Yeah, he wants me to...

Therapist: To him.

Alice: You want me to spend more time with you in the evening and when I don't, you feel bad because you think it means I don't care for you.

The therapist continues working with the couple in this manner until they reach a point when they are able to express to one another what their real concern is and why it is an issue for them. The therapist's main goal is to help the couple eliminate the broad accusatory statements and to replace them with more specific statements which incorporate the individual's feelings about the issues. It is clear from this dialogue between Bob and Alice that their initial statements evoked defensive, angry reactions. Later in the exchange, when Bob talked only about his desire to have Alice spend time with him in the evening and explained his feelings of being uncared for when she does not, Alice was able to hear him better and did not feel the need to counterattack with her own accusatory statements.

During the above dialogue, the therapist noted another issue that was raised: Alice's desire for Bob to help more around the house and with the kids. Consequently, Bob's desire for Alice to spend more time with him and Alice's desire for Bob to help more around the house can become the basis for negotiation and compromise, once these two issues have been clarified.

The following is a dialogue at a later point in the therapy after Bob and Alice have reached the point where both of these issues have been discussed and clarified, and can now be negotiated:

Therapist: Now I'd like to move on and see what we can do about generating some solutions to the two problems which you have raised. Bob, you've raised the issue of wanting Alice to spend some more time with you in the evening. And Alice, you have indicated your desire to have Bob help with the dishes and getting the children to bed after dinner. Let's try and generate some specific ways in which you might be able to meet each other's needs along these lines.

Alice: If he was willing to give me a hand getting the kids to bed after dinner, then there would be no problem with my having some time to sit with him watching television. The problem with this, though, is that when I have done this in the past, no matter how much time I've spent sitting with him, he always complains when I get up that it isn't enough.

Therapist: Bob, can you summarize what you have just heard Alice say?

Bob: Alice, what I just heard you say is that every time you sit with me, I end up complaining that you haven't spent enough time.

Alice: Right.

Bob: Well, if I didn't say anything about how long you stayed, do you think you would sit with me at all?

Alice: Yes, I would. But you have to understand that I don't like to watch TV as much as you do. I like to read a little before I fall asleep.

Therapist: Bob, when you talk about Alice spending some time watching television with you, how long are you talking about?

Bob: I'd be happy if she would stay for an hour with me.

Therapist: Alice, does an hour seem reasonable to you?

Alice: Yes, so long as I get the help with the kids.

Therapist: O.K. Why don't you explain to Bob exactly what kind of help you're asking for?

Alice: You could take Joey and give him his bath right after dinner, put his pajamas on, and clean up the bathroom when you're done.

The negotiation process thus continues with the therapist helping both parties to clarify their requests in very specific terms. This continues until they reach a point where they are both satisfied with the solutions generated. Once this process has been accomplished on a particular issue, it is possible for the therapist to go back and deal with some of the more difficult specific and general issues that had been raised during the course of the discussions. For example, Bob's earlier statement that Alice behaved in a manner just like her mother would need further exploration as would Alice's feelings that Bob is not satisfied with her attempts to meet his needs.

One of the goals of negotiation training is to help the couple to make explicit the problematic issues between them. Learning to communicate unspoken needs and expectations becomes an integral part of the therapy process. Therefore, one of the effects of negotiation training in its early stages is that it helps make salient the actual differences that exist between the two people. In order to negotiate, one must state one's position. When the differences are fundamental differences in philosophy and value, one or both parties may feel extremely hopeless about the long-term stability of the relationship. One goal of communication and negotiation training is to help each spouse at least understand the other spouse's point of view and accept the legitimacy of their differences.

If people can learn to share their disagreements constructively and to understand each other's point of view (thereby validating each other's feelings), then they may not feel the need to defend their own position at all costs or to exaggerate it in an attempt to have it better understood. Once these basic differences are understood and accepted, and not labeled as indicators of the innate badness of the relationship, it is possible to proceed to the next stage of negotiation. The couple can begin to evaluate which aspects of their positions are most important to them and which are less important and, therefore, negotiable. Of course, there is always the risk that once a couple reaches this point, they will find nothing that is negotiable. It is at this point that couples need to make a decision about what they are willing to give up and how many of their individual needs they are willing to sacrifice for the relationship.

CONTRACTING

Negotiation involves: (1) expressing feelings and requests constructively, (2) reducing and clarifying misunderstandings, and (3) problem solving. These skills often have therapeutic impact in their own right. Contracting is the process in which the constructive alternatives generated during negotiation are reviewed and decisions are made about which will be selected for application. This can often be done informally. When there remain, however, strong differences which cannot be resolved informally, formal contingency contracts may be required. In their most structured form, these contracts are written out and actually signed by each spouse.

As noted earlier, there are two general forms of contingency contracting currently used in behavioral marital therapy. The first is the *quid pro quo* (tit for tat) contract. This contract was first introduced into behavioral marital therapy by Stuart (1969). The contract involves each spouse selecting a set of desired behaviors on the part of the partner. The desired behaviors specified by each spouse are then linked with one another, in a contingent fashion, such that the doing of a behavior by one spouse is contingent upon the completion of a behavior by the other. In this way, each spouse is rewarded for complying with their partner's request by having one of their own requests complied with shortly thereafter. This form of contracting is illustrated in Figure 2.3.

The essential aspect of *quid pro quo* contracts that distinguishes them from other forms of contracting is the explicit linking of one spouse's behavior with his or her partner's behavior. For instance, in this example, if Bob does not clear the dinner table and stack the dishes on a particular evening, then Alice is not required to spend 30 minutes watching television with him. In fact, she must actively avoid spending that time with him so that she does not reward him for noncompliance. Similarly, if Bob's lunch is not prepared for him on the prior evening, then he is not to do the grocery shopping again until Alice has prepared his lunch. The compelling nature of *quid pro quo* contracts is the strong desire of spouses to have their partners comply with their stated requests for certain behaviors. The best way for each spouse to influence the likelihood of such changes is to comply with their spouse's requests in the contract. Moreover, spouses pay the price of noncompliance on their part by contingent noncompliance by their partner.

We, Bob and Alice Jones, agree to abide by the following set of agreements for 14 days beginning at 7 A.M., April 14, 1980 and ending April 28, 1980 at 7 A.M.

Bob agrees to:	*In exchange Alice will:*
1. Clear the dinner table and load the dishwasher each night after dinner.	1. Spend 30 minutes watching television with Bob after she has put the children to bed.
2. Inquire about Alice's day and spend at least five minutes discussing his day each weekday evening.	2. Have Bob's lunch prepared to take to work each weekday morning.
3. Do the grocery shopping for the family once each week.	3. Arrange one "date" with Bob each weekend, including scheduling a babysitter.

We understand that completion of an agreement by one of us must be followed by completion of the exchange agreement by the other. If, for any reason, either one of us does not complete one of our agreements, then our partner is not to complete his/her "matching" agreement.

We understand this agreement may be terminated at any time by either partner but only in the presence of the therapist.

_____   _____
        (Date)

_____
      (Witness)

Fig. 2.3. Example of *quid pro quo* contract.

Finally, spouses are not put in the anger-producing position of continuing to contribute to the relationship in the absence of comparable contributions on the part of their partner.

In writing *quid pro quo* contracts, some general guidelines should be kept in mind. First, a behavior which is aversive to either spouse must not be listed among the agreements. A frequent request from males or females is increased sexual contact with their partner. Not uncommonly, decreased sexual interest and frequency is a by-product of marital distress. This is an area of such a high degree of vulnerability and personal investment that some spouses find sexual contact repulsive while their feelings toward their partner remain negative. To write a contract which specifies sexual contact would be a form of coercion, the very mode of behavior change which typifies couples experiencing distress. Though most couples are not so distressed that their reactions are characterized by such strong emotions as repulsion, this somewhat extreme example should make clear the undesirability of incorporating behavior into a contract with which either spouse is very uncomfortable. Issues of a highly emotional, delicate nature should be dealt with through other therapeutic means or put on the "back burner" until a more positive, trusting atmosphere in the relationship has been created.

A second guideline to be used in the selection of behaviors for inclusion in the contract is that both spouses must feel that their reward is equitable. Spouses must feel that their partners are contributing a comparable amount of energy and involvement or they will feel cheated and resentful, and will be unlikely to complete their end of the bargain. Consequently, the matching of behaviors in the contract should be such that balance is achieved between the perceived value of the spouses' behaviors. Returning to our illustration of a *quid pro quo* contract, it is clear that the first two agreements stipulate behaviors for each spouse which require approximately equivalent time investments. If, however, the contract had been written such that Alice would only spend ten minutes watching television with Bob, then Bob would probably end up feeling that all of his after-dinner cleaning is not worth the effort.

Time is not the only dimension for rendering equivalence. Effort and convenience may also be incorporated into the function defining equity. The third agreement in our illustration demonstrates this. Although Alice's agreement to arrange a weekend activity will probably not take 20 minutes each weekday, it is perceived by both Bob and Alice as harder work involving more initiative. Therefore, although Bob will put in a greater amount of time shopping for the family, he feels amply compensated by Alice's completion of her task.

The third guideline addresses the specificity with which agreements are written. The natural language of couples typically involves broad generalizations for classes of behavior. Spouses may request that their partners be more affectionate, considerate, and interested in them. Exactly what spouses mean by these terms, and hence their expectations, is quite variable among different individuals. One spouse might have in mind the partner showing affection by using pet names and playful teasing, whereas another would view those behaviors as childish and would want instead a tender kiss before sleep. As a result, the therapist must help the spouse learn to pinpoint exactly what behaviors they are requesting when they use the more general terms. Without explicit guidance, spouses are left to try to guess the wishes and to read the minds of their partners.

Related to the issue of the specificity of the agreements is the need to eliminate ambiguity. The contract should leave nothing to chance or misinterpretation. Distressed spouses are often characterized by a lack of trust and by misinterpretation of their mate's behavior. Each spouse's behavior should be described precisely so that any observer would recognize its completion. In addition, the duration of the behavior and when the behavior is to be performed should be designated. In this way, questions of compliance with the terms of the contract do not themselves become sources of conflict for the couple.

The *quid pro quo* contract was a major breakthrough in therapy with couples. In spite of its early success, however, a number of problems inherent in it have led therapists to develop other forms of behavioral contracting. One quickly sees how easy it is to sabotage a *quid pro quo* contract. If the husband does not clear the dishes one evening, then his wife is not required to spend a half-hour watching television with him. This is, in fact, one of the major pitfalls in that as soon as one spouse fails to comply with his or her part of the contract, then the partner does not have to perform his or her part. This can result in a sudden and complete cessation of behavior-change activities on the part of both spouses. When new behavior is being learned, it is not at all uncommon for mistakes, misunderstandings, and "weak moments" to occur. Since these are to be expected, it is quite problematic that the intervention is so susceptible to them.

A second problem area in the use of *quid pro quo* contracts is the resistance on the part of spouses to be the first to change. *Quid pro quo* contracts, because they stipulate "if/then" relationships, require one of the spouses to be the first to make a behavior change. In the case of many distressed marriages, both spouses are so angry with and wary of each other that it is unreasonable to ask one spouse to be the first to change.

The second type of contract developed is known as the *Good Faith* contract. Though empirical evidence does not indicate the superior efficacy of good faith contracts over *quid pro quo* contracts (Jacobson, 1978a), clinical practice of the late 1970s clearly favors the use of good faith contracts (O'Leary & Turkewitz, 1978). Just as in *quid pro quo* contracts, each spouse specifies the desired behavior changes in his or her partner. The difference between the two forms of contracting lies in the absence of a contingency between each spouse's performance of desired behaviors. Rather than having the partner's behavior as a reward for completion of the spouse's part of the contract, other rewards which may not involve the partner are provided. Figure 2.4 is an illustration of a good faith contract.

This good faith contract between Judy and Paul has some of the same behaviors specified in the *quid pro quo* contract between Bob and Alice. The important distinction to be noted, however, is that the behaviors of Judy and Paul are not cross-linked as they were for Bob and Alice. Consequently, if a mistake or omission occurs one evening and Paul does not clear the dinner table, then he cannot spend any time in his workshop. Nevertheless, Judy's positive changes may continue to occur since, technically, they are independent of Paul's behavior. One spouse's failure to comply with the contract does not bring all behavior change efforts to a standstill.

We, Paul and Judy Smith, agree to abide by the following set of agreements for 14 days beginning at 7A.M., May 12, 1980 and ending May 26, 1980 at 7 A.M.

1. Paul will clear the dinner table and load the dishwasher each evening after dinner. In return, he may spend one hour each evening in his workshop undisturbed so long as it does not extend beyond 10 P.M.
2. Each weekday evening before dinner, Paul will ask Judy how her day went and spend at least five minutes telling her about his day. In return, he may have a beer with dinner.
3. Judy will have Paul's lunch prepared to take to work each weekday morning. In return for having prepared five lunches, she may make one 15-minute long-distance phone call when evening rates are in effect.
4. Judy will arrange a "date" with Paul for each weekend including obtaining a babysitter. In return, she may plan one evening out when Paul will take care of the children.

We understand that only after the first part of the agreement is completed can we take advantage of the second part.

We understand this agreement may be terminated at any time by either partner, but only in the presence of the therapist.

_____   _____

_____   _____
      (Date)

_____
      (Witness)

Fig. 2.4. Example of good faith contract.

As is the case for *quid pro quo* contracts, there is also a similar set of guidelines which should be followed in drawing up good faith contracts. First, the rewards stipulated for each spouse's completion of certain behaviors should not include things that upset the partner. For example, if one of Judy's concerns is that Paul has a drinking problem, then it would not be advisable to specify a beer at dinner as a reward for Paul. Similarly, if Paul is upset because he thinks Judy is involved with another man, then Judy having an evening out as a reward may be a source of real irritation for Paul.

On the other hand, not all debated issues need to be avoided in contracting. For instance, if one of Judy's complaints is that Paul does not help around the house enough, but finds plenty of time for his own hobbies, then combining help with the dishes with *one hour* of being in his workshop may solve both problems simultaneously. Moreover, Paul will undoubtedly be pleased with his option of one hour of undisturbed activity in his workshop which he can do openly rather than having to sneak off undetected to avoid sharp comments or repeated interruptions from Judy. Another example of including a problem issue as a reward is if Paul feels that Judy is financially irresponsible and is bringing them into more debt by the high phone bills she runs up by calling her out-of-state friends. By specifying one long-distance call of a designated length per week as a reward for Judy, the excessive calling could be eliminated while providing Judy with one call which she could enjoy completely without an angry outburst by Paul at the end of the month when the phone bill arrives. Again, the fundamental importance of teaching spouses to create resolutions to their problems by specifying what can be done rather than what should not be done is underscored. While Paul may have walked into therapy ready to tear the phone off the wall and Judy was ready to set Paul's workshop on fire, both are likely to be more willing to compromise on more moderate use.

The last two guidelines for good faith contracts are identical to those already described for *quid pro quo* contracts. The behaviors written into the contract should be specific and sufficiently overt so that there is a minimum of ambiguity regarding their completion. The rewards listed should be equitable with the designated behavior sufficiently attractive to motivate the spouse. Some good faith contracts also list penalties for noncompliance with desired behaviors. For example, returning to our illustration, if Judy does not prepare Paul's lunch one morning, then the penalty might be for her to clean one of the closets in the house that day. The purpose in adding penalties to a contract is to increase further the motivation of spouses to participate in behavior exchange. It may be particularly effective with recalcitrant spouses or with couples in which either spouse is especially sensitive to inequity of exchange. In this case, a penalty is a way to ensure some degree of constructive effort on the part of spouses even when they are not fully compliant with the contract. Secondly, and as importantly, it may soothe the feelings of the irritated spouse.

Although there may be occasions when penalties are to be recommended, as a rule they are better avoided. Punishment as a penalty for bad behavior is too much a part of many couples' destructive style of relating. Not infrequently, punishment incites anger in the recipient even when he or she acknowledges the fairness of it. But more importantly, lack of compliance with agreements in a contract should suggest to the couple and therapist that there is an unaccounted for element operating in the relationship. Thus, rather than selecting a coercive strategy as a means of obtaining compliance, the terms of the contract should be reevaluated. Special attention should be focused upon rewards that are found insufficiently motivating or that lose their attractiveness with repeated use. Perhaps a "menu" of rewards needs to be specified so that the selection is not quickly exhausted.

A problem often associated with good faith contracts is that the rewards do not involve the spouse, such that behaving "well" toward one's spouse reaps rewards other than those naturally emanating from the relationship. Distressed couples may be too often characterized as obtaining an inordinate amount of their pleasure from sources other than their spouse. To perpetuate this further does not seem to be in the interest of having both spouses maximize the pleasure they can obtain from their partner.

Despite the problems associated with both forms of contracting, they are valuable, if only as a framework in which to specify desired changes for each spouse constructively. A general rule of thumb associated with contracting, be it formal or informal, is that the agreement should specify an increased occurrence of desired behaviors, not decreased occurrence of negative behaviors. The positive set is needed to prevent either spouse from feeling that behavior is being forbidden without replacement with other behavior. For example, instead of specifying, "husband will not go to bar with friends on Friday night" (which husband may be doing to avoid a dull evening with his wife), the contract would state, "husband will come home after work on Friday night and have gourmet meal prepared by his wife along with a bottle of wine." Under normal circumstances, it is easy to see how the husband would be much more likely to follow through with the second agreement rather than the first. In fact, the first would be more likely to elicit a desire on the husband's part also to deprive his wife of something she finds enjoyable.

In spite of the success of negotiation training and contracting in marital therapy, it is not news to anyone who has used these interventions that they are not a panacea. We have found that one-third to one-half of the couples we see respond well to a somewhat straightforward use of some of the above techniques. For these couples, therapy is typically short-term (10–15 sessions) and includes caring days and negotiation and communication training. When contracting is used, it is usually informal in nature because we have found that most couples do not require the structure of the formal, written document. It might also be noted here that it is not necessarily the couples with the least severe problems who respond to these interventions. In fact, it is not uncommon for an extremely distressed couple with one foot in the lawyer's office to be as responsive as a seemingly less distressed couple.

BEHAVIORAL INTERVENTIONS AS A WAY OF CHANGING FEELINGS

One of the problems in the application of these techniques stems from the clients' reaction to them. Caring days and contracting, particularly if the latter is formal, can seem too simplistic and mechanistic to couples who are enmeshed in the complexity of their feelings and behavior. These interventions, many clients believe, seem to ignore the thoughts and feelings which they consider much more important than their behavior. A therapist who focuses on the behavior can seem to the couple to be missing the main point. Sometimes this reaction is appropriate. A whole range of issues (which will be discussed below) complicates the couple's problems and are not effectively dealt with through these techniques alone. But for a fair portion of couples having this reaction, behavioral techniques are relevant and potentially effective. The problem lies in their lack of appreciation for the remarkable impact behavior change can have on cognitive and affective states. A typical diagram and explanation of the concept which we use is the following:

$$FEELINGS \rightleftarrows BEHAVIOR$$

We know that how you feel toward someone affects the way you behave toward them. But we also know that what you do, in turn, affects how you feel. We have found that it is much easier to change how you behave directly than it is directly to affect how you feel. Therefore, since a change in behavior ultimately leads to a change in feelings, which is what you are seeking from therapy, the change in behavior is going to be the focus of therapy.

It will be a disappointed therapist who expects couples to adopt this view of human interactions readily. One reason that we see so many couples encountering problems is their helplessness in knowing how to change a series of interactions that have gone into a negative spiral. Thoughts and feelings are viewed as rightfully preceding behavior such that when feelings are negative, positive behavior cannot be expected. As we graphically indicate to them, their belief is:

$$FEELINGS \longrightarrow BEHAVIOR$$

Consequently, once a negative set has been established, it is self-perpetuating; the bad feelings lead to angry or disinterested behavior which, in turn, reinforces the feelings.

The change of set needed for couples to learn how to gain more control over the quality of their interactions comes from their acceptance of the causal relationship between behavior and feelings. Again, as we depict the process goal to such couples:

$$BEHAVIOR \longrightarrow FEELINGS$$

It is this link in the feedback loop described above which underlies the strategy of behavioral marital therapy. When couples begin to see that they can have an impact on the feelings of their spouse as well as their own through changes in their behavior, they no longer feel helpless or at the mercy of Cupid's whims. Despite the therapist's own adoption of this model, however, it takes time for couples to understand and believe it fully. Experience is the best teacher, so we urge and cajole reluctant spouses to participate in the strategy for a week or two to see for themselves if it will lead to the predicted outcome.

FEAR OR REJECTION OF INTIMACY

As indicated earlier, not all couples' problems are effectively dealt with through the therapeutic methods outlined thus far. Some couples introduce issues that require additional or alternative forms of intervention. Occasionally, we encounter a spouse who feels he or she has been contributing positive behavior to the relationship for a long time in the absence of an equitable exchange on the part of his or her partner. Therapy is frequently viewed by this spouse as a final attempt to coerce the partner to live up to his or her end of the bargain. The spouse, however, is unwilling to "invest" further in the relationship until he or she is convinced that his or her partner is going to contribute equitably. There are also those spouses who, like the one just described, feel as though their dues have been paid and it is now not only their partner's turn to reciprocate, but to suffer as they suffered by providing positive behavior in the absence of reciprocity: "Let him or her suffer for a while to see what it's like!"

These spouses are seeking a revenge which is antithetical to the presumed goal of therapy which is to bring the couple closer together and to help them establish positive ways of relating and constructive problem-solving skills. With vengeful spouses, the therapist's first task is to work with them until their need for revenge as a way of reconciling their anger and hurt is no longer necessary.

Another reason why spouses may enter therapy reluctant to reinstitute emotional intimacy with their mates can also stem from excessive anger or disgust. These couples have allowed hurts, injuries, and disappointments to build up and form tough "scar tissue" without ardently attempting to communicate these feelings to their spouse. Time and again they have experienced negative feelings in their marital interactions and have learned to distance and to isolate themselves in an attempt to reduce their hurt. Meanwhile, they form a personality profile of their spouse which is congruent with their negative experiences and is repeatedly confirmed. Most of all, they lose any closeness and intimacy they may have had with their spouse and often end up feeling that they are sharing their bed with a stranger. The image of the spouse can be so negative that the partner cannot bear to encounter the spouse intimately without experiencing feelings of repulsion and fear of more emotional hurt. The pleading question of these spouses is, "How can you expect me to start acting warmly towards him or her when I don't feel that way? I can't! When he or she changes, then maybe I will be able to feel better toward him or her." Once the destructive process has evolved to the point where one partner harbors extremely negative feelings toward the other which preclude any approach toward the spouse, then exploration of the feelings with an emphasis on their development, impact on the marriage, and current role is a necessary first step in the therapy. With few exceptions this is best done conjointly so that the "accused" spouse may learn how it is that his or her partner has come to feel so strongly. As mentioned above, it is typically with noncommunicating spouses that this situation is most likely to develop. Thus, therapy serves not only to investigate the current problem, but also to move the couple toward open, constructive communication.

INDIVIDUAL PROBLEMS

It is also important to recognize that each spouse may have individual problems that may prevent progress from being made with a behavioral intervention focused on the dyad. For example, a necessary component for successful communication and negotiation is that both parties be rational enough to engage in this activity. It can be extremely difficult for spouses with individual psychopathy to participate in negotiation training. Such people tend to become preoccupied with their own perspectives and find it difficult or impossible to compromise, or to recognize that compromise may be in their best interest in the long run. Sometimes it is necessary for these individuals to work on their individual problems before they can actively engage in constructive work within the dyad.

Individuals bring aspects of their past history to their current marital relationship. Whether one conceptualizes these problems in psychodynamic, behavioral, or other terms, we have found that resentment, anger, and other "old business" revolving around the family of origin are translated into behavior which is disruptive to the marital relationship. An obvious example of this is the daughter of an alcoholic father who is hypersensitive to her husband's drinking, even though this drinking would not be considered a problem in most relationships. While negotiation skills and contracting can be useful to couples such as this, it is naive to believe that teaching of these skills will solve the marital problems if the issues out of the past are not also dealt with and resolved. We are not suggesting long-term psychotherapy, but simply that the therapist should not ignore these factors as important elements in the marital relationship. Kaplan (1974) recognizes this need in her proposal for a "new sex therapy." She proposes that sex therapy with a couple continue until a block is reached and, if it becomes apparent that no more work can be done because of individual problems, for the couple work to stop, and for the blocked individual to be worked with until his or her issues can be resolved. Then couple therapy is resumed.

Another difficulty is the actual "sabotage" of therapy progress by one or both spouses. A prerequisite for change is a mutual motivation to change. In spite of their stated objectives to change, some individuals seem to have an investment in maintaining the dysfunctional marital system. For all its dissatisfactions, there is a certain amount of security and predictability in maintaining a marital status quo. Change can be frightening to people because of the unpredictability it brings regarding the future of the relationship. Some spouses, while requesting behavior change in their partner, seem to do everything in their power to inhibit the process of those changes. An example is the wife who states that she wants her unassertive husband to stand up for his rights, take more responsibility, and "act more like a man," but consistently puts him down when he makes any attempt to assert himself in therapy. Such individuals may, on the one hand, want their spouse to change, but on the other hand, they may not want to give up the power associated with being able to point a finger at their spouse's inadequacy. They may also fear the changes that can come about in their spouse as a result of therapy.

The issue of imbalance of power may also have a negative influence on the effectiveness of negotiation training and contracting as a therapeutic intervention. If one partner in a relationship has absolute or near absolute power, then that person certainly has no reason to negotiate and contract. This can occur when one member of a dyad feels completely dependent on the other, while the other is perfectly willing to function on his or her own if the relationship were to break up. Persons with such power are in a position to request major changes of their spouses while making few, if any, changes in themselves. When we encounter such cases, we find that regardless of how many changes one spouse makes, it does not ultimately result in an increase in overall satisfaction for either spouse.

These issues have to be dealt with either individually or conjointly before negotiation training and contracting, and perhaps even caring days, can be effective in alleviating marital distress.

Trust

We have found that one of the toughest blocks to surmount in marital therapy is a lack of trust on the part of one or both partners. In order for spouses to resolve their differences and become more intimate, they must be willing to acknowledge and attempt better ways of interacting. Moreover, they must be willing to become vulnerable by coming within "striking range" of their partner. Therapists must show sensitivity to this issue in the way they structure and direct sessions. Very high on the list of priorities must be a commitment to minimizing the likelihood that either spouse will take advantage of his or her partner's increased vulnerability. Sometimes, by force of habit, spouses will "jab" their partners. The toll taken when the partner has risked letting his or her armor down is very high and is likely to produce a wariness of becoming vulnerable again. Consequently, we do a few things early in therapy. First, we explain to couples the need to trust and to risk approaching their partners; peace can't be made from a distance. We also specifically address the fear of being hurt again which we anticipate to be at the core of their reluctance to trust. Their initiation of therapy is a statement to each other that they wish to abandon their destructive patterns and to become friends and lovers once again. We see this as a time to lay down arms. We warn them, however, that they will promptly destroy this atmosphere on the first occasion that they attack their spouse while he or she is vulnerable. Thus, it is imperative that they guard against this to the best of their ability. Finally, we warn them that if jabbing occurs in a session, this is the one circumstance in which we, as therapists, will reprimand one spouse. This safeguarding tends to foster trust between spouses and to facilitate opening up to one another, which is fundamental to improved relations.

A second way in which trust becomes an issue is during the actual process of change. Distressed couples are notorious for misinterpreting the intentions of their spouses' statements and behavior. The error usually runs in the direction of assuming a negative intention. This same problem can continue during therapy while spouses are making changes desired by their spouse. Learning new behaviors is typically not error-free and spouses must be patient with one another during this process. It is most frustrating and discouraging to have your spouse presume that you meant to do harm when you have been trying so hard to meet his or her requests and made a blunder in the process. The more willing spouses are to suspend their judgments of presumed guilt and to allow themselves to believe that their partner's motives are worthy, then two things are more likely to happen. First, they will create a more positive, supportive atmosphere that enhances motivation for the behavior change, which can sometimes be quite difficult to accomplish. Second, they can benefit most from the actual behavior changes that occur since they are minimally distorting the events; that is, they see the changes for what they are, rather than remaining skeptical and inferring various hidden motives.

It is probably apparent by this time that when we discuss trust, we are including a certain philosophical view of human potential for change. So often we will be queried by a spouse, "But can you really change someone's personality?" What is meant is that a person views his or her spouse's actions as emanating from his or her personality, that is, God-given, permanent attributes. They are consequently skeptical of the likelihood of anything beyond superficial change. Thus, when we discuss trust with couples, we are trying in part to persuade them to share our largely deterministic view of human behavior. If the proper conditions are designed and contingencies incorporated, then individuals are capable of a wide diversity of behavior patterns. Furthermore, the particular behavior observed in their spouse when they are distressed is a product of the environment and contingencies they have designed for themselves. A change in these will facilitate a change in behavior. The absence of trust or belief in this view of their spouse's potential for change is a compromising factor in therapy.

Intolerance of Differences

This is another instance in which philosophy is encountered. It is quite improbable to find any two persons who share exactly the same beliefs, attitudes, and values in all matters; and it would be significantly more improbable to find two such kindred spirits married to one another. Nevertheless, for some couples, this expectation underlies their distress when they encounter a difference in beliefs or values in their spouse. To many couples, marital harmony means that they should share a common view of the world and priorities for their behavior in it. Invested, as we all are, in our own particular belief system, alternative belief systems are sometimes viewed as wrong, rather than different. Consequently, spouses set out to convince one another of the superiority of their respective views on the issue. "Surely, if he were not so thick-headed, selfish, or neurotic, he could see what I am talking about." Or, "If I only explain it *right*, then she couldn't help but see it my way." These expressions of exasperation, that something must be amiss somewhere since full agreement is not being reached, are typical.

Acceptance of the idea that the same set of events may be evaluated in two completely different, equally legitimate ways is an important step for couples. The person who is like a squirrel in the way money is saved is no better or worse than the person who takes great pleasure in spending money. Undoubtedly though, they will have some compromising to do if they marry. Differences like this are a clear challenge for couples, and it is not our role to trivialize them. They become much less threatening, however, to couples when they abandon their expectation and need to convert their partner to their view point. A major accomplishment has been achieved when a husband and wife can look at one another and calmly acknowledge their differences and accept them as valid. Their task then can be focused upon evaluating the impact of the differences on each of them. The wife may only be able to make large purchases through consistent saving and denial of daily, tiny luxuries, while the husband may feel that "living for the moment" is much more important. In this case, imposition of either philosophy on the other would not be satisfactory. Each spouse would instead have to recognize the legitimacy of the other's position, though different from his or her own, and accept some compromise. The wife would have to accept a slower rate of saving to allow her husband to have a certain amount of cash with which he may enjoy more frequent, smaller pleasures.

Another strategy for dealing with differences does not involve compromise. Take the example of a husband who believes that "cleanliness is next to Godliness," and his wife who feels that her hours after work are better spent with the children than with a vacuum cleaner. If the husband comes to accept his wife's position as a perfectly moral and valid one, he will no longer consider his wife a bad person for having lower standards for household neatness. As a result, he may no longer feel the need to demand this of her. Moreover, he may recognize that it is *his* personal need to maintain a high level of neatness which he has the option of satisfying through his own cleaning and not by demanding it of his wife. Another example is the case of a couple who do not share religious values. The wife believes in God and feels religious training is important for children. In contrast, her husband is an agnostic and thinks that religious training and rituals are useless. Once this couple is no longer bent upon converting one another, then the husband, for example, might feel comfortable with his wife making arrangements for the religious training of their children, since he doesn't think it will do any harm, even if it is not very useful. Thus, the wife's position is the one which is acted upon.

COGNITIVE VARIABLES

Interventions that only consider behavior and do not deal with cognitive and affective variables as well usually have only limited success. Marital distress can often be traced to unrealistic expectations rather than miscommunication, and to attributions rather than behavior itself. For example, if a husband spends a night bowling with friends, his wife could view this as his desire to be with his friends, or as his desire to be away from her. She may not like this weekly behavior in either case, but clearly the latter interpretation is more likely to lead to marital problems. The attributions people make about their spouse's behavior can have a much greater impact on a relationship than the behavior itself.

Unrealistic expectations of how a spouse *should* behave can cause distress when these behaviors are not forthcoming. People often have difficulty differentiating how they would like their spouse to behave from how they know their spouse should behave. When something should happen and it doesn't, we become outraged; when we would like something to happen and it doesn't, we become disappointed. We frequently use an informal, rational restructuring approach to help individuals make this distinction. This may be done in conjoint therapy or individually. When lack of progress in therapy seems to be due to the unrealistic expectations of one of the spouses, we may see them separately for one session to introduce rational concepts that may help them to be more flexible.

Therapist: It seems that every time the subject of Julie's getting a job comes up you get so angry, Dan, that all the work we've done on ways to communicate seems forgotten. Why do you think that you become so angry?

Dan: Because all she's trying to do is get out of her responsibilities at home. She has a job. We have two small kids and a whole house to take care of, and I make good money, and there's no reason for her to work. She's a wife and a mother and she should stay home and take care of her family.

Therapist: I can really understand you having strong feelings about this. It really seems to mean a lot to you. But let me ask you something, Dan. Do you think there are some husbands who don't mind that their wives want to go out to work—maybe even actually like it?

Dan: Well, sure. Some guys don't care what their wives do. And I guess if they really need the money, they may even like it that their wives go out to work. But that's not the way I see it.

Therapist: Okay, I understand that. The reason I asked is because you said before that your wife *should* stay home. But it sounds as if what you really mean is that you would *like* her to stay home.

Dan: Well, what's the difference?

Therapist: Well, it's really just the way you think about it. When you say somebody *should* do something, it's almost as if it were a law or something; as if it were inscribed in stone somewhere that wives *should* stay home. But you yourself said there may be some other men somewhere who wouldn't mind if their wives went to work. So what you're really saying is that you mind when your wife goes to work, and therefore what you really mean is that you're disappointed or unhappy or don't like the fact that she wants to do that. I'm not saying you're wrong in feeling that way. Those are your feelings and you are entitled to them. The point is, when we believe someone *should* do something and they don't, then we are very often extremely angry and outraged because we believe they've broken some kind of a law or rule. But when we think of it in terms of wanting somebody to do something, or liking them to do something, then when they don't, we're disappointed, unhappy, and somewhat angry because we didn't get what we want, but usually we're not quite as outraged.

Dan: Yeah, but that still doesn't change anything.

Therapist: That's true, but when we're less angry and more in control, we have a better chance of communicating about what's bothering us and have a better chance of resolving the issue. Why don't you try this little experiment for awhile. Every time you think that Julie should or should not do something, rephrase it in your head as "I would like her to do or not like her to do something" and see if that changes the way you feel.

Such an intervention can be extremely effective in reducing pressure within the relationship, thus making it possible to introduce some of the behavioral interventions discussed above effectively.

ENDING A MARRIAGE

As marital therapists, we find it important to begin therapy with the assumption that the relationship will last and that it can work. We start with the assumption that the spouses have the potential to make each other happy. For some couples, however, it becomes apparent, once therapy is well under way, that the relationship is not a viable one. This may happen even when some of the interventions discussed previously have been successful. It is important to note that successful negotiation does not necessarily lead to satisfaction. Negotiation usually results in compromise and, even if each individual is able to maximize the rewards and to minimize the costs within the relationship as a result of negotiation, the results may still be far short of what they require to remain in the relationship. Other couples may find that they are so far apart in values, individual relationship goals, and requirements for a successful marriage, that the efforts involved in attempting to make the relationship more satisfactory are just not worth the possible results. Others may find that after successful communication work, when they are finally interacting and dealing with each other as individuals, they don't like each other very much and then choose not to spend their lives together. Other couples enter their marriages with an implicit contract as to their roles in the relationship. Then, as we frequently find in this era of change, one person chooses to deviate from the implicit contract and the other does not. It is not unusual to find a wife who is experiencing personal growth, a new awareness of herself as an individual, and a new sense of self-worth, each of which may lead to behavior at odds with her originally contracted role. If her husband does not experience similar changes or is unwilling to try to make changes in their relationship, the marriage which at one point was satisfactory to both may no longer be viable.

If both therapist and clients agree that divorce seems to be the most viable alternative, some couples may still benefit from therapy. Divorce and separation counseling requires negotiation and contracting skills in the same way as a working relationship does, especially when children are involved. Therapy can help the individuals to clarify issues and to find the strength to face the alternatives of a new life style.

FUTURE DIRECTIONS

Marriages will undoubtedly continue to be the focus of much interest and work by researchers and clinicians in the upcoming years. As we have indicated, stresses on the institution have multiplied in recent decades and there is no sign of a reprieve. New conceptions of women's contributions to home, business, and the community are just beginning to be incorporated into both public and private views of marriage. Flexibility in work schedules, particularly in crowded metropolitan areas, is providing the opportunity for some men to be more involved in child rearing and other homemaking activities. Community-based self-help groups have played an important role in easing individuals' responses to these many changes. They have also been a breeding ground for ideas that have been brought into the public arena to effect legal, economic, and social changes regarding marriage and the family. But for those couples with acute distress, more intensive, individualized help will continue to be sought.

Research is needed to develop methods for assessing those dimensions of a couple's relationship that determine their satisfaction. Strategies that are minimally intrusive, time-consuming, and costly are needed to perform behavioral analyses of couples' daily interactions. This will enable clinicians to pinpoint behavior patterns that instigate and sustain distress. Greater understanding of the interplay between behavior and cognitions is necessary so that negative feeling states, developed by couples, may be addressed more directly. This will predictably lead to a broadening of therapeutic interventions used by behavioral marital therapists. The reciprocal nature of marital and child problems will gain greater recognition and clinicians will find that many families can be maximally helped when both areas are emphasized. Finally, prevention is a concept that must be accepted by the educational system, the media, and young, marrying people. Programs should be designed to teach marital skills early before the mistakes and destructive trial-and-error method of spouse's problem solving require individual, professional attention. Monogamous marriage thus far remains the most viable alternative for heterosexual interactions. Providing individuals with the skills to yield its potential gratifications is the challenge facing researchers and clinicians in the upcoming years.

REFERENCES

Alexander, J. F., & Parsons, B. V. Short-term behavioral intervention with delinquent families: Impact on family process and recidivism. *Journal of Abnormal Psychology*, 1973, **81**, 219–226.
Azrin, N. H., Naster, B. J., & Jones, R. Reciprocity counseling: A rapid learning-based procedure for marital counseling. *Behavior Research and Therapy*, 1973, **11**, 365–382.
Blechman, E. A., & Olson, D. H. L. Family contract game: Description and effectiveness. In D. H. L. Olson (Ed.), *Treating relationships*. Lake Mills, Iowa: Graphic Publishing Co., 1976.
Cookerly, J. R. The outcome of the six major forms of marriage counseling compared: A pilot study. *Journal of Marriage and the Family*, 1973, **36**, 608–611.
Glick, P. C., & Norton, A. J. Perspectives on the recent upturn in divorce and remarriage. *Demography*, 1973, **10**, 301–314.
Greene, B. J., & Solomon, A. Marital disharmony: Concurrent psychoanalytic therapy of husband and wife by the same psychiatrist. *American Journal of Psychiatry*, 1963, **17**, 443–450.
Haley, J. Marriage therapy. *Archives of General Psychiatry*, 1963, **8**, 213–234.
Jacobson, N. S. Problem solving and contingency contracting in the treatment of marital discord. *Journal of Consulting and Clinical Psychology*, 1977, **45**, 92–100.
Jacobson, N. S. A review of the research on the effectiveness of marital therapy. In T. J. Paolino & B. S. McCrady (Eds.), *Marriage and marital therapy: Psychoanalytic, behavioral and systems theory perspectives*. New York: Brunner/Mazel, 1978(a).
Jacobson, N. S. Specific and nonspecific factors in the effectiveness of a behavioral approach to the treatment of marital discord. *Journal of Consulting and Clinical Psychology*, 1978, **46**, 442–452(b).
Jacobson, N. S., & Martin, B. Behavioral marriage therapy: Current status. *Psychological Bulletin*, 1976, **83**, 540–566.
Kaplan, H. S. *The new sex therapy*. New York: Brunner/Mazel, 1974.

Kifer, R. E., Lewis, M. A., Green, D. R., & Phillips, E. L. Training pre-delinquent youths and their parents to negotiate conflict situations. *Journal of Applied Behavior Analysis*, 1974, 7, 356–364.

Lange, A., & Jakubowski, P. *Responsible assertive behavior.* Champaign, Ill.: Research Press, 1976.

Lederer, W. J., & Jackson, D. D. *The mirages of marriage.* New York: W. W. Norton & Co, 1968.

Martin, B. Brief family intervention: Effectiveness and importance of including the father. *Journal of Consulting and Clinical Psychology*, 1977, 45, 1002–1010.

Masters, W. H., & Johnson, V. E. *Human sexual inadequacy.* Boston: Little, Brown, 1970.

Ohrenstein, M. Battered women. *Statewide Task Force Study of Battered Women.* New York Senate publication, available from office of New York State Senate Minority Leader, Albany, N.Y., 1977.

O'Leary, K. D., & Turkewitz, H. Marital therapy from a behavioral perspective. In T. J. Paolino & B. S. McCrady (Eds.), *Marriage and marital therapy: Psychoanalytic, behavioral, and systems theory perspectives.* New York: Brunner/Mazel, 1978.

Olson, D. Marital and family therapy: Integrative review and critique. *Journal of Marriage and the Family*, 1970, 32, 501–538.

Patterson, G. R., & Reid, J. B. Reciprocity and coercion: Two facets of social systems. In C. Neuringer & J. L. Michael (Eds.), *Behavior modification in clinical psychology.* New York: Appleton-Century-Crofts, 1970.

Prochaska, J., & Prochaska, J. Twentieth century trends in marriage and marital therapy. In T. J. Paolino & B. S. McCrady (Eds.), *Marriage and marital therapy.* New York: Brunner/Mazel, 1978.

Robin, A. R., O'Leary, K. D., Kent, R. N., Foster, S. L., & Prinz, R. J. Communication training: An approach to problem-solving for parents and adolescents. *Behavior Therapy*, 1977, 8, 639–643.

Sager, C. *Marriage contracts and couple therapy: Hidden forces in intimate relationships.* New York: Brunner/Mazel, 1976.

Satir, V. Conjoint marital therapy. In B. C. Greene (Ed.), *The psychotherapy of marital disharmony.* New York: The Free Press, 1965.

Straus, M. A. Wife beating: How common and why? *Victimology*, 1978, 2, 443–458.

Stuart, R. B. Operant-interpersonal treatment for marital discord. *Journal of Consulting and Clinical Psychology*, 1969, 33, 675–682.

Stuart, R. B. An operant-interpersonal program for couples. In D. H. Olson (Ed.), *Treating relationships.* Lake Mills, Iowa: Graphic Publishing Co., 1976.

Stuart, R. B., & Tripodi, T. Experimental evaluation of three time-constrained behavioral treatments for pre-delinquents and delinquents. In R. D. Rubin, J. P. Brady, & J. D. Henderson (Eds.), *Advances in behavior therapy, Vol 4.* New York: Academic Press, 1973.

Thibaut, J., & Kelley, H. H. *The social psychology of groups.* New York: Wiley, 1959.

Turkewitz, H. *A comparative outcome study of behavioral marital therapy and communication therapy.* Unpublished doctoral dissertation, SUNY at Stony Brook, N.Y., 1977.

Walker, L. E. *The battered woman.* New York: Harper & Row, 1979.

Walster, E., Walster, G. W., & Berscheid, E. *Equity: Theory and research.* Boston: Allyn & Bacon, Inc., 1978.

Watson, A. The conjoint psychotherapy of marriage partners. *American Journal of Orthopsychiatry*, 1963, 33, 912–922.

Weathers, L., & Lieberman, R. P. Contingency contracting with families of delinquent adolescents. *Behavior Therapy*, 1975, 6, 356–366.

Weiss, R. L., Hops, H., & Patterson, G. R. A framework for conceptualizing marital conflict, a technology for altering it, some data for evaluating it. In L. A. Hamerlynck, L. C. Handy, & E. J. Mash (Eds.), *Behavior change: Methodology, concepts, and practice.* Champaign, Ill.: Research Press, 1973.

Chapter 3
Self-Control
Edward G. Carr and
Jody A. Binkoff

The tempest in my mind
Doth from my senses take all feeling else
Save what beats there . . .
O, that way madness lies; let me shun that.
No more of that.
—Shakespeare, *King Lear*, Act III, Scene IV, Lines 12–14, 21–22

King Lear, of course, is a work of fiction but, unfortunately, what happened to Lear happens every day to real people. His uncontrollable outbursts of anger helped alienate people from him. Soon, he was left with almost nothing. But, as the above passage demonstrates, even the haughty King was, in his own way, able to learn a measure of self-control over his rages.

The notion of self-control was, like so many other ideals, introduced to Western civilization by the Greeks. An individual required both intelligence and *enkrateia*, or inner strength, in order to achieve the ideal state of *sophrosyne*, self-control. Working toward self-control was considered the true path to happiness. This theme is taken up repeatedly by the great Stoic philosophers of the ancient world, Zeno, Epictetus, Marcus Aurelius. Their Stoicism was undoubtedly too rigorous and too fatalistic for most modern people to accept but it did serve to make the important point that even in the face of great frustration and provocation, individuals can learn to retain a measure of control over their thoughts, feelings, and behavior.

In current clinical practice, the Greek ideal of self-control can be found in those approaches that emphasize teaching a client active coping strategies for dealing with problematic situations. In this chapter, we discuss three such strategies: relaxation, cognitive restructuring, and assertion. These interventions all make a common assumption, namely that self-control is a set of learned skills, not an inherent personality trait. That is, a statement such as "I just can't help myself; I'm a hot-tempered type of person" is held to be self-defeating because it is thought that individuals can *learn* to control their anger and aggression. It is assumed that through careful assessment of behavioral, cognitive, and affective variables, coupled with the provision of skills training, a therapist can teach a client to develop self-control. Once clients acquire these skills, they will be in a better position to confront and to handle a variety of new problem situations productively on their own. From this standpoint, self-control can be seen primarily as the acquisition of coping skills (Goldfried, 1980).

RELAXATION

We have all heard the advice that when we are very angry or on the verge of becoming aggressive, we should "count to ten." This strategem is nothing more than an *unsystematic* form of relaxation training. *Systematic* relaxation training is in fact a basic method for the self-control of anger and aggression and we shall discuss this method first.

Training in muscle relaxation is assumed to produce a state of parasympathetic dominance which, because of the mode of functioning of the autonomic nervous system, is antagonistic to the sympathetic arousal that mediates feelings of anger and anxiety (Wolpe, 1958). In lay terms, it is almost impossible to feel both intense anger and deep relaxation at the same time. Thus, it is reasoned that if one teaches an angry client to relax, the feelings that the client has of being overwhelmed by anger should dissipate.

At the outset, we should note that relaxation training is used clinically in anger control primarily to prepare a client for other interventions and/or in conjunction with other interventions. Anger and accompanying aggression, as will be noted below, are usually exacerbated by or arise from certain beliefs that the client holds as well as by a lack of alternative, nonaggressive means for attaining personal and interpersonal goals. Such problems must of course be dealt with in their own right and the cognitive learning and assertive training methods described below specifically address these problems. A client who is in a state of rage, however, is not likely to be able to employ various self-control measures that require patience and planning. One is reminded of the popular admonition to "Calm down and get a hold of yourself." Relaxation training is a systematic method for teaching clients to "calm down" so that they will be able to employ the cognitive learning and assertive training methods alluded to above.

The ultimate objective is for the client to learn *self*-management of intense anger, a goal that is consistent with the general notion of relaxation as an active coping skill (Goldfried & Trier, 1974). As is the case with the other self-control techniques discussed in this chapter, however, it is necessary to begin by having the *therapist teach the client* the various skills. As the client becomes more self-sufficient, the therapist gradually reduces the level of assistance provided to the client.

When learning relaxation, the client is first seated in a large comfortable chair. Clothing is loosened so as to help maximize comfort. At this point, the therapist presents the *rationale* for relaxation training to the client:

> The agitation that you feel when you are angry stems partially from tense muscles. Normally, you are likely not even aware that your muscles are tensing up on you—only that there is a general feeling of discomfort, perhaps queasiness. I am going to help you to recognize the tension and learn how to relax your muscles, in an orderly fashion, so that you will feel calm rather than tense and agitated. Once you've learned the skill, you'll be able to use it on your own in an abbreviated form whenever you start to feel angry. This will help calm you down enough so that you'll be able to more effectively use some of the other techniques [e.g., cognitive restructuring and/or assertion as described in later sections of this chapter] that you'll learn later. The relaxation procedure that we'll work on involves having you purposely tense a set of muscles, then relax those muscles, then tense and relax the opposite set of muscles. We'll begin by trying to relax your hands, then we'll relax your biceps and triceps, your shoulders, and so on until your entire body is relaxed.

The progressive (deep) muscle relaxation exercises described above were initially developed by Jacobson (1948) and Wolpe (1958, 1969). This is the most frequently used type of relaxation procedure and consists, as we have noted, of a number of *tension-relaxation* cycles.

Once the rationale has been presented, the therapist guides the client through the first tension-relaxation cycle. The therapist gives a number of verbal instructions to the client while the client carries out the exercise. The therapist speaks in a slow and calm manner using a soft but audible voice:

> I'd like you to raise your left arm now and hold it out in front of you. Make a fist with your hand. (*Voice grows tense but not loud.*) Clench your fist tight, hard. Notice the pressure and tension in your hand and fingers. (*After about 10 seconds of tensing, the therapist continues in a soothing tone.*) Now relax. Let your hand fall onto your lap just as if it were made of limp spaghetti. Notice the contrast between the tension and relaxation. Focus on the feelings of relaxation in your hand and fingers. Try to flow with those feelings of relaxation. Focus on the warm feeling of calm.

Following about ten seconds of relaxation, the above exercise would be repeated. Next, the entire sequence is performed twice with the right arm. Following this, the client is instructed to tense and relax the opposite set of muscles as follows:

> I'd like you to raise your left arm again and hold it out in front of you. This time bend your fingers back at the wrist so that the muscles in the back of your hand and forearm become tense. Make your fingers point toward the ceiling. Feel the tension in your hand. (*After about ten seconds, the therapist continues in a soothing voice.*) Now relax. Let your hand fall onto your lap. Notice the difference between the tension and the relaxation. Focus on the feelings of relaxation . . . pleasant . . . calm. Let go just a little bit more. You can feel the tension draining out of your hand. Just keep letting go of those muscles further and further.

Again, the tension-relaxation cycle would be repeated. The therapist would move on next to other muscle groups. A standard progression has been outlined by Goldfried and Davison (1976) and Rimm and Masters (1979). Most of the exercises listed below have "a" and "b" parts. Typically, the "a" part is performed twice and then the "b" part is performed twice:

1. *Hands.* This cycle was described above.
2. *Upper arm.* Tense the biceps by making a muscle, then relax. Repeat.
3. *Shoulders.* (a) The shoulders are pulled back and then relaxed; (b) the shoulders are brought forward, then relaxed.
4. *Neck.* Rimm and Masters (1979) suggest a yoga exercise at this point. The head is (a) slowly rolled on the neck's axis three or four times in one direction and then (b) in the other direction.
5. *Mouth.* (a) The mouth is opened to its maximum, then relaxed; (b) the jaws are clenched, then relaxed.
6. *Tongue.* (a) The tongue is extended as far as possible, then relaxed; (b) the tongue is retracted as far as possible, then relaxed.
7. *Tongue.* (a) The tongue is pressed hard against the roof of the mouth, then relaxed; (b) the tongue is pressed hard against the floor of the mouth, then relaxed.
8. *Eyes and forehead.* Goldfried and Davison (1976) suggest wrinkling the forehead, then relaxing, followed by smoothing the forehead as much as possible, then relaxing. With the eyes, they suggest closing the eyes tightly, then relaxing. Rimm and Masters (1979) suggest, instead, imagining a pleasant scene. They recommend this based on their clinical experiences which suggest that a tension-relaxation cycle performed at this point sometimes create, rather than alleviate, muscle tension.

9. *Breathing.* (a) Inhale as much as possible, then relax; (b) exhale as much as possible, then relax.
10. *Back.* With shoulders supported against the chair, the client arches his or her back by pushing the trunk of the body forward, then relaxes. This exercise is dropped in the case of clients who suffer from back injuries since it may induce unwanted strain on the back muscles.
11. *Midsection.* (a) The midsection is raised by tensing the buttocks, then relaxed; (b) the midsection is lowered by pressing into the seat, then relaxed.
12. *Thighs.* (a) The legs are extended and raised six inches off the floor, then relaxed; (b) the client digs his or her heels into the floor, then relaxes.
13. *Stomach.* (a) The stomach is pulled in as if the client is ready to do a sit-up, then relaxed; (b) the stomach is extended as far as possible, then relaxed.
14. *Calves and foot.* (a) The toes are pointed toward the head, then relaxed; (b) the toes are pointed toward the floor, then relaxed.
15. *Toes.* (a) The toes are dug into the bottom of the shoes, then relaxed; (b) the toes are made to touch the upper part of the shoes, then relaxed.

This completes the relaxation sequence. Typically, both before and after the sequence, clients are asked to indicate their degree of tension on a scale of 0 (no tension) to 100 (maximum tension). This helps to assess a client's progress in learning to relax.

Clients should not expect to master the relaxation exercises during the first session. Building the skill requires practice. Therefore, it is useful for the therapist to tape the first session and have clients take the relaxation tape home to practice the exercises for about half an hour a day. After a number of such sessions, clients will become proficient at inducing a deep state of relaxation on their own.

At this stage, clients are ready for a procedure referred to as "letting go." Recall that in the initial phase of training, clients are instructed to tense muscles, then to let the muscles relax. Once clients become skilled at this, the tension-inducing phase can be dropped. The client is now instructed to instate relaxation only:

Focus on the feelings in your left hand and let go of any tensions that you feel there. (*Pause for a few seconds.*) Try to relax just a little bit more (*pause*). Feel the tension draining out of your hand (*pause*). Now relax the muscles in the left forearm (*pause*). Let go of the tension there. Try to relax as much as you can (*pause*). Further and further. (*And so on for the other muscle groups.*)

Of course, both the tension-relaxation cycle and the letting go exercise are rather intrusive and time-consuming. Therefore, clients could not perform such exercises in public in situations where they became angry and wished to induce a state of relaxation preparatory to using other anger control skills. To remedy this problem, two additional relaxation procedures are used with clients who are already skilled in inducing relaxation by the more intrusive methods. First is the method known as *differential relaxation* (Jacobson, 1938). The basic concept underlying this procedure is that clients, while engaged in certain activities, can learn to relax those muscles that are not essential to carrying out the activity. For example, a client may be feeling great anger over another person's comments to him or her. Tension may be evident in the stomach and forehead. Since muscle tension in these areas is not essential in order for the client to respond to the other person, the client may attempt to relax muscles in those areas simply by taking a deep breath and, while breathing out slowly, relaxing the relevant muscles. In this manner, the well-trained client can systematically and differentially relax those specific parts of the body that are most tense.

There is another, nonintrusive option available to help clients relax in day-to-day situations, namely *cue-controlled relaxation* (Paul, 1966). During the full relaxation exercises (described earlier), the client learns to pair a state of deep relaxation with some cue word such as "Calm" or "Easy now." Each time that the deeply relaxed client exhales, he or she repeats the cue word to him or herself. After a number of weeks of such pairing, the cue word alone should induce a state of relaxation. Now, in a problem situation, angry clients can breathe deeply and repeat to themselves "Calm," thereby inducing sensations of relaxation that counteract and help dissipate the tension produced by anger. It should be noted that cue-controlled and differential relaxation are frequently used together; that is, the client repeats the word "calm" while relaxing selected muscle groups. The client will become calm enough to implement other options (to aggression) in the situation, such as cognitive restructuring and/or assertion (discussed below).

Another technique that has been used to control anger is a variant of *systematic desensitization*. This technique has not been employed with great frequency as yet to control anger but research evidence (noted below) suggests it may be helpful for many clients. The procedure incorporates muscle relaxation training as described above. More specifically, the procedure involves having a deeply relaxed client imagine each of a series of increasingly potent anger-eliciting situations. As was true of relaxation training, the goal of systematic desensitization for anger is to help clients to control their arousal or agitation. It then becomes possible for them to employ other techniques to help them express their anger in an effective and nonaggressive manner. Thus, systematic desensitization would normally be applied as part of a treatment package that included provision for altering anger-inducing cognitions and ameliorating behavior deficits to provide nonaggressive response alternatives.

Before beginning the intervention, the therapist must assess two things. First, one must determine whether the client can imagine problematic scenes vividly enough to engender the angry feelings that brought him or her to the clinic. Sometimes it may be necessary for the therapist to provide external prompts in the form of a detailed narrative to help the client imagine the scenes. If the client still cannot perform this task, then desensitization will be ineffective. Fortunately, the majority of clients are able to do this. Second, the therapist should determine whether the client is able to achieve a state of deep muscle relaxation since this too is an integral part of the intervention. Once the client meets these two preconditions, the therapist is ready to present the treatment rationale.

In spite of considerable controversy regarding the effective mechanism underlying desensitization (Wilson & Davison, 1971; Wolpe, 1958), therapists generally introduce the procedure to clients using some variant of a "counter-conditioning" rationale:

> To begin with, we'll work together to get you really relaxed. Then what I'll have you do is imagine various situations related to your anger, starting with ones that arouse only a little bit of anger, and then working up to those that get you really mad. I'll introduce the scenes in a *gradual* way and you'll learn to relax when you imagine them. Because of this, you'll eventually be able to imagine situations related to the anger-provoking scenes and feel calm and under control at the same time. Once you can *imagine* these situations, and still feel calm, you'll find that when you're up against an anger-inducing situation in real life, you'll be able to avoid becoming uncontrollably upset. Do you have any questions about what we're doing before we go on?

The next step involves constructing a *hierarchy*. The hierarchy consists of a graded series of scenes depicting real-life, anger-provoking situations that clients will be asked to imagine while they effect a state of relaxation. The client, not the therapist, is responsible for constructing this hierarchy. The scenes are ordered so that those at the beginning of the hierarchy will induce only slight anger whereas those farther down on the hierarchy will induce intense anger. Clients will typically be given a homework assignment in which they are asked to select scenes that vary in anger-inducing properties on a scale of 0 to 10 from little to none (1–2), to mild (3–4), to moderate (5–6), to strong (7–8), to intense (9–10). The client is instructed to describe the scene in sufficient detail so that when the therapist later presents it during desensitization, there is reasonable assurance that the client is vividly imagining the scene. The items in the hierarchy should be selected to cover the entire range of anger arousal and should be more or less equally spaced along the intensity continuum. Generally, ten items in a hierarchy are deemed adequate (Marquis and Morgan, 1969).

Often, hierarchies are constructed around some theme. The following is an example of an anger hierarchy constructed arount the theme "Disrespect from others makes me angry." The description of each item is abbreviated and is given only to clarify the general nature of a hierarchy. In actual practice, each item would contain more elaborate description.

1. I am waiting in a shoe store for the clerk to help me but he is chatting with a friend.
2. I ask my children to wash up before dinner but they dally.
3. I am sitting at my office desk about an hour before quitting time and my boss drops off two hours worth of work and asks me to finish it before I leave.
4. I am talking to my mother-in-law on the phone explaining why we can't visit her this weekend but she is not listening to me.
5. I am watching my neighbor prune her tree. She is being careless and letting many branches fall into my backyard.
6. I am lying in bed at 2 A.M. and can't get to sleep because my neighbors have decided to play their stereo at full volume.
7. I am sitting at a sales meeting at work. My boss is listening to the advice of my coworkers but barely acknowledges my advice.
8. I am in an auto repair shop picking up my car that was supposed to be ready. The mechanic is explaining that he couldn't get to my car today because there was a backlog and the other cars had priority.
9. I have asked my son to go to his room because he was disruptive at dinner. He is smarting off telling me that he doesn't have to go if he doesn't want to.
10. I am at a cocktail party with friends. My spouse has had too many drinks and is explaining to friends why I'll never amount to much.

It is important to note that the hierarchy constructed above is likely to be valid for one client but not another. That is, other clients may find item #1 extremely irritating but item #8 only mild to moderately irritating. The point is that clients must construct their own hierarchy of anger-inducing situations.

The desensitization itself begins with the first item on the hierarchy. The client is instructed to imagine the first scene (i.e., the therapist uses the description of the scene provided by the client) and to signal the therapist when he or she has generated a clear image of the scene. Typically, the signal consists of raising the index finger (Cautela, 1966; Wolpe, 1969). Also, the client is instructed to signal again if he or she experiences at least some anger (say a level of 1 on a scale of 0–10 where 10 represents intense anger). If the client experiences agitation, he or she attempts to become more relaxed. This can be done via deep muscle relaxation but it is preferable to employ cue-controlled or differential relaxation (as described above). This is because these methods are more generally usable in the natural environment to which we wish such anger-control measures to generalize. When the arousal is brought under control, the scene is repeated after a break of about 30 seconds. Once the client is successful in imagining the scene for 10 seconds without anger, the scene is repeated for 25–30 seconds (Rimm & Masters, 1979). If this longer presentation also fails to evoke intense anger, the therapist moves on to the next item in the hierarchy. Whenever anger is signalled, relaxation is employed until the anger-related arousal is reduced to a negligible level.

As was noted above, desensitization is typically combined with other therapeutic interventions including assertive training and cognitive restructuring (discussed at length below). It is rarely used alone in anger control because clients who suffer from chronic anger problems and related aggression will almost always possess a maladaptive system of beliefs and/or deficits in their repertoire of appropriate, interpersonally successful behaviors. Once the client has undergone effective desensitization and received additional cognitive and assertive training, it is important that he or she practice all these skills in real-life situations in order to promote generalization from the clinic to the natural environment.

The relaxation and desensitization techniques described above have proven useful in anger control. Although the literature is not extensive as of yet, several studies have documented the utility of these procedures (Evans, 1970; Evans, Hearn & Saklofske, 1973; O'Donnell & Worell, 1973; Rimm, deGroot, Boord, Heiman & Dillow, 1971). In an interesting study, Smith (1973) used laughter, rather than relaxation, as a means for inhibiting anger via a desensitization procedure. This study has considerable face validity given the everyday observation that tense, anger-filled situations can often be defused once combatants are induced to see the humorous aspects of what is occurring.

Finally, we may note that in a later section of this chapter, we will outline the important work of Novaco (1975) who employed relaxation concomitantly with several other procedures in order to enhance anger control.

COGNITIVE LEARNING METHODS

The second technique relevant to aggression control that we wish to discuss involves identifying and changing those beliefs a client has that facilitate or set off aggressive behavior.

Theory

The basic rationale behind cognitive methods is that a client's feelings and behavior can be changed by influencing his or her patterns of thinking. One important treatment intervention derived from this notion is referred to as Rational Emotive Therapy (RET), developed intensively by Ellis (1962). RET is based on the assumption that most serious, nonpsychotic psychological disturbances such as those involving intense anger, depression, and anxiety result from faulty or irrational patterns of thought. These ways of thinking, in turn, arise from assumptions that are derived from the client's basic belief system. For example, clients who assume that they must be loved by everyone in order to have value as people, may respond to rejection by having thoughts characterized by a desperate hostility: "It's very important that everybody like me. My neighbor criticized me unfairly the other day. How dare he put me down as if to say that I'm worthless? I'll show him who's worthless. I'm going to storm over to his house and give him a piece of my mind right now." Certain thoughts, then, can help trigger angry emotions and aggressive outbursts. It should be noted that in the above example and in many of the examples that follow, the client may not in fact be self-verbalizing such statements as "My neighbor thinks I'm worthless." Rather, his or her general thinking about a problem may usefully and accurately be summarized by such statements.

RET distinguishes between rational and irrational thoughts, and appropriate versus inappropriate emotions. Irrational thoughts have one of two characteristics: (a) they are empirically false, or (b) they are of a nature that cannot be empirically verified. Thus, if a man is turned down for a date, he may think "Women hate me," and subsequently respond by feeling hostile toward women. This type of thinking is irrational since one usually finds that a number of women in the individual's life have responded to him at one time or another with love and affection. Further, it may be that the woman in the present example did not hate the man but, instead, had another date that evening, or was feeling ill, or was upset by something that happened to her that day and did not feel like going out. The thought, "Women hate me" can thus be empirically proven to be false. But what if women really do hate the client? This leads to a second point of interest, namely that in the face of such loathing, the client may think "Women hate me; therefore, I am worthless." This type of irrational thinking cannot be empirically verified. In what sense can one *rate* the totality of a human being? There is no absolute set of standards that we can invoke that allows us to give ratings to our "selves." A given behavior can be judged desirable or undesirable but it is irrational to conclude that one is good or bad on the basis of a particular behavior or situational outcome. In short, even if women do hate the individual, it does not mean that the individual is worthless, although he certainly may be unhappy.

In contrast to the irrational type of thinking illustrated above, rational thoughts are those that help an individual to survive; they aid the individual in achieving self-selected goals and in acting on values that make life more pleasurable and worthwhile. Thus, in the example cited above, the man might think to himself, "I wonder if there's something that prevents her from going out with me tonight. Maybe she had another date or wasn't feeling well. I'll follow up in a few days with another phone call. If that doesn't work, I'll ask her if she would rather that I not pursue a dating relationship with her at this time. At least then I'll know to look for someone else to go out with." This type of thinking does not involve self-rating nor does it contain empirically false statements. Instead, a sequence of actions is planned that help the individual to achieve personal goals. In sum, irrational thoughts are self-destructive; they engender emotional distress and facilitate maladaptive behavior. Rational thoughts, on the other hand, help the individual to obtain personal satisfaction and effectively prevent or at least mitigate self-defeating emotional and behavioral reactions.

Having noted the difference between rational and irrational thoughts, we may now consider the distinction between appropriate versus inappropriate emotions. The central point is that it is appropriate to feel *concerned* about life events and to *care* about what happens such that one may feel disappointment, frustration, or sadness if things do not go well. These are natural human reactions and are appropriate expressions of emotion. On the other hand, emotional excesses involving deep depression, rage, or extreme anxiety are held to be inappropriate emotional reactions. Ellis hypothesizes that these emotional states are brought on by irrational, self-destructive patterns of thinking and, because they harm us (i.e., by producing emotional distress and by preventing us from achieving important personal goals), they are inappropriate. To put it another way, *others* do not cause our emotional problems, *we* do, namely by the things that we tell ourselves. There are several important clues that signal when irrational thinking and concomitant inappropriate emotions are about to occur (Ellis, 1977):

1. The existence of "awfulizing," that is, self-verbalizations that certain events are awful or catastrophic; for example, "It would be awful if the teacher criticized me in front of my classmates."
2. The presence of "can't stand" or "can't bear" statements; for example, "I can't bear the thought of her not loving me any more."
3. "Musterbating;" for example, "I *must* reach the top of my profession."
4. Damning (blaming) oneself or others; for example, "I'm a gutless nobody because I didn't speak up at that meeting," or "He is disgusting and worthless because he's always trying to win brownie points from his boss."

By engaging in the above types of thinking, individuals immeasurably increase the probability that they will experience inappropriate emotions.

Where do these irrational ideas come from? There are five important sources (Ellis & Harper, 1975). First, in early childhood, we have difficulty distinguishing real from imagined dangers. If we act badly, a monster may sweep down and carry us away. This magical type of thinking, albeit in modified form, frequently survives into adulthood where it continues to plague us. Second, as young children, we experience strong emotional upset when our needs are not immediately gratified. Unfortunately, some people maintain this pattern of emotional reaction in adulthood (i.e., "Isn't it terrible that other people won't give me what I want right away?"), with the result that positive interactions with others are disrupted. Third, as children, we are dependent on others who plan and think for us. Their thoughts, however wrong or irrational, guide our lives. Some adults continue to accept such thoughts as the truth, even when it is self-destructive to do so. A fourth point, related to the third, concerns the possibility that our parents may inculcate in us many prejudices and superstitions. If we do not challenge or question these modes of thinking as we mature, we may be left with a host of untenable hypotheses with which to guide our lives. Fifth, the mass media of our culture may indoctrinate us into believing much that is harmful. If we come to believe that it is possible to be happy only if we have many beautiful women (or men) friends, an expensive sports car, are young, good looking, and own a $300,000 house in Malibu, then the chances are great that rage or depression will be our lot in life.

The link between irrational thinking and inappropriate emotions, noted above, is best expressed in terms of the *A-B-C-D-E* paradigm (Ellis, 1971; 1974). *A* refers to an external event (or activating experience) that the individual encounters. The person responds to *A* with any of several self-verbalizations or patterns of thinking, B, that reflect the individual's belief system. Certain emotional and/or behavioral consequences, C, result from B. D refers to the therapeutic efforts engaged in by the individual (with help from the therapist) to challenge and dispute the irrational beliefs symbolized by B. E represents the favorable consequences (i.e., emotional relief and more appropriate behavior) that are produced once the irrational belief system has been successfully challenged and altered in the direction of greater rationality. In sum, A-B-C represents Ellis' theory of emotional reactivity and D-E symbolizes the therapeutic change process. The example of the man who asks for a date and is refused can serve to explicate this paradigm further. A consists of the man's being rejected by the woman when he asks her for a date. B is represented by the self-verbalization "I am worthless. Good people are not turned down when they ask for dates." C is the emotional consequence of the individual's belief, B, namely a feeling of anger or rage at being turned down. D might involve the therapist's helping the client to dispute the cognitions represented by B, perhaps by teaching the client that humans cannot be rated in a global sense and therefore there is no such thing as worthlessness. Further, the woman may have specific reasons for not going out and it might therefore be worthwhile to ascertain what these reasons are and perhaps ask her out again. E would then follow and consist of a feeling of relief and reduced anger coupled with constructive feelings of hopefulness. Also, E might involve a series of adaptive behaviors aimed at promoting and enhancing the client's social life.

A great deal of effort has gone into explicating the kinds of irrational beliefs that give rise to emotional disturbance and maladaptive behavior. Based on extensive clinical work with hundreds of clients, Ellis and Harper (1975) have isolated those irrational beliefs that are most common to our culture and therefore the ones most in need of remediation efforts. Some of these beliefs are especially relevant from the standpoint of anger and aggression control. It is therefore worthwhile to describe them and briefly discuss their problematic aspects.

One belief concerns the notion that one must prove thoroughly competent. This notion is irrational on several counts. To begin with, it sets the individual up for inevitable failure and possibly for subsequent feelings of anger or rage. It is impossible to master all tasks at all times. Humans must inevitably perform at less than optimal levels if only for reasons of fatigue or illness, not to mention real skill deficits. Secondly, those who are driven to perfection may soon find life empty since in their single-minded pursuit of optimum performance, they will of necessity forego much that is enjoyable and pleasurable in life. This in turn could lead to a feeling of being "cheated" and perhaps manifest itself in short temper. Third, the desperate struggle for achievement is often a reflection of a desire to beat out others and thereby to affirm one's self-worth. But worth in this global sense cannot be measured (as we have seen). Finally, thinking in this manner is apt to produce inappropriately competitive aggressiveness.

A second, aggression-relevant idea noted by Ellis and Harper, pertains to the belief that certain people are bad and must therefore be punished. This usually stems from the idea that there are *inherently* correct ways for people to act. This is irrational because it implies that there is some absolute standard of good and evil. But as Shakespeare noted long ago in *Hamlet*, "There is nothing good or bad but thinking makes it so." We arbitrarily define good and evil or at best arrive at some kind of consensus that reflects local values and specific situations. Thus, it makes no sense to declare another person "intrinsically" bad and therefore worthy of severe punishment. Second, by labeling others as bad, we imply that they possess some immutable trait and that there is no possibility of their changing the behaviors that make us so angry. In fact, this is very often not the case. We are frequently in a position to remove the cause of our anger by rationally deducing a course of action that would alter events (including the behavior of others) in a direction that is more satisfactory from an interpersonal standpoint. Third, blaming others may not only make us angry but may bring about even more unpleasant consequences. For example, by criticizing others, we may in fact elicit further obnoxious behavior and a vicious circle of aggression and counteraggression.

A third irrational belief, namely that it is catastrophic when things do not go the way one wants them to, is problematic on several counts. First, by pouring all of one's energies into ranting against the injustices of the world, one effectively blocks potential constructive action that might be taken to ameliorate the undesirable state of affairs. There are really only two courses of action that can be rationally taken in the face of frustration or unfair treatment. One can either plan how best to resolve the problem or one can decide that the problem is after all insoluble and decide to adjust to an imperfect world. Unfortunately, the latter track is unacceptable to many people who habitually work themselve up into a frenzy of righteous indignation rather than accept the fact that unfair and unethical circumstances arise and that sometimes one's only option is to learn to live with this unhappy reality. But working oneself up is self-defeating since it not only induces aversive emotional states such as rage but in addition prevents the person from planning more constructive alternatives.

Many people believe that emotional misery comes from external pressures and is therefore beyond an individual's control. But as we have seen repeatedly in the examples above, it appears that to a large extent we control our own emotional states by the kinds of statements we verbalize to ourselves. Yet, many people will complain that they cannot help themselves: "When Mr. X says certain things, I automatically fly into a rage." Thus, to some extent, the individual believes that he or she is a marionette and other people are pulling the strings that control emotional states. Although it may be difficult to control one's thoughts, and thus feelings, it is not impossible. Through concerted effort and practice, one can alter ones thoughts and thus avoid being overwhelmed by self-destructive feelings. This outlook is by far the most important one that comes from the philosophy of RET.

Research

A number of investigators have produced data that bear directly on the validity of Ellis' theory of emotional reactivity. According to this theory, one's mood states or emotional arousal should be affected by the kinds of self-verbalizations that one makes. In a direct test of these ideas, Velten (1968) had subjects read statements that varied in content. Some statements reflected elation (e.g., "This is great—I really do feel good"); others reflected depression (e.g., "I have too many bad things in my life"); while still others were neutral (e.g., "Utah is the Beehive State"). Consistent with the theory behind RET, Velten found that an individual's mood (as reflected by self-report and the tempo of one's motor acivities) changed according to the kinds of statements the individual was reading. Similar findings, that emotional arousal can be directly influenced by one's self-verbalizations, have been obtained by other investigators (May & Johnson, 1973; Rimm & Litvak, 1969; Russell & Brandsma, 1974).

Several outcome studies have compared the efficacy of RET to other treatment modalities. In one study, Maes and Heimann (1970) compared the effectiveness of RET, systematic desensitization, and client-centered therapy (a therapy emphasizing the importance of the therapist's understanding the client's subjective experiences and helping the client to gain understanding of his or her feelings and current behaviors). The subjects were test-anxious high school students. On a number of physiological measures (e.g., heart rate, galvanic skin response), subjects treated with desensitization or RET showed much less emotional reactivity, when put in a test situation, than subjects who were given client-centered therapy or subjects who had been in an untreated control group.

A study by Meichenbaum, Gilmore, and Fedoravicius (1971) compared group RET and group desensitization with two control groups as methods for treating speech anxiety. With respect to a variety of objective and self-report measures, the subjects who received desensitization or RET showed the greatest improvement in connection with test speeches. Subjects in both of these groups improved significantly more than subjects in either an attention control group or a waiting-list control group.

In a third study, DiLoreto (1971) treated a number of individuals who suffered from excessive interpersonal anxiety. RET was compared with systematic desensitization, client-centered therapy, a placebo treatment, and a no-treatment control group. Subjects in the desensitization group showed the greatest degree of anxiety reduction. RET, however, produced the greatest effect with respect to increasing the amount of interpersonal activity.

Finally, Moleski and Tosi (1976) treated a group of stutterers using either RET or systematic desensitization. RET was more effective than desensitization in reducing objectively rated speech dysfluencies.

The above outcome studies suggest that RET can be a useful intervention for the reduction of anxiety and anxiety-related disorders. In addition, there are a number of case studies reported that suggest the usefulness of RET in treating problems such as depression and guilt (Ellis, 1971). Finally, and most importantly for our purpose, there are a few reports of the successful use of RET to eliminate fighting among siblings (DiGiuseppe, 1975, 1977) and antisocial acts such as theft and child molestation (Watkins, 1977). In sum, then, there is an empirical basis for the notion that RET might prove clinically useful in controlling a variety of psychological problems including those related to anger and aggression.

Practice

An important question relevant to carrying out RET concerns how best to convince or teach clients to alter the way they think so that they view situations more rationally. There are a number of ways that one can proceed but a particularly useful strategy has been outlined by Goldfried and Davison (1976) and we will describe their approach next in some detail.

Presentation of Rationale. Consider a case that one of the authors dealt with in which a man came into therapy because he was having considerable trouble controlling his temper around his wife and children. The result was that his marriage was in trouble and his children tried to avoid him as much as possible. The therapist suspected that this individual spent a lot of time ruminating about the injustices of life and how people were constantly "screwing him over." The first step is to get this client to realize that he is making himself excessively angry by the kinds of things he keeps saying to himself. We would like him, in short, to accept the basic tenet of RET, namely that one's feelings may be strongly affected by the content of one's thoughts. The following is a typical transcript:

Therapist: You mentioned that you were especially troubled by your inability to control your temper. Tell me a little more about this.

Client: I don't know what the problem is but it just seems to me that people can be really rotten. They can't be trusted. Every time I try to stay calm, somebody does something that really irks me. Like last week I was going through an intersection and this son of a bitch driver cuts me off. Well, I wasn't going to let him get away with that. I followed him for ten blocks, honking my horn, trying to get him to pull over. I don't understand it but my wife became really upset with me.

In talking further with this client, it became clear why the wife was upset. The husband in fact pursued the other driver at high speeds through 30 blocks, not 10. All the while, he was cursing at the top of his lungs, pounding the dashboard, threatening to kill the other driver if he caught up with him. When his wife pleaded with him to pull over and let her and the children out, he accused her of ganging up against him in favor of the other driver. In short, he was prepared to kill himself and his family, if necessary, in order to "teach the other driver a lesson."

We would like this client to consider the possibility that his anger results to a considerable degree from the way in which he thinks about the situation. It is best not to begin by addressing the problem that brought the client to the clinic as this may prove to be too much to deal with right away. Instead, the therapist may select a fairly general example to illustrate the treatment rationale:

Therapist: It seems that some situations really get to you. Often people bring on their own anger by the way the look at a situation. Let me see if I can illustrate this. Suppose you were walking in the park and a person that you knew who had just inherited a large sum of money went by without looking at you or greeting you. What would you think?

Client: That he believed he was too good for me now that he was rich.

Therapist: O.K. So you'd feel snubbed and maybe a little angry.

Client: That's right.

Therapist: Now, what if I told you that he had just found out his son was terminally ill?

Client: Oh, that's different. I'd feel sorry for him and would try to help him out.

Therapist: In other words, now you would feel pity and maybe a little bit of anxiety as well.

Client: Right.

Therapist: But why do you suppose you would have two such different feelings—anger versus anxiety—even though objectively the situation was the same?

Client: Well, its because I wouldn't be looking at things the same way in the two situations.

Therapist: Would it be fair to say that the way a person thinks about things might determine what kinds of feelings he experiences?

Client: Well, the way you just described it, I would say that you're right.

At this point, the client is on the way to recognizing that his thoughts about a given situation may strongly influence how he feels and acts in that situation.

Overview of Irrational Assumptions. Once the client accepts the basic rationale that thoughts influence feelings, the therapist can become more specific by discussing various irrational assumptions related to the problem of anger and aggression per se. The purpose of this step is to help the client recognize that certain beliefs are untenable and self-destructive. The social psychological literature on reactance (Brehm, 1966) suggests that if the therapist attacks the client's irrational beliefs, some clients may respond by clinging even more tenaciously to such beliefs. To avoid this kind of backfire, the therapist may employ the devil's advocate strategy. That is, the therapist may present an irrational belief and ask the client to argue against it. The cognitive dissonance literature (Brehm & Cohen, 1962) would imply that clients might be more apt to change their attitudes in a rational direction if they can be induced to argue in favor of a more rational position.

Therapist: I'd like to do something unusual now. I'm going to present a particular belief. What I want you to do is try to give me as many reasons as you can to convince me that my belief is irrational and can only hurt me. That is, I want you to argue against my ideas and tell me why they just don't hold water.

Client: O.K.

Therapist: I believe that people who criticize me are basically bad and deserve to be punished.

Client: That's ridiculous. If somebody criticizes you, it doesn't automatically mean they're bad.

Therapist: But they were only saying what they did to make me look silly.

Client: Isn't it possible that a person can have an honest difference of opinion?

Therapist: Sure, but I think this time they really meant to get my goat.

Client: Well, that's their problem if that's the way they treat people. You don't have to stoop to their level.

Therapist: But I don't like being treated that way.

Client: Of course you don't, who would? It's unfortunate for both you and them that they've learned to deal with people that way but that doesn't make them bad, irritating yes, but not bad.

Therapist: (*Returning to normal role*) O.K. I think you saw right through the irrationality of that belief. What you said was that people who criticize us aren't intrinsically bad even when their criticisms are ill intentioned.

As pointed out above, it is likely that several other beliefs contribute to excessive anger. For example, the idea that one must be thoroughly competent at everything may produce much frustration and anger when the inevitable failure occurs. Likewise, the belief that it is a catastrophe when things do not work out the way one would like and the belief that emotional misery comes exclusively from external pressures are both examples of ideas that can set off angry reactions given the appropriate situation. It would be useful then for the therapist to play devil's advocate with respect to these beliefs as well.

Analysis of Client's Problem in Rational Terms. Once the client has come to see how certain general beliefs can set off anger reactions, the therapist can start to focus on the specific problems encountered by the client. For example, the irrationality of the client's self-verbalizations can be looked at from the standpoint of how likely it is that the client is interpreting the situation correctly and what the ultimate implications are of the way that the client is looking at the situation. We can illustrate this procedure with respect to the earlier example of the client who had an angry outburst when another driver cut him off at an intersection:

Therapist: When the other driver cut you off, what kinds of things went through your mind?

Client: I thought that this is the last time someone is going to push me around and get away with it.

Therapist: So you thought that perhaps the other driver had no respect for you and regarded you as some kind of nobody.

Client: Yeah, that's right. Just as if I was a nobody. Just as if I was trash.

Therapist: Did you know the other driver?

Client: No.

Therapist: So far as you know, he wasn't doing it to put *you* down personally?

Client: Well—uh—I guess not.

Therapist: When he cut you off, did he yell "You're worthless so I'm cutting in front of you?"

Client: (*Laughing*) No, not really.

Therapist: So far as you could tell, it wasn't particularly likely that he was out to put you down.

Client: I guess not but it did make me angry.

At this point, the therapist has gotten the client to see that his original interpretation of the situation was very likely inaccurate. Now, we would like the client to see how this inaccurate belief can ultimately hurt him:

Therapist: I'm sure the situation made you very angry. But tell me this—did the angry reaction you had reverse what happened?

Client: What do you mean?

Therapist: Did the other driver get out of his car, apologize to you, and offer to back up into the intersecion so that you could go before him?

Client: Of course not, I couldn't catch him.

Therapist: True, but even if you did, there was no guarantee that the situation would have become more favorable. In fact, it sounds as if you would have gotten into a worse fight.

Client: Well, you're right of course. But I couldn't help the way I felt.

Therapist: How did you feel while you were chasing him?

Client: I felt tense and queasy.

Therapist: How did you feel about the fight you had with your wife?

Client: I felt bad later and guilty because I was risking my family's safety just to prove a point.

Therapist: So, what you're saying to me is that by looking at the situation as if the other driver was challenging your worth as a person, you succeeded in making yourself tense, and afterwards guilty, of the way you behaved. That's propably not the outcome you were hoping for.

Client: (*Quietly*) No, it wasn't.

Having gotten the client to see that his irrational beliefs that set off anger are faulty and cause him much emotional distress, the therapist can proceed to teach the client to change his self-verbalizations so that they are more rational and constructive.

Teaching Clients to Modify Self-Verbalizations. The core of this technique is to teach clients to use their anger as a cue to analyze and resolve their problems with rational methods. That is, each time clients feel themselves getting angry, they should stop and ask, "What am I saying to myself that might be irrational? Is there a more rational way of looking at the situation?" Several interventions are possible for teaching clients this new skill.

1. *Imaginal Presentation.* One important type of intervention that can be used is referred to as systematic rational restructuring (Goldfried, Decenteceo, & Weinberg, 1974). With this technique, the therapist helps the client to construct a hierarchy of anger-producing situations such that the client experiences greater intensity of anger with items higher on the hierarchy. In the case of the client described above, it may be that being cut off by another driver produces a level of anger rated at 30 (on a scale of 0 to 100, with 100 as the maximum); the presence of noisy children in the living room produces anger rated at 50; and perceived put downs from his wife produce anger rated at 70. These three situations would be presented to the client sequentially such that he would be taught to deal with the situation that evoked the least amount of anger first and the situation that evoked the greatest amount of anger last. Most importantly, the situations would be presented to the client imaginally in the consulting room, thereby allowing the therapist to prompt the client to engage in more rational self-discourse. Thus, the therapist might, in the example under discussion, prompt the client to view the behavior of the person who cut him off in more rational terms by teaching the client to say to himself, "The other driver is probably in a rush to get somewhere," or "The other driver hasn't learned any manners. I'm glad I'm not like him." Eventually, the therapist would help the client to work his way to the top of the hierarchy. An example of the client-therapist dialogue will illustrate the procedure more clearly:

Therapist: I'd like you to imagine yourself in a particular situation and tell me how angry you feel. Then, I want you to repeat out loud the things you're telling yourself that are fueling your anger and how you might change what you're telling yourself so that you'll experience less anger. Periodically, I'll be interjecting various statements and questions and I want you to treat them as if they were your own thoughts. Any questions?
Client: No.
Therapist: O.K. Close your eyes and imagine yourself in this situation: Your wife would like you to go to a party where all of the people

are friends of hers from work. You tell her that you don't want to go and she responds by asking you why you're afraid of them. How angry do you feel on a scale of 0 to 100?

Client: About 70.

Therapist: (*Simulating the client's thoughts*) O.K. I'm really furious. What is that I'm saying to myself right now?

Client: I hate it when she puts me down like that.

Therapist: But how do I know that she's putting me down?

Client: Her friends are all professionals and I'm not. She's ashamed of me and she's shooting barbs at me because of it.

Therapist: I wonder if I'm overreacting. Whenever I get this angry I tend not to view things too clearly. Let me think a minute. If she was really ashamed of me, why would she want me to accompany her to the party?

Client: Probably she's not ashamed of me.

Therapist: Could it be that I'm ashamed of myself and that's why I'm angry?

Client: That's really possible. I guess I feel I haven't gone far enough in life.

Therapist: But my value as a person doesn't depend on what occupational status I've achieved. First, and foremost, I am a person and I'd like to enjoy life.

Client: I guess I can't do that if I'm always hiding from people.

Therapist: Right, and if a bunch of strangers don't think highly of me, am I therefore a worm?

Client: No! Of course not!

Therapist: So what have I got to lose by going to the party?

Client: Really nothing. I'm beginning to see that perhaps my wife wants me to go because she wants to be with me. That's flattering. It doesn't make sense to explode with anger. I feel pretty good.

The therapist gave the client a lot of help in disputing the irrational cognitions engendered by the wife's request. As the client practices dealing with more and more problem situations, his skills will become better and the therapist can gradually eliminate his or her help altogether. That is, clients will be in a position to carry out the corrective procedure entirely on their own even in new situations.

2. *Modeling*. The therapist's own rational philosophy can function as a model for the client to adopt. Essentially, the therapist-client interaction can be conceived of as an educational process in which the therapist's statements convey to the client the appropriateness and utility of a rational belief system. The technique described above can be explicitly

supplemented by the therapist's disclosing personal experiences to the client and modeling for the client how he or she, the therapist, used rational restructuring to overcome some of his or her own anger-evoking thoughts.

3. *Group Settings.* Occasionally, it is appropriate to carry out rational restructuring in groups. The members of the group will all have similar kinds of problems with anger control. Basically, the group intervention is a form of modeling in which each member can observe, learn from, and provide corrective feedback and impressions to other members of the group.

4. *Behavior Rehearsal.* Rational restructuring may under certain circumstances involve *overt* rather than imagined activities. For example, the client might act out the anger-producing interaction with his wife in the presence of the therapist. This can be particularly useful since some of the wife's misperceptions can be dealt with as well. Thus, both husband and wife can practice more rational ways of dealing with problems. This mode of intervention is likely to be especially beneficial in cases of marital discord and parent-adolescent conflict (see Chapter 2 on negotiation and contracting).

5. *In vivo Assignments.* Once clients have mastered the rational restructuring procedure in the consultation room, they are ready to try it in the real world (*in vivo*), that is, in their homes, neighborhoods, or places of work. Any difficulties encountered there can be discussed later with the therapist and appropriate modifications made.

6. *Bibliotherapy.* Some clients are helped by reading books that outline the rationale and methods that constitute the cognitive change procedures we have been describing (e.g., Ellis & Harper, 1975). Such bibliotherapy can serve as a useful adjunct to direct client-therapist contact and is certainly consistent with the self-help emphasis inherent in this mode of therapy.

ASSERTIVENESS TRAINING

Assertiveness training is a third intervention relevant to aggression control. We will begin by discussing the nature of assertive behavior and how it differs from counterproductive modes of behavior such as aggression and nonassertion.

Theory

Assertive behavior has been defined in a variety of ways by different investigators and practitioners. In the past, assertive behavior was largely synonymous with the notion of standing up for one's rights. More recently, however, the concept of assertion has been expanded to include other forms of interpersonal behavior especially that involving the appropriate expression of thoughts and feelings, both positive and negative. A hallmark of assertive behavior is that it is direct and honest and, equally important, that it takes into consideration the rights and feelings of others. Last, and of considerable significance, assertive behavior involves effective communication with a view to achieving personal goals.

In our culture, assertion and aggression are frequently confused with one another. One of us recently worked with the parents of an aggressive boy. The father boasted that he was proud that his son was aggressive since that was the only way of getting ahead in the world. The more aggressive one was the better. When it was pointed out, *reductio ad absurdum*, that according to this logic, murder should therefore be the most effective and desirable behavior, the father appeared confused. He, and many other people, stress the importance of domination and winning as the most adaptive style of interpersonal behavior. Yet, this aggressive style is frequently a self-destructive one. By means of aggressive behavior, an individual stands up for personal rights but does so in a way that always violates the rights of others (Lange & Jakubowski, 1976). Further, aggressive expression is typically dishonest and socially inappropriate. In fact, then, aggression and assertion are diametric opposites. Thus, individuals who describe their domination or intimidation of another as assertive are confused. Their behavior, quite simply, is aggressive.

If aggression involves violating the rights of others, then nonassertion may be said to violate one's own rights. The nonassertive individual expresses thoughts and feelings in a self-deprecating, apologetic manner that can be readily ignored by others. Or, the individual may fail altogether to express personal needs. It is common for such individuals to confuse nonassertion with politeness or good manners. For example, one of us had a client who could not decline his friend's requests to help them fix their faulty plumbing. He spent most of his free time doing repair work and was thus unable to spend much time with his own family, a matter that was causing considerable friction between him and his wife. The basic problem was his belief that he would not be a "nice guy" if he asserted himself and told his friends that he wanted the time to be with his family.

Confusion between assertion and aggression, or nonassertion and politeness is common among clients who have distressed interpersonal relationships. There are a number of predictable reasons that clients give for their ineffective modes of interpersonal behavior. Several of these have been described at length by Lange and Jakubowski (1976) and are discussed next.

With respect to nonassertive behavior, many clients believe, based on their family upbringing, that any display of firm assertiveness is tantamount to an expression of anger or outright aggression. This is particularly true in the case of women. Traditional socialization practices have emphasized that aggressive behavior is appropriate for men but not women. Thus, a woman who equates assertion with aggression may avoid the former because it is "unfeminine" and likely to precipitate derision from significant others. Secondly, as noted above, some people believe that nonassertion is a form of politeness. They think that only a boor would speak up and express feelings that their rights were being violated by others. In short, they believe that if another person is obnoxious and takes advantage of them, the proper thing to do is to ignore the situation and wait for it to fade away, irrespective of how angry or hurt they might be. A third reason for nonassertion is a belief that an individual does not have personal rights such as the right to attempt to satisfy one's emotional needs. Worse, some individuals deny that they are entitled to express certain feelings such as anger or disappointment. They believe it is wrong to have such feelings. Sometimes one sees this in the case of traditional parents who believe that they must sacrifice their own needs for those of their children. They believe that they are not permitted any feelings of resentment toward their offspring even though a pattern has developed in which the parent explicitly forgoes many activities that once brought enjoyment. By denying any negative feelings in this situation, the parent is acting nonassertively. The sacrifices made may ultimately turn out to be a bitter experience for both child and parent alike unless some explicit recognition is given to the legitimacy of the parent's emotional needs. A fourth, and very common basis for nonassertion, stems from the client's fears that assertive behavior will likely be met with a variety of negative consequences. For example, other people may reject the assertive individual as selfish or unfeeling and subsequently withdraw their affection and friendship. It is believed that still others may become angry and subject the assertive individual to verbal abuse or worse. Fifth, nonassertion is sometimes confused with "rescuing" those who violate our rights. The nonassertive person may rationalize the other person's intrusiveness and unfair behavior by claiming that the offender "could not help himself" or that the other is to be pitied. Of course, once an individual equates nonassertion and helpfulness, he or she becomes an easy target for those who would take advantage. In time, the "helpful" individual may feel used and resentful. Finally, some individuals are nonassertive simply because they never had an opportunity to acquire such skills while growing up. A common case in point concerns individuals who come from families in which both parents are nonassertive. Lacking assertive models, individuals do not learn how to express themselves or stand up for their rights. Instead, they may model the ineffective behavior of their parents.

As the above discussion illustrates, there are a number of reasons that people give for behaving nonassertively in interpersonal situations. Despite the plausible nature of many of these reasons, however, nonassertive behavior generally reaps negative consequences. In the short run, the nonassertive person is able to avoid certain anxiety-producing situations by behaving in a self-effacing manner. Further, others may praise the individual for altruism, or for quiet compliance. Notwithstanding these short-term gains, however, the ultimate, long-term consequences are negative. The nonassertive person suffers a loss of self-esteem and may complain of being taken advantage of. Such an outlook is often correlated with anger and resentment toward others as well as a feeling of being tense or "on edge." Other individuals may avoid the nonassertive person because they feel that such a person is difficult to form an honest relationship with or they may feel revulsion and irritation at the other's constant self-deprecation and palpably ingratiating manner. In the end, the nonassertive person may have few social outlets, and loneliness and frustration may result.

Aggressive behavior, the other self-defeating mode of interpersonal behavior, also occurs as the result of certain common beliefs and reinforcement histories. Some individuals believe that criticism from others is tantamount to a personal attack and the only way to preserve self-esteem is to counterattack. A second factor controlling aggressive behavior is, paradoxically, prior nonassertion. Some nonassertive individuals will allow their feelings and/or rights to be trampled upon by others for a period of time, meanwhile ruminating about these injustices. Then, sometimes quite abruptly, they will "overassert" themselves through an aggressive outburst in an attempt to ameliorate the perceived injustices of the past. Prior nonassertion may also set the stage for "displaced aggression." An individual may be nonassertive in the presence of those who possess greater power, only to respond later with an aggressive outburst directed to others who have less power. The most typical example of this pattern is the parent who returns home after a day of being put down by the boss and responds by verbally attacking his or her children. A third pattern of aggression is mediated through stimulus generalization occurring between a significant other from the individual's past and a significant person from the individual's present. For example, a woman might overreact to her husband's demands for her to adopt a particular viewpoint. On closer examination, one may find that the woman's father forced her to "tow the line" on certain issues and violated her right to have her own opinion. Although her husband may not exert such pressure, the woman perceives a similarity between her husband and her father and reacts to her husband with the same type of angry outburst as she displayed to her overcontrolling father. In some ways, this pattern parallels the psychoanalytic notion of negative transference but the problem is likely more easily remediated by conceptualizing it in stimulus generalization terms. A fourth factor that can set off aggression has to do with the individual's belief that the only way to get anywhere with others is by overpowering them. The philosophy embraced by the client is that it is a "dog-eat-dog world." Finally, as was discussed in Chapter 1, aggressive behavior may be a major part of an individual's repertoire simply because it has "paid off" (i.e., been reinforced). Further, the behavior may have become prepotent because the individual never learned a more appropriate way of carrying on interpersonal relations. In other words, aggression may sometimes reflect a skill deficit; the individual simply does not know how to be assertive.

As was the case with many instances of nonassertion, aggressive behavior often results in short-term gains bought at the price of long-term failure. Frequently, the immediate effect of aggression is that "one gets what one wants." In the long run, however, a pattern of recurrent aggressive acts is typically enough to drive others away, if only because others wish to protect themselves. Thus, developing satisfying interpersonal relationships becomes all but impossible. Alternatively, and not infrequently, the victims begin to counterattack. Ironically, then, individuals who initiate aggressive acts because they perceive the world to be full of threats, in fact create a world that is indeed full of threats—threats of their own making. Finally, those people who are given to only occasional acts of aggression following prolonged periods of nonassertion may feel tremendous guilt upon seeing the hurtful consequences of their aggression. This outcome may then act to strengthen nonassertion, leading the individual to accept higher levels of inappropriate behavior from others. Eventually, though, the individual can no longer remain silent in the face of repeated denial of his or her rights and a new aggressive scene occurs. In this manner, a vicious and upward spiralling cycle of nonassertion followed by aggression is established.

In light of the many drawbacks, described above, to behaving nonassertively or aggressively, one may raise the question of what the presumed benefits of assertion are per se. There are two sets of benefits posited. First, the assertive individual is thought to benefit, phenomenologically, by experiencing feelings of increased self-confidence and well-being. Second, the assertive person is better able to achieve more satisfying, more intimate relationships with others as well as accomplishing goals not directly related to interpersonal relationships as such.

The material reviewed so far may help to define, in broad terms, the elements of a theory of assertiveness. It would be inaccurate to say, however, that a well-developed theory exists at this time. Nonetheless, there are four sets of factors, implicit in the above discussion, that are generally posited to underlie a lack of assertive behavior. We will review and elaborate upon these briefly. First, is the notion put forth by Wolpe (1958) that nonassertive behavior results from a history of punishment for assertion with the result that assertive behavior comes to elicit feelings of anxiety. The individual can avoid the conditioned anxiety by behaving in a nonassertive manner. From this conceptualization, Wolpe deduces a treatment that emphasizes counterconditioning. That is, operating on the assumption that anxiety and assertion are incompatible responses, he advocates training the client to emit assertive behaviors in the face of cues that normally set off anxiety. In this manner, these cues will become discriminative for approach (i.e., assertive) responses that will compete with and eventually nullify the anxiety.

One may acquire anxiety through indirect as well as direct experiences. Often, individuals become anxious in certain interpersonal situations as a result of vicarious learning. That is, many individuals have learned to inhibit assertive behaviors by observing their parents do the same. In fact, it seems that inadequate models may be a source of nonassertion even when anxiety per se is not a factor. Thus, modeling effects are often pointed to as a second variable controlling nonassertion (Wolpe & Lazarus, 1966).

Third, some investigators have advanced the notion that for many clients nonassertion is the result of a skill deficit. The individual does not have the assertive skills that are most effective for a given situation and thus acts nonassertively or aggressively (Gambrill, 1973; MacDonald, 1975).

Finally, an individual's belief system may be such as to impede the expression of assertive behavior (as described in the cognitive learning section above). This set of factors has been discussed at length by Ellis and Harper (1975). Basically, individuals who believe that they have no rights or that certain emotions are forbidden, are not likely to express themselves in an honest and direct fashion.

It is important to note at this point that in spite of the plausible nature of the above four factors in the etiology of nonassertion, relatively little systematic research has been carried out to test such ideas. In what follows next, we will briefly review what research there is on assertiveness training, attempting to tie in some of the above theoretical notions where possible.

Research

The research on assertion can be separated into two types: that dealing with more basic theoretical notions and that dealing with the efficacy of treatment. These two types of research sometimes overlap.

Studies pertaining to the assessment of assertiveness have yielded some interesting results from the standpoint of theory. Before proceeding, however, it is necessary to delineate the nature of these assessment inventories. The inventories are self-report measures that ask clients to indicate whether or not they would carry out a particular activity or to specify the probability that they would carry out the activity. For example, in the Gambrill and Richey Assertion Inventory (Gambrill & Richey, 1975), clients are asked to indicate their degree of discomfort in performing specific responses and the probability of making the response. Items on the scale include: "Tell someone that you like him/her," "Return defective items (e.g., in a store or restaurant)," "Asking a person who is annoying you in a public situation to stop." Other inventories commonly used are the Wolpe-Lazarus Assertiveness Schedule (Wolpe & Lazarus, 1966) and the Rathus Assertiveness Schedule (Rathus, 1973). These scales have good validity data to support them. Thus, Rathus reported a .70 correlation between measures on the Rathus Assertiveness Schedule (RAS) and ratings of assertion in role-played situations. Most important from a theoretical standpoint, however, is the finding of a negative correlation between measures of interpersonal anxiety and RAS scores (Orenstein, Orenstein, & Carr, 1975). Thus, consistent with Wolpe's theory, it appears that anxiety and assertion are incompatible responses. Other research has also demonstrated that clients who behave assertively report feeling less anxious (McFall & Marston, 1970). Of greatest interest is the finding of an inverse relationship between self-reports of anger and assertive expression (Rimm, Snyder, Depue, Haanstad, & Armstrong, 1976). Apparently, anger as well as anxiety may be diminished *following* assertiveness training.

An additional theoretical finding of some interest is that assertion is not a trait. A trait is defined here as a set of behaviors that occurs across situations and is relatively stable over time. A number of studies (e.g., Lawrence, 1970; Gambrill & Richey, 1975) suggest that assertion is situationally specific. Thus, for example, an individual may have no problem being assertive at home and yet be markedly nonassertive at work. Likewise, a woman may be very nonassertive toward her spouse but quite assertive toward other relatives. This specifity supports the learning theory speculations outlined above. That is, if fear conditioning, modeling, or skill deficit analyses have merit, one would expect that an individual's assertion or nonassertion would be dependent on specific environmental cues. This is apparently the case.

Thus far, we have seen that assertive training may be useful in diminishing anger and anxiety. Further, the data suggest that assertion or the lack of it may be situation specific. Therefore, remediation efforts must seek to identify problem situations and to train relevant skills for those situations. Much of the intervention research on assertion has in fact trained clients in specific situations. Notwithstanding this unity of outlook, however, investigators have differed considerably from one another in the particulars of their intervention efforts. There are several general treatment strategies though, which we briefly outline before continuing with our discussion of the research that supports their efficacy.

The therapist begins by attempting to *motivate* the client to change from a nonassertive or aggressive mode of behavior to an assertive one. The rationale for assertion training is presented and the client is helped to develop a more assertive belief system. This is done especially in the case of those clients who deny their own rights of the propriety of expressing certain emotions. Next, the core technique is introduced, namely *behavior rehearsal.* The client and therapist enact relevant interpersonal situations. The client may role play the situation first, then the therapist might step in and *model* a more appropriate (assertive) response. The client may then attempt the role again while the therapist provides *constructive feedback* on the appropriateness and skill of the client's response. In addition to the above, it is typical for the client, with the help of the therapist, to construct, at the start of treatment, a *hierarchy* of interpersonal problem situations. This hierarchy begins with a description of those situations that cause the client the least distress and difficulty, and gradually proceeds to those that are the most problematic. The client and therapist then generate and practice assertive responses to each item on the hierarchy, proceeding from the easiest to the hardest items.

Four principles are involved in determining the content of a given assertive response. First, one begins with the *minimal effective response* (Rimm & Masters, 1979), that is, the response that is the most likely to accomplish the goal with the least effort and the lowest probability of engendering defensive reactions from others. Thus, in dealing with the problem of anger, the therapist teaches the client to communicate in a way that gets the message across but does not unduly upset the listener. A second and related principle is that of *empathic assertion*. Here, the idea is to recognize explicitly the other individual's rights and feelings in addition to getting the point across. For example, one might express one's anger about being pushed by another person while waiting in a line by responding in the following manner: "I know we've all been waiting here for an hour and its hot out (*empathy*), but I don't like being pushed (*assertion*). Could you be more careful (*assertion*)?" A third principle is that of *escalation*, a tactic that is used when the initial assertive statement proves ineffective. The basic idea is for the client to use a stronger statement, remarking on the other person's noncompliance and possibly specifying negative consequences contingent on repeated noncompliance. Finally, assertive training typically employs *in vivo practice* wherein clients try out newly acquired skills in real-life situations returning occasionally to the clinic for additional feedback and training based on the consequences of their *in vivo* efforts.

Some or all of the above strategies have been combined into various assertiveness training packages. The efficacy of these packages is reviewed next.

In one study (Lawrence, 1970), female college students were taught how to express honest disagreement (i.e., disagreement that was consistent with the feelings they experienced in a given interpersonal situation). The students were divided into three groups. The first group was taught how to express disagreement by participating in a behavior rehearsal procedure. The second group was merely given instructions pertaining to the importance of being assertive. The third group listened while the experimenter paraphrased what each subject had said. The primary dependent measure was an objective rating of the subject's ability to disagree while engaged in conversation with two confederates of the experimenter. The behavior rehearsal group showed the greatest improvement, an improvement that was maintained during a two-week follow-up. Interestingly, Lawrence's data also showed that assertive training produced relatively situation-specific effects. In particular, although subjects learned to express honest *disagreement* more readily, there was no change observed for honest *agreement*. This treatment specificity has been noted in other studies as well (e.g., Goldsmith & McFall, 1975) and points to the need for more generalized training experiences.

One question that arises from the above research concerns the relative contribution of each of the various components of assertion training packages. In an influential study, McFall and Twentyman (1973) examined the relative efficacy of behavior rehearsal, modeling, and coaching (i.e., verbal instructions and feedback). On both paper and pencil as well as objective, behavioral measures, rehearsal and coaching appeared to facilitate assertion whereas modeling did not add anything. The behavior involved in this study, however, was a simple one (i.e., making refusals). It is possible that the acquisition of more complex responses would require modeling. This prediction was borne out in a study by Voss, Arick, and Rimm (1976) who found that for simple responses (i.e., refusals), modeling did not enhance assertion whereas for complex responses (e.g., making requests of authority figures), it did. In sum, then, there exists evidence that rehearsal, modeling, and feedback may all contribute to the development of assertion.

Given that assertion training techniques can be effective, one important remaining question concerns the extent to which these techniques can reduce aggression. Several case studies set forth some encouraging results. For example, Foy, Eisler, and Pinkston (1975) treated a client who was given to explosive rages at home and at work. The client's pattern was to hold in anger until he could not stand it anymore and then to engage in some overt aggressive act. Through modeling and verbal instructions, the client was taught assertive responses such as making requests and dealing with demands from others. Following treatment, there was a decrease in hostile remarks and other indices of aggression. Improvement at home and at work was maintained at a 6-month follow-up. In another study, Wallace, Teigen, Liberman, and Baker (1973) treated a psychiatric inpatient who had a 3-year history of violence. Intervention involved a combination of assertive training and contracting. Assaultive behaviors decreased to a negligible level where they remained during a 9-month follow-up. Other researchers have also demonstrated the utility of assertive training in controlling aggression (e.g., Rimm, 1977; Thelen, Fry, Dollinger, & Paul, 1976). In sum, then, assertiveness training has been used successfully to control a variety of aggression-related problems. The components of this intervention do exert a positive influence on the client's behavior and it is these components that we now describe in some detail.

Practice

Assessment. Clients seldom come into a clinic and request assertion training. Therefore, it is up to the therapist to determine whether or not there is a bona fide need for this type of intervention. In short, the first step must be to assess whether a failure to be assertive is contributing to the client's distress. Most commonly, this step can be achieved through one of the following means: structured inventories, the use of interviews, role-playing, or self-assessment.

We have already alluded above to structured inventories. These consist of a series of situations involving interpersonal problems that clients are asked to comment on in terms of whether they would be able to make an effective response. Anger-related items might include situations such as the following: "If someone betrayed your confidence, would you express your disappointment and anger about it?" or, "If someone's smoking is annoying you, are you able to ask the person to smoke elsewhere?" (Wolpe & Lazarus, 1966).

In actual clinical practice, one would seldom use an inventory alone to assess assertiveness. Rather, the inventory would be used in conjunction with a detailed interview. The interview might use the information gathered from the inventory as a starting point for more intensive assessment. It is important to follow up on these leads by questioning the client on specifics. One would like to know, for example, how long the client has had the problem? What were its probable origins? How has the client attempted to cope with the problem? What positive client characteristics (strengths) might be brought to bear to help solve the problem? What are the reactions of others to the client's current behavior in the problem situation? What are the client's expectations and goals in the area of interpersonal relationships? These questions form the core of the interview (Goldfried & Davison, 1976).

Optimally, we would like to observe the client directly in the problem situation in order to get a sample of his or her problem behavior. Although this is rarely possible, we may nevertheless obtain some direct behavioral information by asking the client to role-play the situation. This strategy can often be quite revealing especially in the case of "overcontrolled" anger. That is, some individuals are ashamed to admit that they have angry feelings or thoughts toward another. Their maxim is, "If you don't have something good to say about somebody, don't say anything." Thus, they condemn themselves to a life of internal seething accompanied by guilt. Directly questioning the client about his or her anger may produce defensive reactions. When this situation is anticipated, the therapist might be wise to gather more information by asking the client to role-play the problem. Consider a husband who is angry at his wife. If he is asked to role-play his wife's responses in a disagreement, he might act out an obnoxious Xanthippe without actually labeling his wife's behaviors as shrewish. Or, on the other hand, if the husband is asked to role-play himself, he might speak words that sound rational enough but give his anger away through the sharp tone of his voice, by a disgusted look on his face, with a clenched fist, and so on. In a sense, the therapist becomes like the Bene Gesserit witch in the novel *Dune,* in that he or she judges another person's motives or feelings by the minutiae that accompany speech rather than by the actual content of speech.

Finally, for some clients, those who are more open about their anger and aggressive behavior, a self-assessment procedure may be used. Either through structured inventories, direct interview, or a daily log, a list of problematic situations can be drawn up and the therapist can suggest that the client examine the list at home and reflect upon which items are most upsetting, that is, most predictably set off aggressive patterns of behavior. Bower and Bower (1976) suggest that the client examine the items in terms of the *intensity, duration,* and *frequency* of the emotional reaction accompanying them. Essentially, the self-assessment exercise is a way of beginning to teach clients to become aware of physical, behavioral, and cognitive precursors to anger. Once clients have learned what these cues are, they are in a better position to know what triggers their anger in a given situation, thereby opening the possibility of taking preventive actions before the situation deteriorates. Some clients might experience heart-pounding or butterflies in the stomach at the onset of anger. These physical sensations could then be used as cues that the anger pattern is beginning. In the case of overt behaviors, a client's self-assessment may reveal that anger is correlated with clenched teeth, tensed fists, or disorganized speech. Finally, self-assessment may reveal to the client certain cognitive precursors to anger, thoughts such as "They're out to get me," "He's doing it to make a fool of me," or "She's trying to get my goat." In sum, then, self-assessment can be a learning experience for clients in that they come to recognize the situations that are likely to set off anger. Further, by monitoring these correlates, the client can eventually learn to initiate self-control measures to prevent an aggressive outburst.

Presenting the Treatment Rationale and Preparing the Client. After the therapist has determined that the client can profit from some form of assertion training, the next step is to present the treatment rationale. This is particularly important in working with clients who have a belief system that is incompatible with assertive behavior.

Consider the client who believes that certain people are intrinsically bad and merit punishment. Such a client is likely to be so wedded to the notion that his or her actions are self-righteous and justified that no amount of prodding from the therapist will succeed in moving the client toward more constructive interpersonal relations. Likewise, the passive-aggressive client who fears the negative consequences that might follow assertive behavior will also be unable to practice more interpersonally satisfying behavior. It is common in such cases to help the client develop an *assertive belief system* (Lange & Jakubowski, 1976). Some of the techniques described above in the section on cognitive learning methods may be helpful here. Specifically, the therapist assists clients in challenging the self-defeating nature of their beliefs by: (1) presenting the notion that certain thoughts lead to undesirable emotional states such as intense anger or anxiety; (2) discussing some common irrational assumptions about social behavior; (3) analyzing the client's problems in more rational terms; and (4) teaching the clients to modify their self-verbalizations so as to minimize emotional stress and maximize constructive behavior. With regard to the above, some therapists attempt to convince clients that they absolutely must be assertive. This strategy can backfire, however, since as Ellis suggests, absolutist thinking (e.g., "I *must* be assertive") can lead to frustration and possible anger in situations in which the client's assertion fails or when the client occasionally reverts to nonassertive behavior. The best strategy is to teach clients to emphasize to themselves the adaptiveness of assertive behavior: "By behaving either aggressively or nonassertively, I alienate others; by behaving assertively, I am able to facilitate honest communication and interpersonal relations that are mutually satisfying." It is unlikely that merely by talking with the client, the therapist will convince him or her that such self-statements have merit. A more realistic strategy is for the therapist to have the client focus on the validity of these self-statements *following real-life experiences* in which positive consequences ensued upon the performance of assertive behavior. During the course of assertive training, there will normally be many opportunities for the therapist to point to the usefulness of an assertive belief system.

One cannot stress enough that the goal of assertive behavior is the attainment of satisfying interpersonal relationships, not intimidation, domination, or humiliation of others. Further, the client should be taught that assertive behavior is not valuable in and of itself, but only when it is directed at achieving the individual's goals. In other words, the purpose of treatment is *not* to make the client assertive every second of the day, but only when it is rational and personally meaningful to be so.

Finally, as mentioned above, some clients will require "calming down" exercises prior to implementing assertiveness techniques. A client who is in a "white hot" frenzy is not likely to remember how to behave assertively. Such clients can profit from a program of structured relaxation exercises and/or systematic desensitization as described above in the section on methods of inducing relaxation. The client who is able to restrain the development of extreme anger is in a better position to express assertive behaviors that will change the interpersonal situation to one that is more satisfying.

Those individuals who have begun to develop an assertive belief system and are able to curb extreme emotional reactions through relaxation techniques are ready for more specific assertive training interventions.

Specific Treatment Procedures. It is useful to begin by having the client draw up a hierarchy of situations that make him or her aggressive. The list of problems is ordered so that those requiring the least amount of assertive skill and eliciting the lowest level of emotional upset are dealt with first.

Consider the case of one short-tempered, verbally abusive man who frequently alienated spouse, children, and other relatives through his frequent outbursts of shouting and threats. The items that he generated formed the following hierarchy in order of increasing difficulty:

1. Being cut off in a conversation by my brother-in-law.
2. Children are noisy while I'm trying to watch the news.
3. Children "smart off" when I reprimand them.
4. Wife ties up the telephone by having long conversations.
5. Wife makes put-down remarks concerning my inability to advance professionally.

Working from this hierarchy, the therapist is most likely to begin by using some variant of *behavior rehearsal*. For example, the client may be asked to role-play the problem situation:

Therapist: O.K. What I'd like you to do is imagine that I'm your brother-in-law. I want you to act toward me the way you would act toward him.

Client: Fine.

Therapist: Go ahead and start talking about some topic with me as if I were him.

Client: Alright. I've been thinking about buying a new house but several people have told me that the interest rates . . .

Therapist: (*Interrupting*) No, you'd have to be crazy to buy now. You'd pay an arm and a leg.

Client: (*Glaring at the therapist*) Will you shut up. I can't get a word in edgewise.

This interaction gives the therapist a more concrete and realistic picture of what is going on in the situation and facilitates his or her helping the client to plan a more appropriate response. One way to begin generating such a response is for the therapist to ask clients what features of the behaviors that they role-played were aggressive or nonassertive and how they might alter these behaviors in a more assertive direction. Another tactic is for the therapist to suggest a *role reversal* whereby the therapist becomes the client and the client becomes the brother-in-law. This allows the therapist to model additional assertive responses for the client.

Therapist: O.K. Let's change roles just as I described it. (*Taking on client's role*) I've been thinking about buying a house but . . .

Client: (*Interrupting as the brother-in-law would*) No, you're out of your mind to do it now.

Therapist: I realize that you may have a different opinion but when you interrupt me, I lose my train of thought and I feel myself getting angry. I'd like to hear what you have to say but I'd prefer to have you wait until I'm finished.

The therapist's response, just described, combines three important aspects of a good assertive response. First, the therapist demonstrated a response that was likely to accomplish the goal (i.e., getting the brother-in-law to stop interrupting) with minimal effort and with minimum negative emotion engendered in either the client or the brother-in-law. This has been referred to as the *minimal effective response* (Rimm & Masters, 1979). Second, the therapist demonstrated *empathic assertion* by acknowledging that the brother-in-law might have a different opinion on the matter being discussed. This mode of assertion helps reduce the likelihood that the brother-in-law will perceive himself to be the subject of a threat. In this manner, the possibility of conflict can be kept to a minimum. Third, the therapist used *I-language assertion* (Gordon, 1970). This consists of a description of the anger-arousing situation (i.e., "When you interrupt me"), followed by a statement describing the effects of this situation (i.e., "I lose my train of thought"), followed by a description of the feelings engendered (i.e., "I feel myself getting angry"), and finally followed by a statement of what behavior the client would prefer instead (i.e., "I'd prefer to have you wait until I'm finished"). Typically, all the skills just described would not be taught at the same time, otherwise one might risk overloading the client at the start of training. Thus, the best approach is to teach each skill separately.

At this point in training, the therapist may suggest that the client go back to playing himself and try to use the newly acquired skill:

Therapist: Let's go back to our original roles now. I'd like you to try to express yourself in a manner similar to the way I did but using your own words.

Client: O.K. Like I was saying, I was thinking of buying a house but the interest rates . . .

Therapist: (*Interrupting*) No way! The real estate situation is hopeless now.

Client: (*Clenching his fists and gritting his teeth*) Look, I know you're trying to help me but can't you keep quiet until I'm finished?

Therapist: That's somewhat better! You expressed some empathy and you tried to state more clearly and less offensively what you wanted. But there are still some rough edges. For example, I noticed that you seemed tense and agitated. You were clenching your fists and speaking through your teeth. It's important that the way in which you act doesn't contradict what you're saying. Also, if you're calm, you'll find it easier to think of what you want to say. Try to relax your hands and not grit your teeth together. Look your brother-in-law in the eyes when you talk to him. I think that'll help you get through better.

Essentially, then, the therapist gives the client *feedback* on the adequacy of the assertive response. The feedback consists of reinforcing the client for approximating a good assertive response as well as suggesting modifications for the next practice attempt. As was clear from the example, the therapist provides feedback on both the content and manner of delivery of the client's assertive statements. It is counterproductive for the client to say one thing with his words and something else with his body or tone of voice. The feedback and modeling process continues until client and therapist are comfortable with the final product.

Sometimes, of course, the minimal effective response is inadequate. The other person simply ignores the client's assertive statement. In this case, the strategy would be to teach the client the skill of *escalation*. This simply consists of a stronger and more blunt statement:

Therapist: I want you to play your brother-in-law and I'll be you. Keep in mind that the initial assertive response did not work.
Client: O.K.
Therapist: As I was saying before, I've always wanted to own my own house ...
Client: You and me both kiddo! But who can afford these crazy mortgages?
Therapist: You're interrupting again. Please wait until I'm finished.

This assertive statement is noticably more blunt than the initial one. At this point, the client would be instructed to practice escalation and the therapist would provide corrective feedback. If the stronger statement fails, the therapist would model further escalation including statements that specify negative consequences:

Therapist: (*Modeling for the client*) I've asked you twice not to interrupt. If you won't wait for me to finish, I'll have to break off our conversation.

Once the therapist is satisfied that the client has mastered the above assertive techniques, he or she will generally urge the client to practice them in the "real world," returning to the clinic for further suggestions and feedback following these real-life experiences. If the client has been successful, the therapist will proceed to the second item of the hierarchy. As consecutive items are mastered, the therapist will fade out his or her help as much as possible. Eventually, clients will reach a point where they are able to resolve new problems on their own. That is, they will have acquired an assertive repertoire that enables *self*-control of anger and aggression. One final point should be considered. Some of the more complex items at the difficult end of the hierarchy might best be resolved by using negotiation and contracting techniques. For example, in the case of the wife's "put-down" remarks concerning her husband's lack of occupational achievements (item #5 on the hierarchy outlined above), some intervention aimed at clarifying life goals and differing personal needs might be in order. Generally speaking, negotiation and contracting techniques are often a part of assertive behavior. The mode of implementation of these techniques is discussed at length in Chapter 2.

There is one final point that is worth examining. Many clients find that they become flustered in the real-life assertion situation. They forget what they were going to say. One useful adjunct to assertion training to help remediate this problem involves the use of written "scripts" (Bower & Bower, 1976). A script is essentially a small play in which clients write out their assertive lines for use in the real-life situation. It is useful both as a mnemonic device and as a way to help clients to calm down and develop a sense of control over the problem situation. The script gives clients practice in thinking in assertive terms. Further, by writing a number of scripts, clients should gradually learn to abstract the general rules underlying successful assertion. This process will help facilitate more natural assertion, thereby eventually allowing clients to dispense with written scripts altogether.

The basic formula for writing scripts is summarized in the acronym, *DESC* (Bower & Bower, 1976). This is short for *D*escribe, *E*xpress, *S*pecify, *C*onsequences. We can illustrate each of these components with reference to the example of the rude brother-in-law noted above. First, the client *describes* the other person's behavior in objective, specific terms: "You're interrupting me and making me lose my train of thought." Second, the client *expresses* feelings calmly: "I feel frustrated and angry when you do this." Next, the client *specifies* the desired behavior change on the part of the other person: "I'd appreciate it if you would wait until I'm finished speaking." Finally, the client notes the *consequences* for the other person's behavior: "That way we can both contribute to the conversation and get the most out of it." In line with the discussion on empathic assertion, we would suggest adding to the script a statement that recognizes the other person's position. In the present example, a statement such as the following could be inserted between the describe and express components: "I understand that you want to share your opinion, however . . . ." With this written document in hand, clients can rehearse the "assertive scene" to perfection, or if need be, can modify it with the help of the therapist.

In sum, then, assertive training involves assessing the client's problem and motivating him or her to participate by making sure that the client's beliefs are consistent with stated long-term goals. In addition, assertive training typically involves direct behavior rehearsal and practice and may occasionally entail the use of written scripts as well.

A MODEL PROGRAM FOR THE CONTROL OF ANGER

Recently, Novaco (1975, 1976) has outlined a multifaceted program that can be used to deal with clients who have chronic anger control porblems. The program is of particular interest because it combines the three major procedures discussed at length above: cognitive learning, relaxation, and assertion/behavior rehearsal.

In the initial study, 34 individuals were identified using an anger inventory (Novaco, 1975). The inventory included a variety of items pertaining to the likelihood that an individual would be provoked to anger and aggression should the situation described by the item occur (e.g., "Being called a liar," or "Being stood up for a date"). The individuals that were identified scored much higher than a randomly selected comparison sample of undergraduates. Many of them had recently physically assaulted others or engaged in property damage while in a fit of anger. In short, they evidenced a chronically elevated level of anger.

The 34 clients were divided into four groups: combined cognitive control and relaxation; cognitive control alone; relaxation alone; and attention control. The effectiveness of each intervention was assessed using a pre- and posttreatment analysis of the anger inventory scores. In addition, a number of laboratory measures reflecting changes in blood pressure and self-report (e.g., degree of anger as rated on a 7-point scale) were taken in several situations both pre- and postintervention. These situations included imaginal provocation (i.e., the client was asked to imagine a particular anger-inducing scene); role-play provocation (i.e., the client interacted with an assistant of the experimenter and role-played a situation that was problematic with respect to anger control). In addition, subjects kept a diary of real-life anger-arousing incidents and rated the intensity of their arousal in response to those incidents on a 7-point scale. Subjects made these ratings throughout the course of the study, thereby providing a naturalistic appraisal of the efficacy of the various interventions.

The three treatment groups were presented with a rationale that emphasized the *functional* nature of anger; that is, the rationale that was given did not represent anger as a response totally lacking in adaptive function. Instead, anger was viewed as having both constructive and destructive dimensions. The goal of therapy, therefore, was to help the client identify and use anger in such a way as to enhance the attainment of personal goals while avoiding self-defeating modes of behavior. Anger was conceptualized as having any of six functions (Novaco, 1976): (1) *energizing* behavior by increasing the intensity of responding; (2) *disrupting* behavior by interfering with constructive information processing and facilitating impulsivity; (3) helping to *express* negative feelings, that is, serving to communicate something to others; (4) *defending* against perceived threats by inhibiting anxiety; (5) *instigating* learned patterns of aggressive behavior; and (6) helping in the *discrimination* of provocative events, thereby acting as a cue to initiate coping behaviors. It is apparent, then, that some aspects of anger can be of potential benefit to an individual. In particular, the energizing, expressive, and discriminative functions of anger could serve an adaptive function for the individual if properly channelled.

Clients in the combined cognitive control and relaxation training group received the following interventions. During the first phase of treatment, the rationale for therapy was presented including the important notion that thinking certain kinds of thoughts was likely to produce anger or, more generally, that there is a correspondence between thoughts and feelings. Clients were educated about the different functions of anger just described and were asked to monitor and identify the types of self-statements they made when they were angry as well as the kinds of situations in which they became angry. The stress inoculation model popularized by Meichenbaum and Turk (1976) was used to facilitate anger control. This intervention consists of teaching a series of coping self-statements organized sequentially around four steps as follows (Novaco, 1975):

1. Preparing for a provocation (e.g., "If I find myself getting upset, I'll know what to do.").
2. Confronting the provocation (e.g., "Don't assume the worst or jump to conclusions. Look for the positives.").

3. Coping with arousal and agitation (e.g., "My anger is a signal of what I need to do. Time to talk to myself."). This is a particularly crucial step since it is here that clients learn that they must stay on task and keep their goals in mind.
4. Self-reward (e.g., "I actually got through that without getting angry.").

The above statements were tailored to fit the experiences described in the diary of each client. In addition, each client was taught deep muscle relaxation to cope with successively more intense anger-provoking scenes.

The cognitive control group received only the self-instruction/coping statement components outlined above. The relaxation training group received only the relaxation-desensitization described above. The attention control group visited the clinic and discussed their anger diaries with the therapist but did not receive either the cognitive or relaxation interventions.

The main results were that the combined cognitive-relaxation group was superior to the attention control group on virtually every measure. Also, overall the cognitive-only group showed greater gains than the relaxation-only group.

The above study, then, suggests the utility of teaching clients specific coping skills (either cognitive and/or relaxation) in order to deal with anger. Clients who thus become "task oriented" are able to handle provocations without excessive and uncontrollable anger. In a later publication, Novaco (1977a) noted the importance of assertive training as a method to be added to the treatment package in order to control anger effectively.

The type of multifaceted approach to the treatment of anger and aggression control outlined by Novaco has the potential for application to a wide variety of human problems. First, many parents who engage in child abuse have patterns of beliefs that are conducive to angry outbursts of aggression (e.g., "He wet his pants because he knows I can't stand to change him"). Such parents might profit from a combination of cognitive restructuring (e.g., "He wet himself because he's very young and doesn't know better yet") and relaxation training. Second, the above treatment may also be of use in controlling the anger reactions of police officers who, as part of their occupation, must deal regularly with provocation (Novaco, 1977b). Finally, business executives must often confront high-pressure anger-provoking situations that may set off various types of aggressive behavior. Such high levels of hostility coupled with a drive for upward mobility produce the classic Type A person who is more prone than others to coronary problems as well as angry outbursts. A combination of cognitive restructuring, assertion, and relaxation may help these individuals to cope more adaptively (Roskies & Avard, 1980).

In sum, then, the techniques described in this chapter, when used in combination and individually tailored to the client's needs, are applicable to a wide range of human problems centering on anger and aggression control.

CONCLUDING STATEMENT AND SUMMARY

In the preceding sections, a number of points were made—implicitly or explicitly—pertaining to the acquisition and performance of self-control skills. Since these points form the basis of successful aggression control, it is worthwhile to recapitulate them now:

1. The acquisition of coping skills requires some effort on the part of the client. Clients who are not *motivated* to reduce their aggressive behavior are unlikely to follow through with the training procedures. Therefore, they will probably acquire few if any self-control skills.
2. *Self-assessment* is an important initial step in the acquisition of self-control. This involves the client's determining what he or she is doing and thinking in the problem situation and what consequences accrue to particular modes of responding. Thus, an important aspect of self-assessment involves the client's performing a *functional analysis* of the problem behavior. Rather than merely attending to behavioral topography per se (e.g., "I shout and scream a lot"), the client determines (or is helped to determine) what *function* the problem behavior is serving. The results of this analysis can then serve as a guide in formulating treatment approaches. For example, if a client's anger serves as a way of coping with anxiety, some form of relaxation training might be useful; if the anger results from frustration at not being listened to, the training of assertive skills might be useful.
3. Clients must learn to specify desired goals in terms of *positive behaviors* (i.e., what they *want*) rather than in terms of *negative behaviors* (i.e., what they do *not* want). Thus, a statement such as "I don't want to lose my temper" is too vague to be useful. In contrast, a positive statement such as "I want to be able to discuss a problem with another person and come to a mutually satisfactory solution" aids in the identification of concrete goal behaviors (e.g., com-

munication training, negotiation) that can then become the focus of specific skill training programs.

4. Clients must learn to conceptualize their problems in *situational* terms rather than in terms of traits. For example, the statement "I am an aggressive person" represents aggression as a trait, that is, a pattern of behavior that occurs in a wide variety of settings and is relatively stable over time. A client who thinks in such terms is likely to be discouraged at the outset of treatment since a trait implies a widespread problem that will require an exhausting and time-consuming reconstruction of the entire personality. In contrast, a client who conceptualizes aggression in situational terms (e.g., "I shout at my children when they're noisy") is more likely to see his or her problem as somewhat limited in scope and therefore subject to remediation.

5. Self-control skills are built *gradually*. Component skills are practiced at first with help from the therapist and as circumscribed homework assignments. The therapist emphasizes to the client that mistakes will be made along the way to eventual success and, therefore, rapid resolution of problems should not be expected. As mastery develops with respect to relatively simple situations, the client is encouraged to attempt to apply the skills to more complex, real-life situations. By adopting this "go slow" approach, the therapist facilitates the maintenance of client motivation during the course of therapy.

6. The client must learn to identify and use emotional upset as a *cue for initiating coping skill sequences*. This stands in contrast to the pretreatment pattern of ruminating about the problem, thereby exacerbating it.

7. When the client foresees a problem situation, he or she is taught to *plan in advance* how to handle it effectively rather than simply entering the situation unprepared. In this manner, the client can prevent the development of the kind of intense arousal that so often leads to counterproductive action.

8. Once a client has handled a problem situation effectively, he or she is taught to ask, "*What did I do differently this time that worked?*" By focusing on personally successful strategies and abstracting general rules from them, the client will be in a stronger position for dealing with future problems.

The above principles cut across the various techniques discussed in this chapter. By attending to these points, a client will be better able to anticipate and resolve situations that have in the past evoked anger and aggression. Since such action on the part of the client eventually takes place without guidance from a professional, it is a true example of the *self*-control of anger and aggression.

REFERENCES

Bower, S. A., & Bower, G. H. *Asserting yourself.* Reading, Mass.: Addison-Wesley, 1976.

Brehm, J. W. *A theory of psychological reactance.* New York: Academic Press, 1966.

Brehm, J. W., & Cohen, A. R. *Explorations in cognitive dissonance.* New York: Wiley, 1962.

Cautela, J. R. A behavior therapy approach to pervasive anxiety. *Behaviour Research and Therapy,* 1966, **4,** 99–109.

DiGiuseppe, R. A. The use of behavioral modification to establish rational self-statements in children. *Rational Living,* 1975, **10** (2), 18–20.

DiGiuseppe, R. A. The use of behavior modification to establish rational self-statements in children. In A. Ellis & R. Grieger (Eds.), *Handbook of Rational Emotive Therapy.* Berlin & New York: Springer-Verlag, 1977.

DiLoreto, A. D. *Comparative psychotherapy.* Chicago: Aldine-Atherton, 1971.

Ellis, A. *Reason and emotion in psychotherapy.* New York: Lyle Stuart, 1962.

Ellis, A. (Ed.) *Growth through reason.* Palo Alto, Calif.: Science and Behavior Books, 1971.

Ellis, A. *Rational emotive therapy.* In A. Burton (Ed.), *Operational theories of personality.* New York: Brunner/Mazel, 1974.

Ellis, A. Can we change thoughts by reinforcement? A reply to Howard Rachlin. *Behavior Therapy,* 1977, **8,** 666–672.

Ellis, A., & Harper, R. A. *A new guide to rational living.* Hollywood, Calif.: Wilshire, 1975.

Evans, D. R. Specific aggression, arousal and reciprocal inhibition therapy. *The Western Psychologist,* 1970, **1,** 125–130.

Evans, D. R., & Hearn, M. T., & Sablofske, A. Anger, arousal, and systematic desensitization. *Psychological Reports,* 1973, **32,** 625–626.

Foy, E. W., Eisler, R. M., & Pinkston, S. Modeled assertion in a case of explosive rages. *Journal of Behavior Therapy and Experimental Psychiatry,* 1975, **6,** 135–138.

Gambrill, E. D. *A behavioral program for increasing social interaction.* Paper presented at the meeting of the Association for the Advancement of Behavior Therapy, Miami, 1973.

Gambrill, E. D., & Richey, C. A. An assertion inventory for use in assessment and research. *Behavior Therapy,* 1975, **6,** 550–561.

Goldfried, M. R. Psychotherapy as coping skills training. In M. J. Mahoney (Ed.), *Psychotherapy process: Current issues and future directions.* New York: Plenum, 1980.

Goldfried, M. R., & Davison, G. C. *Clinical behavior therapy.* New York: Holt, 1976.

Goldfried, M. R., Decenteceo, E. T., & Weinberg, L. Systematic rational restructuring as a self-control technique. *Behavior Therapy,* 1974, **5,** 247–254.

Goldfried, M. R., & Trier, C. Effectiveness of relaxation as an active coping skill. *Journal of Abnormal Psychology,* 1974, **83,** 348–355.

Goldsmith, J. B., & McFall, R. M. Development and evaluation of an interpersonal skill-training program for psychiatric inpatients. *Journal of Abnormal Psychology,* 1975, **84,** 51–58.

Gordon, T. *Parent effectiveness training.* New York: Peter H. Wyden, 1970.

Jacobson, E. *Progressive relaxation.* Chicago: University of Chicago Press, 1938.

Lange, A. J., & Jakubowski, P. *Responsible assertive behavior.* Champaign, Ill.: Research Press, 1976.

Lawrence, P. S. *The assessment and modification of assertive behavior.* Unpublished doctoral dissertation, Arizona State University, 1970.

MacDonald, M. L. Teaching assertion: A paradigm for therapeutic intervention. *Psychotherapy: Theory, Research, and Practice,* 1975, **12,** 60–67.

Maes, W. R., & Heimann, R. A. *A comparison of three approaches to the reduction of test anxiety in high school students.* (Final Report, Project 9-1049). Washington, D.C.: Office of Education, Bureau of Research, U.S. Department of Health, Education, and Welfare, 1970.

Marquis, J. N., & Morgan, W. G. A guidebook for systematic desensitization. Palo Alto, Calif.: Veterans Administration Hospital, 1969.

May, J. R., & Johnson, H. J. Physiological activity to internally elicited arousal and inhibitory thoughts. *Journal of Abnormal Psychology,* 1973, **82,** 239–245.

McFall, R. M., & Marston, A. R. An experimental investigation of behavior rehearsal in assertive training. *Journal of Abnormal Psychology,* 1970, **76,** 295–303.

McFall, R. M., & Twentyman, C. Four experiments on the relative contribution of rehearsal, modeling, and coaching to assertion training. *Journal of Abnormal Psychology,* 1973, **81,** 199–218.

Meichenbaum, D. H., Gilmore, J. B., & Fedoravicius, A. Group insight vs. group desensitization in treating speech anxiety. *Journal of Consulting and Clinical Psychology,* 1971, **36,** 410–421.

Meichenbaum, D., & Novaco, R. Stress inoculation: A preventative approach. In C. Spielberger and I. Sarason (Eds.), *Stress and Anxiety, Vol. 5.* Washington, D.C.: Hemisphere, 1978.

Moleski, R., & Tosi, D. J. Comparative psychotherapy: Rational-emotive therapy versus systematic desensitization in the treatment of stuttering. *Journal of Consulting and Clinical Psychology,* 1976, **44,** 309–311.

Novaco, R. *Anger Control: The development and evaluation of an experimental treatment.* Lexington, Mass.: Heath, 1975.

Novaco, R. W. The functions and regulation of anger. *American Journal of Psychiatry,* 1976, **133,** 1124–1128.

Novaco, R. W. Stress inoculation: A cognitive therapy for anger and its application to a case of depression. *Journal of Consulting and Clinical Psychology,* 1977, **45,** 600–608 (a).

Novaco, R. W. A stress-inoculation approach to anger management in the training of law enforcement officers. *American Journal of Community Psychology,* 1977, **5,** 327–346 (b).

O'Donnell, C. R., & Worell, L. Motor and cognitive relaxation in the desensitization of anger. *Behaviour Research and Therapy,* 1973, **11,** 473–482.

Orenstein, H., Orenstein, E., & Carr, J. E. Assertiveness and anxiety: A correlational study. *Journal of Behavior Therapy and Experimental Psychiatry,* 1975, **6,** 203–207.

Paul, G. L. *Insight versus desensitization in psychotherapy.* Stanford, Calif.: Stanford University Press, 1966.

Rathus, S. A. A 30-item schedule for assessing assertive behavior. *Behavior Therapy,* 1973, **4,** 398–406.

Rimm, D. C. Treatment of antisocial aggression. In G. C. Harris (Ed.), *The group treatment of human problems.* New York: Grune & Stratton, 1977.

Rimm, D. C., deGroot, J. C., Boord, P., Heiman, J., & Dillow, P. V. Systematic desensitization of an anger response. *Behaviour Research and Therapy,* 1971, **9,** 273–280.

Rimm, D. C., & Litvak, S. B. Self-verbalization and emotional arousal. *Journal of Abnormal Psychology,* 1969, **74,** 181–187.

Rimm, D. C., & Masters, J. C. *Behavior therapy.* New York: Academic Press, 1979.

Rimm, D. C., Snyder, J. J., Depue, R. A., Haanstad, M. J., & Armstrong, D. P. Assertive training versus rehearsal and the importance of making assertive responses. *Behaviour Research and Therapy,* 1976, **14,** 315–321.

Roskies, E., & Avard, J. Teaching healthy managers to control their coronary-prone (Type A) behavior. In K. Blankstein and J. Polivy (Eds.), *Self-control and self-modification of emotional behaviors.* New York: Plenum, 1980.

Russell, P. C., & Brandsma, J. M. A theoretical and empirical integration of the rational-emotive and classical conditioning therapies. *Journal of Consulting and Clinical Psychology*, 1974, **42**, 389–397.

Smith, R. E. The use of humor in counter-conditioning of anger responses: A case study. *Behavior Therapy*, 1973, **4**, 576–580.

Thelen, M. H., Fry, R. A., Dollinger, S. J., & Paul, S. C. Use of videotaped models to improve the interpersonal adjustment of delinquents. *Journal of Consulting and Clinical Psychology*, 1976, **44**, 492.

Velten, E. A. A laboratory task for induction of mood states. *Behaviour Research and Therapy*, 1968, **6**, 483–492.

Voss, J., Arrick, C., & Rimm, D. C. *The role of task difficulty and modeling in assertive training.* Unpublished Master's thesis, Southern Illinois University, 1976.

Wallace, C. J., Teigen, J. R., Liberman, R. P., & Baker, V. Destructive behavior treated by contingency contracts and assertive training: A case study. *Journal of Behavior Therapy and Experimental Psychiatry*, 1973, **4**, 273–274.

Watkins, J. T. The rational emotive dynamics of impulsive disorders. In A. Ellis & R. Grieger (Eds.), *Handbook of rational emotive therapy.* Berlin & New York: Springer-Verlag, 1977.

Wilson, G. T., & Davison, G. C. Processes of fear reduction in systematic desensitization: Animal studies. *Psychological Bulletin*, 1971, **76**, 1–14.

Wolpe, J. *Psychotherapy by reciprocal inhibition.* Stanford, Calif.: Stanford University Press, 1958.

Wolpe, J. *The practice of behavior therapy.* Oxford: Pergamon, 1969.

Wolpe, J., & Lazarus, A. A. *Behavior therapy techniques: A guide to the treatment of neuroses.* Oxford: Pergamon, 1966.

II

Group Controls and Alternatives

Chapter 4
Social Skill Training
Arnold P. Goldstein

The qualities which an age possesses are not always those it professes to admire. Many Englishmen of noble lineage left edifying counsels for their descendants on how to manage their lives, written while the author was awaiting execution for the conduct of his own. La Rochefoucauld touched upon the point in a maxim well-known in England: "Old men delight in giving good advice as a consolation for the fact that they can no longer set bad examples."

—*The Polite Americans.*

Advising another person how to behave, whether by dictum, suggestion, example, or otherwise, is probably an event as old as man himself. Twenty-five hundred years ago, the *Li Ki* was written, a compilation of Confucian edicts on proper social customs; the *Mahabharata* of India, appeared about 200 A.D., composed of rules and guidance for acceptable personal behavior; the *Old* and *New Testaments* are also major examples of such ancient documents, as is the Roman *Civilitas.* Over the centuries, man advising man on proper, effective, acceptable, or satisfying behavior has taken many forms. There began in France, in the 11th century, the chivalric movement seeking systematically to dictate manners, morals, tastes, social behavior, and ethical standards. In the 15th and 16th centuries a number of highly influential writings known as courtesy books appeared in Italy—among which Guazzo's *La Civile Conversazione* and Castiglione's *Il Cortegiano* (The Book of the Courtier) are two of the more significant. Books such as these, in turn, led to the great profusion and popularity of etiquette books in 18th- and 19th-century England and, later, to the spate of popular good behavior books, decorum manuals, and treatises on manners and social conduct in early 20th-century America.

EDUCATIONAL ANTECEDENTS OF SOCIAL SKILLS TRAINING

In America, in the first few decades of this century, it was not only popular books that sought to influence the form and content of our interpersonal and social behavior. There were also parenting manuals, religious tracts, and a number of major educational movements. Chief among the latter was "Character Education," largely a development of the 1920s, in which ethical interpersonal behavior, the development of leadership skills, effectiveness in groups' decision-making ability and self-control were among the chief pedagogic training targets. Though Character Education as a formal, educational movement had largely disappeared by the mid-1930s, the institutionalized concern of American education with what was optimal in the behavior of its charges has very much continued to the present day—if in various new forms. Moral education (Kohlberg, 1973), affective education (Miller, 1976), human relations training (Bradford, Gibb, and Benne, 1964), confluent education (Castillo, 1974), and identity education (Weinstein and Fantini, 1970) are but some of these forms. Their methods vary—discussion, sensitivity groups, exercise, simulations, games, and others—but their goals are to help shape and foster the behavioral and emotional development and growth of the target trainees involved.

But it is not only in these formal educational senses that there exists in America today such active concern with development of skilled interpersonal and social behavior. There are important but less institutionalized examples also, examples which provide additional fertile context for the growth of the movement which will be the major focus of this chapter—the social skill training movement. There are over 2,000 community colleges in the United States today. In addition, a great many universities have adult education or evening college divisions. Course offerings at a large majority of such institutions include a very considerable and unusually diverse array of interpersonal skill-oriented courses such as, Communication Skills and Self-Awareness, Coping with Difficult People at Home and at Work, Interpersonal Communication, Managerial and Leadership Skills, Assertiveness Training for Women, Managing Stress: The Problem of Our Time, Rational Living in an Irrational World.

This spirit of interpersonal growth; this belief that one's happiness, effectiveness, and satisfaction in life can be enhanced by self- or other-offered instruction is also both massively influenced by and reflected in the vast number of self-help books available in America today.

Clearly, from what is offered children and adolescents in school, from what is offered adults at the community college level, and from what adults may offer themselves from America's immense self-help library, formal and informal education in America today has given its stamp of encouraging approval to the social skills training movement.

PSYCHOTHERAPEUTIC ANTECEDENTS OF SOCIAL SKILLS TRAINING

Beyond its broad historical context and its more recent educational roots, social skill training also grows in major ways from American psychotherapy. In fact, as we will see, an alternative name for social skill training is *psychoeducational therapy*. To understand this source of the social skill training movement best, one ought first to point to the fact that the primary concern of American psychology since its formal inception in the late 19th century has been the understanding and enhancement of the learning process. This readiness to center upon learning processes took major therapeutic form starting in the 1950s, as psychotherapy practitioners and researchers alike came increasingly to view treatment in learning terms. The very healthy and still expanding field of behavior modification grew from this joint learning-clinical focus, and may be viewed as the immediately preceding context in which social skill training came to be offered. In most behavior modification approaches, as is true of social skill training itself, specific target behaviors are selected as the goals for remediation or enhancement, laboratory-derived learning procedures are implemented toward these goals, the change agent functions as teacher-trainer, and the success or failure of the effort is judged in terms of observable, behavioral criteria.

Prior to the 1970s, most of the nonbehavioral approaches to psychotherapy rested firmly on a medical model. In this view, diagnosis must precede treatment, there are hidden and underlying causes to be discerned, removing "mere" symptoms will lead to the appearance of new symptoms, "cure" consists in dealing with underlying causes, and so forth. The influence of the medical model has waned considerably in recent years. Medical model psychotherapies—and especially its major therapy, psychoanalysis—have advanced very little theoretically, have avoided careful research scrutiny, and have failed to yield discernible improvements in technique. The more ahistorical and nonpsychodynamic approaches, such as the behavioral, have been shown to be at least as effective—if not more effective—than are treatments adhering to a medical model. In part, therefore, the emergent weaknesses of medical model treatments have correspondingly enhanced the attractiveness of alternative, newer approaches based on an educational, pedagogic foundation.

Social skill competence, and effective and satisfying interpersonal functioning, are chief among the goals of social skill training. In the 1960s, American psychiatry and psychology more and more insistently proclaimed that remediation was not enough. In this, the Community Mental Health era, prevention became the byword. Let us not wait until inadequacies are demonstrated and then try to undo them. Let us instead, this view held, train persons *in advance* to meet life's challenges, thus hoping to necessitate less remedial concern at later points. Quite clearly, social skill training is a direct expression of such preventive thinking.

Thus, psychotherapy's recent interest in both prevention and learning, its concern with didactically equipping the person not so much with insight into his unconscious processes but, instead, with overt, behavioral skills for effective interpersonal functioning are highly relevant to our focus here. Psychotherapy has clearly joined with the educational forces and events examined earlier to set the stage directly for the advent of social skill training in America.

A Functional Definition

Having provided a contextual overview, a sense of historical roots, we now offer a formal, functional definition of social skills training. *Social skills training is the planned, systematic teaching of the specific behaviors needed and consciously desired by the individual in order to function in an effective and satisfying manner, over an extended period of time, in a broad array or positive, negative, and neutral interpersonal contexts. The specific teaching methods which constitute social skills training directly and jointly reflect psychology's modern social learning theory and education's pedagogic principles and procedures.*

In this definition, we have described social skills training as *planned and systematic* in order to emphasize the organized, premeditated, and stepwise quality of such training, in contrast to the much more typically haphazard, unplanned, and unsystematic way in which most individuals are "taught" social skills, that is, by naturalistic reliance upon the parents, friends, church, school, and other people, institutions, and events that may or may not cross one's path and that may or may not exert positive skill development influence in the course of maturation.

Social skills training seeks to teach *specific behaviors*, and not—at least not directly—values, attitudes, or insight. It is a behavioral approach, designed to enhance the overt actions of the trainee, in contrast to those psychotherapeutic and educational interventions which seek to alter the individual's beliefs about himself, or self-understanding, in the (typically vain) hope that somehow behavior change will follow.

In our definition, it is important that the behavior changes toward which the trainning is oriented be *needed and consciously desired* by the trainee. Overt behavior change in the form of higher levels of skill competence, especially on an enduring basis, will not result—however good the social skills training—if the trainee's motivational level is not adequate. The training may be recommended by a spouse, boss, friend, doctor, or other interested party in the trainee's life, but a definition of successful training must include a perceived skill deficiency, a felt need, a desire for improvement on the part of the trainee. For training to succeed, there must be adequate levels of what we would term trainee "competency motivation."

The goals of social skills training, optimally, are both effectiveness and satisfaction. Effectiveness, we feel, pertains to the impact on others deriving from one's newly enhanced skill level. Effectiveness pertains to the questions, "Does it work?," "Did I succeed?," "Was I competent?" Satisfaction, in our view, is where behavior and feelings meet. Satisfaction is the inner consequence of overtly effective skill behavior. We have included both effectiveness and satisfaction in this definition of social skills training because we are aware of skill training programs in industrial, law enforcement, and other settings in which trainee "productivity" or on-the-job skill competence is the *sole* training program goal. We are also aware of therapies and educational commitments initiated at the urging of, and for the satisfaction of, a spouse, parent, boss, teacher, or other figure, and not of the patient, student, or trainee himself. We strongly feel that this is both insufficient and short-sighted, and urge that the pleasure, gratification, or personal satisfaction of the trainee be accepted as a regular, companion goal of equal importance to effectiveness in all such programs.

For a social skills training program to be satisfactory, in our view it must energetically aspire to lead to trainee effectiveness and satisfaction *over an extended period of time and in a variety of positive, negative, and neutral contexts.* This part of our definition seeks to speak to the issue of transfer. Far too many psychotherapeutic and educational interventions succeed in changing trainee behaviors in the training setting, but fail to yield sustained change where it counts—in the real-world contexts in which the trainee works, plays, and exists. Thus, a satisfactory social skills training program will actively seek to incorporate specific procedures that help the trainee perform the skills he acquired in the training context when he is in both a variety of other contexts (i.e., setting generalization) and over a sustained period of time (i.e., response maintenance).

The skill training targets that constitute the actual content of a social skills training program are optimally both diverse and numerous, and should include both interpersonal and personal skills. Interpersonal skills are the competencies that individuals must bring to bear in their interactions with individuals or groups of individuals. Communication skills, leadership skills, relationship skills, and conflict management skills are but a few examples. Personal skills are emotional, cognitive, observational, or relate to practical aspects of daily living in work, school, or home environments. They include self-control, decision making, goal setting, preparing for stressful conversations, and setting problem priorities.

Finally, a comprehensive definition of social skills training must address not only matters of skill content, as we have done above, but also teaching procedure. Optimally, social skills training consists of *procedures derived from psychology's social learning theory* (e.g., modeling, behavioral rehearsal, performance feedback) *and education's contemporary pedagogic principles and procedures* (e.g., instructional texts, simulation and gaming, structured discussion).

These, then, are the definitional characteristics of social skills training. As best we can discern, 25 programs reflecting most or all of these characteristics currently exist. Table 4.1 provides an overview of these programs, after which we turn to a detailed, in-depth consideration of one of them. In so doing, we will seek to clarify the several ways in which social skills training is fully relevant to the major theme of this book—aggression control and prosocial alternatives to aggression.

All of the programs represented in Table 4.1 meet most or all of the criteria we have included in our formal definition of social skills training. Nevertheless, considerable diversity is represented. Some programs are broadly comprehensive in the interpersonal and personal skill competencies they seek to enhance. Others focus more narrowly, for example, on anxiety or assertiveness. Yet others seem especially concerned with particular interpersonal domains (dating, marriage) or particular settings (school, work). The range of potential trainees across programs is especially broad, varying from early elementary school children through all stages of adolescence and adulthood, and into old age. The trainees represented are also quite diverse in their pretraining levels of overall skill competence, varying from significantly unskilled retarded individuals and chronic, long-term psychiatric patients to essentially "average" individuals whose general skill competence level is adequate, but who seek to enhance a few "weak spots."

Consistent with what has occurred with psychotherapists in psychotherapy and, to a lesser extent, with teachers in education, the range of persons successfully utilized as trainers in these social skills training programs is not only broad and quite diverse, but also includes a substantial number of different types of paraprofessionals. That is, in addition to credentialed teachers or psychologists, we find that teacher aides, mental hospital attendants, college undergraduates, group home parents, and others can and do serve successfully in these programs as, to use Carkhuff's (1974) apt term, "functional professionals."

Somewhat in contrast to the apparent diversity across programs in skills, trainers, and trainees, the training methods involved seem to consist largely of one of two possible procedural combinations. The first, a series of procedures derived from social learning theory principles and research, typically consists of instruction, modeling, role playing, and feedback. The skill training approach described in detail later in this chapter is of this type, and thus the nature of these procedures will be elaborated in depth. The second subgroup of programs—those growing more from strictly educational contexts—usually rely upon a combination of instructional texts, gaming and simulation exercise, structured discussion, and related didactic procedures. Perhaps most striking about both the social-learning-based and education-based procedural combinations is the degree to which they initially grew from, and are continuing to receive careful and extensive experimental scrutiny. This reliance upon a viable and quite substantial research foundation is clearly one of the strongest qualities of the social skill training movement. These investigative roots have been examined in depth in a number of recent review articles. For the reader wishing greater exposure to this research and its critical evaluation, we recommend the articles by Arkowitz (1977); Authier, Gustafson, Guerney, & Kasdorf (1975); Cartledge & Milburn (1978); Combs & Slaby (1977); Curran (1977); Drum & Knott (1977); Gambrill (1977); Goldstein (1973); Hersen & Eisler (1976); McFall (1976); and Nietzel, Winett, McDonald, & Davidson (1977).

Now that we have completed our introduction to social skills training, defined it, and provided an overview of major, individual programs, we turn to an in-depth consideration of one such program in order to provide a concrete and detailed view of rationale, methods, and materials in this aggression-relevant domain.

STRUCTURED LEARNING THERAPY

In 1955, the very year that the patient census in public mental hospitals in the United States reached its all-time high of 559,000 individuals, a series of medications was introduced that were destined to revolutionize patient care. These *ataractic* drugs appreciably reduced

Table 4.1. Social Skills Training Programs.

Developer	Program	Trainers	Trainees	Training Methods	Skills
Adkins (1970, 1974)	Life Skills Education	Professional and para-professional	Disadvantaged adolescents and adults	Instruction, audio/visual demonstration, discussion	• Developing oneself and relating to others Managing a career Managing home and family responsibilities Managing leisure time Exercising community rights
Argyle, Trower, & Bryant (1974); Trower, Bryant & Argyle (1978)	Social Skill Training	Hospital and clinic staff	Psychiatric patients	Modeling, role playing, feedback	• Introductory skills Observation skills Listening skills Speaking skills Meshing skills Expression of Attitudes Social Routines Tactics and Strategies
Burka, Hubbel, Preble, Spinelli, & Winter, (1972)	Communication Skills Workshop	Professional counselors	University undergraduates	Sensitivity group procedures, exercises, relaxation training, role playing, feedback	• Self-disclosure skills Feedback skills Intimacy skills Other interpersonal skills
Carkhuff (1974)	Facilitative Interpersonal Functioning	Professional and para-professional	Psychiatric patients, university undergraduates, disturbed children, parents	Didactic-experiential: modeling facilitative conditions training via practice, feedback, group participation	• Empathy Positive regard Genuineness Concreteness Immediacy Confrontation
Curran (1977)	Dating and Social Skills	Professional, graduate student	University students	Instruction, modeling, role play, coaching, video and group feedback, *in vivo* assignments	• Giving and receiving compliments Nonverbal communication Assertiveness

Reference	Program	Trainers	Trainees	Methods	Skills
Egan (1976)	Interpersonal	Diverse (including trainees)	Unspecified (presumably non–"patient"): in-group format	T-group procedures, contracting, exercises, modeling	Feeling talk Handling silence Planning dates Requesting dates Handling intimacy problems • Self-presentation skills Listening/responding skills Challenging skills Group participation skills
Elardo & Cooper (1977)	AWARE: Activities for Social Development	Teachers	Elementary school children	Structured discussions, exercises, games, role playing	• Getting acquainted skills Recognizing feelings skills Understanding individuals skills Social living skills
Galassi & Galassi (1977)	Assertion Training	Educators, human development specialists, mental health professionals	Unassertive individuals	Programmed text, relaxation, role playing, feedback	• Expressing positive feelings skills Expressing negative feelings skills Self-assertion skills
Goldstein, Sprafkin, & Gershaw (1976, 1979)	Structured Learning	Hospital and clinic staff, teachers	Hospital patients, adolescents	Modeling, role playing, feedback, transfer training	• Conversational skills Expressive skills Responsive skills Dealing with feelings skills Dealing with stress skills Alternative to aggression skills Planning skills
Gottman, Motarius, Gonso, & Markham (1977)	Couples Communication	None	Couples	Instructional text, exercises, *in vivo* practice	• Listening and validation Leveling Editing Negotiating agreements Dealing with hidden agendas

Table 4.1. Social Skills Training (Cont.)

Developer	Program	Trainers	Trainees	Training Method	Skills

Guerney (1977)	Relationship Enhancement	Various professional and paraprofessional	Couples, families	Instructions, modeling, role playing, social reinforcement	• Expressive skills
					  Empathic skills
					  Mode-switching skills
					  Facilitator skills

Hanson (1971, 1972)	Basic Social Communication Skills	Hospital staff	Chronic psychiatric patients	Instruction, modeling, role playing, feedback	• Eye contact
					  Facial expression
					  Affective quality of speech
					  Introducing oneself
					  Listening
					  Asking questions
					  Responding to embarrassing questions
					  Speaking in front of a group

Hare (1976)	Teaching Conflict Resolutions	Teachers	High school students	Exercises, simulation, role play	• Developing awareness of conflict management styles
					  Building trust
					  Alternatives to conflicts

Hawley, & Hawley (1975)	Developing Human Potential	Teachers	Elementary school children	Exercises, games, structured discussion	• Self-awareness skills
					  Communication skills
					  Relationship skills
					  Creativity skills

Heiman (1973)	Interpersonal Communication	Teachers	High school students	Lecture, exercises, role play	• Trust building
					  Sharing of self
					  Communication
					  Listening

Hersen & Eisler (1976)	Social Skill Training	Professional, graduate student student	Psychiatric patients	Instruction, modeling, role play, feedback	• Assertiveness

Johnson (1978)	Interpersonal Career Skills	Self	Diverse	Instructional text, group discussion,	• Cooperating and leading skills
					  Communication skills
					  Relationship skills
					  Conflict management skills

Reference	Program	Trainer	Trainee	Methods	Skills
Liberman, King, De Risi & McCann (1975)	Personal Effectiveness	Hospital and clinic staff	Psychiatric patients	Modeling, behavioral rehearsal, prompting, shaping, feedback	• Language skills Emotional expressiveness skills Social interaction skills Employment skills
McFall & Twentyman (1973, 1975)	Interpersonal Skill Training	Professional, graduate student	Psychiatric patients, university undergraduates	Instruction, modeling, role playing, feedback	• Initiating and terminating conversations Dealing with rejection Self-disclosure Assertiveness Other interpersonal skills
Miller, Nunnally & Wachman (1975)	Alive and Aware	None	Couples	Instructional text, in vivo practice	• Self-awareness skills Awareness of others skills Communication style skills Communication patterns skills
Patterson, Hops & Weiss (1975)	Interpersonal Training Skill	Authors	Married couples	Instruction, role play, feedback	• Pinpointing problem behaviors Negotiation Reinforcement delivery Problem solving
Rhode, Rasmussen & Heaps (1971)	Effective Communication	Teachers	College students	Role play, discussions feedback	• Communication skills
Stephens (1976, 1978)	Directive Teaching	Teachers	Children aged 7–12	Modeling, rehearsal, social reinforcement, contingency contracting	• Environmental behaviors Interpersonal behaviors Self-related behaviors Task-related behaviors
Terkelson (1976)	Parent-Child Communication Skill Program	Counselors	Parents, children grades 4-6	Exercises, role playing, review	• Listening Sending "I" messages Resolving conflict Dealing with value collisions
Thiel (1977)	Habilitation Programs for Mentally Handicapped Adults	Counselors, teachers, group home staff	Physically and mentally handicapped adults and adolescents	Modeling, role playing, feedback, in vivo practice	• Social behavior skills Practical living skills Socialization skills Job skills

patient anxiety, bizarreness, assaultiveness, and a variety of other overt behaviors that ill fit the person for nonhospital living. Thus, the advent and rapid widespread use of these medications set the stage for what was to occur but a few years later—the Community Mental Health movement. With overt manifestations of psychotic conditions reduced, the notion of discharging many (even long-term chronic) patients to live in the community became possible. The fact that in 1978 the national census was 175,000 shows just how successful this deinstitutionalization effort has been.

But there is another, less sanguine side to this movement. Many newly discharged individuals came into the community ill prepared to meet even the routine minor demands of daily living. Many were, after all, persons who in adolescence and early adulthood were too schizoid, incompetent, or unskilled to succeed in effective community functioning. They entered a mental hospital and remaind there for 10, or 20, or even more years. Their "training" during hospitalization involved socialization into the "good patient" role or what others have described as a colonization effect, rather than being taught what one needs in order to function adequately outside the hospital, in the real and often demanding world. Thus, it is not surprising that many of these persons functioned quite poorly, and failed to exercise at even a reasonable level of competence the wide array of interpersonal, planning, communication, personal hygiene, economic, and other daily living skills demanded of us all when we seek to lead effective and satisfying lives. For many of these persons, the "discharge door" at the main entrance of the hospital, the one separating hospital ward from group home or welfare hotel or halfway house became a revolving door. Frequent short stays in the hospital proved necessary; frequent long stays in the community proved impossible.

It was in response to these events that the present writer and his colleagues initially came to develop the skill training approach called *Structured Learning Therapy*. At the outset it became clear to us that our development efforts would have to significantly reflect two concerns. We not only had to decide what to teach (a skill *content* problem), but also how best to teach it (a teaching *methods* problem). It is to this latter topic, i.e., the teaching methods that optimally constitute a skills training approach, to which we first turn.

Teaching Methods

In spite of increased demonstrations of its effectiveness with other types of patients, psychotherapy involving lower socioeconomic class patients has quite frequently proven unsuccessful (Goldstein, 1973; Riessman,

Cohen & Pearl, 1964; Schofield, 1964). Since approximately 85 percent of all public mental hospital patients (the initial trainee group for Structured Learning) are lower or working class socioeconomically, this dismal treatment prognosis is a matter of considerable and relevant concern. This failure grows, at least in large part, from the insistence of most psychotherapists that the treatment to be offered remain essentially the same, almost regardless of significant patient characteristics, i.e., insight-oriented, highly verbal, feeling-centered treatment—a treatment into which the patient simply had to fit. At times, efforts have been made to train, indoctrinate, or socialize the patient into the "competent patient" role (Goldstein, 1971, Hoehn-Saric, Frank, Imber, Nash, Stone, and Battle, 1964; Lorion, 1973), but most of these efforts have failed. This conformity prescription, this decision to make the patient fit the therapy has essentially proven a bankrupt treatment strategy. Was there, we wondered, a viable alternative strategy, one we termed a reformity prescription? Its core is to leave the patient as is and try to develop a treatment to fit the patient, to seek to understand the patient as fully as possible along treatment/training relevant dimensions and then tailor his treatment to be as fully responsive to these characteristics as possible. To determine the nature of such an approach, we turned to developmental psychology research on child rearing, and to sociological writings on learning styles as a function of social class level. These bodies of literature consistently reveal that middle-class child-rearing practices and life-styles—with their emphasis upon intentions, motivation, inner states, self-regulation, and the like—are excellent "basic training" for participation in the traditional, verbal psychotherapies which, in fact, require precisely these qualities of their patients. Lower and, to some extent, working-class child rearing and life styles—with their emphasis upon reliance on authority and external example, action and motor behavior, rather than heavy reliance on verbal behavior, consequences rather than intentions, a restricted verbal code—prepare such persons poorly for traditional psychotherapy but, we felt, might prepare them very well for an intervention which was responsive to such life-style characteristics in the competencies it demanded. As will be seen below, we knew early that it would be a variety of social and other community functioning skills we would teach as the content of our program. With regard to teaching methods, we now felt that we should teach such materials via a program which—in response to patient-preferred living and learning styles—was brief, required imitation of specific, behavioral examples; was authoritatively administered; included role-taking training; provided immediate feedback; and included early, continuing, and frequent reinforcement for correct enactment of the behaviors being taught (Goldstein, 1973).

These were in our view the optimal prescriptive channels of access for the target patients, the learning style characteristics to which we had to respond in an effort to be maximally effective in our training program. It was, then, based upon these patient characteristics and programmatic goals that we selected and developed the teaching components of Structured Learning—modeling, role playing, performance feedback, and transfer.[1] We wish at this point in our presentation to describe these teaching components in some detail. As we do so, it should be noted that we have also used these same procedures, sometimes in slightly varied form, for skill training purposes with a number of aggressive and aggression-relevant populations—delinquent adolescents, child-abusing parents, police being trained to deal with family disputes, and others.[2] We discuss our work with these trainee populations in some depth later in this chapter.

Structured Learning consists of: (1) modeling, (2) role playing, (3) performance feedback, and (4) transfer training. The trainee is shown numerous specific and detailed examples (on audiotape, videotape, film, filmstrip, or live) of a person (the model) performing the skill behaviors we wish the trainee to learn (i.e., modeling); given considerable opportunity and encouragement to rehearse or practice the behaviors that have been modeled (i.e., role playing); provided with positive feedback, approval, or behavior of the model (i.e., performance feedback); and exposed to procedures that increase the likelihood that the newly learned behaviors will in fact be applied in a stable manner at work, in class, at home, or elsewhere in the person's real world (i.e., transfer training).

Modeling

The study of modeling or imitation learning has a long history in psychological research. Imitation has been examined under many names: copying, empathic learning, observational learning, identification, vicarious learning, matched-dependent behavior, and, most frequently, modeling. This research has shown that modeling is an effective, reliable, and rapid technique for both the learning of new behaviors and the strengthening or weakening of behaviors learned earlier. Three types of learning by modeling have been identified:

1. Observational learning effects: the learning of new behaviors which the person has never performed before.
2. Inhibitory and disinhibitory effects: the strengthening or weakening of behaviors which were previously performed very rarely by the person, because to do so would lead to disapproval or other negative reactions.

3. Behavioral facilitation effects: the performance of previously learned behaviors which are neither new nor a source of potential negative reactions from others.

The variety and number of different behaviors that research has shown are learned, strengthened, weakened, or facilitated through modeling are impressive indeed. These include acting aggressively, helping others, behaving independently, career planning, emotional arousal, social interaction, dependency, speech patterns, empathy, self-disclosure, and many more. It is clear from such research that modeling can be a reliable approach to the learning of behavior.

Yet it is also true that most people observe dozens and perhaps hundreds of behaviors in other people every day which they do not imitate. Many persons are exposed every day (by television, radio, magazines, and newpapers) to very polished, professional modeling displays of someone buying one product or another, but they do not later buy the product. And many persons observe expensively produced and expertly acted instructional films but remain uninstructed. Apparently, people learn by modeling under some circumstances but not others. Laboratory research on modeling has successfully identified a number of the circumstances that increase modeling, which we have called "modeling enhancers." These modeling enhancers are characteristics of the model, the modeling display, or the trainee (the observer), which have been shown to affect significantly the degree to which learning by imitation occurs.

Modeling Enhancers

Model Characteristics. Greater modeling will occur when the model (the person to be imitated): (1) seems to be highly skilled or expert; (2) is of high status; (3) controls rewards desired by the trainee; (4) is of the same sex, approximate age, and race as the trainee; (5) is apparently friendly and helpful, and, of particular importance; (6) is rewarded for the given behaviors. That is, we are all more likely to imitate expert or powerful but pleasant people who receive rewards (reinforcement) for what they are doing, especially when the particular rewards involved are something that we too desire.

Modeling Display Characteristics. Greater modeling will occur when the modeling display shows the behaviors to be imitated: (1) in a clear and detailed manner; (2) in the order from least to most difficult behaviors; (3) with enough repetition to make overlearning likely; (4) with as little irrelevant (not to be learned) detail as possible; and (5) when several different models, rather than a single model, are used.

Trainee Characteristics. Greater modeling will occur when the trainee is: (1) told to imitate the model; (2) similar to the model in background or in attitude toward the skill; (3) friendly toward or likes the model; and, most important; (4) rewarded for performing the modeled behaviors.

Modeling—Necessary but Insufficient. The positive outcome in most modeling studies may make the reader wonder about the need for the other components of Structured Learning. If so many types of behavior have been successfully changed by watching a model, why are role playing, performance feedback, and transfer training necessary? Our answer is clear. Modeling alone is insufficient because its many positive effects are very often not lasting effects. For example, we have taught ministers (by modeling) to be more empathic when conducting interviews. They were more empathic immediately after training, but a very short time later their increased empathy had disappeared. We found exactly the same result in our modeling study of empathy with nurses and hospital aides (Sutton, 1970), and in yet others of our investigations in which we use modeling to change patient behavior (Friedenberg, 1971; Walsh, 1971). Others have reported similar results (e.g., Burrs and Kapche, 1969). We noted earlier that learning appears to be improved when the learner has opportunity and encouragement to practice, rehearse, or role-play the behaviors he has seen performed by the model, and when he is rewarded for doing so. Stated otherwise, viewing the modeling display teaches the trainee what to do, but he needs, in addition, enough practice to learn how to do it, and reward to motivate him or, in effect, to answer the question of why he should behave in certain ways. Let us now turn to the "how" question—that is, to the second component of Structured Learning, role playing.

Role Playing

Role playing has been defined as "a situation in which an individual is asked to take a role or behave in certain ways not normally his own, or if his own in a place not normal for the enactment of the role." (Mann, 1956). The use of role-playing acting, behavioral rehearsal, and similar methods to help a person change his behavior or attitudes in the direction of the role he is playing has been a popular approach for many years. Recently, clinical psychologists have shown the value of role playing to increase assertive or independent behavior in unassertive and dependent patients, to reduce smoking, and to change the attitudes of hospitalized mental patients toward treatment staff.

Role playing has also been the target of much research by social psychologists. Perhaps as many as one hundred studies have been done, mostly aimed at discovering the effects of role playing on attitude change. In the typical experiment of this type, the research subjects are first given some sort of attitude questionnaire. One of the attitude dimensions on this questionnaire is selected for the study. The subjects are then placed in one of three experimental groups. Those assigned to the role-play group are requested to make a speech or other public statement on the attitude dimension, in support of attitudes that are opposite to their own actual attitudes. Subjects in the second group, the exposure group, hold the same private attitudes as the role-play subjects but are not requested to make a speech opposed to their real attitudes. They are simply required to listen to one of the speeches made by a role-play subject. Control group subjects neither make nor hear such a speech. All subjects are then given the attitude questionnaire a second time. This type of experiment has consistently shown that role-playing subjects change in their attitudes (away from what they privately believed, toward what they publicly said) significantly more than either exposure or control subjects.

Studies such as these, in clinical, social, or industrial settings, combine to form an impressive demonstration of the value of role playing for behavior and attitude change. We noted earlier, however, that modeling procedures have been shown to lead to substantial behavior change, but that such change is quite likely to disappear unless (1) sufficient attention is given to a broad selection of modeling enhancers when developing and using the modeling procedures; (2) sufficient opportunity for practice or rehearsal is provided; and (3) sufficient incentive or reinforcement is delivered. Likewise with role playing. Behavior or attitude change through role playing either will not occur or will not be lasting if the role player does not have enough information about the content of the role to enact it (or if he is not shown such information by a model) and if insufficient attention has been paid to what may be called role-play enhancers.

Role-play enhancers, like modeling enhancers, are procedures that increase the likelihood of lasting behavior change. Specifically, behavior change from role playing will be greater and more lasting, the greater the role player's:

1. choice regarding whether to take part in the role playing;
2. commitment to the behavior or attitude he is role playing, in the sense that his enactment is public rather than private, or otherwise difficult to disown;
3. improvisation in enacting the role-play behaviors; and
4. reward, approval, or reinforcement for enacting the role-play behaviors.

Role Playing—Necessary but Insufficient. There exists considerable evidence for the value of role-playing procedures in a variety of settings. We said earlier that modeling appears to be a necessary but insufficient procedure for effecting durable behavior change. We would now propose that role playing may also be seen as a necessary but insufficient behavior change technique. Its effects, as seems true for modeling in isolation, often do not appear to be lasting ones. Three investigations reported by Lichtenstein, Keutzer, and Himes (1969) on the effects of role playing on smoking failed to demonstrate any lasting behavioral change. Furthermore, a very careful study reported by Hollander (1970) found no behavior change due to role playing even though choice commitment, improvisation, and reward were all reflected in her procedures. Thus, in most attempts to help a person change his behavior, neither modeling alone nor role playing alone is enough. A combination of the two is an improvement, for then the trainee knows what to do and how to do it, but even this combination is insufficient; the trainee still needs to know why he should behave in new ways. That is, a motivational or incentive component must also be added to the "training package." It is for this purpose that we turn to consideration of performance feedback.

Performance Feedback

Performance feedback or responding to how well a trainee has done may take several forms—reward or reinforcement, criticism, indifference, reteaching, and so forth. In the present discussion of performance feedback we emphasize social reinforcement, that is, praise, approval, and encouragement, because such reinforcement has been shown to be an especially potent influence on behavior change. The nature and effects of reinforcement have received more study than any other aspect of the learning process.[3] Reinforcement has typically been defined as any event that serves to increase the likelihood that a given behavior will occur. Three types of reinforcement have been described: (1) material reinforcement, such as food or money, (2) social reinforcement, such as praise or approval from others, and (3) self-reinforcement, which is a person's positive evaluation of his own behavior. Effective training must give proper attention to all three types of reinforcement. Material reinforcement may be viewed as a necessary base, without which the "higher" levels of reinforcement (social and self) may not function. For many trainees, material reinforcement may be the only class of reinforcement to which they will at first respond. But there is considerable evidence that, although trainee behaviors change as a function of material rewards, such changed behavior typically disappears (or is extinguished) when the rewards are no longer forthcoming. It is for this reason that an effort is usually made to pair social reinforcement with material reinforcement and, eventually, to have the former substitute for the latter. In real-life settings, a job well done (if it receives any reward at all) receives a verbal "nice job" more often than a tangible reward, and helping a friend with a chore elicits "thanks" or approval, not money or objects. Stated otherwise, it is important that a skill-training effort not rely too heavily or too long upon material reinforcers.

Even though social reinforcers may be more likely and hence more valuable than material reinforcers in the real-life sense described above, it is also true that many valuable real-life behaviors go unnoticed, uncommented upon, and unappreciated by others. Therefore social reinforcement, too, may be an unreliable ally at times in the skill-training enterprise. For their own needs and reasons, such potential social reinforcement suppliers as teachers, parents, and friends may often be either nonrewarding or simply unavailable. If, however, we can aid trainees in becoming their own reinforcement suppliers, if we can help them evaluate their own skill behaviors and silently praise or approve their own effective performance, we have made a very major stride toward increasing the chances that newly learned skills will be performed in a reliable and enduring way where they count—in their homes, at work, in school, or in other real-life settings.

So far, we have defined reinforcement, indicated the nature and consequences of different types of reinforcement, and emphasized its importance for human performance. In looking for effective training methods, it is insufficient simply to acknowledge that reinforcement is a crucial ingredient in the training process, for how effective and enduring the influence of feedback in the form of reinforcement is on performance will depend upon several characteristics of the reinforcements used. It is these characteristics or reinforcement enhancers that we now examine.

Reinforcement Enhancers

1. *Type of reinforcement.* As McGehee and Thayer (1961) have observed, "What one person regards as a rewarding experience may be regarded by another as neutral or non-rewarding, or even punishing" (p. 140). While it is obviously true that certain types of reinforcers, such as approval, food, affection, and money, have a high likelihood of serving as effective reinforcers for most people most of the time, this will not always be the case. Both the individual's own reinforcement history and his needs at the time will affect whether the intended reinforcer is in fact reinforcing. It is desirable, therefore, that all training procedures take

into account and respond to the individual reinforcement histories and current needs of the participating trainees. This means choosing not only between and among given material, social, and self-reinforcers when necessary, but making changes in these choices in a continuing and sensitive manner.

2. *Delay of reinforcement.* Laboratory research on learning has consistently shown that behavior change occurs most effectively when the reinforcement follows immediately after the desired behavior. Reinforcement strengthens the behavior which was going on just before the reinforcement took place and makes it likely that the behavior will occur again. Thus, it is possible that delayed reinforcement can lead to the strengthening of inappropriate or ineffective behaviors should such behaviors occur between the desired behavior and the onset of reinforcement.

3. *Response-contingent reinforcement.* Related to the issue of immediate versus delayed reinforcement are other matters of timing that aid or inhibit the effects of reinforcement on performance. Bandura (1969) has commented:

> In many instances considerable rewards are bestowed, but they are not made conditional upon the behavior that change agents wish to promote ... special privileges, activities, and rewards are generally furnished according to fixed time schedules rather than performance requirements, and, in many cases, positive reinforcers are inadvertently made contingent upon the wrong types of behavior (pp. 229–230).

Thus, it is clear that the contingent relationship or linkage between performance and reinforcement must be reflected in training procedures and made sufficiently clear to the trainee.

4. *Amount and quality of reinforcement.* In addition to considerations noted above concerning type, timing, and contingency of the reinforcement provided, the amount and quality of reinforcement will be a major source of its effect upon performance. With certain important exceptions, the greater the amount of reinforcement, the greater the positive effect upon performance. One limitation on this principle is that increases in certain types of reinforcement do increase performance, but in smaller and smaller amounts. Research on amount of reinforcement serves as further illustration of the difference between learning and performance. In the laboratory at least, subjects appear to learn (acquire new knowledge) no more rapidly for large rewards than they do for small ones. Once learning has taken place, however, performance will often be more dependable if larger rewards are provided.

5. *Opportunity for reinforcement.* A further requirement for successful and consistent performance is that the behavior to be reinforced

must occur with sufficient frequency that reinforcement can be provided. If such behaviors are too infrequent, insufficient opportunity will exist to influence them through contingent reinforcement. We may note here that beyond its several types of practice effects noted earlier, role playing provides excellent opportunities to offer appropriate contingent reinforcement.

6. *Partial (intermittent) reinforcement.* Partial reinforcement refers to the reinforcement of only some of the person's correct responses by reinforcing at fixed times (e.g., once every five minutes), at a fixed number of responses (e.g., every fifth correct response), on a variable time or response schedule (e.g., randomly choosing—within limits—the times or correct response to reward), and on other schedules. In all instances, it has been consistently shown that responses acquired under conditions of partial reinforcement are exceedingly resistant to extinction. That is, they continue to occur even when they are not reinforced at all.

In summary of our discussion of reinforcement thus far, research evidence combines to indicate that high levels of performance are likely to occur if the trainee is given enough opportunity to receive immediate reinforcements of a kind that is right for him, in sufficiently large amounts, and offered in a response-contingent manner on an intermittent schedule.

There is considerable evidence supporting the behavior change impact of modeling, role playing, and reinforcement. We held that neither modeling alone nor role playing alone yields results nearly as effective as the two combined. We now take a similar position regarding reinforcement. While it is true that reinforcement alone is more likely to lead to lasting behavior change than either modeling or role playing alone, it is also true that the behaviors to be reinforced must occur with sufficient correctness and sufficient frequency for reinforcement to have its intended effect. Modeling can provide the correctness, role playing can provide the frequency.

Yet there is one further component of Structured Learning to consider, a component responsive to the massive failure of both education program gains and psychotherapeutic gains to transfer from the training site to real-life settings. This component is transfer of training.

Transfer of Training

The main interest of any training program (and where most training programs fail) is not in the trainee's performance at the training site but, instead, in how well he performs in his real-life setting. If satisfactory performance has been developed at the time of training, what procedures are available to maximize the chances that such performance will continue in a durable manner in class, in school hallways, on the street, at home, or at other places or times where it is appropriate? Stated otherwise, how can we encourage transfer of training?

Research has identified five different principles of transfer enhancement. While it may prove difficult to implement all of these principles in any given training program, their combined impact is to increase greatly the likelihood of satisfactory, positive transfer. We describe these principles below and examine their implementation in Structured Learning.

1. *General principles.* Transfer of training has been increased by giving the trainee general principles which cover satisfactory performance in both the training and real-life settings. We refer here to giving the trainee, in a clear and complete manner, the organizing concepts, principles, or rationales that explain or account for successful skill selection and implementation in both places. Concretely, in Structured Learning, trainees are presented skill choice, skill context, skill alteration, and skill-use principles.

2. *Response availability.* Transfer of training has been increased by procedures that maximize response availability. It has been well established by research that, other things being equal, the behavior that has occurred most frequently in the past will be more likely to occur on later occasions. This principle of transfer originates from research on overlearning, which demonstrates that the higher the degree of original learning, the greater the probable level of later transfer. Overlearning may not only increase the likelihood of positive transfer, it may also decrease the chances that negative transfer will occur. When more than one skill is being taught, negative transfer (interference rather than facilitation) is likely to occur if training on the second skill is begun while the first is still only partially learned, an unlikely event if enough practice of correct skill behavior is done to ensure that overlearning had been provided.

3. *Identical elements.* In the earliest experimental work with transfer of training, it was demonstrated that the greater the number of identical elements or characteristics shared by the training and application settings, the greater the later transfer from training to application. This finding has been repeatedly reaffirmed over the years. Ideally what would be identical, or as similar as possible, would include both the interpersonal and physical characteristics of the training and application settings. Thus, if possible, the adolescent trainee would be trained along with other youngsters in *his* class, his friends, or others with whom he interacts regularly; training would take place to the extent feasible in school or at other real-life settings in which youngsters actually interact

rather than at a therapy or training center; the furnishings, materials, and other physical characteristics of the two settings, as well as the nature and schedule of reinforcements would be as similar as possible.

4. *Stimulus variability.* Several investigators have demonstrated that positive transfer is greater when a variety of training stimuli are employed (Callantine & Warren, 1955; Duncan, 1958; Emshoff, Redd & Davidson, 1976). As will be shown later in the chapter, the broad array of interpersonal stimuli represented by the several models, trainers, and role-play coactors utilized in Structured Learning readily provides an example of this principle of transfer enhancement. The diverse styles and behaviors of these several persons all have the potential of serving in application settings as stimuli or cues for the desirable skill behaviors acquired during the Structured Learning sessions.

5. *Real-life reinforcement.* As noted above, in our discussion of response availability, the training needs of the trainee are all too likely to be forgotten once he "graduates" from being a trainee and leaves the training site for his real-life setting. Our efforts until "graduation day" may have been educationally perfect. By whatever training techniques, we may have brought the trainee to an exceedingly high level of performance excellence. We may also have sought to maximize transfer by providing him with general principles, high levels of response availability, maximum identical elements in the training and application settings, and considerable stimulus variability. And yet, given all these successful efforts, our training may fail if we stop at this point. Training provides skills, information, knowledge, and the potential for their successful application. It is primarily real-life reinforcement—by teachers, parents and peers—that will decide what happens at the application site, that determines whether the learning acquired finds *enduring* expression in successful performance. Real-life reinforcement to maximize such transfer must be supplemented by corrective feedback for poor quality performance, and pay full attention to *continued* real-life reinforcement for satisfactory performance. Such reinforcement must take account of all the dimensions of reinforcement (scheduling, source, nature, amount, etc.) noted earlier as crucial aspects of the training process.

We have underscored several times in this chapter the importance of continued (if intermittent) reinforcement for lasting behavior change. Are the new behaviors ignored? Or, as is perhaps more common, are they reinforced at first and then ignored? Continued, if periodic, reinforcement is clearly a very necessary enhancer of enduring transfer of training. Our belief in this principle is sufficiently strong that, when implementing Structured Learning with adult mental patients, we have trained hospital staff, relatives, and others to be reinforcement allies. Similarly, with aggressive adolescent trainees we have (whenever possible) sought to teach teachers, parents, principals, peers, and other real-life reinforcement dispensers for the trainees the value of and procedures for providing the trainee with continued real-life reinforcement. To the extent that efforts such as these have proven successful, a benevolent learning cycle is established whereby the likelihood of continued real-life reinforcement, and thus maximal transfer, is increased.

The Training Procedures in Overview

We have examined in detail four procedures for skill training purposes—modeling, role playing, performance feedback, and transfer training. The nature of each and techniques that maximize their impact have been presented. Yet, in discussing each procedure, our enthusiasm was lessened by one or more cautionary notes. For example, while modeling does indeed result in the learning of new behaviors, without sufficient practice old ways of acting very clearly tend to recur. Practice or role playing is also an important aid to new learning, but one must practice correct behaviors, and without prior modeling or similar demonstration, the trainee's performance is advanced very little. Given both modeling and role playing, the newly learned behaviors have greater likelihood of persisting, but will not do so unless the trainee sees his use of these behaviors as a rewarding experience. Hence, the crucial necessity for reinforcement. Yet, while reinforcement is indeed crucial, and while evidence supporting its impact on behavior change is very impressive, we have held that willingness to offer reinforcement is also frequently not enough for effective human learning. The behaviors to be reinforced must be enacted by the trainee correctly and with sufficient frequency for adequate opportunity for reinforcement to occur. It is procedures such as modeling and role playing that lead to such sufficient frequency of correct enactment. Without such procedures, the new behaviors—even if reinforced—may occur too seldom for stable learning to occur. Combining these three procedures would, and it appears bring us much closer to an effective and widely applicable approach to skill learning. Yet, a truly effective approach to learning must also demonstrate such learning beyond the training setting and must prove to be powerful, broadly applicable, and reliably enduring in the learner's real-life setting. Thus we turned to transfer training. The five principles we have described, and a number of additional potential transfer enhancers of perhaps a more experimental nature, which we have presented in detail elsewhere (Goldstein and Kanfer, 1979), are a comprehensive beginning toward facilitating the endurance of newly learned skills.

The Training Procedures in Action

We have examined the nature and function of modeling, role playing, performance feedback, and transfer training—the major teaching components of both Structured Learning and several other social skills training programs. Our next concern is how these components are implemented in actual practice. In the following sections we describe the procedures in action.

Organizing the Structured Learning Group

Selection of Patients. Each Structured Learning group should consist of trainees who are clearly deficient in whatever skill is going to be taught. If possible, trainees should also be grouped according to the degree of their deficiency in the given skill. The optimal group size for effective Structured Learning sessions consists of 6 to 12 trainees and two trainers. In order for both learning and transfer to occur, each trainee must have ample opportunity to practice what he has heard or seen modeled, to receive feedback from other group members and the trainers, and to discuss his attempts to apply what he has learned in the training sessions at home, on the job, or on the ward. Yet, the duration of each session should typically not exceed two hours, since Structured Learning is intensive and trainees' learning efficiency diminishes beyond this span. A group size of 6 to 12, therefore, is optimal in that it permits the specific training tasks to be accomplished within the allotted time period. If most trainees in a given group show a particularly brief span of attention, the session can be shortened to as little as one half-hour, although in this instance it is advisable to meet more often than the usual two or three times per week.

The trainees selected need not be from the same ward (if inpatients), the same class (if adolescents), nor from the same community area (if abusing parents). Again to maximize transfer, however, trainees are asked to "set the stage" when role playing by enacting the modeling tape's specific behaviors, or behavioral steps, as they fit their real situation on the ward, in class, at home, or at work. Each role play involves at least two participants, the trainee himself (main actor) and another trainee (coactor) chosen by him to play the role of wife, teacher, classmate, husband, boss, nurse, or whatever role is appropriate for the given skill problem. We ask the main actor playing himself to describe in detail an actual situation in which he is having or could be having difficulty performing the skill behaviors that have been modeled. The coactor plays the part of the other person in the main actor's life who is involved in the skill problem area. In this way, the role playing becomes real—that is, it becomes a rehearsal for solving real-life problems. Thus, while participants need not come from the same ward, class, or community, they should be familiar enough with one another's real-life situations so that they can role-play these situations realistically.

Number, Length, and Spacing of Sessions. The Structured Learning modeling tapes and associated procedures typically constitute a training program from 3 to 15 sessions long, depending on the level of the group and the number and complexity of skills being taught. We have developed a different modeling tape for each interpersonal or personal skill we have sought to teach. The specific behaviors comprising the skill are concretely demonstrated on each tape. The order in which the modeling tapes are utilized should (1) give trainees a sense of making progress in skill mastery (thus, the easier skills should come first), and (2) provide them (in each session) with useful knowledge that can be applied in real-life settings between sessions.

It is most desirable that training occur at a rate of two or, at the most, three times per week. Spacing is crucial. Most trainees in all skill training programs learn well in the training setting. As noted earlier, however, most fail to transfer this learning to where it counts—in class, on the ward, at home, at work, in the community. Structured Learning includes special procedures which maximize the likelihood of transfer of training, including between-sessions "homework." To allow trainees ample opportunity to try out in real-life what was learned in the training setting, sessions must be well spaced. One sequence of modeling several role plays, feedback, and assignment of homework is ideally covered in each training session of one to two hours in length. The following session should open with a review of the previous session's homework.

The Structured Learning Sessions

The Setting. One major principle for encouraging transfer from the training to the real-life setting is the rule of identical elements. As we noted earlier, this rule states that the more similar the two settings—that is, the greater number of identical physical and social qualities shared by them—the greater the transfer. Therapy in a fancy office or at a mountaintop work-play retreat may be great fun, but it results in minimal transfer of training. We urge that Structured Learning be conducted in the same general setting as the real-life environment of most participating trainees and that the training setting be furnished to resemble or simulate the likely application settings as much as possible.

In the majority of Structured Learning groups, we have found it useful to provide each trainee with a simplified and structured guide which explains group procedures and is useful for taking notes during and between training sessions. This guide, the *Trainee's Notebook for Structured Learning*, outlines the procedural details for Structured Learning and provides note pages on which the trainee may write behavioral steps, role-play notes, and homework assignments. The *Notebook* also serves as a convenient reference for trainees as they build a repertoire of skills.

The Introduction. The initial session is opened by the trainers first introducing themselves and having each trainee do likewise, being sure that every trainee has the opportunity to tell the group something about his background and training goals. After such an initial warm-up or familiarization period, the trainers introduce the program by providing trainees with a brief description of its rationale, training procedures, targets, and so forth. Typically, the introduction also covers such topics as the centrality of interpersonal skills for effective and satisfying community living, the value of skill knowledge and skill flexibility on the part of the trainee, the variety of skills needed in relation to the complex demands made in contemporary society, and the manner in which training focuses on altering specific behaviors as opposed to attitude change. The specific training procedures (modeling, role playing, etc.) are then described, as is the implementation (dates, time, place, etc.) of these procedures. A period of time is spent discussing these introductory points, and then the actual training begins. It is vital during this introduction that the concepts explained and the language level used to explain them are tailored to the level of understanding and language of the participating patients, adolescents, parents or other trainees.

Modeling. Trainers describe the first skill to be taught and hand out cards (Skill Cards) to all trainees on which the name of the skill and its behavioral steps are printed. The first modeling tape is then played. Trainees are told to listen closely to the way the actors in each vignette on the tape follow the behavioral steps.

To ease trainees into Structured Learning, it is recommended that the first skill taught be one that trainees can master with relative ease. It is particularly important that a trainee's first experience with Structured Learning be a successful one.

All modeling audiotapes begin with a narrator setting the scene and stating the name of the skill and the behavioral steps that make up that skill. Sets of actors portray a series of vignettes in which each behavioral step is clearly enacted in sequence. The narrator then returns on the tape, makes a summary statement, restates the behavioral steps, and urges their continued use. In our view, this sequence of narrator's introduction, modeling scenes, and narrator's summary constitutes the minimum requirement for a satisfactory modeling audiotape. We have found that live modeling by trainers can also often provide those elements that promote satisfactory learning by trainees.

Role Playing. A brief spontaneous discussion almost invariably follows the playing of a modeling tape. Trainees comment on the behavioral steps, the actors, and, very often, on how the situation or skill problem portrayed occurs in their own lives. Since our primary goal in role playing is to encourage realistic behavioral rehearsal, a trainee's statements about his individual difficulties using the skill being taught can often develop into material for the first role play. To enhance the realism of the portrayal, we would have him (now the main actor) choose a second trainee (coactor) to play the role of the significant other person in his life who is relevant to the particular skill problem. One trainer should be responsible for keeping a record of who has role played, which role, and for which skill, to be sure that all participate about equally.

It is of crucial importance that the main actor seeks to enact the behavioral steps he has just heard modeled. He is told to refer to his Skill Card on which the behavioral steps are printed. As noted, the behavioral steps should also be written on a chalkboard for him to see while role playing. Before role playing begins, the following instructions should be delivered:

1. *To the main actor*: Follow and enact the behavioral steps. Do so with the real skill problem you have chosen in mind.
2. *To the coactor*: Respond as realistically as possible, doing what you think the actual other person in the main actor's real-life situation would do.
3. *To the other trainees in the group*: Observe how well the main actor follows the behavioral steps and take notes on this for later discussion.

The main actor is asked to describe briefly the real skill problem situation and the real person(s) involved in it, with whom he could try these behavioral step behaviors in real life. The coactor should be called by the name of the main actor's significant other during the role play. The trainer then instructs the role players to begin. It is the trainers' main responsibility, at this point, to be sure that the main actor keeps role-playing and that he attempts to follow the behavioral steps while doing so. If he "breaks role" and begins to make comments, explaining background events, etc., the trainers should firmly instruct him to resume his role. One trainer should position himself near the chalkboard and point to each behavioral step, in turn, as the role play unfolds, being sure none is either missed or enacted out of order. If the trainers or actors feel the role play is not progressing well and wish to start it over, this is acceptable. Trainers should make an effort to have the actors complete the skill enactment before stepping down. Observers should be instructed to hold their comments until the role play is completed.

The role playing should be continued until all trainees have had an opportunity to participate (in either role) and preferably until all have had a chance to be the main actor, even if all of the same behavioral steps must be carried over to a second or third session. Note that while the framework of behavioral steps for each role play in the series remains the same, the actual content can and should change from role play to role play. It is the problem as it actually occurs, or could occur, in each trainee's real-life environment that should be the content of the given role play. When completed, each trainee should be better armed to act appropriately in the given reality situation.

A few further procedural matters relevant to role playing should be noted, as each will serve to increase its effectiveness. Role reversal is often a useful role-play procedure. A trainee role-playing a skill problem may have a difficult time perceiving his coactor's viewpoint, and vice versa. Having them exchange roles and resume the role playing can be most helpful in this regard.

At times, it has proven worthwhile for the trainer to assume the coactor role, in an effort to expose trainees to the handling of types of reactions not otherwise role-played during the session. It is here that the trainer's flexibility and creativity will certainly be called upon. We might add in this context that while we sometimes suggest that trainers play the coactor role, we urge them to be especially cautious when taking on the main actor role. Errors in the enactment of this live modeling role can be most serious, destroy trainer credibility, and severely decrease their value as trainers for that group of trainees.

Real-life problems very often require effective use of a combination of basic skills for their satisfactory solution. To reflect this fact in our training procedures, we have developed a series of modeling application tapes which portray sequences and combinations of basic skills necessary to deal with such daily living matters as finding a place to live, job seeking, marital interactions, and dealing with crises. The procedures utilized with the application skill tapes are essentially the same as those used for the basic skill tapes, though individualized skill combinations will have to be constructued prior to role playing. Application groups, using basic skills in combination, should only be started once trainees have a firm grasp of basic skills used separately.

Feedback. Upon completion of each role play, a brief feedback period should ensue. The goals of this activity are to let the main actor know how well he followed the behavioral steps or in what ways he departed from them, to explore the psychological impact of his enactment on his coactor, and to encourage him to try out his role-play behaviors in real-life.

In all these critiques, it is crucial that the behavioral focus of Structured Learning be maintained. Comments must point to the presence or absence of specific, concrete behaviors, and not take the form of general evaluative comments or broad generalities. Feedback, of course, may be positive or negative in content. At a minimum, a "poor" performance (major departures from the behavioral steps) can be praised as "a good try," while it is being criticized for its real faults. If at all possible, trainees failing to follow the relevant behavioral steps in their role play should be given the opportunity to re-role-play these same behavioral steps after receiving corrective feedback. At times, as a further feedback procedure, we have audiotaped or videotaped entire role plays. Giving trainees later opportunities to observe themselves on tape can be an effective aid to learning by enabling them to reflect on their own behavior.

Since a primary goal of Structured Learning is skill flexibility, a role-play enactment which markedly departs from the behavioral steps may not be "wrong." That is, it may in fact "work" in some situations. Trainers should stress that they are trying to teach effective alternatives and that the trainees would do well to have the behavioral steps in their repertoire of skill behaviors, available for use when appropriate.

As the final feedback step, after all role playing and discussion are completed, the modeling tape can be replayed. This step, in a sense, summarizes the session and leaves trainees with a final review of the behavioral steps.

Transfer Training. Several aspects of the training sessions described above had, as their primary purpose, augmentation of the likelihood that learning in the therapy setting will transfer to the trainee's actual environment. We would suggest, however, that even more forthright steps need to be taken in order to maximize transfer. When possible, we would urge a homework technique which we have used successfully with most groups. In this procedure, trainees are openly instructed to try the behavioral step behaviors they have practiced during the session in their own real-life settings. The name of the person(s) with whom they will try it, the day, the place, etc., are all discussed. The trainee is urged to take notes on his first transfer attempt on Homework Report 1 provided by the trainers. This form requests detailed information about what happened when the homework assignment was attempted, how well the relevant behavioral steps were followed, the trainee's evaluation of his performance, and his thoughts about what his next assignment might appropriately be.

As is true of our use of the modeling tapes, it has often proven useful (to ensure success experiences) to start with relatively simple homework behaviors and, as mastery is achieved, work up to more complex assignments. The first part of each session is devoted to a presentation and discussion of these homework reports. Trainers should meet patient failure to "do their homework" with some chagrin and expressed disappointment. When trainees do attempt, however, to complete their homework assignments, social reinforcement (praise, approval, encouragement) should be provided by the trainers. It cannot be stressed too strongly that without these, or similar attempts to maximize transfer, the value of the entire training effort is in severe jeopardy.

Of the several principles of transfer training for which research evidence exists, the principle of performance feedback is clearly most consequential. A trainee can learn very well in the training setting, do all his transfer homework, and yet the training program can be a performance failure. Trainees will perform as trained if, and only if, there is some "payoff" for doing so. Stated simply, new behaviors persist if they are rewarded, and diminish if ignored or actively challenged.

As noted earlier in this chapter, we have found it useful to implement several supplemental programs outside the Structured Learning setting which can help to provide the rewards or reinforcements trainees need so that their new behaviors will be maintained. These programs include provision of both external social reward (provided by people in the trainee's real-life environment) and self-reward (provided by the trainee himself).

In several hospitals, schools, and agencies, we have actively sought to identify and develop environmental or external support by holding orientation meetings for staff and for relatives and friends of trainee's— i.e., the real-life reward and punishment givers. The purpose of these meetings was to acquaint significant others in the trainee's life with Structured Learning theory and procedures. Most important in these sessions is the presentation of procedures whereby staff, relatives, and friends can encourage and reward trainees as they practice their new skills. We consider these orientation sessions for such persons of major value for transfer of training.

Environmental support is frequently insufficient to maintain newly learned skills. It is also the case that many real-life environments in which trainees work and live will actively resist a trainee's efforts at behavior change. For this reason, we have found it useful to include in our transfer efforts a method through which trainees can learn to be their own rewarders. Once a new skill has been practiced through role playing, and once the trainee has made his first homework effort and has received group feedback, we recommend that trainees continue to practice their new skill as frequently as possible. It is at this time that a program of self-reinforcement can and should be initiated. Trainees can be instructed in the nature of self-reinforcement and encouraged to "say something and do something nice for yourself" if they practice their new skill well. Homework Report 2 will aid both trainers and trainees in this effort. On this form, trainees can specify potential rewards and indicate how they rewarded themselves for a job well done. Trainees' notes can be collected by the trainer in order to keep abreast of independent progress being made by trainees without consuming group time.

THE SKILLS

We have completed our examination of the major training procedures that constitute Structured Learning and turn to consideration of content and curricula. We present the specific skills we have developed for and taught to diverse populations, for the most part focusing as above on skills especially germane for aggressive and aggression-relevant Structured Learning trainees. In addition to the skills per se, examples of skill behavioral steps and modeling vignettes portraying these steps will be presented.

Mental Hospital Patients

As noted earlier in this chapter, public mental hospital patients were the first target trainees for Structured Learning. Our basic skill and application skill modeling tapes are listed below (skills 1–37 are basic skills, 38–59 are application skills):

Series I. Conversations: Beginning Skills

Skill 1. Starting a conversation
Skill 2. Carrying on a conversation
Skill 3. Ending a conversation
Skill 4. Listening

Series II. Conversations: Expressing Oneself

Skill 5. Expressing a compliment
Skill 6. Expressing appreciation

Skill 7. Expressing encouragement
Skill 8. Asking for help
Skill 9. Giving instructions
Skill 10. Expressing affection
Skill 11. Expressing a complaint
Skill 12. Persuading others
Skill 13. Expressing anger

Series III. Conversations: Responding to Others

Skill 14. Responding to praise
Skill 15. Responding to the feelings of others (empathy)
Skill 16. Apologizing
Skill 17. Following instructions
Skill 18. Responding to persuasion
Skill 19. Responding to failure
Skill 20. Responding to contradictory messages
Skill 21. Responding to a complaint
Skill 22. Responding to anger

Series IV. Planning Skills

Skill 23. Setting a goal
Skill 24. Gathering information
Skill 25. Concentrating on a task
Skill 26. Evaluating your abilities
Skill 27. Preparing for a stressful conversation
Skill 28. Setting problem priorities
Skill 29. Decision making

Series V. Alternatives to Aggression

Skill 30. Identifying and labeling your emotions
Skill 31. Determining responsibility
Skill 32. Making requests
Skill 33. Relaxation
Skill 34. Self-control
Skill 35. Negotiation
Skill 36. Helping others
Skill 37. Assertiveness

Application Skills. Each application tape portrays a model enacting three to eight basic skills, in a sequence and combination chosen to deal completely with a real-life problem.

Skill 38. Finding a place to live (through formal channels)
Skill 39. Moving in (typical)
Skill 40. Moving in (difficult)
Skill 41. Managing money
Skill 42. Neighboring (apartment house)
Skill 43. Job seeking (typical)
Skill 44. Job seeking (difficult)
Skill 45. Job keeping (average day's work)
Skill 46. Job keeping (strict boss)
Skill 47. Receiving telephone calls (difficult)
Skill 48. Restaurant eating (typical)
Skill 49. Organizing time (typical)
Skill 50. Using leisure time (learning something new)
Skill 51. Using leisure time (interpersonal activity)
Skill 52. Social (party)
Skill 53. Social (church supper)
Skill 54. Marital (positive interaction)
Skill 55. Marital (negative interaction)
Skill 56. Using community resources (seeking money)
Skill 57. Using community resources (avoiding red tape)
Skill 58. Dealing with crises (inpatient to nonpatient transition)
Skill 59. Dealing with crises (loss)

Seventeen of the basic skills listed above were designed by us as relevant to either the control of aggressive behavior or as a prosocial alternative to aggression. (Skills 10, 11, 12, 13, 15, 19, 20, 21, 22, 30, 31, 32, 33, 34, 35, 36, 37.) The illustrative material which follows consists of a sampling of six of these skills, their behavioral steps, and the first of the ten vignettes which appear on each of the modeling tapes portraying these basic skills. The reader interested in the corresponding information for the remaining basic skills, or the application skills, should see Goldstein, Sprafkin, & Gershaw (1976).

Skill 11. Expressing a Complaint

Behavioral Steps

1. Define what the problem is, and who is responsible.
2. Decide how the problem might be solved.
3. Tell that person what the problem is and how it might be solved.
4. Ask for his response.
5. Show that you understand his feelings.
6. Come to agreement on the steps to be taken by each of you.

Modeling Vignette Example

Person 1: I bought this toaster last month I think it was . . . it must be about four weeks now. And this morning it's not working right. It only toasts on one side. Wonder if maybe I broke it? I . . . I . . . don't know; I thought I was following the instructions . . . I . . . I don't know whether I broke it or whether there's something wrong with it . . . or . . . No, I'm pretty sure I didn't do anything to it. I've been just toasting bread and, uh, it's broken and . . . and I'm sure there's something wrong with the toaster. If I take it back to the store I can tell them that there was something wrong with the toaster and that they should fix it.

Excuse me. I bought this toaster here four weeks ago . . . Remember when I came into the store?

Person 2: Yeah, . . . that's one of ours.

Person 1: Um, it seems to be broken, and . . . I think there's something wrong with the toaster and I'd like you to . . . it's on warranty . . . I'd like you to take it back and fix it for me.

Person 2: Well, these are good toasters . . . they seldom break down. Um . . . you been using it correctly?

Person 1: Yes, I've been using it correctly. I . . . I'd like you to take it in and check it out and make sure that . . . uh, you know . . . and fix it for me. Or if you have some other way that you can check on it?

Person 2: Well . . . uh . . . we never get complaints about these . . . these toasters. And, uh, I don't know . . . I think that maybe . . . uh . . . you have been plugging it in the right outlet? You don't hold the button down, you just let it down by itself?

Person 1: Yeah, I've been following all the instructions and I know that you usually sell good merchandise. I've been happy with everything I bought here. And . . . uh, I can understand that you would think that maybe I did something wrong, but . . . I do believe that there's something wrong with this toaster because I've been very careful with it and I . . . I . . . I would hope that you could take it and repair it. Or give me another toaster maybe?

Person 2: Well . . . uh . . . let me do this, ma'am. Let me send it off to the shop and have them check it and, uh, see what the problem is. And, uh, we'll send you a card when it comes back.

Person 1: O.K. Thank you.

Skill 13. Expressing Anger

Behavioral Steps

1. Pay attention to those body signals that help you know what you are feeling.

2. Decide which outside events may have caused you to have these feelings.
3. Decide if you are feeling angry about these events.
4. Decide how you can best express these angry feelings.
5. Express your angry feelings in a direct and honest manner.

Modeling Vignette Example

Person 1: Boy, there it is. I've got that throbbing right in my forehead again. Gee, I...I wonder what it is. Boy, that's uncomfortable. It's really upsetting. Wonder...what could be causing that. I don't know...uh, there was a lot of noise this morning, that bothers me, and then in the meeting I wanted to say something and...and...Jane was leading the meeting, and she didn't call on me. I really wanted to say it and she wouldn't call on me. I...that...that must be it. 'Cause I know it bothered me right after that...I've been getting this throbbing ever since then. Boy, that makes me angry, now that I think about it. You know...I...I'm just not going to sit on this anymore. I better tell her about that...tell her that I'm angry about it...and...and that I don't think she was treating me fairly in the meeting. I'll do it when...when we're together and there's time to talk about it...I really have to tell her about it.

Jane, there's something I've got to tell you. I really am angry about the way you ignored me in that meeting. I had something to say, I had my hand up, I...I...wanted to contribute there and...and...you know...you wouldn't even call on me. And I don't think that's fair.

Person 2: Gee, I'm sorry, Bob. I didn't do it intentionally.

Skill 19. Responding to Failure

Behavioral Steps

1. Decide if you have failed.
2. Think about both the personal reasons and the circumstances that have caused you to fail.
3. Decide how you might do things differently if you tried again.
4. Decide if you want to try again.
5. If appropriate, try again, using your revised approach.

Modeling Vignette Example

Person 1: Well I know I'm not going to get that job. I know the interview didn't go well. Boy, I...I...just struck out again. Let's see, I wonder what it was? I know that in some ways I'm not really qualified, and that if I had a little more training, I'd be in a better position and, as he said, the job market's tight, so maybe that's another thing. I don't know ... maybe ... maybe next time I oughta ... at least be better prepared for the interview. I can ... get all the things ready before I go to the interview and tell them exactly what I know how to do and what my skills are and maybe ... maybe try to interview for jobs that are more appropriate. I'm gonna do it again. Um ... it's worth it. I ... I really want a job. In fact, maybe even before I leave here today I'm gonna set up another appointment with the interviewer. That's what I'll do.

Skill 20. Responding to Contradictory Messages

Behavioral Steps

1. Pay attention to those body signals that help you know you are feeling trapped or confused.
2. Observe the other person's words and actions that may have caused you to have these feelings.
3. Decide whether his words and actions are contradictory.
4. Decide whether it would be useful to point out the contradiction.
5. Ask the other person to explain the contradiction.

Modeling Vignette Example

Person 1: Bob, whatta ya want for dinner?

Person 2: Gee, I don't know. Do you have some ... some chops or ... maybe a casserole, or something like that?

Person 1: Mmh ... Are you sure you want chops or a casserole?

Person 2: Yeah ... I love chops. Casserole is good.

Person 1: You always like meat loaf. How about ... how about a meat loaf?

Person 2: There it is again! Boy, I get that tight feeling. I ... I don't understand that. I just don't understand. There's something about ... when she says that ... it just makes me feel uptight and confused. Something's not right there. It ... It ... it doesn't make sense. On the one hand she asks me what I want for dinner and then I tell her what I want for dinner and then she tells me that I can't have that, that she wants to make meat loaf. That ... that ... that just doesn't make sense to me. You know ... I have to ... I've gotta do something about that. I'm gonna have to tell Jane that that's just very confusing to me. And ... that it's gotta stop. This situation just can't go on. It just gets me uptight every time she does this.

Jane, there's something that's been going on and I . . . I've gotta talk to you about it, 'cause I just don't understand it. When I come home at night and you ask me what I want for dinner and I tell you what I want for dinner and then you say "no, you can't have that." Why do you ask me? It doesn't make any sense to me.

Person 1: I guess I'm really doing that, huh?

Person 2: You sure are.

Skill 22. Responding to Anger

Behavioral Steps

1. Listen openly to the other person's angry statement.
2. Show that you understand what the other person is feeling.
3. Ask the other person to explain anything you don't understand about what he has said.
4. Show that you understand why he is feeling angry.
5. If appropriate, express your thoughts and feelings about the situation.

Modeling Vignette Example

Person 1: Laurie, I wish you'd stop bugging me! You're always hanging around here and you know I have a lot to do. I have to be alone some time. You've been here every single day this week.

Person 2: Boy, you're really yelling. I've never seen you so mad. Your face is red. Why don't . . . why don't you sit down. Um, I didn't realize that . . . you know . . . that you had so much to do, and that I'm really bothering you. Um, is it all the time that I bother you, or just . . . just because you're really busy today?

Person 1: Well, it's just that you've been here so much. Uh . . . I . . . like I said—every single day, and I just . . . I don't mind seeing you now and then, but every single day is just too much.

Person 2: Well, no wonder why you're mad. I've been . . . you know . . . I've been kinda lonely lately. That's why I've been doing this but I'll try to stop.

Skill 35. Negotiation

Behavioral Steps

1. State your position.
2. State your understanding of the other person's position.
3. Ask if the other person agrees with your statement of his position.

4. Listen openly to his response.
5. Propose a compromise.

Modeling Vignette Example

Person 1: You know, Sam, there's a very good movie on television tonight that was just at the theater about a year ago ... and ... and I'd ... very much want to see it. Um ... I know that the football game's on tonight and you usually wanna watch football. Is that ... is that what you probably want to do?

Person 2: Yeah, that's right.

Person 1: I wonder ... is there a way that we could work something out so that maybe this week we watch the movie since it's the only time it'll be on, well, football games come on at least three times a week. Could we do something like that?

Person 2: That sounds reasonable.

Aggressive Adolescents

Teenagers consistently displaying overt aggression in regular schools, special schools, residential centers, and correctional institutions have been a major focus of social skill training via Structured Learning.[4] The basic skills we have taught such aggressive youngsters are briefly defined as follows:

Skill 1. *Listening*: Does the adolescent pay attention to someone who is talking and make an effort to understand what is being said?

Skill 2. *Starting a conversation*: Does the adolescent talk to others about light topics and then lead into more serious topics?

Skill 3. *Having a conversation*: Does the adolescent talk to others about things of interest to both of them?

Skill 4. *Asking a question*: Does the adolescent decide what information is needed and ask the right person for that information?

Skill 5. *Saying thank you*: Does the student let others know that he or she is grateful for favors, etc.?

Skill 6. *Introducing yourself*: Does the student become acquainted with new people on his or her own initiative?

Skill 7. *Introducing other people*: Does the student help others become acquainted with one another?

Skill 8. *Giving a compliment*: Does the student tell others that he or she likes something about them or their activities?

Skill 9. *Asking for help*: Does the student request assistance when he or she is having difficulty?

Skill 10. *Joining in*: Does the student decide on the best way to become part of an ongoing activity or group?

Skill 11. *Giving instructions*: Does the student clearly explain to others how they are to do a specific task?

Skill 12. *Following instructions*: Does the student pay attention to instructions, give his or her reactions, and carry the instructions out adequately?

Skill 13. *Apologizing*: Does the student tell others that he or she is sorry after doing something wrong?

Skill 14. *Convincing others*: Does the student attempt to persuade others that his or her ideas are better and will be more useful than those of the other person?

Skill 15. *Knowing your feelings*: Does the student try to recognize which emotions he or she is feeling?

Skill 16. *Expressing your feelings*: Does the student let others know which emotions he or she is feeling?

Skill 17. *Understanding the feelings of others*: Does the student try to figure out what other people are feeling?

Skill 18. *Dealing with someone else's anger*: Does the student try to understand other people's angry feelings?

Skill 19. *Expressing affection*: Does the student let others know that he or she cares about them?

Skill 20. *Dealing with fear*: Does the student figure out why he or she is afraid and do something to reduce the fear?

Skill 21. *Rewarding yourself*: Does the student say and do nice things for him or herself when the reward is deserved?

Skill 22. *Asking permission*: Does the student figure out when permission is needed to do something, and then ask the right person for permission?

Skill 23. *Sharing something*: Does the student offer to share what he or she has with others who might appreciate it?

Skill 24. *Helping others*: Does the student give assistance to others who might need or want help?

Skill 25. *Negotiating*: Does the student arrive at a plan that satisfies both him or herself and others who have taken different positions?

Skill 26. *Using self-control*: Does the student control his or her temper so that things do not get out of hand?

Skill 27. *Standing Up for your rights*: Does the student assert his or her rights by letting people know where he or she stands on an issue?

Skill 28. *Responding to teasing*: Does the student deal with being teased by others in ways that allow the student to remain in control of him or herself?

Skill 29. *Avoiding trouble when with others*: Does the student stay out of situations that might get him or her into trouble?

Skill 30. *Keeping out of fights*: Does the student figure out ways other than fighting to handle difficult situations?

Skill 31. *Making a complaint*: Does the student tell others when they are responsible for creating a particular problem for the student, and then attempt to find a solution for the problem?

Skill 32. *Answering a complaint*: Does the student try to arrive at a fair solution to someone's justified complaint?

Skill 33. *Sportsmanship after a game*: Does the student express an honest compliment to others about how they played a game?

Skill 34. *Dealing with embarrassment*: Does the student do things which help him or her to feel less embarrassed or self-conscious?

Skill 35. *Dealing with being left out*: Does the student decide whether he or she has been left out of some activity, and then do things to feel better about the situation?

Skill 36. *Standing up for a friend*: Does the student let other people know when a friend has not been treated fairly?

Skill 37. *Responding to persuasion*: Does the student carefully consider the position of another person, comparing it to his or her own, before deciding what to do?

Skill 38. *Responding to failure*: Does the student figure out the reason for failing in a particular situation, and what he or she can do about it, in order to be more successful in the future?

Skill 39. *Dealing with confusing messages*: Does the student recognize and deal with the confusion that results when others tell him or her one thing, but say or do things that indicate that they mean something else?

Skill 40. *Dealing with an accusation*: Does the student figure out what he or she has been accused of and why, and then decide on the best way to deal with the person who made the accusation?

Skill 41. *Getting ready for a difficult conversation*: Does the student plan on the best way to present his or her point of view prior to a stressful conversation?

Skill 42. *Dealing with group pressure*: Does the student decide what he or she wants to do when others want him or her to do something else?

Skill 43. *Deciding on something to do*: Does the student deal with feeling bored by starting an interesting activity?

Skill 44. *Deciding what caused a problem*: Does the student find out whether an event was caused by something that was within his or her control?

Skill 45. *Setting a goal*: Does the student realistically decide on what he or she can accomplish prior to starting on a task?

Skill 46. *Deciding on your abilities*: Does the student realistically figure out how well he or she might do at a particular task?

Skill 47. *Gathering information*: Does the student decide what he or she needs to know and how to get that information?

Skill 48. *Arranging problems by importance*: Does the student decide realistically which of a number of problems is most important and should be dealt with first?

Skill 49. *Making a decision*: Does the student consider possibilities and make choices which he or she feels will be best?

Skill 50. *Concentrating on a task*: Does the student make those preparations that will help him or her get a job done?

Child-Abusing Parents

Structured Learning work with physically abusing, sexually abusing, and neglecting parents is not yet as far advanced as that oriented toward either adult mental hospital patients or aggressive adolescents. It is clear from the work already done, however, that the typical range of skill deficiencies in such individuals is considerable indeed. Not only are they particularly lacking in parenting skills per se, but they also very often demonstrate a general imcompetence and impoverishment in all spheres of social and intrapersonal functioning. It is for this reason that, as the following lists indicate, the modeling displays we are currently developing for use with this trainee group include—in addition to parenting skills—self-control skills, marital skills, and peer-oriented social skills.

I. Self-Control Skills

Skill 1. Knowing your feelings
Skill 2. Relaxation
Skill 3. Expressing a complaint
Skill 4. Responding to failure
Skill 5. Assertiveness
Skill 6. Instructing yourself
Skill 7. Rewarding yourself
Skill 8. Seeking alternatives
Skill 9. Problem solving

II. Parenting Skills

Skill 10. Listening
Skill 11. Structuring
Skill 12. Empathy
Skill 13. Offering encouragement

Skill 14. Providing reward
Skill 15. Setting limits
Skill 16. Disciplining
Skill 17. Giving instructions
Skill 18. Expressing criticism
Skill 19. Expressing praise
Skill 20. Expressing affection
Skill 21. Dealing with hostility
Skill 22. Dealing with dependency

III. Marital Skills

Skill 23. Negotiation
Skill 24. Responding to persuasion
Skill 25. Preparing for a stressful conversation
Skill 26. Responding to false accusations
Skill 27. Dealing with anger from others
Skill 28. Expressing affection
Skill 29. Disagreeing
Skill 30. Decision making
Skill 31. Setting goals

IV. Peer-Oriented Skills

Skill 32. Dealing with boredom
Skill 33. Initiating interaction
Skill 34. Maintaining a conversation
Skill 35. Helping others
Skill 36. Asking for help
Skill 37. Expressing disagreement
Skill 38. Expressing praise
Skill 39. Expressing a preference

Police

Family disputes and similar disturbances are dangerous police calls. In fact and perhaps surprisingly, because of the high levels of emotional arousal present and the unpredictability of the aggressive behavior involved, such calls have consistently been the *most* dangerous demand made of police. A number of Structured Learning training programs have been conducted to train police and other law enforcement personnel in a series of skills demonstrated to constitute effective handling of such family disputes and other crisis calls involving high levels of emotional arousal and unpredictable aggressive behavior (mental disturbance, drug and alcohol intoxication, rape) (Goldstein, Monti, Sardino, & Green, 1977). These skills for police crisis intervention and their behavioral steps are listed below:

I. Observing and Protecting against Threats to Your Safety

1. Consider your prior experience on similar calls.
2. Anticipate that the unexpected may actually happen.
3. Form a tentative plan of action.

II. Calming the Situation

1. Observe and neutralize threats to your safety.
2. Create a first impression of nonhostile authority.
3. Calm the emotional citizen.

III. Gathering Relevant Information

1. Explain to the citizen what you want him or her to discuss with you and why.
2. Interview the citizen so as to gain details of the crisis as clearly as possible.
3. Show that you understand the citizen's statements and give accurate answers to his or her questions.
4. Revise your plan of action if appropriate.

IV. Taking Appropriate Action

1. Carefully explain your plan of action to the citizen.
2. Check that the citizen understands and agrees with your plan of action.
3. Carry out your plan of action.

A Structured Learning skill program has also been developed for use in training police and other law enforcement personnel in effective negotiation for the release of hostages (Miron & Goldstein, 1978). These hostage negotiation skills are presented below.

I. Safety

1. Make certain sufficient personnel are both trained in hostage management strategy and tactics and available in adequate numbers for a hostage situation.

2. The hostage management area, inner and outer perimeter personnel, fire power, communications, and related resources must be controlled and coordinated by a single source.
3. Influence media, if possible, so that no mention is made of tactical plans and resources.
4. Maintain communication among responding personnel.
5. All inner perimeter personnel must be readily identifiable.
6. Negotiator should be physically near the perpetrator, but secure enough that he won't become a hostage himself.
7. Make sure there IS a hostage.
8. Do not fulfill perpetrator requests to bring relatives or friends to the scene.
9. Avoid a show of force, especially when a single perpetrator is involved.
10. Do not negotiate for new weapons, alcohol, narcotics, or other items likely to increase the threat to hostage or negotiator safety.
11. If at all possible, avoid movement of the perpetrator and hostages to another location.
12. If it is possible to communicate by any direct means with the hostages, provide them with suggestions designed to increase their safety.

II. Information to Be Obtained

1. Relevant information about the perpetrator should be gathered as completely and rapidly as possible.
2. Relevant information about the hostages should be gathered as completely and rapidly as possible.
3. Relevant information about the hostage site should be gathered as completely and rapidly as possible.

III. Negotiating Strategies

1. At the outset, *contain* and *stabilize* are your two goals. Avoid all precipitous acts.
2. Establish a problem-solving negotiating climate.
3. Establish a compromising climate.
4. Avoid use of a forcing negotiating strategy.
5. Avoid use of a soft-bargainer negotiating strategy.
6. Use the negotiating strategy that your prenegotiation investigation reveals best fits the nature of the perpetrator involved.
7. Use of force should be planned for, but implemented only as a last resort.

IV. Calming the Perpetrator

1. Attempt to calm the agitated perpetrator by showing understanding of his feelings.
2. Attempt to calm the agitated perpetrator by displaying your own calmness to him.
3. Attempt to calm the agitated perpetrator by reassuring him.
4. Attempt to calm the agitated perpetrator by encouraging him to talk.
5. Attempt to calm the agitated perpetrator by distracting him from the source of his concern.
6. Try to anticipate perpetrator violence by being sensitive to nonverbal cues of aggression.
7. Avoid any aggressive, offensive, or humiliating comments to the perpetrator; do not argue with him; avoid outright rejection of all his demands; avoid sudden surprises.

V. Building Rapport

1. Stall for time.
2. Disclose information about yourself to the perpetrator, as it may help build rapport.
3. Show high levels of empathy in your response to what the perpetrator says and does.
4. Show high levels of warmth in your response to what the perpetrator says and does.
5. Help the perpetrator save face.
6. Avoid "talking down" to the perpetrator.
7. Do not criticize, threaten, or act impatiently toward the perpetrator.

VI. Gathering Information

1. Attempt to gather information about the perpetrator by use of open-ended questions.
2. Attempt to gather information from the perpetrator by use of closed-ended questions.
3. Attempt to gather information from the perpetrator by use of good listening skills.
4. Attempt to gather information from the perpetrator by use of restatement of content.
5. Attempt to gather information from the perpetrator by use of reflection of feeling.
6. Attempt to clarify information you receive from the perpetrator by pointing out discrepancies in what he has said.

7. Expect the perpetrator's demands to be presented to you with a threat of specific consequences if all demands are not met, in full, within a specific time period.

VII. Persuading the Perpetrator

1. Start your persuasion attempts by agreeing with part of the perpetrator's views.
2. Try to build a climate of successful negotiation by dealing with smaller, easier to settle items first.
3. Don't just give the perpetrator the facts with the hope that he'll change his mind in your direction; draw conclusions from these facts for him.
4. Encourage the perpetrator actively to imagine or "try on" the position you are trying to convince him of.
5. Present both sides of the argument (yours and his).
6. Consider the perpetrator's motivations.
7. Argue against one or more unimportant aspects of your own position.
8. Point out to the perpetrator any perpetrator-negotiator similarities.
9. Request delayed compliance.
10. Minimize counterarguments.
11. Seek to change the perpetrator's thinking and behavior a small step at a time.
12. Introduce issues into the negotiations yourself so that you can give in to them later as a way of encouraging concessions from the perpetrator.
13. Reward the perpetrator for any statements or steps he makes toward successful resolution of the hostage situation.
14. Use clear, unambiguous, factual evidence to support your position.
15. Avoid negotiating in front of others to the extent such "privacy" is possible.
16. Do not challenge or dare a perpetrator to act.
17. Try to decrease the level of perpetrator irrationality.
18. Agree with clear reluctance to any demands that in reality benefit the police position.
19. Whenever possible, stall on demands that benefit the perpetrator.
20. Offer only those suggestions you feel are clearly necessary, as any suggestions may speed up the time factor in ways not to your advantage.
21. Keep alive the perpetrator's hope of escape.
22. Be open to the possibility that you may have to let the perpetrator escape in trade for the hostages.

Self-Help Trainees

We have developed a self-administered version of Structured Learning, one for which no group of trainees, trainers, or similar others are necessary. The trainee is able to learn about and apply Structured Learning procedures and skill content by use of an instructional self-help text designed for this purpose (Goldstein, Sprafkin, & Gershaw, 1979). Because learning is *self*-administered, a number of procedures, in addition to modeling, role playing, performance feedback, and transfer training, are incorporated into this version of Structured Learning. In particular, the individual engages in self-diagnosis of skill deficiencies, base-rate record keeping, seeking environmental support for skill usage, contracting, graduated skill use, and self-reward.

CRITIQUE AND RECOMMENDATIONS

As we indicated at the outset of this chapter, social skills training as an everyday event is probably as old as man himself. As earlier sections of this chapter have made clear, however, as a systematized, research-based, scientific movement, social skills training is still in its infancy. Many relevant theoretical and applied issues remain unresolved, a number of training methods and curricular concerns remain to be dealt with and, in general, a great deal of necessary research is yet to be conducted. It is to a number of these matters that we now turn.

Assessment

Though its history as a formal, systematic, psychoeducational intervention is quite brief, a wide variety of means have already been utilized to determine the nature and level of a given individual's social skills deficiency. These include projective testing, use of case files or other biographical data, interviews of varying structuredness, skill inventories or questionnaires completed by either the potential trainee or someone familiar with his daily behavior (nurse, teacher, parent), and direct observation of trainee overt behavior in either natural or contrived situations. In all instances, the goal of such assessment has been to estimate the individual's proficiency and deficiency levels reliably across a variety of skills. In our view, most of these procedures—save direct behavioral observation—have largely failed in this effort.

Some have been too inferential, requiring too great a leap from assessment data to the skill behaviors one is seeking to predict. This is especially true of assessment via projective testing and global or comprehensive (nontargeted) interviews and, often, of case files or school records. Skill inventories or questionnaires often do not suffer from this fault, but are typically weak in another regard shared by all but behavior observational assessment. Reliable estimation of skill levels has been thwarted by the failure in the assessment process to reflect sufficiently the fact that skill proficiency-deficiency is not only a characteristic of the person, but also of the situation or context, where and when the use of the skill is appropriate. A youngster may respond with skilled self-control when admonished by a police officer, but with overt aggression to the same admonishment if offered by a teacher. Clearly, an appraisal of his self-control skill level must reflect, at absolute minimum, *both* interpersonal contexts. Such situational assessment may be approximated in inventory or questionnaire assessment, as we have done in an assessment device we designed for one of our trainee populations. For example, our Skill Inventory items included:

10. *Expressing anger*: Communicating your angry feelings to someone in a direct and honest manner.
    a. I express my angry feelings to my spouse for accepting a party invitation when he or she knew I wanted to stay home.
    b. I express my angry feelings to my friend for not telling me about his or her change in plans.
    c. I express my angry feelings to my coworker for leaving the hardest part of the job for me.

17. *Responding to a complaint*: Trying to arrive at a fair solution to someone's justified complaint.
    a. I listen openly and respond to my spouse's complaint about my buying something that he or she thought was unnecessary.
    b. When my boss becomes angry about a detail I have overlooked, I respond calmly and rationally, without becoming sullen.
    c. When my neighbor nastily complains about a problem I am causing, I listen and take appropriate action about the problem.

22. *Self-control*: Controlling your temper so that things do not get out of hand.
    a. I control my temper when my children disobey my requests.
    b. I control my temper when my spouse does something that I find annoying.
    c. I control my temper when a salesperson treats me rudely in a store.

23. *Negotiation*: Arriving at a plan which satisfies both yourself and another person who has taken a different position.
    a. I negotiate with repairmen on a fair price for a job.
    b. When my spouse and I encounter family problems, we compromise on a mutually agreeable solution.
    c. I negotiate with my friend when each of us wants to do something different.

We are, however, considerably more supportive of a behavior observational assessment approach. In our view, such assessment is ideally

conducted to be cross-situational, cross-temporal, and cross-observer—
that is, the potential trainee should be observed in an array of natural
and/or contrived situations in which competent skill use is judged to be
appropriate. This array of assessment situations should reflect diverse
samples of times, places, and stimulus persons. Potential trainee
behavior in given contexts is ideally observed on multiple occasions by
two or more independent observers. When the exigencies of the real-life
school, work, home, or other observational context preclude implementation of such ideally structured behavioral observation, ap-
proximations thereto are still to be preferred over the more inferential
and less situational alternatives noted earlier.

Social Skills Trainers

We have had little to say in this chapter thus far about optimal credentials and characteristics of those persons who serve as trainers in social
skills training groups. We wish to do so now, using our own trainer-
training experience in this domain, as well as conclusions drawn from
relevant research literature as the basis for our trainer recommendations. The role-playing and feedback activities that constitute
most of each Structured Learning session are a series of "action-
reaction" sequences in which effective skill behaviors are first rehearsed
(role playing) and then critiqued (feedback). As such, the trainer must
both lead and observe. We have found that one trainer is very hard
pressed to do both these tasks well at the same time, and thus, we
strongly recommend that each session be led by a team of two trainers.
Their professional credentials are largely irrelevant; on the other hand,
their group leadership skills, interpersonal sensitivity, enthusiasm, and
the favorableness of the relationship between them are the qualities that
appear crucial to the success of training. Furthermore, proficiency in
two types of skills are required of Structured Learning trainers.

The first might best be described as General Trainer Skills—that is,
those skills requisite for success in almost any training effort. These
include:

1. Oral communication skills.
2. Flexibility, resourcefulness.
3. Enthusiasm and adequate energy level.
4. Ability to work well under pressure.
5. Broad knowledge of human behavior and its determinants.
6. Group management skills (e.g., handling resistance).
7. Nurturance.

Specific Trainer Skills, the second category, are those germane to Structured Learning in particular (A parallel set of requisite Specific Trainer Skills can be constructed for other social skills training programs.) They include:

1. In-depth knowledge of Structured Learning, its rationale, background, procedures, and goals.
2. Ability to orient both patients and real-life reward dispensers to Structured Learning procedures, contents, and goals.
3. Ability to communicate material in a concrete, behavioral, and directive form.
4. Ability to initiate and sustain role playing.
5. Ability to reduce trainee resistance.
6. Sensitivity in providing corrective feedback.
7. Imagination in conducting training so that it has real-life-like qualities.

There exists a substantial, if largely speculative, literature pointing to yet other qualities of trainers, therapists, and teachers that are likely to prove success enhancing. Considerable research sorting through these speculations, verifying or rejecting their impact on trainee learning, is an endeavor to be strongly recommended. In doing such research, we would urge the investigators to look for leads not only in the training, psychotherapy, and educational literature. There exist thousands of very competent social skills trainers, persons who—often without premeditation—are regularly able to increase the prosocial skill level of diverse individuals—many of whom characteristically had consistently behaved in antisocial ways. Just as in formal social skill training, the title, position, or credentials of such "natural trainers" seem largely irrelevant. They may be parents, high school athletic coaches, teacher aides, drug store owners, prison guards, clergymen, friends. What we are arguing here is that those interested in maximizing social skills trainer potency, seek out and observe potential "natural trainers," and try to identify the means by which they successfully "train," so that we might seek to incorporate such wisdom formally into planned skill training programs.

For both trainer selection and development purposes, we have found it most desirable to have potential trainers participate, as if they were actual trainees, in a series of Structured Learning sessions. After this experience, we have had them co-lead a series of sessions with an experienced trainer. In doing so, we have shown them how to conduct such sessions, given them several opportunities to practice what they have seen, and provided them with feedback regarding their performance. In effect, we have used Structured Learning to teach Structured Learning. To aid others in this method, we have developed and employed a series of Trainer Preparation tapes portraying Initial, Advanced, and Resistive Structured Learning sessions.

Transfer of Training

Prosocial skill acquisition, which is essentially limited to the training setting, which fails to find consistent expression in the variety of real-life settings that constitute the trainee's world, is in our view a largely worthless accomplishment. We have reviewed evidence elsewhere indicating that a substantial majority of training room, therapy room, and classroom gains do *not* currently maintain in or transfer to real-life settings (Goldstein & Stein, 1976; Goldstein, Lopez, & Greenleaf, 1979). It is a dismal but accurate conclusion, testifying to the largely functionally autonomous manner in which so much training, therapy, and education exists. In our earlier presentation of the procedures that constitute Structured Learning, we began to sound a more hopeful note, and presented five experimentally substantiated procedures which, at least in that social skills training context, have begun to show they can reliably improve the rate of positive transfer.

But this very important research domain, this quest for procedures that can be used as reliable transfer enhancers, is still in its early infancy, at least as far as transfer enhancement in the social skills arena is concerned. Many *potential* transfer enhancers exist. As described earlier, the trainer may provide general skill selection and implementation principles, conduct social skills training *in vivo*, or otherwise reflect in the training transfer enhancement via "identical elements," provide a sufficient number of successful skill-use trials to maximize "overlearning;" see to it—following the transfer principle of "stimulus variability"—that these successful skill practices are done in conjunction with several *different* types of co-role players, maximize, by the numerous means described earlier, the likelihood that the trainee will be rewarded by others and/or himself when he seeks to use his newly learned skills outside the training context. There exist additional potential means for enhancing transfer, means that draw upon research on social support systems, social climates, biofeedback, drug treatment, and other diverse and often novel bodies of experimentation (Goldstein & Kanfer, 1979; Kazdin, 1975; Wildman & Wildman, 1975). Building upon the offerings of these researchers is a most crucial need in the social skills training domain.

Ethical Considerations

In social skills training, as is the case for all psychotherapeutic, educational, or other endeavors that seek to alter human behavior, serious consideration of relevant ethical matters must be an integral part of intervention planning. Ethical issues may be even more of a concern when target trainees are persons who frequently engage in aggressive or other antisocial behaviors, and whose very participation in the skills training program may be less than voluntary. The relevant ethical questions are many, and easy to find. Their answers are often harder to come by. Whose values will the training program try to reflect, especially when behaviors that "society" defines as antisocial are defined as prosocial by the person's smaller reference group? Shall we respond to the trainer's values here? The trainee's? The administrative agency involved (school, hospital, prison)? Who will select the skills to be taught? To be omitted? Will participation be voluntary, and based upon informed consent? What risks—obvious or subtle, immediate or long term—may be associated with program participation? We do not offer our own answers to these ethical questions as necessarily optimal nor, certainly, final. They are, however, our best current attempt.

Skill Selection. Selection of concrete training goals, that is, the decisions about which skills should be taught to a particular trainee and which omitted must, in our view, be a collaborative decision reached via mutual consultation between trainer and trainee. When such decisions are made by the trainer alone they run a serious risk of imposing trainer biases regarding what constitutes "good" or "proper" or "competent" skill functioning on the trainee. Since trainer and trainee often differ in social class, educational background, life style, and aspiration level, the likelihood that serious skill selection biases might actually (if subtly) operate is not negligible. Skill selection made solely by the trainee is, we feel, an equally serious threat to an heuristic set of training goals. By definition, the trainee is deficient in and inexperienced with an array of skills. To place such skills before him, cafeteria-style, and propose that he choose those he wishes as the sole means of skill selection, is to risk serious miscalculation of appropriate and reachable training goals.

With the procedures that constitute academic counseling as our model, we have opted for a "negotiated curriculum" solution to this ethical dilemma. A student seeking to register for an academic program will typically seek an academic counselor or advisor. After a suitable exchange of background and aspirational information, the student will often indicate a desire to enroll in courses *A*, *B*, and *C*. The counselor, responding from his own perspective, may propose that courses *D*, *E*, and *F* are more suitable, or would be more useful for the student. The two negotiate, exchange reasons, consider alternatives, and ideally reach a negotiated curriculum superior in quality for that student than either of the one-person-determined curricula that they brought to their meeting.

Analagously, in our skill selection in Structured Learning, both trainer and trainee complete parallel versions of the Structured Learning Skill Inventory. These Inventories are constructed to reflect a broad array of skills and situational contexts and, at least for the trainer version, can be derived from behavioral observation. After trainer and trainee independently complete their Inventories, they come together and engage in precisely the type of curricular negotiation described above as part of the academic counseling process. In a large majority of instances, we feel, a superior curricular outcome results.

Volition and Informed Consent. The trainee's decision to participate in social skills training must be made on as fully voluntary a basis as his pretraining competencies and capacities permit. We believe that this view is appropriate whether the trainee is a juvenile delinquent on probation, an adult incarcerated in a prison, a mental hospital patient, a moderately retarded individual, or an elementary school pupil. We can identify no compelling examples of appropriate exceptions to this recommendation.

The potential trainee's right to free choice requires that the decision to participate or not be made in response to accurate and adequate information. Thus, potential participants in social skills training should be provided with clear and comprehensive information about the planned training experience and any evaluation associated with it. If it is consistent with the potential trainee's reading ability, this information should be written, worded nontechnically, and should fully explain the content, procedures, and goals of the training program. Particular emphasis should be placed on the voluntary nature of participation and, consistent with such an intent, one should actively seek to avoid the use of subtle pressure by trainers or others vis-à-vis persons leaning toward or electing not to participate. When possible, invitees should be asked to respond to the invitation to participate in writing.

Risks. Risks associated with social skills training do not seem appreciable to us. Those relevant threats to the trainee essentially parallel those that are characteristic of any educational endeavor. Some trainees will learn a given skill more slowly than others in their groups, a discrepancy with some potential for feelings of embarrassment and discomfort. Those trainees who prove to be particularly slow may develop feelings of failure and lowered self-esteem. Good pedagogic practices—homogeneous grouping based upon shared skill deficiencies, appropriate pacing, ample use of reinforcement (even for "just trying")—can effectively minimize such outcomes.

Perhaps a more serious risk ensues from the possibility that an apparently well-learned skill may fail to "work" in the real world and bring the trainee not reward, but either indifference or, worse, some form of punishment. To minimize the likelihood of such outcomes we would recommend:

1. Teach trainees "back-up" skills, e.g., Responding to Failure, Responding to Contradictory Messages, etc., early in their skill training participation.
2. Teach trainees self-reward skills, to compensate at least partially for failures to receive reward from others.
3. Be certain that real-life, skill-use homework assignments are (1) made only when the trainee demonstrates high levels of proficiency in the skill in the training setting, and (2) graduated so that real-life implementation attempts, while always somewhat challenging, start with relatively easy target persons and situations and move *slowly* toward more difficult ones.

SUMMARY

Social skills training is an energetic and growing movement in the United States today. We have examined its remote and contemporary antecedants, its current programmatic representations, its problems and its promise. Aggression control and the development of prosocial alternatives to aggression are complex, multifaceted challenges. Such complex challenges require complex solutions, consisting of a variety of interventions. Social skills training, while no panacea, is in our view one important such intervention. Its potential is considerable when implemented in a preplanned, systematic, and broad manner. It is our hope that the present chapter may serve as both stimulus and guideline for such implementation.

NOTES

1. As we noted in conjunction with Table 4.1, these very same teaching methods are also frequently the core teaching methods of many other social skills training programs. It is of interest that most of these programs appear to have arrived initially at the same selection of methods as we have, but from a rather different route, i.e., clinical practice and experimental research in behavior modification and applied social learning theory.

2. Though we do not feel that the prescriptive utility of Structured Learning is limited to low-income, lower-class and working-class populations—since we and others have also conducted successful skill training of diverse middle-class groups with these methods—most of these aggressive and aggression-relevant trainees are lower- and working-class persons. Thus, we feel what we have said above about the prescriptive relevance of certain learning accessibility channels in adult mental patients is also directly relevant here.

3. In our earlier discussion of the reproduction phase of modeling, we mentioned briefly the difference between learning and performance. Learning refers to acquiring knowledge, to coming to know how to do something, to the perception and storage of stimulus-response relationships. Learning defined this way is an internal process and as such cannot be directly observed. Performance refers to action, to doing what was learned. Many researchers are taking the position that the main effects of reinforcement are on performance—that is, on the occurrence and nature of how and when what is learned is actually enacted.

4. In much of our training and research oriented toward skill-deficient adolescents, we have worked not only with aggressive youngsters, but also with those whose skill incompetencies take form in withdrawal, passivity, immaturity, or other ineffective behavioral patterns (Goldstein, Sherman, Gershaw, Sprafkin, & Glick, 1978).

REFERENCES

Adkins, W. R. Life skills: Structured counseling for the disadvantaged. *Personnel and Guidance Journal*, 1970, **49**, 108–116.

Adkins, W. R. Life coping skills: A fifth curriculum. *Teachers College Record*, 1974, **75**, 507–526.

Arkowitz, H. Measurement and modification of minimal dating behavior. In M. Hersen, R. M. Eisler & P. M. Miller (Eds.), *Progress in behavior modification*. Vol. 5. New York: Academic Press, 1977.

Argyle, M., Trower, P., & Bryant, B. Explorations in the treatment of personality disorders and neuroses by social skills training. *British Journal of Medical Psychology*, 1974, **47**, 63–72.

Authier, J., Gustafson, K., Guerney, B. G. Jr., & Kasdorf, J. A. The psychological practitioner as teacher. *The Counseling Psychologist*, 1975, **5**, 1–21.

Bandura, A. *Principles of behavior modification*. New York: Holt, Rinehart & Winston, 1969.

Bandura, A. Blanchard, E. B., & Ritter, B. The relative efficacy of desensitization and modeling approaches for inducing behavioral, affective and attitudinal changes. *Journal of Personality and Social Psychology*, 1969, **13**, 173–199.

Bandura, A., Grusec, J. E., & Manlove, F. L. Vicarious extinction of avoidance behavior. *Journal of Personality and Social Psychology*, 1967, **5**, 16–23.

Bradford, L. P., Gibb, J. R., & Benne, K. R. *T-group theory and laboratory method*. New York: Wiley, 1964.

Brehm, J. W., & Cohen, A. R. *Explorations in cognitive dissonance*. New York: Wiley, 1962.

Brock, T. C., & Blackwood, J. E. Dissonance reduction, social comparison, and modification of other's opinion. *Journal of Abnormal and Social Psychology*, 1962, **65**, 319–324.

Bryan, J. H., & Test, M. A. Models and helping: Naturalistic studies in aiding behavior. *Journal of Personality and Social Psychology*, 1967, **6**, 400–407.

Burka, J., Hubbell, R., Preble, M., Spinelli, R., & Winter, N. *Communication skills workshop manual.* Fort Collins, Colo.: University of Colorado Counseling Center, 1972.

Burrs, V., & Kapache, R. Modeling of social behavior in chronic hospital patients. Unpublished manuscript, California State College at Long Beach, 1969.

Callantine, M. F. & Warren, L. M. Learning sets in human concept formation. *Psychological Reports,* 1955, **1**, 363–367.

Carkhuff, R. R. *Cry twice.* Amherst, Mass.: Human Resources Development Press, 1974.

Carkhuff, R. R., & Berenson, B. G. *Beyond counseling and psychotherapy.* New York: Holt, Rinehart & Winston, 1967.

Carlsmith, J. M., Collins, B. E., & Helmreich, R. K. Studies in forced compliance: I. The effect of pressure for compliance on attitude change produced by face-to-face role playing and anonymous essay writing. *Journal of Personality and Social Psychology,* 1966, **4**, 1–13.

Cartledge, G., & Milburn, J. F. The case for teaching social skills in the classroom: A review. *Review of Educational Research,* 1978, **1**, 133–156.

Castillo, G. *Left-handed teaching.* New York: Praeger, 1974.

Chesler, M. & Fox, R. *Role playing methods in the classroom.* Chicago: Science Research Associates, 1966.

Chittenden, G. E. An experimental study in measuring and modifying assertive behavior in young children. *Monographs of the Society for Research in Child Development,* 1942, **7**, No. 31.

Cohen, A. R., & Latane, B. An experiment on choice in commitment to counter-attitudinal behavior. In J. W. Brehm & A. R. Cohen (Eds.), *Explorations in cognitive dissonance.* New York: Wiley, 1962.

Combs, M. L., & Slaby, D. A. Social skills training with children. In B. B. Lahey & A. E. Kazdin (Eds.) *Advances in clinical child psychology.* Vol. 1. New York: Academic Press, 1977.

Curran, J. P. Skills training as an approach to the treatment of heterosexual-social anxiety: A review. *Psychological Bulletin,* 1977, **84**, 140–157.

Davis, K., & Jones, E. E. Changes in interpersonal perception as a means of reducing cognitive dissonance. *Journal of Abnormal and Social Psychology,* 1960, **61**, 402–410.

Drum, D. J., & Knott, J. E. *Structured groups for facilitating development.* New York: Human Sciences Press, 1977.

Duncan, C. P. Transfer after training with single versus multiple tasks. *Journal of Experimental Psychology,* 1958, **55**, 63–73.

Egan, G. *Interpersonal living: A skills/contract approach to human relations training in groups.* Belmont, Calif.: Brooks Cole, 1976.

Elardo, P., & Cooper, M. *AWARE: Activities for social development.* Reading, Mass.: Addison-Wesley, 1977.

Emshoff, J. G., Redd, W. H., & Davidson, W. S., Generalization training and the transfer of treatment effects with delinquent adolescents. *Journal of Experimental Psychiatry and Behavior Therapy,* 1976, **7**, 144–148.

Evers, W. L., & Schwarz, J. C. Modifying social withdrawal in preschoolers: The effects of filmed modeling and teacher praise. *Journal of Abnormal Child Psychology,* 1973 **1**, 248–256.

Feshback, S. The function of aggression and the regulation of aggressive drive. *Psychological Review,* 1964, **71**, 247–272.

Friedenberg, W. P. Verbal and non-verbal attraction modeling in an initial therapy interview analogue. Unpublished masters thesis, Syracuse University, 1971.

Galassi, M. D., & Galassi, J. P. *Assert yourself!* New York: Human Sciences Press, 1977.

Gambrill, E. D. *Behavior modification: Handbook of assessment, intervention and evaluation.* San Francisco: Jossey-Bass, 1977.

Goldsmith, J. B., & McFall, R. M. Development and evaluation of an interpersonal skill-training program for psychiatric inpatients. *Journal of Abnormal Psychology*, 1975, **84**, 51–58.

Goldstein, A. P. *Psychotherapeutic attraction.* New York: Pergamon Press, 1971.

Goldstein, A. P. *Structured learning therapy.* New York: Academic Press, 1973.

Goldstein, A. P., Cohen, R., Blake, G., & Walsh, W. The effects of modeling and social class structuring in paraprofessional psychotherapist training. *Journal of Nervous and Mental Disease*, 1971, **153**, 47–56.

Goldstein, A. P., & Kanfer, F. H. *Maximizing treatment gains.* New York: Academic Press, 1979.

Goldstein, A. P., Lopez, M., & Greenleaf, D. O. Introduction. In A. P. Goldstein & F. Kanfer (Eds.) *Maximizing treatment gains.* New York: Academic Press, 1979. Pp. 1–24.

Goldstein, A. P., Martens, J., Hubben, J., VonBelle, H. A., Schaaf, W., Weirsema, H., & Goodhart, A. The use of modeling to increase independent behavior. *Behavior Research and Therapy*, 1973, **11**, 31–42.

Goldstein, A. P., Monti, P. J., Sardino, T. J., and Green, D. J. *Police crisis intervention.* New York: Pergamon Press, 1977.

Goldstein, A. P. & Stein, on *Prescriptive psychotherapies.* New York: Pergamon Press, 1976.

Goldstein, A. P., Sherman, M., Gershaw, N. J., Sprafkin, R. P., & Glick, B. Training aggressive adolescents in prosocial behavior. *Journal of Youth and Adolescence*, 1978, **7**, 73–92.

Goldstein, A. P., Sprafkin, R. P., & Gershaw, N. J. *Skill training for community living.* New York: Pergamon Press, 1976.

Goldstein, A. P., Sprafkin, R. P., & Gershaw, N. J. *I know what's wrong but don't know what to do about it.* Englewood Cliffs, N.J.: Prentice-Hall, 1979.

Gottman, J., Motarius, C., Gonso, J., & Markham, H. *A couple's guide to communication.* Champaign, Ill.: Research Press, 1977.

Guerney, B. G. Jr. *Relationship enhancement.* San Francisco: Jossey-Bass, 1977.

Hanson, R. W. Assertion training program. Unpublished manuscrpit, Palo Alto, Calif.: Veterans Administration Hospital, 1971.

Hanson, R. W. Training program in basic communication skills. Unpublished manuscript, Palo Alto, Calif.: Veterans Administration Hospital, 1972.

Hare, M. A. Teaching conflict resolution simulations. Presented at Eastern Community Assoc., Philadelphia, March, 1976.

Hawley, R. C., & Hawley, I. L. *Developing human potential: A handbook of activities for personal and social growth.* Amherst, Mass.: Education Research Assoc., 1975.

Heiman, H. Teaching interpersonal communications. *N. Dakota Speech and Theatre Assoc. Bulletin*, 1973, **2**, 7–29.

Hersen, M. & Eisler, R. M. Social skills training. In W. E. Craighead, A. E. Kazdin, & M. J. Mahoney (Eds.), *Behavior modification: Principles, issues and applications.* Boston: Houghton Mifflin, 1976.

Hoehn-Saric, R., Frank, J. D., Imber, S. D., Nash, E. H., Stone, A. R., & Battle, C. C. Systematic preparation of patients for psychotherapy. I. Effects on therapy behavior and outcome. *Journal of Psychiatric Research*, 1964, **2**, 267–281.

Hollander, T. G. The effects of role playing on attraction, disclosure and attitude change in a psychotherapy analogue. Unpublished doctoral dissertation, Syracuse University, 1970.

Hubbell, A. Two person role playing for guidance in social readjustment. *Group Psychotherapy*, 1954, **7**, 249–254.

Johnson, D. W. *Human relations and your career: A guide to interpersonal skills.* Englewood Cliffs, N.J.: Prentice-Hall, 1978.

Kazdin, A. E. *Behavior modification in applied settings.* Homewood, Ill.: Dorsey, 1975.

Keller, M. F., & Carlson, P. M. The use of symbolic modeling to promote social skills in preschool children with low levels of social responsiveness. *Child Development,* 1974, **45,** 912–919.

Kirkland, K. D., & Thelen, M. H. Uses of modeling in child treatment. In B. B. Lahey & A. E. Kazdin (Eds.), *Advances in clinical child psychology.* New York: Plenum Press, 1977.

Kleinsasser, L. D. The reduction of performance anxiety as a function of desensitization, pre-therapy vicarious learning, and vicarious learning alone. Unpublished doctoral dissertation, Pennsylvania State University, 1968.

Klinger, B. I. Effect of peer model responsiveness and length of induction procedure on hypnotic responsiveness. *Journal of Abnormal Psychology,* 1970, **85,** 15–18.

Kohlberg, L. *Collected papers on moral development and moral education.* Cambridge, Mass.: Harvard Graduate School of Education, 1973.

Krumboltz, J. D., & Thoresen, C. E. The effect of behavioral counseling in group and individual settings on information seeking behavior. *Journal of Counseling Psychology,* 1964, **11,** 324–333.

Krumboltz, J. D., Varenhorst, B. B., & Thoresen, C. E. Non-verbal factors in the effectiveness of models in counseling. *Journal of Counseling Psychology,* 1967, **34,** 412–418.

Lack, D. Z. The effects of a model and instructions on psychotherapist self-disclosure. Unpublished masters thesis, Syracuse University, 1971.

Lefkowitz, M., Blake, R. R., & Mouton, J. S. Status factors in pedestrian violation of traffic signals. *Journal of Abnormal and Social Psychology,* 1954, **51,** 704–706.

Liberman, B. The effect of modeling procedures on attraction and disclosure in a psychotherapy analogue. Unpublished doctoral dissertation, Syracuse University, 1970.

Liberman, R. P., King, L .W., De Risi, W. J. & McCann, M. *Personal effectiveness.* Champaign, Ill.: Research Press, 1975.

Lichtenstein, E., Keutzer, C. S., & Himes, K. H. Emotional role playing and changes in smoking attitudes and behaviors. *Psychological Reports,* 1969, **23,** 379–387.

Lorion, R. P. Socioeconomic status and traditional treatment approaches reconsidered. *Psychological Bulletin,* 1973, **79,** 263–270.

Mann, J. H. Experimental evaluations of role playing. *Psychological Bulletin,* 1956, **53,** 227–234.

Marlatt, G. A., Jacobson, E. A., Johnson, D. L., & Morrice, D. J. Effect of exposure to a model receiving evaluative feedback upon subsequent behavior in an interview. *Journal of Consulting and Clinical Psychology,* 1970, **34,** 194–212.

Matarazzo, J. D., Wiens, A. N., & Saslow, G. Studies in interview speech behavior. In L. Krasner & L. P. Ullman (Eds.), *Research in Behavior Modification.* New York: Holt, Rinehart & Winston, 1965.

McFall, R. M. *Behavioral training: A skill acquisition approach to clinical problems.* Chicago: General Learning Press, 1976.

McFall, R. M., & Marston, A. R. An experimental investigation of behavior rehearsal in assertive training. *Journal of Abnormal Psychology,* 1970, **76,** 295–303.

McFall, R. M., & Twentyman, C. T. Four experiments on the relative contributions of rehearsal, modeling and coaching to assertion training. *Journal of Abnormal Psychology,* 1973, **81,** 199–218.

McGehee, N., & Thayer, P. W. *Training in business and industry.* New York: Wiley, 1961.

Miller, J. P. *Humanizing the classroom.* New York: Praeger, 1976.

Miller, S., Nunnally, E. W., & Wachman, D. B. *Alive and aware: Improving communication in relationships.* Minneapolis: Interpersonal Communication Programs, 1975.

Miron, M., & Goldstein, A. P. *Hostage.* New York: Pergamon Press, 1978.

Nichols, H. Role playing in primary grades. *Group Psychotherapy*, 1954, **7**, 238–241.

Nietzel, M. T., Winett, R. A., McDonald, M. L., & Davidson, W. S. *Behavioral approaches to community psychology.* New York: Pergamon Press, 1977.

O'Connor, R. D. Relative efficacy of modeling, shaping, and the combined procedures for modification of social withdrawal. *Journal of Abnormal Psychology*, 1972, **79**, 327–334.

Patterson, G. R., Hops, H., & Weiss, R. L. Interpersonal skills training for couples in early stages of conflict. *Journal of Marriage and Family*, 1975, **37**, 295–301.

Perry, M. A. Didactic instructions for and modeling of empathy. Unpublished doctoral dissertation, Syracuse University, 1970.

Rathjen, H., Hiniker, A., & Rathjen, E. Incorporation of behavioral techniques in a game format to teach children social skills. Presented at Assoc. for Advancement of Behavior Therapy, New York, 1976.

Rhode, N., Rasmussen, D., & Heaps, R. A. *Let's communicate: A program designed for effective communication.* Presented at American Personnel and Guidance Assoc., April, 1971.

Riessman, F., Cohen, J., & Pearl, A. (Eds.) *Mental health of the poor.* New York: The Free Press, 1964.

Ritter, B. Treatment of acrophobia with contact desensitization. *Behavior Research and Therapy*, 1969, **7**, 41–45.

Rosenbaum, M. E., & Tucker, I. F. The competence of the model and the learning of imitation and non-imitation. *Journal of Experimental Psychology*, 1962, **63**, 183–190.

Rosenthal, T. L. Modeling therapies. In M. Hersen, R. M. Eisler, & P. M. Miller (Eds.), *Progress in behavior modification*, Vol. 2. New York: Academic Press, 1976.

Ross, D. M., Ross, S. A., & Evans, T. A. The modification of extreme social withdrawal by modeling with guided participation. *Journal of Behavior Therapy and Experimental Psychiatry*, 1971, **2**, 273–279.

Schofield, W. *Psychotherapy, the purchase of friendship.* Englewood Cliffs, N.J.: Prentice-Hall, 1964.

Shoabs, N. E. Role playing in the individual psychotherapy interview. *Journal of Individual Psychology*, 1964, **26**, 84–89.

Spivack, G., & Shure, M. *Social adjustment of young children.* San Francisco: Jossey-Bass, 1974.

Staub, E. The use of role playing and induction in children's learning of helping and sharing behavior. *Child Development*, 1971, **42**, 805–816.

Stephens, T. M. *Directive teaching of children with learning and behavioral handicaps.* Columbus: Charles E. Merrill, 1976.

Stephens, T. M. *Social skills in the classroom.* Columbus: Cedars Press, 1978.

Sutton, K. Effects of modeled empathy and structured social class upon level of therapist displayed empathy. Unpublished masters thesis, Syracuse University, 1970.

Terkelson, C. Making contact: Parent-child communication skill program. *Elementary School Guidance and Counseling*, 1976, **11**, 89–99.

Thiel, S. A. (Ed.) *Inventory of habilitation programs for mentally handicapped adults.* Portland, Oregon: Portland Rehabilitation Center, 1977.

Trower, P., Bryant, B., & Argyle, M. *Social skills and mental health.* Pittsburgh: University of Pittsburgh Press, 1978.

Walsh, W. The effects of conformity pressure and modeling on the attraction of hospitalized patients toward an interviewer. Unpublished doctoral dissertation, Syracuse University, 1971.

Weinstein, G., & Fantini, M. D. *Toward humanizing education: A curriculum of affect.* New York: Praeger, 1970.

Wildman, R. W., II, & Wildman, R. W. The generalization of behavior modification procedures: A review. *Psychology in the Schools*, 1975, **12**, 432–448.

Chapter 5
Problem-Solving Training
Arnold P. Goldstein

In 1939, Dollard, Miller, Doob, Mowrer, and Sears published *Frustration and Aggression*, a classic contribution to our subsequent understanding of aggressive behavior and its instigation. At the heart of their position lay the hypothesis that a universal causal relationship existed between frustration and aggression. In its initial formulation, frustration was posited always to cause aggression; aggression was predicted always to be a consequent of frustration. Early in its history, it was in several ways an attractively simple hypothesis. It turned the thinking of many individuals away from mythological and untestable notions of instinctual bases for aggression, it stimulated literally hundreds of investigations, and ultimately it led to a considerable advance in our knowledge of the antecedants of aggression and the consequents of frustration.

Stated as a universal causality, however, the hypothesis has proven severely limited. Frustration was shown to lead to aggression as predicted in only some instances. In young children, regression was often a more typical response (Barker, Dembo, & Lewin, 1941), and in others it has been shown to lead to fixation or displacement (Johnson, 1972). Wright (1942, 1943), Bateson (1941), Montague (1978), and other anthropologists have identified cultures in which aggression is an unusual consequent of frustration. Buss (1961) and others have shown that only some kinds of frustration lead to aggression, while other kinds do not. And Pastore (1952) demonstrated that how justifiable the frustration seems to the individual is a major determinant of whether he responds to it with aggression. Bandura (1959) presents the multiplicity of potential consequents of frustration well, with his observation:

> When distressed, some people seek help and support; others increase achievement strivings; others show withdrawal and resignation; some aggress; others experience heightened somatic activity; still others anesthetize themselves against a miserable existence with drugs and alcohol; and most intensify constructive efforts to overcome their adversities. [Pp. 53–54]

Not only may frustration have consequents in addition to aggression, aggression has a number of potential antecedents other than frustration.

These latter include one's reinforcement history for aggressive behavior, competing instigative and inhibitory tendencies, opportunity for the displacement of aggression, degree of exposure to aggressive models, previous history of punishment for behaving aggressively, the likelihood of counteraggression, and broader social sanctions for aggressive behavior. As Berkowitz (1969) comments, "In the long run, the frustration-aggression hypothesis contains considerable truth, but it is too simple and too sweeping" (p. 19).

While notions of universal causality have clearly failed to sustain, there are many instances in which frustration *does* lead to aggression, and in which aggression *is* the individual's dominant response to frustration. Aggression is the individual's prepotent response to frustration when he has learned that the thwarting, goal-blocking, or other aversive component of the frustrating circumstance is most rapidly, thoroughly, or expeditiously resolved by aggression. Frustration is likely to lead to aggression when one is rewarded for such behavior. As we have noted many times throughout this book, aggression very often pays. The more frequently it does so, the more likely aggressive responses become in the individual's response hierarchy or repertoire. One means for decreasing the likelihood or prepotency of such a response is to increase the relative potency of other, more socially desirable responses. If some individuals can respond to frustration by, as Handura (1969) notes "increasing achievement striving" and "intensifying constructive efforts to overcome their adversities," perhaps we can actually teach such constructive behaviors to individuals more prone to respond with aggression. It is toward this goal that the present chapter is devoted.

In the previous chapter, we noted that for most individuals the learning of interpersonal and social skills was often a chance affair. The development of such skills, we observed, was rarely the object of concrete and systematic training. One "picked up" interpersonal and social skill behaviors haphazardly, as part of the overall socialization process, or one typically learned them quasisystematically in spurts at home, school, church, or elsewhere. Very much the same inadequate teaching picture exists with regard to the focus of the present chapter, problem-solving skills. Some of the people, some of the time, may be fortunate enough to receive systematic problem-solving instruction, but this is a relatively rare event. As with social skills training, the rather little problem-solving training that does occur tends to be irregular and unsystematic in occurrence and incomplete and inadequate in scope. We can do better. Individuals can be provided systematic training in problem-solving skills both for purposes of building general competence in meeting life's challenges, and as a specific means of supplying one more reliable, prosocial alternative to aggression.

Toward the attainment of these broad goals, in this chapter we will examine two general types of problem-solving training. The first focuses quite explicitly upon *interpersonal* problem solving. Our concern will be how individuals faced with frustrating, aggression-instigating, problematic events involving a spouse, peer, parent, child, boss, or other person may be effectively trained to engage not in aggressive behavior vis-à-vis such important figures in their interpersonal world, but in competent problem solving instead. While this body of literature is not yet very large, what does exist is both substantial and of proven efficacy. It is a body of literature well worth our serious attention.

Our second major focus in this chapter will be upon a body of applied literature best described as *impersonal* problem solving. Here the concern is not directly avoiding or resolving person-to-person hostilities, or learning means for working through other problematic interpersonal events. Instead, impersonal problem solving is more concerned with cognitive events, with solving rational, usually nonemotional problems, with fostering creativity and originality. Whereas interpersonal problem solving is largely the concern of the clinician, the mental health specialist, or the counselor, impersonal problem solving has traditionally been the domain of the educator, the industrial consultant, and the experimental psychologist. As we will illustrate in detail later in this chapter, our own training and research philosophy is in part extrapolatory. We will propose that the procedures, techniques, and materials at the core of impersonal problem solving have, by extrapolation, real and substantial implications for improving the effectiveness of interpersonal problem solving. We now turn, however, to our first concern, direct training in interpersonal problem solving.

INTERPERSONAL PROBLEM SOLVING

The notion that problem-solving ability might be among the factors helping determine the quality of an individual's psychological adjustment and may also be relevant to his level of aggressive and impulsive behavior, is both relatively recent and not frequently advanced. Jahoda (1953, 1958) was an early advocate of this view and, more recently, we see a similar position in Weinstein's (1969) focus on the development of interpersonal competence and the delineation of stages in the problem-solving process by D'Zurilla and Goldfried (1971). The general stance advanced here is that inadequate problem-solving skills in the interpersonal and personal spheres of functioning result in too frequent reliance on socially unacceptable and nonenduring solutions, especially solutions of an acting-out nature. Note that this viewpoint directly parallels our earlier position regarding social skills training. In that chapter we proposed that skilled social behaviors could successfully be taught as viable substitutes for aggression, even in situations in which aggression—at least on a short-term basis—paid off. Similarly with problem-solving skills. In lieu of hitting, grabbing, insulting, pushing, threatening, or other aggressive behavioral solutions to interpersonal problems, individuals can successfully be taught the cognitive, reasoning, delaying skills necessary to reach satisfying, nonaggressive solutions to the same problem situations. We wish in the remainder of this section to examine the specific attempts made thus far to train people in such problem-solving skills. In doing so, we look very briefly at a number of modest preliminary attempts at such training, and then make an in-depth examination of the one effort in this domain that has yielded a comprehensive, elaborate, and seemingly valid series of problem-solving training programs and materials.

Pilot Training Programs

Small, pilot efforts aimed at enhancing problem-solving skills were initiated by Holzworth (1964) and Giebink, Stover, and Fahl (1968). By using game-like and other instructional materials, each sought to teach impulsive children adaptive means for handling frustrating situations. Each found suggestively (small N) positive results. Tentatively positive findings were also found in beginning research efforts to teach problem-solving skills to alcoholic patients (Intagliata, 1976) and to hospitalized psychiatric patients (Coche and Flick, 1975). Branca, D'Augelli, and Evans (1975) provide similarly encouraging early results for their training program in decision-making skills for preadolescents. Not unlike most of the programs we will examine in this chapter, their focus is upon teaching the *process* of decision making or problem solving, and not upon the rightness or wrongness of any particular decision or solution. As is also true of several other programs, the decision-making process is segmented, and viewed as a phase or stepwise process involving problem definition, identification of alternative solutions, choice of one solution as probably optimal, test of this selection, and evaluation of this trial solution. In a similar program named Thresholds (Burglass & Duffy, 1974), trainers have sought to teach a problem-solving process whose sequential steps were:

1. Defining the situation.
2. Expanding possibilities.
3. Evaluating possibilities.
4. Establishing decisional criteria.
5. Making a decision.

6. Acting on the decision.
7. Ratifying the decision.

Whereas Branca et al. (1975), and Burglass and Duffy (1974) implement their training efforts via an array of didactic, discussional, and simulational activities, Blechman (1974) has taught problem-solving skills utilizing a game format. Her Family Contract Game is designed for use by family units experiencing marked conflict and inability to deal successfully with interpersonal problems that involve them. The game is structured to circumvent or minimize the conflictual behaviors that usually characterize the behavior of the participating families—complaining, criticizing, interrupting, unresponsiveness, and so forth. Instead, again following a stage model, participation seeks to teach:

1. Definition of the problem.
2. Collection of relevant information.
3. Examination of alternatives.
4. Selection of course of action.
5. Evaluation of consequences.

In a seminal article, D'Zurilla and Goldfried (1971) explored the manner in which an array of behavior modification approaches, especially those concerned with self-control, might constitute an effective clinical reflection of experimental psychology's efforts in the problem-solving arena. They describe separate behavior therapy procedures for teaching what they view as the essential stages of effective problem solving: (1) general orientation, (2) problem definition, (3) generation of alternatives, (4) decision making, and (5) verification. Goldfried and Davison (1976) have described actual clinical applications of these suggested problem-solving methods, and a few investigators have begun to conduct the necessary evaluation research in order to test the actual efficacy of these applications (Ross & Ross, 1973; Stone, Hinds & Schmidt, 1975; Wagner, Breitmeyer & Bottum, 1975).

Impulsive youngsters have been the target of the problem-solving training effort put forth by Camp and Bash's (1975) *Think Aloud* Program. By use of an extended series of didactic lessons, games, and other activities, trainees are taught a variety of self-instructional procedures aimed at increasing their reflectiveness, as well as such specific problem-solving skills as the ability to develop alternative solutions to interpersonal problems, to consider possible consequences, and to formulate a plan of action based upon this formulation. It is skills such as these, in much more refined and elaborated form, that are the skill development targets of the major, problem-solving training program which we now consider in depth.

The Interpersonal Cognitive Problem-Solving Program

The pioneering work on problem-solving training we wish to examine in this section was conducted over a 15-year period by George Spivack, Myrna B. Shure, Jerome J. Platt, and their coworkers. The fruits of their efforts appear in three volumes, *Social Adjustment of Young Children* (Spivack & Shure, 1974), *The Problem-Solving Approach to Adjustment* (Spivack, Platt, & Shure, 1976) and *Problem-Solving Techniques in Childrearing* (Shure & Spivack, 1978). While we will seek here to do justice to this seminal research and materials development program in our discussion of it, the reader is strongly encouraged to examine the above-cited references directly.

In its earliest phase, training in Interpersonal Cognitive Problem Solving (ICPS) was oriented primarily toward young children. The following comment by Spivack and Shure (1974) communicates a sense of why, in the context of aggressive behavior, they view problem-solving skills as worth teaching.

> What might an adult say to a preschool child who hits another child or grabs a toy or cries? One possible response is, "Kevin, I know you feel angry at Paul, but I can't let you hit him." Another is, "Paul doesn't like to be hit." Sean snatches a truck from Robert and the adult asks him why he has taken the truck. "I want it!" is the answer. "Wait until Robert is finished and then you can play with it," says the adult. . . .
>
> In handling such behaviors as hitting and grabbing, many teachers and parents of young children demand that the behavior stop "because I said so." They often explain why the behavior is unacceptable. ("You can't hit Paul because you might hurt him.") If the hitting persists in school, the child might be isolated from the other children until he calms down or is judged to be ready to play without hitting.
>
> We believe that such techniques have serious limitations if one's goal is to help children develop effective ways of handling personal and interpersonal problems. First, the adult is too often doing the thinking for the child. The child is told he should wait his turn or stay away from another child or not hit. . . . The child neither solves his problem nor is helped to discover a solution of his own. Second, the adult in attempting to help a child often assumes that the child has a real understanding of the language of emotions ("I know you feel angry") or of negation ("but I *can't* let you hit him") or of causal relationships ("because you might hurt him"). Many young children do not have mastery of the language concepts necessary to solve interpersonal problems. . . . Finally, solving a problem for a child does little to help him feel good about himself. He is simply told what he can or cannot do, even though the reasons may be explained and the solution may work in that particular instance. He does not experience mastery that emerges when one has solved a problem. He may feel protected, but not competent. [Pp. IX–X]

It is from this rationale that the ICPS program emerged. Children (and later adolescents and adults), are to be taught *how* to think, not *what* to think. ICPS training teaches the problem-solving process, not problem solutions. In the case of young children trainees, prerequisite language and conceptual skills must also be taught. More generally, from the viewpoint articulated above, there emerged a series of principles or guidelines from which the specific content and procedures of the ICPS program would follow.

Principles underlying ICPS. The first principle concerned prerequisite language and conceptual skills. For later ability to learn to construe alternative solutions, games and other activities are used first to teach the meaning of words such as "or," "and," and "not." To aid in later understanding of individual preferences and interpersonal differences, words such as "some," "same," and "different" must be understood. And in the affective realm, of relevance to interpersonal sensitivity and empathy, notions of "happy," "sad," "mad," and the like are provided.

The second principle underlying ICPS training for young children is that it is easier to teach new concepts with words already familiar to the child. Thus, a major effort is made to utilize previously learned content to teach new materials. The third principle is that program content and situations should center on interpersonal themes, not impersonal problems.

An emphasis on conceptual learning and understanding, rather than the use of specific words or sentences, reflects the fourth principle. Emphasis, for example, is on the *idea* of negation rather than its necessarily accurate grammatical representation in any given sentence. The fifth principle, one lying at the heart of ICPS training, emphasizes teaching the child the habit of seeking alternative solutions and evaluating them on the basis of their potential consequences. Spivack and Shure (1974) observe with regard to this principle that no emphasis is placed in training upon the absolute merits of any given solution. If a child states "hit him" as a solution to getting a toy from another child, the teacher-trainer says (just as she would say if a more socially acceptable solution were offered): "That's one idea. Can you think of a different idea?" (if the trainer is teaching the seeking of alternatives). Or the trainer might comment: "That's one idea. What might happen next if you hit him?" (if the trainer is teaching the seeking of consequences).[1] To buttress the subsequent implementation of this principle further, and thus aid trainee ability to evaluate alternative solutions, additional prerequisite skill words and concepts are taught, e.g., "maybe," "might," "why–because," "if–then."

The sixth guiding principle underlying ICPS training stresses that the child think of and evaluate his own ideas, and be encouraged to offer them in the context of problem situations. This principle, Spivack &

Shure note, rests on the belief that a child is more likely to act on a conclusion he views as his own, than upon problem solutions provided by others.

Finally, ICPS training grows from the principle that the prerequisite language skills and the cognitive problem-solving skills, which together constitute the training goals of this program, are not ends in themselves but, instead, should be conceptualized as antecedent, mediating skills necessary to enhance behavioral adjustment and reduce such maladaptive behaviors as impulsiveness, aggressiveness, and overemotionality.

ICPS Skills. It is appropriate at this point in our presentation that we more fully define and examine the specific problem-solving skills that constitute the focal training targets of the ICPS program. To do so most understandibly we will end at this point our exclusive consideration of ICPS efforts with young children and move on in this and the following sections of the chapter to a more comprehensive consideration of the skills, aggression-relevant research results, and age-related training methods and materials of the ICPS programs across age samples including young children, but also preadolescents, adolescents, and adults.

1. *Alternative Solution Thinking.* A person's ability to generate different options or solutions that could potentially be utilized to solve a problem defines his capacity for alternative solution thinking. ICPS training for this skill has typically centered upon problems in trainee interpersonal relationships with a variety of types of persons, but especially with peers and authority figures. Spivack, Platt, and Shure (1976) observe, in partial explanation of their interest in promoting this skill, that if someone has only one or two solutions available to him in any given problematic situation, his chances of success are less than is the case for individuals who can turn to alternative solutions when the first option attempted fails to succeed in problem resolution:

> Among four- and five-year-olds, for instance, a girl may want her sister to let her play with her doll. She may ask her, and her sister may say no. Of interest is whether the child who wants the toy would conceive of an alternative way to get her sister to let her play with the doll. . . . If the girl's sister consistently says no every time she is asked for something, and no other options are available to the girl, she would soon become frustrated with her sister. She might react aggressively and exhibit impulsive behavior (for example, she might grab the toy) or she might avoid the problem entirely by withdrawing. [Spivack, Platt, & Shure, 1976, p. 19.]

2. *Consequential Thinking.* This second ICPS skill is defined as an ability to consider how one's actions may affect both other people and oneself, as well as the subsequent reactions these behaviors may

engender. The process of consequential thinking includes consideration of pros and cons to an interpersonal act that goes beyond the simple enumeration of alternative events that might ensue. As will be seen in our later examination of ICPS training procedures and materials, consequential thinking is stimulated by having the trainer follow the offering of problem solutions with such questions as "What might happen next?," "How will this make Mary feel?," "What will happen in the short run?," and "What will happen in the long run?"

3. *Causal Thinking.* Causal, or cause and effect thinking associated with interpersonal problem situations is the ability to relate one event to another over time with regard to the "why" that might have precipitated any given act. At the simplest level, to continue the example described above, if the girl wishing to obtain a doll from her sister, hit her sister, accurate cause and effect thinking would make her aware she hit her because she would not let her play with the doll or because of her anger at not being given the doll. If her sister hit her back as a result of having been hit, accurate causal thinking should lead the child to be aware that her sister hit her because she hit first. The inclusion of causal thinking as a skill training goal in the ICPS program was initially based, in part, on the position of Muuss (1960). His concern was social causal thinking across developmental levels. At its optimal levels, Muuss viewed causal thinking as:

> an understanding and appreciation of the dynamic, complex and interacting nature of the forces that operate in human behavior. It involves an attitude of flexibility, of seeing things from the point of view of others as well as an awareness of the probabalistic nature of knowledge. A causally oriented person is capable of suspending judgment until sufficient factual information is available. [P. 122.]

Relevant to our present purposes, in Muuss' view, low levels of causal thinking and its companion, low insight into the dynamics of behavior, make it difficult to react logically and appropriately to the behavior of others and, hence "behavior of others may be misunderstood and perceived as threatening, and such misunderstanding could lead to heightened conflict between the parties involved" (Spivack et al., 1976, p. 75).

4. *Interpersonal Sensitivity.* This problem-solving skill concerns an individual's awareness that an interpersonal problem in fact exists. It is the ability to perceive such problems combined with skill in focusing upon its interpersonal problematic components. Spivack et al. (1976) comment:

> To carry our example of the girl who wanted her sister's doll one step further, it

seems reasonable to assume that if she were aware that a [interpersonal] problem or potential problem could develop once she decides to ask for a doll, her behavior and/or problem-solving strategies may differ from what might ensue in the absence of such sensitivity. [Pp. 33–34]

As we will see shortly, however, empirical evidence examining the degree to which the several ICPS skills discriminate between well-adjusted and poorly adjusted individuals, or between aggressive and impulsive versus nonaggressive and more reflective persons does not support interpersonal sensitivity as among the highly potent ICPS skills.

5. *Means-End Thinking.* Means-ends thinking is careful, step-by-step planning in order to reach a given goal. Such planning, Spivack et al. (1976) observe, includes insight and forethought to forestall or circumvent potential obstacles and, in addition, having available alternative means when needed to deal with realistic obstacles in the way of reaching one's goal. Means-ends thinking involves, in addition, awareness that goals are not always reached immediately and that the timing of one's behavior is also often relevant to goal attainment. Spivack et al. (1976) comment illustratively:

A child adept at means-ends thinking may consider, I can go visit the boy next door [means] but he won't know me and won't let me in [obstacle]. If I call first and tell him I just moved in and ask if I can come over [means], he'll say okay. But I better not go at dinnertime or his mother will be mad [time and obstacle] and he won't like me. [p. 64]

6. *Perspective Taking.* This interpersonal problem-solving skill is reflected by the extent to which an individual recognizes and can integrate the fact that different people may have different motives and viewpoints, and thus may respond differently in a given situation. Perspective taking closely resembles what others have termed role taking or empathy. A fuller sense of the meaning of this ICPS skill can be obtained from an understanding of its measurement. In ICPS research on perspective taking, use was made of Feffer and Jahelka's (1968) Thematic Apperception Test (TAT) procedure. After creating stories to four TAT cards following standard TAT instructions, the trainee is presented the same cards again, and asked to retell the initial story from the viewpoint of each of its characters. Among other qualities of taking the perspective of others, scoring reflects the degree of coordination between the various versions.

Competence in these six problem-solving skills is the overall training goal of the ICPS program. The program's success in achieving these goals, and its impact on the overt aggressive and impulsive behavior of ICPS trainees, as well as their more general adjustment, are the concerns to which we turn.

ICPS Research. A substantial number of evaluative ICPS studies have been conducted. Many have been either comparisons, on each ICPS skill, of trainees who are high versus low in adjustment, aggressiveness, impulsiveness or inhibition. Others, seeking to provide complementary information, have examined the degree of correlation between the skills and these same criterion measures. Table 5.1 summarizes the major results of these experimental and correlational studies. It presents, for each of the major ICPS trainee age groups, indication of the presence or absense of a significant impact of each skill upon the criteria studied.

Before turning to specific results—especially those relevant to aggression and its reduction—with particular trainee samples, an overall comment on Table 5.1 appears appropriate. The developers of ICPS, as will be recalled, set forth as their final guiding principle in undertaking this work the notion that the problem-solving skills are not taught as ends in themselves, but as antecedent, mediating skills necessary to enhance behavior adjustment and reduce aggressiveness, impulsivity, and overinhibition. Table 5.1 tells us that, while not all the skills thus impact in all the samples, Spivack, Shure, and Platt have essentially succeeded in their goal.

With regard to specific findings, let us examine alternative thinking first. Shure, Spivack, and Powell (1972) found that youngsters whose behavior ratings indicated a predominance of either acting-out behaviors or inhibition conceptualized significantly fewer solutions to problem situations than did children rated as well adjusted. Elardo and Caldwell (see Spivack, Platt, & Shure, 1976) found that as alternative thinking improved, disrespect, defiance, inattentiveness, withdrawl, and over-reliance on others all decreased. Two studies demonstrated that increased levels of alternative thinking on posttraining test situations are also paralleled by analogously high levels in real-life contexts. (Larcen, Chinsky, Allen, Lochman, & Selinger, 1974; McClure, 1975). As was true for children, poor levels of adjustment correlates with deficient alternative thinking in both adolescents (Shure and Spivack, 1970), and adults (Platt & Spivack, 1973).

Consequential thinking was examined by Shure, Newman, and Silver (1973), and Spivack and Shure (1975). These studies indicate that four-year-olds rated as behaviorally adjusted conceptualize a greater number of different, relevant consequences to such aggressive acts as grabbing toys and taking objects belonging to others without permission than do children rated as impulsive or inhibited. Shure and Spivack (1975) found

Table 5.1. ICPS Skills Relevant to Training Criteria: Adjustment, Aggression, Impulsivity, Inhibition.

Trainee	Skill					
	Alternatives	Consequences	Causality	Interpersonal Sensitivity	Means-End Thinking	Perspective Taking
Early Childhood (Age 4–5)	yes	yes	no	no	—	—
Middle Childhood (Age 9–12)	yes	no	yes	—	yes	—
Adolescence (Age 13–17)	yes	yes	no	no	yes	yes
Adulthood	yes	yes	yes	no	yes	yes

that the number of consequences given by a youngster increases as a function of ICPS training. Comparisons of normal versus impulsive adolescents (Spivack & Levine, 1963), and normal versus psychiatric patient adults (Platt & Spivack, 1973) reveal that the normal sample in each instance provided significantly more consequences.

Platt and Spivack (1973) report similar differential results favoring the normal adult sample on causal thinking. These individuals were significantly more likely to think in terms of prior causes and the relationship between past and present events than were psychiatric patients, and this quality of thinking was unrelated to IQ. Larcen et al. (1972) found a significant relationship between causal thinking and measures of both impulsivity and inhibition in 9 to 12 year olds, with well-adjusted youngsters identifying causal statements significantly more often than did those displaying behavior deviance. No such result emerged in other examinations of this relationship involving 4–5-year olds or adolescents.

Level of interpersonal sensitivity, in the sense defined earlier—i.e., degree of awareness that an interpersonal problem exists—did not differentiate between adjusted and more deviant child (Spivack & Shure, 1975), adolescent (Platt, Spivack, Altman, Altman, & Peizer, 1974), or adult (Platt & Spivack, 1973) samples. Perspective taking, a separate skill reflecting a different type of interpersonal sensitivity (role taking, empathy) has found greater success in ICPS evaluative research. Platt et al. (1974) found significantly greater ability on this skill in normal adolescents as compared with disturbed youngsters. Platt and Spivack (1973) and Suchotliff (1970) found parallel results at the adult level.

Finally, let us consider research on means-ends thinking. Larcen, Spivack, and Shure (1972), in a sample of 9–12-year-old children, found a significant inverse relationship between the level of means-ends thinking skill and such behavior as social aggression, inability to delay, and emotionality. Working at the same age level, Shure and Spivack (1972) obtained evidence that normal, as compared with disturbed youngsters conceptualized more means (steps) to reach a goal, more obstacles that might be met on the way to that goal, and more consideration of the importance of time. In addition to mentioning fewer means, obstacles, and time considerations in reaching a goal, less well-adjusted youngsters expressed stories more limited to impulsive and aggressive means. As we noted in Table 5.1, means-ends thinking is an equally significant problem-solving skill at the adolescent (Platt, Scura, & Hannon, 1973; Spivack & Levine, 1973), and adult (Platt & Spivack, 1975) levels.

This brief overview of ICPS outcome research confirms the conclusion we drew earlier in our summary of Table 5.1. The skills examined, with only few exceptions, appear meaningfully and significantly to relate to and differentiate among samples varying in levels of adjustment, aggression, impulsivity, and inhibition. Their importance seems well established.

ICPS Training. We have now considered the underlying rationale and guiding principles of the ICPS program, its skill targets, and its supporting research. The final aspect of ICPS we will address is training. In this section we will briefly consider, separately for young child and adult trainees, the specific materials and procedures utilized to teach the ICPS skills.

The ICPS training program for young children (age 4–5) makes use of a variety of age-relevant materials—games, cut-out dolls, face puppets, picture sets, and the like. The program, according to its developers, is optimally implemented for 20 minutes per day over a three-month period. The trainer may be a teacher and/or aide working in a classroom setting (Spivack and Shure, 1974) or a parent teaching his or her own child or children in the home setting (Shure & Spivack, 1978). In content, the program consists of 24 games or lessons devoted to prerequisite language and conceptual skills (phase 1) and a dozen aimed at the ICPS skills directly (phase 2). As mentioned earlier in this chapter, the prerequisite skills include focus on such language concepts as "is," "not," "all," "same," "or," "same–different," emotional awareness, "if–then," identifying feelings in others, identifying preferences in others, what might happen next (consequences), and fairness.

The following excerpt will provide a sense of how a parent or teacher, in the second phase of the program, seeks to teach one of the ICPS skills—in this instance alternative thinking:

> The goal is to stimulate the child to think of as many different solutions as possible to the everyday interpersonal problems presented to him. The emphasis here is on "What else can I do?" when confronted with such a problem.
>
> To elicit solutions, use the following techniques. Show the child a picture, puppets, or other visual materials and state the problem. . . . Say: "The idea of this game is to think of lots of different ways (or ideas) for [repeat the problem]. I'm going to write all your ideas on the board." Despite the fact that the child cannot read, this has been a very useful motivating technique.
>
> After the first idea is given, say: "That's one way. Now the idea of the game is to think of lots of different ways. Can you think of a different (new, another) way? What else can this child [point to picture, puppet, etc] do to [repeat problem]." . . . After a few ideas are given, count on your fingers: "Way number one [repeat solution], way number two" and so on. Then ask: "Can you think of way number three?" If the child has been proposing things for the child character to *do*, switch the question to: "What can he *say*?" If the youngster jumps the gun and offers a consequence to a solution, recognize it, do not discourage it, then continue asking for a solution.

An enumeration is a variation of the same solution but not a different solution. The most common enumerations are giving something (give him candy, give him ice cream, give him potato chips), telling someone (tell his daddy, tell his mommy, tell his sister), and hurting someone (hit him, kick him, bite him). Let the child enumerate for a while, then classify, using the following words: "Giving ice cream and candy and potato chips are all giving something to eat. Can you think of an idea that's different from giving something to eat?"

If an idea is relevant to the problem as stated, it is acceptable, and value judgments are not communicated to the child. "Hit him" is just as relevant as "please." The general dialogue is: "That's one way. Can you think of a different idea? Remember, the idea of the game is to think of lots of ways" [Shure and Spivack, 1978, Pp. 86–87].

Shure and Spivack (1978) report that, beyond the formal ICPS training program outlined and illustrated above, mothers who consistently applied the ICPS skills when actual problems arose involving their children, had children who most improved in the ICPS skills and subsequent behavioral adjustment. They term this trainer problem-solving style "interpersonal problem solving dialoguing." In the example of such supplementary training by dialoguing provided below, note how the mother's statements pointedly encourage, respectively: (1) perspective taking, (2) causality, (3) alternative thinking, and (4) consequences:

Four-year-old Ralph let a friend play with his racing car, but the friend has played with it a long time and Ralph has just grabbed it back.

Mother: How do you think your friend feels when you grab toys? [Encourages perspective taking]
Ralph: Mad, but I don't care, it's mine!
Mother: What did your friend do when you grabbed the toy? [Encourages cause and effect thinking]
Ralph: He hit me but I want my toy!
Mother: How did that make you feel? [Encourages emotional awareness]
Ralph: Mad.
Mother: You're mad and and your friend is mad, and he hit you. Can you think of a different way to get your toy back so you both won't be mad and so John won't hit you? [Encourages alternative thinking]
Ralph: I could ask him.
Mother: And what might happen then? [Encourages consequential thinking]
Ralph: He'll say no.
Mother: He might say no. What else can you think of doing so your friend will give you back your racing car? [Encourages alternative thinking]
Ralph: I could let him have my match-box cars.
Mother: You thought of two different ways. [Pp. 36–37.]

These materials, procedures, and illustrative dialogues, while geared toward young children, serve to show concretely how ICPS skills may be taught optimally. One final example will conclude our presentation of the ICPS programs. Siegel and Spivack (1973) developed an ICPS training program designed to teach the basic problem-solving skills to adult psychiatric patients. It consists of 12 game-like exercises, each of which takes 20 to 45 minutes. They can be used on an individual or small group basis. At the outset of their program participation, the trainee is provided with the following structuring statement:

> The purpose of this program is to help people learn to solve problems that have caused them trouble. Many people do not know how to go about thinking of the ways to solve problems. There are a number of useful steps in the solving of problems. This program is intended to teach you these steps and to give you practice in mastering each of the steps. The steps are:
>
> 1. Recognition of Problems.
>   Problems are a part of real life. Everybody has them. Some people are just better at solving them than others. The first step in successful problem solving is to learn how to recognize problems. In this first step, you will be given a number of exercises to give you practice to be better at recognizing problems.
> 2. Definition of Problems.
>   After you learn how to better recognize problems, you will be given practice in how to define problems clearly by learning how to find out about problems and their solutions.
> 3. Alternative Ways of Solving Problems.
>   The third and possibly most important step in problem solving is looking at alternate ways of solving problems. There may be more ways of solving a problem than one. Some of the ways may be clearly better than other ways. To learn this step you will practice thinking about alternate ways to solve problems.
> 4. Deciding Which Solution is the Best Way to Solve the Problem.
>   The final step you learn is how to evaluate different solutions to a problem, and try to make a decision. In this step you will get practice at looking at the pros and cons of various solutions to problems, and trying to decide which one is best. [Pp. 229–230.]

The first step in this program, termed problem recognition, appears to be designed to teach the ICPS skill, Interpersonal Sensitivity. That is, the adult trainee is helped to see problems where they exist, and to conceptualize them interpersonally. For example, one exercise in this phase of the program, "Magazine Faces," requires the trainee to respond to pictures from magazines of people experiencing some emotion by describing the emotion and constructing a story explaining what might have led up to the feeling depicted. A second exercise, "Finding Problems," involves showing the trainee photographs of people in real-life interpersonal problem situations (e.g., fight at a party; a drunken spouse) and asking the trainee to identify what the problem is.

The activities of the second phase of this ICPS program, problem definition, seem oriented to teaching perspective taking and, to a lesser extent, cause and effect thinking. One exercise in this phase, for example, is "Finding Out About People." In it, the trainee listens to a series of taped playlets illustrating an array of means for learning about the feelings and thoughts of others. These are: (1) asking direct questions of a third party, (2) indirectly bringing up the subject in conversation, and (3) interacting with the person directly.

Training in alternative thinking is the target of the third phase. One exercise in this phase is a picture card sorting task, "Finding Alternatives." In a manner not unrelated to training in means-ends thinking, the trainee is presented with a problem (card with picture of lonely dejected person) and an outcome (card with same person at a party) and a number of other cards depicting the person in situations and activities some of which could reasonably lead (if ordered correctly) from the problem to the outcome. The trainee's task is to select and order the alternative solutions. In this phase, the trainee is taught not only to recognize alternatives, but also to generate them. In the exercise "Creating Alternatives," the trainee is presented with interpersonal problem situations (e.g., getting along with one's boss, changing the annoying behavior of a friend), and encouraged by the trainer to come up with as many solutions as he can.

The final stage, deciding which solution is best, is oriented toward consequential thinking, that is, toward evaluation of the relative strengths and weaknesses of the available alternatives. The exercise "Impulsivity-Reflection Slides" in this stage seeks to accomplish this goal by a series of demonstrations to the trainee that the initial, frequently impulsively chosen solution to an interpersonal problem is often not the best one, and that it is often better to wait and reflect on alternative solutions before taking action. In "Decision Faces," the trainee is given practice in enumerating the pros and cons of each alternative. In the final program exercise, "Plays," the trainee is asked to bring together and sequentially enact all four phases of the problem-solving process as defined by this ICPS program.

This consideration of ICPS program procedures and materials concludes our consideration of the work of Spivack, Platt, and Shure. Their contribution to this domain is substantial and continuing. Aggressive, impulsive behavior, and its alteration have not been their only focus but have been a major one. It is clear from their work that Interpersonal Cognitive Problem Solving training should be considered an important component in developing preventive and remedial techniques that have potential for aiding in the control and reduction of interpersonal aggression.

IMPERSONAL PROBLEM SOLVING

The personal and interpersonal consequences of the mismanagement of aggression, of excessive hostility, of chronic conflict and the inability to control or resolve it, are very much *personal* problems. Yet the remainder of this chapter deals with *impersonal* problem-solving methods. Among our ultimate concerns in this book is aiding the individual to manage his emotional world better, to regulate and reduce his anger, to aid in his efforts at self-control, yet in the following discussion, we deal with methods for the enhancement of the ability to solve intellectual and cognitive problems, to function more creatively, and with higher levels of problem-solving originality. We embark on this consideration of the impersonal to understand the personal better because we have long believed that such an effort might be profitable. We are guided, in effect, by an extrapolatory strategy here. A host of problem-solving and creativity-enhancing methods have been actively used for a number of years in industrial, educational, and laboratory contexts. Their use has not been oriented toward the resolution of personal problems. Instead, these methods have been employed in order to enhance organizational effectiveness, to develop new products, to resolve cognitive dilemas, to improve the on-the-job functioning of managers, teachers, scientists, and other applied problem solvers, and toward the experimental goal of better understanding the intellectual and cognitive processes involved in effective problem solving and creativity.

Whether this vast, and only partially research-based, literature does in fact have significant implications for the enhancement of personal problem solving is as yet unknown, and remains a matter to be examined by substantive research scrutiny. We have been implementing an extrapolatory research philosophy in another context for many years, drawing on social-psychological laboratory research for testable hypotheses relevant to enhancing the effectiveness of psychotherapy (Goldstein, Heller, and Sechrest, 1966; Goldstein & Simonson, 1971). During the course of this extended research program it has become clear that some change-enhancing methods developed in the laboratory context can find direct applied usefulness in a personal framework; some can also find such usefulness, but must be altered or adapted first, and other laboratory procedures have essentially no import for applied concerns. We suspect much the same outcome will in the long run prove true for the extrapolation of impersonal problem-solving methods to the personal problem-solving domain: Which impersonal methods will prove extrapolatable, which will have to be adapted, and which will prove useless for these purposes is a matter for future formal and informal research. It is to stimulate just such inquiry that we have written the following sections. We will examine brainstorming, synectics, morphological analysis, attribute listing, and a number of other techniques purporting to enhance impersonal problem-solving skill and to stimulate creativity. Consistent with the extrapolatory viewpoint we champion here, it is important to note that unlike such personal problem-solving methods as ICPS, none of the impersonal methods considered has been concerned in any substantial way with matters of aggression reduction, anger control, or the like. We urge upon the interested reader the challenge of just such extrapolatory translation and experimental examination.

Brainstorming

Brainstorming is an idea-generating, problem-solving technique developed by Osborn in 1938 and first explicated in detail in his book, *Applied Imagination* (Osborn, 1953). It is a widely used technique, particularly in industrial and educational settings. Osborn differentiated between the idea-finding and solution-finding phases of the creative problem-solving process. Brainstorming is oriented toward the goal of the first phase of this process, i.e., to produce a substantial quantity of high-quality, problem-relevant ideas. The second phase, not relevant to brainstorming, is evaluative. Here, the ideas of phase one are judged, considered, evaluated, winnowed, and eventually adopted.

To promote the overriding idea-generating purpose of brainstorming, two guiding principles have been put forth. The first, *deferment of judgment*—requires participants to verbalize or write down their ideas during the brainstorming session without concern for their value, feasibility, or significance. Within the stipulation that the ideas be problem-relevant, that is, not "free association," the brainstormer is asked to suspend what Osborn (1953) calls the "judicial mind" that analyzes, compares, and chooses. Instead, Osborn urges that the "creative mind" that visualizes, foresees, and generates ideas be encouraged. The second basic brainstorming principle is that *quantity breeds quality*. This principle rests on notions beyond simple ideas of, somehow, the more the better. As Stein (1974) observes,

> The rationale for this dictum originates in associationistic psychology, which assumes that our thoughts or associations are structured hierarchically. The most dominant thoughts in this hierarchy are those which are most habitual, common, or usual, and are therefore likely to be, from other points of view, the "safest" and most acceptable to others. It is necessary to "get through" these conventional ideas if we are to arrive at original ones. [P. 29.]

Four operational rules that grow from these two principles guide the actual conduct of the brainstorming session:

1. Criticism is ruled out. This rule is the operational underpinning for the deferment of judgment principle. In group brainstorming, for example, criticism of another's ideas, or of one's own ideas, or apologizing are all actively discouraged. Evaluation, adverse judgments and the like are kept strictly off limits.
2. Freewheeling is welcomed. As Davis (1973) notes, "The wilder the idea, the better; it is easier to tame down than to think up.... The brainstormer—as any other creative thinker—must be consciously set to be imaginative, to try different and unusual strategies, and to view the problem from novel perspectives—in a word, to suggest anything" (p. 93).
3. Quantity is wanted. This rule directly reflects the second principle described above. In all possible ways, sheer quantity of ideas is to be encouraged.
4. Combination and improvement are sought. Participants are urged to build on the ideas of others, especially by showing how previously offered ideas can be improved, combined, or otherwise transformed for the better.

Brainstorming can be conducted on an individual or group basis. If a group, it is customary for 10 to 12 persons to participate. Ideally, participants are heterogeneous in training, experience vis-à-vis the focal problem, sex, and similar characteristics—except rank or status within the organization, a dimension in which similarity is considered best.

Osborn is among the many writers on creativity, problem solving, and originality who believe strongly in incubation effects, that is, the preconscious progress made by individuals toward idea generation when they seem, to themselves and others, otherwise occupied. To provide systematic opportunity for incubation to occur, it is recommended that participants in a brainstorming group be advised of the problem to be dealt with two days in advance of the actual session. The session itself, usually 30–45 minutes in length, usually involves the participants, a leader, an associate leader, and a recording secretary. Sessions typically open with warm-up activities, a presentation of the four rules, and a call for ideas and suggestions from the group. Osborn comments:

> He [the leader] quickly recognizes those who raise their hands to signify they have ideas to offer. Sometimes so many hands are raised that he simply goes around the table and lets each person present one idea in turn. Participants should never be

allowed to read off lists of ideas which they may have brought to the meeting. . . . Only one idea at a time should be offered by any brainstormer. Otherwise the pace would be badly impeded because the opportunity for "hitch-hikes" [one idea stimulating a related idea] would be precluded [p. 176].

Various techniques, such as use of Osborn's (1963) idea-spurring questions, stop and go brainstorming in which freewheeling periods and evaluative ones are alternated, and ideas put forth by the leaders are used for stimulation when the group seems to be running dry.

Since brainstorming procedures specifically preclude the type of idea evaluation and analysis necessary for problem solution, the total problem-solving process involves submitting the ideas generated by the brainstorming group to an idea evaluation group. This latter panel may or may not contain some of the members of the original brainstorming group. Its members, regardless of whether they were involved in the brainstorming, should be people with direct future responsibility for the focal problem. It is their task to evaluate the raw or edited brainstormed ideas for simplicity, timeliness, cost, feasibility, and other organizational implementation.[2]

These descriptive comments complete our consideration of brainstorming. How the individual, group, or organization may optimally use these procedures for the aggression control purposes at the heart of this book is an as yet untested, empirical question the answer to which requires substantial doses of the very creativity which procedures such as brainstorming are designed to elicit.

Synectics

Synectics is a problem-solving approach initially developed by Gordon in 1944, and comprehensively described in *Synectics* (Gordon, 1961), *The Metaphorical Way* (Gordon, 1971), and *The Practice of Creativity* (Prince, 1970). Synectics, not unlike brainstorming and many other creative problem-solving techniques, rests on a rationale and uses specific procedures that seek both to help the user "break free," and to move beyond evaluative analytical and conventional thinking. "Naturally" creative problem solving does this; synectics seeks consciously to institute such a cognitive state, e.g., detachment, unconventionality, metaphorical word play, apparent irrelevance, empathy. It is, as we will see, a system based largely on the use of metaphor and analogy.

A synectics group typically consists of five to seven members, one of which is the designated leader and one of which is the group's client-expert, a resource person included largely for his or her factual understanding of the focal problem. Meetings typically last an hour. Synectics programs vary in length, but all reflect a three-phase problem-solving process. The steps constituting the first phase of synectics are devoted to defining, elaborating, analyzing, and understanding the problem. This initial phase is followed by one in which the basic operating mechanisms of synectics, metaphors, and analogies are utilized. Finally, in the "force fit" steps of the last phase, the effort is made to use the fruits of the metaphorical and analogical phase to move toward problem solution. The flow of a synectic effort at moving from problem to solution may be clarified by the following pr~sentation of the specific steps involved in synectic problem solving.

1. *Problem as given.* The problem as given is the statement of the focal problem to the synectic group. As Gordon (1961) notes, this statement may prove to be an accurate statement of the problem, or as stated initially it may in part hide or confuse the question to be addressed.

2. *Analysis.* To clarify the nature and substance of the problem, and reduce ambiguities associated with the problem as given, the group's client-expert is called upon to present an analysis of it.

3. *Purge.* A number of problem solutions typically emerge spontaneously from group members during the initial steps of the synectic process. Such solutions, much like the earliest-expressed ideas in a brainstorming session, tend to be superficial and generally obvious. Their verbalization at this time permits the group's expert to explain their inadequacy, thus simultaneously "purging" the inadequate solutions and further clarifying the focal problem.

4. *Problem as understood.* Prince (1970) suggests that at this step each participant be called upon to come up with his own view of the problem and his fantasy solution. This process enables each participant to begin "owning" the problem personally, it takes advantage of the group's diversity, it helps break the problem into manageable sub-problems when needed, and the use of fantasy or wishful thinking at this point begins the transition to the level of thinking required at the next, analogical step of the synectics process. This step ends with the leader, after checking with the expert, selecting one of the group's problems as given as the groupwide problem goal to seek to resolve.

5. *Excursion.* During this step in the synectics process, the different operational mechanisms that lie at the creative core of the program are utilized. These mechanisms are the use by group members of different types of analogies to help move away from the problem into a speculative mode, in order to return to it later with very different perspective. In

fact, in this step, the participants are literally asked to forget the problem per se, to take a mental excursion from it. This step is an effort to evoke, as in all creative problem-solving programs, nonevaluative, nonanalytical thinking of a metaphorical nature. It is, as Gordon terms it, an effort to "make the familiar strange" and thus view the [familiar] problem later from brand new perspectives. He observes further:

> Analogies are developed which are relative to (and evoked by) the problem as understood. This phase pushes and pulls the problem as understood out of its rigid form of impregnable regularity into a form that offers some conceptual finger holds. These finger holds open up the problem as understood. [Gordon, 1961, p. 157.]

The analogical mechanisms thus utilized are of three types. In the first, *personal analogy*, the individual seeks to engage in what Gordon calls "an extensive loss of self" and imagines himself to *be* the object involved in the problem as understood. As Stein (1975) observes, "he 'becomes' the spring in the apparatus and feels its tension, or he 'becomes' the pane of glass and allows himself to 'feel' like the molecules in it as they push and pull against each other" (p. 187). Gordon (1961) stresses that the operative process here is empathic identification, and not a less identity-losing role playing. Four levels of increasingly deep empathic identification, as a result of use of personal analogy, are described in the synectics Teacher's Manual (Synectics, 1968).

1. First-person description of facts. Someone asked to imagine he is a fiddler crab states he would have a hard outside and soft inside, and so on.
2. First-person description of emotions. In the example above, the person responds that he was busily involved in gathering food for himself, and had to be on guard for fear he himself might become food for a bigger fish.
3. Identification with a living thing.[3] This level is viewed as genuine personal analogy, involving both kinesthetic and emotional identification with the object. In the fiddler crab example, the person might state that his big claw was a useless burden, it is heavy and frightens no one when he waves it.
4. Identification with a nonliving object. This level is viewed as the deepest and most difficult to achieve, personal analogy. It apparently requires, in practice, the greatest analogical effort by participants.

A second type of excursion from the problem as understood involves the use of *direct analogy*. For inexperienced participants it is the easiest analogical method to master, and thus often the first introduced. Unlike personal analogy, in which the person is asked to "become" an aspect of the problem, direct analogy requires turning outward. Facts, knowledge or technology from one domain are utilized analogically to view the problem domain more clearly. Gordon (1961) comments:

> Brunel solved the problem of underwater construction by watching a shipworm tunneling into a timber. The worm constructed a tube for itself as it moved forward, and the classical notion of caissons came to Brunel by direct analogy. . . . Alexander Graham Bell recalled, "It struck me that the bones of the human ear were very massive, indeed, as compared with the delicate thin membrane that operated them, and the thought occurred that if a membrane so delicate could move bones relatively so massive, why should not a thicker and stouter piece of membrane move my piece of steel." And the telephone was conceived [p. 42].

A variety of fields have been drawn upon for direct analogical purposes in synectics groups, but it is clear that biology has been most frequently used in this manner. Whatever the field drawn upon, Prince (1970) claims that the greater the logical distance between the problem object and the analogy, the less the apparent relevance of the latter to the former, the more likely it will be helpful in the problem-solving process.

The third analogical mechanism used during the excursion step is *symbolic analogy*, also variously called "Book Title," "Essential Paradox," and "Compressed Conflict." This type of analogy is frequently used to suggest other, direct analogies. Prince (1970) comments:

> The Book Title . . . helps take a more interesting and therefore better vacation from the problem. In form, a Book Title is a two-word phrase that captures both an essence of and a paradox involved in a particular thing or set of feelings. The combination of an adjective and a noun is the most workable form. The usual purpose of a Book Title is to generalize about a particular and then use it to suggest another example [i.e., Direct Analogy]. This procedure also helps hardcase, stay-on-the-problem types get away from the problem [p. 95].

6. *Force fit.* The goal of the next step in the synectics process is to return to the problem from the analogical excursion and try to come up with a practical application of the analogy to the problem. The analogical material has been developed, and in spite of its apparent irrelevance, the group must now force it to fit the problem in a useful manner. Gordon reports the force fit activities of a synectics group dealing with the problem of inventing a better mousetrap. In its analogical excursion, the group came up with "Trojan Horse," reflecting the idea of leaving something around that mice will covet so much that they will pull it into their nests. The force fit interactions led to the notion that lint, which

could be used by mice in this manner, be left around; the lint would be treated so that when warmed by the mice in the nest it would give off a painless but lethal gas.

7. *Viewpoint.* The return to the real problem, seeking workable solutions continues in this next and final stage of the synectics process. This stage, in a sense, involves the evaluation of the analogically derived force fit. Is the fit viable? Has the solution been reached? If answered affirmatively, the synectic problem-solving process is completed.

Creative Problem-Solving

Creative Problem Solving is a comprehensive series of training programs developed by Parnes, and described in detail in *Creative Behavior Guidebook* (Parnes, 1967), and *Creative Behavior Workbook* (Parnes, 1967). Numerous articles in the *Journal of Creative Behavior,* a publication founded by Parnes, further describe and evaluate this approach. It is an approach that relies heavily on fostering the cognitive aspects of the creative process, with considerably less exclusive concern than brainstorming and synectics on promoting the intuitive or preconscious components of this process. It uses a wide variety of techniques and materials rather didactically to teach individuals how to apply "deliberate creative effort." In this view, to be handled effectively, problems must be refined, clarified, and worked on through stages of (1) fact finding, (2) problem finding, (3) idea finding, (4) solution finding, and (5) acceptance finding.

The Creative Problem Solving training program can be implemented by persons working alone (using the two program texts cited above) or in classes of as many as 25 members. The total program consists of 16 sessions, designed as a group to train participants in how to be effective in the five-step problem-solving process enumerated above, and also to give them increasingly autonomous practice in doing so. A better overall sense of this program can be obtained by a brief look at the substance of each session.

Session 1. Training in problem sensitivity or how to become aware of problems that can be worked creatively.

Session 2. Training in problem definition, to arrive at a clearer and more manipulable statement of the problem.

Session 3. Training in brainstorming rationale and technique.

Session 4. Training in "forced relationship" techniques, a technique designed to help the trainee overcome fixed ways of thinking by learning how to force a relationship between, or to combine, two quite unrelated ideas or objects.

Session 5. Training in the development and use of evaluation criteria. The criteria developed are actually applied to the ideas generated in preceding sessions.

Session 6. Training in how to gain acceptance of one's solutions. Use is made here of an implementation checklist that raises questions of possible advantages, objections, anticipated responses to criticism of one's solution, and the optimal time and place for solution implementation.

Session 7. A demonstration by the Creative Problem Solving instructor of the total problem-solving process as taught in the preceding sessions. This is the first of four "experience cycle" sessions in which the participants, with increasing autonomy, have an opportunity to experience the complete problem-solving process.

Session 8. Additional training in fact finding, with particular emphasis on the use of descriptive categories.

Session 9. The second "experience cycle" session focusing on the entire problem-solving process. Rather than being modeled by the instructor (as in Session 7), the trainee works with a small group of other trainees.

Session 10. Additional training in idea finding, with particular emphasis on the use of manipulative categories.

Session 11. Additional training in solution finding. Part of this session deals with the utilization of strange, unusual, and even seemingly silly potential solutions. The remainder focuses on how evaluation criteria may be used as stimuli to enhanced creativity.

Session 12. The third experience cycle session, in this instance the trainee works in two-person teams, as well as alone.

Session 13. Additional training in acceptance finding. Using a "who, what, where, why, and how" checklist, trainees are taught to "sell" their obtained problem solutions.

Session 14. The final experience cycle session, in which the trainee works alone through all steps of the problem-solving process on a problem of his own choosing.

Session 15. Training in the use of the Creative Problem Solving procedures to make rapid, on-the-spot decisions.

Session 16. Review of the program.

Restructuring Techniques

There exists a group of problem-solving techniques that share the common goal of producing novel idea combinations, and the common methodology of part or characteristic changing. We consider these as a group and, following Rickards (1974), term them "Restructuring Techniques."

Attribute Listing. Crawford is the developer of this problem-solving approach, which he explores in his books, *How to Get Ideas* (Crawford, 1950), and *Techniques of Creative Thinking* (Crawford, 1954). According to this approach, any idea, object, or product may potentially be improved by isolating and modifying any of its individual attributes or qualities. Attribute listing literally involves the listing of idea or object attributes, to aid in consideration of their subsequent possible modification. As Davis (1973) comments, "In designing clothes, attribute listing is almost the modus operandi. . . . Consider the creation of a shirt or blouse: the cuffs, sleeves, collar, 'cut', colors and color patterns, material and closure device are separately considered attributes that may be modified or perhaps removed" (p. 104). Stein (1974) provides a second example of attribute listing and modification:

> During the course of time each of the attributes of the screwdriver has undergone some kind of modification. The former round shank now has a hexagonal cross section, which is easier to grip with a wrench to gain more torque. For longer use, the handle is now made of plastic rather than wood. The traditional flat wedge-shaped end has been modified for use with many different types of screws. Electric motors now provide power and there are screwdrivers that develop torque by being pushed rather than twisted [pp. 214–215].

Crawford (1954) captures the essence of his view of attribute listing with his suggestion that "being original is *simply* reaching over and shifting attributes in what is before you." The method we consider next provides a systematic basis for the attribute-shifting process.

Morphological Analysis. This problem-solving approach, a logical extension of attribute listing, was developed by Zwicky and elaborated in *Morphological Astronomy* (Zwicky, 1957), and *Discovery, Invention, Research: Through the Morphological Approach* (Zwicky, 1969). One first identifies two or more major dimensions or attributes of the problem. In the shirt-design problem alluded to earlier, relevant dimensions were cuffs, sleeves, collar, cut, color and color patterns, material, and closure device. Next, one lists alternative ideas or implementations for each dimension. For example, for cuffs, one could readily list one-button, two-button, French, and none. By means of such enumeration of attributes, and then the systematic grouping into all possible combinations of these attributes, Davis (1973) notes that 43,200 different shirts are possible. Or, in a simpler example, Davis (1973) also reports a morphological analysis done by a sixth grade class in which the dimensions of flavors and extras were examined in an effort to develop new ice creams. Fifty-six flavors were systematically paired with 36 extras (nuts, fruits, vegetables, etc.) to yield 2,016 ice creams. A number of variations of this approach have been described, usually under the category of forced relationships techniques. Three of the more frequently mentioned are the catalog technique, the listing technique, and the focused object technique. We refer the reader to the developer of these variants, Whiting (1958), for more detailed information on their character.

Checklists. Two broad types of checklists have been used for problem-solving purposes: specialized and generalized (Whiting, 1958). The specialized, as used in business and industry, are a listing of reminders and guidelines for such purposes as introducing a new product, making a sale, etc. Their general purpose is to remind the user of the essential steps that ideally constitute a given process. The generalized checklist, as its name implies, can ideally be applied to a variety of situations. One frequently used list of this type is Osborn's (1953) checklist of nine basic categories of "idea-spurring questions" for altering an existing idea, object or product:

1. *Put to other uses*? New ways to use as is? Other uses if modified?
2. *Adapt*? What else is like this? What other idea does this suggest? Does past offer parallel? What could I copy? Whom could I emulate?
3. *Modify*? New twist? Change meaning, color, motion, odor, form, shape? Other changes?
4. *Magnify*? What to add? More time? Greater frequency? Stronger? Larger? Thicker? Extra value? Plus ingredients? Duplicate? Multiply? Exaggerate?
5. *Minify*? What to substitute? Smaller? Condensed? Miniature? Lower? Shorter? Lighter? Omit? Streamline? Split up? Understate?
6. *Substitute*? Who else instead? What else instead? Other ingredients? Other material? Other process? Other place? Other approach? Other tone of voice?
7. *Rearrange*? Interchange components? Other pattern? Other layout? Other sequence? Transpose cause and effect? Change pace? Change schedule?
8. *Reverse*? Transpose positive and negative? How about opposites? Turn it backward? Turn it upside down? Reverse roles? Change shoes? Turn tables? Turn other cheek?
9. *Combine*? How about a blend, an alloy, an assortment, an ensemble? Combine units? Combine purposes? Combine appeals? Combine ideas?

In addition to attribute listing, morphological analysis, and the use of idea-stimulating checklists, other lesser-known restructuring, problem-solving techniques have been described. These techniques, which the interested reader may wish to pursue further, include the Vice-Versa Approach (Goldner, 1962), the Input-Output Technique (Whiting, 1958), Use of the Ridiculous (Von Fange, 1959), the Fresh Eye (Whiting, 1958), and Relevance Systems (Rickards, 1974).

Other Sources for Extrapolation

In the second half of this chapter, we have presented the more widely known approaches to impersonal problem solving, and have simultaneously urged upon the reader an extrapolatory frame of reference. This frame of reference seeks to encourage attempts to view techniques designed to enhance problem-solving effectiveness in industry, education, and the experimental laboratory as of potential value for frustration reduction and problem solving in the interpersonal realm. Experimental psychology has long been seriously involved in providing yet another important domain for such possible extrapolation. Investigators have devoted very substantial amounts of effort seeking in laboratory contexts to clarify the problem-solving process. These efforts have generally sought to identify and describe task variables influencing problem difficulty, problem-solving styles and strategies, and personality characteristics that aid or hinder problem-solving effectiveness. Three theoretical viewpoints have emerged. The Gestalt view of problem solving saw this activity as involving directed learning, including conscious and purposive processes. It is a mentalistic theory in which the problem solver actively hypothesizes, reasons, follows leads, encodes, deduces, makes and tests predictions, and especially, gains insight. The associationistic view, in contrast, seeks to explain learning in conditioning, S–R terms. Trial-and-error learning, rather than insight, is the dominant process. Responses are organized in response hierarchies and, in this view, problem solving is a process of rearrangement of responses in such an hierarchy. The third theoretical view, information processing, has been closely tied to computer simulation methodology and technology. Computers can be programmed to simulate significant cognitive processes—forming associations, hypothesis testing, comparison of information, remembering, and so forth. The fact that such complex formulation and evaluation processes can be simulated has enabled information-processing investigators to examine increasingly complex problems and the means by which they may be resolved.

While these bodies of theory and the companion research they have stimulated are quite substantial, it must be stressed again that one is faced here with questions of extrapolatory appropriateness. Laboratory investigators of (impersonal) problem solving study anagrams, maze tests, perceptual problems, logic, chess, checkers, abstract concept development, and a host of problems seemingly far removed from the interpersonal and emotional domains at the heart of this book. Thus, again, we urge an openness of thinking, and the desirability of responding with formal and informal research to the extrapolatory challenge implicit in this state of affairs.

Much the same point can be made regarding the very substantial theoretical and research literature on creativity and its enhancement. A great many creativity enhancement programs exist and are prime extrapolatory targets. These include Torrance's (1975) seminal, long-term program for enhancing creativity in school children, Maltzman's (1960) training for originality, Mearns' (1958) procedures for the reinforcement of original behavior, the Williams Total Creativity Program (Williams, 1972), the Purdue Creativity Program (Covington, Crutchfield, & Davies, 1972), the Myers and Torrence (1965) ideabooks, the Productive Thinking Program (Crutchfield and Covington, 1964), Inquiry Training (Suchman, 1961), and the Inductive Teaching Program (Karlins & Schroder, 1967). Together they constitute a mass of exciting procedures and insights of potential viability for the personal problem-solving domain.

Beyond the formulation and evaluation of creativity-enhancing programs, procedures, and materials, creativity research has yielded two additional bodies of information of potential value for personal problem solving. One concerns the identification of characteristics of creative individuals, and, of course, our concern would be the development and accentuation of these characteristics. They include open-mindedness, nonconformity, assertiveness, independence, perseverance, willingness to consider the irrational, and tolerance for ambiguity and flexibility. The second grows from studies on blocks or inhibitors of creativity, and here, of course, our concern is their diminution or elimination. Such blocks include excessive reliance on logic, overcommitment to a single approach, unwillingness to speculate, excessive deference to experts, stereotyping, a belief that fantasy and playfulness are inappropriate for adults, and other perceptual, cultural, emotional, intellectual, and expressive blocks. These domains, too, we feel might well be explored for their interpersonal problem-solving implications.

SUMMARY

Aggressive behavior is a frequent consequence of the frustration associated with inadequate, personal problem-solving skills. In constructive response to such deficits, we have examined two classes of problem-solving skill development programs in depth. The first bears quite directly on the diminution of aggression, impulsivity, and the like. These programs, especially Interpersonal Cognitive Problem Solving, were described in detail. It is clear that we encourage their wide use. The second type of program examined was those that seek to enhance impersonal problem-solving skills. While these skills have traditionally been the domain of industry, the school, or the laboratory, their substance and their success strongly encourage formal and informal trials of their utilization in more personal and interpersonal contexts.

NOTES

1. Spivack and Shure (1974) have demonstrated, in this context, that well-adjusted and poorly adjusted children do not differ in the frequency with which they verbally offer aggressive solutions such as "hit him" to problems such as these. They do, however, differ significantly in the frequency with which they actually use such aggressive behaviors overtly in attempts to resolve problematic situations.

2. We do not in this chapter present a detailed examination of research exploring the effectiveness of brainstorming. Such research has been critically and comprehensively presented by Stein (1975) and we refer the interested reader to this source. It should be clear, however, that as with all of the concrete interventions presented in this book, their very inclusion here reflects our appraisal that research relevant to the intervention is generally supportive of its efficacy.

3. A problem-solving approach closely resembling this aspect of personal analogy is Bionics (Papanek, 1969). Using "the infinite storehouse of ideas in nature itself," Bionics is the study of the structure, function, and mechanisms of plants and animals to gain design information for analogous manmade systems. As Davis (1973) observes, "The bionicists ... strategy is to examine closely the motor, circulatory, neural, and especially sensory capabilities of organisms from ... the animal kingdom—mammals, birds, reptiles, amphibians, fish and insects. The ambition of each bionicist ... is to achieve an occasional breakthrough in such engineering goals as increasing reliability, sensitivity, strength, maneuverability, or speed, while reducing size, weight, or power requirements. On all counts, the bionicist can easily point to biological systems which overwhelmingly outstrip any man-made analog" (p. 129).

REFERENCES

Bandura, A. & Walters, R. H. *Adolescent aggression.* New York: Ronald Press, 1959.

Barker, R. G., Dembo, T., & Lewin, K. Frustration and regression: An experiment with young children. *University of Iowa Studies in Child Welfare,* 1941, **18**, 1–314.

Bateson, G. The frustration-aggression hypothesis and culture. *Psychological Review,* 1941, **48**, 350–355.

Berkowitz, L. *Roots of aggression.* New York: Atherton, 1969.

Blechman, E. A. The family contract game. *The Family Coordinator,* 1974, **23**, 269–281.

Branca, M. C., D'Augelli, J. F., & Evans, K. L. Development of a decision-making skills education program. Unpublished manuscript. University Park, Penn.: Pennsylvania State University, 1975.

Burglass, M. E., & Duffy, M. G. *Thresholds: Teachers manual.* Cambridge: Correctional Solutions Foundation, 1974.

Buss, A. H. *The psychology of aggression.* New York: Wiley, 1961.

Camp, B. N., & Bash, M. A. *Think aloud program group manual.* Unpublished manuscript. Boulder, Colo.: University of Colorado Medical Center, 1975.

Coche, E. & Flick, A. Problem solving training groups for hospitalized psychiatric patients. *Journal of Psychology,* 1975, **91,** 19–29.

Covington, M. V., Crutchfield, R. S., & Davies, L. B. *The productive thinking program.* Berkeley: Brazelton Printing Co., 1966.

Crawford, R. P. *How to get ideas.* Lincoln, Nebraska: University Associates, 1950.

Crawford, R. P. *Techniques of creative thinking.* New York: Hawthorn, 1954.

Crutchfield, R. S. & Covington, M. V. Programmed instruction and creativity. *Programmed Instruction,* 1964, **4,** 1–10.

Davis, G. A. *Psychology of problem solving.* New York: Basic Books, 1973.

Dollard, J., Miller, N. E., Doob, L. W., Mowrer, O. H., & Sears, R. R. *Frustration and aggression.* London: Kegan Paul, Trench, Trubner & Co., 1944.

D'Zurilla, T. J. & Goldfried, M. R. Problem solving and behavior modification. *Journal of Abnormal Psychology,* 1971, **78,** 107–126.

Elardo, P. T. & Caldwell, B. M. The effects of an experimental social development program on children in the middle childhood period. In preparation.

Feffer, M. H. & Jahelka, M. Implications of decentering concept for the structuring of projective content. *Journal of Consulting and Clinical Psychology,* 1968, **32,** 434–441.

Giebink, J. W., Stover, D. S., & Fahl, M. A. Teaching adaptive responses to frustration to emotionally disturbed boys. *Journal of Consulting and Clinical Psychology,* 1968, **32,** 336–368.

Goldfried, M. R. & Davison, G. C. *Clinical behavior therapy.* New York: Holt, Rinehart & Winston, 1976.

Goldner, B. B. *The strategy of creative thinking.* Englewood Cliffs, N. J.: Prentice-Hall, 1962.

Goldstein, A. P., Heller, K., & Sechrest, L. B. *Psychotherapy and the psychology of behavior change.* New York: Wiley, 1966.

Goldstein, A. P. & Simonson, N. Social psychological approaches to psychotherapy research. In A. E. Bergin & S. L. Garfield (Eds.), *Handbook of psychotherapy and behavior change.* New York: Wiley, 1971.

Gordon, W. J. *Synectics.* New York: Collier Books, 1961.

Gordon, W. J. *The metaphorical way.* Cambridge: Porpoise Books, 1971.

Holzworth, W. A. Effects of selective reinforcement therapy in a miniature situation in nursery school children. Unpublished masters thesis, University of Illinois, 1964.

Intagliata, J. Increasing the responsiveness of alcoholics to group therapy: An interpersonal problem solving approach. Unpublished doctoral dissertation, State University of New York at Buffalo, 1976.

Jahoda, M. The meaning of psychological health. *Social Casework,* 1953, **34,** 349–354.

Jahoda, M. *Current concepts of positive mental health.* New York: Basic Books, 1958.

Johnson, R. N. *Aggression in man and animals.* Philadelphia: Saunders, 1972.

Karlins, M. & Schroder, H. M. Discovery learning, creativity and the inductive teaching program. *Psychological Reports,* 1967, **20,** 867–876.

Larcen, S. W., Chinsky, J. M., Allen, G., Lochman, J., & Selinger, H. V. Training children in social problem solving strategies. Presented at Midwestern Psychological Association, Chicago, 1974.

Larcen, S. W., Spivack, G., & Shure, M. Problem-solving thinking and adjustment among dependent-neglected pre-adolescents. Presented at Eastern Psychological Association, Boston, 1972.

Maltzman, I. On the training of originality. *Psychological Review*, 1960, **67**, 229–242.

McClure, L. F. Social problem-solving training and assessment: An experimental investigation in an elementary school setting. Unpublished doctoral dissertation, University of Connecticut, 1975.

Mearns, H. *Creative power: The education of youth in the creative arts*. New York: Dover Publishers, 1958.

Montague, A. *Learning non-aggression*. New York: Oxford University Press, 1978.

Muuss, R. E. The relationship between "causal" orientation, anxiety, and insecurity in elementary school children. *Journal of Educational Psychology*, 1960, **51**, 122–129.

Myers, R. E. & Torrance, E. P. *Can you imagine?* Boston: Ginn & Co., 1965.

Osborn, A. F. *Applied imagination*. New York: Charles Scribner & Sons, 1953.

Papanek, V. J. Tree of life: Bionics. *Journal of Creative Behavior*, 1969, 3, 5–15.

Parnes, S. J. *Creative Behavior Guidebook*. New York: Scribner, 1967.

Parnes, S. J. *Creative Behavior Workbook*. New York: Scribner, 1967.

Pastore, N. The role of arbitrariness in the frustration aggression hypothesis. *Journal of Abnormal and Social Psychology*, 1952, **47**, 728–731.

Platt, J. J., Scura, W. C., & Hannon, J. R. Problem-solving thinking of youthful incarcerated heroin addicts. *Journal of Community Psychology*, 1973, **1**, 278–281.

Platt, J. J. & Spivack, G. Studies in problem-solving thinking of psychiatric patients. Presented at American Psychological Association, Montreal, 1973.

Platt, J. J. & Spivack, G. *Manual for the means-ends problem-solving procedure.* Philadelphia: Hahnemann Community Mental Health Center, 1975.

Platt, J. J., Spivack, G., Altman, N., Altman, D., & Peizer, S. B. Adolescent problem-solving thinking. *Journal of Consulting and Clinical Psychology*, 1974, **42**, 787–793.

Prince, G. M. *The practice of creativity*. New York: Collier Books, 1970.

Rickards, T. *Problem solving through creative analysis*. Essex: Power Press Ltd., 1974.

Ross, D. M. & Ross, S. A. Cognitive training for the EMR child: Situational problem solving and planning. *American Journal of Mental Deficiency*, 1973, **78**, 20–26.

Shure, M. B., Newman, S., & Silver, S. Problem-solving thinking among adjusted, impulsive and inhibited head start children. Presented at Eastern Psychological Association, Washington, 1973.

Shure, M. B. & Spivack, G. Problem-solving capacity, social class and adjustment among nursery school children. Presented at Eastern Psychological Association, Atlantic City, 1970.

Shure, M. B. & Spivack, G. Means-ends thinking, adjustment and social class among elementary school-aged children. *Journal of Consulting and Clinical Psychology*, 1972, **38**, 348–353.

Shure, M. B. & Spivack, G. *Problem-Solving Techniques in Childrearing*. San Francisco: Jossey-Bass, 1978.

Shure, M. B., Spivack G., & Powell, L. A problem solving intervention program for disadvantaged preschool children. Presented at Eastern Psychological Association, Boston, 1972.

Siegel, J. M. & Spivack, G. Problem-solving therapy. Research Report No. 23. Hahnemann Medical College, Philadelphia, 1973.

Spivack, G. & Levine, M. Self-regulation in acting-out and normal adolescents. Report M-4531, NIMH, Washington, D.C., 1973.

Spivack, G., Platt, J. J., & Shure, M. B. *The problem-solving approach to adjustment*. San Francisco: Jossey-Bass, 1976.

Spivack, G. & Shure, M. B. *Social adjustment of young children.* San Francisco: Jossey-Bass, 1974.

Spivack, G. & Shure, M. B. Maternal childrearing and the interpersonal cognitive problem-solving ability of four-year-olds. Presented at Society for Research in Child Development, Denver, 1975.

Stein, M. I. *Stimulating creativity.* New York: Academic Press, 1974.

Stone, G. L., Hinds, W. C., & Schmidt, G. W. Teaching mental health behaviors to elementary school children. *Professional Psychology,* 1975, **6**, 36–40.

Suchman, J. R. Inquiry training: Building skills for autonomous discovery. *Merrill-Palmer Quarterly,* 1961, **7**, 147–170.

Suchotliff, L. Relation of formal thought disorder to the communication deficit of schizophrenics. *Journal of Abnormal Psychology,* 1970, **76**, 250–257.

Synectics, Inc. *Making it strange—Teachers manual.* New York: Harper, 1968.

Taylor, J. W. *How to create new ideas.* Englewood Cliffs, N.J.: Prentice-Hall, 1961.

Torrance, E. P. *Rewarding creative behavior.* Englewood Cliffs, N.J.: Prentice-Hall, 1975.

Von Fange, E. K. *Professional creativity.* Englewood Cliffs, N.J.: Prentice-Hall, 1959.

Wagner, B. R., Breitmeyer, R. G., & Bottum, G. Administrative problem solving and the mental health professional. *Professional Psychology,* 1975, **6**, 55–60.

Weinstein, E. A. The development of interpersonal competence. In D. A. Goslin (Ed.), *Handbook of socialization theory and research.* Chicago: Rand McNally, 1969.

Whiting, C. S. *Creative thinking.* New York: Reinhold, 1958.

Williams, F. E. *A total creativity program for individualizing and humanizing the learning process.* Englewood Cliffs, N.J.: Educational Technology Publications, 1972.

Wright, M. E. Constructiveness of play as affected by group organization and frustration. *Character and Personality,* 1942, **11**, 40–49.

Wright, M. E. The influence of frustration upon the social relations of young children. *Character and Personality,* 1943, **12**, 111–122.

Zwicky, F. *Morphological astronomy.* Berlin: Springer-Verlag, 1957.

Zwicky, F. *Discovery, invention, research: Through the morphological approach.* New York: Macmillan, 1969.

Chapter 6
Moral Education
Eric M. Edelman and
Arnold P. Goldstein

Today, the way that our society develops the character of its young people is grossly inadequate. In recent decades (the last 70 to 100 years) there has been a steady decline in efforts to teach character in our public schools. This is a basic reason for the explosive increase in crime, violence, alcoholism, drug addiction and other disturbing manifestations of moral decay in our society. Thus, one of the most effective and economical ways to reduce these problems is to quickly improve the quantity and quality of moral instruction in all of our institutions particularly our public schools.

—The Case for Character Education

Rising rates of juvenile delinquency, child abuse, family violence, and other acts of overt aggression, as well as the magnitude of business, union, and political corruption in a post-Vietnam, post-Watergate society have shocked many into realizing the extent of the "moral crisis" in this country. By "moral crisis" we refer to a situation, existing at the individual, group, institutional, and/or societal level, characterized by one or more of the following: (1) use of clearly antisocial behaviors such as criminal activity or other forms of interpersonal aggression as means toward other ends, or as ends in themselves; (2) lack of clearly defined values or value confusion; (3) moral hypocrisy whereby one's behavior contradicts one's professed values; and (4) belief in certain "positive" or prosocial values, but not knowing how to apply those values in certain problematic situations or what to do when these values conflict with each other. The last several years have witnessed an increasing interest and involvement on the part of ordinary citizens in moral issues that affect both our daily interactions as well as matters of national and international importance. This new level of awareness has led to a reexamination of our traditional institutions regarding their role in America's ethical malaise. One result of this reexamination is widespread agreement that much of the responsibility for America's moral crisis lies in the failure of traditional institutions—family, religion, and the schools—to provide the necessary moral example, guidance, and teaching. Another result is that one institution in particular—the schools—have been given a kind of "mandate" to set things straight.

We believe that the schools should have a major responsibility in the moral education of the young. In this chapter, we propose that a renewed commitment to systematic moral education in the public schools should be made, from kindergarten through high school. Such a commitment would constitute a critical step in the learning of constructive alternatives to the varied forms of interpersonal aggression and destructiveness that characterize the "moral crisis" in this country. Nevertheless, we should note that the mandate which the public schools have received is both ambiguous and controversial. In this context, the following five questions have most commonly been raised:

1. Isn't moral education the responsibility of the family and church, rather than the schools?
2. Shouldn't the schools stick to the teaching of basic cognitive-intellectual skills, rather than getting into such peripheral and esoteric matters as the teaching of morality?
3. Wouldn't teaching morality or values in the schools be equivalent to indoctrination of our young, and isn't this impermissible in a democratic society?
4. Aren't all values relative? Isn't it just a matter of personal choice or preference? If so, what's the point of teaching values at all?
5. Just how do you teach morality or values in the schools?

These questions go to the heart of the complex problems involved in moral education in the schools; we therefore address each of them, in turn, in the sections that follow.

Isn't Moral Education the Responsibility of the Family rather than the Schools?

The Family. The critical importance of the family, especially the parents, in the moral development and education of children can hardly be overestimated. The renewed interest in moral education in this country has not ignored the fundamental importance of the family; witness the recent proliferation of parents' guides (Gordon, 1970; Peine & Howarth, 1975; Salk, 1975; Simon & Olds, 1976; Smith 1968). Psychoanalytic, social learning, and most other psychological viewpoints emphasize the importance of parental child-rearing practices on the moral development and behavior of offspring especially with respect to issues of warmth, control, and discipline (Maccoby, 1968; Saltzstein, 1976).

The contemporary American nuclear family as an institution, however, has also come upon hard times. Increasing divorce rates, broken homes, and parents spending less time with their children present considerable problems for the social and moral development of the young. We feel it necessary to add that parents are naturally as confused as anyone else as to how to teach morality and values to their offspring, and that the approaches to moral education covered in this chapter, although written with teachers in mind, will be relevant to parents as well.

The Schools. Throughout history, many societies have realized that parents needed help in the moral education of the young. In ancient Egypt, morals were an essential part of education as the Egyptians sought to teach their young the art of virtuous living. In ancient India, such moral instruction was given to boys belonging to one of the three upper castes. Before World War II, Japanese education had traditionally been more concerned with moral development than with the learning of basic cognitive skills and knowledge (Goble, 1973).

In a more contemporary vein, Bronfenbrenner (1962) reports that authorities in the Soviet Union view the primary objective of education as the development of "socialist morality" rather than the learning of subject matter. Benson and Engemen (1975) report that modern Western democracies such as Britain, France, West Germany, Scandinavia, Switzerland, Canada, and Australia all teach ethics in their schools.

In the United States, many people who believe that moral education belongs in the home or in churches have been under the mistaken impression that the First Amendment doctrine of separation of church and state has historically meant that American schools have not engaged in moral education. This has not been the case. In the early nineteenth century, moral education was a major reason for the existence of American private schools (Benson & Engeman, 1975). It is true that when education in America became public toward the mid-nineteenth century (when the framework for a free system of public education, publicly controlled and supported, was established), it had to reconcile moral instruction as an educational objective with the First Amendment separation of church and state. Nevertheless, in the early years of public education, highly influential educators from Horace Mann to William T. Harris argued forcefully that while public education had to be divorced from narrow denominational ties, moral education remained an important educational task (Benson & Engeman, 1975; Goble, 1973). In 1916, John Dewey, a seminal figure in American educational thinking, wrote that "it is a commonplace of educational theory that the establishing of character is a comprehensive aim of school instruction and discipline" (p. 359). The Character Education Movement of the 1920s, while it owed little allegiance to Dewey, held moral instruction to be a fundamental responsibility of public education (Chapman, 1977). Over the last 50–60 years, the National Education Association has issued periodic statements in support of moral education in the public schools (Goble, 1973).

Shouldn't the Schools Stick to the Teaching of Basic Cognitive-Intellectual Skills, rather than Getting into Such Peripheral and Esoteric Matters as the Teaching of Morality?

This question addresses fundamental issues concerning the nature of "morality," the aims of education in general, and the goals of "moral education" in particular. A full discussion of these issues could easily fill several volumes, and we can hardly do justice to them in this section. In the following discussion, we present a broad-based perspective on these issues and offer a functional definition of "morality" and "moral education."

1. Moral and Cognitive-Intellectual Development are Inseparable as Educational Goals. John Dewey, philosopher and educator, exerted a profound influence on American educational thinking in this century. Especially relevant to moral education are his two volumes, *Moral Principles in Education* (1909), and *Democracy and Education* (1916), although the interested reader is also referred to *The Child and the Curriculum* (1902), *Interest and Effort in Education* (1913), *The School of Society* (1915), and *Experience and Education* (1938). Dewey (1909) maintained that "moral" and "intellectual" education were part of the same process. He believed that the artificial separation of "moral" from "intellectual" education was a result of the erroneous notion that "morality" designated some special, transcendent area of life in which basic cognitive skills had no place.

For Dewey, then, morality involved people's ability to apply their intellectual skills to social situations—that is, their ability to think rationally and reason effectively in social situations (especially problematic or conflictual situations), and to behave in accordance with such reasoning. Thus, the aim of education was not to increase students' cognitive-intellectual skills per se, but rather to develop their capacities to think, reason, and act competently and effectively as social beings in a democratic society. These Deweyan notions concerning the nature of morality and the aims of education have left their mark on a number of contemporary writers in the field of moral education, (e.g., Beck, Hersh, & Sullivan, 1976; Kohlberg & Mayer, 1972; Raths, Harmin, & Simon, 1966).

2. Moral and Intellectual Development are Inseparable from Affective Development as Educational Goals Just as Dewey maintained that it is erroneous to separate "moral" from "intellectual" development, many writers in the field of moral education have maintained that it is equally erroneous to separate "moral" and "intellectual" from "affective-emotional" development (Glasser, 1969; Hall & Davis, 1975; McPhail, Ungoed-Thomas, & Chapman, 1975; Oliver & Bane, 1971; Raths, Harmin, & Simon, 1966; Wilson, 1973a & b). The premise of the contemporary movement toward "affective" or "humanistic" education in the schools is that its central themes (positive self-concept, sense of identity, self-awareness, empathy, caring, loving) are both important as educational goals in themselves, and necessary for the success of cognitive learning and social-moral development (Chase, 1975; Miller, 1976; Ringness, 1975).

For the proponents of "affective education," morality involves not only people's ability to think rationally and reasonably in problematic social situations, but also their abilities to experience constructive feelings vis-à-vis themselves and others in these situations, and to act in constructive ways as social beings on the basis of such feelings. Thus, from this perspective, one of the major aims of education in general, and the defining goal of moral education in particular, is to develop these abilities in the young.

3. The Nature of Morality. The thinking of Dewey and of the various writers in affective and moral education mentioned in the preceding two sections converge on the view that morality, far from reflecting peripheral or esoteric matters, involves issues of fundamental importance in a person's day-to-day thinking, feeling, and conduct as an individual and social being who must somehow create meaning and purpose in life while living cooperatively and constructively with other social beings. This broad perspective on morality has led to widespread criticism of simplistic definitions of morality as "conscience," "self-control," "altruism," "social conditioning," and other such reductive terms. Yet with the rejection of simplistic notions of morality, there still remains the monumental task of providing a clear yet comprehensive definition of morality, a task with which philosophers, educators, and thinkers of all persuasions have struggled for centuries.

4. John Wilson's *moral components.* John Wilson, director of the Far-mington Trust Research Unit in Oxford, England from 1965 to 1973, developed one of the first significant contemporary approaches to moral education in the west (Wilson, 1971, 1972, 1973a, 1973b; Wilson, Wil-liams, & Sugarman, 1968). For Wilson, a clear and precise definition of morality was a prerequisite for a program in moral education. While his approach is somewhat vague with respect to concrete methods and applications in the classroom, his thoughtful philosophical analysis of the nature of morality has provided one of the most incisive yet comprehensive definitions of morality we have found. For Wilson, morality essentially involves the following components (Wilson, 1972, 1973a, 1973b):

A. An attitude of concern and consideration for other people as equals, of giving the same weight to the wishes and needs of other people as to one's own. This includes a belief in the value of "justice"— respecting the equal rights of others, and the value of "benevolence"— making others' interests part of one's own. The process of arriving at such values involves: (1) cognitive aspects—having the concept of a "person," understanding that "human beings" are similar in impor-tant ways, (2) affective aspects—feelings of respect and considera-tion for others as "human beings," and (3) behavioral aspects—help-ing others, treating others as equals on the basis of such feelings and understanding.

B. An ability to be aware of feelings in oneself and other people. This ability also involves both (1) cognitive aspects—having the concept of an "emotion," identifying and labeling emotions in oneself and others, as well as (2) affective aspects—emotional sensitivity to one's own and others' feelings.

C. Knowledge of "hard facts" relevant to moral decisions. This involves the learning of a basic fund of knowledge necessary for making moral decisions (e.g., laws, social norms, and conventional expectations of society and relevant subgroups within society: basic facts concerning physical health, safety, and well-being of people generally).

D. Bringing the above to bear on the actual decision-making pro-cess in particular "moral" situations, i.e., problematic situations in which one's own and others' interests are at stake, so as to arrive at a rational, "moral" decision about what one ought to do in such situations.

E. Bringing the above to bear on one's actual conduct in particular "moral" situations, so as to translate one's "moral" decisions into action.

These "moral components" largely involve specific skills, attitudes, and abilities that are necessary for "being reasonable in morality," that is, for making reasonable moral decisions and acting on them in problematic interpersonal situations. The goal of moral education then, according to Wilson, is to teach and develop these skills and abilities.

5. A Functional Definition of Morality and Moral Education. In line with Wilson's analysis of the skills necessary for "being reasonable in morality," as well as the thinking of Dewey and many affective and moral educators on the inseparability of cognitive, affective, and moral development as educational goals, we offer the following broad-based, functional definition of morality and moral education: *Morality involves those skills, values, and abilities that comprise (1) thinking or reasoning (problem solving, decision making) in a rational way, while (2) showing an awareness of, and consideration or caring for the needs, interests, and feelings of others as well as oneself, and (3) behaving constructively, i.e., in ways that benefit both self and others, in the problematic or conflictual social-interpersonal situations which one encounters in one's daily interactions with other people. Morality, then, involves cognitive (thinking), affective (feeling), and behavioral (doing) aspects which are necessarily interrelated. It follows that the goal of moral education is to teach and develop, or facilitate the development of, the above skills, values, and abilities that define morality. The aim of moral education, then, is development in the cognitive, affective, and behavioral aspects of morality.*

In this way we can see that moral education has some relationship to social skills training and problem-solving training discussed in the previous two chapters. For example, some of the social-interpersonal skills taught in Structured Learning Therapy (Chapter 4), such as responding to the feelings of others, identifying and labeling one's own emotions, determining responsibility, negotiation, helping others, and assertiveness, are relevant to a program in moral education. Other skills taught in the Interpersonal Cognitive Problem Solving program (Chapter 5), such as alternate-solution thinking, consequential thinking, interpersonal sensitivity, and perspective taking, are also relevant. Nevertheless, while we recognize some overlap, we emphasize that by defining moral education as development in the cognitive, affective, and behavioral aspects of morality, we are delimiting an educational domain which is conceptually and functionally distinct from social skills training and problem-solving training. Thus, moral education constitutes another important arena with respect to the learning of constructive alternatives to interpersonal aggression.

Wouldn't Teaching Morality or Values in the Schools be Equivalent to Indoctrination of our Young, and Isn't This Impermissible in a Democratic Society?

There is no more controversial question concerning the school's involvement in moral education than the issue of indoctrination. There is the fear, shared by parents, teachers, and administrators alike, that if schools engage in systematic moral education they will inevitably be involved in indoctrinating the young. We would suggest that this is not necessarily the case, and that such a fear reflects a misunderstanding of the concept of indoctrination.

Indoctrination refers to the teaching of certain values, attitudes, or beliefs *without due regard to thoughtful reflection and direct, open inquiry and discussion concerning their reasonableness and worth in light of other, alternative values or beliefs.* Many thoughtful writers on the subject, then, do not consider the school's teaching of certain values per se as indoctrination. Furthermore, these writers maintain, as we do, that it is both inevitable and desirable that the public schools, as social and socializing institutions, serve at least some value-transmitting functions (Beck, Hersh, & Sullivan, 1976; Benson & Engeman, 1975; Forcinelli & Engeman, 1977; Goble, 1973; Hersh & Mutterer, 1975; Ringness, 1975; Rokeach, 1975). The question of whether or not the schools should engage in the teaching of certain values is a pseudo-question; it is impossible for them not to. More important questions are, how do the schools teach values, and what values would we want the schools to teach in a democratic society?

Schools may teach values (1) overtly, through subject matter contained in curricula and textbooks, and (2) covertly, through various arrangements, rules, and regulations that define the process of *how* one learns in the classroom. On an overt level schools in a democratic society typically seek to promote certain values. For example, a school may teach values such as "democracy," "freedom of speech," "pluralism," and "respect for differences in values," in social studies class; "creativity" and "freedom of expression" in fine arts class; and "critical thinking" and "perspective taking" in English literature. A class in moral education might teach these and other values. Our own definition of moral education would involve the teaching of such values as "rational thinking," "consideration for others," "self-awareness," and "behaving in accordance with one's values." The point we wish to make here is that it is both necessary and desirable that schools in a democratic society help teach some of these values. The manner in which such values are taught will determine whether we are also engaging in indoctrination, which is unwarrantable. We are indoctrinating when we teach such values in a way that limits thoughtful reflection, direct inquiry, and open discussion as to their reasonableness and worth in light of existing alternative values.

Schools also teach values covertly, through the various arrangements that define *how* one learns in school. We are referring to the indirect and implicit value transmission which accompanies the so-called "hidden curriculum" of classroom behavior management, automatized rules and regulations, evaluation and grading procedures, seating arrangements, and teacher-student interactions and role relationships. The "hidden curriculum," with its implicit value-transmitting function, has been rightfully criticized by many writers (Beck, Hersh, & Sullivan, 1976; Fenton, 1975; Hersh & Mutterer, 1975; Kohlberg, 1970a; Ringness, 1975). Values taught covertly and indirectly through the "hidden curriculum" constitute, by definition, a subtle form of indoctrination. Furthermore, a careful examination of the values often indoctrinated through the "hidden curriculum" of many classrooms reveals that some of these values, such as *unquestioning* conformity to rules and obedience to authority, are antithethical to other values consciously desired and taught in a democratic society. The best antidote to such indoctrination, then, is to make the implicit values of the hidden curriculum explicit and to subject them to direct scrutiny and reasoned debate regarding their desirability.

Aren't All Values Relative? Isn't it Just a Matter of Personal Choice or Preference? If so, What's the Point of Teaching Values at All?

Values are attitudes or beliefs concerning what is good and desirable, what has worth. Advocates of "value relativity" maintain that all values are subjective and develop out of one's personal experience and background; that is, values are relative to each culture as well as each person within a culture. There are no valid grounds therefore for proposing that some values are "better" than others, and there are no objective criteria for judging behavior as right or wrong. The implications of the "value relativity" position for moral education is that while educators can teach students a *process* of valuing—i.e., how to develop their own personal value systems—there is no justifiable basis for teaching certain values over others. The authors of "Values Clarification" (Raths, Harmin, & Simon, 1966), a major contemporary approach to moral education in this country, have made "value relativity" one of their guiding principles. While Raths et al. (1966) believe that value relativity is the only justifiable position to take vis-à-vis moral education in a democratic and pluralistic culture, they concede that it is possible for a student to learn the process of valuing taught in their approach and then decide that he values intolerance or thievery.

Since we have already stated our belief that it is necessary and desirable for schools in a democratic society to teach certain values in a nonindoctrinative way, it will come as no surprise that we find "value relativity" an untenable position. We maintain that if a program in moral education is to have implications for social behavior, as it should, it is simply unacceptable that a student can successfully graduate from such a program having decided that he or she personally values violence or prejudice or delinquency. "Value relativity" is itself a value position, and it is logically impossible for it to remain value-neutral with respect to moral education. Rokeach (1975), for example, argues that "Values Clarification" implicitly teaches such nonrelative values as "broad-mindedness is better than narrowmindedness." Furthermore, Kohlberg (1972a, 1975) maintains that "value relativity" is a scientifically unsound value position in light of what he claims is substantial empirical support for the existence of culturally universal values differently conceived according to a universal sequence of stages of moral judgment. We believe that the value position embodied in "value relativity" has destructive implications for moral education, moral behavior, and ultimately, individual and social well-being.

Just How Do You Teach Morality or Values in the Schools?

The rest of this chapter represents an attempt to answer this complex question by presenting an in-depth examination of three important yet fundamentally different approaches to moral education: (1) Character Education, (2) Values Clarification, and (3) Kohlberg's Cognitive-Developmental approach. For each of these approaches we will provide a brief background and rationale, a discussion of theoretical principles, a detailed consideration of teaching methods with examples of classroom applications, and an evaluation and critique. The interested reader is referred to the following for additional approaches to moral education: Beck's Ultimate Life Goal approach (Beck, 1971; Beck, Hersh & Sullivan, 1976; Beck & Sullivan, 1976); McPhail's Learning to Care program (McPhail, Ungoed-Thomas, & Chapman, 1975); Newmann, Oliver, and Shaver's Public Issues program (Newmann and Oliver, 1970; Oliver and Shaver, 1966); Wilson's Moral Components approach (Wilson, 1971, 1972, 1973a, 1973b); Mosher and Sprinthall's Psychological Education (Mosher and Sprinthall, 1970, 1972); Glasser's Classroom Meeting approach (Glasser, 1969); and Weinstein and Fantini's Identity Education (Weinstein & Fantini, 1970).

CHARACTER EDUCATION

The Character Education Movement of the 1920s

Moral education was very much an institutionalized concern of the American public schools in the 1920s. Most of the approaches to moral instruction during this period comprised a major educational movement called Character Education. Although the goals and methods of these various approaches to Character Education were not entirely uniform, the common denominator of this movement was an emphasis on developing the "moral character" of the young. Moral character was typically defined in terms of certain personality traits, virtues, or values generally believed important to the welfare of the individual as well as of society. These desirable character traits included such values as honesty, altruism, self-control, patriotism, responsibility, friendliness, and moral courage. Unfortunately, character educators of this period were more explicit about theoretical aims than they were about concrete procedures for developing such traits in school children. Teaching methods relied heavily on discussion of the importance of such traits or values, and on exhortation to use these values as guides to virtuous conduct.

This period of character education culminated in the important research of Hartshorne, May and their coworkers, reported in their three-volume *Studies in the Nature of Character* (Hartshorne & May, 1928; Hartshorne, May & Maller, 1929; Hartshorne, May, & Shuttleworth, 1930).

Hartshorne et al. investigated the social behavior of thousands of children in various experimental situations, in and out of school, with respect to the character traits of honesty (defined as resistance to cheating and stealing), service (giving up objects for the welfare of others), and self-control (persistence in assigned tasks). Their results were nothing less than shattering to the character education movement of the 1920s. In their first volume (1928) on honesty, they explain that 8,150 public school and 2,715 private school children between the ages of 8 and 16 were given opportunities to lie, cheat, and steal in situations ranging from classroom work to party games to athletic contests. From the results, they concluded that (1) no one is honest or dishonest by nature, i.e., almost everyone cheats some of the time; (2) verbal promises to be honest and verbal formulations of the ideal of honesty do not in themselves lead to honest behavior; (3) honest or dishonest behavior is determined largely though not entirely by situational factors such as expediency, conditions of reinforcement and group approval, and example. Concerning the implications of these findings for character education as it was then practiced in the schools, Hartshorne and May (1928) concluded:

> The mere urging of honest behavior by teachers or the discussion of standards and ideals of honesty, no matter how much such general ideas may be "emotional", has no necessary relation to the control of conduct....
> This does not imply that the teaching of general ideas, standards and ideals is not desirable and necessary, but only that the prevailing ways of inculcating ideals probably do little good and may do some harm [p. 413].

In their second volume, Hartshorne, May, and Maller (1929) reported similar results regarding the importance of situational determinants of "service" (altruism) and "self-control," and spelled out similar implications for moral education. Taken together, all three volumes offered impressive documentation that the prevailing approaches to character education in the schools were not successful in producing cross-situational improvements in moral behavior. The authors maintained that moral behavior could be learned more effectively by students in the context of active experience and practice in concrete situations under appropriate reinforcing conditions.

Hartshorne and May's documentation of the ineffectiveness of character education as commonly taught in the schools dealt a blow to the character education movement as it was practiced in the 1920s from which it never recovered; character education as a formal, educational movement had largely disappeared by the mid-1930s.

Contemporary Character Education: Early Projects of the 1960s

Some 35–40 years after Hartshorne and May's work, character education is again alive and well in a new and revised form. More than any other current approach to moral education, contemporary character education programs have developed in response to widespread concern over disturbing increases in juvenile delinquency, crime, and corruption in America. The goals of the revised form of character education are similar to those of the 1920s—the teaching of values, character traits, and standards of ethical conduct that are considered important for constructive living in a democratic society. Indeed, character educators today lay some of the blame for the alarming increases in crime and delinquency on the public schools' abnegation of responsibility for teaching such traditional values as honesty, altruism, tolerance, justice, kindness, politeness, and convictions. Character educators maintain that the successful inculcation of such values in the schools, especially when accomplished in the formative years of elementary school, will lead to a reduction in the violence and aggression rampant in American society.

Although character educators today agree with the basic aims of the 1920s movement, they recognize the importance of developing more explicit, systematic, and effective methods for teaching such values or virtues. The 1960s witnessed a few beginning pilot programs developed by various individuals and organizations interested in bringing character education back into the public schools. American Viewpoint, Inc., an organization concerned with preventing crime and delinquency, developed a teacher's manual for teaching citizenship values in the elementary grades called "The Good American Program" (Mayer, 1964). This program was based on the premise that direct teaching of specific values at the appropriate time in the development of elementary school children was necessary in order for such values to take hold and influence behavior. The program combined opportunities for experience and practice along with reading and discussion (without "moralizing") in the context of social studies class. The "Good American Program" was tried in elementary schools in Ossining, New York, and Goble (1973) reports impressionistic evidence that the program produced positive results in student behavior, although it was discontinued by subsequent school administrators who were unfamiliar with the program.

In Colton, California, a high school teacher, Virginia Trevitt, out of concern about the rise in juvenile delinquency, developed a program called "As I Am, So Is My Nation," (Trevitt, 1964). Her aim was to help students view both their education and personal behavior as relevant to needs and practices of American society, and to develop in students the moral qualities necessary for constructive contributions to society. Her methods included the study of the ideals of the founding fathers, discussion of moral concepts, and testing these concepts in daily living. Trevitt taught her course to incoming students at Colton High School for several years. She reported striking changes in student behavior in and out of school, ranging from decreases in classroom cheating to return of stolen articles to students becoming more responsive and cooperative at home.

Russell Hill (1965) developed Freedom's Code, a statement of character traits or ideals proposed by the author as comprising (1) the historic American standards of ethical conduct, and citizen responsibility, as well as (2) the standards of virtuous conduct that are necessary for the maintenance of all free and democratic societies. These traits include honesty, generosity, justice, kindness, helping others in need, courage, tolerance, and understanding and fulfilling citizenship obligations.

Bain and Clark (1966) developed a teacher's handbook for developing the character traits of Freedom's Code in elementary school children.

This handbook contains various instructional strategies as well as suggested resource materials such as films, records, and books. Teaching methods include discussion of the general meaning as well as specific examples of each trait, classroom debates, role play, study of historical and contemporary American figures as exemplars of particular traits, written exercises, art and music projects, reinforcement of desired behavior, and various assignments for practicing these values in real-life situations, in and out of school. Unfortunately, there is an absense of empirical research regarding the effectiveness of Bain and Clark's methods.

The Character Education Curriculum

Presently, the most comprehensive and sophisticated approach to character education in the public schools is the Character Education Curriculum (CEC) developed by the American Institute for Character Education (AICE) in San Antonio, Texas. The AICE is a nonprofit organization whose purpose is to help teachers develop the moral character of the young, especially elementary school children. The AICE has been involved in the development and field testing (begun in 1970 throughout the country) of instructional materials and procedures for a comprehensive program of character education in the elementary schools. To date, the result of these efforts has been the development of the Character Education Curriculum (CEC).

Rationale. The rationale of the CEC is that children who are taught to consider the consequences of their behavior in terms of certain traditional values (such as those presented in Freedom's Code) will choose to behave in ways beneficial to themselves and society. Rather that simply indoctrinating students with certain standards of conduct, the CEC seeks to teach particular values in such a way that the student comes to understand their reasonableness and worth as a basis for decision making in interpersonal situations.

Materials. The CEC materials for kindergarten through fifth grade are briefly described as follows:

1. *The Kindergarten Kit* contains a series of teaching units, in English and Spanish, divided into two semesters—"The Happy Life Series" (first semester) and "You and Me" (second semester). "The Happy Life Series" includes six books of animal stories, with accompanying filmstrips and songs, containing lessons on honesty, generosity, helpfulness, kindness, and fairness. "You and Me" contains lessons designed to

help children transfer the values developed in "The Happy Life Series" to their interactions with family members and others in their community.

2. *CEC Kits for Grades 1 through 5.* A separate CEC kit for each grade level contains a teacher's guide, posters, activity sheets, a teacher's handbook, and evaluation instruments. The teacher's guide for each grade level details a sequence of step-by-step lessons, with explicit objectives, divided into two areas—"Living With Me and Others," and "Our Rights and Responsibilities." "Living With Me and Others" involves lessons on such individual virtues as honesty, truthfulness, kindness, helpfulness, generosity, politeness, justice, tolerance, courage, convictions, honor, and constructive use of time and talents. "Our Rights and Responsibilities" contains lessons on values considered important to effective citizenship in American society such as freedom of speech, freedom of choice, citizenship, the right to be an individual, the right to equal opportunity, and economic security. The teacher's guide for each grade level also contains a listing of relevant books, films, and other audiovisual materials. In addition, there are large posters to reinforce the lessons in the teacher's guide, activity sheets to be used with the children during the lessons, a teacher's handbook with suggestions for implementing the lessons and evaluation forms to be used by the teacher to assess the children's level of understanding of the values taught (these forms can be used as pre- and posttest instruments to evaluate the effectiveness of the lessons).

Teaching Methods. The CEC lessons make use of a wide variety of methods such as class discussion, role playing, written exercises, art projects and multimedia presentations, games and activities and projects offering opportunities to experience and practice the value being taught in a variety of group situations. For example, different lessons include such activities as role-playing good manners in particular situations, discussing behaviors that show tolerance, drawing pictures of honest and dishonest behavior, and interviewing classmates about their convictions.

Regarding the implementation of the CEC, the AICE recommends the following (Mulkey, 1977a):

1. CEC lessons should be scheduled on a regular basis: daily for 15–20 minutes with the lower primary grades, two to three times a week for 30–50 minutes with the upper primary grades.

2. CEC lessons can be taught as a separate subject, or can be integrated with regular school subjects, preferably in the areas of social studies or language arts.

3. A child's work resulting from CEC lessons should not be graded or

marked for handwriting, grammar, etc., as such evaluation would inhibit the freedom of expression necessary for effective character education.

4. The way a teacher conducts class discussions is critical to the success of CEC lessons. The teacher should not lecture, moralize, or scrutinize. The teacher's role is that of a "facilitator" whose goal is to help the children in the class learn to think for themselves. The teacher should use discussion as a means for improving children's problem-solving and decision-making skills.

5. Role playing is an especially important instructional method and should be used as often as possible. Discussion is necessary immediately after role playing in order to provide feedback to the participants.

The AICE recognizes the need for teacher preparation in implementing the CEC and has developed a program for in-service training (Mulkey, 1977b). The goals of this experimentally based training program, which can be conducted over a one-and-a-half- to three-day period are to help teachers (1) understand the importance of improving children's self-concept before attempting to aid their character development, (2) recognize the importance of values and value conflicts in themselves and their students, (3) become acquainted with techniques for assisting students in identifying and clarifying their values, (4) learn how to conduct group discussions in a manner that will facilitate the goals of the CEC, (5) understand the purposes and procedures involved in role playing, and (6) become acquainted with the CEC materials (kits) relevant to their grade levels and begin planning the implementation of these materials in their classrooms.

Examples of CEC Lessons

1. *Teaching Kindness, Helpfulness, Generosity, and Politeness in the First Grade.* The following is the third lesson in a sequence of three lessons, taken from the teacher's guide for the first grade (Anon., 1974a). The explicit objective of this sequence is for students to be able to describe their feelings when someone is nice to them.

Step I.   Introduce a new game to the children called "Tell Me." Explain that it is played in this way:

   1. A particular topic or idea is chosen for a lesson.
   2. In relation to the topic, the children tell about something that really happened to them or someone they know. (No names shall be used.)
   3. When the person telling the story gets to the end, instead of

finishing it, he or she says to the group, "How would you feel? Tell Me!"

4. Class members make up different endings and share their feelings as if they were the characters themselves.

Step II.   Explain that today the topics and stories will be about one of the following ideas: Politeness, helpfulness, generosity, or kindness. List these words on a chalkboard.

Step III. Go over the rules in Step I again.

Step IV. Give the following examples as you, the teacher, start off by telling the first two or three stories:

1. It's your birthday today. Your friends brought you a present, and you really liked it. How would you feel? Tell Me!

2. You're playing out on the playground. You fall down and really scare yourself. You want to cry, but some of the other children come to see what they can do for you. How would you feel? Tell Me!

3. You have been at home sick for several days and now that you're back in school you can't run outside with the other children. You go over to sit down by yourself. In a little while, two or three classmates come over and sit down with you and begin to talk to you. How would you feel? Tell Me!

Step V.   Seek volunteers to relate stories from their own experience when someone showed them kindness, politeness, helpfulness, or generosity.

Step VI. After each story ask these questions:

1. Which of the four qualities was shown? Check on the board.
2. How was it shown?
3. Why did you feel the way you did?

2. *Teaching Tolerance in the Fifth Grade.*   The following lesson is taken from the teacher's guide for the fifth grade (Anon., 1974a). The objective is for students to be able to describe ways in which people can work to become more tolerant.

Step I.   Have each student select from magazines two pictures—one which she or he thinks is ugly and the other, beautiful. Have the class write their descriptions (ugly or beautiful) on the back of the pictures and pin them on the bulletin board.

Step II. Number each picture.

Step III. Ask each student to select five pictures from those displayed on the bulletin board which she or he thinks are ugly and five, beautiful. Have them write their choices on paper.

Step IV. Allow two or three students at a time to check to see how the person who put the picture up considered it.

Step V. Tally the marks for each picture on the chalkboard using the following form:

	Picture	Ugly	Beautiful
1.			
2.			
3. . . .			

Step VI. Discuss with the class whether or not they can accept what other people think is beautiful and what they think is ugly. If they can, why? If they can not, why not? What are the consequences of each?

Evaluation and Critique

Thousands of teachers have used the CEC materials in their classrooms. Questionnaire surveys conducted by the AICE reveal widespread approval by teachers and favorable student interest and involvement. The AICE has received numerous reports and testimonials from various teachers and educators claiming that use of the CEC has led to a reduction in violence, vandalism, cheating, and stealing in the schools. There is, however, an absence of carefully controlled empirical research examining the effectiveness of the CEC. This void is also a major problem with other character education programs discussed in this section. Beyond the CEC in particular, a number of criticisms have been leveled against the character education approach in general. Objections have been raised on empirical, philosophical, ethical, and practical grounds.

The empirical argument is that character traits such as honesty are merely labels used by other people to describe or evaluate a person's behavior in certain situations, rather than a reflection of any consistent dispositions or internal structures in the person who is labeled. This is the "situationist" argument against the existence of any internalized, cross-situational personality traits, moral or otherwise. Hartshorne and May's research 40 years ago provided a great impetus to the situationist movement in psychology when the authors concluded that people do not possess general traits of honesty of dishonesty, but rather, learn to behave "honestly" in some situations and "dishonestly" in others as a function of differentially reinforced experiences in these situations.

The "trait" versus "situationist" controversy has been a source of great debate in the field of psychology for many years, with both sides offering empirical support for their positions. While a fuller exposition of this controversy is beyond the scope of this section, we can say that current thinking and research in this area is beginning to converge on a middle ground or "interactionist" position (Ekehammar, 1974; Endler & Magnusson, 1976; Mischel, 1973). Briefly stated, this position maintains that a person's internal dispositions interact with his or her learning experiences in particular situations to determine his or her behavior in these situations. For example, Burton (1976) reanalyzed the original intercorrelations of the Hartshorne and May (1928) data with multivariate methods. He concluded from this as well as other studies that a "small but consistently manifested factor" (Burton, 1976, p. 176) that differentiates individuals interacts with their differential learning experiences in specific situations to determine how honest or dishonest they are in these situations. The implications of the "interactionist" position for character education is that, while a person could develop a character "trait" of some generality such as "honesty," he could not learn by being taught either the meaning of "honesty" per se or how to behave honestly in general. He would have to be taught the meaning of honest behavior in certain situations and then to generalize this behavior to a class of situations perceived as similar.

The philosophical objection to CEC is related to the empirical argument discussed above; it is that character traits are vague constructions open to differing interpretations as to their meaning, depending on one's perspective. Kohlberg and Turiel (1971) observe:

What is one man's integrity is another man's stubborness; what is one man's honesty in expressing his true feelings is another man's insensitivity to the feelings of others. . . . Those sympathetic with a social movement, such as that of student protesters, view their behavior as reflecting the virtues of altruism, idealism, awareness, and courage. Those in opposition to the movement regard the same behavior as reflecting the vices of irresponsibility and disrespect for law and order [p. 431].

Even if one were to arrive at clear definitions of different character traits through consensual agreement regarding their behavioral referents, there is the further objection that it is simply not plausible to assume that in a pluralistic and democratic culture there exists or can ever exist a societal consensus regarding which traits are "desirable" and should be taught. We would agree that certain traits, such as some of the "Boy Scout virtues" (reverence, loyalty, cleanliness, bravery), are subject to much divergence of opinion concerning their moral worth. We wonder, however, if there are not some traits or values that can be both operationally defined and subject to general societal agreement on their desirability. "Thinking rationally" (e.g., taking alternatives into consideration and weighing the consequences of alternatives) "self-awareness" (e.g., an ability to identify and label one's feelings), "getting along with others" (e.g., empathy and considering the needs of others) are just three that come to mind.

Perhaps the most serious criticism of character education is an ethical criticism—namely that the teaching of certain values, such as those taught in the CEC, constitutes indoctrination. We have explicated our own position that the teaching of certain values in the schools is desirable and does not necessarily constitute indoctrination; we are certain that the blanket condemnation of character education programs as indoctrination is unfair and misguided. Whether or not character education or any other approach to moral education involves in-doctrination depends on the *manner* in which certain values are taught. For example, if CEC lessons could be taught in a nonindoctrinative way, and subsequent empirical research should provide evidence that they indeed lead to reductions in violence and vandalism in the schools, then we would maintain that it would be unethical not to teach them.

Finally, an objection has been raised that the teaching of individual values or virtues, as in the CEC, does not realistically prepare the student to deal effectively with the difficult choices and decisions he or she must make in many problematic situations that involve a conflict of values. How does a student who has been taught the desirability of honesty, tolerance, and kindness, for example, decide what to do in a situation where these 3 values might be in conflict? How does this student solve the dilemma presented by a particular situation where being honest would involve being unkind or intolerant? The argument here is that character education programs do not give sufficient attention to the explicit teaching of those cognitive processes involved in rational problem solving and decision making. We believe this objection has some merit. In terms of our functional definition of morality and moral education, we would judge the character education approach to be somewhat lacking with respect to the teaching and development of cognitive skills necessary for effective problem solving and decision making in value-conflict situations. In this regard we wonder whether character education might be more appropriate for younger than for older children. We see the nonindoctrinative teaching of individual values such as kindness, honesty, helpfulness, justice, or tolerance as beneficial to children in the early primary grades. Older children, however, from the upper primary grades through high school, are more likely to understand the inherent conflict among individual values in many situations, and are likely to be faced with increasingly complex choices and decisions in such conflictual situations. Other approaches with a greater emphasis on cognitive processes and development might be more appropriate for these children.

VALUES CLARIFICATION

Rationale

In 1966, Raths, Harmin, and Simon wrote a book, *Values and Teaching*, which was to exert a profound influence on values education in the schools. In it, the authors strongly oppose any program in moral education the objective of which is the direct teaching of certain "desirable" values or which otherwise offers learning experiences that facilitate the understanding and acceptance of particular values. In raising ethical and practical objections to such programs similar to those discussed in the preceding section, Raths et al. delineated a set of assumptions and guiding principles for a radically different approach to moral education.

1. *Values are relative to subgroups within societies, and to individuals within subgroups.* It is impossible for pluralistic society such as ours to reach a general consensus as to which "desirable" values ought to be taught. The young of today find themselves increasingly exposed to a bewildering array of divergent values from parents, peers, television, newspapers, teachers, and other sources. Those values considered "desirable" by one source may be "undesirable" to another. There are no universally "correct" values to guide the young in their daily living; they have to learn to develop their own values.

2. *Values are relative to time, place, and circumstances in a rapidly changing world.* In a rapidly changing technological society, the values that one finds useful and satisfying one year may become obsolete and unsatisfying the next. Desirable values in one situation may not be desirable in another. The young have to learn thoughtfully to examine, evaluate, and revise their values as necessary in light of changed circumstances.

3. *Values often conflict with one another.* The young of today are faced with increasingly complex value choices in situations where there

are no simple answers and where values may conflict. They must learn to choose what they value in given situations among competing alternatives.

4. *Values are a matter of personal discovery and choice.* A person's values develop—indeed, they are discovered—from personal experience and must be freely chosen by the person if they are to become effective guides for living. A teacher cannot teach certain values to a student directly. The teacher can, however, help the student discover and develop his or her own values.

5. *The young need help in developing and clarifying their own values.* Values are those beliefs, attitudes, and goals that one especially cherishes and that give meaning, direction, and purpose to one's life. They are guideposts in one's continued efforts to make sense of and adapt to one's world in a constructive and satisfying way. It is becoming increasingly difficult for the young in our society, bombarded as they are by contradictory and constantly changing values from a multitude of sources, to develop a clear and coherent set of values of their own. Many young people today suffer from a common malady—value confusion or lack of values.

6. *Value confusion in the young leads to certain kinds of behavioral problems.* Value confusion can lead to one or more of the following destructive behavior patterns:

a. *apathy*—youths who are listless and uninterested in things.
b. *flightiness*—youths who are interested in many things for brief periods of time, but who never get deeply involved in anything.
c. *great uncertainty*—youths who are perpetually unable to make up their minds about the many life choices before them.
d. *great inconsistency*—youths who express contradictory values or whose behavior is contradictory to stated values.
e. *drifting*—youths who are planless and aimless in life, unenthusiastically drifting from one thing to another.
f. *overconformity*—youths who, not knowing what they want to do with their lives, conform to what they see as the dominant values and life styles of important others.
g. *overdissension*—youths who are chronic and irrational dissenters, as if, lacking their own value systems, they get their identity by opposing others.
h. *role playing*—youths who "cover their lack of clarity about what life is for by posturing in some role or other that is no more real for them than a made-up cardboard image" (Raths et al., 1966, p. 6).

7. *The schools have a responsibility to help the young clarify and*

develop their own values. The consequences of rampant value confusion in the young are too deleterious for individual and societal well-being for the schools to adopt a laissez-faire position toward value education. Young people need and want help in developing, clarifying, and applying their values and the schools have a responsibility to provide this help.

The Valuing Process

With these guiding principles in mind, Raths et al. (1966) developed what has become perhaps the most widely used approach to moral education in the schools, Values Clarification. The authors maintained that although students could not be taught certain values, they certainly could learn a *process of valuing*, how to develop and to clarify their own values. Raths et al. defined this process of valuing as consisting of seven subprocesses:

1. *Choosing freely.* If [a value] is in fact to guide one's life ... it must be a result of free choice. If there is coercion, the [value] is not likely to stay with one long, especially when out of range of the source of that coercion.
2. *Choosing from among alternatives.* . . . there can be no [free] choice if there are no alternatives from which to choose.
3. *Choosing after thoughtful consideration of the consequences of each alternative.* . . . For [a value] to intelligently and meaningfully guide one's life, it must emerge from a weighing and an understanding. Only when the consequences of each of the alternatives are clearly understood can one make intelligent choices. There is an important cognitive factor here. A value can emerge only with thoughtful consideration of the range of the alternatives and consequences in a choice.
4. *Prizing and cherishing.* When we value something, it has a positive tone. We prize it, cherish it, esteem it, respect it, hold it dear. We are happy with our values.
5. *Affirming.* When we have chosen [a value] freely, after consideration of the alternative, and when we are proud of our choice ... we are likely to affirm that choice when asked about it. We are willing to publicly affirm our values. . . .
6. *Acting upon choices.* When we have a value, it shows up in aspects of our living. . . . We budget time or energy for our values. . . . Nothing can be a value that does not, in fact, give direction to actual living. The person who talks about something but never does anything about it is dealing with something other than a value.
7. *Repeating.* Where something reaches the stage of a value, it is very likely to reappear on a number of occasions in the life of the person who holds it. It shows up in several different situations, at several different times. . . . Values tend to have a persistency, tend to make a pattern in a life [pp. 28–29].

To simplify, these seven subprocesses can be grouped into three categories of choosing, prizing, and acting; and, in turn, these three categories involve cognitive, affective, and behavioral components respectively:

Choosing (cognitive):
1. freely,
2. by generating alternatives, and
3. thoughtfully considering the consequences of each alternative.

Prizing (affective):
4. cherishing, feeling proud enough of one's chosen values,
5. to be willing to affirm or stand up for them publicly.

Acting (behavioral):
6. behaving in accordance with one's chosen values,
7. repeatedly, in one's pattern of living.

Thus, the goal of Values Clarification is to help students develop, clarify, and apply their own values by learning to use these seven subprocesses of valuing in their own lives.

To accomplish this, Raths, Simon, and their associates have provided teachers with a tremendous variety of suggested methods, materials, activities, and exercises that help students learn, practice, and apply the seven subprocesses of valuing. It is this provision of numerous, clear, and easy-to-implement classroom activities or value-clarifying exercises that has made values clarification such a popular and widely used approach. The creative teacher can choose from these many activities or develop his or her own, always with the goal of providing students with opportunities for practicing one or more of the seven subprocesses of valuing.

Teaching Methods: The Value Clarifying Response

Fundamental to the success of all the Values Clarification activities is a certain method of discussing value-related issues and problems with students. This method is the "value-clarifying response," and more than any other technique, it captures the spirit of the Values Clarification approach. Although originally designed as a way for the teacher to respond extemporaneously to value-related comments made by individual students in relatively informal situations (e.g., in the hallways between classes), it is critical for conducting value-clarifying classroom discussions in general.

The clarifying response is a way of responding to a student so as to raise questions in his or her mind, to encourage him or her to examine his or her beliefs and actions, and thus to stimulate him or her to clarify his values. The clarifying response avoids moralizing, sermonizing, advice giving, or evaluating. Proponents of values clarification are passionate in their insistence that the teacher avoid any and all traces of moralizing in his or her comments. With value issues, the teacher should avoid all "why" questions, which tend to make a student feel defensive or judged, "yes-or-no" questions which limit a student's choices, and leading questions to which the teacher already has a predetermined "correct" answer in mind; there are no "correct" answers or values in values clarification. The teacher's comments must place the responsibility on the student to think about his or her own behavior and ideas and decide for him or herself what it is that he or she values. The teacher must genuinely be ready to accept any value decisions that the student makes as a result of their discussions, including the student's choice *not* to think about or clarify his or her values. It should be noted that Raths et al. believe there is nothing wrong with the teacher eventually sharing his or her own values on an issue, as long as he or she lets the student think about it for him or herself first, and is careful to present his or her opinion as just another alternative that the student might want to consider.

1. Examples of Value-Clarifying Responses. Raths et al. (1966) list numerous kinds of clarifying responses that teachers might use. Some of these responses are oriented toward promoting one or more of the seven valuing components, others encourage reflection more generally. The following are some examples of clarifying responses suggested for stimulating each of the seven valuing components or subprocesses:

a. *Choosing freely.*
 1. Where do you suppose you first got that idea?
 2. Are you the only one in your crowd who feels this way?
 3. What do your parents want you to do?
b. *Prizing and cherishing.*
 1. Are you glad you feel that way?
 2. Should everyone do it your way?
 3. In what way would life be different without it?
c. *Acting upon choices.*
 1. I hear what you are for; Now is there anything you can do about it? Can I help?
 2. Are you willing to put some of your money behind this idea?

2. Examples of Value-Clarifying Exchanges. The following examples of brief impromptu value-clarifying exchanges in action are taken from Raths et al. (1966):

a. *Teacher:* You say, Glenn, that you are a liberal in political matters?
  Glenn: Yes I am.

Teacher: Where did your ideas come from?
Glenn: Well, my parents I guess, mostly.
Teacher: Are you familiar with other positions?
Glenn: Well, sort of.
Teacher: I see, Glenn. Now class, getting back to the homework for today . . . (returning to the general lesson). (Pp. 54–55.)

b. *Clara*: Some day I'd like to join the Peace Corps.
   Teacher: What are some good things about that, Clara?
   Clara: Oh, the chance to be of service excites me and going to faraway places does too.
   Teacher: Of those two, which would you put in first place?
   Clara: I guess the faraway places part.
   Teacher: Are you glad that that one is first?
   Clara: No, I guess people would respect me more if the service part was first. (P. 75.)

In this example, the authors observe that at this point in the dialogue the teacher has several alternatives which he or she could explore with Clara: (1) how important is it for Clara to feel respected; (2) what services has she performed and might she perform right now; (3) what other possibilities does she have for getting to faraway places; or (4) the teacher might sense that Clara was beginning to feel uncomfortable and decide to postpone any further discussion until a later time.

Teaching Methods: Value Clarifying Classroom Strategies

Raths, Simon, and colleagues have suggested that teachers make use of a broad array of methods, including numerous types of class and small-group discussions, written exercises, homework assignments, role playing, and interviewing, as well as other activities in and out of class. In *Values Clarification: A Handbook of Practical Strategies for Teachers and Students* (Simon, Howe, and Kirschenbaum, 1972), the authors provide 79 classroom activities, each designed to promote one or more of the seven subprocesses or components of valuing.

1. Guidelines for Implementation. Simon and his coworkers recommend the following guidelines for implementing these value-clarifying classroom strategies (Simon et al., 1972; Simon & Harmin, 1973):

a. Most values clarification strategies can be used with any age levels, from elementary school through high school and adult groups, as long as the activities are adapted to the particular age group.
b. Many activities can be used with the entire class and/or small groups in the class.

c. Values clarification can be taught as a separate subject, with teachers setting aside five minutes to an hour or more each day or week, depending on goals and circumstances. Some schools may offer elective courses in values clarification.

d. Alternatively, values clarification can be integrated with standard subject matter taught in many regular courses such as social studies, history, literature, science, and health education. Most courses or subject matter can be taught on a facts level, a concepts level, and a values level. For example, Simon and Harmin (1973) illustrate these three levels with respect to teaching the United States Constitution in social studies class: *On a facts level* the teacher might want the class to know such information as (1) where and when the Constitution was drawn up, and (2) how the Constitution differed from the Articles of Confederation. *On a concepts level*, the teacher might discuss with the class (1) how the Constitution was a landmark in the evolving concept of a democracy, or (2) the concept of amendment and how it has operated in Congress. *On a values level*, the teacher might ask the class to consider some of the following issues: (1) many student governments are really token governments controlled by the "mother country," i.e., the administration. Is this true in your school? What can you do about it? If not you, who should do it? (2) When was the last time you signed a petition?; and (3) Where do you stand on wire tapping, financial aid to parochial schools, censorship of pornographic magazines?, etc.

e. Although the strategies are very explicit and easy to implement, it is up to the creative teacher to decide which of them he or she wants to use, how to adapt them to the particular needs of his or her class and how much time to spend on each activity and the discussion following the activity.

f. When using these activities, it is critical that the teacher facilitates a classroom atmosphere of openness, acceptance, respect, and trust. The teacher must model this in his or her own behavior.

g. The teacher should share his or her values (or value confusion) on a particular issue *after* the students have had a chance to think for themselves and to express their own points of view. The teacher's particular values should be presented as just another alternative point of view, holding no more weight than anyone else's.

2. Examples of Classroom Strategies

A. *Forced Choice Ladder.* This activity promotes the valuing components of choosing from alternatives and choosing by considering the consequences of alternatives. The teacher asks students to construct a "forced choice ladder," with 8 to 16 steps. Then the teacher presents a series of alternatives which reflect particular values. Using a key word, the student ranks each alternative in terms of whether he or she is for or against the value. In the following example, taken from Miller (1976), the student ranks the following eight alternatives ranging from "the person I'd least like to be like" at the bottom of the ladder, to "the person I'd most like to be like" at the top:

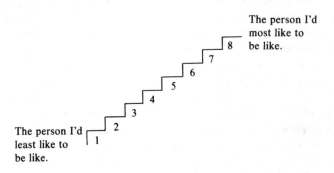

1. A rich person who gives very generously to charities. (Philanthropist)
2. A person whose prime concern is conserving the environment so that he becomes involved in various conservation projects. (Ecologist)
3. An individual whose main concern in life is integrating himself through self-help techniques, such as meditation and yoga. (Meditator)
4. An individual whose main focus in life is getting involved with and helping other people through the Salvation Army. (Helper)
5. An individual whose main value is serving his country through the armed forces. (Patriot)
6. A person whose primary focus in life is his small business. He devotes most of his energy toward running an efficient and profitable business. (Business person)
7. An individual whose primary concern is taking care of and spending time with his family. (Family head)
8. A person who feels that the only hope for humanity is through world organizations and who commits his life to working for the World Federalists. (Internationalist) [Miller, 1976, p. 53.]

After the students complete this exercise individually, they can be divided into small groups to compare their choices. This gives them an opportunity to clarify the reasoning behind their value choices.

B. Public Interview. This popular strategy gives the student the opportunity to affirm and explain his stand on various value issues publicly. The teacher asks for volunteers who would like to be interviewed in front of the class about some of their beliefs, feelings, and actions. The volunteer sits in front of the room, with the teacher asking questions from the back of the room.

The following are some examples of interview questions suggested by Simon et al. (1972) for secondary school students:

1. How do you feel about grades in school?
2. What are some of the things you really believe in?
3. What do you see yourself doing five years from now? Ten years? Twenty?
4. Would you bring up your children differently from the way you are being [were] brought up?
5. Can you think of something you would like to say to the group that you think might be good for them to hear?

C. Alternative Action Search. In this strategy students learn to consider alternatives for action in various situations and to make their everyday actions more consistent with their values. The student is presented with a specific vignette that calls for some proposed action. The teacher then asks "Now, given all your beliefs, feelings, and values related to this vignette, ideally, what would you want to do in this situation?" The following is a sample vignette provided by Simon et al. (1972):

> You are on a vacation trip and are driving to the beach with your parents. You would like to go to the amusement park, but you are concerned because you have spent most of the money you had saved for your vacation earlier. Your father stops for gasoline and you get out and walk around. A lady is walking back to her car and you see her purse fall open and her wallet fall out. You walk over, pick up the wallet just as the lady gets into her car to drive away. The edges of several ten dollar bills are sticking out of the wallet. No one saw you pick it up. What would you do? [P. 200.]

Evaluation and Critique

The popularity of Values Clarification is beyond dispute. The many strategies and activities developed by its proponents are interesting, highly structured, and easily applied and integrated into the school curriculum. Nevertheless, there is considerable confusion as to what this approach to moral education actually accomplishes, that is, what behavioral and attitudinal changes it facilitates in students. Unfortunately, the empirical research conducted has not done much to clarify this confusion.

The original hypotheses proposed by Raths et al. (1966) were that (1) certain kinds of behavioral problems often seen in school—e.g., chronic apathy, flightiness, overconformity, overdissension—are related to a lack of values or value confusion in students; (2) values-clarification activities, by helping students develop and clarify their own values, would lead to a reduction in frequency and severity of these destructive behavior patterns; and (3) these activities would also lead to an increase in such constructive behaviors as active interest and involvement in school, more positive attitudes toward learning, persistence in school tasks, improved decision-making abilities, and greater self-esteem and confidence. Empirical research has provided some tentative and partial support for the effectiveness of Values Clarification in decreasing some of the destructive behaviors and increasing some of the constructive attitudes and behaviors mentioned above in students ranging from primary grades to college level (Raths et al., 1966; Kirschenbaum, 1975). Much of this research, however, is methodologically weak. There have been inadequate control groups, measurement problems, and assessment of constructive behaviors and attitudes by simplistic scales of questionable reliability and validity.

There is also the theoretical and empirical problem of identifying the active ingredients in a values-clarification program. Are all seven valuing subprocesses proposed by Raths et al. (1966) necessary? Are there other operative subprocesses or components? For example, Kirschenbaum has rejected Raths original seven components and has constructed a more elaborate framework which includes the components of feeling, thinking, and communicating (each with its own set of subprocesses), in addition to choosing and acting as critical in the valuing process (Kirschenbaum, 1973). Alternately, one might ask whether *any* of these proposed valuing components are necessary. Raths et al. (1966) claim that an open and trusting classroom climate facilitated by a warm, nonjudgmental teacher is a prerequisite for an effective values-clarification program. Could this classroom climate be more important than the actual learning of the valuing components in helping students become less apathetic, more actively involved in learning, more purposeful and confident, etc.? These are questions that only further, more rigorous research will answer.

The confusion in the Values Clarification movement over just what kinds of changes or behavioral outcomes this approach facilitates in students is made more acute by the "value relativity" issue. Proponents of this approach maintain, as a major guiding principle, that values are relative to the individual, that no values are better or more desirable in general than others and that there are no valid, nonrelativistic criteria for judging behavior as right or wrong. The teacher must accept the student's right to arrive at any values he or she chooses through the valuing process. In the introduction to this chapter, we proposed that "value-relativity" (1) is a value position in itself, (2) is an empirically unsupported value position, and (3) has deleterious practical implications for moral education in particular and social behavior in general. The "value relativity" position is antithetical to the very premise of this book. In emphasizing the importance of learning constructive alternatives to violence and aggression, we are assuming that these various alternatives constitute more desirable values than violence and aggression. We believe that a general societal consensus does exist on this issue, and that the schools have a responsibility to teach students alternative values to violence and aggression in a nonindoctrinative way.

KOHLBERG'S COGNITIVE-DEVELOPMENTAL APPROACH

Lawrence Kohlberg believes that the direct teaching of particular values, as in character education, constitutes indoctrination. He also believes that the principle of value relativity, embodied in values clarification, is philosophically and scientifically unsound and that it leaves teachers as well as students in a morass of value confusion as to the meaning of morality and the aims of moral education. Over a span of 20 years, Kohlberg has elaborated an alternative position on moral development and education which he claims is philosophically justified, empirically supported, and which escapes the quagmires of indoctrination and value relativity. Kohlberg's position, based on cognitive-developmental principles, represents the most theoretically sophisticated contemporary approach to moral education and has generated much needed debate as well as empirical research.

Contrary to the belief of some writers (Bensen and Engeman, 1975; Forcinelli and Engeman, 1977), Kohlberg's complex theoretical treatment of moral development has not been at the expense of the development of explicit methods for concrete application in the schools. While we will discuss the cognitive-developmental approach in some detail, we cannot hope to do full justice to the intricacies of this position. The interested reader is referred to the following articles concerning theory, research, and applications by Kohlberg and colleagues: Beyer, 1976; Blatt & Kohlberg, 1975; Colby, Kohlberg, Fenton, Speicher-Dubin, & Lieberman, 1977; Fenton, 1977; Kohlberg, 1968, 1969, 1970a, 1970b, 1971a, 1971b, 1972a, 1972b, 1973, 1975, 1976; Kohlberg & Kramer, 1969; Kohlberg & Mayer, 1972; Kohlberg, Scharf, & Hickey, 1972; Kohlberg & Turiel, 1971; Rest, 1973, 1974; 1976; and Wasserman, 1976. For critiques on philosophical, theoretical and empirical grounds, see Alston,

1971; Fraenkel, 1976; Kurtines & Grief, 1974; Peters, 1978; Simpson, 1974; and Sullivan, 1977.

Rationale and Background

To understand Kohlberg's theory we must first understand the meaning and implications of a "cognitive-developmental" approach to morality. A cognitive perspective on morality emphasizes the notion that there are qualitatively different ways in which people think about, reason, and make sense of basic moral issues (e.g., value of life, truth, or justice) in their continual attempts to relate effectively to other human beings in their world. A developmental perspective on morality emphasizes the notion that these fundamentally different ways of reasoning about and making sense of basic moral issues change over time, that is, over the course of a person's growth. Central to a cognitive-developmental perspective is the notion of stages. Stages are structured or organized systems of thought. When we say that there are qualitatively different ways of thinking about moral issues over the course of a person's growth, we are saying that there are distinct *stages* of moral reasoning characterizing a person's development. Critical to the cognitive-developmental concept of stages are the following:

1. *The final or "highest stage" represents the theoretically "ideal" endpoint of development.* As a person develops from a young child to a mature adult, his or her ways of reasoning about moral issues progress through a series of stages toward a final or highest stage that may or may not be reached.
2. *Stages form an invariant sequence.* As a person develops, his or her ways of reasoning about moral issues progress through a series of stages (to the hypothesized final stage) in a fixed order or sequence. Although a person may progress through this sequence of stages more slowly or more rapidly than others, and although his or her development may become arrested or fixated at a particular stage (which may then become the highest stage that that person achieves); if that person *does* progress, it is always to the next stage up. This invariant sequence of stages is assumed to be true for all people; that is, there is a hypothesized universally invariant sequence of stages of moral development.
3. *Stages are "hierarchical integrations:" Higher stages are "better" than lower stages.* Each successive stage represents an increasingly integrated and effective mode of moral reasoning and problem solving than the previous stage.
4. *The motivation for stage transition is cognitive conflict.* During

certain critical periods in a person's development, he or she experiences his or her current mode of moral reasoning (his or her current stage) as increasingly inadequate for understanding and resolving more complex problems and dilemmas in value-conflictual situations. This induces a state of cognitive conflict, doubt, or uncertainty and dissatisfaction which in turn induces him or her to begin experimenting with modes of reasoning characteristic of the next higher stage.

According to Kohlberg, the cognitive-developmental approach to moral education is nonindoctrinative since it involves the stimulation of a natural progression of development in the direction in which a person is already heading. Furthermore, it is contrary to the premise of value relativity since the notion of a universally invariant sequence of stages or moral reasoning implies that (1) there are universal modes of reasoning about moral issues or values and, thus, for judging behavior as right or wrong, and (2) that some of these modes of reasoning are "better" or more adequate than others.

The background for this approach to moral develoment and education lies in the educational philosophy of John Dewey and the developmental psychology of Jean Piaget. We have already discussed Dewey's belief that cognitive-intellectual and moral development were inseparable as educational goals. In further suggesting that (1) development, both cognitive and moral, occurs in an invariant sequence of stages, and (2) developmental progression requires the stimulation of the child's critical thinking processes through the arousal of cognitive conflict (intellectual uncertainty, confusion, doubt), Dewey laid the foundation for a cognitive-developmental approach to moral education. In so doing, Dewey looked to psychology to provide the necessary knowledge about the stages and processes of cognitive and moral development.

Piaget's Theory of Moral Development. For some 50 years, Jean Piaget has been engaged in theorizing and research concerning the process of cognitive-intellectual development. According to Piaget, intelligence or logical thinking develops in the following universally invariant sequence of four hierarchically integrated stages: sensorimotor (birth–2 years), pre-operational (2–7 years), concrete operational (7–11 years), and formal operational (12–adult). While discussion of these stages is beyond the scope of this chapter, we should note that Piaget's theory of cognitive development represents one of the landmark achievements in the field of psychology. We refer the interested reader to Flavell's *The Developmental Psychology of Jean Piaget* (1963), and Ginsburg and Opper's *Piaget's Theory of Intellectual Development: An Introduction* (1969).

Piaget has also investigated the development of thinking or reasoning concerning explicitly moral situations. In his seminal work in this area, *The Moral Judgment of the Child* (Piaget, 1932), Piaget theorized that there were two major stages of moral development: (1) an earlier stage—heteronomous morality (or moral realism or morality of constraint), and (2) a later stage (beginning roughly at 10–11 years)—autonomous morality (or moral relativism or morality of cooperation). Discussion of these stages is, again, beyond the scope of this chapter. We wish only to comment that in addition to certain conceptual ambiguities (Ginsberg and Opper, 1969), an extensive review of the research by Lickona (1976b) indicates that Piaget's two-stage theory is lacking empirical support as a comprehensive theory of moral development. Nevertheless, it provided the basis for Kohlberg's more elaborate and systematized six-stage perspective.

Kohlberg's Six Stages of Moral Reasoning

1. Kohlberg's Hypothesis. Kohlberg's consideration of moral philosophy led him to conclude that (1) the moral domain is essentially delimited to those situations wherein conflicting interests and values—the competing claims of different parties—are at stake; (2) morality involves those modes of reasoning and problem solving necessary for resolving such competing claims in value-conflictual situations; and (3) the essence of morality is the principle of justice—the primary regard for the value and equality of all human beings, and for reciprocity in human relations—that is, the principle of "justice" is philosophically the most justifiable criteria or standard for resolving conflicting claims and interests in problematic social situations. Thus, Kohlberg used moral philosophy to hypothesize that moral development proceeds through a universally invariant sequence of stages of moral reasoning based primarily on increasingly adequate conceptions of "justice"—toward a postulated "ideal" endpoint (highest or final stage) of a fully differentiated, hierarchically integrated, and universalized sense of justice.

2. Research Methods: The Moral Judgment Interview. To investigate his hypothesis, Kohlberg studied the development of moral reasoning through a "moral judgment interview." In this method, a trained interviewer presents the interviewee with a series of brief stories, each of which contains a moral dilemma involving value-conflicting alternative actions with which the protagonist is confronted. The interviewee is asked which action the protagonist *should* take and why, and a series of probe questions attempt to ascertain the nature of the interviewee's reasoning and decision-making processes vis-à-vis certain moral issues such as the value of human life, laws and rules, punishment and justice.

3. Longitudinal and Cross-Cultural Research: Kohlberg's Six Stages. In 1957, Kohlberg began investigating the moral reasoning of 72 lower and middle-class urban American boys aged 10–16 through moral dilemmas. He classified their responses on the basis of the similarity of the reasoning process used and was able to distinguish six basic types of moral reasoning that he felt corresponded to a developmental sequence of stages. Subsequent retesting of 50 of these same subjects every three years (Kohlberg, 1969, 1976; Kohlberg and Kramer, 1969) essentially confirmed his hypothesis that the development of moral reasoning progressed through an invariant sequence of six stages, although the rate of development and the highest stage achieved varied somewhat (e.g., many subjects did not progress to the final one or two stages). We would like to make two comments concerning this longitudinal research: (1) Results indicate that at any given time, a person reasons predominantly at one stage and secondarily at adjacent stages above and/or below the predominant stage; thus, for example, when we say a person is "at stage 3," we mean that he or she is reasoning predominantly, but not solely, at that stage. (2) Through the course of this research, Kohlberg has changed his system of scoring subjects' responses to moral dilemmas to account for results that were discrepant with his invariant sequence hypothesis, provoking considerable methodological criticism in the process.

Kohlberg and his colleagues have also conducted research in a number of different countries including Mexico, Turkey, Taiwan, India, Canada, and Israel. Kohlberg interpreted results from this cross-cultural research as supporting his hypothesis that the invariant sequence of six stages found in the United States was culturally universal, despite considerable cultural variations in rates of development and highest stages achieved. (Kohlberg, 1969; Kohlberg and Turiel, 1971). For example, in his studies of boys (ages 10, 13, and 16) in the urban middle class of the U.S., Taiwan, and Mexico as well as in two isolated villages in Yucatan and Turkey, Kohlberg found that age-related changes in predominant stage usage, *when such changes occurred*, followed in the predicted direction. In the same studies, however, Kohlberg also found that *at age* 16, (1) stage 5 reasoning predominated among middle-class boys in America, while (2) stages 3 and 4 still predominated among middle-class boys in Mexico and Taiwan (although stage 5 usage did increase), and (3) stages 1 and 2 still prevailed over stages 3 and 4 among isolated-village boys in Yucatan and Turkey with stage 5 reasoning totally absent. Kohlberg's interpretation of such data as consistent with his hypothesis of a universally invariant sequence of six stages has aroused considerable criticism, some of which will be addressed later in our critique and evaluation.

Perhaps even more controversial are Kohlberg's conclusions, based on his cross-cultural research, that (1) people in all cultures and sub-cultures reason about the same basic moral concepts or values—e.g., the value of life, love, and affection, contract and trust, laws and rules, authority, punishment, property, truth, liberty, and most fundamentally, justice, and (2) each successive stage in his universally invariant sequence represents an increasingly differentiated and hierarchically integrated mode of reasoning about these universal moral concepts or values. It is difficult to overemphasize the significance of such conclusions. For one thing, if valid, they would put the final "nail in the coffin" of value relativity. Needless to say, "No issue has stirred more heated debate in the ranks of social scientists engaged in the study of values" (Lickona, 1976a, p. 9). While we submit that there is not enough sound empirical research at present either to support or refute Kohlberg's cross-cultural conclusions, we wish to emphasize that they are fundamental to his theory. To summarize: Kohlberg claims to have provided empirical support for the existence of a universally invariant sequence of six stages of reasoning about certain fundamental, universal moral values, the most fundamental of which is justice. The following description of these six stages, hierarchically ordered in three levels of two stages each, is taken from Kohlberg (1971b):

I PRECONVENTIONAL LEVEL

At this level the child is responsive to cultural rules and labels of good and bad, right or wrong, but interprets these labels in terms of either the physical or the hedonistic consequences of action (punishment, reward, exchange of favours) or in terms of the physical power of those who enunciate the rules and labels. The level comprises the following two stages:

Stage 1 punishment and obedience orientation. The physical consequences of action determine its goodness or badness regardless of the human meaning or value of the consequences. Avoidance of punishment and unquestioning deference to power are valued in their own right, not in terms of respect for an underlying moral order supported by punishment and authority (the latter being stage 4).

Stage 2 instrumental relativist orientation. Right action consists of that which instrumentally satisfies one's own needs and occasionally needs of others. Human relations are viewed in terms similar to those of the market place. Elements of fairness, or reciprocity, and equal sharing are present, but they are always interpreted in a physical pragmatic way. Reciprocity is a matter of "you scratch my back and I'll scratch yours," not of loyalty, gratitude, or justice.

II CONVENTIONAL LEVEL

At this level, maintaining the expectations of the individual's family, group, or nation is perceived as valuable in its own right, regardless of immediate and obvious consequences. The attitude is one not only of *conformity* to personal expectations and social order, but of loyalty to it, of actively *maintaining*, supporting, and justifying the order and of identifying with the persons or group involved in it. This level comprises the following two stages:

Stage 3 interpersonal concordance or "good boy—nice girl" orientation. Good behavior is that which pleases or helps others and is approved by them. There is much conformity to stereotypical images of what is majority or "natural" behavior. Behavior is frequently judged by intention: "he means well" becomes important for the first time. One earns approval by being "nice."

Stage 4 "law and order" orientation. There is orientation toward authority, fixed rules, and the maintenance of the social order. Right behavior consists of doing one's duty, showing respect for authority, and maintaining the given social order for its own sake.

III POST-CONVENTIONAL, AUTONOMOUS, OR PRINCIPLED LEVEL

At this level there is a clear effort to define moral values and principles that have validity and application apart from the authority of the groups or persons holding these principles and apart from the individual's own identification with these groups. This level again has two stages:

Stage 5 social-contract legalistic orientation. Generally, this stage has utilitarian overtones. Right action tends to be defined in terms of general individual rights and in terms of standards that have been critically examined and agreed upon by the whole society. There is a clear awareness of the relativism of personal values and opinions and a corresponding emphasis on procedural rules for reaching consensus. Aside from what is constitutionally and democratically agreed upon, the right is a matter of personal "values" and "opinion." The result is an emphasis upon the "legal point of view," but with an emphasis upon the possibility of changing law in terms of rational considerations of social utility, (rather than freezing it in terms of stage-4 "law and order"). Outside the legal realm, free agreement, and contract is the binding element of obligation. This is the "official" morality of the United States government and constitution.

Stage 6 universal ethical-principle orientation. Right is defined by the decision of conscience in accord with self-chosen *ethical principles* appealing to logical comprehensiveness, universality, and consistency. These principles are abstract and ethical (the Golden Rule, the categorical imperative); they are not concrete moral rules like the Ten Commandments. At heart, these are universal principles of justice, of the reciprocity and equality of human rights and of respect for the dignity of human beings as individual persons. [Kohlberg, 1971b, pp. 86–88.]

The Relationship between Kohlberg's Stages and Behavior

The relationship between Kohlberg's stages and behavior remains, in many respects, problematic. Nevertheless, Kohlberg and his colleagues have provided evidence showing that there is a positive relationship between (1) preconventional moral reasoning (stages 1 and 2) and certain forms of antisocial behavior, and (2) postconventional moral reasoning (stages 5 and 6) and certain kinds of principled, prosocial behaviors.

1. The Importance of Conventional Moral Reasoning. Research indicates that in the United States, preconventional moral reasoning is characteristic of children under age 10, some adolescents, and the *vast majority of adolescent delinquents and adult criminals* (Kohlberg, 1976).

A. Preconventional Moral Reasoning and Antisocial Behavior. The relationship between preconventional moral reasoning and delinquency and crime is especially relevant to us. A study by Freundlich and Kohlberg (see Kolhberg, 1973) found that 83 percent of 15 to 17-year-old working-class delinquents were at preconventional stages, compared with only 23 percent of working-class nondelinquent adolescents. Subsequent studies have shown that adolescent delinquents or adult inmates almost invariably scored at the preconventional level (Fodor, 1972; Hudgins & Prentice, 1973; Kohlberg, Scharf, & Hickey, 1972). These studies suggest that preconventional moral reasoning may well be a critical factor in consistent delinquent and criminal behavior. This should not be surprising since the preconventional individual, by definition, has not yet developed to the point where he or she can really understand, let alone consistently uphold, conventional societal rules, laws, and expectations. For the stage 1 individual, the reason for doing right is simply to avoid punishment from powerful authority figures; for the stage 2 individual the reason for doing right is to "serve one's own needs or interests in a world where you have to recognize that other people have their interests, too" (Kohlberg, 1976, p. 34). Thus, for preconventional individuals, there simply are no adequate reasons for obeying and conforming to societal rules and laws in the absence of powerful authority figures or concrete payoffs.

B. Critical Period for the Transition to Conventional Moral Reasoning. Kohlberg's research suggests that in this country pre- to early adolescence (roughly ages 10–13) seems to be a developmentally "critical period" for the transition from preconventional (i.e., stage 2) to conventional (i.e., stage 3) moral reasoning. Those children who do not begin to evidence *at least some* stage 3 moral reasoning during this period may get "locked into" or fixated at the preconventional level. For example, it is very difficult for a 17-year-old at stage 2 to move to stage 3 compared with a 12-year-old at stage 2. Thus, for Kohlberg, one important goal of moral education would be to prevent preconventional level fixation in those upper elementary and junior high school students whose moral development is beginning to lag behind.

2. The Importance of Postconventional Moral Reasoning. Research indicates that in this country *conventional moral reasoning (stages 3 and 4) is characteristic of the vast majority of adolescents and adults.* Stage 3 is reached as early as age 9, but usually later, while stage 4 is usually reached by middle or late adolescence. *Postconventional moral reasoning (stages 5 and 6) is attained by only a small minority of the adult population,* with perhaps 10–15 percent reaching stage 5 in their late teens, early twenties, or even later; very few people reach stage 6 at all, and those who do may be older than 30 (Fenton, 1977).

For Kohlberg, such findings have particularly important implications for moral education in that he maintains postconventional moral reasoning is critical for (1) effective citizenship in a just and democratic society, and (2) the consistent performance of certain kinds of prosocial behaviors in situations where conventional rules and expectations are ambiguous or actually oppose such prosocial behaviors.

A. Postconventional Moral Reasoning and Effective Citizenship. While the achievement of conventional moral reasoning may be laudable for adolescent and adult criminal offenders, it is not, according to Kohlberg, a satisfactory long-term goal for the majority of citizens in a participatory democracy such as ours. For example, the conventional individual believes in obeying and upholding societal laws as an end in itself. The postconventional individual believes that society's laws are rules of conduct designed to protect the fundamental rights (e.g., life, liberty, truth) and well-being of its members; these fundamental rights are in turn based on the universal principle of justice, that is, "of the reciprocity and equality of human rights and respect for the dignity of human beings as individual persons" (Kohlberg, 1971b, p. 88). For the conventional individual, the law is right because it is the law; there is a confusion between the legal and the moral. For the postconventional individual, the law is right if it is just; the moral is differentiated from and considered superordinate to the legal. The postconventional person believes in changing those laws that are contrary to the principle of justice and, thus, to the welfare of society's members. Thus, Kohlberg and his colleagues maintain that it is the postconventional rather than the conventional citizen who is necessary for the development and maintenance of a free and just democracy. The very structure of our government as embodied in the social contract of the Constitution is based on postconventional (specifically stage 5) conceptions of the values of justice, life, liberty, contract and trust, laws and rules, and authority. Since only a small minority of adults in this country reach stage 5 moral reasoning, we are left with the alarming conclusion that the vast majority of adult American citizens do not fully understand the principles of justice, contract, and law on which their government is based. Fenton (1977) proposes that a major goal of high school social studies and civic education courses should be to graduate students who are able to understand the Constitution as a stage 5 document.

B. Postconventional Moral Reasoning and Principled, Prosocial Behavior. Kohlberg and colleagues have provided empirical support for a positive relationship between postconventional moral reasoning and such principled prosocial behaviors as honesty (resistance to cheating), nonviolence (refusal to inflict pain on another person), and altruistic bystander intervention (intervening to help someone in distress) in situations where conventional authoritative rules and social expectations are ambiguous or even opposed to such prosocial behaviors.

Concerning honesty, studies by Brown (Kohlberg and Turiel, 1971, p. 458) with college students and Krebs (1967) with children found that a much greater percentage of postconventional than conventional students actually refrained from cheating in experimental situations characterized by an absence of explicit authoritative or group sanctions against cheating. Kohlberg and Turiel (1971) explain that only the postconventional student can formulate adequate reasons for not cheating in the absence of *explicit* conventional rules against cheating. Such reasons, based on postconventional conceptions of justice, contract, and trust, involve an understanding that (1) a mutual trust, agreement or contract not to cheat is *implicit* in such a situation, (2) while it doesn't seem that bad if one person cheats, what holds for all must hold for one, and (3) in cheating, one is taking unfair advantage over those who do not cheat.

Concerning nonviolence, Kohlberg (Kohlberg & Turiel, 1971, p. 459) gave the moral judgment interview to subjects in Milgram's (1963) classic study. In Milgram's study, undergraduate subjects were required, in the guise of a learning experiment, to administer increasingly severe electric shock punishment to a "stooge victim" (an experimental confederate). Kohlberg found that 75 percent of the stage six subjects refused to continue shocking the "victim," compared with only 13 percent of all the subjects at lower stages (including stage 5). Kohlberg and Turiel (1971) explain that only stage 6 students could formulate a clear reason for not shocking the "victim" under orders from the experimenter—i.e., the experimenter did not have the moral right to ask them to inflict pain on another person. Even stage 5 students were unable to reach a clear decision as to what to do in this situation since, according to stage 5 principles of social contract, the "victim" as well as themselves (as subjects) had voluntarily contracted to participate in the experiment.

Concerning altruistic bystander intervention, McNamee (1977) created the following experimental situation in which it was necessary to violate the experimenter's authority to help someone. The experimenter and subject (college student) enter a room where the latter is to receive the moral judgment interview. An experimental confederate arrives, presents himself as the next subject, and tells the experimenter he cannot do the experiment because he has just taken drugs and is having "a bad time." In the real subject's presence, the confederate persists in asking the experimenter for help with his distress, with the experimenter refusing until, finally, the confederate leaves the room. Thus, the subject is faced with the choice of remaining an uninvolved bystander or intervening to help the confederate. McNamee (1977) found that 100 percent of stage 6 subjects and 68 percent of stage 5 subjects actually intervened in some way (e.g., offering a referral or personal assistance) to help the confederate, as compared with only 38 percent of stage 4 subjects and 28 percent of stage 3 subjects. Again, only stage 6 subjects could consistently formulate a clear reason for intervening, as expressed in the following representative stage 6 response: "I felt an obligation to the experimenter to finish, but in this case, helping a person in trouble took priority." Representative stage-based responses from those subjects who did not intervene were: (1) stage 3—"I was concerned about what the experimenter would think of me—her disapproval"; (2) stage 4—"My role was that of a subject. I'm not qualified as a psychologist. I had to trust the experimenter's judgment"; and (3) stage 5—"I wanted to help, but I had an obligation to the experimenter to finish the experiment" (McNamee, 1977, p. 30).

C. Critical Period for the Transition to Postconventional Moral Reasoning. Kohlberg's research suggests that, in this country, late adolescence to early adulthood (roughly ages 16–20) appears to be a developmentally "critical period" for the transition from conventional (i.e., stage 5) moral reasoning. Those people who do not begin to use *at least some* stage 5 moral reasoning during this period may fixate at the conventional level, making it increasingly difficult to develop postconventional reasoning as they get older. Thus, for Kohlberg, another major goal of moral education would be to prevent conventional level fixation in those high school and college students whose moral development is beginning to lag behind.

3. The Goal of Moral Education: A Recap. We have spent considerable time elaborating the background, rationale, and some of the theoretical principles of Kohlberg's perspective. We feel this is necessary in order to provide an understanding of the basic goal and teaching strategy of this most complex approach to moral education. The goal, to recapitulate, is the facilitation of the development of moral reasoning through each of the stages, to the eventual attainment of postconventional reasoning (at least stage 5, although ideally stage 6). The aim is also to prevent developmental fixation or retardation at preconventional and conventional levels, especially during the critical transitional periods of pre- to early adolescence and late adolescence to early adulthood, respectively.

We now turn our attention to methods for achieving this goal. In the next section we (1) discuss conditions that facilitate moral development, and (2) introduce a specific teaching strategy designed to provide these conditions.

Facilitative Conditions for Moral Development and a Teaching Strategy for Moral Education

1. Facilitative Conditions for Moral Development. Kohlberg and his colleagues have explored the question of which conditions are facilitative of the development of moral reasoning. The following represent some pertinent generalizations from their thinking and research.

A. Role-Taking Opportunities Through Reciprocal Social Interaction. Moral problems arise when the differing interests, values, and perspectives of different individuals come into conflict. It follows that moral reasoning about such problems requires the ability to perceive and to comprehend the differing perspectives of other people. This ability to take the role or perspective of others, to put oneself in their shoes and see the world through their eyes has been variously referred to as role taking, social perspective taking, or empathy (in the cognitive rather than affective sense). Selman (1976), a colleague of Kohlberg, defines role taking in terms of the way in which a person differentiates his or her perspective from other perspectives, and the way in which he or she relates these perspectives to one another. Selman has defined stages of role taking that parallel the stages of moral reasoning, and has provided empirical research to support the notion that the former is a necessary though not a sufficient condition for the latter (Selman, 1976). Kohlberg concurs with Selman and maintains that the development of role-taking abilities (vis-à-vis a sequence of stages such as Selman's) through the provision of *role-taking opportunities* is a major determinant of moral development. Role taking opportunities involve an exposure to and active exchange or sharing of differing perspectives and ways of thinking in a context of reciprocal or mutual social interaction. Such opportunities are provided by the family, school, and other societal institutions.

Concerning moral education, then, the provision of role-taking opportunities—that is, exposure to and mutual exchange among students (as well as between teacher and student) of different ways of reasoning about moral problems—is necessary for moral development, although it is not sufficient in itself.

B. Cognitive Conflict over Genuine Moral Dilemmas. As previously discussed, it is axiomatic to Kohlberg's theory that the motivation for transition from one stage to the next higher stage is the subjective experience of cognitive conflict. Cognitive conflict, it will be recalled, is a state of intellectual doubt, uncertainty, and dissatisfaction arising out of the felt inability of one's current mode of moral reasoning (one's current stage) to resolve moral problems adequately. This can only happen, the theory holds, if during certain developmentally optimal or critical periods, the person is repeatedly confronted with moral problems that represent genuine moral dilemmas—that is, situations involving a conflict of fundamental human values and interests with no clear-cut, culturally approved right or wrong answers. The resulting experience of cognitive conflict is heightened if these moral dilemmas, whether actual or hypothetical, are (1) genuinely meaningful or relevant to the person, (2) cognitively stimulating and challenging to him or her, and (3) are presented *in a social context that provides for role-taking opportunities*—that is, for exposure to and exchange of conflicting opinions and different modes (stages) of reasoning about these dilemmas. In such a social context, the cognitively conflicted person will begin experimenting with some of these different modes or stages of moral reasoning.

C. Exposure to the Next Higher Stage of Reasoning. If the cognitively conflicted person is exposed to a mode of moral reasoning one stage above his own, this will increase his sense of conflict still further and will induce him or her to begin experimenting with that stage of reasoning in particular. This is because it is also axiomatic to Kohlberg's theory that the cognitively conflicted person is attracted to the next higher stage of reasoning since it appears more integrated, logical, and adequate for resolving moral dilemmas. Kohlberg and colleagues have provided empirical evidence in support of this axiom. Specifically, Rest (1973), and Rest, Turiel, and Kohlberg (1969) have demonstrated that people subjectively prefer the highest stage of reasoning about moral dilemmas that they can comprehend (paraphrase without distortion), which is typically one stage above the one they predominantly use.

2. A Teaching Strategy for Moral Education: Classroom Discussions of Moral Dilemmas. On the basis of these considerations concerning facilitative conditions for moral development, Kohlberg and his colleagues developed a specific teaching strategy designed to provide these conditions in the classroom. Whereas character education and values clarification use numerous instructional methods and strategies for achieving their respective objectives, Kohlberg's approach to moral education, insofar as it is limited to the confines of the classroom, relies exclusively on one basic strategy—classroom discussions of moral dilemmas (Kohlberg's approach also involves intervention strategies aimed at the structural-organization level of the entire school as a moral educational institution). In this strategy, meaningful and cognitively stimulating moral dilemmas are used to trigger teacher-led moral discussion and debate among student peers, especially in social studies and English classes. Since the typical upper elementary, junior high, senior high, or college class consists of students who are at two or three adjacent stages of moral reasoning, such moral discussions are likely to induce the most cognitive conflict in the relatively lower-stage students in the class and to provide them with critical role-taking opportunities, particularly in the form of exposure to modes of reasoning one stage above their own. If such moral discussions are continued over a period of time and across numerous dilemmas, the "lower-stage" students should begin gradually to make the transition to the next higher stage of reasoning. This is consistent with the goal of moral education as preventing fixation or retardation in the moral development of students who are beginning to lag behind their peers during critical transitional periods, as opposed to accelerating the development of "higher-stage" students who are progressing satisfactorily.

Within the last several years, several experimental investigations have attempted to facilitate stage change through moral dilemma discussion programs, ranging from upper elementary through college levels (Blatt & Kohlberg, 1975; Boyd, 1973; Colby, Kohlberg, Fenton, Speicher-Dubin & Lieberman, 1977; Rest, 1974). Results generally indicated that a greater percentage of students in the "experimental" classrooms (i.e., who participated in teacher-guided peer discussion of moral dilemmas) made notable progress toward the next higher stage of reasoning than did students in various types of control-group classrooms.

An important investigation in this context was conducted by Blatt and Kohlberg (1975). After a smaller pilot project, Blatt personally led moral discussions (18 45-minute sessions held twice weekly) with 44 public school students divided into four "experimental" classrooms varying systematically in age (sixth graders, ages 11–12, and tenth graders, ages 15–16) and race-related socioeconomic status (lower-class blacks and lower middle-class blacks and lower middle-class whites). Results indicated that students in these "experimental" classrooms showed significant upward change in moral reasoning (they moved an average of one-third of a stage up) compared with students in various control-group classrooms (who remained essentially unchanged); furthermore, "experimentals" maintained this upward-change advantage over "controls" at one-year follow-up. Blatt and Kohlberg (1975) also found the following: (1) almost all changes in moral reasoning occurring through moral discussions were in the direction of the next higher stage (e.g., students at stage 2 moved in the direction of stage 3, while students at stage 3 moved in the direction of stage 4); this suggested that these changes were due to genuine stimulation of the "natural" sequence of moral development rather than mere verbal learning of phrases and concepts at other stages of reasoning; and (2) about as much overall change in moral reasoning occurred in lower-class black children as in lower middle-class white children; this suggested that moral discussions, although relying heavily on verbal exchange, were effective regardless of differences in verbal skills and social background.

Colby, Kohlberg, Fenton, Speicher-Dubin, and Lieberman (1977) essentially replicated Blatt and Kohlberg's (1975) findings although this time with regular high school teachers leading moral discussions in their social studies classes. Although their results were somewhat more modest than Blatt and Kohlberg's (1975), Colby et al. (1977) demonstrated that students in "experimental" classrooms (where teachers, with a minimum amount of special training in Kohlberg's theory, led moral discussions in the context of their social studies classes) showed an overall significant upward change in moral reasoning compared with students in "control" classrooms (where teachers taught their social studies classes without moral discussions). Importantly, Colby et al. (1977) also found that, compared with students in the "experimental" classrooms who showed minimal change in moral reasoning, students who showed the greatest degree of upward change were more likely to have (1) initially begun the experiment at some optimal or critical period for stage transition (e.g., 13-years old preconventional students showed more upward change than older preconventional students who "may have been at stage 2 long enough to have 'fixated' at that level" [p. 102]), (2) been in "experimental" classrooms consisting of students who represented an initially wider range of adjacent stages (e.g., three as opposed to two) of moral reasoning, (3) had teachers who used a greater number of moral dilemmas or discussion periods, and (4) had teachers who were more skillful in eliciting moral reasoning from students at adjacent stages during discussion.

Now that we have established the rationale, principles, and research base for conducting classroom discussions of moral dilemmas, we will examine the concrete implementation of this teaching strategy.

Conducting Classroom Discussions of Moral Dilemmas: The Teaching Process

Most of the material in this section comes from Galbraith and Jones' (1976) book, *Moral Reasoning: A Teaching Handbook for Adapting*

Kohlberg to the Classroom, and Beyer's (1976) article "Conducting Moral Discussions in the Classroom." The interested reader is encouraged to consult these sources for further information as well as for variations on the basic teaching strategy. This strategy requires that the teacher help students engage in the following four-step process: (1) confront a moral dilemma, (2) state a tentative position, (3) examine the reasoning, and (4) reflect on an individual position. In discussing each of these four steps, we will include recommendations for implementation as well as illustrations of the teaching process with reference to discussion of a particular moral dilemma. The following points should be kept in mind for a clearer understanding of this discussion:

a. Although the teaching process as illustrated in this section is geared to a standard 45-minute class period, a given moral dilemma discussion can be organized in advance by the teacher to extend over a number of class periods, or, alternately, can spontaneously arise within the context of teaching regular subject matter and take only 10–15 minutes.
b. Moral dilemma discussions can take place at any level of education, from upper-elementary to college, and in the context of almost any regular subject-matter course. Indeed, it is recommended that such discussions, rather than being taught as "pure" moral education lessons, be integrated within the regular school curriculum, particularly in social studies, English literature, history, and civic education classes.
c. Teachers do *not* have to be able to identify the stages of reasoning their students use in order to lead moral discussions. Unless a class is extraordinarily homogeneous, it will usually contain students who reason predominantly at two or three adjacent stages. It is the mutual interaction and confrontation among students at adjacent stages which is critical.
d. The teacher's primary roles, then, are to promote such interaction and confrontation among students, as well as to keep the focus of the discussion explicitly on those moral issues involved in the particular dilemma. The teachers' skills in communication and group facilitation are more important in leading moral discussions than is their skill in stage identification and interpretation.
e. It is critical that the teacher be able to facilitate a nonjudgmental classroom climate that reflects trust, informality, and tolerance. It is recommended that students sit in a large circle so that everyone can face and hear each other. By joining this circle, a teacher can assume the role of discussion leader, mediator, or facilitator, rather than of an authority figure who has established a separate "teacher space."

1. Confront a Moral Dilemma. There is no basic difference between moral dilemmas used for class discussion and dilemmas used to assess students' stage(s) of reasoning in Kohlberg's moral judgment interviews. Let us present the dilemma we will be using for purposes of illustration throughout this section:

> Sharon and her best friend Jill, walked into a department store to shop. As they browsed, Jill saw a sweater she really liked and told Sharon she wanted to try the sweater on. While Jill went to the dressing room, Sharon continued to shop.
>
> Soon Jill came out of the dressing room wearing her coat. She caught Sharon's attention with her eyes and glanced down at the sweater under her coat. Without a word, Jill turned and walked out of the store.
>
> Moments later the store security officer, sales clerk, and the store manager approached Sharon. "That's her, that's one of the girls. Check her bags," blurted the clerk. The security officer said he had the right to check bags, and Sharon handed them over. "No sweater in here," he told the manager. "Then I know the other girl has it," the clerk said. "I saw them just as plain as anything. They were together on this." The security officer then asked the manager if he wanted to follow through on the case. "Absolutely," he insisted. "Shoplifting is getting to be a major expense in running a store like this. I can't let shoplifters off the hook and expect to run a successful business."
>
> The security officer turned to Sharon. "What's the name of the girl you were with?" he asked. Sharon looked up at him silently. "Come on now; come clean," said the security officer. "If you don't tell us, you can be charged with the crime or with aiding the person who committed the crime."
>
> Question: Should Sharon tell Jill's name to the security officer? Why, or why not?
> [Colby et al., 1977, p. 104]

A dilemma story such as the above includes the following components:

a. *central character*—students make moral judgments about what the central character should do.
b. *choice*—the central character should have two action alternatives which present a definite conflict. Neither action choice should represent a culturally approved "right" answer.
c. *moral issues*—a dilemma should involve a conflict between two or more fundamental moral issues or values. In Sharon's dilemma, for example, Sharon's affectional relationship and implicit contract and trust with Jill conflict with issues of authority, property, truth, and punishment. Sharon faces the prospect of being punished herself if she fails to give Jill's name or of bringing punishment on Jill if she does tell her name. Also, Sharon faces the possibility of losing Jill's friendship if she tells or of losing the affection of her own family if she becomes a party to the shoplifting.
d. *"Should" question*—asking what the central character *should* do keeps the ensuing discussion focused on moral judgments or reasoning, for it asks students to decide what is the "right," "correct," or "good" thing to do.

In general, dilemmas may be derived from three main sources: (1) current issues in contemporary society (e.g., should a terminally ill patient be allowed to die or be kept alive by a life support system?), (2) the real-life experiences of students (e.g., should a student let another student copy test answers?), (3) the specific content of a course such as social studies (e.g., should Thoreau have gone to jail rather than pay taxes to support a war of which he disapproved?). Such dilemmas may be used as they are found or recast as hypothetical incidents involving fictional characters.

Dilemmas may be presented through written handouts, readings from novels, role playing, films, filmstrips, audiotapes, newspaper articles, or other media. While most dilemmas for secondary students are presented via written handouts or various readings, it is suggested that dilemmas for elementary students make more use of story telling, role playing, and a variety of audiovisual means of presentation.

The teacher begins a moral discussion by presenting the dilemma to the class. It is often helpful to precede presentation of the dilemma with comments or questions designed (1) to prepare students for the kind of situation or character(s) described in the dilemma, (2) to help students see the relationship between the dilemma and what they have been studying, and (3) to build up student interest in the dilemma. (This kind of "warm-up" is especially important for younger, elementary students). For example, before presenting Sharon's dilemma to the class, the teacher might (1) point out that crimes involving property are a major type of teenage crime today, and (2) ask if students have known of someone who actually stole something from a store, or of someone who had to decide whether or not to tell on a friend.

After presenting the dilemma, the teacher should ask questions in order to help students clarify the circumstances involved, define terms, identify the characteristics of the central character, and state the exact nature of the dilemma and the action choice open to the central character.

2. State a Tentative Position. Once students have understood the nature of the dilemma, the teacher should give them the opportunity to state a tentative position on what action alternative they think the central character should take. This is accomplished in the following sequence of steps:

a. Students should be given time to think quietly about where they stand.
b. Each student should then individually write down what action alternative he or she tentatively recommends for the central character, as well as his or her reasons for this position.

c. The teacher then needs to find out what action positions were taken by the students. A good dilemma usually generates a division within the class on the action that the central character should take; this division is necessary for engendering the kind of confrontation that motivates a critical evaluation of moral reasoning. Students can indicate by a show of hands how many support each position, as well as how many are initially undecided. If students divide on action on at least a 70–30 basis, discussion can begin. If the class fails, however, to divide satisfactorily, the teacher should be prepared to add one or more alterations to the original dilemma to create the necessary class division. For example, concerning Sharon's dilemma, if almost the entire class agrees that Sharon *should* tell, the teacher might add this twist: Suppose that Jill has done Sharon many favors and that Sharon knows that she will lose many of her friends if she tells on Jill; what should she do in that case? Or, alternately, if nearly the entire class agrees that Sharon should *not* tell, the teacher might add this: suppose that instead of being a best friend, Jill was only a casual acquaintance; what should Sharon do in that case?

d. After determining that there is a satisfactory class division on action, the teacher should spend a few minutes asking different students to volunteer their reasons for their action positions. This will help prepare students for the discussion to follow as well as indicate to them that people have many different reasons for recommending a particular action position.

3. Examine the Reasoning. This step involves the actual discussion of the moral dilemma and represents the heart of the teaching process. As previously stated, the teacher's two main tasks are (1) promoting student-to-student interaction, and (2) keeping the discussion focused on the moral issues involved in the dilemma. Student interaction can be promoted by the way student seating is arranged, by the classroom climate, and by using questions or comments to draw students into the discussion. The teacher can keep the discussion focused on the moral issues involved by (1) not permitting students to dwell on comments, arguments, or speculation about the *facts* and *circumstances* of a dilemma; the teacher can simply restate what the facts are and return the discussion to *reasoning*; and (2) using *probe questions* to help students examine issues they had ignored or to think about reasoning at a higher stage. The following types of probe questions can be used, along with examples specific to Sharon's dilemma:

a. *clarifying probes* call on students to define terms or explain comments that do not convey reasoning. For example, if a student says, "I think stealing is immoral," the teacher might ask "What do you mean by immoral?"

b. *issue-specific probes* encourage students to examine their reasoning about a fundamental moral issue involved in the dilemma. For example, to get at the issue of affectional relations, the teacher might ask, "What obligations do you owe to a friend?"

c. *inter-issue probes* encourage students to think about what to do when a conflict occurs between two separate yet critical moral issues or values; e.g., "Which is more important, loyalty to a friend or the obligation to obey the law? Why?"

d. *role-switch probes* encourage the students to take the perspective of another figure in the dilemma in order to help them see another side of the problem; e.g., "From the point of view of Jill's parents, should Sharon tell?"

e. *universal consequence probes* ask students to consider what might happen if such a position or such reasoning were applied to everyone; e.g., "Is it ever right to tell on a friend?"

Effective use of probe questions are critical to a teacher's efforts in leading a successful moral discussion. Probe questions facilitate movement to the next higher stage of moral reasoning by helping students (1) focus increasingly on the more fundamental, universal moral issues and values implicit in a moral dilemma, (2) develop an ability to empathize with and understand other perspectives on a moral issue, and (3) reason in increasingly generalizable ways. The teacher should prepare in advance a list of specific probe questions relevant to the particular dilemma (such as the above questions regarding Sharon's dilemma) as part of his or her teaching plan.

The recommended procedure for moral dilemma discussions involves small-group discussions followed by a discussion involving the entire class. The small-group discussions are less critical, and serve more as "warm-ups" for the entire class discussion. Nevertheless, small-group discussions are helpful in that they (1) maximize student-to-student interaction, (2) generate thinking about a variety of reasons for supporting a particular position, and (3) allow each individual to share his or her own reasoning with a few other class members with less fear of failure or disapproval than might otherwise be felt in an entire class discussion. Any of several different small-group strategies may be used. The following are two of the most common: (1) *homogeneous groupings*, in which all members within a group hold the same action position—they list all the reasons they have for their position, choose the best two reasons, and then state why these reasons are the best; and (2) *heterogeneous groupings*, in which members within a group represent opposing positions ("undecided" students can be included too)—they discuss their positions and reasons and then make a list of the two best reasons for each position represented.

While students meet in small groups, the teacher should move from one group to another, helping students focus on the assigned tasks, facilitating group interaction, and asking occasional probe questions to help them clarify and examine their reasoning. Students should feel free to switch their positions as the group discussions develop. When the group tasks have been completed, students can then convene as an entire class to continue their dicussion.

4. Reflect on an Individual Position. During the final phase of the class discussion, the teacher should help students to reflect once again on the positions considered and then to choose individually the reason(s) and/or positions they now find most persuasive. Although some students may indicate that they have changed their thinking during the discussion, the objective is *not* to form a consensus or to try to reach a conclusion regarding the "correct" action for the dilemma character. The process remains open-ended; students should be encouraged to continue thinking about positions taken and reasons heard in the discussion. The teacher might also ask students to (1) question their parents about how they would respond to the class dilemma, or (2) find dilemmas in newspapers and television shows involving moral issues similar to the class dilemma. Finally, in subsequent weeks students can discuss other dilemmas that involve similar issues and compare their reasoning across these dilemmas.

Beyond the Classroom: The Creation of the "Just Community School"

Writers from nearly every contemporary approach to moral education, including character education and values clarification, have discussed with great concern how their objectives in integrating moral education within the formal curriculum of the classroom are often subverted through the so-called "hidden curriculum" of arbitrary rules and regulations, authoritative administration (and teacher)-student interactions, and homogenizing evaluation and grading procedures. This "hidden curriculum" is derived from, and reflects, the organizational and governance structure of the school as an institution. Thus, the explicit goals of moral education in the classroom are often diametrically opposed by the implicit goals of the "hidden curriculum" of the school. Indeed, the implicit goals of the "hidden curriculum"—such as unquestioning obedience and conformity to authoritative rules and conventional expectations—are seen by many educators as deleterious to the functioning of a free, just, and democratic society.

Kohlberg and his colleagues have been especially articulate in their discussions concerning the dangers of the "hidden curriculum" and have been bold and imaginative in developing intervention strategies aimed at changing it (Kohlberg 1970a, 1972a; Fenton, 1975, 1977; Wasserman, 1976). From their perspective, the "hidden curriculum" often hampers, rather than facilitates moral development. Kohlberg proposes that the school as a moral educational institution—the "moral atmosphere of the school"—should facilitate moral development by providing students with opportunities to try out and consolidate their developing moral reasoning (their developing conceptions of justice, laws and rules, authority, etc.) through exposure to and participation in real-life moral dilemmas and decisions faced by the school community. For Kohlberg, classroom discussions of moral dilemmas should be part of a "broader, more enduring involvement of students in the social and moral functioning of the school" (Kohlberg, 1972a, p. 16). These considerations led Kohlberg to develop as well as to implement the concept of a "Just Community School" (Fenton, 1975, 1977; Wasserman, 1976). Here the administration, teachers, and students work together to (1) establish a school with a governance structure based on a participatory democracy, (2) develop a school community based on principles of justice or fairness, and (3) examine the hidden curriculum and make it congruent with the explicit curriculum; for example, if the explicit curriculum stresses the importance of participatory democracy vis-à-vis the issue of school rules, then students as well as staff are involved in the process of developing the school's rule structure. In 1974, the Kohlberg group opened the first "Just Community School," called the "Cluster School," by setting up a self-governing, participatory, democratic, alternative school unit within a traditional urban public high school in Cambridge, Massachusetts (Cambridge High and Latin School). About 70 students were voluntarily recruited for this school-within-a-school; students were drawn from all four high school classes and from the varied socioeconomic and racial groups of the wider school population. Eight staff members (representing a variety of academic backgrounds) volunteered and were accepted without screening. Early in the school year, students and staff together drew up a constitution by making a set of rules and developing a system to enforce them.

Staff and students in the "Cluster School" govern themselves through community meetings in which each person has one vote. During these community meetings, members constantly confront and discuss real-life moral dilemmas such as (1) how should you punish a student who has broken the rule against stealing when you know that other students have also stolen and not been caught? or (2) should you suspend a member of the community who constantly disrupts classes but who has found for the first time a real home in the community? The students take their social studies and English courses within the "Cluster School," and take the rest of their courses with other students from Cambridge High and Latin School. Both the social studies and English courses include class discussions of moral dilemmas. In a preliminary progress report on the "Cluster School," Wasserman (1976) indicates that (1) Students have assumed increasing responsibility for their own behavior and that of others; (2) a genuine sense of community has emerged; (3) many students have become competent at participating in community meetings and a smaller number have learned to lead these meetings skillfully; (4) the staff reports positive changes in the behavior of students with long histories of difficulty in school; and (5) the staff believes that many students have begun to progress in moral reasoning, although actual research has only begun.

Following the lead of the "Cluster School," other "Just Community School" programs have since been established (Fenton, 1977; Wasserman, 1976). The Kohlberg group has also implemented the "Just Community" approach within a woman's prison (Kohlberg, Scharf & Hickey, 1972).

Critique and Evaluation

We begin our evaluation by stating our belief that, with respect to our functional definition of moral education, Kohlberg's classroom discussions of moral dilemmas represents the best approach we have found for the facilitation of the development of those *cognitive* skills and abilities necessary for rational reasoning, problem solving and decision making in value-conflictual social situations. Some writers, though, have argued that exclusive reliance on moral dilemma discussions represents too limited a teaching strategy (Fraenkel, 1976; Miller, 1976). Specifically, they maintain that students may get bored with hypothetical moral dilemmas that may be too narrow in scope, too simple, or too remote from their real-life experiences and problems, and constant verbal discussion of dilemmas to the exclusion of other, more varied instructional methods. We believe that these criticisms underscore the importance of using moral dilemmas that are more real-life than hypothetical in origin and that confront students with complex moral issues that are directly relevant to their day-to-day experiences, and of using other instructional methods such as role playing within the context of the basic teaching strategy.

While we feel confident that Kohlberg's classroom teaching strategy is facilative of the development of moral reasoning and problem solving *in general*, we are less certain that this strategy stimulates moral reasoning in the specific direction that Kohlberg's theory postulates, especially vis-à-vis the final two stages. Our uncertainty is well founded; in fact,

Kohlberg's theory of moral development rests on rather limited empirical grounds and has generated considerable empirical, philosophical, and theoretical criticism. A full discussion of these criticisms would take a separate book, and we can only briefly touch on some of them here. Nevertheless, in Kohlberg's defense, we wish to say that these criticisms have arisen largely because Kohlberg has been bold enough to elaborate a complex and controversial theory in great depth, and has attempted to provide empirical support for it—something that very few writers in the field of moral education have done. Regardless of the ultimate outcome of Kohlberg's theory, it has provided the impetus for much needed debate in this field; for this alone, he deserves much credit.

Much of the empirical and philosophical objections to Kohlberg's theory are directed toward his fundamental hypothesis that there exists a universally invariant sequence of six stages of moral reasoning, culminating in postconventional reasoning in general, and in the "ideal" final stage of a fully universalized and hierarchically integrated sense of justice in particular.

This fundamental hypothesis rests on longitudinal and cross-cultural research that is methodologically problematic. Kohlberg's contention that there exists an invariant sequence of six stages is based on his 17-year longitudinal study of the moral development of a sample of lower and middle-class urban American males. There are basic problems throughout this research regarding Kohlberg's Moral Judgment Interview as an instrument for assessing the predominant stage of his subjects. From 1958 to around 1972, Kohlberg's Moral Judgment Interview was based on a certain system for scoring subjects' responses to moral dilemmas and determining modal stage (called the aspect scoring system). Kurtines and Greif (1974) have roundly criticized this aspect scoring-based Moral Judgment Interview on several grounds: (1) lack of standardized administration, (2) lack of evidence for reliability and validity, and (3) lack of a published scoring manual, making independent validation of Kohlberg's theory next to impossible. Kurtines and Greif (1974) also criticized Kohlberg's omission of such basic information as the number of dilemmas used, and interrater reliability in the reporting of his longitudinal research.

Kohlberg himself found data discrepant with his "invariant sequence" hypothesis (e.g., stage regression) in his longitudinal research using the aspect scoring system. In addition, Holstein (1973), using the same scoring system, also found such theoretically unexpected findings as skipping of stages and stage regression. As a result, Kohlberg began to develop and refine a new scoring system (issue scoring) which could account for his own as well as for Holstein's discrepant data, in effect making such data "fit" his "invariant sequence" hypothesis. Critics have charged that Kohlberg cannot keep changing and refining his scoring system (Fraenkel, 1976), while Kohlberg supporters counter that such methodological refinement is critical to the process of validating his theory (Broughton, 1978). Perhaps the greatest objection in this regard, though, concerned Kohlberg's failure to clarify, until recently (Kohlberg, 1976), the properties and implications of his newer issue scoring system publicly, thereby making it difficult for anyone outside his immediate circle to make sense of discrepancies between his earlier research (longitudinal or otherwise) using aspect scoring and his later research using issue scoring. The unavailability of a published scoring manual is simply inexcusable, although Fenton (1977) reports that the Kohlberg group is currently developing a "definitive" scoring manual for publication in which they describe standardized procedures for conducting and scoring a Moral Judgment Interview.

Kohlberg's cross-cultural research, which led to his claim that there exists a culturally universal invariant sequence of stages of reasoning about certain universal moral values or concepts, has been criticized on the following grounds:

a. The failure to report important information such as subject characteristics or sample sizes, or to describe fully the method used to determine stages of reasoning in the various cultures (Kurtines and Greif, 1974).
b. The failure to investigate enough cultures to support claims of universality (Fraenkel, 1976; Simpson, 1974).
c. The use of an assessment instrument (the Moral Judgment Interview) that may be invalid in cultures where analytical modes of thinking and language are not valued or developed (Simpson, 1974).
d. The a priori scoring of moral dilemmas vis-à-vis certain moral values or concepts (e.g., "property rights," "justice") without consideration as to whether such values concepts were valid or relevant to the particular culture studied, and then using results of such scoring to claim that these moral values or concepts are culturally universal (Simpson, 1974). We maintain that this kind of methodological "self-fulfilling prophecy" is unjustifiable; thus, the issue of whether there are universal moral values remains an empirically open question.
e. The relative scarcity (and sometimes total absence) of postconventional moral reasoning (especially stage 6) in the various cultures studied (Simpson, 1974).

It is intrinsic to the "invariant sequence" hypothesis that not everyone necessarily reaches the higher stages. Nevertheless, because of the general lack of postconventional reasoning in the various cultures studied, there simply does not exist at present a sufficient data base to support or refute empirically Kohlberg's theorizing concerning the nature and universal existence of the final two stages. In particular, the paucity of empirical data on Stage 6 has, in effect, confined discussion of this ideal stage to the level of philosophical presupposition and speculation.

In this regard, a number of writers have objected on philosophical grounds to Kohlberg's a priori definition of the highest stage of moral development in terms of a universalized sense of justice (Fraenkel, 1976; Peters, 1978; Simpson, 1974; Sullivan, 1977). Kohlberg's stage 6, "ideal" moral individual is someone who, in a totally rational and impartial way, considers and reasons through the conflicting interests and values of different individuals on the basis of an abstract respect for the universal equal rights of all people. The problems several writers have with this definition of the "ideal" moral individual is best expressed in Sullivan's (1977) comment that this "ideal principled person is a moral entity without flesh or bones" (p. 21). Specifically, objections converge on the notion that this definition of the highest stage of moral development neglects or minimizes the importance of concrete moral habits, and basic moral feelings (e.g., compassion, caring, guilt)—two aspects of morality which, along with moral reasoning, are necessary for actual moral *behavior*.

Concerning moral habits, Alston (1971) argues that in dismissing conventional character traits (e.g., cooperative, sympathetic, polite) as an irrelevant "bag of virtues," Kohlberg has thrown out the critical concept of "habits"—regularities in the way people behave or respond to certain social situations. Peters (1978) maintains that certain conventional moral habits or codes of conduct are critical for the moral behavior of the vast majority of people (e.g., the non- "postconventional" people) and essential to "the maintenance of social life under almost any conceivable conditions" (p. 155).

Concerning moral feelings, Peters (1970) maintains that people have to be passionately and emotionally devoted to their moral principles in order for these principles to influence behavior. Peters (1978) also criticizes Kohlberg for subordinating the affective-based moral principle of concern for human welfare (consideration or caring for others) to the cognitive-based moral principle of universalized justice. In a biting critique, Sullivan (1977) remarks that Kohlberg's stage 6 individual "will ultimately have to face the dilemma that thinking thoughts of universal brotherhood and sisterhood is a far cry from the passion, care, and commitment that will bring that ideal into being" (p. 31).

These philosophic objections to Kohlberg's stage 6 conception of morality have extremely important practical implications for a comprehensive program in moral education. Such a program would include yet transcend Kohlberg's approach. Its goals (which are in line with our own functional definition of moral education) are development in the explicitly behavioral and affective, as well as the cognitive, aspects of morality. For example, we have reviewed research suggesting that preconventional moral reasoning is a necessary though an insufficient condition for consistent and repetitive delinquent and criminal behavior; for example, while adolescent criminal offenders almost invariably reason at preconventional levels, many preconventional adolescents do *not* engage in repetitive delinquent or antisocial behavior. This would suggest that, compared with the former group, the latter group has learned more alternative, prosocial behavior habits and/or has developed more positive feelings toward themselves and others. Thus, a comprehensive program of moral education for repetitively delinquent adolescents would aim to (1) teach certain alternative, prosocial behavioral habits directly (what the character educators would call prosocial "character traits") so that they have the behavioral competence and skills to *be able to engage in prosocial behavior*, (2) facilitate the development of conventional moral reasoning à la Kohlberg so that they *understand why they should engage in prosocial behavior* even when there simultaneously exist other reasons for engaging in antisocial behavior (e.g., self-advantage, crime pays)—for if they cannot formulate good reasons for behaving prosocially, it is unlikely that they will do so consistently (e.g., in the absence of a powerful authority figure or in lieu of a concrete payoff), and (3) facilitate the development of a positive self-concept, and of sensitivity to and caring for the needs of others so that they will *want to engage in prosocial behavior*.

SUMMARY

We began this chapter with the proposition that a renewed commitment to moral education in the schools is a critical step in the learning of constructive alternatives to the varied forms of interpersonal aggression that characterize society today. We discussed three important and highly influential approaches in depth: character education, values clarification, and Kohlberg's cognitive-developmental approach. It is our belief that these three approaches, despite philosophical and theoretical differences, need not be seen as mutually exclusive in practice, and offer important possibilities toward a comprehensive program in moral education.

We suggest that the direct and nonindoctrinative teaching of certain prosocial values through a character education curriculum such as the one discussed in this chapter would be most valuable in the early primary grades. Such prosocial "character traits" as taught in character education are neither abstract principles nor general personality dispositions; rather, they reflect concrete moral habits or prosocial behavior patterns—regularities in the way people can behave in certain kinds of social situations. Children should be given opportunities to practice such moral values or habits and to learn about their desirability at an early age so that they can develop a foundation of prosocial behavioral skills and attitudes.

Unfortunately, the early primary grade child often confronts a value-conflicted society as he or she progresses through childhood and adolescence, and the simple moral values and habits learned through character education, while they provide a necessary foundation, are not likely to suffice. With his expanding social awareness, the person will encounter constructive values such as nonviolence, cooperation, and generosity existing side-by-side with their respective destructive opposites—aggression, cut-throat competition, and greed. Furthermore, with his increasing cognitive capacity, he will be able to understand rationales in favor of destructive values (e.g., aggression may be the easiest way to get what you want, "do unto others before they do unto you") as well as constructive ones. This is why Kohlberg's approach to the development of moral reasoning becomes so important, from the upper primary grades through high school and college. Unless the student can rationally arrive at "better," subjectively preferred reasons for constructive values and behaviors (e.g., conventional and postconventional moral reasons) than for destructive ones (e.g., preconventional moral reasons), the former may not prevail in situations in which they conflict with the latter.

Yet, even if the student has learned constructive moral values and habits, appreciates their desirability, and can formulate good reasons for putting them into practice in problematic social situations, he is still unlikely to behave accordingly unless he is motivated to do so. Such motivation can come from the kind of affective learning and development that results in a predominantly positive feeling toward oneself and others—in feelings of self-esteem as well as respect and caring for the needs and feelings of others. It occurs to us that it is in this area that values clarification can make an important contribution. While we reject the premise of value relativity, we believe that learning to feel proud enough of one's beliefs and values ("prizing and cherishing") to be willing to stand up for them ("affirming") and to act on them consistently ("acting upon choices," "repeating") encourages and develops self-respect, confidence, and self-esteem.

It is our view that if we are to meet the challenge of the development of constructive alternatives to interpersonal aggression, then the schools must get involved in the moral education of our young. The aim of the present chapter has been to provide some helpful considerations and practical suggestions for such involvement.

REFERENCES

Alston, W. P. Comments on Kohlberg's "from is to ought." In T. Mischel (Ed.), *Cognitive development and epistemology*. New York: Academic Press, 1971, pp. 269–284.

Anon. *Living with me and others*. San Antonio, Texas: American Institute for Character Education, 1974(a).

Anon. *Our rights and responsibilities*. San Antonio, Texas: American Institute for Character Education, 1974(b).

Bain, O. & Clark, S. *Character education: A handbook of teaching suggestions based on freedom's code for elementary teachers*, San Antonio, Texas: The Children's Fund, 1966.

Beck, C. *Moral education in the schools: Some practical suggestions*. Toronto: Ontario Institute for Studies in Education, 1971.

Beck, C., Hersh, R., & Sullivan, E. *The moral education project (year 4): Annual report*, 1975–1976. Toronto: Ontario Institute for Studies in Education, 1976.

Beck, C. & Sullivan, E. *The reflective approach in values education: the moral education project, year 3*. Toronto: Ontario Institute for Studies in Education, 1976.

Benson, G. C. & Engeman, T. S. *Amoral America*. Stanford, California: Hoover Institution Press, 1975.

Beyer, B. K. Conducting moral discussions in the classroom. *Social Education*, 1976, **40**, 194–202.

Blatt, M. & Kohlberg, L. The effects of classroom moral discussion upon children's level of moral judgment. *Journal of Moral Education*, 1975, **4**, 129–161.

Boyd, D. Education toward principled moral judgment: An analysis of an experimental course in undergraduate moral education applying Lawrence Kohlberg's theory of moral development. Unpublished doctoral dissertation, Harvard University, 1976.

Bronfenbrenner, U. Soviet methods of character education. *American Psychologist*, 1962, **17**, 550–564.

Broughton, J. The cognitive-developmental approach to morality: A reply to Kurtines and Greif. *Journal of Moral Education*, 1978, **7**, 81–96.

Burton, R. V. Honesty and dishonesty. In T. Lickona (Ed.), *Moral development and behavior: Theory, research, and social issues*. New York: Holt, Rinehart & Winston, 1976, pp. 173–197.

Chapman, W. E. *Roots of character education*. Schenectady, N.Y.: Character Research Press, 1977.

Chase, L. *The other side of the report card: A how-to-do-it program for affective education*. Santa Monica, Calif.: Goodyear, 1975.

Colby, A., Kohlberg, L., Fenton, E., Speicher-Dubin, B., & Lieberman, M. Secondary school moral discussion programmes led by social studies teachers. *Journal of Moral Education*, 1977, **6**, 90–111.

Dewey, J. *The child and the curriculum*. Chicago: University of Chicago Press, 1902.

——*Moral principles in education*. Boston: Houghton Mifflin, 1909.

——*Interest and effort in education*. Boston: Houghton Mifflin, 1913.

——*The school and society: Second edition*. Chicago: University of Chicago Press, 1915.

——*Democracy and education*. New York: MacMillan, 1916.

——*Experience and education*. New York: MacMillan, 1938.

Ekehammar, B. Interactionism in personality from a historical perspective. *Psychological Bulletin*, 1974, **81**, 1026–1048.

Endler, N. S. & Magnusson, D. Toward an interactional psychology of personality. *Psychological Bulletin*, 1976, **83**, 956–974.

Fenton, E. A developmental approach to civic education. In J. R. Meyer, B. Burnham, & J. Cholvat (Eds.), *Values education: Theory/practice/problems/prospects*. Waterloo, Ontario: Wilfrid Laurier University Press, 1975, pp. 41–50.

Fenton, E. The implications of Lawrence Kohlberg's research for civic education. In F. Brown (Ed.), *Education for responsible citizenship: The report of the national task force on citizenship education*. New York: McGraw-Hill, 1977, pp. 97–132.

Flavell, J. H. *The developmental psychology of Jean Piaget*. New York: Van Nostrand Reinhold, 1963.

Fodor, E. Delinquency and susceptibility to social influence among adolescents as a function of level of moral development. *Journal of Social Psychology*, 1972, **86**, 257–260.

Forcinelli, J. & Engeman, T. S. Value education in the public school. *Thomas Jefferson Research Center Newsletter*, Pasadena, Calif. 1977 (March), no. 132.

Fraenkel, J. R. The Kohlberg bandwagon: Some reservations. *Social Education*, 1976, **40**, 216–222.

Galbraith, R. E. & Jones, T. M. *Moral reasoning: A teaching handbook for adapting Kohlberg to the classroom*. Anoka, Minn.: Greenhaven Press, 1976.

Ginsburg, H. & Opper, S. *Piaget's theory of intellectual development: An introduction*. Englewood Cliffs, N.J.: Prentice-Hall, 1969.

Glasser, W. *Schools without failure*. New York: Harper & Row, 1969.

Goble, F. *The case for character education*. Pasadena, Calif. Thomas Jefferson Research Center, 1973.

Gordon, T. *Parent effectiveness training*. New York: Wyden, 1970.

Hall, R. T. & Davis, J. U. *Moral education in theory and practice*. Buffalo, N.Y.: Prometheus Books, 1975.

Hartshorne, J. & May, M. A. *Studies in the nature of character. Vol. I: Studies in deceit.* New York: MacMillan, 1928.

Hartshorne, J., May, M. A., & Maller, J. B. *Studies in the nature of character. Vol. II: Studies in service and self-control.* New York: MacMillan, 1929.

Hartshorne, J., May, M. A., & Shuttleworth, F. K. *Studies in the nature of character. Vol. III: Studies in the organization of character.* New York: MacMillan, 1930.

Hersh, R. H. & Mutterer, M. Moral education and the need for teacher preparation. In J. R. Meyer, B. Burnham, & J. Cholvat (Eds.), *Values education: Theory/practice/problems/prospects*. Waterloo, Ontario: Wilfrid Laurier University Press, 1975, pp. 65–69.

Hill, R. C. *Freedom's code: The historic American standards of character, conduct, and citizen responsibility*. San Antonio, Texas: The Children's Fund, 1965.

Holstein, C. B. Moral judgment change in early adolescence and middle age: A longitudinal study. Paper presented at the Society for Research in Child Development, Philadelphia, 1973.

Hudgins, W. & Prentice, N. Moral judgments in delinquent and non-delinquent adolescents and their mothers. *Journal of Abnormal Psychology*, 1973, **82**, 145–152.

Kirschenbaum, H. Beyond values clarification. In H. Kirschenbaum & S. B. Simon (Eds.), *Readings in values clarification*. Minneapolis, Minn.: Winston Press, 1973, pp. 92–110.

Kirschenbaum, H. Recent research in values education. In J. R. Meyer, B. Burnham & J. Cholvat (Eds.), *Values education: Theory/practice/problems/prospects*. Waterloo, Ontario: Wilfrid Laurier University Press, 1975, pp. 71–78.

Kohlberg, L. The child as a moral philosopher, *Psychology Today*, 1968 (Sept.), **7**, 25–30.

Kohlberg, L. Stage and sequence: The cognitive-developmental approach to socialization. In D. A. Goslin (Ed.), *Handbook of socialization theory and research.* Chicago: Rand McNally, 1969, pp. 347–480.

Kohlberg, L. The moral atmosphere of the school. In N. Overley (Ed.), *The unstudied curriculum.* Washington, D.C.: Association for Supervision and Curriculum Development, National Education Association, 1970, pp. 104–127(a).

Kohlberg, L. Education for justice: A modern statement of the platonic view. In N. F. Sizer and T. R. Sizer (Eds.), *Moral education: Five lectures.* Cambridge, Mass.: Harvard University Press, 1970, pp. 57–83(b).

Kohlberg, L. From is to ought: How to commit the naturalistic fallacy and get away with it in the study of moral development. In T. Mischel (Ed.), *Cognitive development and epistemology.* New York: Academic Press, 1971, pp. 151–235(a).

Kohlberg, L. Stages of moral development as a basis for moral education. In C. M. Beck, B. S. Crittenden, & E. V. Sullivan (Eds.), *Moral education: Interdisciplinary approaches.* New York: Newman Press, 1971, pp. 23–92(b).

Kohlberg, L. A cognitive-developmental approach to moral education. *The Humanist,* 1972 (Nov-Dec.), **32**, 13–16(a).

Kohlberg, L. Indoctrination versus relativity in value education. *Zygon,* 1972, **2**, 285–310(b).

Kohlberg, L. *Collected papers on moral development and moral education.* Cambridge, Mass.: The Center for Moral Education, Harvard University, 1973.

Kohlberg, L. The relationship of moral education to the broader field of values education. In J. R. Meyer, B. Burnham, & J. Cholvat (Eds.), *Values education: Theory/practice/problems/prospects.* Waterloo, Ontario: Wilfrid Laurier University Press, 1975, pp. 79–85.

Kohlberg, L. Moral stages and moralization: The cognitive-developmental approach. In T. Lickona (Ed.), *Moral development and behavior: Theory, research, and social issues.* New York: Holt, Rinehart & Winston, 1976, pp. 31–53.

Kohlberg, L. & Kramer, R. B. Continuities and discontinuities in childhood and adult moral development. *Human Development,* 1969, **12**, 93–120.

Kohlberg, L. & Mayer, R. Development as the aim of education. *Harvard Educational Review,* 1972, **42**, 449–496.

Kohlberg, L. Scharf, P., & Hickey, J. The justice structure of the prison: A theory and an intervention. *The Prison Journal,* 1972, **51**, 3–14.

Kohlberg, L. & Turiel, E. Moral development and moral education. In G. S. Lesser (Ed.), *Psychology and educational practice.* Chicago: Scott Foresman, 1971, pp. 410–465.

Krebs, R. L. Some relationships between moral judgment, attention and resistance to temptation. Unpublished doctoral dissertation, University of Chicago, 1967.

Kurtines, W. & Greif, E. B. The development of moral thought: Review and evaluation of Kohlberg's approach. *Psychological Bulletin,* 1974, **81**, 453–470.

Lickona, T. Introduction. In T. Lickona (Ed.) *Moral development and behavior: Theory, research, and social issues.* New York: Holt, Rinehart & Winston, 1976(a). Pp. 3–28.

Lickona, T. Critical issues in the study of moral development and behavior. In T. Lickona (Ed.), *Moral development and behavior: Theory, research, and social issues.* New York: Holt, Rinehart & Winston, 1976(b).

Maccoby, E. E. The development of moral values and behavior in childhood. In J. A. Clausen (Ed.), *Socialization and society.* Boston: Little/Brown, 1968, pp. 227–269.

Mayer, H. C. *The good American program: A teacher's guide to the direct teaching of citizenship values in the elementary grades.* New York: American Viewpoint, 1964.

McNamee, S. Moral behaviour, moral development and motivation. *Journal of Moral Education,* 1977, **7**, 27–31.

McPhail, P., Ungoed-Thomas, J. R., & Chapman, H. *Learning to care: Rationale and method of the lifeline program*. Niles, Ill.: Argus Communications, 1975.

Milgram, S. Behavioral study of obedience. *Journal of Abnormal and Social Psychology*, 1963, **67**, 371–378.

Miller, J. P. *Humanizing the classroom: Models of teaching in affective education*. New York: Praeger, 1976.

Mischel, W. Toward a cognitive social learning reconceptualization of personality. *Psychological Review*, 1973, **80**, 252–283.

Mosher, R. & Sprinthall, N. Psychological education in the secondary schools. *American Psychologist*, 1970, **25**, 911–916.

Mosher, R. & Sprinthall, N. Psychological education: A means to promote personal development during adolescence. In R. E. Purpel & M. Belanger (Eds.), *Curriculum and the cultural revolution*. Berkeley, Calif.: McCutchan, 1972, pp. 117–132.

Mulkey, Y. J. *Character education and the teacher*. San Antonio, Texas: American Institute for Character Education, 1977(a).

Mulkey, Y. J. *Teacher training for character education*. San Antonio, Texas: American Institute for Character Education, 1977(b).

Newmann, F. & Oliver, D. *Clarifying public issues: An approach to teaching social studies*. Boston: Little/Brown, 1970.

Oliver, D. & Bane, M. J. Moral education: Is reasoning enough? In D. M. Beck, B. S. Crittenden, & E. V. Sullivan (Eds.), *Moral education: Interdisciplinary approaches*. Toronto: University of Toronto Press, 1971, pp. 252–271.

Oliver, D. & Shaver, J. *Teaching public issues in the high school*. Boston: Houghton Mifflin, 1966.

Peine, H. A. & Howarth, R. *Children and their parents*. Harmondsworth, Middlesex: Penguin Books, 1975.

Peters, R. S. Concrete principles and the rational passions. In N. F. Sizer & T. R. Sizer (Eds.), *Moral education: Five lectures*. Cambridge, Mass.: Harvard University Press, 1970, pp. 29–55.

Peters, R. S. The place of Kohlberg's theory in moral education. *Journal of Moral Education*, 1978, **7**, 147–157.

Piaget, J. *The moral judgment of the child*. London: Routledge and Kegan Paul, 1932.

Raths, L. E., Harmin, M., & Simon, S. B. *Values and teaching: Working with values in the classroom*. Columbus, Ohio: Charles Merrill, 1966.

Rest, J. The hierarchical nature of moral judgment: A study of patterns of comprehension and preference of moral stages. *Journal of Personality*, 1973, **41**, 86–109.

Rest, J. Developmental psychology as a guide to value education: A review of "Kohlbergian" programs. *Review of Educational Research*, 1974, **44**, 241–259.

Rest, J. The research base of the cognitive developmental approach to moral education. In T. C. Hennessy (Ed.), *Values and moral development*. New York: Paulist Press, 1976.

Rest, J., Turiel, E., & Kohlberg, L. Level of moral development as a determinant of preference and comprehension of moral judgments made by others. *Journal of Personality*, 1969, **37**, 225–252.

Ringness, T. A. *The affective domain in education*. Boston: Little/Brown, 1975.

Rokeach, M. Toward a philosophy of value education. In J. R. Meyer, B. Burnham, & J. Cholvat (Eds.), *Values education: Theory/practice/problems/prospects*. Waterloo, Ontario: Wilfrid Laurier University Press, 1975, pp. 117–126.

Salk, L. *What every child would like his parents to know*. London: Fontana/Collins, 1975.

Saltzstein, H. D. Social influence and moral development: A perspective on the role of parents and peers. In T. Lickona (Ed.), *Moral development and behavior: Theory, research, and social issues*. New York: Holt, Rinehart & Winston, 1976, pp. 253–265.

Selman, R. L. Social-cognitive understanding: A guide to educational and clinical practice. In T. Lickona (Ed.), *Moral development and behavior: Theory, research, and social issues.* New York: Holt, Rinehart & Winston, 1976, pp. 299–316.

Simon, S. B. & Harmin, M. Subject matter with a focus on values. In H. Kirschenbaum & S. B. Simon (Eds.), *Readings in values clarification.* Minneapolis, Minn.: Winston Press, 1973, pp. 113–119.

Simon, S. B., Howe, L. W., & Kirschenbaum, H. *Values clarification: A handbook of practical strategies for teachers and students.* New York: Hart, 1972.

Simon, S. B. & Olds, S. W. *Helping your child learn right from wrong: A guide to values clarification.* New York: McGraw-Hill, 1976.

Simpson, E. L. Moral development research: A case of scientific cultural bias. *Human Development,* 1974, **17**, 81–106.

Smith, L. J. *Guiding the character development of the preschool child.* New York: Association Press, 1968.

Sullivan, E. V. *Kohlberg's structuralism: A critical appraisal.* Toronto: Ontario Institute for Studies in Education, 1977.

Trevitt, V. *The American heritage: Design for national character.* Santa Barbara, Calif.: McNally & Loftin, 1964.

Wasserman, E. R. Implementing Kohlberg's "just community concept" in an alternative high school. *Social Education,* 1976, **40**, 203–207.

Weinstein, G. & Fantini, M. *Toward humanistic education: A curriculum of affect.* New York: Praeger, 1970.

Wilson, J. *Education in religion and the emotions.* London: Heinemann Educational Books, 1971.

Wilson, J. *Practical methods of moral education.* London: Hienemann Educational Books, 1972.

Wilson, J. *A teacher's guide to moral education.* London: Geoffrey Chapman, 1973(a).

Wilson, J. *The assessment of morality.* Windsor, Berks.: National Foundation of Educational Research, 1973(b).

Wilson, J., Williams, N. & Sugarman, B. *Introduction to moral education.* London: Penguin Books, 1968.

III

Community Controls and Alternatives

Chapter 7
Prevention of Aggression
Craig Blakely and
William S. Davidson, II

The earth was corrupt before God, and the earth was filled with violence—*Genesis*, 6:11

Time marched on and eventually modern humans—*homosapiens sapiens*—emerged, creatures who, to an extraterrestrial observer, must seem to be more than a little perverse. Unlike no other animal, we wage war on each other. We knowingly exploit limited resources in our environment and seem to expect that our profligacy can go on forever. And we choose to ignore deep chasms of injustice, consciously inflicted both between nations and within nations. In a sense it is humans who rule the world: our extraordinary creative intelligence gives the potential to do more or less anything we want. But, an extraterrestrial observer may wonder, isn't the ruler just a little bit crazy?—Leakey & Lewin, 1977, p. 10.

Earlier chapters have noted that excessive aggression has been a problem plaguing human beings since the beginning of recorded history. Civilizations have constantly searched for methods of reducing the prevalence of aggressive behavior. Given the current official crime rates, the effectiveness of our efforts at preventing aggressive behavior has been a source of ongoing debate. Notions of preventing, rather than correcting, aggression hold great promise and appeal. In fact, many have argued that only through prevention can aggression be dealt with effectively. The negotiation, contracting, self-control, skill training, problem-solving and moral education methods examined in earlier chapters are all concrete expressions of such a preventive orientation. It can be argued that once aggressive behavior has occurred, it is often too late for effective intervention.

Hirschi and Selvin (1969) have noted that one's definition of a problem will to a great extent determine its explanation. At first glance, the statement seems obvious and simple. The point, however, is that in order to assess the efficacy of preventive efforts and to explain their success or lack of success, one must carefully define one's terms.

THE DEFINITION OF PREVENTION

Aggression was defined in an earlier chapter so as to exclude desirable and competitive aggressiveness. That is, the definition was restricted to *behavior* that was likely to result in personal injury against a person or property destruction of a sufficiently serious magnitude to warrant a societal consideration of legal sanctions (Bandura, 1969). As Megargee (1976) suggests, this working definition should include the threat of violent behavior as well. The notion of "likely" was included such that attempted violent behavior, whether successful or not, would fall within the bounds of the definition (Monahan, 1980).

The goal of a preventive intervention is to reduce the initial incidence of delinquent or violent behavior rather than simply to react to it after it has occurred. The emphasis is on the modification of factors likely to produce aggression. Johnson, Bird, & Little (1979) suggested that preventive intervention should refer to activities designed to reduce the incidence of aggressive behaviors among individuals not already in contact with the legal system. The current authors, however, do not wish to exclude those individuals who have already had contacts with the system. That is, many interventions described as preventive are carried out with offenders who have had previous contacts with the system (designed to reduce the incidence of *subsequent* aggressive/violent behavior).

Prevention, then, can be seen as any intervention effort undertaken with the goal of reducing the prevalence of future aggressive or violent behavior. Preventive intervention can vary along several dimensions. This chapter involves a discussion of these varying modes of prevention.

GENERAL CONCEPTS

Society's response to the incidence of violent aggressive crime has taken on many forms. Examples include imprisonment, hospitalization, increased police patrols, environmental impact statements, and government regulation. Most prevention efforts can be categorized into primary, secondary, and tertiary prevention. Primary prevention approaches typically reflect the assumption that "intervention is best attempted before manifest signs of psychological disturbance are evident" (Zax & Specter, 1974, p. 144). This assumption is based on the position that problematic behavior is a function of broad conditions that affect groups or individuals differentially. Differential income distribution is a commonly cited example. Primary prevention is an attempt to optimize the conditions for everyone, thus minimizing the probability of aggressive behavior in anyone.

Secondary prevention, on the other hand, singles out individuals most likely to be aggressive and provides for a direct intervention. There are two distinct components to a secondary prevention effort: early detection and preventive intervention. The Gluecks distinguished between primary and secondary prevention in the following manner.

> As we reflect on the complexities and implications of etiologic involvement in delinquency and criminalism, the wide ranging central problem is seen to fall into two major areas of possible preventive attack: general immunology and special immunology. Broad and permeative causal forces such as poverty, urban decay, racial conflicts, general weakening of family life, or religious-moral convictions, call for general societal and governmental attack on many fronts; and they entail a great deal of time before they are initiated and before their results can be assessed. Specific immunology is more concrete; it deals with timely recognition of children who are especially vulnerable.... It is this latter area that the predictive device can become a route to prevention [Glueck and Glueck, 1972, pp. 125–126].

The bulk of the work reported in the literature focuses on prediction and prevention, that is, secondary prevention.

The notion of early detection brings up the heated controversy of clinical versus actuarial/statistical prediction. Over 20 years ago Meehl (1954) distinguished between these two methods by defining clinical prediction as the formulation of "some psychological hypotheses regarding the structure and dynamics of this particular individual ... on the basis of interview impressions" (pp. 3–4). While actuarial or statistical prediction was defined as "the mechanical combining of information for classification purposes, and the resultant probability figure which is an empirically determined relative frequency" (p. 3), in practice, most schemes combine the two strategies. In other words, attention is paid to the probability of aggression given a set of events *and* an individual human judgment based on interactions.

In nearly every study comparing the two overall strategies (clinical versus actuarial), actuarial tables have proved to be more accurate (Monahan, 1980; Meehl, 1954). Others (Holt, 1978) have disputed the quality of this evidence by summarizing that "No matter how impressively high it is piled, garbage remains garbage" (p. 12). This criticism was based on the notion that "it hardly makes any more sense to expect it [clinical prediction] to grind out numerical averages of course grades than to expect an actuarial table to interpret dreams" (Holt, 1978, p. 27). Allport, another strong proponent of the clinical assessment/prediction strategy, has suggested that the downfall of the actuarial method can be found in its outcome. That is, the method yields a figure that is the probability that a certain class of people will commit an aggressive act. The problem arises when one applies this reasoning to a single case. In actuality, the individual has either a 100 percent or a 0 percent probability of committing the given act. Allport suggested that the chance of occurrence is determined by the individual's experience, not the frequency in some subpopulation. Therefore, psychological causation is always personal and never actuarial (cited in Monahan, 1980).

Gottfredson summed up this issue well by suggesting the use of a weather report as an analogy (Gottfredson, Wilkins, & Hoffman, 1978). It is suggested that a report of a 60 percent chance of rain does not mean that it will rain 60 percent of that day, but that on similar days in the past it has rained 60 percent of the days. Though it does not provide us with a prediction that is 100 percent certain, it does provide some useful information. The critical factor is a causal linkage or theory connecting the predictor variables with the outcome. Monahan further suggested: "What is necessary to make the inferential leap from membership in a class that has in the past been violent to the prediction that this member of the same class will in the future be violent, is a *theory* linking the conditions operating to produce violence in the past class of cases with the conditions operating to produce violence in this specific present case" (1980, pp. IV–6).

While the debate concerning the validity of predictions about the future incidence of violence rages, an accurate assessment of current methods of prediction as a basis for secondary prevention intervention yields disappointing results. As shall be seen in later sections of this chapter, the extent to which such interventions have potential iatrogenic effects or are costly in fiscal terms is the extent to which secondary prevention becomes a questionable strategy.

Tertiary prevention aims to reduce the future incidence of aggression among those groups of individuals already officially identified as aggressive. Basically, tertiary prevention encompasses a wide variety of programs aimed at the rehabilitation of individuals who have already been labeled aggressive. It is, however, the goal of reducing overall aggression rather than the rehabilitative treatment of individuals per se which is the focus of tertiary prevention. The emphasis of tertiary prevention is on improving the quality and quantity of intervention. A common example of tertiary prevention in the area of aggression control is prison reform (Nagel, 1973). It is also, however, implied in such strategies as fines for corporate environmental abuse, retraining chronic traffic violators, and others. While many parts of this volume contain theoretical propositions, program descriptions, and recommendations that may be applied in the tertiary prevention context, the primary focus of this chapter is on activities typically described as primary or secondary prevention in their approach.

Regardless of the type of prevention attempted, each can be carried out within varying theoretical and philosophical positions. By examining the theoretical and philosophical base of these strategies, alternative prevention approaches can best be understood.

CONTEMPORARY CAUSAL LINKAGES

A full spectrum of both social scientific and political positions have impinged upon the design and selection of strategies for the prevention of aggression. In fact, the theoretical positions that underlie contemporary approaches to the prevention of aggression are not in any way unique. Namely, they are the same propositions commonly employed as explanations for a wide variety of "human deviance." The same positions have provided the basis for most of our contemporary programmatic approaches to a wide variety of social problems. Since many of these positions have been reviewed in some detail earlier in this volume, the brief review that follows focuses primarily on the implications of these major theoretical-political positions for the prevention of aggression.

Intraindividual Explanations

To date, the most prevalent explanations offered for aggression are intraindividual in their focus. In a recent review of the literature, Rappaport and Holden (in press) found that nearly three-fourths of the literature suggested a person-blame ideology. The range of specific theoretical explanations for aggressive behavior is quite expansive when specifics are considered. The bulk of these positions, however, argue that something *within* the individual is the source of aggression.

The roots of most intraindividual explanations of aggression are typically traced to earlier instinctual positions. Whether the ultimate cause is traced to the inherent aggressive nature of the human race (e.g., Lorenz, 1963) or traced to the formation of agricultural society (e.g., Leakey & Lewin, 1977), these positions would argue that human beings are inherently aggressive. Only through extreme social controls can these instinctual aggressive tendencies be minimized. While this is no longer widely accepted as the central cause of aggression, the preventive implications of such positions are not very dissimilar from many prominent contemporary views. With the rare exception of chromosomal typing (e.g., Court Brown, 1968), such positions have not played a major role in contemporary approaches to the prevention of aggression. They remain primarily philosophical positions for debates concerning the ultimate causes of aggression (Gibbons, 1970; National Institute of Juvenile Justice and Delinquency Prevention, 1977).

Personality disorders have long been considered the central causes of delinquency. Some have merely allowed that personality disorders are necessary but insufficient of themselves to produce aggressive behavior. It is clearly the case that a wide variety of studies have demonstrated statistically reliable differences between offenders and nonoffenders (e.g., Waldo & Dinitz, 1967; Schuessler & Cressey, 1950; Kassebaum, 1974). Typically, the prevention paradigm implied necessitates the identification of those individuals with personality or character disorders likely to lead to aggressive or delinquent behavior. A wide variety of predictive methods have been employed including objective tests, projective tests, interviews by clinical experts, observations and ratings by significant others, etc. Within this paradigm both intraindividual and environmental factors are cited as the ultimate cause of the violence or aggression. Namely, the violence-prone individual may be a product of inappropriate upbringing, environmental stress, or inherent character flaws. The implications of this position for the prevention of aggression are classically described as secondary prevention as outlined in the preceding section. The basic position suggests that if the products (individuals) of psychologically and socially harmful environments can be identified early in life, preventive interventions can then be applied.

As mentioned earlier, the classic work in the area was carried out in the 1940s by the Gluecks. In comparing 500 institutionalized delinquent youths with 500 matched nondelinquents on over 400 physical, psychological, and social variables, the Gluecks identified dimensions that differentiated delinquents early in elementary school. It was felt that such predictors could then be used as a basis for identification and preventive intervention. After several analyses of the data, the Gluecks concluded that five factors, descriptive of problematic parenting strategies, were the best predictors of delinquency (Glueck & Glueck, 1970). This highly influential work is representative of a large body of work that focuses on individual and microsocial differences. The criterion group model, in which differences between those who have been identified as aggressive and those who have not, has led to a myriad of "individual difference" explanations for aggression proneness. Specific work has focused on issues of socialization, mental illness, moral immaturity, and cognitive deficits (Smith & Austrin, 1974; Adams, 1974; Prentice, 1972; Jordan, 1974).

The approach of early detection and prevention has met with less than positive results when the accuracy of prediction and further involvement in official deviance are used as criteria. A project designed to examine the credibility of this position was carried out by the Washington D.C.

Youth Council. The major conclusions of Tait & Hodges (1971) were that delinquents could be identified using the Gluecks' five-factor method accurately (about 75 percent valid positives), but that the resulting interventions to identified families had no impact on future delinquency. Further, when the high base rate in the population examined was considered (71 percent delinquent) and the large proportion of false positives (88 percent), even the first conclusion is questionable. Review of a large number of similar studies led three authors to conclude that, at present we lack sufficient knowledge of delinquency, preventive intervention effectiveness, or intervention processes to allow us to engage in efforts of early detection and prevention for projected future aggression among young people (Kahn, 1965; Berleman & Steinburn, 1969; Venezia, 1971).

Despite the conflicting evidence concerning the accuracy of predictions and the efficacy of preventive interventions, personality-based intraindividual explanations of the precursors of violence and aggression remain prominent. For example, in summarizing major reviews of the literature, Kassebaum (1974) stated, "it is striking then that two of the reviews of published studies of personality differences between the law-violating and the law-abiding, which taken together reviewed 207 studies ranging over several decades of research, are unable to provide any firm basis for the claim that there are distinguishable and characteristic features in the personality of the offender" (p. 52). Similarly, Johnson et al. (1979) concluded a discussion concerning the existence of a relationship between personality disorder and delinquency by stating that "an assumption that no relationship has been documented appears prudent" (p. 37).

Social Factors and Precursors of Aggression

Positions that espouse the macrosocial bases of aggression are based primarily on the work of sociologists (e.g., Merton, 1957). Heavy emphasis is placed on the role of social structures, milieu, and opportunity. Such classic early studies as that of Shaw and McKay (1942) had demonstrated the proportional distribution of various social and physical problems among socioeconomic and geographic groups. The combination of such information with the propositions of anomie theory led to conclusions that aggression was a result of differential access to legitimate and illegitimate means to attainment of socially defined personal and particularly material goals.

As with the intraindividual approaches, a myriad of specific macrosocial factors have been cited as precursors of aggression. Two specific examples will suffice for the purposes of our discussion. First, the general social class differences in official aggression mentioned above led to suggestions that social disorganization produced excessive aggression. In other words, the cluster of social, physical, economic, and other problems typically found in the lower class, all produced a breakdown in the basic fabric or "control mechanism" of society. Whether for internal or external reasons, the resulting disorganization led to the development of "undesirable" behavior patterns. In other words, the typical social structures that keep all individuals "in line" were so destroyed that increased violence and other forms of deviance were prevalent.

A second specific explanation of the role of society in producing deviants was the blocked opportunity approach (e.g., Cloward & Ohlin, 1960). According to this position, society emulates middle-class ideals and values but is structured in such a way that legitimate modes of access to these cultural and societal goals (particularly material goals) are not equally available. Inadequate schools, racial discrimination, the squalor of slums, and numerous other manifestations of unequal economic, social, and political opportunities are all cited as evidence supporting the blocked opportunity position. The socially defined importance of acquiring material goods and middle-class status can pressure large groups of individuals into aggressive means of attaining these goals, since other more legitimate means of access are not available.

Like intraindividual explanations of aggression, those that focus on social factors have direct implications for prevention. In fact, many of the "war on poverty" and "delinquency prevention" programs are based on just such propositions. While it is certainly the case that most such programs have not used these theoretical positions as a base of their operating procedures (e.g., Klein, 1979), they are often based vaguely on the notions of equalizing opportunity structures and reducing societal alienation. The implication of the social factors position is that broad changes need to be made in society and its structures if aggression is to be minimized.

It is also true that the social factors positions have come under attack as viable models for prevention strategies. They have been seriously criticized owing to their inherent dependency upon official measures of aggression (e.g., Williams & Gold, 1972; Krohn, Waldo, and Chiricos, 1975). The most frequently mentioned criticism of the use of official record data (e.g., arrests for aggressive behavior) as a dependent measure is that it is far more a measure of police behavior than a measure of aggression (Gold, 1966; Farrington, 1973; Williams & Gold, 1972). An equally plausible explanation is that the correlations between official records and socioeconomic status stem from differential treatment by the police following detection of aggressive behavior.

Those preventive interventions that derive from macrosocial explanations are often equally intraindividual in their focus (e.g., Monahan & Splane, 1980). In other words, while focusing on social forces and structures, they are all ultimately reduceable to individuals who possess the "by-products" of such harmful social structures. While this is probably a disciplinary argument that can not be settled here, it is safe to say that many attempts at delinquency prevention from a social factors position have been implemented in such a way that the real focus is on changing aggressive individuals.

OTHER PROMINENT POSITIONS

There are two additional positions that have had impact on the prevention of aggression which do not really fit into the dichotomy discussed above. Namely, they are really neither intraindividual nor societal in their focus.

Labeling Theory

Rather than focus on relatively static characteristics of the individual or the environment, labeling theory looks at the critical role of the interaction between labelers and "aggressive actors." In other words, primary focus is placed on the observation that in order for a behavior to be labeled aggressive, it must first be observed and then labeled by one in a sufficient position of power to define the act as aggressive. While considerable discussion in this volume and others has been devoted to the definition of aggression and violence, from a labeling perspective, aggression is only a form of behavior that is so labeled by others. Similarly, aggressive behavior is behavior performed by those who have been labeled aggressive (e.g., Becker, 1963). The focus of this position is on the actions of the labelers (most typically the criminal justice system), the characteristics of those likely to be labeled, and the resulting processes. The labeling theory position, coupled with the previously discussed data that suggested that individuals are differentially labeled aggressive as a function of socioeconomic status, race, sex, etc., has resulted in a good deal of debate in this area.

Social labeling theory is highly inconsistent with other prominent views of the aggression problem. According to the propositions of social labeling theory, most individuals drift in and out of aggressive behavior patterns. Most such behavior is not officially noticed, nor is a formal label applied. If an individual is apprehended and a negative social label is conferred, the processes of this position are put in motion. It is suggested that the conferring of such negative social labels has adverse affects on the future incidence of aggressive performances. In other

words, one of the effects of the symbolic interactions involved in
formally labeling an individual as aggressive is the production of additional aggressive behavior. From this point of view, extensive use of
formal control mechanisms as a means of preventing aggression are
contraindicated (Faust, 1973; Lemert, 1974; Matza, 1964; Schur, 1969,
1973; Johnson, et al., 1979).

The primary implications of the social labeling position for the prevention of aggression are also contrary to other alternatives. In short,
what is suggested is a minimal formal social response to aggression. It
certainly does not rule out preventive interventions completely, but
suggests that expansive use of primary or particularly secondary prevention may have more negative side effects than positive benefits. In
other words, if identifying individuals as aggression prone sets in motion
powerful social forces that can in fact produce aggression, then the
overuse of such strategies is not desirable.

There have been very few systematic attempts to implement the
implications of social labeling theory in the prevention of aggression
(Klein, 1980). In addition, investigators typically have had difficulty
producing consistent support for the proposition of labeling theory.
Most studies have attempted to operationalize the labeling process into a
single critical incident (e.g., adjudication or sentencing) and examine its
effects cross-sectionally (Davis, 1972). For example, in a series of
studies, a strong association between being on probation in a juvenile
court and negative school evaluations were reported. Discrepancies,
however, between probationers and nonprobationers were as great prior
to as after a supposed critical courtroom labeling event (Fisher, 1972).
Another study reported a survey of 200 adjudicated youths as to their
perceptions of the social liability that had resulted from their involvement with the juvenile court and law enforcement agencies. For the
most part, no liability was perceived on the part of the youth (Foster,
Dinitz, & Reckless, 1972).

Control Theories

Control theories suggest that the critical variables in preventing aggression lie in the consequences or costs of the commission of aggressive
acts. Individuals who have positive family, career, home, and peer group
ties have a good deal invested in appropriate and socially desirable
behavior. To decide to perform deviant or aggressive acts has the
potential to place those investments in jeopardy. Not only is there the
threat of socially defined punishment or consequences, but the loss of
status and involvement in other settings is a more grave consequence.

The degree to which individuals are committed to these investments
defines the extent to which they are "controlled." Hirschi (1969) sees the

critical control processes as made up of four mechanisms. The first, commitment, refers to the extent to which the individual has investments that might be jeopardized by aggression. The second, attachment, refers to the degree of ties to others. A low level of attachment would allow one to violate socially defined norms at minimal cost. The third control mechanism in Hirschi's model is involvement. The more involved the individual is in socially desirable roles and behaviors, the greater the allocation of time to conventional activities. The fourth mechanism Hirschi suggested is the belief in the validity of the rules laid out by the dominant social group.

In short, the stronger the ties (through these four mechanisms) to the norms of society, the greater society's control over the individual. This perspective clearly suggests preventive interventions, particularly with young people. Youth have fewer established investments in the community and therefore, following this logic, the community has less potential control over youth. Johnson et al. (1979) have suggested that control theories outline a clear need for increased efforts to improve the image of community control agents, increased employment opportunities for young, and reducing obstacles to attachment with the schools. The labeling perspective discussed above would appear to serve only to reduce the control over those negatively labeled by reducing their attachment and involvement in desirable social systems. While the perspective of control theories is both individual and social in nature, it clearly demands policy-level change likely to impact on the totality of individual involvement in desirable social subsystems.

Examination of the validity of social control theory as a potential conceptual framework for the prevention of aggression is essentially untested. While there have been specific attempts to translate the propositions of social control theory into the procedures used in certain intervention strategies such as behavior modification, there has been no widespread examination of its effects. This is not particularly surprising since the propositions of social control theory were put forth primarily as descriptive statements in order to contrast the social phenomena leading to nonaggression. There has also been no systematic predictive work applying the propositions of social control theory to the prevention of aggression.

COMPARATIVE EFFECTIVENESS OF PREVENTION STRATEGIES: THE CASE FOR CONFUSION

At this point in the volume, the authors felt it would be appropriate to provide a review based on comparison of the differential effectiveness of the varying approaches to prevention suggested by the above positions.

Various other reviews of relevant work (e.g., Monahan, 1980; Tait & Hodges, 1971; Rappaport, 1977), however, have concluded that no such statement is possible. In fact, when the plethora of theoretical positions are reviewed in combination with the empirical work to date, a state of confusion is the logical outcome.

At a basic level, there is no comparative information that would allow us to conclude that one or more of the above approaches are particularly effective. Each of the above positions is much more a philosophical base than a clearly articulated plan for action. In other words, it is extremely difficult at this point in their development for any of the above positions to be operationally translated into programs for preventing aggression. The principles of preventive intervention for aggression are an amalgam of poorly understood concepts, each with hidden social intentions, that are difficult to translate into operational terms, and are often aimed at an inappropriate level of analysis. Most specifically, we have seen that many prominent positions are ultimately reduced to an individual focus on training, retraining, or rehabilitating the bottom third of our society. In short, the area of prevention of aggression is a disaster from a policy standpoint.

To those involved in the field of the prevention of aggression, this may come as no surprise. To the outsider, the above paragraph may be shocking indeed. There are, however, a number of reasons that lead to this confusion.

The first issue that is not directly addressed by most of the prevention work to date is, "What violence is being prevented?" The theory of prevention, resting heavily on such work as that of Caplan (1964), would demand a conceptually clear-cut definition of aggression. Implied by the prevention ideology is the notion of a dynamically developing phenomena, with identifying precursors and concomitants, amenable to *a priori* intervention. The question at hand is whether or not the medical analogy of disease is appropriate in the area of preventing aggression. There is clearly no consensus as to what are the precursors or concomitants of aggression. Second, and perhaps more important, is the question of what behaviors are worthy of intervention. As noted above, most of the research literature, and hence, resulting interventions to date have focused on the prevention of "aggression" within the same social groups whose intellect we have attempted to upgrade, whose mental health we have attempted to repair, whose neighborhoods we have tried to renew. In short, little attention has been paid to corporate, white collar, environmental, or other forms of aggression and violence. It can certainly be argued that unsafe automobiles annually cause more violence than do all the inmates in maximum security settings for the "dangerous." The point is that our conceptions of and programmatic approaches to prevention have become inextricably entwined with our philosophical and political positions. Not surprisingly, social and behavioral sciences have followed the lead. A broader discussion of these issues indicates that these criticisms about the prevention of aggression have characterized our approaches to other social problems as well (e.g., Ryan, 1971; Rappaport, Davidson, Mitchell, & Wilson, 1975; Caplan & Nelson, 1973).

TWO EXAMPLES OF PREVENTING AGGRESSION

In order to illustrate the kinds of conceptual and pragmatic difficulties alluded to above, two specific examples of contemporary approaches to the prevention of aggression will be described in some detail. In one sense, the two approaches selected represent extreme ends of a continuum of prevention activities. First, a review of society's response to juvenile delinquency will be provided. Essentially, this country's approach to juvenile delinquency can be viewed as a broad-based policy approach to the prevention of aggression among adults. At the other end of the continuum, contemporary approaches to the prevention of dangerousness will be reviewed.

PREVENTING DELINQUENCY

The juvenile justice system represents an approach to the prevention of violence in American society that has spanned the last 80 years. Empey (1978), noted the prevalence of aggressive behavior since medieval times and concluded that rates have not changed to a great extent. What has changed, it was argued, is society's reaction to aggressive behavior. In tracing the history of the juvenile court, and hence concepts of delinquency, he noted that this was particularly obvious in that notions of childhood and delinquency were invented together. In one very real sense then, the development and current status of the juvenile court provides an excellent example of a prevention of aggression procedure. Juvenile delinquency and society's response to the problem can be traced to the precolonial days in Europe. For the present purposes, however, the most meaningful place of departure would be the dawn of the industrial revolution in America around the turn of the 19th century. The social control system of the day, based on strong family ties, was deteriorating with increasing child labor. These trends, coupled with the move toward urban areas and the resultant increase in population density, led to a drastic increase in the juvenile crime rate. These conditions led to the first house of refuge, opened in New York City in 1825. The houses of refuge sprang up across the country within the next several years. The houses themselves served essentially as prisons for delinquent youth though they were viewed as schools for instruction (e.g., the mode of preventing subsequent delinquency) rather than places of punishment. Since they were founded as preventive institutions, they accepted delinquent, dependent, and neglected youth, a practice continued to this day by the juvenile court. During the latter half of the 19th century, the states took over jurisdiction of the houses and they became known as state reform schools. Prevention during the 1800s then, can be seen as an attempt to punish offenders by removing them from their immediate environment and attempting to reduce the probability of subsequent offenses. It was an individual strategy based on the identification of known offenders. The definition was, however, considerably broadened to include all troubled or troublesome youth. In other words, youth who had committed crimes were placed together with other troublesome youth out of their own community. The idea was that such treatment would reduce the probability of aggression in adulthood.

The twentieth-century version of the juvenile justice system began in Illinois in 1899 with the passage of the first comprehensive child welfare legislation. The legislation was an attempt to protect the youth from the mistreatment that had historically been a part of the houses of refuge and state reform schools while at the same time protecting the community from the aggressive activities of delinquent youth. The thrust of the *parens patriae* doctrine was at the base of juvenile court operation. The initial goal of the juvenile court was that it should provide care for the youth in a manner as similar as possible to that provided by a responsible parent. In other words, good parenting in a good environment would reduce the probability of future delinquent and aggressive behavior. There were minimal due process safeguards involved in the juvenile court from the beginning. Rules of evidence, procedure, etc., were all extremely lax compared with their counterparts in the adult system. The youth were essentially required to trade their constitutional rights to due process for the parentlike concern and individualized justice and treatment provided by the juvenile court.

The court's sphere of influence quickly expanded. By 1901, status offenses (those offenses unique to juvenile offenders such as truancy, violation of curfew, incorrigibility) were included in the court's jurisdiction. By the mid-1920s, virtually every state in the union had its own separate juvenile justice system. Though these court systems were heavily influenced by the leading theorists of the day, they continued in this preventive, substitute parent role through the mid-1960s. Prevention was increasingly seen as a process of increasing earlier identification and intervention. It was theorized that the inclusion of status offenders within the court's legal realm allowed for the identification of youth prior to their commission of adult offenses.

During the 1960s, the juvenile court came under critical attack on many fronts. Major stumbling blocks included the very procedural informality upon which the court system was based. In addition, the punitive confinement strategies used in the juvenile court, the high recidivism rate among juvenile offenders, the rising crime rate, and resultant political and public outcry all led to demands for change. Three major sets of criticism were central in attacks on the effectiveness of the juvenile justice system in preventing juvenile delinquency and aggression.

The first line of criticism attacked the juvenile court's justification for acting with procedural informality. The argument had been that there was little danger in the court "over including" wayward youth since they would act with parentlike interest and concern. Characterized by the Supreme Court decision in the case of Gault (1967), it was suggested that the entire juvenile court movement had been a disaster. The majority opinion of the court stated that, laudatory intentions aside, "the condition of being a boy does not justify a kangaroo court." The failure of the juvenile court to provide either effective treatment or preventive services or constitutional safeguards struck at the very heart of its operations. Evidence presented created serious concern. For example, Scarpitti & Stephenson (1971) surveyed 1,200 juvenile court decisions in the late 1960s and found that rather than providing for individualized justice, the severity of disposition handed down by juvenile court judges was related to the socioeconomic standing of the young person. Further, Langley, Graves, & Norris (1972), in surveying cases of over 200 youth in a state training school, found that rather than considering the individual merits of the case, the judges typically placed youth in out-of-home institutional settings as a function of community pressure.

A second set of criticisms focused on the effectiveness of juvenile courts in preventing delinquency. Rather troublesome recidivism data have been presented by various authors. For example, Wolfgang et al. (1972) report the following data: of all youth arrested for the first time, 54 percent commit a second offense; for all youth arrested a second time, 65 percent commit a third offense; and for all youth arrested a third time, 75 percent commit a fourth crime. Further, Scarpitti and Stephenson (1968) report that recidivism among youth on probation tends to run about 50 percent. Finally, varying authors, in calculating recidivism rates of youth who were in juvenile treatment institutions, have found recidivism rates to fall between 50 and 85 percent (e.g.,

Griffin & Griffin, 1978; Jesness, 1975). A third and somewhat more pervasive flaw attributed to the juvenile court was the insistence on viewing delinquency as unique to apprehended and convicted youth. This problem relates to the general problem of the criteria for aggression presented earlier in this chapter; namely, there is serious disagreement as to what are the appropriate criteria for determining necessary intervention in prevention. As pointed out earlier, viewing the problems of delinquency from the perspective of apprehended and convicted youth usually led to the conclusion that delinquency, and hence delinquency proneness, was centered among lower-class groups. The focus of delinquency prevention efforts among lower-class groups, particularly given the labeling effects of such interventions discussed above, may be highly inappropriate and may only exacerbate the problem. For example, if self-report studies indicate widespread commission of unlawful acts quite unrelated to social standing, it seemed inappropriate that juvenile courts had focused their attention on primarily lower-class youth. In other words, officially labeled delinquent youth may have been more representative of the actions of the juvenile justice system than of the behavior of youth per se.

Each of these attacks led to arguments for the juvenile court getting out of the "prevention" business. Essentially, the President's Crime Commission on Law Enforcement and Criminal Justice (1967) argued that the court be avoided at all costs. As a result, the concept of diversion was born as the "new prevention" approach. The Commission jointly challenged the juvenile justice system and the community to seek alternatives in the prevention of delinquency. Essentially, we have come full circle in the prevention of aggression by dealing with juvenile offenders. Within 80 years, we have seen it argued that we should create a separate juvenile justice system to prevent adult crime. Part of the original argument was that a separate system was necessary in order to avoid the pitfalls and ineffectiveness of the adult criminal justice system. Over half a decade later, it was argued that it was necessary to find an alternative to the juvenile justice system. Essentially, the "new juvenile court" has been born.

Proponents of the diversionary approach found immediate support in several areas. Many base strong appeals for diversion on the conclusions of labeling theorists (e.g., Lemert, 1971), who stated that "in many cases the harm done to children and youth by contacts with these courts outweighs any benefits thereby gained. Moreover, the interaction between child and court in unanticipated consequences of the processing of a child in many instances contributes to or exacerbates the problem of delinquency" (p. 1). Given the newness of the diversion alternative, sound evaluations have only existed in recent years. The results have been extremely conflicting. Lincoln conducted an evaluation of a series of diversion programs located in Southern California and failed to find positive effects in terms of official recidivism or self-reported delinquency (Lincoln, Teilmann, Klein, & Labin, 1977). In fact, the study findings suggested that the diversion programs yielded higher recidivism rates and simpler release procedures (Carter & Klein, 1976). In a similar study, Elliott (1978) found that recidivism rates for a diverted group did not differ from those rates of youth treated in the usual juvenile court. Others have reached more positive conclusions. Collingswood, Douds, and Williams (1976), in evaluating the Dallas Police Department and youth service program, found that diverted youth receiving counseling and skills programming were less likely to be arrested than were those who did not participate in the program. Though the evaluation was not based on a strong experimental methodology, it does provide some promising support. In a truly randomized experimental evaluation of a similar program, Binder, Monahan & Newkirk (1976) reached mixed conclusions. A series of studies conducted by Davidson and colleagues (Seidman, Rappaport, & Davidson, 1976; Davidson, Seidman, Rappaport, Berck, Rapp, Rhodes, & Herring, 1977; Kantrowitz, 1979) indicate that diversion programs produce less recidivism than either outright release or referral to juvenile court. Across all studies, however, no differences in actual self-reported delinquent behavior are observed.

Despite the above evidence and rationale, diversion has already come under attack. These attacks are exemplary of the types of concerns and criticisms that will face preventive efforts in the area of aggression. First, it has been suggested that diversion programs provide a means of side-stepping the Gault (1967) decision, by forcing youth to choose less consequential diversional alternatives rather than employing legal safeguards (Nejelski, 1976). Any secondary prevention program that aims at the reduction of aggression will be faced with this issue: to what extent is the intervention justifiable given the constitutional safeguards employed? The other side of this apparent dilemma is to what extent constitutional safeguards can be employed while still maintaining a preventive focus. In other words, highly formalized proceedings are traditionally reserved for criminal procedures in our society. Were we to begin employing them in the use of all preventive programs, the nature of prevention would change dramatically. Their appeal would also be severely restricted. To what extent prevention approaches for aggression can in the future unravel or side-step this dilemma is unclear.

A second criticism of diversion programs is that they have engaged in "creaming." In other words, the diversion programs have dealt with youth who are not really likely to be engaged in aggressive acts. The core question here is one of false positives. Have restrictive preventive interventions been employed on behalf of individuals who would not be expected to commit aggressive acts if left alone? Any preventive interventions focused on the control of aggression must address this issue.

Finally, it has been suggested that diversion programs may in fact contribute to delinquency. If diversion programs are involving youth who would otherwise be left alone in service programs, the following problem arises. To the extent to which such programs have iatrogenic effects (i.e., produce aggression), their effectiveness is attenuated. Worse, they have contributed to the very problem they are expected to ameliorate.

The history of our society's interventions with young people through means of the juvenile justice system represents many of the problems currently plaguing the prevention policy area. On the one hand, the broad preventive impact of the juvenile justice system on reducing aggression among adults is impossible to assess. While most juvenile offenders do not in fact become adult offenders, to what extent this would occur without juvenile justice system intervention is unknown. At the specific individual level, a number of difficult issues have arisen that characterize preventive interventions at the secondary level. Namely, when preventive interventions involve the restriction of freedoms, constitutional and procedural safeguards are demanded. This presents the inherent dilemma described above. In addition, the question of false positives is again prominent. It is quite clear that many of the youth who receive the preventive interventions of the juvenile court do not need such intervention. Finally, it has been argued that the juvenile justice system creates more problems than it solves. This is also a parallel attack of secondary prevention approaches. To the extent that such interventions contribute to the future incidence of aggression in young people who would not otherwise be expected to be aggressive, is a devastating criticism.

PREDICTION OF DANGEROUSNESS

A second common contemporary example of approaches to preventing aggression might be labeled the prediction of dangerousness. The term, "prediction of dangerousness," implies a host of procedures that have been practiced in this country for some time. Generally involved are procedures that call for the involuntary incarceration of an individual based on a prediction, usually both clinical and judicial, that the individual is likely to be highly dangerous in the future. Although occurring less frequently in recent years, such individuals are typically (these procedures vary from state to state) incarcerated for long periods of time without judicial review or trial. A common way in which these decisions are made is through criminally insane commitment procedures. In other words, individuals who have been charged with a (usually violent) crime are civilly committed as criminally insane. The attempt is to reduce the incidence of aggression by removing "highly aggressive" individuals from this society. The incapacitative effect is the desired prevention strategy.

There is little question that such predictions of dangerousness are in common practice today (Meehl, 1970; Monahan, 1976, 1980; Rappaport, 1977; Shah, 1978). The prediction of dangerousness represents an excellent example of an instance in which available evidence to date has had little or no policy impact. It is generally concluded (e.g., Monahan, 1976) that violence is vastly overpredicted in the long term. In other words, we commonly make "dangerousness" decisions about individuals and incarcerate them for long periods of time in a highly erroneous fashion. This appears to be true whether the predictors used are behavioral observations, clinical interviews, or psychological test batteries. There is little question that once again the problem of false positives (e.g., predicting someone to be dangerous and incarcerating them when in fact they are not) rears its ugly head. Three particular studies will illustrate this problem. Kozol et al., (1972) followed 592 patients that were admitted to a diagnostic center. During the period of the study, 435 of the patients were released. Of these 435, 386 were released with the approval of the professional staff after careful diagnostic procedures. Forty-nine were released against the wishes of the staff. In a five-year follow-up Kozol, et al., found that 8 percent of those released with the approval of the staff recidivated (i.e., committed a violent act). On the other hand, 35 percent of those released against the diagnostic predictions of the professional staff recidivated. At first glance, this study provides some promising evidence for the predictive ability of the professional staff, and the diagnostic procedures used. It has to be pointed out, however, that 65 percent of those predicted to be violent did not commit an illegal violent act during the five-year follow-up interval.

The Baxtrom case (*Baxtrom* vs. *Herold*, 1966) is one of the more famous examinations of the prediction of dangerousness question. In this case, Baxtrom was sentenced to a specific sentence for the commission of a violent act. He was detained, however, beyond the specific duration of the sentence in an institution for the criminally insane on the basis of a prediction of dangerousness. The court ruled that Baxtrom must either be released outright or provided a civil commitment hearing. The decision resulted in the release of many patients from institutions for the criminally insane. Many of the "Baxtrom patients" were ultimately transferred to civil mental hospitals, while others were eventually released outright. In a four-year follow-up of these patients reported by Steadman & Keveles (1972), only 20 percent of these patients were assaultive in the civil institution or the community setting. Only 3 percent committed subsequent offenses of a sufficiently serious nature to warrant their return to an institution for the criminally insane. Fewer than 1 percent were actually convicted for a violent assaultive act.

A similar case is reported by Thornberry & Jacoby (1979). In *Dixon vs. The Attorney General of the Commonwealth of Pennsylvania* (1966), similar issues about the constitutionality of commitment for the criminally insane were raised. As a result of the Dixon case, 586 individuals were released. In a five-year follow-up, they found that 23.7 percent of the Dixon group were rearrested while 14.5 percent committed crimes against a person. Monahan (1980) summarized these and similar research efforts by concluding that professionals are "accurate in no more than one out of three predictions of violent behavior over a several year period" (p. III–11).

Given that the prediction of violent behavior is no more accurate than the above study suggests, it is extremely difficult to defend a strategy of labeling certain individuals as predisposed to the commission of aggressive behavior and defining preventive intervention strategies in an attempt to protect society from these "aggressive individuals." Mischel (1968) suggests that "predictive validity tends to decrease as the gap increases between the behavior sampled and the predictive measure in the behavior that is being predicted" (p. 323). This gap is extreme in the contemporary predictive framework. Trying to predict the likelihood of an institutionalized individual committing a violent act in the next three to five years in the community environment is difficult indeed. Similarly, trying to predict the aggressive behavior of an adult by viewing that individual 10 or 12 years earlier during their adolescence or childhood seems equally difficult. Not only are the attending stimuli drastically different in the various settings, but there is a long time interval involved as well. Monahan (1980) has noted that this is analogous to trying to predict the weather. The U.S. Weather Bureau is able to predict with 80 percent accuracy over a four-hour interval. That predictive accuracy, however, drops below 30 percent as the time interval is increased to 12 hours (Federal Aviation Agency, 1965; Monahan, 1980).

The above analogy to the weather bureau may not be sufficiently severe. In other words, attempts at long-term prediction from social demographic variables, individual variables, or the presence of aggression itself is extremely difficult. Not only are the predictors unclear, but specifiable criteria are extremely difficult to define. Even when we examine the severe case of predicting extreme dangerousness we find that to date, predictive accuracy has been severely lacking. As Monahan (1976) stated several years ago, such approaches to prevention still remain a question of how many people do we want to incarcerate, treat, etc., unnecessarily at the cost of protecting ourselves from the few individuals likely to be accurately predicted as violence prone. Further, the political and philosophical debates raised by such person-oriented prevention efforts are intense and complex. It is not likely that any of us would want to live in a society where such predictions were made systematically.

In the case of preventing and predicting dangerousness in "severe adult" populations we have again met with the same difficulties. These difficulties parallel those outlined in describing the history of the juvenile justice system; namely, in each case the validity and accuracy of the dangerousness prediction has been called in to question owing to the high rate of false positives. In other words, we are detaining and imposing severe interventions on a good number of individuals who will not really be aggressive. It has also been the case that too often procedural safeguards have been ignored. Further, the interventions applied have done little to truly prevent the incidence of aggression but have been "removal" strategies.

FUTURE DIRECTIONS IN PREVENTION

It is clear from the above review that our approaches to prevention must be drastically altered. In fact, given the above review it may seem curious to the reader why our approaches to aggression prevention have suffered from such serious errors for so long. The most obvious explanation is that our continued willingness to overpredict is a function of political and interpersonal events. The "safe thing to do" is to overpredict aggression and to intervene. In short, false positives are much less damaging than false negatives. One young person who commits a violent act after having been ignored by a juvenile court or one inmate who murders his wife after having been paroled is extremely damaging. Assigning young people and their families, however, to casework services or holding the criminally insane for many years in prison when such interventions are in fact unwarranted is unlikely to produce backlash. This built-in lack of corrective feedback is to a great extent a function of the groups of individuals who have typically been the subject of such overpredictions. Namely, as long as powerless groups are predicted to be violent there are few viable or powerful mechanisms available for correction. When however, powerful groups are targeted for preventive intervention, they have a wide variety of resources available to fight such identification. It is a common occurrence that when the Environmental Protection Agency wants to restrict the output of pollutants from a manufacturing company for purposes of preventing violence on people's health, there is a long series of debates (often court battles) over the validity of the predicted violence. Similar examples abound in attempts to add safety devices to automobiles, safety devices in the work place, auditing requirements for government contracts, and so on. In each of these cases, the validity of the prediction is demanded *a priori*. No such mechanisms have existed in our traditional approaches to preventing aggression and violence. In addition to such social and political complications there are a number of specific technical problems that currently face the field of aggression prevention. The general prevention model necessitates measurement at two time points. The predictor variables are assessed at the first time point and an individual or group is categorized as a function of a composite score or subjective summation of the evidence accumulated at this point in time. In the case of the prediction of violence, it has been noted that predictor variables have included broad social conditions, socioeconomic variables, demographic variables, community ties, previous history of aggressive acts, and others. As noted in the earlier review, a good deal of the evidence suggests that these predictors may in fact not be particularly useful; that is, their relationship to aggressive behavior has not been of sufficient strength to warrant their use in an applied setting.

A more specific pressing problem is the specification, in a technical sense, of exactly what behavior is to serve as a dependent variable (i.e., aggression). Perhaps the greatest criticism of prediction methods is that they typically underestimate the actual occurrence of aggressive behavior. The typical dependent variable is official court or police detection of illegal or aggressive behavior. It has been suggested that in many cases, false positives are actually underestimated considerably owing to the failure of the official justice system to detect a great deal of actual illegal behavior (Monahan, 1980). To the extent that this is true, the resulting unreliability in criteria may account for some of the attenuated relationships that have been demonstrated. Monahan (1980) concluded that roughly two-thirds of all violent crimes in this country are reported to the police while only one-third actually result in an arrest. This clearly demonstrates the criteria problem present in prediction paradigms. With only two-thirds of the criteria variable observed it is no wonder that the prediction studies have fairly low hit rates.

A major problem that has been mentioned several times in this chapter is that of base rate. The traditional example frequently used to demonstrate this phenomena was stated by Livermore, Malmquist, &

Meehl (1968):

> assume also that an exceptionally accurate test is created which differentiates with 95 percent effectiveness those who kill from those who will not. If one hundred thousand people were tested, out of the 100 individuals who will kill, 95 would be isolated. Unfortunately, out of the 99,900 who would not kill, 4,995 people would also be isolated as killers. In these circumstances, it is clear that we could not justify incarcerating all 5,090 people. If, in the criminal law, it is better that 10 guilty men go free than that one innocent man suffer, how can we say in the civil commitment area that it is better that 54 harmless people be incarcerated least one dangerous man be free? [p. 84].

The pervasive base rate problem creates two serious problems for the prevention paradigm. In the first instance, it renders the strategies of secondary prevention and tertiary prevention hopeless. We do not now have, nor are we likely to have in the future, prediction procedures of sufficient accuracy to warrant the widespread use of interventions that we see prominent today. Second, when examining broadly construed primary preventive strategies, the hope of having measurable impact is severely limited.

In light of these considerations "perhaps the most serious problem that prevention programs face is that planned intervention in the lives of others 'before' they are clearly in need of help violates a cultural norm of privacy" (Heller & Monahan, 1977, p. 151). The labeling effects of the false positives can have a devastating effect in and of themselves.

Accurate prediction of violent behavior, and effective programmatic response thereto are not easily accomplished tasks. As Rappaport & Holden (1980) observe:

> It is clear that the willingness to predict violence is not a function of scientific success. But our focus here is on the implications of our inability to predict with regard to programs of prevention, rather than on why we continue to do it. If we are unable to predict who is violent, who will commit a violent act, and if we are unclear as to the etiology of what we are trying to prevent, specific programs of preventive intervention are neither possible nor justifiable. Rather, more general strategies of social policy are required [Rappaport & Holden, 1980, p. 29].

The implications of this position are twofold. Strategies of secondary and tertiary prevention as currently practiced ought to be abandoned on a widespread basis. Until techniques of both prediction and prevention show far more validity and effectiveness than has been the case to date, their continued use appears unconstitutional. Second, moves in the direction of primary intervention will need to change their focus. Broad systems-oriented interventions aimed at social conditions will have to be used. Many of the methods outlined in other parts of this volume are worthy of careful examination in the prevention domain.

More specifically, both the particular techniques outlined in the first six chapters of this volume and the generic programmatic strategies outlined in the five chapters below are cases in point. What is obvious from this discussion is that the context, purposes, and expected outcomes may have more to do with actual effectiveness than the particular techniques employed. In terms of prevention, considerable attention ought to be paid to including the prevention of aggression goals in policies aimed at improving the human condition. In addition, the largest impact of prevention programs will be felt if more prevalent forms of aggression are targeted. This should also take prevention programs into the arena of target groups who have the power to resist. The resulting demands for validity of the predicted aggression and desirable outcomes of the interventions will put in place checks and balances. This should guarantee the appropriate level of caution in instituting preventive intervention.

REFERENCES

Adams, K. A. The child who murders: A review of theory and research. *Criminal Justice and Behavior*, 1974, **1**, 51–61.

Bandura, A. *Principals of behavior modification*. New York: Holt, Rinehart, & Winston, 1969.

Baxtrom v. Herold, 383 U.S. 107 (1966).

Becker, H. S. *Outsiders*. New York: Free Press, 1963.

Berleman, W. C. & Steinburn, T. W. The value and validity of delinquency prevention experiments. *Crime and Delinquency*, 1969, **15**, 471–478.

Binder, A., Monahan, J., & Newkirk, M. Diversion from the juvenile justice system and the prevention of delinquency. In J. Monahan (Ed.) *Community mental health and the criminal justice system*. New York: Pergamon Press, 1976, 131–140.

Caplan, G. *Principles of preventive psychiatry*. New York: Basic Books, 1964.

Caplan, G. & Nelson, G. D. On being useful: The nature and consequences of psychological research on social problems. *American Psychologist*, 1973, **28**, 199–211.

Carter, R. M. & Klein, M. W. (Eds.). *Back on the street: The diversion of juvenile offenders*. Englewood Cliffs, N.J.: Prentice-Hall, 1976.

Cloward, R. A. & Ohlin, L. E. *Delinquency and opportunity: A theory of delinquent gangs*. New York: Free Press, 1960.

Collingswood, T. R., Douds, A., & Williams, H. *The Dallas police diversion project*. Exemplary Project Report: U.S. Dept. of Justice, 1976.

Court Brown, W. M. Males with an XYY sex chromosome complement. *Journal of Medical Genetics*, 1968, **5**, 341–359.

Davidson, W. S., Seidman, E., Rappaport, J., Berck, P. L., Rapp, N. A., Rhodes, W., & Herring, J. Diversion programs for juvenile offenders. *Social Work Research and Abstracts*, 1977, **1**, 40–54.

Davis, N. J. Labeling theory in deviance research: A critique and reconsideration. *Sociological Quarterly*, 1972, **13**, 447–474.

Dixon v. Attorney General of the Commonwealth of Pennsylvania, 325 F. Supp. 966 (1966).

Elliott, D. S. *Diversion: A study of alternative processing practices.* Final Report to the Center for Studies of Crime and Delinquency, NIMH, Boulder, Colo.: Behavioral Research Institute, 1978.

Empey, L. T. *American delinquency: Its meaning and construction.* Homewood, Ill.: Dorsey Press, 1978.

Farrington, D. Self-reports of deviant behavior: Predictive and stable? *Journal of Criminal Law, Criminology and Police Science,* 1973, **54,** 456–469.

Faust, F. L. Delinquency labelling: Its consequences and implications. *Crime and Delinquency,* 1973, **19,** 41–48.

Federal Aviation Agency. *Aviation weather for pilots and flight operations personnel.* Washington, D.C.: U.S. Government Printing Office, 1965.

Fisher, S. Stigma and deviant careers in schools. *Social Problems,* 1972, **20,** 78–83.

Foster, J. D., Dinitz, S., & Reckless, W. C. Perceptions of stigma following public intervention for delinquent behavior. *Social Problems,* 1972, **20,** 202–209.

Gault, 387 U.S. 1, 55, 81 S. Ct. 1428, 1458 (1967).

Gibbons, D. C. *Delinquent behavior.* Englewood Cliffs, N.J.: Prentice-Hall, 1970.

Gleuck, S. & Gleuck, E. *Toward a typology of juvenile offenders.* New York: Grune & Stratton, 1970.

Gleuck, S. & Gleuck, E. (Eds.). *Identification of predelinquents validation studies and some suggested uses of Gleuck table.* New York: Intercontinental Medical Book Corporation, 1972.

Gold, M. Undetected delinquent behavior. *Journal of Research in Crime and Delinquency,* 1966, **13,** 127–143.

Gottfredson, D., Wilkins, L., & Hoffman, P. *Guidelines for parole and sentencing.* Lexington, Mass.: Lexington Books, 1978.

Griffin, B. S. & Griffin, C. T. *Juvenile delinquency in perspective.* New York: Harper & Row, 1978.

Heller, K. & Monahan, J. *Psychology and community change.* Homewood, Ill.: Dorsey Press, 1977.

Hirschi, T. *Causes of delinquency.* Berkeley: University of California Press, 1969.

Hirschi, T. & Selvin, H. Delinquency research: An appraisal of analytic methods. *Journal of Criminal Law and Criminology,* 1969, **43,** 177–200.

Holt, R. *Methods in clinical psychology, Volume 2: Prediction and research.* New York: Plenum, 1978.

Jesness, C. F. Comparative effectiveness of behavior modification and transactional programs for delinquents. *Journal of Consulting and Clinical Psychology,* 1975, **43,** 759–779.

Johnson, G., Bird, T., & Little, J. W. *Delinquency prevention: Theories and strategies.* Office of Juvenile Justice and Delinquency Prevention, L.E.A.A., U.S. Department of Justice, U.S. Government Printing Office, 1979.

Jordan, V. E. The system propagates crime. *Crime and Delinquency,* 1974, **20,** 233–240.

Kahn, A. J. A case of premature claims. *Crime and Delinquency,* 1965, **11,** 217–228.

Kantrowitz, R. E. Training nonprofessionals to work with delinquents: Differential impact of varying training/supervision/intervention strategies. Unpublished doctoral dissertation, Michigan State University, 1979.

Kassebaum, G. *Delinquency and social policy.* Englewood Cliffs, N.J.: Prentice-Hall, 1974.

Klein, M. W. Deinstitutionalization and diversion of juvenile offenders: A litany of impediments. In N. Morris & M. Tonry (Eds.), *Crime and justice.* Chicago: University of Chicago Press, 1979.

Klein, M. W. Diversion as operationalization of Labeling theory. Final report to the Center of Studies in Crime and Delinquency, NIMH, Los Angles: University of Southern California, 1980.

Kozol, H., Boucher, R., & Garofalo, R. The diagnosis and treatment of dangerousness. *Crime and Delinquency*, 1972, **18**, 371–392.

Krohn, M., Waldo, G., & Chiricos, T. G. Self reported delinquency: A comparison of structured interviews and self-administered checklists. *Journal of Criminal Law and Criminology*, 1975, **65**, 545–553.

Langley, M. H., Graves, H. R., & Norris, B. The juvenile court and individualized treatment. *Crime and Delinquency*, 1972, **18**, 79–92.

Leakey, R. E. & Lewin, R. *Origins*. New York: Dutton, 1977.

Lemert, E. M. *Instead of court: Diversion in juvenile justice*. Washington, D.C.: U.S. Government Printing Office, 1971.

Lemert, E. M. Beyond Mead: The societal reaction to deviance. *Social Problems*, 1974, **21**, 457–461.

Lincoln, S. B., Teilman, K. S., Klein, M. W., & Labin, S. Recidivism rates of diverted juvenile offenders. Paper presented at the National Conference on Criminal Justice Evaluation, Washington, D.C., 1977.

Livermore, J., Malmquist, C., & Meehl, P. On the justification for civil commitment. *University of Pennsylvania Law Review*, 1968, **117**, 75–96.

Lorenz, K. *On aggression*. New York: Basic Books, 1963.

Matza, D. *Delinquency and drift*. New York: Wiley, 1964.

Meehl, P. *Clinical versus statistical prediction: A theoretical analyses and a review of the evidence*. Minneapolis: University of Minnesota Press, 1954.

Meehl, P. Psychology and the criminal law. *University of Richmond Law Review*, 1970, **5**, 1–30.

Megargee, E. The prediction of dangerous behavior. *Criminal Justice and Behavior*, 1976, **3**, 3–21.

Merton, R. K. *Social theory and social structure*. New York: Glencoe Press, 1957.

Mischel, W. *Personality and assessment*. New York: Wiley, 1968.

Monahan, J. The prevention of violence. In J. Monahan (Ed.), *Community mental health and the criminal justice system*. New York: Pergamon Press, 1976.

Monahan, J. *The clinical prediction of violent behavior*. Washington, D.C.: U.S. Government Printing Office, 1980.

Monahan, J. & Splane, S. Psychological approaches to criminal behavior. In E. Bittner & S. Messinger (Eds.), *Criminology review yearbook*. Beverly Hills: Sage Publications, 1980.

Nagel, W. G. *The new red barn: A critical look at the modern American prison*. New York: Wackor, 1973.

National Institute of Juvenile Justice and Delinquency Prevention. *Preventing delinquency: A comparative analysis of delinquency prevention theory. Volume I of IX*. Washington, D.C.: U.S. Department of Justice, 1977.

Nejelski, P. Diversion: The promise and the danger. *Crime and Delinquency*, 1976, **22**, 393–410.

Prentice, N. M. The influence of live and symbolic modeling on prompting moral judgement of adolescent delinquents. *Journal of Abnormal Psychology*, 1972, **80**, 159–211.

Presidents Commission on Law Enforcement and the Administration of Justice. *Task force report: Juvenile delinquency and youth crime*. Washington, D.C.: U.S. Government Printing Office, 1967.

Rappaport, J. *Community psychology: Values, research, and action*. New York: Holt, Rinehart & Winston, 1977.

Rappaport, J., Davidson, W. S., Mitchell, A., & Wilson, M. N. Alternatives to blaming the victim or the environment: Our places to stand have not moved the earth. *American Psychologist*, 1975, **30**, 525–528.

Rappaport, J. & Holden, K. Prevention of violence: The case for a nonspecific social policy or "We have seen the enemy and he is us." In J. R. Hays, T. K. Roberts, & K. S. Solway (Eds.), *Violence and the violent individual.* Englewood Cliffs, N.J.: Spectrum Books, 1980.

Ryan, W. *Blaming the victim.* New York: Vintage, 1971.

Scarpitti, F. R. & Stephenson, R. M. A study of probation effectiveness. *Journal of Criminal Law, Criminology, and Police Science,* 1968, **39**, 361–369.

Scarpitti, F. R. & Stephenson, R. M. Juvenile court despositions: Factors in the decision making process. *Crime and Delinquency,* 1971, **17**, 142–151.

Schuessler, K. E. & Cressey, D. R. Personality characteristics of criminals. *American Journal of Sociology,* 1950, **55**, 476–484.

Schur, E. M. Reactions to deviance: A critical assessment. *American Journal of Sociology,* 1969, **75**, 309–322.

Schur, E. M. *Radical non-intervention: Rethinking the delinquency problem.* Englewood Cliffs, N.J.: Prentice-Hall, 1973.

Seidman, E., Rappaport, J., & Davidson, W. S. Adolescents in legal jeopardy: Initial success and replication of an alternative to the juvenile justice system. Invited address: 1976 National Psychological Consultants to Management Consulting Psychology Research Award, Meeting of the American Psychological Association, Washington, D.C., 1976.

Shah, S. A. Dangerousness: A paradigm for exploring some issues in law and psychology. *American Psychologist,* 1978, **33**, 224–238.

Shaw, C. R. & McKay, H. D. *Juvenile delinquency and urban areas.* Chicago: University of Chicago Press, 1942.

Smith, P. M. & Austrin, H. R. Socialization as related to delinquency classification. *Psychological Reports,* 1974, **34**, 677–678.

Steadman, H. & Keveles, G. The community adjustment and criminal activity of the Baxtrom patients: 1966–1970. *American Journal of Psychiatry,* 1972, **129**, 304–310.

Tait, E. C. & Hodges, E. F. Followup study of predicted delinquents. *Crime and Delinquency,* 1971, **17**, 202–212.

Thornberry, T. & Jacoby, J. *The criminally insane: A community follow-up of mentally ill offenders.* Chicago: University of Chicago Press, 1979.

Venezia, P. S. Delinquency prediction: A critique and suggestion. *Journal of Research in Crime and Delinquency,* 1971, **8**, 108–117.

Waldo, G. P. & Dinitz, S. Personality attributes of the criminal: Analysis of research studies from 1950–1965. *Journal of Research in Crime and Delinquency,* 1967, **4**, 185–202.

Williams, J. R. & Gold, M. From delinquent behavior to official delinquency. *Social Problems,* 1972, **20**, 209–229.

Wolfgang, M., Figlio, R., & Sellin, T. *Delinquency in a birth cohort.* Chicago: University of Chicago Press, 1972.

Zax, M. & Specter, G. A. *An introduction to community psychology.* New York: Wiley, 1974.

Chapter 8
Community and Organizational Level Change
Martin G. Kushler and
William S. Davidson, II

The history of the great events of the world is little more than a history of crime—Voltaire, L. Ingenu.

Archeological evidence indicates that the occurrence of excessive aggression is a problem that has plagued mankind from the beginning of civilization. Similarly, the earliest recorded history reveals that even primitive societies were faced with the problem of controlling and responding to undesirable aggression. It is a rather obvious comment on the futility of these past efforts to note the widespread incidence of crime and violence exhibited in today's society. With the ever-increasing technological sophistication of the tools of aggressive behavior, one must hope that the near future will produce a better record of achievement in the effort to curb unwanted aggression.

DEFINING AGGRESSION AS A SOCIAL PROBLEM

At the outset, it is appropriate to provide the working definition of aggression that we have used in this chapter. It should be made clear that what we mean by aggression are those activities that are both undesirable and harmful, as opposed to what some would consider desirable and competitive aggressiveness. Perhaps the following definition by Albert Bandura (1976) is an appropriate one to consider here: "Aggression is defined as behavior that results in personal injury and in destruction of property. The injury may take the forms of psychological devaluation and degradation as well as physical harm" (p. 203). As our use of this definition may imply, it is our intention to confine this chapter to the consideration of acts or behaviors that are or might properly be considered criminal. (Criminal in this sense implies that society would consider formal, legal sanctions in response to the commission of such acts.) Indeed, it is only in the consideration of those acts for which society deems a social response required that this chapter on organizational change takes meaning.

There are two features of Bandura's definition that have particular importance with respect to this conceptualization. First, by including psychological injury and the destruction of property, the definition of aggression becomes somewhat broader than the commonly visualized example of a direct physical assault of one person by another. Second, as Bandura goes on to detail in the above-cited reference, the social labeling process (including the consideration of such factors as demographic characteristics, socioeconomic level, and the judgment of intent) is a major factor in determining which injurious acts are in fact labeled aggressive. One might expect that this is even more true with respect to definitions of "criminality" that may or may not be attached to particular incidents of aggression. Clearly these are important considerations in developing societal efforts to curb undesired aggression and they will be returned to later in this text.

HISTORICAL PERSPECTIVES ON CRIME AND AGGRESSION

Perhaps the earliest known philosophy of response to crime was simply the concept of personal revenge or retaliation to a perceived offense. "Justice" in this sense was a matter for individual or family concern. As early cultures matured, however, the anarchistic nature of unrestrained individual vengence became dysfunctional. Emerging norms of collective behavior gave rise to the beginning of a true "social response" to deviance and undesirable aggression. Personal retribution gave way to collective response, often in the form of a decision-making body of tribal elders. While these early "judges" often ruled from a base of spiritual or mystical power, their decisions nonetheless carried the full force of law, and the punishments were frequently brutal.

Early attempts at codification (e.g., "an eye for an eye") retained the distinct quality of revenge, but with the increasing influence of organized religion, matters of crime began to be considered as much a transgression of God's as of man's law. Ironically, although the New Testament is regarded as championing the "new" concept of divine forgiveness, punishments administered under Church rule for centuries thereafter were often unspeakably harsh for even minor offenses.

This state of affairs led to one of the earliest "reform" movements. During the 1700s and early 1800s, social philosophers such as Voltaire and Rousseau began to question the domination of secular matters by the religious hierarchy and also spoke of the philosophies of rationality and free will. In this emerging conceptualization, behavior was regarded as a result of rational choices rather than of supernatural forces. With the notion of free will as a cornerstone, the "classical school" of criminology was born.

Although the concept of total free will seems a bit eccentric today, the classicists were responsible for a major reform in the fostering of the concept that, in contrast to previous arbitrary and severe treatment of offenders, a punishment should fit the crime that has been committed.

Indeed, the classical school produced the basic concepts that have become the dominant frame of reference for modern correctional policy. The widespread use of imprisonment, with the ability to impose sentences of varying lengths, stems directly from the classical contribution of "punishment to fit the crime." At the time, the policy of imprisonment was regarded as a reform of great significance. In the early 19th century, penal reformers from around the world came to the United States to study that American invention, the penitentiary (Silberman, 1978).

In spite of its many contributions toward the reform of earlier correctional practices, however, the classical point of view also contained its share of distasteful features. As the nineteenth century progressed, the classical assumptions of free will were challenged by the "Positivist School of Criminology," which argued that criminals were not wholly responsible for their acts. Criminal acts were determined, it was argued, at least partially by factors beyond the control of the actors themselves. As a result, reform of disadvantageous social and environmental conditions (e.g., poverty, inequality, lack of education) was seen as a promising approach in contrast to the narrow punishment and deterrence philosophy espoused by the classicists.

With greater or lesser degrees of sophistication, these two major philosophical positions have persisted to this day. It can probably be safely said that the classical school has made its major impact in terms of the operation of the actual correctional system and its penal institutions, while the positivist school, thus far, has had its major influence in the theoretical explanation of crime and its causes. Together, however, they certainly illustrate how deep run the roots of society's efforts at correctional reform.

THE AMERICAN EXPERIENCE

From its very inception as a nation, America seems to have had a special relationship with violence and aggression. Indeed, it would not be much of an exaggeration to say that this country was, by and large, settled by a combination of European paupers, criminals, and social outcasts. Further, the nation itself was created through a bloody and violent revolution that has been dutifully and boisterously celebrated every year ever since. Finally, there is, of course, the example of the "Wild West" with its mythological heroes (ironically both lawmen *and* criminals) who seemed to need only a fast gun and a good horse. Although relatively few Americans actually experienced that short period of history, the folklore surrounding it has had a tremendous impact on American culture.

Yet, the American relationship with violence has been a peculiar one, with many contradictory elements which persist to this day. On the one hand, the founding fathers were very sensitive to the need to safeguard civil liberties and to avoid persecution by the state, as the Bill of Rights demonstrates. On the other hand, however, the violent struggle for independence and the often violent "taming of the wilderness" have created a tradition of the use of violent aggression to achieve desirable ends, the expression of which by individuals in the form of crime has necessitated repressive reaction on the part of the state. Nowhere is this conflict of values and traditions more evident or more heated than in the on-going debate over gun control laws. While we will return to the specific issue of gun control later in this chapter, suffice it to say at this point that this nation certainly presents a curious paradox in its simultaneous allegiance to both "law and order" and "rugged individualism." How to achieve the first goal while preserving the desirable elements of the second is a challenge with which the United States must come to terms.

THE CRIME PROBLEM

A broad-based and relatively enduring consensus has developed in America concerning the seriousness of the problem of crime. The degree of concern is visible both in terms of governmental emphasis (e.g., the 1967 President's Commission on Law Enforcement and the Administration of Justice; the 1973 National Advisory Commission on Criminal Justice Standards and Goals), and of public opinion (Gallup, 1973; Roper, 1977). Indeed, in the last 15 years American society has from one point of view seen a previously unparalleled rise in the crime rate, as well as in the political concern over the crime rate and the resultant funding of crime control activities.

Certainly, by almost any indicator, crime is a social problem of great magnitude. On the other hand, however, a case can be made that much of the recent public and official response is overreaction. Critics could argue that, in fact, the relative extent of the crime problem has increased only moderately in the past 20 years, and that much of the aroused public concern is more likely due to politically self-serving comments by governmental leaders and economically self-serving sensationalism by the media (Morris & Hawkins, 1970; Quinney, 1975).

Violent Crime

Nowhere is the situation represented by that viewpoint better illustrated than in the public perception (or misperception) of violent crime. Consider the following scenarios: "A man/woman finishes working late downtown one night and walks to the parking lot. On the way he/she is suddenly assaulted/robbed/raped/murdered (choose one or more) by a criminal waiting in the shadows." Or, "A man holds up an all night gas station, and in the process beats/shoots the attendant." These scenarios are common representations of crime as portrayed by the entertainment and news media. Yet, they are a misrepresentation of the phenomenon of violent crime and can serve to generate unjustified fear and misplaced concern on the part of the public.

From an actuarial point of view, the physical risk to an individual from street crime is much smaller than the risks in riding in or driving a car, going swimming, or even working around the house. For example, ten times as many Americans are killed in automobile accidents each year as are murdered by strangers; and three times as many Americans die in falls. Further, accidents also cause many more injuries than does street crime. Four times as many Americans are seriously injured in home accidents as are injured in all robberies and aggravated assaults combined. Automobile accidents cause five times as many injuries as robberies and assaults (Silberman, 1978).

In addition, even if one restricts the discussion to street crime, the above scenarios are a very misleading representation of the nation's crime problem. The FBI's *Uniform Crime Reports* provide an "Index of Serious Crimes" which includes seven offenses: willful homicide, forcible rape, aggravated assault, robbery, burglary, larceny over $50.00, and motor vehicle theft. The first four offenses, which are considered "violent" in that they include the use or threat of force, have accounted for only 13 percent of all Index crimes (President's Commission, 1967). Willful homicide and forcible rape together account for less than 2 percent of all Index crimes. (It would be interesting to see the relative percentages for crimes portrayed in the entertainment and news media).

Finally, the common conception of crime represented by the above scenarios is also erroneous and misleading with respect to the perpetrators of violent crime. The fearful image of assault by an unknown criminal is simply inaccurate for the majority of violent crime. Indeed, the President's Commission on Law Enforcement and Administration of Justice (1967) cited the results of several studies indicating that approximately "Seventy percent of all willful killings, nearly two-thirds of all aggravated assaults and a high percentage of forcible rapes are committed by family members, friends, or other persons previously known to their victims" (p. 14). Morris and Hawkins (1970) later estimated that "taken together, murders involving spouse killing spouse, parent killing child, other family killings, romantic triangles and lovers' quarrels, and arguments between those previously acquainted with one another account for about 80 percent of all homicides in America," which led the authors to quip only somewhat sarcastically; "You are safer on the streets than at home; safer with a stranger than with a friend or relative." (p. 57).

Quips aside, however, these rather astonishing figures have profound implications for the conceptualization and design of social responses to criminal aggression. Unfortunately, one can anticipate many road blocks to using this information actually to design policy. No politician ever got elected by warning voters about spouses, families, and friends. In addition, the criminal justice system is well entrenched and content with traditional definitions of crime. Still, as will be discussed in a later section, some promising alternative strategies are available and will, it is hoped, be pursued.

The Statistical Crime Wave

The FBI's seven Index crimes, as reported in *Uniform Crime Reports* (UCR) are usually cited to illustrate the extent of the nation's crime problem. Although this index also includes property crimes, the broad definition of aggression presented at the beginning of this chapter allows a consideration of such offenses as well as "violent" crimes. (Indeed, recent data shows that the relative percentage of nonviolent property crimes has increased to 90 percent of the FBI Index crimes. Thus, despite their more limited publicity, such offenses are much more likely to represent the actual experience of most Americans with criminal aggression—at least in terms of street crimes—than are the violent crimes discussed earlier).

At first glance, the UCR figures concerning the incidence of crime are definitely alarming. From 1940 to 1950 the number of "Index" crimes rose by more than 11 percent; from 1950 to 1960 by over 98 percent; and from 1960 to 1976 by over 230 percent! Many a stirring speech has been made about these and similar figures.

It is, however, fortunately premature to mark the demise of law and order in America. Such data are misleading in that they only consider absolute totals of crime rather than totals relative to population growth. After correcting for this simple factor (e.g. expressing crime *per* 100,000 *persons*), one finds that the number of index crimes actually declined by 5 percent from 1940 to 1950 (Wolfgang, 1963); increased by only 22 percent from 1950 to 1960 (Morris & Hawkins, 1970); and increased by a somewhat lower 180 percent from 1960 to 1976 (Nietzel, 1979). In fairness to the FBI, it should be pointed out that the UCR is typically reported both in number of offenses and as a rate per population base. The FBI has consistently emphasized, however, the absolute frequencies, the consequence of which has been to inflate the reported volume of crime artificially (Harris, 1968).

Yet, what of the 180 percent increase from 1960 to 1976? That surely is upsetting by itself. Critics of UCR data, however, would find much to be skeptical about even in that figure. First, it has been pointed out that crime statistics are usually gathered and published by the same agencies whose budget may be affected by the results. Indeed, Inciardi (1976) reported that arrest figures were used to support police budgetary demands as early as 1858. Modern criminal justice agencies are probably less likely to engage in outright deceit than their predecessors. (Although occasional incidents are discovered; see for example, Silberman's 1978 report of the incredible manipulation of drug addiction statistics by the Nixon administration in the early 1970s.) Still, the art of skillful presentation of crime statistics is a flourishing one.

Second, and more important, are the developmental changes that have occured in the past two decades in both police and public perceptions of crime. "Professionalization" of police agencies has led to an increase in formal handling of offenders, and record-keeping procedures have drastically improved. Both of these developments have contributed greatly to the amount of officially reported crime (President's Commission, 1967; Quinney, 1975; Sutherland and Cressey, 1970). Similarly, certain segments of the population (particularly poor and minority areas) have had rising expectations in terms of police protection and thus have increased their tendency to report crimes to authorities (President's Commission, 1967). Even in society at large there has been a trend toward relying on police and courts to handle formally what were often previously regarded as interpersonal conflicts that would have been resolved informally (Pepinsky, 1977).

Finally, perhaps the major reason that the crime increases reported by the UCR are misleading is that they are not adjusted for demographic variables such as age. It is widely acknowledged that the 16- to 24-year-old age group has by far the highest total incidence of Index crimes. Over the period of greatest rise in crime rates (1960 to 1975), this segment of the population has been rapidly increasing. Between 1960 and 1970, the 15- to 19-year-old age group increased by 45 percent and the 20 to 24 age group by 56 percent (Morris & Hawkins, 1970). The impact of this trend on crime has been substantial. For example, the President's Commission (1967) estimated that for 1960 to 1965, approximately one-half of the total increase in UCR Index crime was explainable by this population shift. Interestingly, as the "baby boom" generation now moves on toward middle age, its effects on the crime rate are even more clearly visible. For the first half of the 1970s, in spite of a mostly continuing crime increase, the rate of growth for the 14- to 24-year-old population had slowed to 10 percent. By the second half of the decade, it appears that this demographic shift began to catch up, as crime rates actually leveled off or even declined (Nietzel, 1979). The prognosis for the near future is even better, as the rate of growth in the 14- to 24-year-old population will only have been 1.5 percent in the second half of the 1970s, and that age group will actually decline by 6.6 percent over the following five years (Silberman, 1978). Some have projected that a trend toward the reduction in crime could be visible for some time, as by 1990 the number of Americans between 14 and 25 will be approximately 16 percent less than it was in 1975 (Schellhardt, 1977).

A Case for Rationality

Viewed in the context of the above remarks, the seemingly alarming statistics that have surfaced repeatedly in the last ten to twenty years can receive a much more reasoned response. In addition, it may be helpful once again to consider an historical perspective. The President's Commission (1967) had the following to say: "There has always been too much crime. Virtually every generation since the founding of the Nation and before has felt itself threatened by the spectre of rising crime and violence" (p. 19). As an example, they offered the following passage, which was written in 1910: "Crime, especially its more violent forms, and among the young is increasing steadily and is threatening to bankrupt the Nation" (p. 19). Silberman (1978) describes how in 1872, *Wood's Illustrated Handbook* "warned visitors to New York not to walk around the city at night except in the busiest streets and urged them to take particular pains to avoid Central Park after sundown" (p. 23). He adds that even Abraham Lincoln, in 1838, decried "the increasing disregard for law that pervades the country" (p. 21). Indeed, it appears that a concern for law and order and a fear of rising crime are recurrent if not in fact permanent phenomena in the United States.

Policy Implications

It should be made abundantly clear, however, that the intent of the
preceding comments is not to deny or minimize the problem of crime.
The special fear of street crime is understandable and real. One does not
think of statistical probabilities when worried about the violation of
one's person or property by a stranger. Society's institutions should
rightly be concerned with correcting the problem that produces not only
that fear, but a substantial amount of both physical and emotional
suffering as well as property loss.

Yet it should also be clear that the special fear of street crime should
not be exploited beyond the bounds of reasoned response. The United
States has much too much to lose in the form of its long heritage of the
protection of civil rights to allow this to happen. Quotes such as the
following, however innocently offered, are beginning to represent the
views of at least a vocal minority in this country:

> If the crime control model can be likened to an assembly line, the due process
> model can be likened to an obstacle course. As Packer describes it, "each of its
> successive stages is designed to present formidable impediments to carrying the
> accused any further along in the process" [Rossman, 1978, p. 85].

Indeed, this is why the issue of crime statistics and the misrepresentation of the parameters of crime is so important. The policy implications of a "moderate yet serious" rise in crime are very different
from those of a "runaway crime wave." The latter implies hasty and
possibly ill-conceived action. The former implies deliberate yet reasoned
action allowing for the safeguarding of civil rights and the thoughtful
consideration of alternative policies.

For example, any thoughtful review of the nation's crime problem
would include consideration of the fact that reforms in the detection and
prosecution of white-collar crime have the potential to save citizens
much greater amounts of money, with much less expenditures of tax
dollars, than policies of increasing deterrent force used against street
crime. (See for example, the relative costs of street crime and white-
collar crime discussed in the President's Commission 1967 report, *Crime
and its Impact: An Assessment*.) Further, a quick mathematical comparison suggests that gun control and auto safety legislation have the
potential to save far more lives and prevent far more serious injuries,
again at lower cost, than a policy of mandatory life sentences for violent
criminals. It is irresponsible to discuss the problem of crime and criminal
aggression in the United States without considering these issues. Indeed,
they will each be discussed further at a later point in this chapter.

Nevertheless, the central focal point of any discussion of the response to crime in America is and will continue to be the criminal justice system. In view of this, the following section will briefly review the major contemporary approaches to crime control, including their theoretical rationale, some programmatic examples, a consideration of research evidence, and a critique and prognosis for their role in the future.

MAJOR CONTEMPORARY APPROACHES TO THE PROBLEM OF CRIMINAL AGGRESSION

The Deterrence Approach

By now Americans, I believe, have learned the hard way that a society that is lenient and permissive for criminals is a society that is neither safe nor secure for innocent men and women.

—Richard M. Nixon, 1974.

The central concept of the deterrence approach, stated quite simply, is that punishment deters crime. Zimring and Hawkins (1973) cite C. S. Kenney's classic text *Outlines of Criminal Law*, which "defines 'deterrence by punishment' as a 'method of retrospective interference; by holding out threats that, whenever a wrong has been actually committed, the wrongdoer shall incur punishment.' The object is 'to check an offense by thus associating with the idea of it a deterrent sense of terror'" (p. 1).

In earlier times, the notion of terror was taken quite literally. In 17th- and 18th-century Europe for example, perpetrators of even fairly common crimes were often killed and left hanging in chains for the public to view, sometimes with the corpse soaked in tar so as to lengthen its time on display (Sutherland and Cressey, 1970). Fortunately, in recent times, most civilized nations have given up or greatly reduced the use of death as a penalty and imprisonment has become the predominant form of punishment.

Theoretical Rationale. The theoretical rationale for deterrence is largely attributable to the classical school of criminology and its doctrines of rational thought and psychological hedonism, which together concluded that an individual calculates pleasures and pains in advance of action and regulates his conduct by the results of this calculation. Hence, the proper societal reaction should be to administer "pain" to the offender in some specified amount such that individuals could take this measure of pain into account in governing their actions. Imprisonment began its heightened popularity at this point, partly because it was viewed as more humane than earlier more grisly punishments and partly because it was a perfect vehicle for meting out specific lengths of punishment for specific crimes. Jeremy Bentham, the classical criminology scholar and reformer, went so far as to work out precise mathematical formulas for the infliction of proper amounts of punishment (Sutherland & Cressey, 1970).

The modern correctional system has continued the use of imprisonment as the cornerstone of its policy and practice. Criminologists have expanded on earlier theory and have identified various categories of deterrent effect that are accomplished by imprisonment. Special or specific deterrence refers to the effect of punishment on the offender, in terms of the implied threat of similar or greater punishment for future transgressions. General deterrence refers to the effect of punishment of an offender on the public at large. In this sense a case is made that the general fear of punishment prevents potential offenders from becoming actual offenders. Another part of the rationale for imprisonment that can conceivably be included under deterrence theory, is the concept of the effect of incapacitation. In other words, the imprisoned offender is, in a sense, incapacitated and thus prevented from committing additional crimes during the period of imprisonment. Some have pointed out, however, the high rate of crime (particularly violent crime) in prisons and claimed that imprisonment does not deter crime through incapacitation but merely displaces it from one setting to another (Goldstein, 1975).

A final factor that is often cited as a rationale for punishment, though not necessarily for deterrence itself, is the concept of retribution. Punishment by the legal system provides a legitimized outlet for revenge. Although many writers choose to ignore or to minimize this somewhat darker side of human behavior, some have gone so far as to say that retribution performs a vital deterrent role by increasing group cohesion through the collective affirmation of group norms and group sanctions for undesirable conduct.

Programmatic Examples. The principles of deterrence are the foundation of virtually every system of criminal law in the world. Within the United States, court fines, imprisonment, and occasionally the death penalty are all concrete examples of deterrence theory put into practice. For street crimes at least, however, the punishment of choice is clearly imprisonment. Indeed, the United States has one of the highest incarceration rates in the world (Waller and Chan, 1974). With problems of crowding in both prisons and courts, probation has also been used as a sentencing option. Determined deterrence theorists, however, would argue that probation is not a sufficient punishment to serve as a deterrent. Conversely, "treatment" theorists would argue that probation as practiced today hardly qualifies as a form of remedial activity. As such, it may be best at this point to classify probation as a bureaucratic necessity rather than a deterrent strategy.

Finally, a wide variety of largely psychological techniques designed to increase the perceived threat to punishment might also be categorized as products of the deterrence approach. Such techniques would include: publicity efforts such as "crime doesn't pay" or "shoplifters go to jail" campaigns; technological deterrents such as camera monitors or the procedure of marking identifying numbers on personal property; or the recently popular practice of police "sting" operations, whereby undercover officers buy stolen merchandise from unsuspecting thieves, film the transaction, and later round up dozens of identified criminals for prosecution.

Research Evidence The effect of punishment as a deterrent to crime is probably one of the most debated issues in all of social science. Most of the research conducted in this area has been of poor quality or simply weak owing to methodological restrictions. Zimring and Hawkins (1973) discuss many of the methodological problems which have plagued deterrence research in some detail, particularly the frequent reliance on retrospective data and on comparison of unequivalent groups for analysis (e.g., states with different punishment practices). Not surprisingly, some very discrepant conclusions have been drawn.

The area of perhaps the greatest attention has been the death penalty and its effect as a deterrent on homicide rates. Numerous comparative statistical studies have been published supporting each side of the debate. In comparative studies of states with different laws, Gibbs (1968) and Tittle (1969) concluded that those areas with the highest penalties for homicide tend to have the lowest rates of that offense. Zimring and Hawkins (1973), however, point out that if one compares within similar regions of the country, that relationship disappears. Also, Chiricos and Waldo (1970) used similar data but examined *changes* in crime rate in relation to *prior changes* in punishment practices and found no support for the conclusion that severe penalties influenced the rate of crime. Sellin (1959), in a classic study, used matching techniques to avoid regional differences and concluded that capital punishment did not appear to have any influence on homicide rates. Another example of the common cycle of publication followed by refutation is the recent paper by Ehrlich (1975), which examined homicide rates from 1933 to 1969 and claimed to "prove" that capital punishment deters murder more effectively than other sanctions. Silberman (1978) discusses how critics using Ehrlich's own equations, depending on the years selected for study, were able to "prove" that the death penalty actually encourages crime.

Aside from the obvious problems with methodology, sampling, and historical confounds, an additional problem with such comparative studies is the question of causality (Minor, 1977). Clearly, crime rates can influence severity of punishments utilized just as well as punishments can affect crime rates. This problem of causality is seldom dealt with in comparative studies of deterrent effect (Bowers & Salem, 1972).

One rare example of an actual field experiment examining the effect of deterrence was that conducted by Schwartz and Orleans (1967). They took a sample of taxpayers and randomly assigned them to four groups: one receiving a threat appeal, one recieving a neutral message on taxpaying behavior, one receiving an appeal to conscientious motives for tax paying, and one receiving nothing at all. The data for the subsequent year showed that the conscience and threat appeal groups both tended to pay more taxes than the neutral or no appeal groups. Further, the appeal to conscience appeared to have a greater influence than the threat appeal. Of course, one should keep in mind that this study is probably more noteworthy as an example of desirable methodological design than as a definitive statement on the effects of deterrence.

While the above examples center on the concept of general deterrence, the issue of specific deterrence has also been examined to some extent. The primary area of research in this endeavor has been the study of the effect of length of prison stay on recidivism. Lipton, Martinson, & Wilks (1975), in a comprehensive review of the effectiveness of various correctional strategies, conclude that the effect of sentence length is curvilinear. It appears that the lowest rate of recidivism is achieved with either very short (a few months) or moderately long (over two to three years) sentences. It also appears, however, that age may be an interacting variable in this relationship. Glaser (1964) found in a study of all adult federal offenders, that inmates aged 23 or younger at release failed more if held over two years than those who had been held less than two years. Glaser also reports that older inmates (36 and over) have much lower recidivism rates regardless of length of confinement (a finding which Lipton et al. confirm has been replicated repeatedly over the past 50 years). These findings themselves have policy implications for the sentencing of offenders of different ages, but taken together they raise the possibility that the second part of the observed curvilinear relationship (i.e., that longer sentences produce less recidivism than moderate ones) may be due to the advanced age of inmates serving longer sentences. Irrespective of this issue, however, the evidence appears stronger for the efficacy of very short prison stays than it does for longer lengths of stay (e.g., Glaser [1964] found 73 percent success for those who served 12 months or less; 65 percent for 13 to 24 months; 56 percent for 25 to 36 months and 60 percent for more than 36 months— regardless of previous record). Of course, cost considerations also favor shorter prison confinement.

Glaser also examined the effect of different levels of custody in federal prisons (maximum, close, medium, minimum) while controlling for rating of "honor stratification" (i.e., level of freedom from surveillance and restriction within the institution granted to an individual). He found a linear relationship between level of custody and recidivism such that lower levels of custody produced less recidivism. These findings held true for both adult and juvenile populations. Unfortunately, since he could not control for initial assignment of individuals to different custody levels, the findings are confounded by the correctional system's original assignment of inmates, which reflect judgments of risk, crowding levels at various institutions, and other variables. Hence, the linear relationship observed could also be regarded as a result of successful prediction, labeling effects, or some combination of such factors. At a minimum, however, the results can be taken as general evidence that lower level custody can be effective.

Finally, a few researchers have attempted to predict, through complex statistical analyses, the effect of a substantial increase in incarceration rates and sentence lengths on overall street crime. Once again, the results have been discrepant. Greenberg (1975), and VanDine, Dinitz, & Conrad (1977) have demonstrated how even large increases in incarceration rates or lengths of imprisonment would have only a modest effect on crime. Conversely, Shinnar & Shinnar (1975) have tried to show that substantial but not extreme increases in the prison population would produce dramatic reductions in crime. Silberman (1978), however, takes issue with Shinnar & Shinnar's definition of "substantial, but not extreme," saying that the proposed increase applied to the New York state prison population (needed to bring about a major reduction in violent crime) turns out to be a growth from 9,000 inmates to between 40,000 and 60,000, an increase of 350 to 550 percent!

In summary, the situation may be best expressed by Silberman when he concluded:

> We simply do not know enough to predict with confidence how much crime will be deterred by any given change in punishment, or even whether stepped-up punishment will have any effect at all. There are too many other factors affecting the crime rate, in both directions, and the statistical techniques for estimating the separate influence of each of them are too crude [p. 195].

Given this lack of research evidence, it is likely that decisions concerning the increase or decrease of punitiveness will continue to be made on some combination of political, emotional, moral, and economic grounds.

Criticisms. Criticisms of the punishment/deterrence approach are numerous. Perhaps the central criticism is one that has guided correctional reformers for centuries, the fact that the severe punishments utilized (imprisonment and the death penalty) are inhumane. Although conditions and treatment in America's prisons cannot rival the grotesque stories of Medieval Europe, it would be difficult to argue that developments in the standard of living of prisoners have kept pace with those of the general public. Indeed, many have detailed the miserable, overcrowded conditions of contemporary American prisons (Silberman, 1978). Conditions recently became so bad in prisons in six southern states that the United States government had to file suit to stop the overcrowding and the abuse of prisoner rights. One judicial opinion described the conditions as "philosophically, psychologically, physically, racially, and morally intolerable" (Silberman, 1978, p. 375). Clearly, although much of the rhetoric of the 1960s about prison reform has disappeared, the oppressive conditions within prisons continue.

With respect to the death penalty, the author feels it best to avoid a prolonged philosophical discussion. Briefly stated, critics argue that the death penalty is inhumane for practice by a civilized nation, is irrevocable in the cases of discovered error in conviction, improperly models aggression and a disregard for human life, is administered in a racially biased manner, and, at any rate, has no demonstrated value as a deterrent to homicide (Shaw, 1961; Sutherland & Cressey, 1970). Further, critics point out that juries tend to change verdicts or vote to convict of a lesser offense if they know that the death penalty is a punishment option (Silberman, 1978).

A second major criticism of the deterrence approach is the issue of costs. Incarceration of offenders is very expensive (over $17,000 a year per offender in federal prisons). Indeed imprisonment costs approximately ten times as much per offender as community alternatives such as probation (Morris & Hawkins, 1970; Fox, 1977). Further, there are hidden costs that are not usually considered in comparisons of imprisonment with alternative strategies, such as the cost of welfare assistance to the family of the prisoner, the loss of productivity of the individual in the work force, and the loss of income taxes that might otherwise be paid. Critics add that since experimental demonstration projects in intensive intervention have shown that for a large number of institution candidates incarceration is clearly unnecessary (NIMH, 1971) less expensive options such as probation, parole, and other community treatment programs should be more readily utilized. This is particularly true since such noninstitutional alternatives have been shown to be equal and at times superior to imprisonment in terms of recidivism (Lipton et al., 1975).

A third major set of criticisms of the deterrence approach revolve around the contention that punishment is not a desirable means of deterring unwanted behavior. Although laboratory studies have demonstrated that punishment, under certain circumstances, can serve to inhibit various behaviors, a whole host of laboratory and field investigations have shown that the use of punishment has numerous undesirable side effects including withdrawal from social contact, counteraggression toward the punisher, modeling of punishing behavior, selective avoidance (i.e., learning to refrain from the undesirable behavior only when under surveillance), and stigmatizing labeling effects (Azrin & Holz, 1966; Milan & McKee, 1974). Indeed, there is ample evidence to support the fact that aversive treatment actually produces aggression (Bandura, 1976). Also, it has been pointed out that punishment tells the offender what behavior is forbidden but does nothing to train or teach about the nature of proper behavior, a particularly important consideration for the ability of an offender to function successfully after undergoing punishment (Johnson, 1968). Finally, as discussed in somewhat more detail previously, there continues to be substantial doubt as to whether there is any empirical support for the belief that increasing punishment reduces crime (Greenberg, 1977; Riedel & Thornberry, 1978).

A fourth criticism is that the deterrence approach ignores the root causes of crime and mistakenly focuses on the individual's "decision" to perform a criminal act. This is essentially the same criticism that the positivists had of the classical school of criminology in the 19th century. Critics who have this perspective would argue that adherents of deterrence theory are unaware of, or are choosing to ignore, three-quarters of a century of social science contributions to the understanding of social or environmental impact on human behavior. Simply stated, such critics would advocate that increased emphasis be put on remedying the undesirable social and environmental factors that contribute to crime rather than on punishing criminals after the fact.

A fifth and final criticism of deterrence theory, and particularly of its current revitalization, is that in spite of the reformist rhetoric of the past 15 to 20 years, the actual criminal justice policy in this country during that time period has remained steadfastly oriented toward punishment and deterrence. For example, the National Council on Crime and Delinquency reports that the average federal prison sentence rose from 17.5 months in 1950 to 29.6 months in 1960 to 41.1 months in 1970 to 45.5

months in 1975. If one were simply to correlate this data with the previously discussed statistics on incidence of crime, one might conclude that the rising sentence lengths actually caused an increase in crime. Obviously this is a methodologically and logically weak argument, but perhaps no more weak than an argument to increase prison sentences further as a deterrent.

Similarly, although three prestigious national committees have recommended decreasing the use of incarceration and increasing community-based treatment, including favoring a reduction or an outright moratorium on building new prisons (President's Commission, 1967; President's Task Force on Prisoner Rehabilitation, 1970; National Advisory Commission, 1973), the nation's heavy emphasis on imprisonment has continued. Including both adult and juvenile institutions, approximately four-fifths of the correctional system budget and nine-tenths of correctional employees are devoted to institutional programs. Although the national prison population did decline by a modest 15 percent during the early 1960s, the trend was soon reversed and by the mid-1970s, the prison population was 40 percent above its low point of 1968 and the rate of new commitments to prison had risen steadily each year to a 1975 figure of 80 percent above the 1968 level (Silberman, 1978). The Federal Bureau of Prisons today operates 50 percent more prisons than it did in 1970 and has received an increase in budget over that time from 70 million to nearly 400 million dollars. Indeed, government policy toward crime is best illustrated by the legislative centerpiece Omnibus Crime Control and Safe Streets Act of 1968, which launched the politically popular "War on Crime," and whose prime creation, the Law Enforcement Assistance Administration (LEAA), has subsequently funneled billions of dollars into crime control efforts of federal, state, and local agencies. Critics focusing on this perspective would argue that deterrence has been the medicine prescribed all along, and that rather than continue to increase the dosage, it might be time to see a new doctor.

Further Directions

> Those who cannot remember the past are condemned to repeat it.
> —George Santayana, *Reason in Common Sense*

Despite the most recent of many episodic resurgences of deterrence theory, one ought not to forget that the punishment approach to crime control has been, with good cause, the target of reformers for centuries. In what may be one of the earliest and most literal examples of the detrimental effects of "labeling," Sutherland and Cressey (1970) describe how an English statute of 1698, which provided for the branding of criminals on the left cheek, was repealed after only eight years because the penalty

> had not had its desired effect of deterring offenders from the further committing of crimes and offenses but, on the contrary, such offenders, being rendered thereby unfit to be entrusted in any service or employment to get their livelihood in any honest and lawful way, became the more desperate [p. 37].

Similarly, it was recognized very early that the effect of prisons was detrimental, particularly for juveniles. John Howard, an English prison reformer, wrote in 1777:

> If it were the wish and aim of magistrates to effect the destruction present and future of young delinquents, they could not devise a more effectual method, than to confine them so long in our prisons, those seats and seminaries ... of idleness and every vice [p. 13].

Clearly, dozens of such quotations could be provided from correctional reformers throughout the years. Perhaps such a historical perspective is useful for those who think that the "liberal" criticisms and proposed solutions of the previous decade were some kind of unusual aberration whose relevance has passed.

Indeed, the persistence of the problem of criminal aggression in the face of centuries of correctional policies based on deterrence is ample testimony that if progress is going to be made, new approaches to the problem must be developed. This, of course, is not to say that no deterrent system is necessary. Few would disagree that some system of laws, including methods of enforcement and means of sanction, are necessary and do serve to regulate behavior to some extent. The deterrence debate, however, is not between no criminal penalties and some criminal penalties. Rather, the issue is one of "marginal" deterrence (Morris & Hawkins, 1970). In other words, would a stricter penalty for a given offense deter more effectively? Would more money spent on police patrols lead to an effective reduction of crime? The issue is very much an economic one in the sense that there are substantial costs associated with attempts at increased deterrence. Also, there are social costs that must not be ignored, such as the impact on the public of increased surveillance or other restrictions of personal freedom. Many would argue that the marginal costs of attempting to increase deterrence are simply too high (i.e., the value of the possible reduction in crime to be achieved is not worth the value of additional economic and social costs to be incurred). From this perspective, the following recommendations for future directions in deterrence practice are offered.

Prisons. It is suggested that the original recommendations of the National Advisory Commission (1973) be followed and that a ten-year moratorium on the construction of new prisons be instituted. Overcrowding in existing prisons should be eased by the release, early parole, or transfer to minimum security institutions of nonviolent offenders. (It should be noted that the Congressional Budget Office in 1977 found that only 11 percent of federal prisoners were committed for violent crimes.) Such alternative placement of nonviolent offenders should save considerable amounts of money (particularly if construction costs of new prisons are considered) and should result in no higher recidivism rates than a strategy of continued imprisonment. Indeed, many authorities agree that as many as one-half of the nation's inmates would function better outside the prison (McCorkle & Korn, 1954; Glaser, 1970; Dominguez, Rueda, Makhlouf, & Rivera, 1976).

A similar moratorium should be extended to institutions that house juveniles. If anything, the moral, practical, and economic rationales cited for avoiding adult imprisonment are even truer for youthful offenders. Many viable alternatives to institutionalization exist, with demonstrated ability to produce equivalent or superior outcomes at reduced cost, including probation, court-related services, or outright diversion from the legal system (Empey, 1967; Lemert, 1971; Schur, 1973; Jordan, 1974).

A final point of support for a moratorium on the construction of new adult or juvenile correctional institutions is the fact of the declining numbers of persons in the age groups most at risk. As the previously cited population figures make clear, the 14- to 25-year-old age group should show a substantial decline in relative numbers through the 1990s. In fact, problems of crowding could potentially turn into underuse within the next decade. But that outcome is not likely. Indeed, Zolton Ferency, a well-known civil rights attorney and criminal justice critic in Michigan has referred to a kind of "Parkinson's Law" that operates with correctional institutions, such that any available bed will always be filled regardless of the absolute level of crime. It is this kind of "system inertia" which led to Massachusetts' ultimate decision simply to close down its state juvenile institutions, a policy which has worked out fairly successfully (Rutherford, 1978).

Psychological Techniques. A number of psychological techniques of enhancing deterrence referred to earlier (e.g., publicity campaigns, monitoring devices, etc.) are likely to see much greater utilization in the future, particularly as the sophistication of such techniques improves. Three factors make the use of such psychological deterrents attractive. First, by their very nature, these techniques function prior to the commission of any crime. Hence, no injury to person or property occurs and no one need be incarcerated for the deterrent effect to occur. This is clearly more favorable than punishment after the fact. Second, to the extent that many criminal acts are very much a function of rather spontaneous reactions to situational opportunities (especially for delinquents and other noncareer criminals), the removal of crime-eliciting stimuli (e.g., a campaign to "lock your car and take your keys") or the addition of crime-suppressing stimuli (e.g., camera monitors in department stores) can be effective and should be encouraged. Third, such techniques cost very little compared with the costs of arrest, prosecution, and imprisonment of an offender after a crime has occurred.

There are, however, some reservations that should be mentioned. In particular, psychological deterrence techniques should be carefully scrutinized and monitored to avoid unpleasant (e.g., two-way mirrors in clothing-store fitting rooms) or illegal (e.g., telephone tapping) invasions of privacy. Also, these measures should be rationally and fairly applied. Adding a camera surveillance system to a store with counters full of highly advertised, glistening pocket-sized items at best creates a terrible approach-avoidance conflict, and, at worst, creates a situation guaranteed to produce apprehended offenders. The latter product is sometimes mistaken as a legitimate goal of security and law enforcement efforts, which of course it is not.

This notion of potential "entrapment" also surfaces with the recently popular police "sting" operations to which we referred above. Indeed, this issue deserves separate comment.

Sting Operations. This author's personal, albeit limited experience with "sting" operations suggests that, for a variety of reasons, their net impact may in fact be to increase crime. Because of their recency in entering the market, inability to pay top dollar and lack of established "credentials," police-operated fencing operations may be much more likely to attract "marginal" criminals (e.g., inexperienced persons and juveniles) than those thieves who have established criminal careers. Hence, owing to the provision of a new market (or "demand") for goods, marginal criminals who hear of the market are led to begin or to increase their criminal activities, while established criminals with established fencing connections are unaffected. (Indeed, in terms of market theory one might question why a better strategy is not devised to put fences out of business, thus reducing the demand for stolen goods.)

Of course, sting operations are not without other obvious benefits. For example, impressive numbers of arrests during the "round-up" following a sting operation make for excellent publicity for the local police agency. Most would agree, however, that such a benefit is not adequate justification for pursuing a questionable police practice. Clearly the popular strategy of conducting sting operations needs to be evaluated carefully through such methods as well-controlled time series analyses before it can be recommended as a means of reducing crime.

The Treatment Approach

The treatment or rehabilitative approach to criminal aggression, as discussed in this chapter, is distinguished by two main features. First, by definition, it is only applied to identified offenders. Second, and partially as a result of the first feature, it implies that the criminal justice system maintains some degree of control over the individual being treated. The extent of control can range from direct custody in an institution to various types of supervision in the community. Within these parameters, the form of treatment is largely unrestricted and can be psychological, educational, medical, vocational, recreational or some combination thereof, in nature.

The rehabilitative approach to corrections has its roots in the major criminological reform movements of the past two centuries. Carter, McGee, & Nelson (1975) refer to Daniel Glaser's classification of the philosophical mix in the American system of corrections as being composed of the three "Rs": retribution, restraint, and reform. Retribution was the primary operating philosophy up into the 18th century and was intended first to punish and, secondarily, to deter others from crime. The second "R" of restraint was the product of the classical school of criminology and was the principle under which imprisonment grew in practice. The third "R" of reform grew out of the positivist school of criminology and led to various efforts to rehabilitate or reform the offender rather than merely to extract revenge or simply to restrain offenders from further misconduct. To these three "Rs" the authors add a fourth, reintegration of the offender back into the community. This is a fairly recent emphasis of the criminal justice system that we will discuss further below.

Carter et al. also trace the origins of the modern practices of parole (suspension of a portion of an institutional sentence to release the offender to the community, subject to continued good behavior) and probation (suspension of any institutional sentence, conditional upon the offender observing the laws and any other restrictions imposed by the court). Probation, it appears, has its roots in the practice of early Anglo-Saxon courts of suspending sentences if the criminal would agree to "keep the peace." The American tradition of probation appears to have begun with the volunteer efforts of a Boston shoemaker in 1841, and by the early 1900s, the use of probation for both adult and juvenile offenders had spread to all states. The concept of parole also originated in Europe in the early 1800s and was brought to America as part of the "ticket of leave" or conditional-pardon movement around 1870. The method of indeterminate sentences, sometimes referred to as the "Irish System," has been incorporated into the correctional systems of all states and of the federal government.

The American tradition of "rehabilitation" programs within prisons also has a long history. The Pennsylvania Quakers (originators of the term "penitentiary") of the early 19th century felt that prisoners kept in solitary confinement with nothing to do but read the Bible, would reflect on their sins and through penitence and prayer, would experience a reformation in character. The history of institutional "treatment" programs since that time, while perhaps not as austere, has often been of similarly dubious value.

Programmatic Examples. The modern emphasis on treatment as a part of the purpose of the criminal justice system has had the result that virtually every correctional program has at least some component or activity that is labeled rehabilitation. The extent to which the real intent, or at least the end result, of many of these activities is the maintenance of order rather than any true rehabilitation is a matter of question. Nonetheless, the range of treatments utilized is considerable.

Individual Therapy. The clinical model of individual treatment is one of the most widely accepted and widely practiced rehabilitation strategies. The convicted offender is liable to experience (or be subject to) psychological testing, interviews, and diagnosis from the time of presentence investigation to intake into an institution to time of consideration for parole or release. Virtually all institutions have psychological and/or psychiatric staff whose responsibility is to treat prisoners, in addition to lower level professionals who function as counselors. The reality of large inmate populations and limited staff size, however, usually dictates that counseling and/or psychological treatment is infrequent, of limited duration, and often reserved for those who exhibit "problems" within the institution. The focus of individual therapy is typically on helping the inmate gain insight into his problems and personality as well as on tempering undesirable impulses (*id*) and strengthening self-control (MacKinnon & Michels, 1971).

Group Therapy. Owing to the previously mentioned manpower shortages, the practice of group therapy has become an attractive option for fulfilling the therapeutic model of treatment. In addition, there is something to be said for at least involving an inmate's peers in the rehabilitation process. This can be a first step toward dealing with the need to consider social and environmental factors in attempting to rehabilitate an offender. Institutional group therapies can include simple opportunities for semistructured social interaction, "strong leader" types of therapist-led and directed learning sessions, psychoanalytic models of relaxing and examining repressed feelings and building ego strength, and types of "peer influence" groups such as "guided group interaction," in which the therapist attempts to bring about group problem solving and the establishment of new and positive social norms.

Behavior Modification. Behavior modification programs are also present in many correctional institutions in one form or another. A popular example is the "token economy" (Ayllon & Azrin, 1968) whereby inmates earn "points" for performing various tasks or maintaining good behavior and can subsequently exchange those points for various materials or privileges. In adult prisons, points are often replaced by the earning of actual cash for various jobs (although at greatly reduced pay scales) which can be used to buy goods at the prison "store." It is sometimes difficult to discern to what extent behavior modification programs are actually oriented toward rehabilitation as opposed to toward prison maintenance. One of the more notorious programs in this sense was that implemented at a federal prison in Missouri, called START (Special Treatment and Rehabilitative Training). As described by the Federal Bureau of Prisons, its purpose was "to provide care, custody, and correction of the long term adult offender" and "to develop behavioral and attitudinal changes in offenders who have not adjusted satisfactorily to institutional settings" (Quinney, 1975, p. 252). For a description of numerous contemporary institutional behavior therapy programs, the reader is referred to Michael T. Nietzel's recent book, *Crime and its Modification: A Social Learning Perspective* (1979).

Educational Programs. Lack of education has always been a key factor associated with street crime. More than one-half of all prison inmates have only an eighth grade education or less (Johnson, 1968; Carter et al., 1975). This fact, combined with the heavy emphasis that American culture places on education as a path to success, has resulted in the widespread adoption of educational rehabilitation efforts in correctional institutions. Participation is generally optional, except for juveniles. Techniques that have been utilized include fairly standard classroom settings, tutoring (by professionals, peers, or volunteers), and a variety of behavioral techniques ranging from contingency management to programmed learning packages. Occasionally, prisoners at lower security institutions are allowed to attend adult education or community college courses off the prison grounds, although relatively few inmates are educationally qualified for such programs.

Vocational Training/Work Programs. It has also been observed that most persons committed to prison, even for the first time, have deplorable work records; over 40 percent have *no* previous sustained work experience (National Advisory Commission, 1973). Further, upon release from prison, the criminal stigma combines with weak or nonexistent job experience to give parolees and released offenders a severe employment problem. These facts (combined with a realistic need for a variety of prison maintenance activities to be performed) have led to the use of work and/or work-training programs as common rehabilitation strategies. Typical examples of work programs include agricultural, food service, clothing and laundry, building and grounds maintenance, and clerical jobs. Again, especially in lower security institutions, daytime work release programs are sometimes available for job experience in actual community locations.

Probation and Parole. While the practices of probation and parole are not necessarily defined as a "treatment" in the sense of rehabilitation, they are generally considered more benign alternatives to incarceration. Hence their inclusion in this discussion of treatment strategies.

The use of probation and parole is indispensable to the criminal justice system and is in fact the predominant form of handling convicted offenders. Slightly more than one-half of all offenders sentenced to correctional treatment are placed on probation, and more than 60 percent of imprisoned adult offenders are released on parole prior to completion of their maximum sentence (Morris & Hawkins, 1970). Both probation and parole typically involve the assignment of an offender to a probation or a parole officer under the understanding that the offender will obey the law as well as any other requirements that are made a condition of that disposition. Actual practices differ and optional services are sometimes provided directly or by referral, but the typical practice is one of minimal supervision, where the individual is one of at least 60 persons in an officer's caseload.

Community Placements. A final correctional strategy that grew out of both a desire for more humanitarian treatment as well as the reality of crowded jails and prisons, is the trend toward community residential programs. Similar to the fourth "R" proposed by Carter et al. (1975), the major goal of community treatment is the reintegration of the offender back into the community in a productive way. According to this philosophy, if satisfactory adjustment to society is a goal, persons are best treated in a setting located within that society and not in isolation from it (Alper, 1974; Dodge, 1975). Community alternatives such as group homes and halfway houses have been used both as direct sentencing options as well as prerelease programs from prison. There are also nonresidential community treatment alternatives such as presentence diversion projects or various rehabilitation programs that might be associated with parole or probation.

Research Evidence. Taken as a whole, the research evidence on correctional programs presents a somewhat dismal picture. In the most pessimistic view, it has been contended that no correctional strategy, from imprisonment to outright release, has demonstrated itself to be capable of reducing recidivism (Robison & Smith, 1971). The prevalent opinion, from several social scientists who have reviewed the field (e.g., Bailey, 1966; Martinson, 1974; Lipton et al., 1975) seems to be well represented by the following quotation from Riedel and Thornberry (1978):

> While a few rehabilitative programs have produced changes in intervening variables and recidivism, these isolated examples do not demonstrate the overall effectiveness of such programs [p. 429].

Reidel and Thornberry, however, go on to acknowledge the generally poor methodological quality of most research conducted in this area and conclude that it would be a mistake to "repudiate the rehabilitative ideal on the basis of such scant evidence" (p. 430). Instead, they recommend the strong pursuit of further quality research, matching specific crime and delinquency control techniques to particular problem areas. In this sense it is useful to consider some of the research evidence that has been gathered concerning various treatment alternatives.

Counseling. With respect to professional counseling and psychotherapy with offenders, the results are fairly clear. It is apparent that individual counseling for adult prisoners can produce positive results in terms of institutional adjustment, but that such treatments are unrelated to post-institutional performance (Lipton et al., 1975). These findings hold true for both general counseling (Fox, 1954) and psychotherapy (Persons, 1965). For delinquent youth, however, individual counseling is unrelated to either institutional adjustment or recidivism. Psychotherapy in particular may actually produce negative results (Guttman, 1963).

For group counseling techniques the research findings are very similar. Although the study was confounded by the use of volunteers only, Kessemeier (1966) found that inmates in a maximum security prison who participated in group counseling had significantly fewer and less serious rule violations. In better controlled studies that included random assignment, both Seckel (1965) and Levinson & Kitchner (1966) found improved institutional adjustment for juveniles involved in group counseling (particularly when instituted early in the youth's stay at an institution). Once again, however, there was no evidence for group counseling for adults or juveniles having any effect on post-release recidivism (Lipton et al., 1975).

In terms of nonresidential psychotherapy, the results are similarly negative. Research on the effects of noninstitutional psychotherapy with adult offenders is rare, but what has been published has shown no support for any positive impact on recidivism (Nietzel, 1979). For juveniles, the evidence suggests that psychotherapy is at best noneffective and at worst seems to produce adverse results (Grey & Dermody, 1972).

One might conclude from these results that counseling for offenders is unproductive, particularly in terms of helping them to achieve success in the community. In their review, however, Lipton et al. (1975) are careful to differentiate between "individual counseling" which is "directed toward developing the client's insight into his problems," and "casework" which is "client-need oriented and involves a broad range approach" (p. 172). Indeed, the latter more comprehensive approach appears to produce much more positive results. They cite a Danish study (Bernstein & Christiansen 1965) that used random assignment of offenders being released from prison, in which it was found that a program of extensive casework produced significantly less recidivism (41 percent versus 58 percent) than the no treatment control group through a three- to five-year follow-up. Of major importance, it appears, is the fact that the extensive casework program included assistance in obtaining jobs, residence, clothing, union and health insurance membership, financial aid, and financial counseling in addition to more traditional supportive counseling.

Similar but somewhat less pronounced effects were found by Ericson (1965), who randomly assigned adult male felon parolees to a combination of psychological, social, and vocational services versus standard parole. He found positive recidivism effects for one year, but no difference thereafter. Dombross (1966) contrasted intensive casework in lieu of prison for minor offenses and found that the treatment group had better recidivism figures than a matched control group (21.1 percent versus 30.5 percent) but that the difference did not reach statistical significance. Finally, research on two much less extensive casework programs, one for juveniles (Hood, 1966), and one for young adults (Shelley & Johnson, 1961), indicated that there was some limited evidence of success, perhaps favoring youths considered to be poorer risks (Lipton et al., 1975).

Behavioral Techniques. Methods of treatment involving behavioral strategies appear to fare somewhat better in the research than the more traditional counseling techniques. Prison token economies have been shown to produce positive results in numerous studies. In one of the best designed and evaluated investigations, Milan and McKee (1974) conducted a series of experiments at the Draper Correctional Center in Alabama. These studies demonstrated the positive effects of a cell-block token economy on such variables as institutional behavior and inmate participation in various desirable activities. It is interesting to note that in one study, using an ABA design, they were able to demonstrate the often referred to negative consequences of a punishment model of control. During the "punishment" phase of their study, although the directly targeted behavior of self-maintenance was satisfactorily achieved, undesirable "behavioral incidents" increased fourfold over the baseline period, while returning to just over one-half the punishment phase rate during the second baseline.

In another quasi-experimental evaluation in Ohio (McNamara & Andrasik, 1977), a program involving the common practice of successive "steps" or "tiers" of behavior change (with commensurate freedoms and privileges at each level) was examined. Results indicated a desirable improvement in self-maintenance (e.g., dressing properly and cleaning living area) and self-improvement (e.g., education and employment activities) behaviors and a decrease in problematic behaviors. In addition, for the 64 residents released during this four-year study, recidivism rates were at only 28 percent. This is a fairly desirable short-term recidivism rate. Unfortunately, no control group was available for direct comparison in this instance.

Paradoxically, despite some very positive results for institutional adjustment and some promising indications in terms of eventual recidivism, prison behavioral strategies have been widely abandoned owing to strong criticism from ethical and legal standpoints (Nietzel, 1979). This issue is discussed further below.

Behavioral strategies have also been widely utilized in noninstitutional settings. For the most part, community-based correctional programs using behavioral techniques have been largely confined to juvenile offenders (Davidson & Seidman, 1976; Nietzel, Winett, MacDonald, & Davidson, 1977). Some successful adult probation utilizing behavioral strategies has been performed, for example, with drug offenders (Polakow & Doctor, 1974) and sexual deviants (see Nietzel, 1979 for a review). The greatest successes, however, have been with juveniles, particularly through the methods of behavioral contracting, which have demonstrated positive results in the family setting (Tharp & Wetzel, 1969; DeRisi & Butz, 1975), at school (Bailey, Wolf, & Phillips, 1970), and in terms of police and court contacts (Davidson & Seidman, 1976; Davidson et al., 1977).

Educational and Occupational Skill Development Lipton et al. (1975) reviewed eight *ex post facto* studies evaluating the effect of prison "skill development" programs, including five that considered educational programs and three that examined vocational training programs. While acknowledging the methodological problems associated with *ex post facto* studies, they conclude that regular institutional academic or vocational training programs, like the counseling programs previously discussed, have little or no relationship to success on parole. Some of the studies (e.g., Glaser, 1964; Gearhart, Keith, & Clemmons, 1967) found, however, that such factors as the type of employment training received and the extent to which parolees receive initial employment in their area of training, do impact on probabilities for success. These findings led the authors to conclude that institutional training programs that are not adjusted to the actual employment market are of little value (Lipton et al., 1975).

In contrast, it appears that skill development with juveniles is somewhat more successful. Lipton et al. (1975) review six studies and conclude that both institutional and community programs that include skill development techniques are more successful at lowering recidivism than are similar programs without skill development. Again, the findings suggest that it is most important to focus on readily marketable skills.

Probation. Probation is a correctional strategy that is so widely practiced, with so many variations, that it would do little good to discuss individual examples. To summarize the research results, it has been found that several empirical studies have shown lower recidivism rates for probation than for commitment to prison (Rumney & Murphy, 1968; Sparks, 1971; Empey & Rabow, 1970). Indeed, numerous examinations of probation programs have revealed that anywhere from 60 to 90 percent of probationers complete their terms without revocation (Morris and Hawkins, 1970). Although direct comparison of probation and prison recidivism is often difficult owing to selection differences based on perceived risk, even if one accepts the common assumption that probation is no less effective than imprisonment in lessening future recidivism, the greatly reduced cost makes probation a desirable alternative.

Parole. Similar to probation, parole is so widely used and varies so greatly in use between states that discussion of individual examples is unfeasible here. (Although the previous discussion of counseling and casework strategies does suggest some relevant factors to consider in examining any particular parole program.) The general nationwide success rate of parolees after one to two years in the community is 60 to 70 percent (Nietzel, 1979). It is important, however, to realize that approximately only one-third of those returned (roughly 10 percent of all parolees) are returned on new felony convictions. Most are for minor offenses and/or technical violations of parole (Morris & Hawkins, 1970; Carney, 1977).

A final area that has received much attention in discussions of parole and probation is the issue of caseload sizes. It has been argued that the typical caseload sizes of 60 to 100 cases per parole or probation officer are too large to provide meaningful contact. Lipton et al. (1975) reviewed five studies, all of which used random assignment, that compared small caseload sizes (averaging 15 cases) to large caseloads (50 to 100 cases) in the supervision of juvenile offenders. They found consistent evidence that the smaller caseloads produced less recidivism. Interestingly, the evidence suggests a different conclusion for adults. Lohman (1967) compared "standard" (50 cases) and "intensive" (15 cases) caseloads with "minimal supervision" (meeting at probationer's request only). He found no difference between the three methods in the number of new crimes, but that the intensive group actually had a higher rate of technical violations (most often related to increased surveillance and visibility).

Community Placements Despite the growing popularity of community residential treatment, Lipton et al. (1975) could find only a handful of suitably evaluated programs. Kirby (1966) experimentally compared the effectiveness of a halfway house with that of a work camp for adult, low-risk offenders. At three months of follow-up, there were no significant differences in recidivism or community adjustment. On the other hand, Hall, Milazzo, & Posner (n.d.) used an *ex post facto* study to evaluate a federal halfway house program and found that participants had significantly lower failure rates than the "expected rate" of failure for federal parolees. The methodological weaknesses in this design, however, limit the usefulness of its findings. Reed (1967) evaluated the effectiveness of a halfway house for juveniles (including counseling, vocational training, recreation, etc.) with conventional probation and found the somewhat perplexing results that the halfway house boys had both higher failure rates (43 percent versus 31 percent) and a higher rate of constructive activities (training or employment in the community) than the controls. This suggests the possible influence of some moderating variable or characteristic but none is offered in the review. In general, Lipton et al. conclude that the inconsistent results, small number of studies, and noncomparability of the studies that have been done necessitate further research in this area.

Criticisms. One central criticism of the "treatment" model as practiced is that it actually lacks a true emphasis on rehabilitation. Modern trends in corrections, in spite of the rhetoric of rehabilitation, are still dominated by the objectives of punishment and incapacitation. What prison treatment does exist is liable to be primitive in nature and oriented more toward maintaining order within the institution than on true rehabilitation (Shah, 1972; Quinney, 1975). This criticism has certainly been leveled at many behavioral management programs (see Nietzel, 1979 for a review) but could also be directed at many prison work programs, for example, where the jobs are often low skill and might be seen as more related to the maintenance needs of the prison (e.g., laundry, food service, etc.) than to the inmates' needs for job training and experience. Similarly, the various counseling and therapy programs have been criticized as being oriented more toward control and satisfactory adjustment of the inmate to imprisonment than to the actual rehabilitation of the person. The following quote from Mitford (1973) is illustrative of this critical perspective:

> In prison parlance, "treatment" is an umbrella term meaning diagnosis, classification, various forms of therapy, punishment as deemed necessary, and prognosis, or the prediction of the malfeasant's future behavior: will/won't he err again? While the corrections crowd everywhere talk a good line of treatment ... very few prison systems have actually done much about implementing it in practice. Nationwide, only 5 percent of the prison budget goes for services labeled "rehabilitation," and in many states there is not even the pretense of making "therapy" available to the adult offender (p. 97).

Indeed, many feel that incarceration is simply incompatible with rehabilitative objectives and that community-based alternatives must be developed (Klapmuts, 1975).

The lack of true rehabilitative emphasis is also put forward as a criticism of probation and parole, at least as they are most frequently practiced. One problem with the current system of parole and probation is the inherently conflicting dual role that the parole/probation officer must fill. The National Advisory Commission (1973) refers to this conflict as that between the "surveillance" function and the "helping" function (p. 393). In any balancing of these two roles, the surveillance function is bound to win because the penalty to the parole/probation officer for failure (e.g., one of those infrequent but greatly publicized cases in which a parolee commits a violent crime) is substantially greater than any rewards for helping a client to avoid recidivism. Further, the person under supervision is well aware of the dual role and is therefore reluctant to trust the officer.

A second major problem with probation and parole is the greatly over-crowded caseloads. It is difficult indeed to argue that much treatment is occurring when an individual is one of 60 or more persons being supervised by a single officer. Carter et al. (1975) trace the historical development of the general consensus that 50 cases is the proper size caseload for efficient management. They point out that this number was more or less arbitrarily arrived at and has become established as a management goal simply by the weight of tradition rather than through any empirical test. The President's Commission (1967) felt this number was too high and recommended a goal of 35-person caseloads. Actual practice, however, has taken quite the opposite direction. Adult parole caseloads have averaged 68 persons and juvenile probation caseloads 64 persons. Most shockingly, 76 percent of all misdemeanants and 67 percent of all felons on probation were on caseloads of 100 or more persons (Morris & Hawkins, 1970).

While it is clear that not much service can occur in caseloads of that size, the severest critics might argue that at least not much surveillance can occur either. Given that over half of all parole failures are for technical violations rather than for new crimes, perhaps they have a point. At any rate, all but the hardline deterrence advocates would agree that at least parole and probation do allow the offender to remain in the community, even if he or she is not receiving much treatment.

A second set of criticisms of the treatment model, somewhat related to the first, is based on moral or ethical objections. Critics from this perspective argue that most "treatments" are in fact punitive in the sense of being generally mandatory and often unpleasant (Opton, 1974, 1975; Quinney, 1975). In addition, various scholars have called attention to the ethical dilemma presented by the uncritical use of the tools of social science to impose control within institutions that reinforce individual conformity and, indirectly at least, maintain inequities in the social status quo (Rappaport, Davidson, Wilson, & Mitchell, 1975; Rappaport, Lamiell, & Seidman, 1978). Indeed, many have commented on the unethicality as well as the impracticality of trying to change an individual while ignoring the wider social change needed to correct causal factors contributing to the individual's criminality (Sutherland & Cressey, 1970; Shah, 1972; Quinney, 1975). The following quote from Reid and Patterson (1973) is representative of this criticism of the treatment approach:

> The traditional psychotherapeutic goal to teach the delinquent child to live happily in a destructive social environment appears not only of dubious moral merit but impossible to achieve. If behavioral psychologists are truly to address themselves to the problem of delinquency in children they must develop methods for changing the structure of the social systems that elicit, shape, reinforce, and maintain delinquent behavior. Instead of a symptomatic treatment (i.e., trying to treat the delinquent child, who is the end product of the system that creates delinquency), a successful solution to the problem of delinquency requires a frontal assault on the homes, neighborhoods, and classrooms in which these behaviors are taught [p. 124].

A third major criticism of the treatment approach is its record of ineffectiveness. From this perspective, one of the most heavily criticized treatment strategies has been the use of psychotherapy. For many years criminality was seen as having its primary roots in mental illness and consequently, psychiatric diagnosis and treatment was widely recommended and practiced. In the past two decades, however, both theoretical and empirical criticisms have rocked the therapy approach. For example, the focus of the "medical model" represented by psychotherapy has been severely criticized for focusing on individual differences and individual correction to the exclusion of environmental and social variables (Ullmann & Krasner, 1975; Krisberg & Austin, 1978). From an empirical perspective, repeated studies have shown the ineffectiveness of therapy approaches with delinquent and criminal populations (Teuber & Powers, 1953; Meltzoff & Kornreich, 1970; Martinson, 1974; Adams, 1975). Critics declare that this is not surprising since these populations rarely exhibit the YAVIS (Young—Attractive—Verbal—Intelligent—Successful) syndrome that often seems to be a prerequisite for benefiting from psychotherapeutic techniques (Nietzel et al., 1977; Nietzel, 1979).

Other treatment strategies, however, have not escaped similar criticism. For example, group counseling and therapy methods (Grosser, 1958; Johnson, 1968; Lipton et al., 1975), as well as institutional behavioral management programs (Burchard, Harig, Miller, & Amour, 1973; Nietzel, 1979) have also been criticized for simply being unable to produce effects that can be generalized to the external environment after release. Indeed, such criticisms are not unique to the criminal justice system but seem to pertain more generally to any form of institutional treatment that purports to prepare individuals for re-entry into the community. Indeed, this same problem has been identified by critics in the mental health field (Fairweather, Sanders, Maynard, & Cressler, 1969; Fairweather, Sanders, & Tornatzky, 1974). The answer, it seems, is more community-based treatment. Unfortunately, in the criminal justice field at least, much more research needs to be done to establish consistently effective means of such treatment.

In summary, it can safely be said that despite instances of individually successful programs, no treatment or rehabilitation strategy has reliably demonstrated itself superior to incarceration in reducing future recidivism. While advocates of treatment programs could turn that argument around and say that alternative programs are just as good as simple imprisonment and cost a lot less, that is still not an impressively strong argument. Clearly, much further research and more carefully planned and administered innovations are necessary before the rehabilitative ideal can be realized.

A final criticism of the treatment approach within corrections is that advanced by strict deterrence theorists: that the function of the criminal justice system should not be expected to include rehabilitation but rather, should simply focus on punishment, incapacitation, and general deterrence. The lack of strong positive research results demonstrating the effectiveness of various treatment strategies has recently added impetus to this critical perspective and made its proponents more vocal. Critics of this persuasion decry the perceived "leniency" toward criminals and advocate a "get tough" policy (Rossum, 1978). As James Q. Wilson (1975) states: "We have trifled with the wicked, made sport of the innocent, and encouraged the calculators. Justice suffers and so do we all" (p. 209).

Of course, this position is not new. Rossum himself, in a critique of rehabilitation, refers to a passage from C. S. Lewis, published in 1953:

> Because proponents of rehabilitation tend to take the position that all crime is more or less pathological, mending becomes healing and curing, and punishment itself becomes therapeutic.... In doing so, however, rehabilitation removes the idea of desert from punishment and with desert, so too, justice.... As Professor C. S. Lewis brilliantly states it, "If crime is only a disease which needs cure, not sin which deserves punishment, it cannot be pardoned. How can you pardon a man for having a gum boil or a club foot?"...[Rehabilitation] wants simply to abolish justice and substitute mercy for it [p. 232].

Aside from demonstrating once again that the degree of perceived brilliance is relative to the darkness of the room in which one is standing, the above quotation is ironically noteworthy for illustrating what many innovative social scientists have known for some time. The "medical model" is an inappropriate approach to the problem of crime. Unfortunately, the choice offered by the above passage is one of illness or sin. In contrast, more enlightened social scientists have long argued that neither of these choices were satisfactory, but that criminal behavior must be understood in a larger context. The implications of this understanding are that rehabilitative efforts must involve preparing the person for reintegration into the community, including active involvement in modifying the individual's environment where possible. All of this is ignored when one simply poses the alternative of "medicine" or "just deserts."

Despite the periodic upsurge of the punishment/deterrence rhetoric, however, it is doubtful that the United States will abandon the goal of rehabilitation of its criminals. Public opinion polls demonstrate that in spite of media attention and the cries of outspoken critics, when questioned about specific issues of individual rights versus police procedure, or about causes of crime, or particularly about crime prevention, the response of the American public is in fact much closer to the rehabilitative ideal than the punitive approach (see, for example, the series of polls outlined in the President's Commission report, 1967). Indeed, the rehabilitative alternative has demonstrated itself to be at least as effective and far less expensive than more punitive approaches.

Future Directions. The future of rehabilitation strategies in the correctional system can be summed up in one word: reintegration. By now the past experience and research evidence have made it abundantly clear that attempts to change the individual in isolation from the environment to which he or she will return are misguided and bound to fail. While numerous rehabilitation strategies have been successful at producing institutional adjustment, those strategies are not doing the job in terms of producing eventual successful community adjustment. For example, it is estimated that at least 90 percent of the inmates released from federal prison seek legitimate careers for a month or more after they leave prison. Yet, the reimprisonment rates eventually reach 20 to 40 percent or more for these offenders (Glaser, 1964). What happens to these individuals between the date of release and the time of their subsequent reincarceration? Why can't they sustain the impetus they had in their first few post release weeks? It is here that the need for an emphasis on reintegration is most obvious.

The need for successful reintegration of an offender back into the community is a goal that should pervade every level of the criminal justice system. The following quotation from Glaser (1973) well illustrates the general tone of the reintegration approach:

> these methods ... have numerous implications for the entire criminal justice system, beginning at arrest and pretrial processing. All of these implications can be consolidated well by the general maxim: never set apart from the community, any more than can possibly be avoided, those whom you wish some day to bring safely back into the community [p. 116].

The movement toward the goal of successful reintegration implies that rehabilitative efforts must move beyond the traditional focus on the offender to include an emphasis on the environment into which the offender is to be placed and on his or her interactions with that environment. This new emphasis can be easily adapted to each of the major areas of rehabilitative effort outlined previously.

Counseling and Therapy. The traditional treatment modes of counseling and therapy need to broaden their focus from institutional adjustment to the types of interpersonal skills and understanding needed for proper community adjustment. In this respect, group counseling methods may be preferable to individual therapy. For those offenders in the community or nearing release from an institution, counseling strategies should be much more closely aligned with the "casework" model of comprehensive service provision mentioned earlier in this chapter.

Behavioral Strategies. Similar comments can be made about behavioral treatment strategies. The focus must move beyond efficient institutional management and into the development of behaviors that will facilitate community adjustment. Once in the community, a variety of behavioral methods are available for use in sustaining productive and prosocial behavior. Such methods as contingency management and behavioral contracting have been shown to be particularly effective with problem children and youthful offenders (Tharp & Wetzel, 1969; Stuart, 1971). Although noninstitutional behavioral interventions with adult offenders have been somewhat limited, the success of such techniques with similar target populations compels the further study of these methods in probation, parole, and post release settings.

Skill Development. Clearly, an emphasis on reintegration of offenders demands that these individuals be given the skills necessary to successfully survive in the community in a legitimate career. Obviously, both educational and vocational training are a necessity in this respect, as demonstrated by the figures for level of schooling and prior work experience of prisoners cited earlier. Methods have been developed for increasing both participation and achievement in skill development programs and should be more widely utilized. Particularly attractive in this sense are programs that utilize naturally available reinforcers (including the use of the "Premack Principle" of reinforcing low probability behaviors such as studying, with high probability behaviors such as increased recreation time). Several such programs have experimentally demonstrated their success (Clements & McKee, 1968; Bassett, Blanchard, Harrison, & Wood, 1973; Dominguez et al., 1976).

In addition, adequate attention must be given to the community. As Lipton, et al. (1975) point out, it does little good to train individuals for jobs that do not exist. Furthermore, the correctional system need not confine itself to passive anticipation of employment trends. Active recruitment of employers for "rehabilitated" offenders should be practiced, perhaps including incentive systems such as tax benefits or positive publicity (where appropriate).

Probation and Parole. Probation and parole should continue to be endorsed as highly preferable alternatives to incarceration. As discussed previously, many current institutional candidates could just as well be handled through these noninstitutional alternatives. Hence, it is recommended that the practice of probation and parole be expanded. One interesting system-level innovation that might accelerate this process is a method of "probation subsidy" developed in California. It is, in effect, a contingency management approach to institutional change whereby the state pays counties a share of the amount of money saved in institutional costs for each juvenile or adult offender placed on probation rather than incarcerated in a state institution (Nietzel, 1979). Such systems-level contingency management is recommended as an excellent way to overcome the resistance or simple inertia that often hinders change in large organizations.

We have a second and perhaps somewhat more controversial suggestion for the reform of probation and parole methods. Stated briefly, it is suggested that the traditional conflict of parole and probation supervision, that between surveillance and assistance, be resolved by separating the two functions. The existing network of supervision within the corrections system would be retained to serve the surveillance function. (Many would argue this would result in few practical changes in operations.) A separate and independent system of parole and probation "advocates" would be set up to provide the much needed assistance in financial, occupational, educational, and other personal areas. It is imperative that this system be independent, both for the development of trust by the offender as well as to ensure freedom from institutional pressures toward surveillance for the caseworker. It is recommended that an entirely different agency handle the advocacy duties, such as the state department of social services.

Participation in the advocacy segment of the system would be entirely voluntary, as opposed to the surveillance segment. It is, however, strongly recommended that some type of incentive structure be established to encourage participation in the advocacy program. Also, care must be taken to ensure that caseload sizes are low enough to allow caseworkers to give meaningful attention to each case on a regular basis. (The appropriate size for such caseloads would have eventually to be determined through experimentation.)

There are operating advocacy type programs that serve as successful precedents for such an effort, particularly in the area of juvenile delinquency (Davidson & Rapp, 1976; Westman, 1979). Also, although the costs of such a two-track system should still be substantially lower than imprisonment, the possibility exists of even further savings by utilizing volunteers as advocates for juveniles and other low-risk offender groups. A substantial amount of research indicates the effectiveness of volunteers for this and similar public service purposes (National Advisory Commission, 1973; Schwartz, Johnson, & Mahoney, 1977). Of course, it is recommended that this new system be implemented on an experimental basis and in selected locations. But the rationale for such a system is sound and it is anticipated that the results would positively reflect the effort to bring true reintegration into the handling of legal offenders.

Institutions. The spirit of Glaser's quote on maintaining proximity to the community is recommended as the guiding principle for correctional institutions as well. A gradation of institutional options should be established, similar to the federal prison system's minimum through maximum security prisons, except that it should be much more weighted toward community placement. Once parole, probation, and release have screened off all suitable candidates, the next preference would be for the smallest and most community-integrated option, such as halfway houses and group homes. In particular, it is recommended that all prison inmates who have suitable prison performance ratings and are approaching consideration for parole be placed in such community placements for the last two or three months of their prison term. This would provide a transition period that should help reintegrate the offender into community life prior to being placed on parole officially. Similar placement or even outright release is recommended for inmates who are approaching their release date. Indeed, research has shown that inmates could simply be released from their terms 90 days early with no additional risk to the community and substantial savings to the taxpayer (Lipton et al., 1975).

Even offenders who need a moderate amount of structure and supervision should be considered for community placement. Nietzel (1979) describes a residential program in Minnesota that utilizes behavioral step-levels, a token economy, and group decision making and has successfully supervised offenders who had been considered unsuitable for probation.

One factor that needs to be considered, however, and that has plagued many recent attempts at community placement, is resistance to the establishment of such community treatment centers by local residents. State and local authorities need to assume a much stronger role in educating community residents as to the realistic levels of risk as well as perhaps providing financial or other incentives for neighborhoods that volunteer to accept such treatment centers. Cities routinely provide such incentives for businesses to locate within their boundaries; it is certainly time that cities took some responsibility for the reintegration of citizens who have become legal offenders.

Finally, even with those offenders who must be placed in large, centralized prisons, steps can be taken to maximize the potential for eventual successful reintegration. For example, Silberman (1978) describes a prison in southern Illinois in which a series of architectural and staff training innovations were successfully used to maximize the inmate's personal responsibilities. The following statement illustrates the views of the warden of that institution concerning the philosophy that is needed:

> The fatal flaw in the traditional approach to prison government, Housewright believes, is that by expecting the worst, it succeeds in bringing out the worst in people's attitudes and behavior. Traditional prison rules are geared to the lowest common denominator. Because some inmates will try to escape, every inmate is kept behind bars and guard towers; because some inmates may attack guards or other inmates, every prisoner is kept under close and rigid surveillance. In fact, Housewright argues, only a minority of prisoners are unwilling to abide by prison rules; instead of gearing everything to that minority, it makes more sense to erect a prison government around the majority of conforming inmates, and then to zero in on those who refuse to conform [Silberman, 1978, p. 421].

Indeed, it is recommended that all but the highest security prisons be operated under similar principles. Housewright, the warden of the southern Illinois prison in question, believes that conversion of existing prisons is possible and has suggested ways that such conversion might be accomplished (Silberman, 1978). Prison policy should begin now to move in that direction.

ALTERNATIVE ORGANIZATIONAL AND SOCIAL SYSTEM CHANGES

Although the preceding section of this chapter rightfully devoted considerable attention to the traditional correctional system, it is clear that if effective, long-term solutions to the problem of criminal aggression are to be found, one must widen the range of potential societal responses to be considered. The best-designed programs of deterrence, rehabilitation, and reintegration of offenders still leave many larger but very important issues unaddressed. In view of this fact, the remainder of this chapter will attempt to introduce some broader organizational and social system changes that might properly be considered a part of any societal response to the problem of undesirable aggression.

Owing to the nature of this document, the purpose of this section will be to provide a brief introduction to each of the concepts rather than an exhaustive or authoritative review. The intent is not to provide the final word on these subjects, but to broaden the arena of debate to include a more thorough conceptualization of the problem of criminal aggression and a more comprehensive repertoire of societal responses.

Systemic Transformations

Having outlined and critiqued the full range of traditional correctional system responses, from both the deterrence and rehabilitation perspectives, we now consider some more far-reaching and somewhat controversial systems-level options that also exist. These alternative responses might be considered as the four "Ds" of criminal justice renovation: decriminalizing, diverting, disarming, and democratizing.

Decriminalizing: Taking the crime out of victimless crime.

> When the criminal law invades the spheres of private morality and social welfare, it exceeds its primary tasks. The unwarranted extension is expensive, ineffective and criminogenic [Morris and Hawkins, 1970, p. 2].

Reformers have argued for some time that the criminal justice system in the United States has a tendency to impose itself on a variety of areas of human conduct that are not necessarily the proper domain of criminal law. This process has been referred to as "over criminalization" (NIMH, 1971) and has most often been criticized in connection with the attempt to regulate such behaviors as drunkenness, drug use, gambling, disorderly conduct, vagrancy, and various sexual behaviors between consenting adults. These offenses have been dubbed "victimless crimes" and have been criticized as improper attempts to regulate "morals" through criminal law (Schur, 1965).

Aside from being offensive to philosophical considerations of individual freedoms, the criminalization of these victimless offenses has several other distinctly negative effects. First, these laws are often differentially enforced, resulting in discrimination against poor and subcultural minorities. Second, these laws frequently lack solid social backing and thus lack legitimacy in the eyes of many, and their enforcement breeds disrespect and indifference to criminal law. Third, these laws have frequently led to the emergence of organized crime to fill the obvious demand for these activities, and in this respect may have created more crime than they have surpressed (Kadish, 1967). Finally, the most damaging effect may be the extent to which the tasks of apprehension and prosecution of these crimes are literally over-whelming the criminal justice system and thus preventing needed resources from being directed toward serious crime. Indeed, the burden is clear; over one-half of all nontraffic arrests in this country are for such victimless crimes (Nietzel, 1979).

Despite increasing rhetoric about the need to move in the direction of decriminalization, little progress seems to have been made thus far. One current example is the much discussed option of the decriminalization of marijuana offenses. Although criminal penalties for possession and use of marijuana have generally been lessened from their earlier, incredibly harsh levels, the criminal justice system continues to arrest and to prosecute these offenses in record numbers. The most recent FBI *Uniform Crime Reports* reveals that well over 400,000 persons were arrested for marijuana offenses in 1978, accounting for 70 percent of all drug arrests. Furthermore, lest one think that the relative overemphasis on minor offenders has changed, 87 percent of all the arrests were for simple possession.

These figures, and the similar continuing attention of the criminal justice system on other victimless crimes, are clearly in opposition to dominant social trends toward liberalized social norms and moral codes. Presumably, legislation will eventually respond to these trends (un-doubtedly spurred on by increasing crises of crowding and expense in the criminal justice system) and decriminalization of victimless offenses will proceed.

Finally, however, it must be acknowledged that there are cases where such offenders present a legitimate danger to themselves or the com-munity (e.g., severe cases of drug or alcohol addiction). In these situa-tions, a combination of voluntary and mandatory treatment options should be pursued through civil court actions. But these cases should be a tiny fraction of the current caseloads comprised of such offenders. Furthermore, such civil action should include careful attention to due process standards and to the assurance that effective treatment is utilized rather than mere civil commitment for custody purposes. (See Quinney, 1975, for an overview of objections to current civil inter-vention.)

Diverting.

A marketplace wherein a negative community image is unwillingly purchased, consumer protection is minimal, and all sales are final.

—A description of juvenile
court, found in a 1973 HEW report, *The Challenge of Youth Service Bureaus.*

The concept of diverting offenders from the criminal justice system is based on some of the same rationales as decriminalization. In particular, overcrowded courts and correctional facilities and the negative effect of the criminal justice system itself on those with whom it comes in contact (e.g., labeling effects, association of low-risk persons with more "hard-core" criminal types) are most frequently cited as reasons for diversion (Lemert, 1971; Schur, 1973).

There are two major alternative forms of diversion. The first, and most "ideologically pure," is the diverting of an offender from all further official contact, or, in other words, an outright release. The rationale for this approach is that noncriminal justice contacts can be just as coercive as the system itself and moreover, have so failed to demonstrate their effectiveness that individuals are better off on their own (Klein, 1979).

The second and most popular form of diversion is the diverting of apprehended offenders from the criminal justice system into some alternative form of service or treatment. The exact nature of the process used and the extent or nature of treatment provided vary greatly, but the underlying rationale is that the offender has certain needs for supervision, counseling, and/or supplemental services which, if provided, will do more to prevent future crimes by that individual than will aversive, stigmatizing formal correctional-system handling.

Numerous diversion programs are in operation throughout the United States for both juvenile and adult offenders (Fox, 1977). The concept is perhaps more widespread with juveniles, however, for whom diversion has become so popular in such a short time that some have referred to it as a fad and have quite correctly pointed to serious shortcomings in many operating programs (Carter & Klein, 1976). Nonetheless, the widespread adoption of this concept illustrates the validity and the seriousness of the needs that gave rise to its popularity. What is needed now is high quality experimental research to investigate the diversion process and to demonstrate operational principles that will maximize successful outcomes.

One such effort with which the author has been personally involved is an on-going experimental examination of diversion strategies for juvenile delinquents. Operating around a core model of diverting youth from the legal system to a trained volunteer who works on a one-to-one basis with the youth in the youth's natural environment, this project has systematically varied several components of the diversion process in an effort to determine their relative effectiveness. The variables that have been examined have included: type of training provided to the volunteer; type of supervision provided to the volunteer; intensity of training and supervision; focus of the intervention (e.g., on youth only; on youth and his or her family; and on youth, family, and relevant community systems); size of supervision groups; and types of volunteers. Although this project has been quite successful in demonstrating effective intervention techniques, and has been cited by the LEAA as an "exemplary project," it is perhaps most noteworthy as an example of the type of comprehensive research that must be done if diversion programs (and societal responses to aggression in general) are to be effective in the purposes for which they are designed. (For further information on this project, see Davidson et al., 1977.)

Disarming: The Case for Gun Control.

The most recent reported comparison between countries in relation to rates of homicide by gunfire indicates that, out of the fifteen countries reporting, the United States ranked first. The present American gunfire homicide rate is 2.7 per 100,000; that of the Netherlands, 0.03; Japan, 0.04; West Germany, 0.12; Canada, 0.52; and the United Kingdom, 0.05. To the student of criminal statistics, the United States may or may not be the land of the free, but it is certainly the home of the brave [Morris & Hawkins, 1970, p. 57].

Amongst the plethora of texts on criminology published in the United States, very few even mention, let alone elaborate on, the potential of gun control as a strategy for reducing violent crime. Yet, a brief glance at some rather astounding statistics can reveal the potential for positive impact in this area. (Most of the following information was obtained from Morris & Hawkins, 1970).

Since the beginning of this century, over three-quarters of a million people have been killed in the United States by privately owned guns. This total is 30 percent more than the number of individuals who have died in all the wars in which this country has been involved in its entire history. In 1968, a fairly typical year, 8,870 persons were murdered with guns, over 10,000 committed suicide, and over 2,500 died in "accidental" gunfire. In addition, there were over 100,000 nonfatal gun injuries in that year. The most incredible fact of all, however, is that the overwhelming majority of murders and nonfatal shootings occurred not in predetermined homicidal attacks and not even in the act of commission of a felony, but simply as a by-product of family quarrels, domestic disputes, arguments between acquaintances, brawls, and other clashes of personality. Indeed, known felony murders—those resulting from robberies, planned homicides, and other felonious activities—constitute, on the average, only about 14 percent of all murders.

While these interpersonal disturbances and domestic quarrels often precipitate violence, there is no reason that they require a death for their resolution. The fact that a gun was handy and available was the causal factor in perhaps a majority of those deaths. UCR data comparing relative fatality rates for various weapons in serious assault situations reveal that firearms are over four times as likely to produce death of the victim than knives and over seven times as likely as attacks with hands, fists, or feet. Moreover, these are rates per assault, and do not even consider that without guns, which require little skill or strength and no contact with the victim as compared with other weapon options, many impulse assaults might not even occur or would be quickly terminated with a nonfatal expenditure of physical energy.

The policy implications here are obvious. Currently popular solutions such as mandatory minimum sentences for crimes committed with a gun may in fact be desirable, but they are only going to affect less than 15 percent of homicides. Murders of impulse—the vast majority of gunfire homicides—are largely unaffected by such a law. Statutes limiting access to guns, on the other hand, deal with both types of homicides, but particularly the much more prevalent crimes of impulse. Furthermore, they have the added advantage of being preventive in focus.

The parameters of the problem are somewhat awesome. The best estimate of the number of guns in private hands in this country is roughly 100 million. Many have recommended, and this author agrees, that the focus should most properly be on handguns. Handguns are by far the most overrepresented weapon of homicides, suicides, and severe or fatal accidents. Handguns are virtually worthless for hunting and sport shooting. Their only conceivable purposes are to threaten, wound, or kill people. Yet, their numbers are also overwhelming. For the ten years ending in 1968, 10 million new handguns were sold in the United States. In only five more years, 10 million more had been sold (Silberman, 1978). The United States is literally becoming an armed camp and it is likely that only severe restriction of handgun ownership (e.g., handguns restricted solely to on-duty use by police and licensed security personnel) can hope to make a dent in the growing violence. Restriction of the so-called "Saturday Night Special" is a popular recommendation and is probably a useful first step. Research indicates, however, that most guns confiscated by police when they make arrests are in fact more expensive, higher-quality weapons (Zimring, 1976).

Progress on this issue will be difficult. Still, the task is far from impossible. Public opinion polls repeatedly show that a majority of Americans are favorable toward some form of gun control legislation. It is conceivable that newly formed pro-gun-control coalitions may be able to overcome traditional lobbying groups opposed to such legislation and effective laws could result. Whatever the outcome, there may be no more important, nor more controversial issue in this nation's efforts to eliminate violent aggression than the issue of gun control.

Democratization: A Broader View of Criminal Aggression

dem-o-crat-ic 3: of, relating to, or appealing to the broad masses of the people 4: favoring social equality.

—*Webster's Third New International Dictionary*

The dominant conceptualization of crime and criminal aggression in the United States is deeply and fundamentally limited in scope to what is commonly called street crime. This is true in spite of the fact that those categories of crime clustered under the title of white-collar crime probably account for substantially more economic loss and loss of health and well-being than all street crimes combined (President's Commission, 1967). An interesting illustration of this skewed perception of crime is represented by this very chapter, where discussion of crimes by business and government is confined to this small subsection.

Indeed, academia has shared and perhaps helped to perpetuate the public ignorance of the parameters of white-collar crime. Until Edwin H. Sutherland published his landmark works in 1940 and 1949, virtually all criminological literature dealt with street crimes—crimes most prevalent among lower socioeconomic classes. As defined by Sutherland, white-collar crime was "crime committed by a person of respectability and high social status in the course of his occupation" (President's Commission, 1967, p. 102). It was Sutherland's contention that criminality was learned, largely through a process of differential association, and that it was furthermore distributed across all social classes. He went into considerable detail in providing examples of white-collar criminality to illustrate his thesis.

Sutherland's contribution to the understanding of white-collar crime was immeasurable. Donald Cressey, in his introduction to the 1961 edition of Sutherland's *White Collar Crime*, wrote that

The lasting merit of this book...is its demonstration that a pattern of crime can be found to exist outside both the focus of popular preoccupation with crime and the focus of scientific investigation of crime and criminality [p. xii].

Somewhat ironically, it is the lasting *de*merit of the American social science community that this pattern of white-collar crime has *remained* outside the focus of both popular preoccupation and scientific investigation. As an example, one may look at any typical text on criminology. If it even includes a section on white-collar crime, one can most assuredly find disclaimers similar to the following (which began the section entitled "The Impact of White Collar Crime" in the 1967

President's Commission Report):

> There is little systematic data available regarding the incidence of white collar
> crime. There are, for example, no consolidated statistics comparable to the F.B.I.'s
> Uniform Crime Reports ... it is very difficult to obtain statistics about ... it is very
> difficult to discover the existence of ... [p. 103].

Why the country's finest research bodies and government commissions know so little about such an important phenomena is an issue
in and of itself and is a question one would hope that criminological
researchers will ask themselves.

The Commission did conclude nonetheless that "such information as
is available, though not systematically compiled, indicates that white
collar crime is pervasive in our society and causes enormous economic
and social harm" (p. 103). Indeed, beneath the surface of public perception and academic pursuit, the dim outlines of the tip of a veritable
iceberg of corporate and governmental crime and corruption have been
detected. The remainder of this section will attempt to outline briefly the
parameters of these crimes and how they relate to the larger problem of
determining societal responses to criminal aggression.

Incidence. As the comments of the Commission make clear, the data on
the incidence of white-collar crime is scanty. Again, one must turn to
Sutherland's classic work. He surveyed 70 of America's largest corporations over a 45-year period and found that every corporation had
received at least one adverse decision (on such laws as restraint of trade,
infringements, labor laws, advertising laws, etc.), and that the average
was 14 adverse decisions per corporation. In a fine example of gallows
humor, Sutherland & Cressey (1970) observed that if the "habitual
criminal" laws of many states were applied, over 90 percent of the major
American corporations surveyed would be considered "habitual" white-
collar criminals.

A variety of other small-scale and somewhat dated studies are available (President's Commission, 1967), but in the interest of conciseness,
only one more will be discussed. In this survey (Baumhart, 1961) nearly
half the respondents agreed with the statement that "the American
business executive tends to ignore the great ethical laws as they apply
immediately to his work. He is preoccupied chiefly with gains" (p. 161).
Four out of seven respondents believed that businessmen "would violate
a code of ethics whenever they thought they could avoid detection."
Were these respondents college students or even the public at large,
these results would not be particularly surprising. The fact that they
were business executives subscribing to the *Harvard Business Review*,

however, makes the study's implications for the incidence of white-collar crime even more noteworthy.

Costs. The costs of white-collar crime can be conceptualized in three main categories; economic, physical, and what for lack of a better term can be called sociocultural. Economic costs can include costs to the public from overpricing or from shoddy or defective materials and services as well as costs to other businesses that are injured by illegal conduct. The President's Commission (1967) made some conservative estimates of the economic costs of several categories of white-collar crime. Roughly adjusted for inflation, they would amount to the following yearly totals today: unreported taxable income of $50 to $80 billion; securities frauds of $1 to $2 billion; $1 billion on "worthless or extravagantly misrepresented drugs"; $1 to $2 billion on fraudulent home repair and improvement; and over $200 million in fraudulent auto repair. This list obviously includes only a few major industries, but it is enough to serve as an illustration. The President's Commission itself concluded: "While no reliable estimates can be made of the financial burdens produced by white collar crime, they probably are far greater than those produced by traditional common law theft offenses—robbery, larceny and burglary" (p. 104).

While most often thought of in terms of monetary losses, white-collar crimes also result in substantial physical harm to the public. Violations of the Pure Food and Drug Act, building code violations, pollution violations, and the marketing of hazardously defective products all represent white-collar crimes that have direct adverse impact on the health and safety of the public. Perhaps the most serious and currently publicized examples of this problem are in the area of toxic substances and pollution. Indeed, names such as DDT, PCB, PBB, Kepone, and Love Canal have practically become household words in recent years, and not without reason. Cancer has become the number two cause of death in the United States (behind heart disease) and it is estimated that between 60 and 90 percent of all cancers are environmentally caused. In addition, a variety of other fatal illnesses, including respiratory and heart diseases, can be caused and/or substantially aggravated by pollutants. Even more at risk than the public at large is the nation's work force. Violations of the Occupation Health and Safety Act (OHSA) and other work-place standards can be very serious. The National Institute of Health estimates that approximately 100,000 Americans die of job-related illnesses every year (which is roughly 20 times the number of persons who die in felony murders per year).

Finally, there are the sociocultural costs of white-collar crime. These might be most properly conceptualized as the effects of white-collar crime on the public consciousness and behavior. Indeed, the examples set by corporate leaders affect the whole moral climate of society. As the President's Commission stated: "Derelictions by corporations and their managers, who usually occupy leadership positions in their communities, establish an example which tends to erode the moral base of the law and provide an opportunity for other kinds of offenders to rationalize their misconduct" (p. 104).

Perhaps even more important in this process is the role of government. As Supreme Court Justice Louis D. Brandeis wrote:

> Our government is the potent, the omnipresent teacher. For good or for ill, it teaches the whole people by its example. Crime is contagious. If the government becomes a law breaker, it breeds contempt for law.

As the National Advisory Commission (1973) put it nearly a half-century later:

> No one can fail to realize the impact of public corruption on street crime. The gas station robber, the burglar, and the mugger know that their crimes are pale in comparison with the larger criminality "within the system"... A sense of injustice is endemic among prisoners, and it stems in large measure from the inmates' belief that they are the unlucky victims of a hypocritical system that tolerates lawlessness among its officials but makes scapegoats of less well-placed offenders.

They concluded:

> In short, official corruption stands as a serious impediment to the task of reducing criminality in America. As long as official corruption exists, the war against crime will be perceived by many as a war of the powerful against the powerless; "law and order" will be just a hypocritical rallying cry, and "equal justice under law" will be an empty phrase [p. 207].

It might be noted, furthermore, that all this was written before the revelations of Watergate and such more recent examples as the Bert Lance affair and the Senator Talmadge scandal.

The Question of Societal Response. It is quite obvious that, at least in terms of official response, society clearly differentiates between white-collar crimes and street crimes. As Sutherland (1940) described it in his early work:

> The crimes of the lower class are handled by policemen, prosecutors, and judges, with penal sanctions in the form of fines, imprisonment, and death. The crimes of the upper class either result in no official action at all, or result in suits for damages in civil courts, or are handled by inspectors, and by administrative boards or

commissions, with penal sanctions in the form of warnings, orders to cease and desist, occasionally the loss of a license, and only in extreme cases by fines or prison sentences. Thus, the white collar criminals are segregated administratively from other criminals, and largely as a consequence of this are not regarded as real criminals by themselves, the general public, or the criminologists [p. 7].

Numerous investigative bodies have since examined the issue of the differential response to white-collar crime and have suggested that stricter penalties, including imprisonment, may be in order. For example, the President's Commisson (1967) reported that the U.S. Department of Justice was recommending increased use of imprisonment (albeit for short terms) in white-collar crimes such as price fixing. They added that the current system of criminal fines and civil damages (virtually unchanged today) was inadequate for several reasons. Specifically, they stated that such monetary penalties were "trivial for corporations in proportion both to their ability to pay and to the profits resulting from the criminal violations"; and that "in a number of states corporate executives may be lawfully reimbursed for fines imposed on them"; and finally, "since discovery of criminal violations of the antitrust laws is very difficult, even substantial civil penalties may not constitute adequate deterrents" (p. 105). They added that prison terms, even of short durations, are liable to be a substantially greater deterrent to this target population than to those engaged in more routine street crime.

Is it appropriate to toughen the penalties for white-collar crime? Many would argue that the present discrepancy in the handling of various types of offenses is desirable and, at any rate, represents the will of the public as manifested through their legislative representatives. Indeed, it is a kind of unspoken criminological assumption in many circles that a society's correctional and punishment systems are a direct reflection of the public's perception of the seriousness of various crimes. Some empirical evidence that has been gathered, however, suggests that this is not necessarily the case. Consumers, for example, have overwhelmingly recommended harsher punishment of violators of the Federal Food, Drug and Cosmetic Act than the courts have typically handed out (Newman, 1957) and the public's level of "moral indignation" has been found to be substantially higher for such offenses as bribery and oil-price fixing than for street crimes such as burglary, larceny, and auto theft (Scott & Al-Thakeb, 1977).

With respect to white-collar crimes that result in injury and death, the verdict is liable to be even more severe. Although there has long been a great difficulty in tracing the effects of such crimes as pollution or toxic substances violations, technology is making the detection of such impacts much more feasible. If a corporate executive takes a gun and shoots someone, the legal response is clear and severe in nature. If that same person makes a business decision to dump hazardous wastes, which may eventually result in the death of many individuals, the legal response is both unclear and incomparably less severe.

Another example—this time not hypothetical—is the recent controversy involving the Ford Motor Company and its automobile, the Pinto. It was alleged that Ford executives continued to produce millions of Pintos in full knowledge that an inadequately designed gas tank system made the car a severe fire risk in rear end collisions, and that the decision to continue production was actually based on a calculation of the cost to the company of repairing the problem versus handling damage claims. Ford has already been subjected to several substantial civil suits (which is the traditional legal response in such cases) but in a precedent-setting case, criminal charges were pressed in connection with the deaths of three girls in an Indiana crash. The case generated a great amount of public attention and a good deal of outrage. Although the jury eventually ruled that speed and not the Pinto design itself was responsible for the fatalities in this specific situation, the case was precedent setting in more than just the legal sense.

Are the above examples cases of criminal aggression? How should they be dealt with and what steps can be taken to prevent this type of aggression against society? These are indeed legitimate questions for both social scientists and the public at large. It is quite possible that their resolution will have greater impact on the future of American society and the well-being of its citizens than any decisions regarding the more traditionally discussed "Index" crimes.

CONCLUSION

This chapter has attempted to provide a review of the phenomenon of criminal aggression. This review has included a discussion of possible causes of this phenomenon. More specifically, however, this review has attempted to examine society's response to criminal aggression, both historically and at the current time, and has offered some suggestions for more appropriate societal responses in the future.

As is true for most texts on criminology, the majority of this document was devoted to the particular problem of "street crime." The historical development of the response to this type of crime was outlined, from the earliest days of revenge and religious persecution through the major "reforms" of the past few centuries, and up to the recent trends toward rehabilitation. It was observed that although the empirical evidence does not demonstrate superior recidivism rates for the present rehabilitative programs, the theoretical rationale is still sound and the substantial deleterious effects of the punitive/in-carcerative model have been unquestionably demonstrated. Further-more, in addition to being more humanitarian, community-based alter-natives are also substantially cheaper than incarceration (a factor that is becoming increasingly important in these days of government budget cutting). The recommendation was made to go beyond the many current attempts at "person-change" rehabilitation toward vigorous pursuit of the concept of reintegration, targeting efforts not only at the individual but also at the social environment in which that individual must function successfully.

Indeed, perhaps the most important point that this chapter has attempted to convey is the need to look beyond the relatively narrow traditional definition of criminal aggression and beyond traditionally individual-centered responses to this multifaceted problem. There is a need for a broader definition of criminal aggression and a willingness to consider organizational and social system variables as root causes, or at the very least, as substantial contributors to many types of criminal aggression. Coupled with this is the need for a commitment to consider actual intervention strategies at an organizational and social system level. Several examples of such approaches—including those referred to as "decriminalizing, diverting, disarming, and democratizing"—were included in this text.

Finally, a recommendation included at various points throughout this chapter deserves re-emphasis here. Briefly stated, it is strongly recom-mended that any and all interventions pursued in the area of criminal aggression be soundly and thoroughly evaluated (preferably, whenever possible, with the use of a true experimental design). As has been detailed elsewhere (Davidson & Kushler, 1979), it is clearly time for a systematic, data-based approach to investigating the problem of crime and its possible solutions. This nation can ill afford to base its policy decisions in this crucial area solely on the "pendulum swings" of public opinion and/or political pressure. The long-term solutions to the problem of criminal aggression are going to require a broadly focused longitudinal program of scientific and experimental exploration of alternatives. Without a commitment to such an organized search, public policy decisions in this realm will continue to blow like so many straws in the wind, veering sharply (depending on the audience) from vengeful and destructive punishment to ill-conceived and wasteful treatment pro-grams, while actually coming no closer to the goal of reducing or ending criminal aggression in this society.

REFERENCES

Adams, S. *Evaluative research in corrections: A practical guide.* U.S. Department of Justice, Law Enforcement Assistance Administration, 1975.

Alper, B. *Prisons inside-out: Alternatives in correctional reform.* Boston, Mass.: Ballinger, 1974.

Ardrey, R. *The territorial imperative.* New York: Dell, 1966.

Ayllon, T. & Azrin, N. *The token economy.* New York: Appelton-Century-Crofts, 1968.

Azrin, N. & Holz, W. Punishment. In W. K. Honig (Ed.), *Operant behavior.* New York: Appelton-Century-Crofts, 1966.

Bailey, W. Correctional outcome: An evaluation of 100 reports. *Journal of Criminal Law, Criminology, and Police Science,* 1966, **57**, 153–160.

Bailey, J., Wolf, M., & Phillips, E. Home-based reinforcement and the modification of pre-delinquents' classroom behavior. *Journal of Applied Behavior Analysis,* 1970, **3**, 223–233.

Bandura, Albert. Social learning analysis of aggression. In E. Ribes-Inesta and A. Bandura (Eds.), *Analysis of Delinquency and Aggression.* Hillsdale, N.J.: Lawrence Erlbaum Associates, 1976.

Bassett, J., Blanchard, E., Harrison, H., & Wood, R. Applied behavior analysis on a county penal farm: A method of increasing attendance at a remedial education center. Proceedings of the 81st Annual Convention of the American Psychological Association, Washington, D.C., 1973.

Baumhart, R. How ethical are business men? *Harvard Business Review,* 1961, **39**, 156–176.

Bernstein, K. & Christiansen, K. A resocialization experiment with short-term offenders. *Scandinavian Studies in Criminology,* 1965, **1**, 35–54.

Bowers, W. & Salem, R. Severity of formal sanctions as a repressive response to deviant behavior. *Law and Society Review,* 1972, **6**, 427–441.

Burchard, J., Harig, P., Miller, R., & Amour, J. New strategies in community-based intervention. In E. Ribes-Inesta & A. Bandura (Eds.), *Analysis of delinquency and aggression.* Hillsdale, N.J.: Lawrence Erlbaum Associates, 1973.

Carney, L. *Probation and parole: Legal and social dimensions.* New York: McGraw-Hill, 1977.

Carter, R. & Klein, M. *Back on the street: The diversion of juvenile offenders.* Englewood Cliffs, N.J.: Prentice-Hall, 1976.

Carter, R., McGee, R., & Nelson, E. *Corrections in America.* Philadelphia: J. B. Lippincott, 1975.

Chiricos, T. & Waldo, G. Punishment and crime: An examination of some empirical evidence. *Social Problems,* 1970, **18**, 200–217.

Clements, C., & McKee, J. Programmed instruction for institutionalized offenders: contingency management and performance contracts. *Psychological Reports,* 1968, **22**, 957–964.

Cohen, A. The sociology of the deviant act: Anomie theory and beyond. *American Sociological Review,* 1965, **30**, 5–14.

Davidson, W. & Kushler, M. Social science contributions to crime and delinquency control: Alternatives to watching the pendulum. Paper prepared under special contract to the National Science Foundation, 1979.

Davidson, W. & Rapp, C. A multiple strategy model of child advocacy. *Social Work,* 1976, **21**, 225–232.

Davidson, W. & Seidman, E. Studies of behavior modification and juvenile delinquency. In A. Graziano (Ed.), *Behavior therapy with children.* New York: Academic Press, 1976.

Davidson, W., Seidman, E., Rappaport, J., Berck, P., Rapp, N., Rhodes, W., & Herring, J.

Diversion program for juvenile offenders. *Social Work Research and Abstracts*, 1977, 13, 40–49.

DeRisi, W., & Butz, G. *Writing behavioral contracts.* Champaign, Ill.: Research Press, 1975.

Dodge, C. The halfway house as an alternative. In C. Dodge (Ed.), *A nation without prisons.* Lexington, Mass.: D.C. Heath & Company, 1975.

Dombross, E. & Silver, J. Excerpt from final report of the San Francisco rehabilitation project for offenders. San Francisco: Northern California Service League, 1966.

Dominguez, B., Rueda, M., Makhlouf, C., & Rivera, A. Analysis and control of activities in custodial human groups. In E. Ribes-Inesta and A. Bandura (Eds.), *Analysis of delinquency and aggression.* Hillsdale, N.J.: Lawrence Erlbaum Associates, 1976.

Ehrlich, I. The deterrent effect of capital punishment: A question of life and death. *American Economic Review*, 1975, **65**, 3.

Empey, L. *Alternatives to institutionalization.* Washington, D.C.: U.S. Government Printing Office, 1967.

Empey, L. & Rabow, J. The Provo experiment in delinquency rehabilitation. In T. Laswell, J. Burma, & S. Aronson (Eds.), *Readings in sociology.* Glenview, Ill.: Scott Foresman, 1970.

Ericson, R. The application of comprehensive psycho-social, vocational services in the rehabilitation of parolees. Minneapolis Rehabilitation Center, 1965. (mimeo)

Fairweather, G., Sanders, D., Maynard, H., & Cressler, D. *Community life for the mentally ill.* New York: Pergamon, 1969.

Fairweather, G., Sanders, D., & Tornatzky, L. *Creating change in mental health organizations.* New York: Pergamon Press, 1974.

Fox, V. The effect of counseling on adjustment in prison. *Social Forces*, 1954, **32**, 285–289.

Fox, V. *Community-based corrections.* Englewood Cliffs, N.J.: Prentice-Hall, 1977.

Gallup, G. "Crime is rated worst urban problem." *The Washington Post*, January 16, 1973.

Gearhart, W., Keith, H., & Clemmons, G. An analysis of the vocational training program in the Washington State Adult Correctional Institution. Research Review No. 23. State of Washington, Department of Institutions, May, 1967.

Gibbs, J. Crime, punishment and deterrence. *Southwestern Social Science Quarterly*, 1968, **48**, 515–530.

Glaser, D. *The effectiveness of a prison and parole system.* Indianapolis: Bobbs-Merrill, 1964.

Glaser, D. *Crime in the city.* New York: Harper & Row, 1970.

Glaser, D. Correction of adult offenders in the community. In Lloyd Ohlin (Ed.), *Prisoners in America.* Englewood Cliffs, N.J.: Prentice-Hall, 1973.

Goldstein, J. *Aggression and crimes of violence.* New York: Oxford University Press, 1975.

Greenberg, D. The incapacitative effects of imprisonment: Some estimates. *Law and Society Review*, 1975, **9**, 541–580.

Greenberg, D. *Corrections and punishment.* Beverly Hills, Calif.: Sage Publications, 1977.

Grey, A. & Dermody, H. Reports of casework failure. *Social Casework*, 1972, **53**, 534–543.

Grosser, G. The role of informal inmate groups in change of values. *Children*, 1958, **5**, 25–29.

Guttman, E. Effects of short-term psychiatric treatment on boys in two California youth authority institutions. Research Report No. 36. California Youth Authority, December, 1963.

Hall, R., Milazzo, M., & Posner, J. A descriptive and comparative study of recidivism in pre-release guidance center releases. U.S. Department of Justice, Bureau of Prisons, n.d.

Harris, L. *The public looks at crime and corrections.* Washington, D.C.: Joint Commission on Correctional Manpower and Training, 1968.

Hood, R. *Homeless Borstal boys: A study of their after-care and after-conduct.* Occasional Papers on Social Administration No. 18. London: G. Bell & Sons, 1966.

Inciardi, J. The role of criminal statistics and victim survey research in planning and organizing for more effective law enforcement. In E. Viano (Ed.), *Victims and society.* Washington, D.C.: Visage Press, 1976.

Johnson, E. *Crime correction and society.* Homewood, Ill.: Dorsey Press, 1968.

Jordan, V. The system propagates crime. *Crime and Delinquency,* 1974, **20**, 233–240.

Kadish, S. The crisis of overcriminalization. *Annals of the American Academy of Political and Social Science,* 1967, **374**, 157.

Kessemeier, L. Does group counseling pay its way? *Correctional Review,* 1966, March–April, 26–30.

Kirby, B. Crofton house: A community oriented halfway home for local offenders. The Crofton House Study: Progress Report. San Diego State College, 1966.

Klapmuts, N. Community alternatives to prison. In C. Dodge (Ed.), *A nation without prisons.* Lexington, Mass.: D.C. Heath, 1975.

Klein, M. Deinstitutionalization and diversion of juvenile offenders: A litany of impediments. In N. Morris & M. Tonry (Eds.), *Crime and justice.* Chicago: University of Chicago Press, 1979.

Krisberg, B. & Austin, J. *The children of Ishmael.* Palo Alto, Calif.: Mayfield Press, 1978.

Lemert, E. *Human deviance: Social problems and social control.* Englewood Cliffs, N.J.: Prentice-Hall, 1971.

Levinson, R. & Kitchner, H. Treatment of delinquents: Comparison of four methods for assigning inmates to counselors. *Journal of Consulting Psychology,* 1966, **30**, 364.

Lewis, C. The humanitarian theory of punishment. *Res Judicatae,* 1953, **6**, 224–230.

Lipton, D., Martinson, R. & Wilks, J. *The effectiveness of correctional treatment.* New York: Praeger, 1975.

Lohman, J. The intensive supervision caseloads: A preliminary evaluation. The San Francisco Project: A Study of Federal Probation and Parole, Research Report No. 11, School of Criminology, University of California, 1967.

Lorenz, K. *On aggression.* London: Methuen, 1966.

MacKinnon, R. & Michels, R. *The psychiatric interview in clinical practice.* Philadelphia: W. B. Saunders Company, 1971.

Martinson, R. What works? *The Public Interest,* 1974, **35**, 22–54.

McCorkle, L. & Korn, R. Resocialization within walls. *Annals of the American Academy of Political and Social Science,* 1954, **293**, 88–98.

McNamara, J. & Andrasik, F. Systematic program change: Its effects on resident behavior in a forensic psychiatry institution. *Journal of Behavior Therapy and Experimental Psychiatry,* 1977, **8**, 19–23.

Meier, R. *Theory in criminology: Contemporary views.* London: Sage Publications, 1977.

Meltzoff, J. & Kornreich, M. *Research in psychotherapy.* New York: Altherton Press, 1970.

Merton, R. Anomie, anomia and socia interaction. In M. Clinard (Ed.), *Anomie and deviant behavior.* New York: Free Press, 1964.

Milan, M. & McKee, J. Behavior modification: Principles and applications in corrections. In D. Glaser (Ed.), *Handbook of criminology.* Chicago: Rand McNally, 1974.

Minor, W. A deterrence-control theory of crime. In R. Meier (Ed.), *Theory in criminology.* Beverly Hills, Calif.: Sage, 1977.

Mitford, J. *Kind and usual punishment: The prison business.* New York: Alfred A. Knopf, 1973.

Morris, N. & Hawkins, G. *The honest politician's guide to crime control.* Chicago: University of Chicago Press, 1970.

National Advisory Commission on Criminal Justice Standards and Goals. *Report on corrections.* Washington, D.C.: U.S. Government Printing office, 1973.

National Institute of Mental Health (NIMH). *Community based correctional programs: Models and practices.* Rockville, MD.: NIMH, 1971.

Newman, D. Public attitudes toward a form of white collar crime. *Social Problems*, 1957, **4**, 228–231.

Nietzel, M., Winett, R., MacDonald, M., & Davidson, W. *Behavioral approaches to community psychology.* New York: Pergamon Press, 1977.

Nietzel, M. *Crime and its modification.* New York: Pergamon Press, 1979.

Opton, E. Psychiatric violence against prisoners: When therapy is punishment. *Mississippi Law Journal*, 1974, **45**, 605–644.

Opton, E. Institutional behavior modification as a fraud and a sham. *Arizona Law Review*, 1975, **17**, 20–28.

Pepinsky, H. Despotism in the quest for valid U.S. crime statistics: Historical and comparative perspectives. In R. Meier (Ed.), *Theory in criminology*. Beverly Hills, Calif.: Sage, 1977.

Persons, R. Psychotherapy with sociopathic offenders: An empirical evaluation. *Journal of Clinical Psychology*, 1965, **21**, 205–207.

Price, R. H. & Denner, B. (Eds.) *The making of a mental patient*. New York: Holt, Rinehart & Winston, 1973.

Polakow, R. & Doctor, R. A behavioral modification program for adult drug offenders. *Journal of Research in Crime and Delinquency*, 1974, **11**, 63–69.

President's Commission on Law Enforcement and Administration of Justice. *Crime and its Impact: An Assessment.* Washington, D.C.: U.S. Government Printing Office, 1967.

President's Task Force on Prisoner Rehabilitation. *The criminal offender—What should be done?* Washington, D.C.: U.S. Government Printing Office, 1970.

Quinney, R. *Critique of the legal order.* Boston: Little, Brown & Co., 1974.

Quinney, R. *Criminology: Analysis and critique of crime in America.* Boston: Little, Brown & Co., 1975.

Rappaport, J., Davidson, W., Wilson, M., & Mitchell, A. Alternatives to blaming the victim or the environment: Our places to stand have not moved the earth. *American Psychologist*, 1975, **30**, 525–528.

Rappaport, J., Lamiell, J., & Seidman, E. Know and tell: Conceptual constraints, ethical issues, and alternatives for psychologists in (and out of) the juvenile justice system. Paper presented for the APA Task Force on the Role of Psychology in the Criminal Justice System, 1978. (mimeo)

Reckless, W. *American criminology: New directions.* New York: Appleton-Century-Crofts, 1973.

Reed, A. The MacLaren vocational center: A special demonstration project conducted by the MacLaren School for Boys. Portland, Oregon, 1967. (mimeo)

Reid, S. *Crime and criminology.* Hinsdale, Ill.: Dryden Press, 1976.

Reid, J. & Patterson, G. The modification of aggression and stealing behavior of boys in the home setting. In E. Ribes-Inesta & A. Bandura (Eds.), *Analysis of delinquency and aggression*. New York: Wiley, 1973.

Riedel, M. & Thornberry, T. The effectiveness of correctional programs: An assessment of the field. In B. Krisberg & J. Austin (Eds.), *The children of Ishmael*. Palo Alto, Calif.: Mayfield Press, 1978.

Robison, J. & Smith, G. The effectiveness of correctional programs. *Crime and Delinquency*, 1971, **17**, 67–80.

Roper Organization, Inc. *Roper reports.* New York: June, 1977.

Rossman, R. *The politics of the criminal justice system: An organizational analysis.* New York: Marcel Dekker, Inc., 1978.

Rumney, J. & Murphy, J. *Probation and social adjustment.* New York: Greenwood Press, 1968.

Rutherford, A. The dissolution of the training schools in Massachusetts. In B. Krisberg & Austin (Eds.), *The children of Ishmael.* Palo Alto, Calif.: Mayfield Press, 1978.

Schellhardt, T. "Arresting forecast: U.S. crime will drop as population matures." *The Wall Street Journal,* October 3, 1977, **1**, 20.

Schur, E. *Crimes without victims.* Englewood Cliffs, N.J.: Prentice-Hall, 1965.

Schur, E. *Radical non-intervention.* Englewood Cliffs, N.J.: Prentice-Hall, 1973.

Schwartz, I., Johnson, D., & Mahoney, M. *Volunteers in juvenile justice.* Washington, D.C.: U.S. Department of Justice, 1977.

Schwartz, I. & Orleans, S. On legal sanctions. *University of Chicago Law Review,* 1967, **34**, 274–300.

Scott, J. & Al-Thakeb, E. The public's perceptions of crime: Scandinavia, Western Europe, the Middle East, and the United States. In R. Huff (Ed.), *Contemporary corrections,* Beverly Hills, Calif.: Sage, 1977.

Seckel, J. Experiments in group counseling at two youth authority institutions. Research Report No. 46. California Youth Authority, 1965.

Sellin, T. *The death penalty.* Philadelphia: American Law Institute, 1959.

Shah, S. Foreword to Marguerite Q. Warren, *Correctional treatment in community settings: A report of current research.* Rockville, MD: NIMH, 1972.

Shaw, G. *The crime of imprisonment.* New York: Citadel Press, 1961.

Shelley, E. & Johnson, W. Evaluating an organized counseling service for youthful offenders. *Journal of Counseling Psychology,* 1961, **8**, 351–354.

Shinnar, S. & Shinnar, R. The effects of the criminal justice system on the control of crime: A quantitative approach. *Law and Society Review,* 1975, **9**, 581–611.

Short, J. (Ed.) *Gang delinquency and delinquent subcultures.* New York: Harper & Row, 1968.

Silberman, C. E. *Criminal violence, criminal justice.* New York: Random House, 1978.

Sparks, R. The effectiveness of probation. In L. Radzinowicz & M. E. Wolfgang (Eds.), *The criminal in confinement.* New York: Basic Books, 1971.

Stuart, R. Behavioral contracting within the families of delinquents. *Journal of behavioral Therapy and Experimental Psychiatry,* 1971, **2**, 1–11.

Sutherland, E. White collar criminality. *American Sociological Review,* 1940, **5**, 1–12.

Sutherland, E. & Cressey, D. *Criminology,* Eighth Ed. Philadelphia: J. B. Lippincott Co., 1970.

Teuber, H. & Powers, E. Evaluating therapy in a delinquency prevention program. *Psychiatric Treatment,* 1953, **21**, 138–147.

Tharp, R. & Wetzel, R. *Behavior modification in the natural environment.* New York: Academic Press, 1969.

Tinbergen, N. On war and peace in animals and man. In T. McGill (Ed.), *Readings in animal behavior.* New York: Holt, Rinehart & Winston, 1973.

Tittle, C. Crime rates and legal sanction. *Social Problems,* 1969, **16**, 409–423.

Ullmann, L. & Krasner, L. *A psychological approach to abnormal behavior.* Englewood Cliffs, N.J.: Prentice Hall, 1975.

U.S. Department of Health Education and Welfare. *The challenge of youth service bureaus.* Washington, D.C.: U.S. Government Printing Office, 1973.

VanDine, S., Dinitz, S., & Conrad, J. The incapacitation of the dangerous offender: A statistical experiment. *Journal of Research in Crime and Delinquency,* 1977, **14**, 22–34.

Waller, I. & Chan, J. Prison use: A Canadian and international comparison. *Criminal Law Quarterly,* 1974, **17**, 47–71.

Westman, J. *Child advocacy.* New York: Free Press, 1979.

Wilson, J. *Thinking about crime.* New York: Basic Books, 1975.

Wolfgang, M. Uniform crime reports: A critical appraisal. *University of Pennsylvania Law Review,* 1963, **111,** 708–738.

Zimring, F. Street crimes and new guns: Some implications for firearms control. *Journal of Criminal Justice,* 1976, **4,** 95–107.

Zimring, F. & Hawkins, G. *Deterrence: The legal threat in crime control.* Chicago: University of Chicago Press, 1973.

Chapter 9
Social Support and Aggression

James G. Emshoff, Donald D. Davis, and William S. Davidson, II

When you're weary, feeling small
When Tears are in your eyes,
I will dry them all.
I'm on your side, when times get rough
And pain is all around
Like a bridge over troubled waters
I will lay me down

—Paul Simon, "Bridge Over Troubled Waters"

The use and effects of social support have recently received a considerable amount of attention, especially in the social and community psychology literature (Bar-Tal, 1976; Bloom, 1980; Caplan & Killilea, 1976; Heller & Monahan, 1977; Rappaport, 1977; Staub, 1974, 1978). Papers at the 1979 American Psychology Association convention addressed the use of social support with children and adolescents (Miller, 1979), job placement (Davis, Johnson, & Overton, 1979), neighborhoods (Berck & Williams, 1979), families (Avgar, 1979), and divorced people (Smyer, 1979), as well as the assessment of perceived social support (Procidano & Heller, 1979).

As any term becomes popular, writers and researchers often expand upon its original use to describe a specific concept or phenomenon. Like other broad conceptual notions, mutual consensus upon definition becomes problematic. Consequently, the first task in explaining the relationship between social support and aggression will be to define social support.

Several definitions of social support are commonly used. These definitions generally include two dimensions: (1) providing information and/or material aid, and (2) delivering such aid in a supportive style. It is actually the stylistic dimension that distinguishes social support as a strategy of change. Cobb (1976) focused on several contents of communication that convey social support. These included:

a. information leading the subject to believe that he is cared for and loved;
b. information leading the subject to believe he is esteemed and valued; and
c. information leading the subject to believe he belongs to a network of communication and mutual obligation.

Caplan (1974) stated that social support helps satisfy the social and psychological needs of the individual. Interpersonal relationships continually provide needed information and feedback. Caplan (1976) defined support systems as "continuing social aggregates (namely, continuing interactions with another individual, a network, a group, or an organization) that provide individuals with opportunities for feedback about themselves and for validation of the expectations about others, which may offset deficiencies in these communications within the larger community context" (p. 19).

Kahn and Quinn (1977) provided a definition that includes several elements of Cobb's including the expression of affection and the acceptance of the individual's beliefs and values. In addition, they added the "provision of aid, including materials, information, time and entitlements."

While it is given less attention in the literature, the provision of aid mentioned by Kahn and Quinn (1977) is an important component in social support. Social support may be conceptualized therefore as having two basic components that exist together or individually. The first component includes the psychological needs of the individual satisfied through the provision of affection and esteem. The second component concerns the material needs of the individual. These two areas have provided the focus for the majority of the literature discussing social support. To these can be added a third objective for the provision of social support—integration of the individual into society. The societal integration process includes the perception on the part of the individual that he or she has a rewarding role in society. The individual's perception of the role is concomitant with the real role characteristics and is equally important to the integration process (see Berger & Luckman, 1967). Thus, this third focus of social support involves some of the internal/psychological characteristics of the first focus mentioned, as well as the provision of material supports that aid an individual in social functioning.

We define social support as a combination of the following characteristics. Social support:

a. satisfies the need an individual has for affection and esteem;
b. implies a mutual obligation among individuals to exchange material
   resources;
c. implicitly and/or explicitly includes the societal integration of the
   individual through the acquisition of rewarding roles; and
d. implicitly and/or explicitly assists the individual in validating expectations about others, contributing to the individual's construction of
   social reality.

Examples of groups that provide social support will further clarify the
ideal of social support. Natural support groups or systems include the
family, other communal living groups (e.g., fraternities, communes,
retirement homes), neighbors, church groups, social clubs, and friends.
Friends are perhaps the most obvious and frequent source of social
support. In fact, social support is fundamental to the concept of friendship. According to *Webster's Collegiate Dictionary*, a friend is defined as
"one attached to another by affection and esteem," and can be distinguished from an acquaintance by the reliable provision of caring,
affection, and trust during times of need.

In the above examples, social support is central to the relationships of
the people involved (members of families, neighbors, friends, social
groups, etc.). The provision of social support in most of these cases,
however, is a by-product rather than a cause of the relationship. Family
members are born into relationships; neighbors are related usually by
coincidental proximity. There are also, however, "artificial" sources
formally designed for the specific purpose of providing such support.
These could include psychotherapy, group counseling, community and
government social services, and group living settings such as halfway
houses for ex-offenders or mental patients. The term "artificial" should
not imply lower quality of support. They involve the formal role of
support provider, usually including such characteristics as a professional
identity, or job description. In addition, the support provider usually
receives material remuneration from the recipient or a third party (e.g.,
government, insurance, etc.). In fact, it could be argued persuasively
that all of these groups exist because the natural systems of support
have failed for some people. People who feel rejected by their families
might enter therapy. People who have no means of economic support and
are not attended to by neighbors or friends may seek government aid.
There is theoretical and empirical support for the belief that people may
become identified as criminals and mental patients owing to a lack of

either psychological or material support (e.g., Price & Denner, 1973; Rutter, 1971).

This chapter will discuss the relationship between social support and aggression. For the purposes of this discussion, Bandura's (1973) definition of aggression will be considered appropriate: "Aggression is defined as behavior that results in personal injury and in destruction of property. The injury may take the form of psychological devaluation as well as physical harm" (p. 5). For the most part, the chapter will focus on the more specific instances of aggression that are considered criminal. The relationship between social support and aggression will be established by examining how aggression often appears to result from a lack of social support. Conversely, it will also be shown that the provision of social support often is associated with low levels of aggression. After establishing the relationship between social support and aggression, the need for increased levels of social support will be discussed. Suggestions for social policy will then be presented. These suggestions will take two forms. First, we will discuss policies designed to facilitate the provision of social support in order to prevent aggression. Second, we will describe proposals for the creation of settings that foster social support for use with identified aggressors.

THEORIES OF CRIME AND AGGRESSION

In order to understand the role that social support plays in aggression, it will be useful to understand first the major theories regarding the causes of aggression. We will discuss the relationship of social support to major theories of aggression. Finally, we will integrate theories of crime and aggression with proposals for social policy and programs.

Individual Differences

Theorists who maintain that internal factors are the cause of criminal behavior focus on the individual differences among people: people who possess certain physiological or psychological characteristics become, or tend to become, criminal or deviant.

The basic paradigm for research in individual differences is the criterion group study in which delinquents and nondelinquents are compared and differences are noted. The classic study of this type was done by Glueck and Glueck (1951). In an ambitious effort they examined 500 institutionalized delinquent youth with 500 nondelinquents (matched on age, IQ, and race). Comparisons were made on over 400 physical (size and condition of body parts), psychological (a variety of personality, intelligence, and projective variables) and social (mostly parenting style and family composition) variables. From the large number of statistically reliable differences they were able to identify, the Gluecks designed a statistical means of early identification of children who were likely to become delinquent. These findings spurred a series of studies. Craig and Glick (1963) and Trevett (1965) attempted to validate empirically the predictive power of the Glueck method, but Kahn (1965) pointed out several methodological problems with these two studies. Noteworthy criticism of the Glueck method concerns the fact that it identifies a large number of nondelinquents (false positives).

Psychological comparison studies have found differences between delinquents and nondelinquents using a variety of objective personality tests, performance measures, and projective techniques (Waldo & Dinitz, 1967). Similar studies have concluded that delinquents are undersocialized (Smith & Ausnew, 1974), psychologically abnormal, and morally immature (Prentice, 1972). A dissenting opinion comes from Gibbons (1970) who concludes that delinquents do not differ from nondelinquents in psychological adjustment.

Biological and physiological explanations of criminal behavior have existed for centuries, but most notably began with the nineteenth-century Italian army physician, Ceasare Lombroso. Krisberg and Austin (1978) have grouped contemporary biological attributions of delinquency into brain tumors, epileptic seizures, gland disorders, prenatal or birth complications, brain dysfunction, genetic factors, chromosome disorders, and physique.

Two explanations, not mutually exclusive, are offered for the great number of studies that focus on individual differences in the cause of delinquent behavior. First, the comparison studies are relatively simple to conduct and the number of potential variables for observation is nearly infinite, especially when considered in combination with each other. Second, as Krisberg and Austin (1978) point out, focusing on the individual appears to depoliticize delinquency and encourages the avoidance of the social issues involved.

Social support is directly relevant to the individual differences explanation of criminal behavior. The most salient psychological explanation concerns the lack of adequate socialization that the criminal received. Socialization is the "process whereby individuals learn and internalize the attitudes, values, and behaviors appropriate to persons functioning as social beings and responsive, participating members of society" (*Encyclopedia of Sociology*, 1974, p. 272). The complete socialization process involves the internalization of these attitudes, values, and behaviors. The individual who receives little social contact and support fails to achieve adequate internalization.

Lack of attachment to parents has been shown to prevent the development of morals (McKinley, 1964) and to increase the probability of the development of psychopathology and other deviant behavior. Hirschi (1969) has stated that "the lack of attachment to others is not merely a symptom of psychopathy, it is psychopathy; lack of conscience is just another way of saying the same thing; and the violation of norms is (or may be) a consequence" (p. 7). From this perspective, attachment and commitment depend upon the provision of social contact and support, specifically the aspect of support concerning the provision of affection and caring. The growing child must get support for adherence to the norms in his or her environment. If an individual gets no support from his or her social environment, there is less reason for this individual to internalize and develop concern for these norms.

Similar arguments can be made concerning many psychological explanations of criminal behavior. Most of these explanations center on some form of psychopathy, which can be related in turn to a lack of social support. Only those rare theories that are completely internal (i.e., genetic; see, for example, Jacobs, Brunton, and Melville, 1965) and unrelated to the environment are immune to a social support explanation.

Sociological Explanations

Norms. Aggression also may be seen as a response to social norms. Social norms, the shared expectations in a society, may foster or retard the demonstration of aggressive behavior. These expectations regarding the appropriateness of aggressive behavior are external to the individual and exist in the reality defined within a particular culture.

We will briefly discuss ethnographic data from the study of aggression in several cultures. We will then show how the breakdown of social norms—a state defined as anomie—may be related to aggressive behavior.

Culturally Defined Aggression. Some societies are remarkable owing to their almost complete absence of aggression. For example, Viniaminov reported no cases of homicide during the 20 years he lived among the Aleutian people (Pelto and Pelto, 1976, p. 450). Homicide is also rare among the Tanala people of Madagascar. Linton (1933, pp. 154–155) reported that murder was so rare among the Tanala that no juridicial procedure existed for murder. Fights between adults were considered disgraceful. Negligible amounts of aggression are also demonstrated among the Hutterites of the United States and Canada (Bennett, 1967; Hostetler, 1974), and the Semai of Malaya (Dentan, 1968).

The Semai seem to be one of the most nonviolent cultures in the world. Dentan (1968, pp. 55–56) discussed how the Semai conceive of themselves as nonviolent; each Semai person thinks of himself as nonviolent. This self-image is not an ideal to strive for but an actual reality construct (Berger and Luckman, 1967). The Semai do not say, "Anger is bad." They say, "We do not get angry." The Semai do not say, "It is forbidden to hit people." They say, "We do not hit people." As Dentan (1968, p. 56) pointed out, while individual Semai might violate the nonviolent norm, as a group, they conceive of themselves as nonviolent. Violent behavior violates the social norm.

Violence seems completely alien to the Semai. It terrifies them. The Semai meet force with passivity or flight. The Semai have no institutionalized method for controlling or preventing violence. They have no social controls, no police, no courts (Dentan, 1968, p. 59). Violence is largely controlled through internalization of the norm of nonviolence. Children are socialized to believe in nonviolence.

The Semai coddle their children (Dentan, 1968, pp. 59–60). Everyone in the village cuddles and plays with infants. If infants cry, someone will always comfort them or direct their attention elsewhere.

As a child grows older, less attention is given. The nonviolent image becomes stressed to children through association with frightening natural events (*Terlaid*), particularly thundersqualls (Dentan, 1968, p. 60). Violent actions may invite a natural calamity like a thundersquall. Thus, Semai parents teach self-control based on threats of natural calamities.

Semai children have little experience with violence; they do not punish their children (Dentan, 1968, p. 61), nor do they object when children refuse to obey. The absence of punishment means that Semai children have no role models for violent behavior. Further, adults express open shock when children do behave aggressively (Dentan, 1968, p. 61). This expression of shock is contrary to the ordinary noninterventive orientation of the Semai (Dentan, 1968, pp. 63–64); Semai do not interfere with the activities of others. Thus, this expression of shock no doubt alerts the child to the inappropriateness of aggressive responding.

The Semai maintain their nonviolence with social norms. It is also possible, however, for social norms to encourage violence. This is true for the Yanomamö people of Venezuela.

Just as the Semai conceive of themselves as nonviolent, the Yanomamö see themselves as fierce (Chagnon, 1968, p. 1). Aggression and war are a way of life for the Yanomamö; they are not simply tolerated, they are indulged in almost gleefully. The state of chronic warfare is reflected in their mythology, values, settlement pattern, political behavior, and marriage practices (Chagnon, 1968, p. 3).

An example of the extent of violence in daily affairs of the Yanomamö may be seen in husband-wife relationships.

> Women must respond quickly to the demands of their husbands. In fact, they must respond without waiting for a command. It is interesting to watch the behavior of women when their husbands return from a hunting trip or visit. The men march slowly across the village and retire silently to their hammocks. The woman, no matter what she is doing, hurries home and quietly but rapidly prepares a meal for the husband. Should the wife be slow in doing this, the husband is within his rights to beat her. Most reprimands meted out by irate husbands take the form of blows with the hand or with a piece of firewood, but a good many husbands are even more brutal. Some of them chop their wives with the sharp edge of a machete or axe, or shoot them with a barbed arrow in some nonvital area, such as the buttocks or leg. Many men are given over to punishing their wives by holding the hot end of a glowing stick against them, resulting in serious burns. The punishment is usually, however, adjusted to the seriousness of the wife's shortcomings, more drastic measures being reserved for infidelity or suspicion of infidelity. Many men, however, show their ferocity by meting out serious punishment to their wives for even minor offenses. It is not uncommon for a man to injure his errant wife seriously; and some men have even killed wives.
>
> Women expect this kind of treatment and many of them measure their husband's concern in terms of the frequency of minor beatings they sustain. I overheard two young women discussing each other's scalp scars. One of them commented that the other's husband must really care for her since he has beaten her on the head so frequently! [Chagnon, 1968, pp. 82–83].

Yanomamö children learn at an early age to behave violently. Chagnon (1968, p. 84) states, "Male children are encouraged to be fierce and are rarely punished by their parents for inflicting blows on them or on hapless girls in the village." Children learn as early as at the age of four that the appropriate response to anger or frustration is to strike out with a hand or object at the source.

When children become adults, frustration or anger is answered by club-fighting duels. The tops of most men's heads are covered with many scars. Some adult males are so proud of their scars that they keep their head shaved, rubbing a red pigment onto their scalp to define the scars more clearly (Chagnon, 1968, p. 119).

We see then that violence and aggression are defined as normal behavior among the Yanomamö. Children learn to respond aggressively to achieve goals. A nonviolent response when feeling angry would be viewed as deviant, providing some evidence for a learning theory interpretation of aggression.

Norms are related to the development and control of aggression in yet a different way. The absence or breakdown in social norms also may explain aggressive behavior.

Anomie. Anomie (a sort of social vacuum marked by the absence of social norms or values) is a concept used by early sociologists (Durkheim, 1951; Merton, 1938, 1957) to explain crime and other forms of deviance:

> Anomie is apt to rise when certain preconditions for the individual's successful integration into his society are lacking...(preconditions) that individual behavior should be governed by social norms, that the norms themselves should form a consistent and coherent value system, and that each individual should be morally involved with others so that the permissable boundaries of individual self indulgence are clearly demarcated. If social norms break down, if there is a conflict of norms, or if the individual is detached from his moral relationship to his fellows, anomie will tend to result [*Encyclopedia of Sociology*, 1974, p. 11].

Anomie is associated particularly with rapid or major social change, resulting in a major alteration of the traditional normative pattern. Anomie originally was believed to result from the emergence of industrialism, which affected the move from traditional rural values and social organization (*Gemeinschaft*) to urban values and social organization (*Gesellschaft*) (see Tönnies, 1940).

The concept of anomie has been expanded to include the social disorganization view of deviance (Cloward & Ohlin, 1959, 1960; Cohen, 1955; Faris, 1955; Merton, 1938, 1957). High rates of officially reported crime, delinquency, addiction, prostitution, and mental illness in lower-class areas of the city were believed to be due to the state of social disorganization in these neighborhoods (Faris, 1955).

The concept of anomie also takes the form of the "blocked opportunity" notion of deviance (Cloward & Ohlin, 1960). Anomie is believed to be particularly prevalent when there is a large gap between cultural ends and goals and the means for accomplishment that a group's location in the social structure makes available to its members (Akers, 1973, p. 14; Merton, 1957). Society emulates only middle-class ideals and values but is structured so that the legitimate modes of access to these cultural goals are not available to individuals of lower socioeconomic classes. Between these lower-class individuals and cultural goals stand unemployment, inferior schools, racial discrimination, the squalor of the slums, and numerous other characteristics associated with unequal economic, social, psychological, and political opportunities. The socially defined importance of acquiring material goods and middle-class status, especially success defined in monetary terms (Merton, 1957, p. 136), acts to pressure people into acting in deviant ways because illegitimate modes of access are often more available. One can more easily succeed on the street, can more easily learn middle-class business skills from selling drugs or pimping than from participating in Junior Achievement.

The concept of social support is compatible with the blocked opportunity theory of criminality. In this case, the emphasis may include those aspects of social support concerning the provision of material goods and resources. Any behavior by which a person advocates for another may be considered an instance of social support. In this case, such advocacy behaviors might include assistance in finding employment, the provision of education or other skills training, housing assistance, financial aid, or any other means by which an individual can be given legitimate access to societally defined and approved goals.

Social support reduces the necessity to use illegitimate means. The outcome of this form of social support is a social role and position for the individual, one of the goals of social support listed in the definitions introduced earlier. Below we suggest methods for developing a broad social support system designed to reduce feelings of anomie.

School. Other sociological explanations of crime attempt to link the school to delinquency. The basic tenet in this literature was put forth by Polk & Schafer (1972). They argued that underachievement, misconduct, and dropping out are not the result of student characteristics in isolation, but also result from factors in the student-school relationship. The school's contribution to delinquency lies in the low involvement (and therefore low commitment) it allows students, a belief in the limited potential of disadvantaged students, irrelevant teaching and curricula (i.e., that do not correspond to adult success). The student experiences frustration and a consequently high chance for failure in an atmosphere that emphasized success. These criticisms can be summarized accurately as the school providing very little support for students, especially those students not doing well at the start. Elliot and Voss (1974) present data that lend some credence to the theories about the school's role in delinquency. Specifically, they found that students who had been involved in delinquency while in school quite often decreased their delinquent behavior after dropping out of school. Again, the lack of support within the school appears to act as a catalyst in the creation of delinquency. We will discuss the use of accelerative educational programs designed to address these issues later.

Labeling Theory. Another environmentally based theory of delinquency is more direct. Instead of centering on the environment's role in causing an individual to commit deviant behavior, some theorists have pointed out that it is the environment itself—society—that defines deviance, and therefore makes "deviants" deviant (Becker, 1963):

> Labeling may place the person in circumstances which make it harder for him to continue the normal routines of everyday life and thus provoke him to "abnormal"

actions (as when a prison record makes it harder to earn a living at a conventional occupation and so disposes its possessor to move into an illegal one) [p. 179].

What is important to understand is that deviance is *created* by certain people's reaction to an act (Matza, 1969). Erickson (1962) called these certain people the "influential audience." Certain behaviors were "designated as crimes when they were repugnant to persons with sufficient political power to have the law impose their standards of conduct on others" (Glaser, 1975). The behavior and the behaver are labeled deviant.

In 1956, Garfinkel pointed out the use of this labeling process to lower the social standing of certain groups. Richette (1972) applied this idea to delinquency by pointing out the use of the juvenile courts' conception of deviancy to rid society of its "undesirable citizens." In Hagan's (1972) review of the labeling literature, he stated that the law enforcement system reacts to the need of an act being negatively categorized. Similarly, in a survey of presiding judges in 229 cases resulting in the placement of a youth in a state training school, the judge's perception of community demand was an important factor in his decision (Langley, Graves, and Norris, 1972). In developing their argument that student deviance is a function of the student-school interaction, Polk and Schafer (1972) stressed the important role of the school in being able to define what *is* deviant.

The labeling of deviance is often an irrational and an unjust process. The extent of deviance attributed to an act depends on how widely that act varies from the influential audience's experience. The location of definitive power among dominant members of the influential audience allows political and social ideology to weigh more heavily than the actual danger to society resulting from the commission of the act. Social institutions such as formal law may lead to the creation of a universalistic morality incompatible with social systems based on structured inequality (Habermas, 1975, p. 86ff; Mulloy, 1976). To the extent that inequality in a social system contributes to the segregation of subcultures and their respective shared experiences, and to the extent that social values and norms derived from shared experiences become defined exclusively by a single subculture (e.g., white middle-class males), it becomes more inevitable that the behavior of members of other subcultures might be labeled as deviant. It appears irrational to assume that members of different subcultures with concomitantly different shared experiences would always agree on acceptable behavior. Another irrational characteristic of the labeling process is that deviants (of any group) are considered to be members of a homogeneous group, defined and made alike by their deviance.

How does the labeling theory of criminality relate to social support? Labeling theory is not concerned with the behavior itself but, rather, with society's reaction to it. Network members may assist in the validation of the individual's expectations regarding others, thus aiding the understanding of others' potential reaction to one's behavior. A person who is a member of a social support network is more likely to be able to avoid labeling by minimizing the reaction to the behavior. Social support also may help the individual labeled deviant by presenting the appearance of a stable, middle-class-like home environment. For example, discretion is practiced at all levels of criminal justice processing, from police to courtroom decision making. Discretion is more likely to favor the offender if he has a stable family or an employer who is willing to vouch for him. Community support for an individual will affect a judge's disposition.

When social support is related to financial resources, its affect on system processing is even greater. Members of higher social classes are typically those who define deviance as opposed to those who are labeled deviant. Financial resources are also necessary for the superior legal representation required to avoid being labeled.

There is a great deal of evidence indicating a large degree of prejudice in the distribution of justice. At the level of the police, youth of lower socioeconomic classes are arrested more, but do not actually commit more delinquent behavior (Akers, 1964; Erickson, 1962; Erickson & Empey, 1973; Hirschi, 1969; Nye, Short, & Olsen, 1958; Williams & Gold, 1972). Secondly, at the level of the courts, youth of lower socioeconomic status receive dispositions more severe than others for the same offense (Erickson, 1973; Scarpitti & Stephenson, 1971; Williams & Gold, 1972). Jordan (1974) has argued that courts punish people who are victims of social inequalities, that the court is a political tool operating separate justice systems for the rich and poor. Thus the appearance of an overly criminal lower socioeconomic population may be the result of differential use of the enforcement and judicial systems, which is related in turn to various forms of social support.

Learning Theory

The learning theory of criminal behavior involves both the individual (the focus of the psychological theories) and the environment (the focus of the sociological theories). A variety of such theories agree that crime is a learned behavior much as any other behavior is learned, through processes of social interaction and rewards (support) for deviant behavior.

Sutherland and Cressey's (1970) differential association theory is a good explanation of crime based on social interaction. This theory states that crime is learned through interactions with others who hold values that encourage crime. These others can include peers (Hackler, 1970; Hirschi, 1969), or family members, particularly parents (McCord & McCord, 1958; Sutherland & Cressey, 1970).

Other learning theories focus on the principles of operant conditioning (Skinner, 1938, 1953). Simply stated, such principles explain that criminal behavior occurs because the consequences of this behavior are rewarding to the youth. Delinquent behavior is learned in the same manner in which any other behavior is learned. "When an individual has acquired a functional connection between an environmental stimulus and a response on his part, learning has taken place. Learning continues from birth to death" (Ullmann & Krasner, 1975).

Criminal behavior can be learned in both social and nonsocial situations. An example of nonsocial reinforcement is the acquisition of material goods through stealing. Much has been written about the social learning of criminal behavior (Bandura, 1969). Deviance is learned when the response of others to a deviant act is rewarding to the person committing the act. It is more specifically suggested that delinquency occurs when parents and teachers fail to reward positive behaviors while differentially attending to and modeling antisocial behaviors. Peers also may model and reinforce criminal behaviors (Patterson & Reid, 1970). A more complete explanation of delinquency based on learning principles and the theory of differential association was presented by Akers (1973; Burgess & Akers, 1969).

In the case of differential association or social learning, social support is offered to the person committing criminal behavior, but this support is contingent on the criminal behavior itself. Thus social support in this case contributes to the deviance because it is offered in response to the deviance, not in response to prosocial behaviors.

Social Support and Criminal Behavior

There clearly appears to be a relationship between social support and criminality. The strength of this association lies in the fact that social support may be included in many theoretical explanations of criminal behavior. In the case of internal psychological theories, a lack of social support may result in a lack of attachment to others and in the development of psychopathology. Blocked opportunity theory claims that lack of legitimate access to socially defined goals leads to the use of illegitimate means. Social support can help to provide legitimate access to societal goals. Labeling theory is based on the social reaction to behavior. Social support can act to minimize negative reactions to some behavior. Finally, learning theories would maintain that social support, when given for antisocial behaviors, will increase the frequency of such behaviors; social support given for prosocial behavior will increase the frequency of prosocial behaviors.

Problems in operationally defining and measuring the level of social support make empirical research supporting the above logical arguments difficult. Nevertheless, several authors have found that a lack of social support from parents may lead to criminal behavior. The process by which this occurs depends on which theoretical explanation and corresponding intervening variables are chosen. Wright and James (1974) noted that parents of delinquents tend to use verbal and physical punishment as a means of control, though the use of punishment to control behavior may be social-class specific, resulting in more frequent use among lower- and lower-middle-class parents (Eshleman, 1974). Similarly, others have said that parents of delinquents show their children little affection, are hostile toward their children (Glueck & Glueck, 1962), and tend to reject them (McCord & McCord, 1958). As we saw in the examples of the Semai and Yanomamö, parental social support may retard or foster aggression.

We see then that aggressive and criminal behavior may be explained with a variety of theories. All of these theories implicitly or explicitly address the existence of social support. For the most part, the lack of social support appears to increase the likelihood of aggressive behavior. Social rewards for aggressive behavior may also increase its frequency. Thus, what is needed is the integration of social rewards and social support such that aggressive behavior is reduced and prosocial behavior is increased. The following section will discuss the levels of social support presently existing in American society.

PRESENT SOCIAL SUPPORT NEEDS

The 1970s was a decade noted for its inordinate focus on the individual. Such an emphasis led to the labeling of.this period as the "me" decade or the "me" generation. While the 1960s was noted for its concern for human welfare, civil rights, sharing of resources, and the building of the Great Society, the 1970s closed with tax cuts and disco dancing as major preoccupations.

The current trend is toward a stylized egoism. A perusal of the shelves of popular bookstores indicates the pervasiveness of this phenomenon. Such titles as *Looking Out for Number One, How To Be Your Own Best Friend, How To Say No*, all reflect the attitude that one should be concerned most with one's self, with little regard or need for others.

Such an attitude certainly does not facilitate the provision of social support to others. Social support requires the mutual exchange of assistance and resources. Caplan (1976) stated that reciprocity is a crucial characteristic of support systems. Consequently, an unwillingness to share and to support results in an enforced self-reliance. This consequence is evident in the growth of the self-help movement and the increasing numbers of books and classes designed to allow an individual to satisfy primarily his or her own needs. This self-support ranges from psychological support (again, *How To Be Your Own Best Friend* is a good example) to the material (instruction in do-it-yourself carpentry, auto maintenance, etc.).

Concurrently, historically primary sources of social support—the family and neighbors—are no longer reliable sources. Less time is spent in the home today. There is a smaller incidence of extended families in single households. Increased rates of divorce also make the traditional family unit less stable. In addition, neighbors no longer exercise many of their traditional social functions. This might be the result of the increased self-reliance and emphasis on the self, increased desire and need for privacy in an age when more of our personal lives are subject to public or semipublic scrutiny, as well as increased mobility and changes in residence which hinder the formation of the kind of close and stable relationships that are usually required for the development of social support.

There is not only a lower level of social support, due to an increased emphasis on the self and a reduction in the roles of the family and neighbors. The social support that is currently available is often less potent because it is more diffuse and decentralized. Historically, the people who provided social support were members of more than one group. Thus, there often was considerable overlap between members of the family, coworkers, church members, neighbors, schoolmates, and friends. Whole families and neighborhoods often worked, went to school, went to church, and attended social gatherings together, thus providing a real sense of community (*Gemeinschaft*). In our present society, there is less integration of these groups; they are more distinct and overlap less in membership. People commute long distances to jobs so that residence in a neighborhood often has little correspondence with place of employment. Children are bussed to schools, often in a manner which disregards neighborhoods. There are fewer family businesses that employ all or most of a family. People lead segmented lives in which there is little relationship among the various components and the corresponding roles that an individual must play. The decentralized sources of support tend to weaken the quality of the support given. Each individual who acts to provide support is likely to relate to only a small

area of the recipient's life. Just as an individual's life becomes segmented, so do the individual's sources of support. A coworker is
unlikely to provide assistance with a family problem if the coworker is
unfamiliar with the family. Similarly, a student cannot do homework
with a neighbor if they go to different schools and have different
teachers and assignments.

The great physical mobility of our society also contributes to this
situation. People change residences at an increasing rate, commute
longer distances, travel more often for pleasure, and travel over a wider
area just to meet basic needs. Consequently, the physical self is too
multilocal, making it more difficult to receive and develop any centralized source of support. The effect of this mobility on the reduction in
neighborhood support can be seen when a serious snowstorm makes
travel impossible for a few days. Neighbors suddenly get to know each
other. Social gatherings occur. Neighbors share resources such as food
and other necessities if travel to a store is impossible. In short, the
neighborhood residents begin to provide the level of support that was
once more common.

Modern transportation allows a spreading of the physical self. Modern
mass communication allows a spreading of the psychological self.
People's awareness and concerns are spread over a wider area. Television
allows the world to enter our living rooms. The telephone allows
interactive communication with the rest of the world. The wider
awareness of the world causes people to identify and care about a wider
range of people who do not share geographic proximity (and thus the
opportunity for the provision of direct social support), but who rather
share some particular interest, characteristic, or belief. Identification and
interaction become restricted to the cognitive domain. People relate too
cognitively to their world. Interpersonal and more involving interaction
becomes less frequent and more difficult.

There appears to be a decreasing level of social support available,
especially from what have been historically natural sources. People
seem less interested in providing support and sharing resources. The
potential sources of support have lost some of their potency and range.
Individuals lead segmented lives and the coactors (who act to support
the individual) vary from role to role. Modern transportation and communication further separate the individual from a common base of
support. The result is a tendency toward less commitment, attachment,
and loyalty to significant others. This in turn seems to lead toward social
disorganization and anomie acting as a catalyst for crime. This lowered
commitment to others is especially relevant to other family members
and neighbors since the home and neighborhood are by far the most
frequent settings for violent crime. Individuals with a lowered

identification and support with a group are more likely to perpetrate aggression upon the members of that group. Individuals are more likely to inflict injury upon disassociated victims.

This decrease in the natural provision of social support is reflected in the development of formalized procedures for the provision of social support. Examples of these newer sources of support include group therapy, singles groups, government social services, and social security. These professional services and support were all previously provided by natural support systems, most typically family and neighbors.

Rural society has not undergone as many changes as has urban society. Consequently, many of the factors leading to the decrease in support described above have not been as pronounced in rural areas. A recent newspaper story illustrates the provision of social support and how it operated in one rural setting.

A midwestern farmer was known to be dying of cancer. His illness made it impossible to attend to the annual business of harvesting his corn and wheat. The family could not afford to hire others to do so, yet neglecting to harvest the crops would mean complete financial ruin for the family. Neighboring farmers, knowing of the family's plight, organized a mass gathering at the farm and completed the harvest in a single day. While the neighboring men worked in the fields, the women prepared a large meal for the end of the day. While the story explicitly did not mention it, it is highly likely that a great deal of psychological support was provided. Information probably was provided allowing each individual to feel that he or she had a legitimate social role.

Information regarding the legitimacy of new social roles is often offered to widows or widowers (see Abrahams, 1976; Silverman, 1976), and could consist of neighbors, say, inviting the widow to participate in social and other community activities. This acts to confirm for the widow the fact that she has a social position beyond the role that she has lost, the role of being a wife.

INCREASING THE PROVISION OF SOCIAL SUPPORT

The above discussion showed the relationship between social support and the incidence of crime. It was also shown that the levels of social support present in our society appear to be decreasing over time and becoming less potent owing to their increased diffuseness and decentralization. Given this trend, the promotion of policies and programs that increase levels of social support would seem appropriate for the benefit of not only the individuals involved but for society as a whole.

In trying to strengthen social support systems, two foci appear practical. The first must be preventive in nature; that is, existing social support systems must be strengthened and expanded. Intervention loci might include the individual, the family, the school, and the neighborhood. Intervention at these levels should be buttressed with the development of more general social policy. These strategies should attempt to prevent the development of aggression, particularly among members of subcultures subject to a higher likelihood of becoming aggressive.

The second focus for the development of social support systems must include identified aggressors (delinquents and criminals). Intervention loci might include the individual, the family, and the neighborhood. Intervention at these levels also should be accompanied by the development of more general social policy. These socially supportive settings should be designed to aid the individual in the development of nonaggressive modes of response to their social environment.

Rappaport (1977) has persuasively argued that social change agents must have the locus of their intervention clear in mind. Interventions focused at the level of the individual will probably have no impact at more macrosocial levels. In fact, an intervention at a larger aggregate level, such as a small group or an organization, might be more successful in attempting to induce change at the individual level. His analysis attempted to implement the change principles of Watzlawick, Weakland, & Fisch (1974). Davis and Markman (1980) showed further that the type of intervention technique selected, (e.g., consultation) shapes the type and amount of social change.

Social change agents consequently must choose the level of their intervention carefully—individual, small group, organizational, institutional and community, or societal. Additionally, social change agents must choose their intervention techniques carefully in order to increase the likelihood of appropriate social change.

The strategies for the creation of social support discussed below are seen to be part of a comprehensive effort designed to (1) limit the likelihood that children will develop and depend on aggressive responses to their environment, and (2) assist already identified aggressors in the development of nonaggressive modes of response to their environment. These strategies direct interventions at the individual, small group, community, and societal levels of analysis.

Preventive Social Support

Preventive social support refers to the attempt to develop social settings (Heller & Monahan, 1977, pp. 161–200) aiming to facilitate supportive and prosocial behavior. It is assumed that the development of preventive social support systems will also reduce the incidence of aggressive behavior among members of the target population. Caplan (1964, p. 16) refers to prevention designed to reduce already occurring disorders as *secondary prevention*. *Primary prevention* includes those efforts that are aimed at the prevention of disorder from occurring among members of a population (Caplan, 1964, p. 16). We will follow Cowen's (1977) suggestion of "baby-steps toward primary prevention," and include the analysis and modification of social environments and competence building as two components of a primary preventive intervention. Thus, (1) *Primary preventive social support* refers to interventions directed at populations or community groups that do not currently manifest measurable levels of aggressive behavior. The intention is designed to prevent aggressive behavior from developing by focusing on the presumed antecedents of aggressive behavior. (2) *Secondary preventive social support* refers to interventions directed at populations or community groups already demonstrating a measurable incidence of aggressive behavior. Interventions are meant to reduce the frequency of aggressive behavior and to increase the frequency of responses serving as alternatives to aggression.

Primary Preventive Social Support. Strategies engendering social support must simultaneously focus on many antecedents. This is true because disorders are the result of several causes or risk factors (Price, 1974), and combinations of multiple risk factors increase the likelihood of deviant behavior (Rutter, 1966, 1979). The social organizations and institutions addressed by the following interventions are representative of the components of a primary preventive social system. They are not meant to exhaust the number of legitimate components for a possible intervention program. The following foci are suggested as possible components of a primary preventive social support system: (1) young individual, (2) family, (3) school, and (4) neighborhoods.

1. *Young Individual.* Rolf (Klemchuk, Rolf, & Hasazi, 1975; Rolf & Hasazi, 1977) designed an interesting intervention for preschool children at high risk for the development of psychopathology. Although he was not interested in the prevention of aggressive behavior in itself, his program offered an interesting prototype that might prove heuristic in the development of interventions designed to prevent the development of aggressive behavior. Rolf examined the impact of therapeutic daycare settings on vulnerable children. The therapeutic intervention addressed the child's classroom teachers, specialized needs such as speech therapy, remedial work in areas such as perceptual motor development,

and training in social competence, affective expressiveness, and response to stress or conflict.

A preschool day-care preventive social support program would intervene at the individual level of analysis (Rappaport, 1975). The global aim would be the development of nonaggressive responses to stressful or conflictive situations. Its objectives would include (a) partial satisfaction of the individual's need for affection and esteem, (b) the development of a sense of mutual obligation, (c) assistance in the acquisition of the rewarding roles of helper and one being helped, and (d) assistance for the individual in the validation of perceptions and expectations of a benign environment.

A curriculum designed to teach prosocial and nonaggressive methods for dealing with conflictive situations could be implemented. The prosocial curriculum could be implemented in day-care centers. The curriculum would stress altruistic and sharing behavior using social reinforcement (e.g., Bryan, 1971, 1972; Bryan, Redfield, & Mader, 1971; Midlarsky, Bryan, & Brickman, 1973), modeling (Bryan et al., 1971; Midlarsky et al., 1973), and role-playing (Staub, 1971) techniques.

A curriculum in prosocial and altruistic behavior would accompany more comprehensive efforts to develop a social support system. The prosocial curriculum would attempt to teach the child how to acquire social support by demonstrating helping behavior instead of aggressive response. The demonstration of social support is more likely than is aggression to elicit social support from others; the ability to repay with prosocial behavior the supportive behavior given by others is more likely to maintain supportive interaction (Walster, Berscheid, & Walster, 1973, pp. 166–170).

2. *Family.* Caplan (1976) has provided a trenchant analysis of the support system functions of the family. He suggests that an ideal type of family support system might include the following modal patterns:

(1) Collector and disseminator information about the world, the fundamental support function.
(2) Feedback guidance system concerning social events.
(3) Source of ideology, viz., beliefs, values and codes of behavior.
(4) Guidance and mediation in immediate problem solving and the provision of long term skills for seeking problem solving help from other social sources.
(5) Source of practical service and concrete aid, particularly during crisis and periods of transition.
(6) Haven for rest and recuperation.
(7) Reference group and social control.
(8) Source and validation of identity.
(9) Contributes to emotional development [pp. 22–30].

Curricula in prosocial behavior can be developed with the family providing the focus for the intervention. The participation of all family members would complement and facilitate the development of prosocial skills for each individual family member. The efficacy of modeling prosocial behaviors could be shown to family members in the context of a program designed to reduce the incidence of aggressive behaviors among one or more individuals.

Localized interventions, like training in prosocial behavior, must be augmented by more comprehensive approaches to the promotion of familial mutuality. These more global approaches should attempt to reduce aggressive behavior by increasing the levels of social support through increasing the intactness of the extended family network.

Caplan (1976) continues with his analysis of the social support functions of the family by offering four suggestions for the promotion of intactness, integration, and mutuality:

(1) Income maintenance programs should allow the family as a group to be responsible for their disbursement to members.
(2) Housing programs should facilitate the proximity of older adults and their families; housing for seniors should be distributed throughout the community.
(3) Special rates should be allowed for the use of telephone and public transportation by older adults to facilitate communication.
(4) The Census Bureau should alter its definition of family from kin living in the same residence, to kin who interact frequently and are bound together by positive concern [p. 32].

We will demonstrate, as an example, how housing programs can be used to develop the social support functions of the family. Existing federal programs sponsored by the U.S. Department of Housing and Urban Development (HUD) and the Farmer Home Administration (FMHA—U.S. Department of Agriculture), might be used more comprehensively to buttress the social support functions of the family.

The Section 8 program, funded under the Housing and Community Development Act of 1974 (Public Law #383, 1974), is administered by HUD. The purpose of this program is to provide existing, new, and rehabilitated housing for families with low and moderate incomes, families with incomes below 80 percent of the median income of the surrounding community. HUD contracts with the owner of the building to pay the difference between the fair market rent for the unit and the amount of money paid by the tenant. The tenant's payment may not exceed 25 percent of gross income.

The Section 8 program could be expanded to favor extended, multigenerational families. Families in which older adults such as grandparents, other extended family members such as uncles and aunts, or other non-blood-related individuals providing skills often provided by kin (e.g., babysitting, child rearing, household maintenance, etc.) could receive preferred treatment in funding allocations, or could be allowed to pay a smaller proportion of gross income for rent. Preferential funding might increase the number of single household extended families. Important here is the use of roles to define extended family members. The actual supportive behavior of the individuals is more important than their lack of consanguinity.

3. *School.* Present school practices often act to prevent the school from contributing to a sense of community and neighborhood. Youth are often assigned to schools that are not in their own neighborhoods. The most predominant instance of this is the use of bussing to achieve racial integration of the school system. Integration should be encouraged through means that do not result in the disintegration of the neighborhood. For instance, housing policies should be developed that encourage residential integration. If a neighborhood is already integrated, educational integration would be achieved without forcing the children of a neighborhood to leave it. School boundaries should be drawn so that integration is accomplished as completely as possible while keeping a school district contiguous. In general, keeping the school an integral part of the local community should act to prevent the diffusion of existing support groups.

Within the classroom, practices and policies should be implemented to encourage a supportive atmosphere. The present system is largely competitive, encouraging individual achievement with little concern for the group as a whole. For example, relative grading, by definition, prevents the entire group from being successful. Students can only succeed by being better than others. Such a practice hardly encourages students to aid each other and to provide support for one another. Similarly, the majority of assignments given to students are meant to be carried out individually. Cooperation is not only not encouraged, it is usually prohibited. Such competition may encourage aggressiveness. The role that the school plays in contributing to delinquency (Elliot & Voss, 1974; Polk & Schaffer, 1972) is relevant here.

Alternative practices should be developed that would contribute to a supportive atmosphere. Group projects can be used to facilitate interaction and support among students. Such a style of teaching and assigning work is also more realistic in terms of representing a typical work situation. Most jobs are accomplished in groups. Not everyone does the same task, but tasks fit together to produce an outcome. School assignments reflecting this reality would better prepare students for such work situations. Peer tutoring programs also provide direct means of support among students. Students should be taught how to aid other students in reaching their goals, as in "buddy systems" (Fo & O'Donnell, 1975).

Curricula designed specifically to address the development of prosocial behavior and to decrease the demonstration of aggressive behavior might also be developed and implemented in schools. Allen, Chinisky, Larcen, Lochman, & Selinger (1976) have developed a program for elementary schools designed to promote peer-related social competence through teaching social problem-solving skills, based on work done by George Spivack (Spivack, Platt & Shure, 1976; Spivack & Shure, 1974). Goldstein, Sprafkin, Gershaw, & Klein (1980) describe a detailed method of teaching prosocial skills to adolescents. Allen et al. (1976) have also provided an excellent example of a multilevel preventive approach designed to increase behavioral adjustment among young children. These multilevel preventive programs provide excellent models for the development of prosocial interventions.

4. *Neighborhoods.* The development of primary preventive social support must also focus on neighborhoods. In order for neighborhoods to become a source of social support, they need to be strengthened and designed such that residents act in a more unified and cohesive manner.

Neighborhoods today do not often share the same employers, schools, or other social loci. Neighborhood organizations can act to bring people who otherwise might have few interactions together. Such organizations can focus on a variety of issues that are common to a neighborhood and can do so in a manner that is both efficient and useful in terms of providing support. Sorrentino (1977) describes Clifford Shaw's Chicago Area Project of the early 1930s:

> Shaw felt that the residents could accomplish much to improve the neighborhood by working cooperatively and in collaboration with all the social groupings and institutions in the area. In other words, he envisioned everyone working together on a mutual basis. Through informal groups in which the ordinary citizen would be free to participate, everyone would have a direct voice in the affairs of the organization [p. 241].

One possible method for focusing neighborhood cooperation involves local community development. Title I of the Housing and Community Development Act (Public Law #383, 1974) provides Community Development Block Grant Funds to communities (cities, townships, or counties). Community Development Block Grants (CDBG) can be used to provide (1) housing rehabilitation assistance; (2) acquisition of property that is blighted, appropriate for preservation or restoration (historic sites), or used for public purposes; (3) the acquisition, construction, reconstruction, or installation of public works, neighborhood facilities including senior citizen centers, historic properties, utilities, streets, street lights, water, sewer, and other public works, pedestrian malls, playgrounds, and recreation facilities; (4) code enforcement in deteriorating areas; and more than a half dozen other community development activities (Public Law #383, Section 105). The objectives of the Act are the elimination and prevention of slums and blight and the elimination and prevention of conditions detrimental to health, safety, and public welfare (Public Law #393, 1974, Section 101).

Every neighborhood can benefit from participation in a community development program. Federal regulations (Federal Register, 1978, p. 8462) require citizen participation in the application development and the selection of target neighborhoods and community development objectives. This process would provide an exceptional focus for neighborhood organization. Some cities (City of Lansing, 1978) already provide excellent opportunities for neighborhoods to organize and participate in the selection of target areas and objectives. Strategies for neighborhood organization (Warren & Warren, 1977) exist for those who reside in areas where citizen participation may not be already built in. Thus, neighborhoods may become more cohesive at the same time as residents improve housing, recreation facilities, etc. This might approximate such cooperative activities as the harvesting that occurs in rural areas.

Neighborhoods could also become greater sources of support and have more reason for interaction if they had more political power and decision-making ability (e.g., Alinsky, 1972). This would require decentralization of the control of resources. Instead of relying on the government to provide social services, neighborhoods should be allowed to determine what kinds of services are needed and how they should be distributed (Schön, 1971). This would allow a greater cultural diversity, as individual neighborhoods would be allowed to practice their values.

Economic measures should also be taken to strengthen neighborhoods. Policies and legislation that favor small neighborhood businesses and co-ops would help to develop the neighborhood into more autonomous units. Economic development strategies first suggested by Schumacher (1973) and Henderson (1978) should be used to provide local, labor-intensive community-oriented occupations. Again, neighborhood interaction opportunities and control over neighborhood affairs should all act to increase the importance of the neighborhood as a social group and as a source of social support.

Network Building. There is a final way in which policies should be implemented to encourage primary preventive social support. This should be accomplished through the building of networks across groups that share resources, people, time, and ideas. Such networks should be built among organizations that have similar goals and needs but individually have limited resources. For example, three community schools may all desire an improved library, swimming pool, and vocational training program. Each individual school does not have the resources to obtain all three. A supportive network and increased sense of community could be obtained if each school developed one program and shared access with students at the other schools. In addition, networks should be developed among different types of organizations that serve a similar area. For instance, a school, a neighborhood organization, and a youth service group can work cooperatively to meet the needs of local youth. The neighborhood organization is likely to have many people but may be limited in other resources. The school has space available for various activities such as community meetings. The youth service organization may have financial resources available.

Such networks help to meet the goals and needs of the individual organizations involved more efficiently. In addition, and equally important, they serve to develop what Sarason has called "the psychological sense of community" (Sarason, 1974), a group of individuals having a consensual agreement about their relatedness, and common values, needs, and goals. Individuals must feel a sense of belonging. Sarason, Carroll, Maton, Cohen, and Lorentz (1977) described the development of a network composed of a variety of social service organizations serving a common area. The major outcomes were an increased productivity of the individual organizations, as well as an increased sense of support and worthiness on the part of all the individuals involved in the network. The network acted as a support group that reduced general feelings of alienation and loneliness on the parts of the individuals attempting to provide service to others.

It seems clear that the development of networks is an activity that must be performed concomitantly with the above-suggested strategies. The building of networks would facilitate all of the above intervention activities, particularly neighborhood development.

Primary preventive social support attempts to develop prosocial and nonaggressive modes of responding among groups not yet demonstrating aggressive behavior. Programs and policies directed at already identified aggressors must also be implemented. Social support among identified aggressors is discussed next.

Secondary Preventive Social Support. Social support systems must also address identified aggressors (delinquents and criminals). Secondary preventive social support includes interventions directed at populations already demonstrating measurable levels of aggressive behavior. Interventions are meant to reduce the frequency of aggressive responding and to increase the frequency of nonaggressive responding to events that have historically elicited aggressive behavior. Again, as discussed by Rappaport (1975, 1977), change agents must focus on appropriate levels of social organization to ensure the occurrence of desired change. We will discuss secondary preventive social support effects aimed at inducing change at the individual, small group, and network levels of analysis. The interventions discussed below are meant to represent the kind of components a comprehensive program should include to foster secondary social support.

Individual. The underlying assumption in using the individual as the intervention target is that he or she fits inadequately into the larger social structure because of some type of deficit (Rappaport, 1977, p. 164). Interventions attempt to remediate the existing inadequacies in the individual. Examples include remedial reading programs, employment and skill training programs, and counseling and psychotherapy. All of these types of programs have been used with identified aggressors. Among many criminologists, in fact, prison is seen as a global attempt to rehabilitate the individual by restoring him or her to some accepted state of normalcy. The belief is that the individual must be resocialized so that their behavior comes under the control of the same social stimuli controlling the behavior of other members of society.

As with primary preventive social support programs directed toward young children, training in social problem-solving skills (e.g., Spivack et al., 1976) might prove beneficial. In many respects, aggression is a pattern of responding to events that has proved successful in the removal of noxious stimuli. Aggressive responding terminates a source of irritation in the environment or increases the probability of success in the pursuit of individual goals. Training in social problem-solving skills might give the individual an alternate means for coping with uncomfortable situations or for achieving personal goals.

Problem-solving training should focus additionally on the reduction of felt deindividuation (Festinger, Pepiton, & Newcomb, 1952; Zimbardo, 1970) and the increase of understanding and adherence to the norm of reciprocity (Gouldner, 1960). Individuals should be shown how they are personally responsible for their aggressive actions. Further, individuals should be shown how to reciprocate prosocial behavior. Structured curricula, modeling, and social reinforcement could be used to train identified aggressors while they were institutionalized; or better yet, individuals should be assigned to training programs instead of incarceration.

Criminal behavior has been theorized (Cloward & Ohlin, 1960) as a response to inadequate access to more legitimate means of achieving social and monetary success. Individual-level interventions must also include components addressing personal deficits in skills necessary for success in American society. For example, individuals must be able to read and to write and must have marketable job skills. In addition to curricula teaching problem-solving skills, accelerative programs teaching reading, mathematics, and employment skills should be implemented. The work of Charles D. Johnson and William D. Crano at Michigan State University (Johnson & Crano, 1977a, 1977b; 1978; Crano & Johnson, 1976, 1977) provides an example. These researchers designed programs addressing the special educational and employment needs of poor youth. The programs stressed the strengths of each individual. Further, every effort was taken to ensure that the exercises fit the unique social experiences of the youths. These accelerative programs did not possess many of the more unrealistic characteristics often basic in standard educational curricula; they improved the individual's reading and mathematic skills much faster than standard educational curricula. Johnson & Crano (1978) demonstrated that youth with as little as 100 hours of instruction typically increase two grade levels in reading and one grade level in mathematics. Youths who read at about the fourth-grade level, and thus were unable to read newspapers, achieved a level of reading competence sufficient to allow them to participate in the verbal culture. The ability to read allowed even individuals with a history of long-term failure in school finally to interpret the written information necessary to increase access to common social reinforcers such as esteem and money.

These and other individual interventions are related to the concept of youth advocacy described by Davidson & Rapp (1976). Such interventions provide direct support in the form of generating and mobilizing community resources for the youth and acting to protect the youth's rights and interests.

The usefulness of advocacy and support efforts with identified aggressors was discussed by Lipton et al. (1975). As reviewed in the previous chapter, they found that casework focusing on clients' external needs was more effective than attempting to develop client insight. For inmates leaving prison, recidivism for ex-inmates was reduced through provision of assistance in obtaining jobs, housing, clothing, union and health insurance benefits, financial aid and financial counseling, and supportive counseling (Bernstein & Christiansen, 1965). Finally, the Adolescent Diversion Project, described in the previous chapter, compared delinquents receiving an intervention based on advocacy with delinquents receiving normal court processing. Delinquents participating in the Diversion Project had fewer court and police contacts (Kushler, Emshoff, Blakely, & Davidson, 1979).

Interventions focusing on the individual, however, must be accompanied by efforts directed at other levels of social organization. A most effective way for doing this is by using the power intrinsic to small group processes.

Small Support Groups. Small groups composed of identified aggressors and helping professionals might also be used to increase levels of social support, creating mutual help groups (Killilea, 1976, p. 67). Necessary here is a redefinition of the helping process. All members of the small group must serve equally in the roles of helper and of recipient of help. While individual deficits may be acknowledged, all members of the group, including professionals, are seen to demonstrate the deficits. Further, each member is shown to possess strengths.

Mutual help support group members must be composed of peers who have similar experiences. Sorrentino (1977), an ex-delinquent, comments:

> ...the fundamental problem of aiding the delinquent or the mentally ill or any person who is out of tune with his environment is to find a person or a group that will receive and welcome the individual and in a friendly, helpful, understanding spirit give that person the feeling he is liked, wanted, and respected. If that person is dealt with in this manner and in addition furnished constructive guidance—new and better incentives, ideals, and opportunities—his rehabilitation would seem to be assured [p. 65].

The role of peers in mutual help support groups has been described by many professional helpers. Peers who have experiences similar to those of the help recipient can offer suggestions grounded in the credibility associated with having "been there," from "knowing the ropes." Killilea (1976, p. 67) further discusses why this is true, particularly among drug addicts and alcoholics. Thus, identified aggressors should be encouraged to band together.

In a similar vein, Skovolt (1974) suggested that when the recipients of help become the dispensers of help, they may in fact gain more from the helping process, and cites several possible explanations: (1) The effective helper often feels an increased level of interpersonal competence as a result of making an impact on another's life; (2) The effective helper often feels a sense of equality in giving and taking between himself or herself and others; (3) The effective helper is often the recipient of valuable personalized learning acquired while working with the helper; and (4) The effective helper often receives social approval from the people he or she helps.

The necessity for identified aggressors to band together to support each other is contrary to conventional theory and practice. For example, differential association theory (Sutherland & Cressey, 1970) would argue that association with other identified aggressors would increase the occurrence of aggression. This belief underlies the rule that restricts individuals on parole from prison from associating with other known criminals. While association with other aggressors might increase individual aggressive behavior, we do not believe that this is an inevitable consequence. Rather, we argue that other aggressors may communicate better with the aggressive individual. We argue further that what is required is not the cloistering of the identified aggressor among professionals, but the creation of mutual help support groups composed of identified aggressors.

Mutual Help Support Groups for Identified Aggressors. The use of a small group deliberately structured to rehabilitate criminals was also suggested by Cressey (1955). Cressey discussed five principles to be followed when creating such groups. Most germane to the present argument is the following principle:

> This most effective mechanism for exerting group pressures on members will be found in groups so organized that criminals are induced to join with noncriminals for the purpose of changing other criminals. A group in which criminal A joins with some noncriminals to change criminal B is probably most effective in changing A, not B; in order to change criminal B, criminal A must necessarily share the values of the anticriminal members [p. 119].

A small group whose purpose is to provide social support to identified aggressors should be composed of a helping professional, individuals who have a long history of aggression and contact with criminal justice agencies, and individuals with perhaps a history of aggressive behavior but only a recent contact with criminal justice agencies. The two types of aggressors might include older and younger adolescents or older criminals and adolescents. The most important aspect of the group composition is that the helper must have extensive experience as an aggressor and the helper must have developed new alternative strategies for coping with events that previously elicited aggressive responses. The helper must also have developed antiaggressive values and have demonstrated nonaggressive behavior.

In addition to the provision of social support and reinforcement for nonaggressive modes of response, the mutual help social support group should also assist with more instrumental tasks such as assistance with housing and job search. This additional help is especially important for members of stigmatized groups (Goffman, 1963) such as ex-convicts.

Azrin (Azrin, 1978; Azrin, Flores, & Kaplan, 1973) has shown that individuals engaged in job search as members of a small group called a "job club" were more successful than individuals searching alone. Variations of the job club have been shown to be effective in helping such stigmatized groups as the physically disabled to find jobs (Davis et al., 1979). One of the critical functions the job club serves is to allow members to provide motivational support to each other during the inherently frustrating course of job search (Wegmann, 1979). For stigmatized groups such as ex-convicts and handicapped individuals, the frequent job search necessary for successful job placement becomes less likely owing to the high incidence of rejection, arising in part from the stigma attached to them by employers and other members of society.

Other functions that might be served by members of the mutual help support group include the supervision of behavioral contracts (e.g., Stuart, 1971) between members of the group and the group as a whole. Behavioral contracts should include problematic situations typically responded to in an aggressive fashion. Behavioral contracts could be monitored by a single group member acting as a "buddy" (Fo & O'Donnell, 1975), serving as a general bridge between the individual, the support group, and the larger social environment.

The mutual help social support group might prove most useful for individuals who are about to be released from institutions. Support groups would be organized both within and outside the institution. The group within the institution would allow members to discuss their feelings about release and their subsequent plans. Upon release, the individual would become a member of an existing support group composed of already released individuals. The second group would provide concrete direction, supervise job search activities, provide housing and other information, and provide general social and motivational/emotional support.

Social Support Networks and Settings. The boundary between the small group and the creation of networks and settings to provide social support is equivocal. The two levels of analysis, however, are distinguished by their longevity and range. Small support groups usually last only long enough to complete a task; what Caplan (1974) would call a "specialist system." Support networks, however, are usually longer lasting, though an individual might not continually draw upon the network for resources. The range of the small group is usually limited to a small number of members, all of whom are known to the individual members. Networks and settings, on the other hand, may be composed of hundreds of individuals, many of whom may not be known immediately to all members (Sarason, 1976). Personal networks include those persons who are connected through intermediaries to a central person, sometimes called an anchor person or ego (Fischer, 1977, p. 34).

Network members may be the source of many kinds of resources including social support. For example, networks have been shown to reduce the negative consequences of rural-to-urban migration in developing nations (Fischer, 1977, pp. 22–23). Craven and Wellman (1973) discussed several characteristics of networks that affect the type of resources available to members:

> 1. Relatively dense (ratio of actual to potential linkages) networks are small; linkages among members are quite strong. Dense networks may increase access to emotional support resources.
> 2. Loose and less dense networks tend to be large; members are less deeply involved with one another. Loose networks may increase access to material resources [pp. 73–74].

A secondary preventive program of social support must develop both loose and dense networks; loose networks to generate general resources such as job leads, information, etc., and dense networks to provide emotional and motivational support. The dense network may overlap with the small group described above. In fact, the small group might act as a nucleus for a larger, looser network. An extended example of how small groups and larger supportive networks might complement each other is seen in the work of George W. Fairweather (Fairweather, 1964; Fairweather, Sanders, Maynard, & Cressler, 1969).

Fairweather created small autonomous groups within the psychiatric ward of a Veteran's Administration hospital. These groups were allowed considerable decision making and responsibility. They also created an atmosphere of mutual support among members. After demonstrating problem-solving ability and group cohesion, members of the small groups earned the right to live in an autonomous community setting known as a "lodge." The lodge included a residential setting and maintenance business that employed the members of the lodge. Lodge members gradually assumed control of both the lodge and the business, and eventually became self-sufficient.

Central to the philosophy of the lodge was the notion that "marginal persons" need a legitimate social status, different from that allowed in the typical mental hospital setting. The lodge was designed to be a setting where an independent and legitimate status was fostered. The lodge structure helped members to provide support and aid to each other, concentrating on their individual skills and strengths. Individuals not demonstrating "normal" behavior were allowed to create their own role within the lodge, fitting their deviance into the looser structure of the lodge.

Fairweather et al. (1969, pp. 199–237) found that members of the lodge lived and worked more productively, stayed out of the hospital longer, and were generally more adjusted than randomly assigned members of the control group. The importance of the support among the lodge members can be seen by examining the reasons given for return to the hospital—control group members simply living in the community returned most frequently because of pressure from significant others; lodge members seldom returned for this reason—their behavior was more tolerated and supported by other lodge members. In the more supportive atmosphere of the lodge, unusual behavior was permissable.

Fairweather et al. (1969) described 13 rules that should be followed when creating settings that attempt to improve the social status of members. While all of the rules are interesting, several deserve special attention:

1. Members must be allowed to participate in the operation of the system in order to feel a sense of pride and belonging.
2. Members should be allowed and helped to perform whatever tasks and roles are possible.
3. The system should establish norms that are tolerant of deviant behavior characteristic of the population involved.
4. Participants should perform as groups.
5. Systems should be designed so that they encourage close interpersonal relationships and an atmosphere of support [pp. 321–336].

Fairweather provides a very interesting example of the deliberate creation of a mutual help support group. His work is valuable because it provides one of the few experimentally evaluated attempts to create supportive settings. His lodge society provides an excellent prototype for change agents wishing to address the social support needs of identified aggressors. Lodges could be used to house and employ identified aggressors while other individually focused remedial efforts like accelerated educational programs are used. The members of the lodge could help the individual become independent of the lodge by assisting in job search, integration into other neighborhoods, etc.

In the area of criminal justice, Goldenberg (1971) established a residential program for delinquents that embodied some of Fairweather's principles. The Residential Youth Center was designed to be supportive in terms of both the content of the intervention and the style in which it was provided. The program aimed to help youth become legitimately involved with the community. Considerable emphasis was placed on assisting the youth in securing employment and providing aid necessary to doing a satisfactory job. The administration of the program was also important. Goldenberg emphasized the need for the youth to be involved in the administration of the program. The youth and the staff all shared equal responsibilities and exchanged tasks and roles. An atmosphere of mutual support and personal growth was developed and considered crucial to the success of the program.

Mutual help support groups like the lodge and the Residential Youth Center must be organized for identified aggressors when they leave institutions. As Sorrentino points out:

> We do not abandon the offender; we continue to show our concern for his welfare by keeping in touch with him while he is in the institution. We visit him personally, send him a copy of our community newspaper, write him letters, give him a little money to purchase candy, cigarettes, or personal items, and in other ways try to keep up his spirit and morale and give him the feeling that some of his neighbors have not forgotten him. These personal contacts enable us to keep up a continuing relationship so that when he is released we can work with him, his family, the parole agency, and other persons who are interested in his welfare [Sorrentino, 1977, p. 159].

While these supportive efforts are useful in institutions, they become even more important upon the offender's return to society. The previous chapter presented the arguments for the necessity of reintegrating the offender into the community. Such a reintegration effort requires a great deal of support from a variety of sources. Chief among these are the reactions and behavior of family and peers. Again, Sorrentino (1977) states:

> It is the community's responsibility to welcome him back to the neighborhood upon his release from an institution and try to incorporate him into the conventional life of the community. ... It is heartening to see experts in this field proposing that ordinary citizens be allowed to play a meaningful role in helping delinquents become re-integrated in the community. There is now at last a recognition of the value of volunteers, businessmen, ex-offenders, and youths who have never been in trouble to serve as advocates for youths in trouble [p. 160].

Reintegration requires, by definition, social support. In order to be integrated in a community, a person must feel a part of that community and must have a responsible role to play within it.

SUMMARY

Several different definitions of social support have been developed. They tend to focus on the following characteristics: Social support (1) satisfies the need an individual has for affection and esteem; (2) implies a mutual obligation among individuals to exchange material resources; (3) implicitly and/or explicitly includes the societal integration of the individual through the acquisition of rewarding roles; and (4) implicitly and/or explicitly assists the individual in validating expectations about others, contributing to the individual's construction of the surrounding social reality.

Major theories of crime and aggression were shown to fall into three broad categories: individual differences, sociological, and social learning. Those theorists who maintain that internal factors are the cause of criminal behavior focus on the individual psychological differences among people. Social support is directly relevant to the individual differences explanation of criminal behavior. Most of these explanations center on some form of psychopathy, which can be related in turn to a lack of social support. The most salient psychological explanation concerns the lack of adequate socialization that the criminal received. Attachment and commitment depend upon the provision of social contact and support, specifically the aspect concerning the provision of affection and caring.

The "blocked opportunity" theory is a leading sociological explanation of criminal behavior. According to this theory, society emulates only middle-class ideals and values but is structured so that the legitimate modes of access to these cultural goals are not available to members of lower socioeconomic classes. Aspects of social support that stress the provision of material goods and resources are relevant to this theory. The outcome of this form of social support is a social role and position for the individual, one of the goals of social support listed above.

Labeling theory, another major sociological theory, points out that society, through its reaction to behavior, defines deviance and therefore makes "deviants" deviant. A person who is a member of a social support network is more likely to be able to avoid labeling by minimizing the reaction to the behavior.

Finally, a social learning theory explanation of criminality can also be interpreted in terms of social support. A variety of such theories agree that crime is a behavior learned much as any other behavior is learned, through processes of social interaction and rewards (support) for deviant behavior. In the case of differential association or social learning, social support is offered to the person committing criminal behavior, but this support is contingent on the criminal behavior itself instead of on prosocial behavior.

The relationship between social support and aggression is particularly important given the general decline in present levels of social support available from traditional sources. The "Me" decade of the 1970s represents an inordinate focus on the individual and the rise of a self-help movement. At the same time, the dwindling social importance of the family unit has reduced its ability to provide support. Not only are there generally lower levels of support available, but support tends to be more diffuse and decentralized. Historically, there was a great overlap between members of the family, coworkers, church members, neighbors, schoolmates, and friends. In our present society, these groups are less integrated and more distinct.

The lack of social support tends to increase the incidence of crime and the levels of social support present in our society are decreasing. Given this reasoning, the promotion of policies and programs that increase levels of social support would be appropriate for the benefit of not only the individuals involved, but for society as a whole. By using the model developed in community mental health, these policies can be considered primary prevention of aggression, while programs for identified aggressors can be considered secondary prevention. Primary preventive social support includes interventions directed at groups that do not demonstrate currently aggressive behavior. Aggressive behavior is prevented by addressing the presumed antecedents of aggressive behavior. Secondary preventive social support focuses on the needs of probable aggressors. The purpose is the reduction of the frequency of aggressive responding and the increase of responses serving as alternatives to aggression.

A preventive social support program for young individuals should teach prosocial and nonaggressive methods for dealing with conflict situations. Its objectives should include (1) partial satisfaction of the need an individual has for affection and esteem, (2) the development of a sense of mutual obligation, (3) assistance in the acquisition of the rewarding roles of helper and one being helped, and (4) assistance for the individual in the validation of perceptions and expectations of a benign environment.

Programs in prosocial behavior should also be developed with the family. Family-focused approaches should attempt to reduce aggressive behavior by increasing the levels of social support, through increasing the intactness of the family with redefined housing policies and less reliance on the notion of consanguinity for defining extended families.

Present school practices often act to prevent the school from contributing to a sense of community and neighborhood. Such practices should be modified to allow maximum integration between the school and the neighborhood. Within the classroom, practices and policies should be implemented to encourage a supportive atmosphere. The present system is largely competitive, encouraging individual achievement with little concern for the group as a whole. Such practices should be changed to include group projects, peer tutoring programs, and curricula designed to address the development of prosocial behavior specifically and to decrease the demonstration of aggressive behavior.

The development of primary preventive social support must also focus on neighborhoods. In order for neighborhoods to become a source of social support, they need to be strengthened and designed such that their members act more cohesively. This can be accomplished through the use of community development, an increase in political power and decision-making ability, and economic measures to strengthen neigh-borhoods.

There is a final way in which policies should be implemented to encourage primary preventive social support. This should be accomplished through the building of networks across groups that share resources, people, time, and ideas. Such networks should be built among similar institutions (schools, neighborhoods, service organizations, etc.) that have similar goals and needs but individually have limited resources. In addition, such networks should be developed among different types of organizations that serve a similar area.

Interventions directed at populations or community groups already demonstrating a measurable incidence of aggressive behavior can be considered as secondary preventive social support. These interventions are meant to reduce the frequency of aggressive behavior and to increase the frequency of prosocial behavior and responses serving as alternatives to aggression.

We discussed three levels of intervention for a prototype of a comprehensive secondary social support system, including components addressing the individual, small groups, and networks. The first model discussed the application of individually oriented programs such as accelerative educational programs. The second model discussed the development of mutual help social support groups. Finally, the development of secondary preventive social support networks was discussed.

Secondary preventive social support programs should be created for identified aggressors residing both in institutions and the community. Identified aggressors should be shown how to band together and provide mutual support upon release from institutions.

REFERENCES

Abrahams, R. B. Mutual helping: Styles of caregiving in a mutual aid program—The widowed service line. In G. Caplan & M. Killilea (Eds.), *Support systems and mutual help.* New York: Grune & Stratton, 1976.

Akers, R. L. Socioeconomic status and delinquent behavior: A replication. *Journal of Research on Crime and Delinquency,* 1964, 1, 38–46.

Akers, R. L. *Deviant behavior: A social learning approach.* Belmont, Calif.: Wadsworth, 1973.

Alinsky, S. D. *Rules for radicals.* New York: Vintage Books, 1972.

Allen, G. J., Chinisky, J. M., Larcen, S. W., Lochman, J. E., & Selinger, H. V. *Community psychology and the schools: A behaviorally oriented multilevel approach.* Hillsdale, N.J.: Lawrence Erlbaum Associates, 1976.

Avgar, A. Family stresses and supports as a function of ecological factors. Paper presented at the 87th Annual Meeting of the American Psychological Association, New York, 1979.

Azrin, N. H. The job finding club as a method for obtaining employment for welfare-eligible clients: Demonstration, evaluation and counselor training. Final report to the U.S. Department of Labor, Grant #51-17-76-04, July 28, 1978.

Azrin, N. H., Flores, T., & Kaplan, S. J. Job finding club: A group assisted program for finding employment. *Behavior Research and Therapy,* 1973, **13,** 17–27.

Bandura, A. *Principles of behavior modification.* New York: Holt, Rinehart, & Winston, 1969.

Bandura, A. *Aggression: A social learning analysis.* Englewood Cliffs, N.J.: Prentice-Hall, 1973.

Bar-Tal, D. *Prosocial behavior: Theory and research.* Washington, D.C.: Hemisphere, 1976.

Bernstein, K. & Christiansen, K. A resocialization experiment with short term offenders. *Scandanavia Studies in Criminology,* 1965, **1,** 35–54.

Becker, H. S. *Outsiders: Studies in the sociology of deviance.* New York: Free Press, 1963.

Bennett, J. W. *Hutterian brethren: The agricultural economy and social organization of a communal people.* Stanford: Stanford University Press, 1967.

Berck, P. L. & Williams, L. J. Neighborhood organization: An empirical examination of psychosocial support. Paper presented at the 87th Annual Meeting of the American Psychological Association, New York, 1979.

Berger, P. L. & Luckman, T. *The social construction of reality.* Garden City: Doubleday, 1967.

Bloom, B. L. Social and community interventions. In M. R. Rosenzweig, & L. W. Porter (Eds.), *Annual review of psychology,* Vol. 31. Palo Alto, Calif.: Annual Reviews Inc., 1980.

Bryan, J. H. Model affect and children's imitative altruism. *Child Development,* 1971, **42,** 2061–2065.

Bryan, J. H. Why children help: A review. *Journal of Social Issues,* 1972, **28**(3), 87–104.

Bryan, J. H., Redfield, J., & Mader, S. Words and deeds about altruism and the subsequent reinforcement power of the model. *Child Development,* 1971, **42,** 1501–1508.

Burgess, R. C. & Akers, R. L. A differential association-reinforcement theory of criminal behavior. In D. R. Cressey & D. A. Ward (Eds.), *Delinquency, crime, and social process.* New York: Harper & Row, 1969.

Caplan, G. *Principles of preventive psychiatry.* New York: Basic Books, 1964.

Caplan, G. *Support systems and community mental health.* New York: Behavioral Publications, 1974.

Caplan, G. The family as a support system. In G. Caplan & M. Killilea (Eds.), *Support systems and mutual help: Interdisciplinary explorations.* New York: Grune & Stratton, 1976.

Caplan, G. & Killilea, M. *Support systems and mutual help: Multidisciplinary explorations.* New York: Grune & Stratton, 1976.

Chagnon, N. A. *Yanomamö: The fierce people.* New York: Holt, Rinehart & Winston, 1968.

City of Lansing, Citizen Participation Plan, August 1, 1978.

Cloward, R. & Ohlin, L. Illegitimate means, anomie, and deviant behavior. *American Sociological Review,* 1959, **24,** 164–177.

Cloward, R. & Ohlin, L. *Delinquency and opportunity.* Glencoe, Ill.: Free Press, 1960.

Cobb, S. Social support as a moderator of life stress. *Psychosomatic Medicine*, 1976, **38**, 300–314.

Cohen, A. K. *Delinquent boys.* Glencoe, Ill.: Free Press, 1955.

Cowen, E. L. Baby-steps toward primary prevention. *American Journal of Community Psychology*, 1977, **5**, 1–22.

Cowen, E. L. The wooing of primary prevention. Distinguished Contribution Award, Division 27, 87th Annual Meeting of the American Psychological Association, New York, 1979.

Craig, M. M. & Glick, S. J. Ten years experience with the Glueck Social Prediction Table. *Crime & Delinquency*, 1963, **9**, 249–261.

Crano, W. D. & Johnson, C. D. Facilitative effects of map interpretation on reading skills. Paper presented at 1976 convention of the American Psychological Association, Washington, D.C.

Crano, W. D. & Johnson, C. D. Applying cognitive principles in remedial instruction. Paper presented at the 1977 NATO International Conference on Cognitive Psychology and Instruction, Amsterdam, The Netherlands.

Craven, P. & Wellman, B. The network city. *Sociological Inquiry*, 1973, **43**, 57–88.

Cressey, D. R. Changing criminals: The application of the theory of differential association. *American Journal of Sociology*, 1955, **61**, 116–120.

Davidson, W. S. & Rapp, C. Child advocacy in the justice system. *Social Work*, 1976, **21**, 225–232.

Davis, D. D., Johnson, C. D., & Overton, S. R. Job placement for handicappers: Developing a natural helping system. Paper presented at the 87th Annual Meeting of the American Psychological Association, New York, 1979.

Davis, D. D. & Markman, H. Community psychology interventions and the planning of change. Unpublished manuscript, Michigan State University, 1980.

Dentan, R. K. *The Semai: A nonviolent people of Malava.* New York: Holt, Rinehart & Winston, 1968.

Durkheim, E. *Suicide: A study in sociology.* In J. A. Spaulding & G. Simpson (Trans.). Glencoe, Ill.: Free Press, 1951.

Elliot, D. S. & Voss, H. L. *Delinquency and dropout.* Lexington, Mass. Lexington Books, 1974.

Encyclopedia of Sociology. Guilford, Conn.: The Dushkin Publishing Group, Inc., 1974.

Erickson, K. T. Notes on the sociology of deviance. *Social Problems*, 1962, **9**, 308.

Erickson, M. L. & Empey, L. T. Class position, peers, and delinquency. *Crime and Delinquency*, 1973, **19**, 41–48.

Eshleman, J. R. *The family: An introduction.* Boston: Allyn & Bacon, 1974.

Fairweather, G. W. (Ed.), *Social psychology in treating mental illness: An experimental approach.* New York: Wiley, 1964.

Fairweather, G. W., Sanders, D. H., Maynard, H., & Cressler, D. L. *Community life for the mentally ill.* Chicago: Aldine, 1969.

Faris, R. E. L. *Social disorganization.* Rev. ed. New York: Ronald Press, 1955.

Federal Register, Vol. 43, no. 41, March 1, 1978.

Festinger, L., Pepitone, A., & Newcomb, T. Some consequences of de-individuation in a group. *Journal of Abnormal and Social Psychology*, 1952, **47**, 382–389.

Fischer, C. S. Network analysis and urban studies. In C. S. Fisher (Ed.), *Networks and places: Social relations in the urban setting.* New York: Free Press, 1977.

Fo, W. S. O. & O'Donnell, C. R. The buddy system: Relationship and contingency conditions in a community intervention program for youth with nonprofessionals as behavior change agents. In C. M. Franks & C. T. Wilson (Eds.), *Annual review of behavior therapy and practice.* New York: Brunner/Mazel, 1975.

440 In Response to Aggression

440 In Response to Aggression

Gans, H. J. *The urban villagers: Group and class in the life of Italian-Americans.* Glencoe, Ill.: Free Press, 1962.

Garfinkel, H. Conditions of successful degradation. *American Journal of Sociology*, 1956, **61**, 421–422.

Gesten, E. L., DeApodaca, R. F., Rains, M., Wissberg, R. P., & Cowen, E. L. Promoting peer related social competence in schools. In M. W. Kent & J. E. Rolf (Eds.), *Primary prevention of psychopathology.* Vol. III. Hanover: University Press of New England, 1979.

Gibbons, D. C. *Delinquent behavior.* Englewood Cliffs, N.J.: Prentice-Hall, Inc., 1970.

Glaser, D. *Strategic criminal justice planning.* Washington, D.C.: U.S. Government Printing Office, 1975.

Glueck, S. & Glueck, E. *Unravelling juvenile delinquency.* Cambridge: Harvard University Press, 1951.

Glueck, S. & Glueck, E. *Family environment and delinquency.* London: Routledge and Kegan Paul, 1962.

Goffman, E. *Stigma: Notes on the management of spoiled identity.* Englewood-Cliffs, N.J.: Prentice-Hall, 1963.

Goldenberg, I. I. *Build me a mountain.* Cambridge: Mass. MIT Press, 1971.

Goldstein, A. P., Sprafkin, R. P., Gershaw, N. G., & Klein, P. *Skill-streaming the adolescent.* Champaign, Ill.: Research Press, 1980.

Gouldner, A. W. The norm of reciprocity. *American Sociological Review*, 1960, **25**, 161–178.

Habermas, J. *Legitimation crisis.* Boston: Beacon Press, 1975.

Hackler, J. C. Testing a causal model of delinquency. *Sociological Quarterly*, 1970, **11**, 511–523.

Hagan, J. L. The labelling perspective, the delinquent, and the police. A review of the literature. *Canadian Journal of Criminology and Corrections*, 1972, **14**, 150–165.

Heller, K. & Monahan, J. *Psychology and community change.* Homewood, Ill.: Dorsey Press, 1977.

Henderson, H. *Creating alternative futures: The end of economics.* New York: Berkley Publishing, 1978.

Hirschi, T. *Causes of delinquency.* Los Angeles: University of California Press, 1969.

Hostetler, J. A. *Hutterite society.* Baltimore: Johns Hopkins Press, 1974.

Jacobs, P. A., Brunton, M., & Melville, M. M. Aggressive behavior, mental sub-normality and the XYY male. *Nature*, 1965, **208**, 1351–1352.

Johnson, C. D. & Crano, W. D. Influence of spatial skills on reading attainment. Paper presented at the 1977 convention of the Midwestern Psychological Association, Chicago, Illinois (a).

Johnson, C. D. & Crano, W. D. Map interpretation, spatial reasoning, and comprehension. Paper presented at the 1977 convention of the American Psychological Association, San Francisco, California (b).

Johnson, C. D. & Crano, W. D. Effects of spatial skills training on reading performance. *Journal of Experimental Education*, 1978, **46**, 25–31.

Jordan, V. E. The system propagates crime. *Crime and Delinquency*, 1974, **20**, 233–240.

Kahn, A. J. The case of the premature claims—public policy and delinquency prediction. *Crime and Delinquency*, 1965, **11**, 217–228.

Kahn, R. L. & Quinn, R. P. Mental health, social support and metropolitan problems. Research proposal, University of Michigan, 1977.

Killilea, M. Mutual help organizations: Interpretations in the literature. In G. Caplan & M. Killilea (Eds.), *Support systems and mutual help: Multidisciplinary directions.* New York: Grune & Stratton, 1976.

Klemchuk, H., Rolf, J. E., & Hasazi, J. E. Preschool children at risk: A multilevel approach to developmental pathology. Paper presented at the 83rd Annual Meeting of the American Psychological Association, Chicago, 1975.

Krisberg, B. & Austin, J. *The children of Ishmael.* Palo Alto, Calif. Mayfield, 1978.

Kushler, M., Emshoff, J. G., Blakely, C., & Davidson, W. S. Youth advocacy: A strategy for service to troubled youth. Paper presented at APA convention, New York, 1979.

Langley, M. H., Graves, H. R., & Norris, B. The juvenile court and individualized treatment. *Crime and Delinquency,* 1972, **18,** 79–92.

Linton, R. *The Tanala: A hill tribe of Madagascar.* Chicago: Field Museum of Natural History, 1933.

Matza, D. *Becoming deviant.* Englewood Cliffs, N.J.: Prentice-Hall, 1969.

McCord, J. & McCord, W. Effects of parental role model on criminality. *Journal of Social Issues,* 1958, **14,** 66–75.

McKinley, D. G. *Social class and family life.* New York: Free Press, 1964.

Merton, R. K. Social structure and anomie. *American Sociological Review,* 1938, **3,** 672–682.

Merton, R. K. *Social theory and social structure.* Rev. ed. New York: Free Press, 1957.

Midlarsky, E., Bryan, J. H., & Brickman, P. Aversive approval: Interactive effects of modeling and reinforcement on altruistic behavior. *Child Development,* 1973, **44,** 321–328.

Miller, B. A. Prerequisites to a community support system for children and adolescents. Paper presented at the 87th Annual Meeting of the American Psychological Association, New York, 1979.

Mulloy, P. J. Conflict, consensus, and critical approaches to law. Unpublished manuscript, University of Toronto, 1976.

Nye, F. E., Short, J. F., & Olsen, V. J. Socioeconomic status and delinquent behavior. *American Journal of Sociology,* 1958, **63,** 381–389.

Patterson, G. R. & Reid, J. B. Reciprocity and coercion: Two facets of social systems. In C. Neuringer & J. L. Michael (Eds.), *Behavior modification in clinical psychology.* New York: Appleton-Century-Crofts, 1970.

Pelto, G. H. & Pelto, P. J. *The human adventure.* New York: Macmillan, 1976.

Polk, K. & Schafer, W. E. (Eds.) *Schools and delinquency.* Englewood Cliffs, N.J.: Prentice-Hall, 1972.

Prentice, N. M. The influence of live and symbolic modeling on promoting moral judgment of adolescent delinquents. *Journal of Abnormal Psychology,* 1972, **80,** 157–161.

Price, R. H. Etiology, the social environment, and the prevention of psychological disorders. In P. Insel & R. Moos (Eds.), *Health and the social environment.* Lexington, Mass.: D. C. Heath, 1974.

Price, R. H. & Denner, B. (Eds.) *The making of a mental patient.* New York: Holt, Rinehart & Winston, 1973.

Procidano, M. E. & Heller, K. Toward the assessment of perceived social support. Paper presented at the 87th Annual Meeting of the American Psychological Association, New York, 1979.

Public Law #383–93rd Congress, S. 3066, August 22, 1974.

Rappaport, J. From Noah to Babel: Relationships between conceptions, values, analysis levels, and social intervention strategies. Paper presented at a symposium: Report of the Austin Conference: The Future of Community Psychology, Ira Iscoe, Chair. 83rd Annual Meeting of the American Psychological Association, Chicago, 1975.

Rappaport, J. *Community psychology: Values, research, and action.* New York: Holt, Rinehart & Winston, 1977.

Richette, L. A. *The throwaway children.* Philadelphia: Lippincott, 1972.

Robins, L. N. *Deviant children grown up.* Baltimore: The Williams & Wilkins Company, 1966.

Rolf, J. E. & Hasazi, J. E. Identification of preschool children at risk and some guidelines for primary prevention. In G. W. Albee & J. M. Joffee (Eds.), *Primary prevention of psychopathology.* Vol. I. Hanover: University Press of New England, 1977.

Rutter, M. *Children of sick parents.* London: Oxford University Press, 1966.

Rutter, M. Parent-child separation: Psychological effects on the children. *Journal of Child Psychology and Psychiatry,* 1971, **12,** 233–260.

Rutter, M. Protective factors in children's responses to stress and disadvantage. In M. W. Kent and J. E. Rolf (Eds.), *Primary prevention of psychopathology.* Vol. III. Hanover: University Press of New England, 1979.

Sarason, S. B. *The psychological sense of community: Prospects for a community psychology.* San Francisco: Jossey-Bass, 1974.

Sarason, S. B. Community psychology, networks, and Mr. Everyman. *American Psychologist,* 1976, **31,** 317–328.

Sarason, S. B., Carroll, C. F., Maton, K., Cohen, S., & Lorentz, E. *Human services and resource networks.* San Francisco: Jossey-Bass, 1977.

Scarpitti, F. R. & Stephenson, R. M. Juvenile court dispositions: Factors in the decision-making process. *Crime and Delinquency,* 1971, **17,** 142–152.

Schön, D. A. *Beyond the stable state.* New York: Random House, 1971.

Schumacher, E. F. *Small is beautiful: Economics as if people mattered.* New York: Harper & Row, 1973.

Silverman, P. R. The widow as a caregiver in a program of preventive intervention with other widows. In G. Caplan & M. Killilea (Eds.), *Support systems and mutual help.* New York: Grune & Stratton, 1976.

Skinner, B. F. *The behavior of organisms.* New York: Appleton-Century-Crofts, 1938.

Skinner, B. F. *Science and human behavior.* New York: Free Press, 1953.

Skovolt, T. M. The client as helper: A means to promote psychological growth. *Counseling Psychologist,* 1974, **4,** 58–64.

Smith, P. M. & Ausnew, H. R. Socialization as related to delinquency classification. *Psychological Reports,* 1974, **34,** 677–678.

Smyer, M. A. Divorce and family support in later life: Emerging trends. Paper presented at the 87th Annual Meeting of the American Psychological Association, New York, 1979.

Sorrentino, A. *Organizing against crime.* New York: Human Sciences Press, 1977.

Spivack, G., Platt, J. J., & Shure, M. B. *The problem solving approach to adjustment.* San Francisco: Jossey-Bass, 1976.

Spivack, G. & Shure, M. B. *Social adjustment of young children.* San Francisco: Jossey-Bass, 1974.

Staub, E. The use of role playing and induction in children's learning of helping and sharing behavior. *Child Development,* 1971, **42,** 805–816.

Staub, E. Helping a distressed person: Social, personality, and stimulus determinants. In L. Berkowitz (Ed.), *Advances in experimental social psychology,* Vol. 7. New York: Academic Press, 1974.

Staub, E. *Positive Social Behavior and Morality.* New York: Academic Press, 1978.

Stuart, R. B. Behavioral contracting within the families of delinquents. *Journal of Behavior Therapy and Experimental Psychiatry,* 1971, **2,** 1–11.

Sutherland, E. H. & Cressey, D. R. *Principles of criminology.* 8th Ed. Philadelphia: J. P. Lippincott, 1970.

Tönnies, T. F. *Fundamental concepts of sociology.* New York: American Books Co., 1940.

Trevett, N. B. Identifying delinquency-prone children. *Crime and Delinquency,* 1965, **11,** 186–191.

Ullmann, L. & Krasner, L. *A psychosocial approach to abnormal behavior.* Englewood Cliffs, N.J.: Prentice-Hall, 1975.

Waldo, G. P. & Dinitz, S. Personality attributes of the criminal: An analysis of research studies, 1950–1965. *Journal of Research in Crime and Delinquency,* 1967, **4**, 185–202.

Walster, E., Berscheid, E., & Walster, E. New directions in equity research. *Journal of Personality and Social Psychology,* 1973, **25**(2), 151–176.

Warren, R. B. & Warren, D. I. *The neighborhood organizer's handbook.* Notre Dame: University of Notre Dame Press, 1977.

Watzlawick, P., Weakland, J. H., & Fisch, R. *Change: Principles of problem formulation and problem resolution.* New York: Norton, 1974.

Wegmann, R. G. Job search assistance: A review. *Journal of Employment Counseling,* 1979, **16**, 197–226.

Williams, J. R. & Gold, I. M. From delinquent behavior to official delinquency. *Social Problems,* 1972, **20**, 209–229.

Wright, J. & James, R. *A behavioral approach to preventing delinquency.* Springfield, Ill.: Charles C. Thomas, 1974.

Zimbardo, P. G. The human choice: Individuation, reason and order versus de-individuation, impulse, and chaos. In W. J. Arnold & D. Levine (Eds.), *Nebraska symposium on motivation,* 1969. Lincoln: University of Nebraska Press, 1970.

IV

Societal Controls and Alternatives

Chapter 10
Conflict Intervention Strategies
Paul Wehr, A. Paul Hare, and Susan Carpenter

Social conflict usually involves aggressive feelings and behavior. This is especially true of conflicts in which values and life-stake issues are prominent. In such conflicts, parties are so emotionally involved and defensive that they are usually unable to control or resolve the dispute without external assistance. In such conflicts the third party intervenor becomes essential.

UNDERSTANDING THE CONFLICT

The intervenor in a conflict must first understand both the general principles of conflict dynamics and structure, and then those characteristics of the specific conflict in question. On the basis of such a conflict analysis, one decides whether, how, and when to intervene.

The interactive nature of conflict is perhaps its central dynamic. This interaction among the conflict parties is inevitably altered and usually complicated by the intervention of a neutral third party. The intervenor must be fully conscious of this consequence.

Conflict's interactive nature leads to what has been called *reciprocal causation*. One party's act elicits a like action from its opponent. In all likelihood, each such response will be at a higher level of aggressiveness and strength than that which evoked it. Thus the dynamic of *spiralling escalation* is set in motion. Escalation is one of several "runaway processes" identified by Coleman. These include: (1) *polarization,* as a number of parties organize into bipolar opposition to one another; (2) *personalization,* in which attacks come to be directed at leaders of the conflicting parties and away from specific issues; and (3) *issue trans-*

formation and proliferation, by which original issues are often super-seded by others. Each runaway process tends to reflect increasingly aggressive behavior and intent in the conflict. These processes can, however, be decelerated, reversed, and even prevented altogether by a skillful intervenor.

CONFLICT MAPPING

Mapping a conflict is an important preliminary step in conflict inter-vention. It involves investigating the *historical and political contexts* of the conflict, its *structure,* its various *dimensions,* and the most ap-propriate *methods of regulating* the dispute (Fig. 10.1). Mapping not only prepares the mapper for a decision whether or not to intervene, but provides the intervenor with a holistic view of the conflict. Too often intervenors are familiar with one, or at the most, two of a conflict's four major dimensions: communication, values, facts, and interests. Under-standing and working at only one or two dimensions may cause the intervention to fail. Each dimension influences the others and each suggests a different, complementary approach to resolution. Some com-bination of those four types of resolution strategies will be necessary for settlement of the dispute.

An intervenor must view a conflict in all its complexity, seeing its four dimensions clearly. This is not to say that a particular conflict will not be primarily interests-based or facts-based, for the dimensions of a conflict are rarely equal in weight. Dimensions of lesser weight may nevertheless be crucial for settlement. Mediation of a primarily interests-based conflict, for example, may be unsuccessful if adequate attention is not paid to communication, or sufficient factual information.

APPROACHES TO INTERVENTION

Once the conflict has been assessed, if a neutral third party concludes that intervention has a reasonable chance of succeeding, an appropriate approach or combination of approaches is selected. Where physical violence characterizes the conflict, third party intervention may take the form of *interposition*—with the intervenor physically separating the disputants. Interposition has been successfully used in a variety of violent conflicts ranging from United Nations peacekeeping in Cyprus and in the Middle East (Rikhye, Harbottle & Egge, 1974) to controlling gang warfare in Philadelphia (Schonborn, 1975). Even in nonviolent conflict, interposition can be an important part of the resolution strategy.

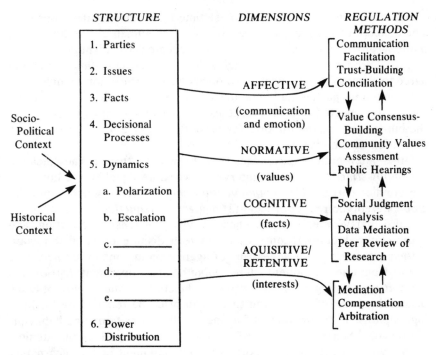

STRUCTURE   DIMENSIONS   REGULATION
                                       METHODS

1. Parties   Communication
                                       Facilitation
2. Issues   Trust-Building
                    AFFECTIVE   Conciliation
3. Facts
                    (communication
Socio-   4. Decisional   and emotion)   Value Consensus-
Political   Processes   Building
Context   Community Values
          5. Dynamics   NORMATIVE   Assessment
                                       Public Hearings
             a. Polarization   (values)

                    COGNITIVE   Social Judgment
Historical   b. Escalation   Analysis
Context   (facts)   Data Mediation
                                     Peer Review of
             c._____   AQUISITIVE/   Research
                          RETENTIVE
             d._____   Mediation
                          (interests)   Compensation
             e._____   Arbitration

          6. Power
             Distribution

Fig. 10.1. The conflict mapping process. The different dimensions of a conflict are, of
course, interactive as are the methods of resolving it.

In some cases of mediation, the physical separation of the parties in
different rooms with the mediator as the intermediary link can be useful
in both functional and symbolic ways. Of course, interposition by itself
can do no more than interrupt the conflict. It must be paralleled by other
techniques that remove the stimulus for the conflict and tension.

Mediation is perhaps the most common form of third party intervention. It has been used for a half-century in the United States to
resolve labor disputes (Douglas, 1962). In the past two decades it has
been increasingly applied in community conflict over racial issues (Laue
& Cormick, 1974). Currently it is also being used in environmental
disputes (Lake, 1980). Here the third party intervenor, assuming the role
of mediator, brings together parties willing to negotiate the resolution of
a dispute. The process requires concessions from all sides that result in a
negotiated settlement. The concept of the trade-off is extremely important—that is, the process by which the mediator arranges the matching of gains and concessions. Sometimes, compensation is used by
which a settlement is made possible through compensation whereby one
party's loss is made acceptable.

Arbitration may well be the most time-tested third party approach. The concept of the impartial judge is as old as human civilization. In its modern application, a third party is accepted by disputants as an impartial arbiter. They present their sides of the issue to this arbiter and agree to accept the judgment of who gets what. Arbitration assumes that the conflicting parties have confidence in both the political system and the person selected to arbitrate. It also relieves the conflicting parties of the burden (but of the opportunity as well) of active involvement in the resolution of the dispute.

Other intervention approaches used by neutral third parties include: (1) *empowerment*, where the intervenor works to equalize the power of the conflict parties; (2) *communication enhancement*, which would include stereotype reduction; and (3) *aggression reduction*.

Third party intervention relies heavily on tension-reduction and aggression-reduction techniques to move a dispute or conflict toward settlement. Four major generators of aggression in conflict are *perceived threat* from one's opponent, *stereotyping* of one's opponent, *tension and frustration* building up within parties to the conflict, and a sense of being *personally attacked*. Perceived threat can often be reduced by facilitating empathy in the opponents for one another's positions and behavior. Understood behavior is generally though not always less threatening. Stereotyping, which usually portrays one's opponent as the incarnation of all that is evil in the world, can often be reduced through reperception exercises such as those used in the Burton (1969) experiments in controlled communication. Tension can often be reduced through *venting*, where the intervenor acts as a sounding board, so to speak, for each disputant's hostility and frustrations. The intervenor as "active listener" performs an important therapeutic function as each of the conflict parties has the opportunity to express fully the conflict viewed from its perspective.

A third party intervenor can often depersonalize a conflict, moving it away from direct attack on the personalities involved and toward the underlying issues, thereby getting disputants to realize a common interest in dealing with and resolving these issues. A conflict is something like an orange. Its subjective "skin" needs to be penetrated or peeled back before the objective core issues can be resolved. Depersonalizing a conflict is an important part of that penetration process.

Increasingly in recent years, the community has become a conflict locus in which third parties have intervened with growing frequency. Two major sources of this increased conflict have been interracial friction and environmental issues.

Two approaches to third party intervention not as well known as mediation and arbitration are now gaining some currency. *Conflict anticipation* and *conciliation* both show considerable promise, and each of the authors of this chapter has been involved in developing one or the other of them.

Some conflicts can be avoided altogether or can be made less intense if they are anticipated. The objective of conflict anticipation is to forecast the emergence of a conflict situation and to develop and implement alternatives acceptable to all parties. One such intervention might involve a third party entering a community likely to experience intense conflict and helping potential conflict parties to avoid or moderate it. In this chapter we describe how this can be done in rural western communities where energy-related development stimulates rapid community growth, which in turn raises conflict and tension levels. The third party intervenor facilitates a community's awareness of how future growth will generate conflict and how, by planning wisely, it can substantially reduce that conflict.

When conflicts are insufficiently structured for mediation, *conciliation* may be appropriate. The conciliator may not have the well-defined parties, issues, and established social and political structures with which to work. The conciliator acts primarily as a catalyst, to get the conflict parties to "stop shouting and start talking," so to speak, or even to start talking while "combat" continues. Conciliation is required, for example, where intercommunal violence and serious communication breakdown have so polarized the conflict that parties may not even concede their opponent's right to exist, at least not in the same community. Family and marital counseling usually uses conciliation as well. It does often seem that the more intimate the relationship between parties to a conflict, the more intractable the conflict. Third party conciliators working with family and marital conflict need special skills since encompassing personal issues are involved—a fact that heightens its intensity (see Chap. 2 for specific negotiation and contracting procedures relevant to marital conflict). Often the conciliator performs some humanitarian service in the conflict which enhances his or her peace-making role. Further on, we will show how conciliation as an intervention technique has been applied in communities rent by racial and ethnic hostility. In the cases we present here, the environmental disputes reflect the experience of Susan Carpenter and Paul Wehr, and the racial and ethnic conflict that of A. Paul Hare.

ANTICIPATING ENVIRONMENTAL CONFLICTS

Industrialized nations have experienced a steady institutionalization of the management of social conflict over the past century. In the United

States, this process began in earnest with the New Deal expansion of the federal government in the 1930s. At that time, federal intervention in industrial relations through the National Labor Relations Act replaced bloody industrial warfare with mandatory collective bargaining. As bureaucratic organizations proliferated—federal regulatory and management agencies, educational institutions, corporations—and shaped more and more aspects of the lives of citizens, the latter have demanded more direct participation in the policy process. This, of course, has raised the level of citizen-involved conflict. In addition, as policy-making bodies have become increasingly specialized with correspondingly diverse goals, conflict between and within these organizations has greatly increased. Thus, while conflict has become more institutionalized, there also seems to be more of it to manage. Nowhere is the heightened level of controversy more evident than in the area of environmental policy. Certain trends have brought this about.

Pollution and Regulation. The almost geometric increase in the use and conversion of natural resources in both manufacturing processes and energy production has produced a growing volume of pollutants that threaten to exceed the limits of tolerance of ecosystems. Commoner (1971) believes the central problem is the recent industrial processing revolution, which produces wastes that are more important than the intended product itself. Inefficient use of energy is another dimension of the ecological crisis. As Lovins (1977) has noted, since 1963 electrical power consumption in the United States has doubled, though national living standards may actually have declined. This rapidly increasing energy addiction exerts new pressures on such resources as land, air, and water.

A series of federal laws were enacted in response to this growth of resource exploitation and corresponding environmental pollution. They provide both the opportunity for increased conflict and new procedures for managing that conflict. The National Environmental Policy Act (NEPA), the Clean Air Act, amendments to the Federal Water Pollution Control Act, the Noise Control Act, and the Coastal Zone Management Act are some of the tools of federal environmental policy that have emerged in the past decade. Agencies such as the Environmental Protection Agency (EPA) and the Council on Environmental Quality, were created to make and to implement that policy. Already existing agencies, such as the Fish and Wildlife Service and the Water and Power Resources Service (formerly U.S. Bureau of Reclamation) found themselves with new bases for interagency conflict.

As competition over resource allocation intensifies, new types of conflict appear. The direction policy should take will be one conflict arena as special interests attempt to influence both general policy directions and specific decisions in their favor. The administration of that policy will also generate conflict with different interpretations of regulations and possibly conflicting regulations established by different agencies.

Controversy will intensify over values judged most beneficial for society. How clean should a city's air be? Communities are already polarized over how much air pollution should be permitted before substantial changes in personal transportation habits and lifestyles are required by law. The focus of future environmental conflict may well shift away from industrialist versus environmentalist toward personal lifestyle versus government regulation.

Long-standing policies controlling resource use are now being challenged as the principles on which they were founded seem increasingly obsolete. For instance, do nonhumans have a right to water? The concept of "beneficial use" in Colorado water law, which has for a century permitted human users to dry up rivers completely, is now being modified by minimum stream-flow law—through not without protracted conflict between conservationists and water users.

New policy data requirements, such as those imposed by NEPA in the Environmental Impact Analysis procedure, have heightened controversy over the amount and type of information necessary for environmental planning, monitoring, and secondary impact analysis. Scientists may disagree, for example, on the effects a proposed coal mine will have on local water supplies and adjacent agricultural land, or on its impact on the economic and social health of the supporting community, or about who should be financially and administratively responsible for preventing or mitigating those impacts.

Environmentalism and Citizen Participation. A second influential trend has been the growing participation of environmentalists in shaping policy. The Earth Day tradition begun in 1970, and the United Nation's Stockholm conference on the environment held in 1972 offered forums for public discussion of the magnitude and immediacy of environmental problems.

There has developed, in the past decade, a citizen participation trend by which environmental, consumer, firearms, wildlife, and other interests intervene in the environmental policy process. Despite the comparatively low level of citizen participation in national elections, our environmental policy has become very much a participatory one, and this trend is likely to continue into the future.

Aside from the development of environmental organizations with politically sophisticated leaders, large memberships, and seven figure

454 In Response to Aggression

budgets, the most forceful impetus for participatory environmentalism has been mandatory citizen review of proposals involving federal action. NEPA, for example, requires citizen hearings on all Environmental Impact Statement (EIS) drafts. Recent federal and state legislation calls for increased citizen involvement at each stage of environmental decision making. This has moved agencies, such as the U.S. Forest Service with its Roadless Area Review program, to restructure their policy making to include citizen judgments.

Ironically, NEPA has both generated conflict and institutionalized its management. Much of this has taken place in the courts. Through a series of cases since 1970, environmentalists have established the authority of the courts to determine whether an agency has sufficiently addressed NEPA's procedural and substantive guidelines.

Organizations like the Natural Resources Defense Council (NRDC) and the National Wildlife Federation can now force or forestall federal action. They have become major factors to be reckoned with in national resource management policy. The *NRDC* v. *Hughs* case, for example, effectively tied up federal coal leasing for years.

Conflict strategies of such environmental organizations have been largely adversarial, relying on litigation and the courts. While important for the establishment of legal precedent, adversarial conflict is a win-lose approach to problem solving, an approach that does not encourage identification of a range of acceptable policy options. Nor do NEPA procedures necessarily encourage examination of alternatives. Our experience with federal environmental impact analysis has been that the legally mandated "alternatives analysis" segment of the EIS is not normally given serious attention by the impact analysis team, and appears in the report somewhat as an afterthought. The procedure seems to be stacked against any serious consideration of alternatives to the proposed action and thus is inherently supportive of it. It becomes a mere formality, a part of the procedure justifying the action. As the team director for the Bureau of Land Management's (BLM) Northwest Colorado Coal impact analysis stated before the draft EIS was released, "There is no way that that coal isn't going to be developed."

Interagency and Interdepartmental Conflict. While the more visible conflict has occurred between environmentalists and developers, much conflict occurs within the federal government itself as it takes an increasingly active role in regulating pollution and resource management. The Interior and Energy departments, for example, have now divided the policy-making and administrative responsibility for the coal program—a division which has already produced serious interagency disagreements.

One agency's policy may contradict that of another. By way of illustration, EPA regulations requiring catalytic converters to reduce auto emissions may decrease vehicle fuel economy, thereby working against the energy conservation goal of Energy. Governmental units may also disagree on the appropriate role of the citizen in making public policy. Some strongly support citizen participation while others will do anything to avoid it.

Finally, federal agencies conflict over environmental policy as they increasingly find themselves cast as advocates for different nongovernmental "constituencies" whose interests they are expected to protect. In the Chikaskia dispute described later in this paper, the U.S. Fish and Wildlife Service found itself acting on behalf of likely (environmentalists, fish and game interests) and unlikely (wheat farmers) constituents, while the Water and Power Resources Service (WPRS) represented, not unexpectedly, the interests of Wichita planners and water users. Even within agencies such as WPRS, conflicts over priorities, and value and judgment differences are increasingly alienating soft from hard scientists, thus making effective planning more difficult.

Institutionalizing Conflict Management

Future environmental conflict must be more effectively regulated. As the number and complexity of environmental problems and attendant conflicts increases, it becomes ever clearer that adversary conflict management is insufficient. Litigation, even where appropriate, is costly in time, money, and other scarce resources. A growing number of environmental disputes do not at all lend themselves to judicial resolution. Increasingly, conflict over environmental policy involves not one group of interests against another, but the larger task of striking an acceptable balance of economic health on the one hand and ecological health on the other. These two conditions are seen more and more as interdependent. A balance can be achieved only through cooperative policy making. The courts are not up to this task for they have no mechanisms, in a particular case, for exploring alternative solutions, or for addressing long-term implications of one action over another. Other means must be found.

Enlightened leadership in industry no longer perceives economic and ecological health as incompatible. Yet it often has difficulty pursuing them simultaneously. The National Coal Policy Project is a pioneering model for environmentalist-business agreement on acceptable methods of coal utilization (Murray, 1978). Nevertheless, neither corporate-environmentalist collaboration nor litigation can meet the diversity of conflict regulation requirements at the different levels at which environmental policy is made and implemented.

In some instances, environmental disputes can be terminated merely by the intervention of technology, by the introduction of what is known as a *technical fix*. It does so by expanding the range of policy options to include a corporation moving beyond the best available pollution control requirements stated in federal law. For example, a coal-fired power plant is a noxious facility primarily because of its emissions into the surrounding air basin. Governments and citizens may conflict vigorously with utilities wishing to build new plants. In recent years the inclusion of electrostatic precipitators and wet scrubbers have in many instances sufficiently reduced a plant's adverse air quality impacts to permit its construction. In the future, technological advances may lower plant water requirements, reduce plant noise, or moderate other common objections that local communities may have to such installations.

Such technological intervention, however, also has its limitations as a conflict management device. The fix is only as effective as the technology. Malfunctioning scrubbers at the Hayden, Colorado power station have been a continuing source of friction between the operator-utility and the Colorado Air Pollution Control Commission. After three years, the plant is still not operating as projected. The fix, as in this case, may generate as much conflict as it resolves. Then too, technological intervention works better to reduce environmental impacts than it does social costs such as uncontrolled growth.

Where the technical fix is not sufficient to eliminate the conflict, *compensation* may work. Communities bearing the social and environmental costs of hosting a noxious facility such as a power plant, can be paid in order to offset those costs. O'Hare (1977) has developed the bidding auction by which communities set the level of compensation at which they would agree to host a noxious facility. This is one technique for compensating for nonquantifiable variables such as quality of life. Compensation, however, may have limited utility in that certain resources such as clean air and water, and open space are becoming so scarce that in a growing number of communities no acceptable level of compensation will be found. Even if a community agrees to accept the facility, such a decision may not maximize the public interest. New schools and a cultural center, for example, may not compensate for serious air quality degradation.

While environmental conflict management is at an early stage of development, it can draw upon a substantial body of knowledge and proven practice in other fields. Conflict research and conflict regulation are now established fields (Wehr, 1979). University research on conflict regulation has been building for decades (Dedring, 1976). Theory about how and why social conflict occurs has been fairly well accepted throughout the social sciences (Boulding, 1962). Conflict management research within universities has been turning recently toward resolution of policy conflict (Hammond & Adelman, 1974) and within that broader field, more toward resolution of conflict over environmental policy (Gladwin, 1978). Several promising methods have emerged from the application of conflict management research to environmental disputes.

Mediation of environmental disputes is a prominent method now being developed (Mernitz, 1980). Much of the mediation technique applied to environmental conflict has been transferred from industrial collective bargaining and community dispute settlement. It has been modified for and applied to certain environmental disputes with some success (Cormick & Patton, 1977) and a group of experienced mediators is developing as a consequence. Mediation, like compensation, has limitations. It is useful only at certain stages in a conflict and only in certain non-zero-sum conflicts where compromise is possible. It is also a voluntary process, all major parties must engage in it willingly.

Conflict assessment, another approach, is an effort by a third party to evaluate specific dimensions of a conflict and offer recommendations, to move the dispute away from impasse. The method differs from mediation in that the third party does not suggest a complete solution. Rather, the intervenor's assessment and recommendations provide a new perspective on the conflict from which the disputants can fashion a workable solution.

Conflict Anticipation: Procedures and Techniques

The conflict intervention methods discussed thus far are normally applied after the dispute is under way. It is often possible, however, to anticipate a conflict and therefore to moderate it in its early stages, or in some cases to remove the conditions for its emergence altogether. In Colorado, we have worked with two types of conflict anticipation:

1. *Third-party intervention in potential disputes* before opposing sides form and before social and economic disruption occurs. Once identified, the potential dispute becomes the focus of efforts to preclude its development.
2. *Conflict-warning devices* built into the environmental policy-making process. These may include: (a) techniques for identifying important values and interests of populations to be impacted by a policy, and (b) anticipating policies which will contradict values and interests of one group or another. Where such contradiction threatens to produce severe conflict, the proposed policy can be discarded at the conceptual stage or

modified to meet the basic values and interests of all seriously impacted parties.

In both (1) and (2), conflict can be precluded or moderated. Let us look at each of these approaches more closely.

Intervention in Potential Disputes. By intervening in potential disputes and organizing early discussion among interested parties, conflict anticipators seek, as do mediators, to replace an adversary, win-lose approach with one of locating alternatives that best meet the needs of all parties. Negotiation here, as in mediation, is essential. Often anticipation will be preferable to mediation since it enables interested parties to work together before mistrust develops and serious costs are incurred. It encourages communities to identify. the widest range of options for solving an environmental problem, thereby allowing for economies in terms of social, economic, environmental, and legal costs.

Delta County is a community that illustrates this anticipation process. Located on Colorado's Western Slope, it is being impacted by energy development. Eleven coal companies have submitted letters of intent to develop underground mines there. The county is characterized by a dramatic natural setting, isolation from urban centers, a highly diversified economic base, and a self-reliant population. A rapid expansion of that population will cause sharp conflict over redistribution of limited resources such as water, clean air, and agricultural land. Already, many perceive the interests of farming and mining to be mutually exclusive.

In January of 1977, ROMCOE, a center for environmental problem solving, was invited by the Delta County League of Women Voters to help citizens deal with expected changes in economic and social life as coal development occurs in the county. At the outset, some local officials were indifferent to these imminent problems and hostile to a program for anticipating them. Nevertheless, ROMCOE and its local partners, with much volunteer time, created a countywide, nonpartisan citizens network where none had existed before.

The program culminated in a workshop, "Quality of Life in Delta County: The Price Tag?" The process leading to it was equally important as it brought together potentially conflicting interests—coal company executives, ranchers, orchardists, and commercial people. At the workshop they learned of one another's values and goals, in a process that supplied objective information on the county's past, present, and projected future.

In preparation for the workshop, community groups gathered information about the possible effects of energy-related growth on the quality of life there, and ways of managing that growth. The local press and community organizations disseminated this information over a period of months. A slide presentation on the quality of life in Delta County was shown to 30 different groups. At the workshop itself, 270 participants with the help of outside resource people, produced over 90 action recommendations for improving the quality of life through (1) governmental planning, (2) economic balance, (3) environmental protection, (4) public services, and (5) community integration. Since conflict anticipation concerns potential rather than actual conflict, it is not easy to evaluate a particular intervention. If one is working on a potential dispute, at least some success can be claimed if the dispute does not materialize. Where one is concerned with an interrelated complex of potential disputes, however, evaluation is more difficult. The Delta County intervention produced a set of conditions that may well reduce conflict and enhance cooperative problem solving: (1) a new sense of being a community with common goals; (2) new patterns of communication and cooperation; (3) new awareness of growth problems to come and of new options for responding to them; (4) the same factual information provided to all interests; and (5) specific plans for action developed by local inhabitants themselves, not by corporate or governmental outsiders. Delta County is aware at least to the extent that objective information reached citizens simultaneously and from the same source. Since miscommunication often exacerbates conflict, the Delta County project no doubt precluded much conflict for that reason alone. This community effort at anticipating problems and conflicts can create an environment conducive to cooperation and conflict resolution, in much the same way that "caring days" may do for a marriage in trouble (see Chapter 2).

Nevertheless, one cannot claim that this form of conflict anticipation necessarily reduces conflict. It could in some respects increase it. Awareness of a problem, while it is a prerequisite for cooperative solutions, is also a first stage in the emergence of a conflict. Potential conflict parties realize their divergent interests, where they may not have before, and set out to win. Whether awareness reduces or induces conflict in a particular case depends on how the intervention is structured.

Conflict-Warning Systems. Environmental policy planning can be structured to avoid policies that will generate conflict. Governmental agencies can use methods for needs assessment and values identification that will flag highly conflictual policy proposals before they go beyond preliminary consideration. Freeman (1977), working with the U.S. Forest

Service, has developed a method that combines a Delphi process to clarify conflicts among forest-user groups, with alternatives analysis. Each policy alternative that produces less rather than more polarization is comparatively judged by citizen panelists according to the number of future use options each would provide. The alternative producing the most options with the least conflict is selected.

Other federal agencies, such as the Water and Power Resources Service (WPRS) are experimenting with citizen participation in values and needs assessment through the imaging of alternative futures (Creighton, 1976). The State of Colorado has created the Joint Review Process (CDLA, 1976) in which proposals for substantial mining, energy facility siting, and winter recreation areas pass through a systematic review. This review provides early warning of conflict-ridden or environmentally unacceptable proposals before substantial proponent investment is made. Initial experience with the JRP has not been that promising, but it is far too early to evaluate it fairly. Researchers in the Environmental Conciliation Project at the University of Colorado have applied conflict-warning methods in two environmental disputes, one involving water impoundment, the other recreational development.

The Chikaskia Conflict. The first intervention was made in cooperation with WPRS in a decision concerning a proposed dam and reservoir on the Chikaskia River southwest of Wichita (Lord & Adelman, 1979). WPRS was deciding whether the project was the most feasible way to provide for Wichita's future water needs. It would inundate 17,000 acres of prime wheat land, displace 100 farm families, and disrupt the flow and riparian ecology of the only scenic river in Kansas (Fig. 10.2). On the other hand, the alternative, serving the projected water needs of Wichita from aquifers northwest of the city, would threaten irrigation farming there. WPRS analysis suggested that the dam and the pumping were the most cost-effective options. Alternatives to increasing the supply such as conservation, price restructuring, and recycling had been examined but not very seriously.

The University of Colorado conflict intervention team, composed of psychologists, sociologists, and an economist, entered the conflict at the invitation of the WPRS. The latter was in a serious bind, confronted by two hostile agricultural communities, urban water planners pressing for WPRS committment to a specific alternative, and environmental advocates. The agency had been considering the Chikaskia alternative in one form or another for 30 years or more and for that reason alone, if for no other, was leaning toward the Chikaskia option. While WPRS was genuinely interested in assistance from our team, it was unprepared for

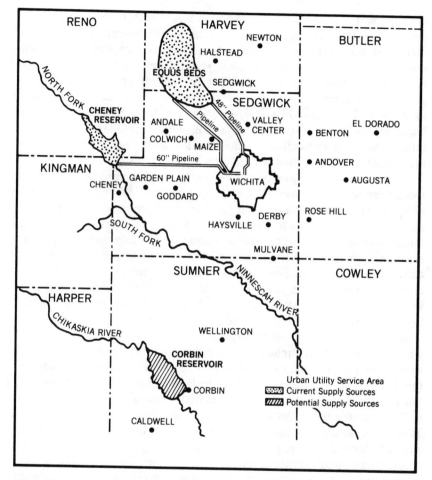

Fig. 10.2. Regional map showing existing and potential Wichita area water supplies.

Source: Lord & Adelman, 1979, p. 42, reprinted by permission.

the substantial changes and delay in its planning procedures and schedule that our intervention strategy would require.

The team first set about mapping the conflict, using interviews with representatives of major parties, press accounts, and reports from various government agencies. A map was drafted, shared with those interviewed, and corrected according to their feedback.

There were four primary parties in the conflict, each with well-defined interests. The *irrigation farmers* northwest of Wichita opposed any plan that would draw down the Equus Beds aquifer, the pumping from which is the lifeblood of the intensive, multicropping agriculture practiced in the region. These farmers saw a serious threat both to their rural way of life and to their substantial investment in equipment and land, from increased pumping by Wichita. They claimed that such an increase would permit the intrusion of saline water from the west, which would permanently contaminate the aquifer for agriculture. Their claim was ultimately validated by hydrological modeling done at the University of Kansas. The irrigation farmers were organized into a regional ground water management district and had considerable influence. Their basic interest was the protection of their fresh water source, their economic investments, and a valued way of life.

The *dryland wheat farmers* to the southwest felt more threatened still, since they would be physically displaced by the Corbin reservoir. Many of the families had been on their land for four generations. These wheat farmers were allied with commercial interests in nearby towns whose businesses depend on agricultural production. In addition to a threat to economic security and their rural way of life, these people were deeply concerned about what they refer to as the "common sense issue." The county in question has some of the most productive wheat land in the world. If the Corbin Dam should be built, 17,000 acres of it would be beneath a reservoir with an average depth of perhaps six feet. They claim the annual evaporation loss from the reservoir would exceed the water storage gained annually from damming the river. Regardless of the validity of such claims, they reflect the lack of respect this group had for the water development people. The dryland farmers were well organized but far fewer in number than the irrigated farming interests to the north.

Water development interests were the third party—WPRS, the Wichita Water Department, and Sedgewick County officials. Engineers and planners for the most part, this group was strongly motivated to produce conventional solutions to water supply problems. They held the levers of governmental power, even by controlling citizen input through public hearings. These men had a mission to perform and were determined to do so with as little controversy and as much public support as possible. Yet, the methods of conflict management that had worked for federal water engineers for more than half a century—credibility of experts, monetary compensation, building a consensus through distributive politics, persuasion—were no longer working. The era of citizen participation and revolt was upon them.

The fourth party grouped the *environmental, wildlife, and scenic river interests* in the state. These included state and federal wildlife agencies, urban environmental organizations, and hunting and fishing associations. Since the Chikaskia is Kansas' only free-flowing scenic river and provides many miles of riparian wildlife habitat, the interests of this party were self-evident.

Issues. The influential issues in this conflict were many and illustrative of the mapping scheme in Figure 10.1. To begin with, there were serious empirical questions that remained unanswered. Were the population growth projections for metropolitan Wichita accurate? These provided the basis for the predicted future water needs. All parties except the water developers pursued that issue.

All parties were likewise concerned about the aquifer drawdown that would result from both sinking additional wells and increased pumping by the City of Wichita. Unknowns included the actual rate of recharge of the aquifer through surface percolation, how much saline water would intrude from the periphery of the aquifer, and how much of that contamination the aquifer could tolerate and still produce usable agricultural water.

A third facts-based issue concerned the unknown degree to which wildlife and fishlife in and along the river would be adversely affected by the dam and reservoir. This concerned areas upstream of the dam, which would be inundated, and downstream from it, where the river's flow would be modified. The size of fish and wildlife populations and habitat area were unknown at that point. Would the reservoir boundaries produce sufficient replacement habitat?

Though facts-based issues seemed to receive the most attention from government officials, it was apparent to the careful observer that serious *value* differences between conflict parties and individuals were exacerbating the conflict. There was the classic opposition of natural resource conservation on the one hand and urban growth on the other. Interestingly enough, this did not divide parties along urban and rural agricultural lines of demarcation. Dryland farmers and urban-based environmentalists agreed that if nonconstruction alternatives for supplying water for urban growth could not be found, that the values of conservation of agricultural land, wildlife habitat, scenic waterways, and a rural way of life should all take precedence over urban growth. Opponents of the Corbin alternative claimed that building the dam would encourage urban growth rather than respond to it. In other words, they said, if the water is available, markets for it will be more likely to develop—the self-fulfilling prophecy. The general conservation value active in this dispute was conversely set against waste of any sort— waste of productive farmland through flooding, waste implied in current Wichita water policy which consistently looks for more supply rather than using present supply more efficiently, waste of federal funds on water projects that do not produce sufficient return on the investment. Countering these values were the preferences of the water developers for structural solutions to water problems, supported by values of (1) the predominance of specialized expertise, (2) the inherent goodness of demographic, economic, and industrial expansion, and (3) the responsibility of urban government to provide adequate services for its population.

The *communication* aspects of the conflict were very prominent. Stereotypes were extremely well developed among the different parties with perhaps the most clear being the images of the slick urban planner well trained in achieving objectives honestly or dishonestly, the backward-looking farmer who won't listen to reason, the federal bureaucrat meddling in people's lives, and the rabid environmentalist or "dicky bird watcher" standing in the way of progress. High levels of mutual suspicion and sense of threat reinforced the stereotyping that extended further to confuse the factual issues.

Finally, divergence of *interests* fueled the dispute. The dryland farmers threatened by inundation with the Corbin Dam alternative would lose their homes, farms, communities, livelihoods, and a highly valued way of life. Monetary compensation, whatever the level, was not a reasonable exchange for such a loss in the view of these people. They felt that they were "fighting for their very lives," as one of them expressed it. To a somewhat lesser degree, the irrigation farmers to the north perceived a similar threat. Though physical elimination of their farms was not a prospect, they saw economic disaster as a likely consequence of Wichita's increased pumping. This perception of one's personal existence being threatened is the most powerful interest imaginable.

For the urban planners, water engineers, and federal officials involved, mission accomplishment appeared to be the most influential interest. For some, that accomplishment would mean career advancement, for others enhanced prestige in the profession. More important, perhaps, was a sense of duty; they are trained and paid to solve that problem, and their training leads them inevitably to structural solutions. Reinforcing that strong sense of mission was the momentum toward closure in the decisional process. The engineers had been studying the problem for years, felt that they had thoroughly studied all feasible alternatives, and that they would make a wise decision.

A third major set of interests centered in environmental protection. The coalition of specialized interests included government agencies such as the U.S. Fish and Wildlife Service, whose professional mission is to preserve nonhuman populations and their habitats, environmental groups such as the Sierra Club, whose avocational interest is similar, outdoor recreation professionals, and sportsmen of various shades and hues.

The conflict management method designed by the University of Colorado team to resolve the conflict included three elements: (1) the mapping of citizen values; (2) the identification of all alternative solutions to the Wichita water supply problem; and (3) the judging by technical experts of the likely social and environmental impacts of each alternative.

A panel of citizen judges was selected from each of the communities most directly impacted by proposals—the dryland wheat farmers to the south, the irrigation farmers to the north, and Wichita residential and industrial water users. Each group of impactees would provide a panel that would judge the desirability of a number of alternative *futures*, and in so doing would reflect the value priorities of its group. A panel of technical experts would examine each alternative proposed and would judge its probable effects on each of the communities. It would also evaluate which alternative might best meet the composite values and interests priorities of the potential impactees.

This approach could indicate which of the alternative policies would be most conflictual—naturally that which most severely disadvantaged one or more of the impacted communities. It could tell us, as well which would produce the fewest conflicts—probably that which would spread the costs and benefits most evenly across these communities and would contradict values least. This method would address social, environmental, and economic costs equitably, something which current procedures do not permit.

Alternative ways of supplying the future water demands, which the conflict map identified included, in addition to the Corbin Dam and increased pumping from the Equus Beds aquifer: (1) several smaller reservoirs on rivers already dammed, (2) recycling of nondomestic water in Wichita, (3) conservation policies such as price restructuring and consumer education, and (4) pumping water from the Chikaskia for storage in the Equus Beds for subsequent use in Wichita (Lord & Adelman, 1979).

The intervention team was not able to carry the test of its method to completion. Citizen value panels were selected, alternatives were identified, technical experts were approached for the technical panel, but the WPRS decisional process became closed to the research team when pressure for closure in favor of Corbin became too great. We had judged WPRS officials to be more open to nonconstruction alternatives than they actually were. The feasibility of a dam on the Chikaskia had been studied intermittently for nearly a half-century within WPRS and the political and administrative decisional processes had created an irresistible momentum toward closure. There was additional pressure from the Sedgewick County planning staff to select the Corbin option and get on with it.

In its final report on the Chikaskia intervention, the conflict management team suggested that the basic problem lay in the decisional procedures used by federal, state, and local water developers. Those procedures, termed by the team, a *descriptive* process, had worked well for many years in the past but given changes that have occurred in the past decade, now produce irreconcilable conflict more often than not (Table 10.1). The descriptive process limits the definition of the problem and the identification of possible solutions at an early point in the decision. This tends to close out of the decisions important constituencies (e.g., Chikaskia wheat farmers, Equus Beds irrigation farmers, fish and wildlife interests). The team suggested an *analytic* decisional mode to replace current procedures. This, we felt, would reduce conflict by involving all relevant parties in defining the problem and selecting an alternative solution which best matched the values and interests of those who would be impacted.

The Adam's Rib Dispute. Values mapping to identify citizen preferences on environmental policy was used in a somewhat different way in a dispute over a proposal to build a ski resort in a pristine mountain valley in the Colorado Rockies (Rohrbaugh & Wehr, 1978). When the research team intervened, opponents and proponents were already organizing for a protracted struggle. The county commissioners were responsible for accepting or rejecting the proposal but had no clear sense of how the project's impacts would fit with citizen value preferences. A values survey was made of a representative sample of the county's population using respondent judgments of the desirability of alternative futures for the county. Analysis of the results produced a values map, with six clusters of respondents, each suggesting a different value profile. Descriptions of these profiles and the size of each profile group were made available to county officials. This information would respond to two questions the commissioners should ask. How would the impacts from the resort fit with the composite county value profile? Would development of the project tend to divide or to integrate the county as a political unit?

Additionally, the value profiles were used by the research team to select a values-representative panel of citizens who had been interviewed in the survey. This panel met in a series of sessions to examine the likely positive and negative impacts of the project for nearby towns, ranches, and forests. The panel was to consider all relevant information, to reach consensus on the advisability of the project, and to report its conclusions to county policy makers. Before this process could be completed, however, the Governor of Colorado announced his opposition to the ski area largely because of the intense conflict surrounding it, and both the decision and the conflict were suspended.

As in the Chikaskia case, the team entered the dispute too late, after proponents had already invested too much in the proposal. Had we been able to intervene earlier with values mapping as a conflict-warning device, the developer could have assessed the potential conflict in good

Table 10.1 Comparison of Analytic and Descriptive Versions of the Planning Processes.

CHARACTERISTIC	ANALYTIC VERSION	DESCRIPTIVE VERSION
Problem Definition		
1) Timing	Redefinition throughout process	Initial definition soon becomes inflexible
2) Nature	Open	Restricted by agency expertise
3) Participants	All those potentially affected	Interest-agency-politician alliance only
Establishment of Objectives		
1) Timing	Redefinition and augmentation throughout process	Initial objective largely predetermined
2) Nature	Multiple	Water development only
3) Participants	All those potentially affected	Water users only
Consideration of Alternatives		
1) Timing of identification	Any time after objective established	Any time, although those defined early are considered more thoroughly
2) Nature	Open to any alternatives potentially affecting objectives	Confined to those which meet water supply objective, biased towards federally subsidized alternatives, limited to mission of Federal water agency
3) Participants	All those potentially affected	All those potentially affected

Source: Lord & Adelman, 1979, p. 63, reprinted by permission.

467

time to seek another site. The U.S. Forest Service, squarely in the middle of the controversy, would have welcomed such a forecast.

Values mapping as a method of conflict anticipation has definite limitations. It is for use only in the early stages of conflicts or for before they actually surface. Its function is to forecast and to help avoid them. While values mapping is most effective in the early stages of policy making, it is difficult to gain entry to that process unless a conflict is already visible and officials are desperate for assistance. In addition, values mapping can be costly and its results may be only temporarily valid since values change over time. Such limitations notwithstanding, this technique has a contribution to make.

We have examined some methods of conflict intervention now being applied to environmental controversy. Mediation, compensation, assessment, and litigation are all useful at certain stages of certain types of conflict. If an ounce of prevention is really worth a pound of cure, however, anticipatory methods of conflict management could be more effective than more conventional techniques. Conflict anticipation could permit economies of time, money, and energy. Communities better equipped, as Delta County is now, to forecast impacts of resource exploitation, and to be aware of alternative strategies to ensure the economic and environmental well-being of its citizens, can handle conflict more effectively.

Government agencies which make and implement environmental and natural resource policy should be giving more attention to anticipatory conflict management. In particular, federal agencies—the Bureau of Land Management, the U.S. Forest Service, the Water and Power Resources Service, the Department of Energy—should be investing more heavily in research that builds conflict anticipation into their policy structures. Values mapping, alternatives analysis, citizen alternative futures planning, and other anticipatory methods should be early-stage components of policy making.

A central goal of resource management policy must be a balance of ecological and economic well-being for local populations, bioregions, and the nation. Conflict anticipation may help suggest in the early stages of planning which policy alternative is most likely to produce that broader well-being.

CONCILIATING IN RACIAL AND ETHNIC CONFLICT

Third party intervention has been increasingly used in conflicts characterized by racial and ethnic tension. In such conflict the interests and values in contention, real as they may be, tend to be overshadowed by the effective dimensions of the conflict—the hatred, the miscommunication, the sheer emotion. Intervenors in racial and ethnic disputes often concentrate on methods that we have called *conciliation*—getting the conflict parties to agreement that each has a right to exist—then to negotiate conflicting interests and values.

Much pioneering work in conciliation has been done in American communities over the past two decades by federal agencies (e.g., Community Relations Service, U.S. Department of Justice; Federal Mediation and Conciliation Service) and a few private organizations (e.g., National Center for Dispute Settlement; Institute for Mediation and Conflict Resolution). A lesser-known but nevertheless significant effort has occurred through transnational intervention teams formed to intervene in particularly intractable intercommunal disputes. Interventions in Cyprus and South Africa will serve to illustrate this approach.

Before the invasion of Cyprus by the Turkish Army in 1974, it appeared that nongovernmental third party intervention might facilitate the resolution of conflict between the Greek and Turkish sides that had existed since 1963. By contrast, before the wave of Black protest in South Africa beginning with the Soweto riots in 1976, there seemed to be little call for nonviolent conflict resolution. In fact many would assert that the Sharpville incident in 1960, when police fired on demonstrators, killing 69 and wounding 180, had effectively put an end to nonviolent protest, and with it a role for third party conflict resolution.

The comparison of Cyprus and South Africa is not complete since the Greek and Turkish communities on Cyprus remain open to initiatives, although it may be harder to find common cause. Also, work was being done in South Africa before Soweto, which formed a basis for contact among the various ethnic groups. The main point is that just as those who seek violent revolution continually try to "make the revolution," hoping that each time that the conditions will be right and their spark will light the fire, so those who wish to bring about nonviolent revolutionary change will find that public opinion and other circumstances are more auspicious at some times than at others.

The open conflict between Greek and Turk in Cyprus has a longer history than that between White and Black in South Africa. There are, however, some similarities. For example, in both we find that democracy and majority rule are not an arrangement acceptable to all parties. In each case, too, there is a nationalism that is not inclusive of all population segments. There are some differences as well. For instance, the United Nations has intervened in the Cyprus conflict and has maintained a physical presence there for many years. Although the United Nations has the right to intervene directly in the South West Africa case, it has not done so.

One seeking to finance a third party team to work on these two conflicts encounters different responses from foundations and other concerned agencies. They *understand* why one would want to work on Cyprus, but think the problem is *not important*. With respect to South Africa, the agencies agree that the problem is *important* but do *not understand* why one would want to go there to work on it.

The Model

A model for third party intervention was proposed by the founders of the World Peace Brigade in 1962 (Walker, 1977). An international group of volunteers was recruited to be on standby status, to provide a presence in a conflict situation anywhere in the world. Members of the Brigade were involved in only two actions before interest in and financial support for the project waned. The first action was to participate in the organization of a mass march of Africans in support of Zambian independence (Walker, 1977). The second was to support, through the presence of several members, the team monitoring the ceasefire in the Nagaland region of India over a period of many years (Aram, 1974).

The largest body of experience in third party intercommunal conflict resolution comes from India, especially from the work of the Shanti Sena (Desai, 1972, 1977). The Shanti Sena, or Peace Brigade, evolved out of the Gandhian movement and trains teams to intervene directly in intercommunal violence involving different castes, Hindus and Muslims, and other antagonistic groups. Intervention techniques include conciliation, medical and other services to all groups involved, and the dispatching of individual Shanti Seniks to towns and villages as resident peacemakers and development workers.

At the time of the Bangladesh crisis in 1971, after observing the work of the Shanti Sena in the refugee camps in India, Narayan Desai, Charles Walker, and A. Paul Hare agreed that its activity could provide a model for other national and international projects. Desai was then the director of Shanti Sena and Walker, a Quaker with long experience in nonviolent direct action, had written the first training manual on the subject (Walker, 1961). Later, these three were members of the first third party team on Cyprus. There, President Makarios was especially interested in Desai's experience with nonviolence in India—Desai had grown up in Gandhi's ashrams while his father was Gandhi's personal secretary. In South Africa, Walker and Hare also joined Cape Town Quakers in their consideration of the Shanti Sena model. This led to the formation of an ambulance unit.

Activities of the World Peace Brigade, the Shanti Sena, and other similar approaches to third party intervention are described in *Libera-*

tion Without Violence: A Third Party Approach (Hare and Blumberg, 1977). The cases are grouped into four categories according to whether the intervenors are (1) primarily nationals working in their own country, (2) a transnational team involved in another country, and whether their role is primarily (3) partisan or (4) nonpartisan.

The principles of third party intervention are very much the same no matter what the composition of the team and its degree of partiality. The approach used in the Cyprus and South Africa interventions can be summarized in the four guidelines used by the team:

1. Use consensus as a decision rule both within the team and in reaching decisions with the first and second parties (i.e., find non-zero-sum solutions to problems so that all parties derive some benefit).
2. Compose a team with the requisite skills for the aspect of the conflict with which they will be concerned.
3. Involve all relevant levels of society and government in the planning and execution of the work.
4. Include the conditions, time, and mode of team withdrawal in the initial planning.

Finding creative solutions through consensus often requires more information about the problem than the opposing sides will present in briefing the third party. Representatives of the parties may well have been trained in or influenced by law and will tend to use the adversary method that forms the basis of legal procedure. Each side gives the facts to back up its own case. Neither side may say anything that is untrue. It is, rather, that some true facts may be omitted which, if known, would lead to a different conclusion. Then too, the parties involved may not have all the facts, especially those that emphasize their common concerns. "Gandhi's truth," as Erikson (1969) has noted, was based not so much upon the facts about the ways people behave in the present but on the ways they might behave in the future when they had discovered more just and equitable solutions for their common problems.

Interventions: Cyprus and South Africa

On Cyprus, a "direct approach" was used when in 1972 the first of several transnational nonpartisan teams were brought together to explore third party intervention possibilities (Hare and Wilkinson, 1977). The time and place for the intervention was suggested by International Peace Academy staff who had served with the United Nations forces and thought that a civilian initiative might supplement the work of those forces (Harbottle, 1978). With a United Nation's force of up to 7,000 in Cyprus since 1963, in addition to specialists involved in United Nation's development projects, it would seem that an additional 5 to 20 persons might make little difference as third parties dealing with local problems.

This was not the case, however, for several reasons. Excepting a few high-ranking officers, U.N. soldiers in Cyprus served six-month tours of duty and personnel at observation posts in the villages were rotated every two weeks to avoid fatigue. Thus, it was difficult for U.N. personnel to help find solutions to problems requiring continuity of approach over time. In addition, problems at the village level were handled by the U.N. Military Police, at the provincial level by the seven U.N. Force Economic Officers, and at the national level by the U.N. Head of Mission and the U.N. Political Officer. Thus, any problem involving several levels of society was dealt with by different personnel. No one set of persons had direct experience with a problem at all levels. Rather, U.N. representatives had to rely on reports and briefings for their facts and impressions. Also, the U.N. staff had to respond to a wide range of issues while the transnational team could focus on one issue as a first step in working out a method for reconciliation of the Greek and Turkish sides. At the suggestion of Mr. Osorio-Tafall, then U.N. Head of Mission, the teams first helped with the resettlement of displaced Turkish persons in their villages, a project that had support in principle from both sides. Given its relatively narrow focus, with the assistance of Greek and Turkish officials, the "Cyprus Resettlement Project" gathered more information about the housing needs of the displaced Turks in a few months than the U.N. forces had been able to collect over a period of years.

One of the minor problems the intervention team solved on Cyprus, which illustrates the consensus method, concerned the issue of "trouble makers." As noted earlier, both the Greek and Turkish sides agreed "in principle" that Turks should be resettled in their villages. The U.N. representatives had urged the reconstruction of houses for many years but without success.

Various problems had to be solved before building could begin. Greek officials maintained that there were Turkish "trouble makers" who would agitate in the villages while Turks were being moved back in. After hearing a Greek statement of the problem, the team went to the Turkish sector of Nicosia, through the military checkpoint, to suggest a possible solution. "How would it be," team members asked, "if the Turkish 'trouble makers' were not allowed to return to the villages?" "No," said the Turks, "we cannot have any of our people 'branded' as 'trouble makers'." The team returned to the Greek side to try again and was told that the "trouble makers" were only a problem when the villagers were first moving back. After most people had returned to a village, the "trouble makers" would have little influence.

By this time the team had surveyed the deserted Turkish villages and empty Turkish quarters in formerly mixed villages and knew how many houses were destroyed or damaged. It also had estimates of repair costs and knew that the Greeks would have difficulty funding a complete rehabilitation of the Turks. In fact, both sides had agreed that it would be enough to start in a few villages. The team suggested to the Greeks that, instead of rebuilding a smaller number of villages completely, they begin by rebuilding half of the houses in a large number of villages. In this way, once they were given a complete list of the Turks who wished to return, the Greeks could designate the families to move in first without having to identify a small set of families likely to cause trouble. The Greeks thought this might work, the Turks agreed, and the team had a solution. No Turks need be branded "trouble makers" and the Greeks need not actually identify those "trouble makers" said by them to be preventing the return of the Turks for so many years.

In South Africa, by contrast, an "indirect approach" was used. Several years before the 1976 Soweto incidents, Bob Steyn and Paul Hare had proposed to the South African Government that a special corps be established that might intervene in time of natural or social crises. In addition, the corps would provide the opportunity for alternative service for conscientious objectors to war. The proposal was not accepted. Nor had the proposers any luck in recruiting members of the Indian community who, inspired perhaps by Gandhi's campaigns in South Africa, might form the basis for a version of the Shanti Sena. Hare was told that there were no Gandhians left in South Africa.

Many of the protest demonstrations in South African cities in the weeks following the unrest in Soweto were completely nonviolent and were carried out without police interference. Others were nonviolent only until the riot police arrived, and still others included violence from the outset. A common form of violence in the Cape Town area involved stoning cars of whites along highways in or near black areas. On these occasions being white was enough to draw hostility from crowds. Early in the Soweto rioting a white social worker had been hacked to death as he sought to find some peaceful resolution to the conflict. The victim was known professionally for his understanding of the problems of black youth and had published a book on the subject. Apparently, these facts were either not known or not considered by his attackers.

It was evident that in South Africa an "indirect approach" was warranted for at least two reasons. On the government side, it was assumed that the riot police and other agencies of law and order would supply the necessary control in situations of conflict. On the side of the black population, interventions by well-meaning whites would have to be clearly understood. Apparently, blacks expected little help from the white quarter. Whites in general were being seen more as part of the problem than the solution.

In the Cyprus intervention, volunteers were recruited largely from organizations with long experience in consensus and other methods—for example, the Quakers in the United States and England, and the Shanti Sena in India. In South Africa as well, the Quakers supplied ideas and volunteers. As Hare and Steyn discussed possible responses to the unrest with Cape Town Quakers, medical professionals serving in local hospitals suggested that help might be needed to transport and treat blacks injured in the disturbances. The tradition of the Friends Ambulance Units (The formal name of the Quakers is The Religious Society of Friends) in World War II was recalled. It had been a form of alternative national service for conscientious objectors. The group then proceeded to organize and to raise money for an ambulance unit, hoping to have three vehicles supported by teams of drivers and persons trained in first aid. Ultimately, funds were found for only one vehicle, but this was sufficient to provide some aid in a crisis and to serve as a model for future operations.

For over a year the Friends Ambulance served various African and colored communities and squatter areas. During this period, one series of events exemplifies the third party service that was possible. As Christmas 1976 approached, the African students in the Cape Town area decided that it should be celebrated as a day of mourning for the students killed earlier by the police. Black families in the segregated areas near Cape Town cooperated. No Christmas cards were sent, no presents exchanged, and on Christmas day people wore black and many attended a memorial service in the local cemetery. There was one notable exception to this mass protest. The single men living in barracks for migrant laborers did not want to interrupt their Christmas holiday which provided a few days for drinking and relaxation. When the students went to reason with these men, they were attacked, as were the homes of some of the families supporting the demonstration. The police were called but did not arrive until injuries had occurred and 187 homes had been partially or wholly burned. Unfortunately, when the police did arrive and interposed themselves, they gave the appearance of siding with the men from the singles quarters.

Although no whites other than government officials, police, and possibly press were allowed in the area at the time, the Friends Ambulance was on the scene, manned by two black members of the committee who lived in the area. They gave some people first aid and took others to clinics and hospitals. Later, when members of some of the white churches donated food and clothing to the families who had lost their homes, the ambulance transported the relief supplies from the white churches to the distribution points within the black community. Still later, a white organization was prepared to construct prefabricated houses as temporary shelters for the displaced families. It wanted to erect one in a black area so that residents could decide if this type of temporary accommodation was suitable. But some of the white members of the organization were unable to obtain passes from the police since a report it had published earlier on housing conditions for blacks was judged to be unfavorable to the government. Black members of the intervention committee used the ambulance to recruit and transport black youths to help erect the sample home. Since Hare had a pass allowing him to enter the area at any time, he was also able to participate.

Once basic needs were met, the intervenors discovered through their responding to crisis that other community services, such as roads, lighting, and shopping areas, also needed attention. Since improvements in these areas would require governmental decisions, they arranged for discussions between black community spokesmen and white Members of Parliament. As the intervenors had hoped, once they found a way to be on the scene at a time of crisis, other possibilities for third party intervention presented themselves. Since that time, the ambulance unit has been used for more routine medical transportation. Persons from the black areas near Cape Town who are not entitled to government medical transport, and who cannot afford private transportation, are driven to clinics and hospitals. The drivers of the vehicles are prepared to take part in third party intervention once again should the need arise.

Two examples of third party resolution of racial and ethnic conflict have been discussed. On Cyprus between 1972 and 1974, a direct approach was used by a transnational team working toward reconciliation of Greeks and Turks through resettlement of displaced Turks. In South Africa after 1976, an indirect approach was used by providing services for the black community, especially through the formation of an ambulance unit to operate in riot-affected areas.

In both cases the example of the Shanti Sena of India guided the approach with information and inspiration. In both cases the intervenors chose a humanitarian problem as point of entry into the conflict situation. Two aspects of third party intervention have been illustrated: on Cyprus the use of consensus in decision making, and in South Africa the multilevel, multifaceted resolution approaches needed to deal with the complexities of intercommunal conflict.

CONCLUSION

We have examined four major aspects of conflict intervention: conflict mapping, diverse intervention strategies, conflict anticipation, and conciliation. Understanding the dynamics, structure, and other characteristics of a conflict can be done effectively by mapping it. The most efficient strategy for resolving it is that which responds adequately to its factual, values, communication, and interests dimensions.

Certain approaches to third party intervention have been more highly developed than others. Interposition is used to stop or preclude physical conflict. Mediation involves a third party as intermediary who facilitates negotiation and bargaining between the disputants. Arbitration, on the other hand, places the responsibility for producing a settlement not on the disputants but on the third party acting as judge. Empowerment to equalize the power relationship in a conflict, communication enhancement to clarify issues and perceptions of disputants, and aggression reduction techniques were also discussed as intervention modes.

We emphasized most heavily two intervention approaches that are less well known but have developed rapidly in recent years. Conflict anticipation, particularly as it is being tested in environmental disputes, involves neutral third party intervention to moderate or avoid future conflict. Anticipation includes such techniques of intervention as third party involvement in a potential conflict situation, conflict-warning devices such as values mapping and judgment analysis, and the restructuring of decisional modes to involve significant constituencies in defining the problem and its possible solutions.

Finally, we discussed conciliation applied in racial and ethnic conflict. Cyprus and South Africa were the cases examined, conflicts in which intergroup animosity is a major obstacle to conflict resolution. In both cases, multinational or multiracial teams, operating by consensus and working with different levels of government, intervened as conciliators. As neutrals, using their ability to perform useful functions for those in need of an important service such as housing or medical care, team members made a significant contribution to moderating at least local segments of the larger conflict.

In closing, we should note that among the most important skills of the third party intervenor is that of patience. Settlement may be a long-delayed payoff. In fact, it may never come in a recognizable form. The intervention team in Cyprus was not successful in 1973 when the strengths of the Greek and Turkish communities were grossly disparate. Since the Turkish invasion, which equalized that strength, the personal contacts and traditions of conciliation initiated by the team have facilitated progress toward intercommunal tolerance and coexistence. We are not suggesting here that one may need a war in order to make peace, only that conflict intervention may not always provide the intervenor with an immediate result. This is especially true where conflict is characterized by deep-seated animosities and mutual mistrust.

REFERENCES

Aram, M. *Peace in Nagaland.* New Delhi: Arnold-Heineman, 1974.

Boulding, K. *Conflict and defense.* New York: Harper & Row, 1962.

Burton, J. *Conflict and communication.* New York: Free Press, 1969.

Colorado Department of Local Affairs. *Manual for the Colorado review process.* Denver, August, 1976.

Commoner, B. *The closing circle.* New York: Knopf, 1971.

Cormick, G. & Patton, L. "Environmental mediation: Potentials and limitations," *Environmental Comment,* May, 1977.

Creighton, J. *Alternative futures planning.* Denver: U.S. Bureau of Reclamation, August, 1976.

Dedring, J. *Recent advances in peace and conflict research.* Beverly Hills, Calif.: Sage, 1976.

Desai, N. *Towards a nonviolent revolution.* Rajghat, Varanasi, India: Sarva Seva Sangh Prakashan, 1972.

Desai, N. Intervention in Riots in India. In A. Hare & H. Blumberg (Eds.), *Liberation without violence.* London: Rex Collings, 1977.

Douglas, A. *Industrial peacemaking.* New York: Columbia University Press, 1962.

Erikson, E. *Gandhi's truth: On the origins of militant nonviolence.* New York: Norton, 1969.

Freeman, D., Tremaine, J., & Madson, P. Social well-being: A conflict approach. *Journal of Environmental Management,* 1977, **5**, October, 319–332.

Gladwin, T. The management of environmental conflict: A survey of research approaches and priorities. Graduate School of Business Administration, New York University, #78–09, Working Paper Series, mimeo, 1978.

Hammond, K. & Adelman, L. Science, values and human judgment. *Science,* 1974, **194**, 22 October, 389–396.

Harbottle, M. "Peacekeeping, peacemaking, peace building: A multi-professional experience in nonviolent action," *Social Dynamics,* 1978, **4**, 1 June, 17–34.

Hare, A. & Blumberg, H. (Eds.). *Liberation without violence: A third party approach.* London: Rex Collings, 1977.

Hare, A. & Wilkinson, E. Cyprus: Conflict and its resolution. In A. Hare & H. Blumberg (Eds.), *Liberation without violence.* London: Rex Collings, 1977.

Lake, L. (Ed.) *Environmental mediation: The search for consensus.* Boulder, Colo.: Westview Press, 1980.

Laue, J. & Cormick, G. *The ethics of social intervention: Community crisis intervention programs.* St. Louis: University of Missouri, Urban Center, 1976.

Laue, J. Training and research in community conflict intervention: Current status. Department of Sociology, Washington University, St. Louis, Mimeo, 1976.

Lord, W. & Adelman, L. *Conflict management in federal water resource planning.* Monograph #28, Program on Technology, Environment and Man. Boulder, Colo.: Institute of Behavioral Science, University of Colorado, 1979.

Lovins, A. *Soft energy paths: Toward a durable peace.* Cambridge: Ballinger, 1977.

Mernitz, S. *Mediation of environmental disputes*, RESOLVE, 360 Bryant St., Palo Alto, Calif., 94301, 1980.

Murray, F. (Ed.). *Where we agree: Report of the national coal policy project*. Vols. I and II. Boulder, Colo.: Westview Press, 1978.

O'Hare, M. "Not on my block you don't: Facility siting and the strategic importance of compensation." *Public Policy*, 1977, **25** (4). 13–17.

Rikhye, I., Harbottle, M., & Egge, B. *The thin blue line: International peacekeeping and its future*. New Haven: Yale University Press, 1974.

Rohrbaugh, J. & Wehr, P. "Judgment analysis in policy formation: A new method for improving public participation." *Public Opinion Quarterly*, 1978, **42**, 521–532.

Schonborn, K. *Dealing with violence*. Springfield, Ill.: Charles C. Thomas, 1975.

Walker, C. *Organizing for nonviolent direct action*. Cheney, Penn.: C. C. Walker, 1961.

Walker, C. Nonviolence in East Africa 1962–1964: The World Peace Brigade and Zambian independence. In A. Hare & H. Blumberg (Eds.), *Liberation without violence*. London: Rex Collings, 1977.

Wehr, P. *Conflict regulation*. Boulder, Colo.: Westview Press, 1979.

Chapter 11
Aggressive Nonviolence*
Paul Wehr

Many events occur in social and international relations for which the natural collective response is an aggressive one. Unprovoked attack by a neighboring nation-state naturally evokes aggressive behavior in one's own self-defense. Colonial occupation eventually brought about an openly aggressive reaction from the colonized population. Repression of peoples by their own despotic regimes, or of minorities by majority governments, likewise calls forth at the least, aggressive feelings if not in fact aggressive behavior in the repressed.

In situations where entire classes, peoples, even nations are subjected to violence and restriction, the range of healthy behavioral responses that the underdogs can safely employ may be narrow indeed. Passivity and submission may be effective initially but the psychological costs and ultimately the physical risks of them are great. Witness the disastrous consequences of the fascist conquest and occupation of Europe.

On the other hand, a violent aggressive response, as finally developed in colonial Algeria and Indochina, may result in great harm to those who resist. Even where violent resistance ultimately triumphs, the human costs and the legacy of trauma may be so great that future societal and personal health is seriously impaired, as we have seen in both Indochina and Algeria.

The development of nonviolent aggressive response to violent aggression may be one way to broaden the range of response options beyond those of submission and violent aggression. Such a response will not always be suitable or effective. But if human survival depends on our maximizing adaptive responses to crisis, we should not ignore its potential usefulness.

---

*Research for this paper was supported by a fellowship from the North Atlantic Treaty Organization.

RESEARCH ON NONVIOLENCE

In the past two decades, violence and its nonviolent alternatives have been the focus of research by a growing number of social scientists and humanists. One branch of this research has concentrated on the costs of violent aggression. Quincy Wright's (1965) monumental study of the social costs of war is a benchmark work. Internal violence organized by and against the state has also proven to be extremely costly (Schonborn, 1975; Gurr, 1970). The degree to which state-perpetrated violence can be legitimized is illustrated in the genocide policies of the Nazis. It can even be "sanitized," one learns from a careful reading of the *Pentagon Papers*.

A second group of researchers has concerned itself with nonviolence as a social psychological process. In the microview, nonviolent action is a dyadic or small group process and can be studied as such (Hare and Blumberg, 1968). Bondurant's (1965) classic analysis of Gandhian nonviolence clearly outlined the aggressive and coercive elements within the Gandhian method when it was translated into a political movement. Viewing that method even more microscopically, Erikson (1969) showed us how that nonviolence emerged from the contained aggressive impulses that Gandhi was struggling to control within himself. What we know of nonviolence leads us to conclude that it is, or at least that it can be, as aggressive a form of social interaction as other forms.

Finally, a substantial number of European social scientists are studying the potential of nonviolent action as a strategy for national defense. To what degree could planned unarmed civilian resistance to external attack be used to deter such an attack, or to resist an occupation successfully if it failed to deter? Sharp (1973) has provided us with the most complete history to date of nonviolent action, tracing its development over more than a millenium. Several studies of nonviolent movements resisting military occupation (Wehr, 1979(b); Keyes, 1978) add to our knowledge of resistance techniques possible under such conditions. Others have applied what we know of past nonviolent resistance to the present and future defense needs of such nations as Denmark (Boserup & Mack, 1975) and Sweden (Roberts, 1972). The consensus emerging from recent reviews of social or civilian defense problems and prospects is that nonviolent collective aggression against an invader is a serious concept, but is also one that needs a good deal more development before it can be applied in policy.

THE NATURE OF AGGRESSIVE NONVIOLENCE

What precisely is meant by the term aggressive nonviolence? For our purposes here it can be defined as defensive behavior having a hostile intent but using nonviolent means to achieve its goals. More often than not, this abstention from violence has at least three roots: (1) what seems to be a natural reluctance of humans, even those in military combat, to do physical injury to fellow humans not physically threatening them; (2) the lack of access to weapons of violence; and (3) the fear of retaliatory violence.

While there are often restrictions on a people's capacity and willingness to do violence when threatened or repressed, they nevertheless experience aggressive feelings. A threat to one's personal security and national institutions will inevitably generate psychological estrangement from and hostility toward those who threaten. While, as Blakely and Davidson note in Chapter 7, students of human behavior disagree about the origins of aggression, none would deny that one prepotent response to threat and repression is aggressive feelings, if not overt aggressive behavior. Such is the case with a population under military occupation. While aggressive feelings toward the occupiers is a normal response, that aggression must be acted out in such a way that it avoids reprisal, protects individuals and national institutions, and sustains individual and collective self-respect.

Aggressive nonviolence is one way of responding to state violence or societal repression. It has been particularly useful for racial and political minorities and for peoples under colonial domination or military occupation, in other words, adversaries with lesser military and political power. Usually, aggressive nonviolence practiced collectively is a response of last resort. The occupied or oppressed cannot safely respond otherwise. On occasion, as in the Gandhian movement, moral conviction and principled nonviolence play a central role. Usually, the natural aversion to do physical violence is involved. The "last resort" character of aggressive nonviolence, however, does not mean that it is less natural than aggressive violence. It may be, shall we say, only a less institutionalized response in social and international relations at this point in human development.

I wish to examine now an instance in which an entire population under military occupation developed some effective modes of aggressive nonviolence. The case of Denmark under German occupation in World War II can suggest for us some of the strengths and weaknesses of such a response.

THE DANISH RESISTANCE

On April 9, 1940, the Wehrmacht invaded Denmark to begin a military occupation of five years duration, and an effort to integrate Denmark culturally and militarily into the Third Reich. The effort failed primarily because of Danish civilian resistance.

Any resistance movement is a mix of paramilitary activity of an organized and often violent nature, and civilian resistance of a largely spontaneous and nonviolent sort. As a movement develops, these two activities become increasingly interdependent as repressive violence by the occupying forces drives them closer together. It is possible, for analytic purposes, however, to distinguish one from the other.

The Danish resistance is known outside of Denmark primarily for its spectacular paramilitary aspects, namely sabotage and political assassinations. The Danes themselves have unwittingly emphasized the violent aspects of the resistance, we would suggest, out of a sense of guilt for not having resisted more militantly and for cooperating too much with the Germans.

In actuality, the nonviolent civilian aspects of the resistance were as effective as the paramilitary ones in obstructing German objectives, though they have received much less attention. While the civilian resistance indirectly contributed to the Allied war effort, its primary function was the protection of Danish social and political institutions. I will concentrate, then, on the process by which this occurred and on the special role that communication played in it.

Benchmarks in the Resistance

There appears to have been little organized civilian resistance to the occupation before 1943. This was partly because Denmark's social and political institutions were not sufficiently threatened during the first years of the war. The nation had lost its sovereignty, of course, but the state remained intact under German tutelage and the occupiers interfered minimally in domestic affairs. As long as troop security and public order were maintained, the Danes were permitted to govern themselves under the limitations of military occupation. The Communist Party was outlawed and its leaders imprisoned following Denmark's signing of the Anti-Comintern Pact in 1941, but otherwise:

> A legal government, based upon still functioning parliamentary institutions, demanded from the people that they accept the situation and adapt themselves. . . . at the same time, economic conditions were relatively favorable, life had a semblance of normality, and the German soldiers behaved correctly. The psychological and political background for resistance was black in the extreme [Haestrup, 1960, p. 151].

While there occurred a gradual German encroachment on the powers of the Danish state before 1943, it was not until the government was forced to resign in August of that year that the Danes began to resist openly. A second reason for the lack of early resistance was the high level of technological and economic development in Denmark at the time. The nation had a vested interest in maintaining a high living standard and this could only be done through agreement not to oppose the occupation.

There is also an essential aspect of the Danish culture which moderated public response to the occupation. This is *hygge* or coziness—a dislike of disagreement, unpleasantness, and of course, even the suggestion of violence. All of these make Danes very nervous. They preferred to go along with the occupation with minimal resistance because it was more *hyggelig* to do so. Reasonableness seems to play an important role in the Danish ethos as well. Given the military situation in the first two years of the war, it seemed inevitable that the Third Reich would triumph. Danish resistance would be pointless and self-defeating.

It is hardly surprising that large numbers of people who were little affected directly by the occupation preferred to go about business as usual. Even in Holland, where national institutions were directly threatened from the beginning, most Dutch cooperated with the occupation and resisted in large numbers only when labor drafts began to threaten their personal security in 1943 (Warmbruun, 1963).

Another factor inhibiting resistance was, ironically, the tradition of legal passive resistance in Denmark. During the German occupation of southern Jutland after 1864, the local population mounted an effective legal resistance movement. This experience combined with a strong Danish attachment to observance of the law to encourage public accommodation with the occupiers. As long as Danish law was in force, even though it was often bent by the Germans to their own purposes, it was obeyed. Only gradually did the distinction between legality and a higher morality develop in the public mind. It was not until Danish law was replaced by German martial law that widespread resistance occurred.

A counterforce, though, constrained the people's acceptance of the Government's cooperation policy. For 80 years a Danish-German antagonism had developed over what Danes saw as German imperialistic policy in southern Jutland. The Danish government had waged a subtle campaign for years prior to 1940 to make Danes aware of historical instances in which they had stood against Germany. Without this, the accommodation policy of the Government might have been even more widely accepted than it was.

Early Resistance. There was some isolated resistance during the early years of the occupation growing out of the tradition of passive resistance cited above. Two political parties, both of which were later driven underground, encouraged active resistance from mid-1941 on. Both the

Communists and the Dansk Samling, the most radical of the legitimate opposition parties, openly criticized the government's cooperation policy and called for open resistance (Haestrup, 1963). These two organizations later supplied much of the leadership for active resistance, but in 1941 their demands were viewed with extreme skepticism by most Danes and as subversive by the Government. The Communists produced the first clandestine newspaper and their cell form of organization was later adopted by the resistance movement.

Two national religious organizations, the *Ungdomsamvirke* and the Council of Elders, encouraged early legal resistance to the occupation but in the most subtle ways. The *Ungdomsamvirke*, through its youth brigades, work camps, sports organizations, and cultural programs strengthened the national consciousness of Danish youth when Naziism and the idea of the greater German *volk* could have been attractive to them. The organization's leader, Hal Koch, wrote openly against Naziism and the occupation but criticized those groups urging illegal resistance as well. Through its member groups and national sports associations, *Ungdomsamvirke* discouraged fraternization with occupation forces and Danish Nazis (Poulsen and Nissen, 1963).

In another respect, however, the *Ungdomsamvirke* inhibited active resistance by counselling only resistance within the law. The police and labor leaders likewise encouraged support for the cooperation policy. Because of their concern for keeping resistance within Danish law, these groups, along with most Danes, opposed active resistance groups such as BOPA. The legalists and the activists never did successfully integrate their resistance. Even after the war, the passive resisters condemned the violence used by some activist groups.

Resistance Within the Government. One type of occupation resistance occurring before August, 1943 has been given little attention. This was the quiet defense of parliamentary and administrative institutions by politicians and civil servants within the framework of cooperation. Under the cooperation policy, Danish control over domestic affairs was an act of precarious balance. If the government resisted German demands too strenuously, the occupation high command would merely dismiss it and assume direct control of the state, with negative consequences for the Danes. By remaining in place, the government acted as a buffer, cushioning the effect of the occupation. The problem of legal jurisdiction is a case in point. The government agreed that German forces had extraterritorial status and that German soldiers would be judged by German courts. But it fought successfully for the judging of Danes by Danish authorities, even in cases involving hostile acts against Germans. In theory the Germans denied such jurisdiction though in practice they permitted it until 1942. In this way politico-administrative resistance protected Danes and their legal institutions to some degree. Nevertheless, stricter penalties for Danish crimes against occupation forces were demanded by the Germans.

A second form of governmental resistance involved the barring of Nazis from positions of power in the government and administration. There was no nazification of the state as had occurred in Norway although this was partly a consequence of the pitiful condition of the Danish Nazi party. The government resisted continuous German pressure to include Nazis. "Why," was the eternal question from Hitler's representatives, "if this is a coalition government, are there no Nazi members?"

Resistance also characterized the way civil servants performed their duties. Even after German authorities took control in 1943, many Danish officials continued in their posts and often frustrated occupier objectives. With few exceptions, one being the 1941 arrest of Communists in which Danish officials were disgracefully obliging, the government was as slow and unhelpful to the Germans as possible. Leaking information such as impending arrests and potential targets for sabotage, and slowing down orders that would hinder resistance was common. Many officials became skilled in unobtrusive obstruction, or what came to be known during the 1968 invasion of Czechoslovakia as "schweikism."[1]

During the last months of the occupation, civil servants became more open in their resistance, even to the extent of cooperating in several major sabotage actions. Relief efforts such as the export of prohibited parcels to Jews and Communists in prison camps were effectively hidden from the German authorities.

Officials resisted the cooperation policy in the economic sector as well. Every three months the German and Danish governments negotiated the amounts and prices of food and other products that Danish agriculture and industry would supply. At each negotiating session, the Danes had strong arguments why the nation could not possibly produce the amounts demanded. Such arguments inevitably forced a compromise. The Danish proposals were sometimes based on misleading or incomplete information. For example, the 1941–42 grain harvest was a poor one and the Danish proposal reflected this. The following year's substantial increase in production was concealed. By such methods Danish production for Germany was kept lower than it might otherwise have been.

Popular Discontent. While Danes remained politically quiescent during the first three years of the occupation, they did show their discontent with it and with the threat that Naziism posed to Danish society. It was common practice to isolate the occupiers socially, to treat them as if they did not exist. This was a demoralizing tactic. German greetings and salutes were not returned. German films, concerts, and other cultural events were poorly attended. Danes would often leave when Germans entered public places such as restaurants.

Social quarantine was more strictly enforced still with regard to Danish Nazis, who were forced to live more and more within their own ingrown circles. Non-Nazis who permitted their businesses to be used in the German war effort were somewhat less isolated. There developed an intensity scale of disapproval for acts of cooperation. Contributing to the German war effort in Denmark was viewed with less antagonism than was going to work in Germany, which in turn was more acceptable than going to Norway to work. In short, working directly for Germans was bad enough but helping them to oppress Nordic compatriots was contemptible.

An important act of civil disobedience occurred immediately after the German invasion. Most of the merchant marine fleet defected to the Allies, defying the legitimate but hardly independent government.

> From Copenhagen [the crews] were ordered to seek Danish, German-controlled or neutral harbors. From London they were called upon to join the Allied cause and go the nearest Allied harbor. For a great many of them the choice was quite open [Haestrup, 1964, p. 287].

One further example of nascent resistance in this early period were the *alsang* and *algang* movements. On July 4, 1940 the first mass singing event was held in Alborg (Haestrup, 1966). Within two months the activity had spread throughout Denmark. On one Sunday in September more than 700,000 persons were involved, perhaps a quarter of the population. The action was innocent enough. Citizens merely gathered to sing. The act of gathering itself, and the significance of the nationalistic songs that were sung caught the imagination of the entire population. Many of the songs dated from the anti-German passive resistance period. Every significant line and possible nuance was emphasized to reinforce Danish patriotism.

Algang became another communal ritual. Group after group, friends and strangers alike, gathered to walk between towns, through forests, anywhere and everywhere. Like *alsang*, *algang* was more a social than a political act. They met a need for comradeship and national solidarity. They were a kind of spiritual affirmation during a period of extreme hopelessness and helped to prepare Danes for subsequent active resistance.

Popular discontent was also reflected in the negligible numbers recruited in Denmark for the German armed forces. While the one person per thousand was similar to that in Holland and Norway, a proportionately large number of the Danish recruits were drawn from families of German descent in Jutland.[2] Recruitment for a Nazi home guard proved to be much more difficult than it had been in Norway. The Schalburg Korps was a miserable failure and an object of national ridicule.

Danes resisted the political development of Naziism. While the Danish Nazi Party quadrupled its membership between 1940 and 1943, the number of votes cast for Nazi candidates in national elections did not increase during that time. In both the 1939 and 1943 elections, the Nazis won only one seat of 150 in the Folketing (Haestrup, 1960). Party growth, then, was merely an institutionalization of sentiment present before the occupation.

The Strikes of 1943. By mid-1943, popular resistance was becoming more active. Allied successes and Axis reverses had kindled new hope of eventual liberation. Socialists and Communists were active among laborers, who increasingly resented a deterioration of their wages and working conditions while management did exceedingly well with German war contracts. Occupation rule was becoming increasingly severe and the Government's cooperation policy became less and less attractive. Popular resistance began to surface.

The strike of 1943 began as early as February in certain industries. The major series began on August 7 in Esbjerg on the west coast of Jutland, then spread to other industrial cities such as Odense, Frederikshaven, Alborg, Skagen, Helsingor, and Aarhus (Haestrup, 1966). The strikes were usually organized by strike committees and some lasted for 20 days. The government condemned the strikes and the Labor, Foreign Affairs, and Justice ministers, along with national union leaders, tried unsuccessfully to terminate them.

The industrial strikes spread to other sectors of the economy and ultimately, even tradesmen, civil servants, and businessmen were persuaded to join. Oppressive curfews and harsh penalties for sabotage helped gain public support for the strikes, which were often accompanied by public demonstrations. The political consequences of these events were extremely important, for they undermined the government's cooperation policy. After consultation with Berlin, German occupation officials presented the government with an ultimatum that it could not accept and continue to govern. German demands amounted to a declaration of martial law: no meetings of more than five persons, no strikes, no German press censorship, and other stringent measures. The Danish government resigned at once although many Danes continued in civil service positions.

With the collapse of the cooperation policy, Denmark's political institutions could no longer be defended passively. The dissolution of the government and parliament, the primary symbols of nationhood, pushed many Danes toward active resistance. Subsequent repressive measures taken by the Germans further galvanized popular support for resistance.

The Rescue of Danish Jews. Another national institution was threatened shortly thereafter—namely, Danish citizenship. Until late 1943, Danish Jews had not been attacked. This was in part because of the high degree of integration of the 8,000 Jews within the total population. Denmark's status as a "protectorate" was also a factor. The political and judicial systems were under Danish control. The Germans would have disrupted an important marriage of convenience had they attacked the Jews, despite mounting pressure from Berlin to do so. When the Danish government resigned, however, the major restraint on Nazi Jewish policy in Denmark was removed. Plans were rapidly set in motion for mass arrests and deportations.

Advance word of the impending arrests was leaked by a compassionate German official and a massive effort to transport the Jewish population to neutral Sweden was begun.[3] With extraordinary organization and with the assistance of thousands of Danes who had not before participated in illegal activity, 7,000 Jews were sent to Sweden. Only 450 were arrested and deported by the Germans.

Danish editor Kate Fleron recounts the experience of one Dane converted to active resistance during this event:

> Ellen [Christensen] became involved in illegal activity during the persecution of the Jews in October 1943, when Bispebjerg Hospital was for two weeks a refugee center and one of the dispatching points. At that time Ellen did not sleep for five days. Many of (those assisting) gave support at that time for humanitarian reasons, when it was a question of helping a few Jews out of the country, happy to return thereafter to their bourgeois existence ... but it was not like that with Ellen. This humanitarian relief work had caught her up and the resistance movement held her fast from then on [Fleron, 1964, p. 52].[4]

The success of the rescue operation rested on the commitment of Danes to the deeply rooted traditions of democracy and "taking care of one's own." The Germans were attacking Danish citizens who had to be protected. Not even Danish Nazis would inform about the location of Jews. Money was collected from anonymous donors to finance the expensive transporting of refugees across the Oresund to Sweden.[5]

The rescue was accomplished through a number of groups, or *ringen*, each of which had its own communication and transit systems for contacting, hiding, and transporting refugees. Certain occupations played special roles: medical personnel who hid and cared for them in hospitals while transportation was arranged; taxi drivers who drove escapees to coastal departure points; and fishermen whose boats carried them across the channel (Yakil, 1967). Persons with relatives or friends to whom they could entrust refugees were likewise essential to the operation.

The *Jodeaktion* was an ideal means for moving the Danish population into open resistance. It was clandestine, therefore the risk was minimal. It did not require violence on the part of those involved. It was a humanitarian operation, which lent it great legitimacy in the public mind. It was an important transitional event in the growth of civilian resistance.

The rescue was doubly important. The system of clandestine routes set up for the Jews was then maintained and used increasingly for daily illegal press communication, courier traffic, and for the eventual escape of 18,000 Danes sought by German authorities (Haestrup, 1966). Swedish marine, customs, and police officials continued to protect the Oresund routes. Communication centers were set up in Gotenborg, Halsingborg and Malmo.

This route system used to evacuate Jews later permitted a similar escape of downed Allied pilots. Formerly, most had been delivered to the Germans by the Danish police. After August 1943, they were smuggled to Sweden by way of the "underground railroad." The disguised pilots were passed from post to post, some of which were resistance workers on the move, others that were ordinary citizens who provided hiding places. This too increased the involvement of ordinary Danes in the organized resistance movement. To ride the railroad successfully, one had to make initial contact prudently with a person who had access to it. Teachers and ministers were likely prospects as these groups were heavily involved in the resistance. Through this system, 102 of the 450 surviving pilots reached Sweden during the occupation.

People's Strike of 1944. The Copenhagen People's Strike was the most dramatic example of open civilian resistance during the occupation. As did the rescue of the Jews, it arose partly in defense of Danish tradition. The Allied invasion of Normandy had encouraged Danish saboteurs to make new and daring attacks on weapons factories. The German commander responded with repression. On June 22, the Danish Nazi SS group known as the Schalburg Korps destroyed the Tivoli Gardens, the municipal student center, and the Royal Porcelain Factory, all beloved cultural symbols for the people of Copenhagen. Eight Danes were executed on June 23. On June 25, Commander Werner Best ordered additional repressive measures: a dusk-to-dawn curfew, interdiction of meetings of more than five persons, and the death penalty for strikers. Protesting these measures, workers at Denmark's largest shipbuilding works went home in the early afternoon the following day.[6]

Other factors provided the appropriate background for the strike and its escalation from a localized to a general one. The Normandy invasion, accompanied by Eisenhower's appeal for the rising up of occupied peoples, certainly encouraged open resistance. Liberation suddenly seemed less remote and execution threats less credible. The image of the invincible occupier was fading fast in the public mind. Weather conditions were influential too, as unusually high temperatures drew people into the streets and raised tempers.

In spite of the labor union council's condemnation of this action, the strike spread rapidly from factory to factory. It encouraged people throughout Copenhagen to defy the new restrictions. Street demonstrations occurred with increasing frequency, violating both the curfew and the edict forbidding public meetings. Forbidden symbols such as the hammer and sickle, and the RAF bullseye were openly displayed. Businesses of some known collaborators were sacked and burned. Bonfires and street barricades appeared all over the city. German troops responded brutally, often firing into the crowds. The German commander sealed off the city.

The subsequent siege had important consequences for the inhabitants of Copenhagen. The city was totally isolated from the rest of Denmark. All utilities had been shut off, no one could enter or leave, and no supplies were permitted to come in. The crisis transformed a city into a community. Rather than demoralizing the population, the siege increased its solidarity and determination. Communal and cooperative activity brought people together out of necessity. With food and fuel in short supply, thousands of unacquainted residents of large apartment buildings formed cooking cooperatives. Cooking fires were built, with each family bringing what they had for the meal. Resources were pooled for weekly menus. The cooperation and closeness of that week changed the lives of many who experienced it. They describe it now as one of the most meaningful experiences of their lives because of the comradeship, interdependence, and sense of common purpose.[7]

The *folkestrejke* ended successfully on July 4. While the uprising had been largely nonviolent, 102 Danes had been killed and between 600 and 700 wounded (Bronsted and Gedde, 1947). The Germans had no effective weapons against such resistance. Isolating the city had had the opposite of the effect they desired. Berlin wanted industries back in operation with the least delay. In the end, all of the Danish demands were granted.

The executions were stopped, the curfew and siege were lifted, meetings were once again permitted, and the hated Schalburg Korps was moved outside the city (Haestrup, 1966).

More important, perhaps, was the impetus the strike gave to the resistance movement. Increasing numbers of Danes were thereafter willing to become involved. The primary resistance organization, the Freedom Council, gained considerably from the strike in its role as spokesman for the city. Since it formulated and presented the demands, it received much of the credit for the strike's successful outcome.

The Role of Communication

The major events in the growth of resistance have been presented. Underlying this evolution, spreading the discontent and techniques of protest, informing Danes of what was happening in and outside of Denmark, was a complex system of communication. It provided for a nationwide exchange of ideas, information to counteract German propaganda, and communication between resistance groups. From the beginning, communication was the most vital function of the resistance movement as well as its sine qua non.

The initial problem was one of getting information to large numbers of people, information that would encourage them to resist the occupation. The early occupation was relatively benign and the Danish government was cooperating with it. The press and broadcasting media were largely at the service of the occupiers but under Danish control. This lent a veneer of legitimacy to the mixture of factual and fictional information given out that was difficult to counteract:

> In spite of the censorship . . . the legitimate press was able to print much accurate news and a good deal of reading and writing between the lines and double-entendre occurred before German censors developed a skill in detecting it. During the last two years of the occupation, of course, when German censorship was direct, news was completely slanted [Frederiksen, 1960, p. 72].

To build a base for national resistance, doubt in the accuracy and objectivity of the official media had first to be sown among the people. That done, superior alternative sources of information had to be provided.

The Illegal Press. The underground press was the single most important stimulus in the formation of the resistance. It functioned primarily to (1) provide a counter-source of news and opinion, and (2) supply leaders for resistance organizations. Many resistance leaders became involved through the clandestine press. Mogens Fog, Aage Schock, Borge Outze, and Kate Fleron began their resistance careers as editors and reporters for illegal papers.

As Jorgen Haestrup, the foremost student of the Danish resistance, notes:

> The outlines of a Resistance programme began to emerge in the illegal press. At the same time, of course, this provided the indispensable propaganda machine, while becoming an organizer itself. Editing, printing, distribution, and financing entailed cooperation, and the creation of the underground press led logically to the formation of Resistance groups with concrete and defined objectives [Haestrup, 1963, p. 21].

Publishing as early as 1940, the illegal press peaked in 1945 when 550 separate papers were published. These ranged from *Frit Danmark* with a national circulation, to local newsletters reaching a few hundred readers (Lund, 1970b).

In the first two years, most resistance literature was in the form of handbills or leaflets, not newspapers. Danish police were too efficient in tracing illegal papers. Nevertheless, flysheets were influential in shaping public opinion. For instance, German troop instructions for winning over the Danish population were obtained and circulated widely in Denmark. This helped prepare people to resist collaboration. Handbills regularly informed the public of discussions within the government of new cooperation proposals, such as a Danish-German customs and monetary union. The release of such information influenced government decisions, for adverse public reaction might endanger the entire cooperation policy.

Danish Communists took the lead in forming the underground press. The party's own press organs were declared illegal on June 22, 1941 and those of its members who were not then arrested were forced underground. The Communists' *Land og Folk* led the field of illegal publications. The circulation of underground papers escalated steadily from 40,000 in 1941 to 301,000 in 1942, 2.6 million in 1943, 10.9 million in 1944, and 10.1 million for the first four months of 1945 (Haestrup, 1963). Each province and region developed a major publication. The staffs of these papers were often in their twenties. Initially, the editorial and production staffs were integrated, but as papers grew in size, a division of labor developed. Duplicating equipment ranged from primitive hectographs, to mimeograph machines, to electric offset presses. Frequency of publication varied as well, with a full range of monthlies, weeklies, and dailies appearing by early 1943.

The first issue of *Frit Danmark* appeared in April 1943. It was to become the largest paper, with a circulation of 150,000 by 1945. Its staff and contributors included such resistance leaders as Ole Chievitz, Mogens Fog, Borge Houmann, and Ole Kilerich. *Frit Danmark* began as a compilation of occupation and resistance news. Its primary function was to integrate resistance activity, which was highly fragmented as late as mid-1943. Initially, the paper was sent to 40 locations where it was further duplicated or used in local papers.

Illegal papers were expensive to produce. They were financed largely through private contributions and through the sale of leaflets and books also published by illegal presses. Locating sites for the larger presses was a problem. They had to be isolated because of the noise, and inconspicuous so that staff and supplies entering the building would go unnoticed. In Bjorring, a printing group solved the problem by bricking in all openings in a house, and reaching the press through a trap door in the ceiling (Buschardt & Tonnesen, 1963).

Distribution of the papers involved a complex operation. Most were sent by mail, a rather reliable means since postal officials were cooperative. Volunteer addressing "teams" would deliver the papers to contacts who in turn fed them into the postal system. Great care was necessary, for large quantities of addressed materials would attract attention. Another method relied on centers throughout Denmark which distributed all sorts of illegal literature. Some large papers had their own systems, distributing in bulk at various contact points. Once the Freedom Council was established, newspapers were also distributed through its network. Finally, papers made their way to readers through places of employment, libraries, and individual Danes who passed their copies along to friends. However it occurred, distribution itself strengthened the resistance. Receiving or exchanging an illegal paper was in itself a modest act of resistance.

The illegal press was invaluable for resistance groups. Even a people ripe for resistance will rarely resist openly without word from an authoritative source. The Freedom Council gained influence in shaping resistance through use of the underground press. The rescue of the Jews illustrates this. The Council formulated a position on Danish Jews and circulated a proclamation just as the rescue was getting underway:

> In Danish society, Jews are not some special class, but countrymen in the same sense as all other Danes. We Danes ask the entire population to stand behind resistance to German oppression. The Council calls upon the Danish population to support in every way their Jewish fellow citizens, who may not yet have been shipped to foreign areas. Any Dane who assists the Germans in their manhunt is a traitor to Denmark and will be punished as such, when Germany is defeated [Yakil, 1967, p. 207].

This combined appeal and threat, distributed through the illegal press network, provided a clear ideological fremework for public behavior and gave people some direction.

The illegal papers also worked to form a public consciousness that would be supportive of specific public acts of resistance. First, the argument that only legal resistance was permissible had to be dispatched. *Frit Danmark*, for example, criticized what it felt was the fallacious reasoning behind the legal resistance position of Hal Koch and his *Ungdomsamvirke*:

> Koch does not understand that a genuine defense of our freedom and interests requires not only sharing but active resistance as well, and that his position of formally opposing the Government's cooperation policy, yet supporting this policy's representatives, dissipates our youth's will to resist [Fleron, 1967, p. 95].

With such attacks on vulnerable points of the cooperation policy, underground editors did much to stimulate resistance.

The Illegal News Service. The clandestine press received its information from diverse sources: informants within the Government; British, Swedish, and German radio broadcasts; local correspondents throughout Denmark; the legal press; and tapped telephones. By April, 1944, however, these sources had been fully integrated for the papers in a unique news service. INFORMATION was initiated in 1943 by Borge Outze, a crime reporter and editorial secretary for a major Copenhagen daily, *National Tidende*. At that time, the supply of information to illegal papers was spotty and uncoordinated. Efforts at coordination then produced the Illegal Joint Press Association, and subsequently the Nordic News Service (NNS) (Lund, 1970b). Outze's INFORMATION absorbed the NNS in March, 1944 and became the semiofficial service of the Freedom Council.

Outze was central to the development of the clandestine media for it was through his organization that accurate information reached it. As an editorial secretary, he had access to news that the legitimate press was not permitted to print. He would edit this news daily and send it in digest form to the editors of legitimate papers. This was quite legal (Lund, 1970b). It became illegal, though, when Outze produced additional copies for underground editors. With legitimate messengers bringing unprintable news to Outze and illegal couriers delivering it from him to underground papers, a rather effective mix of legal sources and illegal destinations for news was created. This arrangement collapsed in February, 1944 when Outze and his associates were forced underground. His illegal service then expanded to become the major news source not only for clandestine papers but for foreign news services and individual subscribers as well.

From whom and to whom did this information flow? Major Danish papers and their foreign correspondents conveniently funneled unprintable news to INFORMATION through the Foreign Ministry's press department. Outze himself would collect the manuscript from the censor's office at the Ministry, use it, and return it the following morning to be sent on its legitimate way. Outze also had a direct communication link with the Danish police, many of whom knew him personally as a crime reporter. Members of other government organizations such as the parliament (Folketing), the treasury, hospitals, the state railways, and intelligence section also passed information to him. There were even informants at German military and Gestapo headquarters. The Freedom Council and its network supplied continuous data, and local resistance groups gave INFORMATION advance notice of sabotage raids. Extremely important was the reciprocal information flow that was established. Local papers began to feed new information back to Outze's group as they received its bulletins. This closed system was essential for the integration of the larger resistance movement.

INFORMATION reached its Danish subscribers by mail and courier. To avoid detection, never more than a thousand copies per day were sent out. Envelopes with addresses and logos of both existing and fictional organizations were used to allay suspicion. Among these were the return address of Dagmar House, the Gestapo headquarters, and one advertising a manufacturer of illuminated keyholes. The envelopes were usually addressed to fictitious persons or to box numbers in the smaller towns, and later delivered to editors of illegal papers.

Sweden was the major relay point for INFORMATION news on its way to Allied nations:

> The material was ferried, sailed, flown, telephoned and telegraphed out, amid constant rivalry between these various services to see which could get it across to Sweden first [Lund, 1970b, p. 17].

The news was received three times daily in Stockholm by the Danish Press Service. It was then dispatched to Swedish news media, foreign news services, and directly to the BBC.

The INFORMATION news service helped to shape resistance to the Germans in several ways. First, it created a vastly expanded market for the illegal press by supplying it with credible and accurate news:

> Our job was to use the truth as a weapon. The truth was enough. It was in such contrast to the lies and exaggerations in the legal media. Everybody believed the illegal papers because they were small, credible and had proven their credibility.[8]

The greatest care was taken to cultivate that credibility. Careful attention was paid to verification of facts before news was released. British and Swedish broadcasting were asked to include much "small news" in their broadcasts, supplied of course by INFORMATION. There would be stories with local significance that inhabitants of a certain town or region could themselves verify—for example, that a B-17 had actually crashed nearby killing three of the seven crew members. If their local news reporting was accurate, the illegal papers would be accepted as the believable source of all news. Precision and contrast were the determinants of success. The small truths countered the big lie.

INFORMATION was also influential through its involvement in such popular uprisings as the People's Strike. Outze's letter to Commander Best concerning the allotment gardens has already been mentioned. This powerful bit of imagery—Danish workers leaving work at grave personal risk to tend their beloved gardens—was influential in spreading the strike:

> This was a brilliant psychological tactic in the strike . . . which was not really a strike, but a form of unshakeable obstinacy. [The workers] did not formally defy the German curfew, they took advantage of an unexpected consequence of it. The allotment gardens excuse gave the massive conspiracy a tinge of bourgeois innocence, which provided a cover for the real struggle. Responding to the workers' action, the entire population acted similarly. It refused, quite simply, to be closed in on the hot summer evenings and it became popular sport to disobey the curfew [Haestrup, 1959, p. 297].

Once the strike was underway, INFORMATION encouraged it. It issued detailed news of the strike and supporting actions in other cities three times daily. It was important news. For the first time in the occupation, Danes were resisting openly and en masse. The citizens of Copenhagen could follow the course of the strike on the BBC which was receiving continuous reports from INFORMATION. There were accounts of events which only a few hours earlier they had perhaps witnessed themselves.

The BBC coverage spurred the strike on. Now aware that the occupiers were vulnerable and that the strike was considered part of the Allied effort, the people were ever more determined to continue it. Detailed BBC reports of events in all parts of the city not only encouraged the strike, they demoralized the occupation forces. It was as if the enemy could penetrate their defenses at will. This accurate news, made available the same day it happened by INFORMATION, gave the resistance a sense of control and confidence it would not otherwise have had. Often, news from elsewhere in Denmark would reach Danes via the BBC before they read it in the illegal press the following day. The sense of geographical and political isolation from the allies was fast fading.

INFORMATION dispelled rumor and misunderstanding as well. An illustration of this was its response to sabotage by the Schalburg Korps.

Their destruction of Tivoli and other beloved public buildings in June, 1944 was a German attempt to arouse the population against sabotage. They assumed either that the people would blame Danish saboteurs directly, or would view it as a Nazi reprisal for Danish sabotage. To clarify the origin of the act, INFORMATION created the term "Schalburgtage" and public antagonism toward Nazis and German occupiers increased. Once again, a German tactic for derailing resistance brought the opposite of the desired effect.

Finally, INFORMATION isolated the wider resistance movement from ideological conflicts within the Freedom Council. It maintained a fierce independence from any well-defined political line. It refused to become the mouthpiece for any faction in the resistance front, remaining nonpartisan. It thereby reduced the temptation within the Council and other groups to seek postwar political advantage. It kept leaders focused on the common goal of providing maximum factual information to fuel resistance.

Books, Pamphlets, Tracts. Illegal books were in great demand during the occupation. Two hundred and ninety-eight separate publications with a total volume of nearly one million copies were printed by the Frie Danske Forlag and other underground publishing houses. Most illegal books were written to reinforce Danish culture and thus to encourage resistance. These included a national songbook and several books of poetry of Kaj Munk, who became a symbol of resistance when he was murdered by Nazi terrorists in 1944. An anthology of poems and novels by well-known Danish authors, *There Burns a Fire*, reflected the growing resistance of nazification (Haestrup, 1966).

Leaflets and posters were used to announce resistance events, to encourage resistance among specific occupational groups, and generally to reinforce the public will to resist. Two leaflets in the archives of the Danish resistance museum read:

> The ninth of April is a day of national mourning. On that day all street traffic will halt for two minutes at 12 noon. There will be no Danish participation during the afternoon and evening in any kind of public amusement.

> To Danish businessmen:
> The German robbers are everywhere
> Stealing from and plundering Danish shops
> Join the fight so Hitler goes down
> Say "no sale" to German customers.

Leaflets were also scattered from the air by Allied planes. From 1941–43, 23 different leaflets and booklets were dropped into Denmark by the British Psychological Warfare Executive.

In summary, then, the underground press in its many forms was an influential medium for the development of popular resistance in Denmark:

> It broke through the censorship, provided the basis for uncensored public discussion, from 1942 on influenced public opinion and eventually dominated it, and maintained continuous incoming and outgoing communication with the press of the free world. Paradoxically, its absolute success tended to militate against its intentions, the wealth of material being in inverse ratio to the amount of reading. When the underground paper became an ordinary everyday thing, the appetite for reading it and the eagerness to distribute it diminished correspondingly [Haestrup, 1963, pp. 33–34].

Telecommunications. Radio was both a stimulating and a restraining influence on the Danish resistance movement. Official Danish broadcasting served to check resistance. Censorship and propaganda supported the myth of German invincibility which helped to keep the lid on resistance sentiment. British and Swedish broadcasting, however, tended to stimulate resistance, particularly from 1942 on with the increase in Allied military success. The Germans never attempted to control listening to Allied broadcasts as they did in Norway, although jamming of broadcast reception was common. Listening became for Danes not only a relatively safe form of popular dissent, but their major source of war news as well. Denmark had the second highest distribution of radios in occupied Europe (Bennett, 1966). Allied broadcasting also functioned as the major amplifier of the information services working in Denmark.

The BBC played a major role in determining the pace of Danish resistance. Until late 1941, the Danish Section of the BBC had no clear policy objectives in its programming. The ambiguity created by the Danish government's cooperation policy discouraged such objectives. By mid-1941, however, the BBC was actively encouraging resistance. Its initial strategy was to convince Danes that their governmental institutions had not been protected from German control and were increasingly forced to make concessions in the interests of the occupiers rather than the Danes. BBC attacks on certain government figures such as Foreign Minister Scavenius were designed to undermine faith in the government and its policies. The Danish Section continually contrasted the firmness of King Christian and the Danish people, with the weakness of their government, hoping to strengthen commitment of Danes to certain institutions while separating them from others. The progressive emasculation of the Danish legal system was emphasized and the murders of the priests, Munk and Johannesen, were portrayed as an attack by occupation forces on Danish religious institutions.

The BBC made heavy use of Danes who had escaped to England. The

Danish Council in London, the closest approximation to a parallel government during the occupation, was used to exemplify what free Danes were doing for the Allied cause. The broadcast speeches of popular Conservative politician John Christmas Moller, urging civilian resistance, were quite effective. Inciting Danes to resist was not, however, a continuous policy of the BBC. Its programming responded both to Allied political objectives and to the political situation within Denmark. In 1941, program content emphasizing the Danish Council was shifted when feedback from Denmark indicated that Danes were beginning to mistrust the BBC, as it seemed to be engaging in Danish partisan politics (Bennett, 1966).

In 1942, by agreement with the League of Danish Army Officers, the BBC changed its policy of encouraging resistance to one more favorable toward maintaining the status quo in Denmark, while resistance groups were organizing there. In April, 1943, when the Special Operations Executive broke with the League, the BBC resumed its encouragement of active resistance. Yet it urged Danes to participate in the 1943 parliamentary elections, to show their resistance by choosing leaders who would refuse further concessions to the Germans. Supporting such participation, which was in fact cooperation with the occupying forces, was in sharp contrast to earlier BBC policy. It examplified the BBC's sometimes confused responsiveness to changes in the Danish political climate.

British propaganda, generally of a subtle, moderate nature, did undoubtedly stimulate Danish resistance to some degree. Such propaganda was largely

> An attempt at influencing ideas in Denmark by the presentation of news and commentaries, by stimulating Danes to thought, and by exposing the falsity of German propaganda. By this method it was hoped that the Danish population would see the situation as it really was. When this happened, the Danish Section . . . hoped the people would act upon its new realization [Bennett, 1966, p. 129].

Most influential, however, was the BBC's credibility, which was established through its reliable and accurate news programs. The gravity of the Allied position early in the war was reported candidly by the BBC. This candor fostered a growing trust among Danish listeners. With information fed to it by the illegal news service, the BBC gained acceptance as an objective source.

Objective news was not sufficient, though, to ensure BBC influence on Danish public opinion. Presentation of the news was also important. Announcers had to speak correct and cultivated Danish, as foreign accents would decrease listener receptivity. News stories were often shaped to engage the emotions of the listener, to sell the story. The human interest rule of journalism was continually applied. For example, a relatively insignificant event such as a resistance worker steering a busload of fleeing saboteurs, seated on the lap of the dead driver, becomes a news item that captures the imagination of large numbers of people. Thus, the news was managed for maximum impact but its essentially factual nature was retained. Accuracy was the other key to influence.

BBC programming was also designed to spur resistance in a negative way through the use of the subtle threat. Suggestions that Denmark would be commercially isolated by the Allies after the war, that she would be excluded from the United Nations if resistance were not more active, that Danish factories producing war material would be bombed if sabotage were not more extensive, all were designed to strengthen the public will to resist.

Other means of persuasion included the broadcast of a blacklist of Danish firms producing for the Germans, and an emphasis on the physical danger from Allied air raids involved in working in German factories. Attempts to attract Danish skilled labor to Germany may well have been hindered by such broadcasts.

While the exact degree of influence British broadcasting had on Danish resistance is debatable, evidence of influence on specific events is strong. It did influence the strikes of August, 1943. There had been continuous BBC emphasis on the issues that led to the initial workers' revolt: the reprisal executions, the abuses of the legal system, the insecurity of Danish workers' economic future. Special broadcast lectures from July 9–August 29 had been directed at Danish labor. These emphasized its importance to the German war effort, the usefulness of the strike as a means of protest, and they urged Danish workers to fight for the better wages and working conditions they deserved (Bennett, 1966). On August 12, the BBC directly encouraged all manner of labor disruption.

Telecommunication was important for getting information out of Denmark as well. Information supplied to British and Swedish broadcasting came mainly by short wave from various parts of Denmark. Such information could be news destined for mass audiences, or messages in code for other resistance groups inside Denmark. The latter often reached their destination more rapidly by way of London and the BBC than they could travel by courier between Jutland and Copenhagen (Haestrup, 1966).

High-frequency channels were used for all types of coded messages. Telegraph-radio sending spots were changed after each transmission and decoy transmissions provided "shielded" broadcasts. The resistance broadcasting section recruited former merchant marine radiomen and telegraphers. It produced its own portable equipment and perfected automatic transmission, with tape recorders to accelerate it and to lessen the possibility of detection. In contrast to radio, the telephone was rarely used for resistance work. Lines were tapped, particularly after 1943, and courier and letter were more secure means of communication.

National Symbols. Certain elements of a national culture—specific words, institutions, music, buildings—have symbolic meaning for citizens of a nation-state. Such symbols performed an essential function in the development of Danish resistance. They brought the people together in deeply rooted nationalistic sentiment, enabling the resistance movement to make an ever clearer distinction between cooperator and loyal Dane. As resistance grew, the symbols became less implicit and historical, more explicit and contemporary.

The monarchy, which for a century had been viewed by most Danes as a charming anachronism, suddenly took on new meaning. King Christian X became a key figure in the resistance, both because of his office and for his exemplary conduct in it. His daily rides on horseback through Copenhagen lent a new accessibility and significance to the royal office. The King's direct contact with his people and his "cold shoulder" for the occupation forces were extremely influential in shaping public attitudes. A royal example of resistance was set by Christian in September of 1942 when he sent a curt telegraphed response, "Sprache meinen besten Dank aus. Christian Rex," to Hitler's annual birthday congratulations (Haestrup, 1966). This calculated discourtesy produced both a strengthening of resistance and increased tension with the Germans. Conciliation from then on became less and less attractive to the Danes. While Christian did encourage resistance by his demeanor, the charming story about his wearing the Star of David to protest anti-Semitism seems to have no basis in fact.

A second person who was especially important as a symbol was the martyred pastor-poet Kaj Munk. Strangely enough, Munk had been somewhat of a crypto-fascist in the 1930s, with a naive hero worship of authoritarian leaders of the 19th century. By 1942 he had reversed his thinking and had begun to write patriotic poetry that was widely circulated later by the underground press. His assassination by the Nazis made his poetry and plays important symbols of Danish nationalism.

Visual marks of resistance were an important form of communication. The "King's mark," a silver and enamel lapel button with the crown and the letters CX, was produced in honor of Christian's 70th birthday. There was little risk involved in wearing these pins since the royal house remained a legal institution. Their resistance message was recognized by all Danes.

The Danish flag and its colors were displayed everywhere. Bookmarks in the form of small national flags were widely distributed. In the last year of the war resistance symbols proliferated, with the more daring persons wearing knitted stocking caps with the RAF bullseye or colors. One of the most effective symbols of resistance originated with the BBC. This was the "V for victory" sign and its Morse code equivalent, dot-dot-dot-dash. "Vi Vil Vinde" became the watchword. The letter V itself, easily painted on walls, scratched on coins, or traced in the dust on German military vehicles, became powerful psychological warfare for demoralizing the occupation forces (Bennett, 1966). The audial symbol, the tapping out of the coded V, was a spontaneous signal of Danish solidarity.

Certain nations took on new meaning. England symbolized active resistance and eventual liberation for the Danes. Her ability to withstand German air attacks eroded the myth of German invincibility. Norway exemplified resistance to German occupation for the Danes. The term "Norske Tilstande," meaning a strong resistance to occupation, was commonly used throughout Denmark. Certain public buildings also became foci for resistance as we saw when the destruction of Tivoli by the Nazis helped precipitate the People's Strike.

Symbols from Denmark's past were reactivated to sharpen the sense of threat to national institutions. The south Jutland resistance to German hegemony, when passive resistance, nationalism, and democracy converged in the formation of the Danish political ethos, was relieved. At the mercy of Bismarck's Germany, Denmark had been small and weak. Danes had sought protection in the development of democratic institutions. The origins and history of those institutions were suddenly topics of lively discussion and renewed study. The evolution of parliamentary government and the development of the Grundtwig folk high school movement were glorified, and contrasted with the truncated political institutions under German occupation.

Finally, music was a unifying symbol system for the Danes. As already noted, songs written during the national revival period of the 19th century were the basis for *alsang* and an essential part of the resistance culture. An internee in the Froeslev concentration camp later told of fellow prisoners producing the greatest sense of solidarity from singing songs of that period.

Interpersonal Communication. The ultimate impact of both mass media and national symbols communication occurred through face-to-face interaction, which produced something of a multiplier effect. The occupation produced new impetus for group activity of all sorts. Several illustrations of this increase in groupness, in addition to *alsang* and *algang*, are worth mentioning. Parlor meetings were very important for the building of a resistance organization. Large meetings were prohibited during the occupation but smaller meetings in homes were often used to introduce the resistance. A group of trusted friends would be invited to a home for an evening's discussion of some quite innocent topic. A resistance worker would be present and gradually the focus of discussion would shift to resistance. The information given would be general and not incriminating. In these intimate contexts where people felt free to share their opinions, resistance sentiment deepened. Danes introduced to the movement in this way often contacted it later to volunteer their service.

Another important "institution" developing earlier in the occupation was the listening group, friends and neighbors meeting for the Danish program of the BBC. It has been suggested that the Germans did not confiscate radio sets as they did in Norway, for fear that the listening function of these groups might be replaced by more dangerous activity. Nevertheless, out of them came solidarity and firm interpersonal relationships that proved important later on for the resistance movement.

Voluntary associations such as field-sports groups provided additional opportunity for face-to-face exchange of ideas. The Germans made no effort in Denmark to institute a corporate state, and these associations remained intact. The sports associations later became essential for the resistance, where six-person field groups were initially drawn from participants in field-sports clubs where they had received paramilitary training of sorts.

Resistance-stimulating communication occurred in the course of daily life at natural communication points: laborers in the factories; civil servants and commercial employees in their offices; and everyone in their allotment gardens in the evenings. The physical arrangement of these gardens, or *kolonihaver*, brought people together quite naturally. Fifty families in a neighborhood might have garden plots in the same area, each with its hut for summer living and flagstaff with Danish flag flying. This pattern facilitated interpersonal communication during the summer months.

By 1943, when resistance became more open, public demonstrations permitted yet another type of face-to-face communication. The silent demonstrations in Copenhagen's city hall square marking the anniversaries of the invasion and the arrest of the Danish police were particularly effective. The open release of anti-German feelings in the People's Strike reached far beyond those tens of thousands participating in the street activity. People communicated in special ways through these public experiences (Bronsted & Gedde, 1947).

Humor. Humor was an important communication medium for mobilizing resistance. It was more difficult to fear or respect an invading enemy if one could make fun of him. As in the 1968 occupation of Czechoslovakia, resistance humor drew upon a highly developed national sense of humor. The Danes enjoy practical jokes and used them as a weapon. Two examples will illustrate the point:

> A German sentry was posted continuously in front of a major public building in Copenhagen. He paced up and down behind a chest-high wall of sandbags. One night a crude sign was placed on the outside of the wall, attracting crowds of delighted Danes until it was discovered and removed. It read simply, "He has no trousers on."

> Shortly after the German invasion, machine gun emplacements surrounded with sandbags were placed in front of Dagmar House, the Gestapo headquarters. Guards lay behind their guns in combat-ready positions. Passersby merely crowded around the emplacements staring down in amusement at the soldiers in what became such a fiasco that the emplacements were removed.

A population's refusal to take an occupation force seriously is both demoralizing to the troops and encouraging to resisters. An enemy made to look ridiculous can hardly maintain its credibility over time. Humor as a weapon is another technique of aggressive nonviolence. Jokes, anecdotes, and political cartoons undermining the occupier's credibility were widely circulated. To pass them along was to identify oneself as a resister and to create a bond between transmitter and receiver.

Ecological Influentials. Communication in the resistance movement was facilitated by what Arnold Rose (1968) has called ecological influentials. Certain occupations were central for the growth of resistance because of access or regular contact they provided with large numbers of people. Persons in these occupations acted as disseminators of information and molders of public opinion.

Journalists were the most important group of influentials. Their numerous contacts with news sources made them natural communicators. In addition to providing leadership, they brought other potential leaders into contact with one another. Outze's INFORMATION was valuable initially because of his extensive network of personal contacts. Kate Fleron, editor of *Frit Danmark*, provided a similar network. Her apartment became the meeting place for persons, both above and underground, whose friendships thenceforth laid the foundation for the Freedom Council. Fleron and her apartment were an important communications juncture.

The Resistance Organization

The development of the Freedom Council and its branches throughout Denmark further demonstrates the essential role of communication in resistance. The Council was formed primarily to improve communication among existing resistance groups. The large ones—the Communists, Dansk Samling, Frit Danmark, Ringen—had substantial memberships. Each had its own system of contacts for distributing information. Communication between these groups, however, was so poor that Frode Jakobsen of Ringen, following the 1943 national election, made plans to journey to England to broadcast a personal appeal to other resistance leaders. He could not locate them in Copenhagen. The Freedom Council integrated these four networks with that of the Special Operations Executive (British Intelligence). It thereby created a unified network for sending and receiving information between levels, and for bringing local representatives into contact with one another.

It is striking how directly the resistance leadership emerged from the writing and journalist professions. Of the six original members of the Frihedstradet, or Freedom Council, three (Fog, Houman, Schoch) were editor-journalists, a fourth (Staffeldt) was a publisher of illegal books, and a fifth (Foss) represented a major underground newspaper. Only Jakobsen seems to have had no direct tie with the underground press. These leaders began to interact before 1942 while still working in legitimate positions. As press censorship increased, they grew more and more dissatisfied, and began to establish a community to which they later gravitated as they were forced off legitimate papers. These people were communication centers in touch with one another. Each had a set of contacts in diverse occupational groupings useful to the resistance. These networks became unusual mixtures, highly personalized in one sense but in which false names were used and where one could not be sure of the true identity of even one's closest contacts. Locally too, resistance leaders were often persons who were connected with the communications media or who had become involved as distributors of illegal papers or as couriers.

The press shaped resistance leadership in yet another way. Illegal papers such as *Frit Danmark* provided a forum in which ideological differences were forged into a common front. As a framework for discussion among disparate political views, it facilitated an integrated leadership. Such unlikely bedfellows as Aksel Larsen (Communist), Christmas Moller (Conservative), Borge Houman (Communist), Ole Killerich (Conservative), Mogens Fog (Liberal), and Kate Fleron (Conservative) buried their ideological differences in writing for a united front. For the duration of the occupation, this front sought the res-

toration of the old order and was unconcerned with bringing about basic
social and political changes within Danish society (Fleron, 1967):

> The Danish illegal press was partly a carrier of news and partly an instrument of
> propaganda . . . confined to urging resistance. The papers had no marked political
> colours, and [the] resistance did not develop substantial new ideas as far as internal
> policy was concerned. Generally speaking, the movement aimed at liberation and
> restoration [Haestrup, 1960].

Largely as a consequence of good communication, the Danish resistance maintained a united front. It avoided the civil/military split of the
Norwegians, and the political, religious, and personal factionalism that
hindered the Dutch resistance (Warmbruun, 1963).

The Freedom Council was both a product of underground communication and dependent upon it and foreign broadcasting for its
growing influence. The Council was a relatively unknown group suddenly proclaiming itself the legitimate directorate of the resistance
movement and representative of the Danish people. With the resignation
of the government in 1943, a legitimacy vacuum was created into which
some group had to move. The continuity and stability then promised by
the Freedom Council no doubt encouraged its acceptance by the
majority of Danes. Just as important, though, were the Council's trusted
sources of information, the illegal press and the BBC. With *Frit Danmark* as its semiofficial organ and with BBC support, the Council gained
the necessary authority and legitimacy.

The Freedom Council's dependency on the illegal press gave the latter
priority in its strategy. An early effort was made to establish contact
with all papers in Denmark. The Council would use them to disseminate
its directives and to standardize information sent out to local groups. A
Council press committee was formed early in 1944 to formalize this
arrangement. Transmission of information from local contacts back to
the Freedom Council was of equal importance. Again the press and the
illegal news service were essential.

Those communicating within the organization itself had to be
extremely cautious. Even so, the attrition rate among resistance workers
was high. Word was generally sent by courier or mail and was always in
code. The rule was to be frugal in communicating with others, with as
little talking as possible. An effort was made to adapt the cell system to
minimize the number of people each person knew. Members of regional
resistance councils were forbidden to participate in other resistance
activities for fear they might meet too many others. The contending
needs to maximize the flow of information along friendly channels, on
the one hand, and minimize the leaking of such information to the
enemy on the other, set up an inner tension.

Assumed names were one technique for protecting the network. A friend unaware of your true identity could hardly be tortured to reveal it. Constant mobility was another means. A rule was established that persons arrested and tortured might tell what they were forced to after 24 hours. Since revelation would quickly lead to other arrests, a person's being taken was a signal to others who knew him or her to move their residence immediately and never to return to it. Indeed, there were special "contact persons" whose sole responsibility was to keep informed of the changing addresses of those moving frequently to escape arrest.[9] The Freedom Council met weekly in a private home, sometimes more often in time of crisis.

One additional communication link within the movement was through local representatives sent out by the Council. Such people would organize regional resistance, returning to Copenhagen regularly to report. These antennae were vital for the Council since it was never able to establish a centralized movement. There was always spontaneous local action, such as the strikes of 1943 and 1944, which was impossible to coordinate through a single organization. Yet the Freedom Council's authority depended on its being aware of such actions and controlling them as much as possible in the interest of the total movement. Precise local information was therefore essential.

Formal Structure. The structure of the resistance organization headed by the Freedom Council (Fig. 11.1) did delineate formal lines of communication, but these existed more in theory than in practice. Control from the top was limited. Communication between levels was too slow to permit top-level decisions on tactical matters. Local units generally acted on their own initiative in accordance with policy directives from the Council. In fact, regional leaders in Jutland often had closer contact with the SOE in England than with the Council in Copenhagen. Not until December, 1944 did the Council receive an adequate report from its Jutland units. A 1944 leadership crisis in Jutland was resolved from London because Copenhagen had insufficient information to make a decision.

Difficult interlevel communication made communicating within regions even more important. A critical aspect of this was nonverbal, that which told resistance workers who could be trusted. Haestrup speaks of an ultrasensitivity, a sixth sense developed during that period, an intuitive feeling about another's trustworthiness.[10] Remarks, facial expressions, and other clues would place a person somewhere on a continuum from potential saboteur, to one who would at least keep quiet, to one who could not be trusted at all.

Ease and effectiveness of communication depended, as it did at the

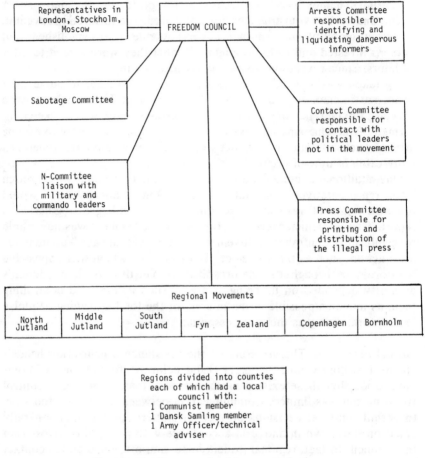

Fig. 11.1 The structure of resistance organization.

national level, on personal networks converted to resistance activity. Often, friendships developed in the Scouting movement and in sports associations formed the basis of such networks. Geographical configuration was also a determinant. In Fyn, an island with a major central city, communication was good. In neighboring Jutland, by contrast, it was poor even at the moment of liberation.

Paroles. The Freedom Council devised a system of *paroler* similar to that of the Norwegian resistance, but used it in a somewhat different way. It rarely issued directives to segments of the population as was done in Norway. Perhaps the Council was uncertain of its position during its first year and thus assumed a coordinating role rather than risk failing a credibility test. Following the People's Strike, however, the Council did issue a parole. It called for a mass sympathy demonstration for those killed during the strike. The population responded en masse and the test demonstrated the Council's authority to both the people and political leaders who had publicly opposed the strike.

Directives were infrequent but guidelines in the form of suggestions were often sent out as paroles. When orders were sent, they were usually to regulate rather than stimulate resistance. As the resistance movement gained momentum in 1944, it inevitably attracted some less desirable elements. Discipline was enforced largely through paroles; for example, that looters would be shot, or that liquidations were to be ordered whenever possible only by top leaders. All things considered, the paroles were to some degree influential in controlling violence and other excesses within the movement.

When the Council sent out a parole directed at the population, it took great care not to go beyond what loyal Danes' better instincts would lead them to follow. This restraint helped maintain the Council's authority. From late 1943 onward, it also used the parole for deterrence purposes, to discourage fence-sitting and collaboration. Its *Naar Danmark Atter er Frit* described how collaborators and traitors would be identified and dealt with after the war, and how democratic institutions would be reestablished.[11] Paroles were most often distributed through the same channels as illegal papers, though sometimes by courier and the BBC as well.

The Danes' less frequent use of the paroles as compared with the Norwegians was in large part a consequence of the dissimilar communication systems each movement used. The Norwegian Home Front communicated primarily through voluntary associations, whose networks lent themselves to a clandestine form of the paroles used in peacetime. It was the natural means of communication in a setting where the underground press was limited. In Denmark, by contrast, the clandestine press was highly developed but there were not the extensive networks of voluntary associations.

CONCLUSIONS

The Danish resistance suggests something of the nature, potential, and limitations of aggressive nonviolence as a method of responding to aggression. Several propositions emerge from the Danish experience.

1. *Political power and authority are given to, not taken by, those in command.* Once the Danes decided to defy occupation authority in large numbers, that authority was seriously diminished. The willingness to

submit to military occupation can be withdrawn, either entirely or in part. In that sense, the governed, the ruled, the occupied are always in charge. Conditions, however, that lead a population to withdraw the authority, to cease submitting, and to begin massive resistance, may rarely be present. This leads us to a second proposition.

2. *Resistance to an occupying force develops in proportion to the degree of psychological polarization between occupier and occupied.* In the Danish case, it required much provocation from the Germans to bring the Danes to the point where they felt sufficiently hostile and threatened to resist openly. Without those basic elements of aggression, hostility, and threat, even the most sophisticated communication system could not have activated them. The necessary psychological polarization that creates a clear we/they dichotomy in the public mind develops more rapidly when the occupier threatens valued institutions. In Denmark, a sequence of unmistakable threats to national institutions began in 1943 to stimulate the polarization process. First, the government resigned, ending the illusion of national sovereignty and self-government. This climaxed a tense summer of increasingly frequent sabotage and German reprisals. The attack on Danish Jews capped the sequence. The physical and institutional threats were then sufficiently clear. Threat to the national future also played a part as the Allies emphasized the undesirable political and economic consequences of a failure to resist openly.

This need for polarization is a definite drawback of aggressive non-violence as a strategy for national defense, as we see in the case of Denmark when the occupation was relatively gentle. The problem might be alleviated if citizens were trained so that the necessary hostile responses were brought into play more or less automatically. Training a population to resist, then, would involve both the stimulation of aggressive feelings and the provision of safe means of using them to resist.

3. *The intensity of both violent and nonviolent resistance correlates positively with external assistance and encouragement.* We must keep in mind that violent and nonviolent aggression in the Danish resistance were part of a single continuum, not discrete activities. Aggressive nonviolence in the Danish resistance was successful in large measure because it was part of a larger Allied effort. How long would it or the violent resistance have continued had the Allies not begun to win the war? The Czechoslovak resistance of 1968 (Wehr, 1979b) illustrates the limits of aggressive nonviolence practiced in isolation from external encouragement and assistance. On the other hand, the alternatives of violent resistance or submission in that case would have been more costly still.

It is difficult to measure the success of aggressive nonviolence in such cases. How does one do it? By the condition of a nation's social and political institutions when it is liberated? By the costs of the nonviolent resistance as compared with other possible techniques? By the number of occupation troops tied down and the state of their morale?

This said, one could argue that aggressive nonviolence of the Gandhian type, which is largely generated from within a society's religious and political contexts, does not depend much on external encouragement and could continue and even grow in relative isolation. This might conceivably have happened even in the Danish case. The Freedom Council member responsible for its paramilitary activity has stated that when he became involved in 1940, he believed Germany would win the war and he anticipated a protracted resistance through nonviolent means.

4. *An effective communication system is a requisite for civilian resistance.* Both internal and external communication were essential to the Danish resistance. Communication was also its primary function. The illegal news service and underground press produced initial leadership, which in turn melded the illegal press, intelligence services, escape route networks, and other elements. The Freedom Council's success in coordinating these various activities was the key to establishing its authority and maintaining its credibility. Its maintenance of communication with the outside world was important as well. By bringing Danes into contact with the outside, such links countered the sense of isolation and hopelessness so pervasive during that time.

The technological base of this communication was complex. Presses, telecommunication, and rapid transportation were all essential. Without this base, individual aggressive impulses would never have become the collective ones necessary for effective resistance. At the same time, modern communication technology could be a limiting factor because of its vulnerability and centrality. Counter-strategies could be developed effectively to close off such facilities. It would be difficult to do so, however, given current trends in miniaturization and solid state electronics.

Civilian resistance of this sort also uses an existing communication network, modified for resistance purposes. The press, the mails, public gatherings and transportation, workplaces, schools, churches, health centers—the Danes used these in everyday life. Resistance merely required using them in new ways for new purposes. People could resist within social networks that were familiar and comfortable.

5. *An equitable social structure and strong democratic institutions are supportive of nonviolent resistance.* Danish social structure was a fairly equitable one. With muted class differences, interpersonal communication could be maximized and political factionalism minimized. The population was homogeneous, relatively small, relatively concen-

trated geographically, and economically secure. The Danes had suffered less economically than most Europeans during the interwar years. This had permitted a political stability to reinforce democracy, while it was being weakened elsewhere in Europe. Once they were clearly threatened, the protection of these democratic institutions became a patriotic duty. Under the threat of nazification, Danes felt an important stake in preserving state and society as they were. This discouraged factionalism and increased solidarity within the resistance movement. Such conditions as obtained in Denmark are actually rather rare within nationstates. Studies of successful national nonviolent resistance suggest, though, that such factors as homogeneity, size, strength of national institutions, and values are major determinants of success.

For occupied Denmark, aggressive nonviolence seemed to work. It was impossible for the Germans to counter effectively. It used weapons quite unlike their own: mass noncooperation, humor, social quarantine and ostracism, humanitarian sacrifice, clandestine rescue, music, unobtrusive obstruction. The usual aggressive/repressive measures, siege, executions, interrogation and torture, just did not work against such behavior.

Aggressive nonviolence was a more acceptable response to their situation for most Danes than violent aggression would have been. As noted earlier, this might not be true for every culture, but for Denmark it was. Generally, it is difficult to move people to commit violence, except where they are under physical attack and flight is impossible. Aggressive nonviolence, to the contrary, responded to normal impulses for self-defense, political independence, and justice, and provided a means by which large numbers of Danes could act on those impulses. They broke laws, disrupted plans, frustrated occupier objectives, ridiculed—all healthy behavior under such provocation. These were means by which the bulk of the population could be personally and directly drawn into the struggle, within the limits of their natural inclinations.

To return to an earlier point, nonviolent and violent aggression coexist in any social movement, whether it seeks to liberate an oppressed people, to overthrow a legitimate government, or to resist a military occupation. A movement can be categorized by which end of the violence/nonviolence spectrum it tends toward. Even within aggressive nonviolence, the amount of aggressive impulse varies. Among the Danish resistance actions, some were more anti-German and some more humanitarian in motivation. Aggressive nonviolence permitted Danes to keep an integrated set of national and personal values intact in a time of dislocation, tension, and uncertainty.

Was this a low-risk option for the Danes? Would such aggressive nonviolence have been a dismal and costly failure in "non-Aryan" areas where the Nazis would raze a Lidice[12] in reprisal for an assassination? It is true that Germany had initially hoped to integrate the Scandinavian populations into the Third Reich. Those occupations were therefore initially less harsh, though they hardened as resistance grew. The Germans gave no indication, however, that they were not prepared to engage in wholesale terror in the Nordic states if they felt pushed to it. Many Danes were executed, transported, or interned. Their use of aggressive nonviolence had less to do with risk perhaps, than with what seemed to work and suited their needs. The Danes needed a method of resistance that would (1) preserve and strengthen national community; (2) not provoke reprisals by the Germans; and (3) permit them to contribute to the Allied effort. Whether it can objectively be said to have worked remains a debatable point.

POSTSCRIPT

Experience with aggressive nonviolence suggests that it is not a panacea, nor is it an approach suitable in all cases under all conditions. It is, nevertheless, a realistic option that has been underexplored as an aggressive strategy for winning in struggles for self-defense. Analysis of historical cases of nonviolent resistance has led scholars to ask whether it could provide a basis for a carefully planned national defense strategy. Could a nation build a credible defense policy relying heavily on a resistance-trained civilian population?

Forty years ago, before the development of nuclear arms, complex weapons, and chemical-biological warfare, this question might have been easily dismissed. National defense has become such a rubber concept, though, that nonmilitary defense is no longer unthinkable. Given the convoluted logic supporting the concept of defense through nuclear deterrence, nonmilitary defense seems not beyond credibility. It too rests on a deterrence theory, one that assumes that a nation will not invade another that it is convinced will be ungovernable. A nation totally prepared for nonmilitary defense might well have greater deterrence capability than one whose deterrence rests on its opponent's belief in its willingness to engage in mutual nuclear suicide.

Before aggressive nonviolence can be seriously considered, however, we would need to know: (1) if it can be taught to a population; (2) if the necessary planning and preparation could be successfully melded with the spontaneity so essential in such resistance; and (3) if a mixed military-civilian strategy such as that being tested by Sweden will work. In smaller, more homogeneous nations with a long history of pacific relations with other states, aggressive nonviolence would have a greater chance of success. If a mixed or nonmilitary defense strategy were shown to be workable on a smaller scale, however, it might be more attractive to larger, more complex states.

Global survival in the nuclear age requires an appropriate mix of institutional continuity and institutional innovation. We must be innovative about handling collective aggressive behavior, of both offensive and defensive motivation, in less injurious ways. A large part of the answer lies in building into national, group, and individual defensive behavior nonlethal yet effective means of struggle.

NOTES

1. Such deliberate ineptitude, disguised bungling, delay in the performance of one's duties with intention to frustrate is named for the Czech anti-hero Josef Schweik, the central character of Jaroslav Hašek's *The Good Soldier Schweik*.

2. Information supplied by Mag. Henning Poulsen, Department of History, Aarhus University.

3. The most reliable first-hand account of this is Aage Berthelsen's *Oktober, 1943*. Berthelsen was a leader of the rescue operation.

4. Unless otherwise noted, translations from the Danish in this paper are the author's.

5. Personal communication from Aage Berthelsen.

6. Erik Lund (1970a) has clarified the origin of this incident. It was long believed that workers at the Burmeister and Wain shipyard sent Commander Best an open letter, explaining that the work stoppage was not to strike but to permit them to work in their allotment gardens. Because of the curfew they could no longer do this in the evening. It has now been learned, however, that INFORMATION's Outze sent the letter to protect the workers who were in fact striking, and therefore liable to be executed. While garden tending was not a motive for the strike, strikers did spend much of the released time in their gardens, which because of their location, facilitated the spreading of open resistance.

7. Wechsberg (1969) notes similar attitudes recorded among Czechs and Slovaks during the 1968 invasion of Czechoslovakia, when a sense of euphoria, joy, and comradeship pervaded the major cities.

8. This quotation and much of the other material on the development of INFORMATION comes from the author's personal interviews with Borge Outze.

9. Personal interview with Kate Fleron.

10. Personal interview with Jorgen Haestrup.

11. In an interview with this author, Freedom Council member Frode Jakobsen expressed his feeling that the deterrence value of such threats had been negligible. The worst offenses of Dane against Dane, he pointed out, were committed in 1944, after the threat of the death penalty was made and by which time it had become quite clear that Germany would lose the war.

12. Lidice was the Czechoslovak village that was totally destroyed by the Germans in retaliation for the assassination of a Gestapo officer.

REFERENCES

Bennett, J. *British broadcasting and the Danish resistance movement, 1940–45*. Cambridge: Cambridge University Press, 1966.

Berthelsen, A. *Oktober, 1943*. Copenhagen: Gyldendal, n.d.

Bondurant, J. *Conquest of violence.* Berkeley: University of California Press, 1965.

Boserup, A. & Mack, A. *War without weapons: Nonviolence in national defense.* New York: Schocken, 1975.

Bronsted, J. & Gedde, K. *De fem lange aar.* Copenhagen: Gyldendal/Nordisk, 1947.

Buschardt, L. & Tonnesen, H. The illegal press in Denmark during the German occupation. *Gazette,* 1963, **9**, (2).

Carpenter, S. *A repertoire of peacemaking skills.* COPRED, Bethel College, North Newton, Kansas.

Erikson, E. *Gandhi's truth.* New York: Norton, 1969.

Fleron, K. Det illegale frit Danmark . . . Og andet illegalt. In *Presse historisk arbog,* 1967.

Fleron, K. *Kvinder i modstands kampen.* Copenhagen: Sirius, 1964.

Frederiksen, L.B. *Pressen under besaettelsen.* Aarhus: Universitets Forlaget, 1960.

Gurr, T. *Why men rebel.* Princeton: Princeton University Press, 1970.

Haestrup, J. *Hemmelig alliance.* Vol. 1. Copenhagen: Thoning og Appels, 1959.

Haestrup, J. Exposé. In *European resistance movements: 1939–45.* Vol. 1. Oxford: Pergamon Press, 1960.

Haestrup, J. *From occupied to ally.* Copenhagen: Berlingske, 1963.

Haestrup, J. Denmark's connection with the Allied powers during the occupation. In *European resistance movements: 1939–45.* Vol. II. Oxford: Pergamon Press, 1964.

Haestrup, J. *Besaettelsens Hvem, hvad, hvor.* Copenhagen: Politikens Forlag, 1966.

Hare, A.P. & Blumberg, H. *Nonviolent direct action.* Washington, D.C.: Corpus, 1968.

Hasĕk, J. *The good soldier Schweik.* Harmondsworth: Penguin, 1951.

Judson, S. *A manual on nonviolence and children.* Philadelphia: Friends Peace Committee, 1977.

Keyes, G. Strategic nonviolent defense in theory; Denmark in practice. Unpublished Ph.D. dissertation, 1978.

Lund, E. *Fire millioner frie ord.* Aarhus: Instituttet for Presse Forskning og Samtidshistorie, 1970 (a).

Lund, E. *A girdle of truth.* Copenhagen: Danish Ministry of Foreign Affairs, 1970 (b).

Poulsen, H. & Nissen, H. *Pa Dansk friheds grund.* Copenhagen: Gyldendal, 1963.

Roberts, A. *Total defence and civil resistance: Problems of Sweden's security policy.* Stockholm: Research Institute of Swedish National Defense, 1972.

Rose, A. The ecological influential: A leadership type. *Sociology and Social Research.* 1968, **52**, (2).

Schonborn, K. *Dealing with violence.* Springfield, Ill; Charles C. Thomas, 1975.

Sharp, G. *The politics of nonviolent action.* Boston: Porter Sargent, 1973.

Warmbruun, W. *The Dutch under German occupation.* Palo Alto, Calif. Stanford University Press, 1963.

Wechsberg, J. *The voices.* Garden City, N.Y.: Doubleday, 1969.

Wehr, P. *Conflict regulation.* Boulder, Colo. Westview Press, 1979 (a).

Wehr, P. Nonviolent resistance to occupation: Norway and Czechoslovakia. In S. Brun & P. Rayman (Eds.), *Nonviolent action and social change.* New York: Irvington Publishers, 1979 (b).

Wright, Q. *A study of war.* Chicago: University of Chicago Press, 1965.

Yakil, L. *Et demokrati pa prove.* Copenhagen: Gyldendal, 1967.

Chapter 12
Learning about Conflict and Aggression
Paul Wehr

In American society, conflict is generally viewed as a pathological condition, a disruptive and destructive force. This may be why learning about it is so difficult and why teaching about it is so poor. Were conflict seen more as a neutral process, that one learns to manage productively, we would better regulate it. In the same sense, aggression is too often viewed as a behavior to be glorified in some settings, and totally unacceptable in others. Were aggression characterized somewhat more objectively as an often functional response to a set of conditions, we might learn to work with it and use it more constructively.

Strong forces reinforce these extreme, distorted views of conflict and aggression. Presentation of conflict and aggression by the mass media as either exalted or unacceptable behavior exemplifies this distortion. Aggression is normally presented as part of a constellation of behaviors—violence, goal attainment, authoritarianism, physical force, conquest and submission. It is little wonder that the image of aggression and conflict that reaches the television or film viewer is a highly confusing one. Is it an end in itself or a means to an end? Is it highly desirable or undesirable? Are you rewarded or punished for engaging in it? The consequences of these confusing images seem particularly important for children in our society.

Aggressive competition is almost universally reinforced in our society. This is perfectly illustrated by the games people play. According to one games company executive, "All games must be competitive. We once had a game called Happiness, which stressed the need to help one another out and was not competitive. It bombed." (Mariani, 1979, p. 42) One can argue whether television, the press, and toy manufacturers respond to basic needs of the consuming public or actively shape its wants by what they provide. Of course, they do both to some degree, but entertainment industries often seem to shape more than they respond. The disturbing thing is the degree to which aggression is so often linked to winning or losing, to violence, or to inevitable destructive consequences for some of the "players." It is seldom portrayed as a behavior which, controlled within a neutral process of conflict, can often pay off for everyone concerned. Rarely are cooperation and conflict presented as compatible, complementary processes in social relations. More seldom still are aggression and conflict presented without being closely linked to violence. In short, treatment of conflict and aggression is unhealthy to say the least.

Nowhere are unhealthy conflict attitudes and practices more evident than in two child-centered institutions, the family and the school. In the family, extremes are the rule, not the exception—either parental violence and authoritarianism which eliminate overt conflict, or the abdication of parental responsibility for child guidance and restraint, which likewise eliminates most parent-child conflict.

In the school the general rule is: order and control, yes; controversy and conflict, no. There is little possibility for the student to learn either the basis of peacemaking or techniques for creatively using conflict and aggression for personal growth and societal health. They do, however, often learn violence in school as recent investigations of corporal punishment have suggested.

I do not deny that there are many exceptions to this general rule, but our society has no formal explicit means by which we are taught how to manage conflict, handle aggression, and eschew violence in creative ways. Conflict management must be among the skills society trains its members to use, and at an early age if possible. Further, as Goldstein urges in Chapter 4, this training must be in specific skill behaviors. But where and how should such learning take place? The major socializing agents of society must be involved—the schools and universities, the press and electronic media, the family, the church.

Over the past two decades there has been some progress made toward revising our societal view of conflict and violence. Most of the peace and conflict education has occurred within our formal educational institutions but in the past decade, communities, government agencies and families have increasingly experimented with violence abatement and conflict management methods as well. In the following pages I will discuss how learning about conflict and conflict regulation is now going on first in our educational institutions, and then in society beyond the schools and universities.

PEACE AND CONFLICT EDUCATION

In recent years a modest yet significant counterforce to our unhealthy approach to conflict has developed in the form of a new pedagogy and literature on peacemaking. It has had some influence on teaching in public and private schools. The literature of peace education is steadily increasing in both breadth and depth.

There now exists a substantial group of classroom materials. Resource works by Stanford (1976), Abrams and Schmidt (1974), Nesbitt (1972), and Judson (1977) provide a base for elementary and secondary level peace education. Numerous audiovisual materials have also been produced over the past decade. Both the National Education Association and the National Council for Social Studies have developed directories and catalogs of peace and conflict studies resources. There are even occasional teacher training programs, such as that at Wayne State University, that offer a curriculum emphasis in peace education, and materials such as the workbook on dealing with aggressive behavior produced by the Ohio Department of Education (1971).

While there are teachers interested in peace and conflict education and materials for them to use, there is little support for it among administrators or local school boards, perhaps because of its controversial nature. The suspicion that peace education contradicts or questions values propagated in the school—patriotism, self-defense, authoritarian structures—builds resistance to it among educators and politically conservative school board members. Peace educators, for example, would argue that military recruiting in and around secondary schools should be balanced with discussion of alternative methods of conflict resolution and civilian national service opportunities. They would also request that the social and physical science curricula present a balanced view of the costs and benefits of violent conflict. Clearly, such suggestions require more than cosmetic curriculum changes. Institutional inertia alone would offer resistance even were the suggestions not controversial.

Besides the lack of support for peace and conflict education among most educators, there is as yet no supporting structure for it outside the schools. Such a structure would include expanded treatment of peacemaking in children's literature, and a linking of in-school and family conflict management training. I will discuss nonformal conflict education later in the chapter.

CONFLICT STUDIES IN HIGHER EDUCATION

The study of peace and conflict processes is more developed in colleges and universities than it is at the lower levels of the educational system.

Curriculum in higher education is less directly controlled by government and one is therefore freer to innovate and to critique existing social, political, and economic structures. For three decades, peace and conflict research has been growing steadily in North American and European universities (Dedring, 1976; Wehr, 1979b). Before 1970, this occurred primarily at the graduate level and provided a literature base for the undergraduate programs that have developed in the 1970s (Wehr, 1979a). The Vietnam War and its repercussions within the university motivated the initiation of most of these programs. Their growth was facilitated by national organizations such as the Consortium on Peace Research, Education and Development (COPRED). New courses were created and faculty specializing in peace and conflict research were sometimes hired. In a few cases, off-campus programs were started in which students gained work experience in conflict management (Wehr and DeHaan, 1978). Antioch College established a Master's degree in peace studies. Friends World College and Earlham College both built their peace and conflict studies curricula around field experience for their students. A third Quaker institution of higher learning, Haverford College, through its Center for Nonviolent Conflict Resolution established an off-campus program in urban studies and conflict management, in which I was deeply involved. The following discussion is based on my experience of this program.

The Haverford Project

The Educational Involvement Program (EIP) was designed to help students understand urban problems, experience the conflict associated with them, and develop skills in urban problem solving and conflict management. It was funded by the Ford Foundation and in addition to Haverford students included some from Bryn Mawr College, Swarthmore College, and Lincoln University. The EIP evolved in response to several undercurrents in undergraduate education in the late 1960s. Many students were concerned about what they felt was the remoteness of their academic learning from the world beyond the campus. They were uncomfortable with the discontinuity between their course work and the rest of life as they saw it. At Haverford, these troubled students were diverse in background—upper- and middle-class whites, blacks, Puerto Ricans. All were impatient to learn how society operates more directly, and to apply their learning in favor of purposive social change.

Simultaneously, a number of university social scientists were seeking opportunities for their students to test theory in the field. These teachers valued the integration of theory and practice and were critical of the distance of their teaching from direct experience.

Lastly, minority leaders were challenging the urban universities which were physically displacing their communities, studying them in exploitive ways, and doing little to help them solve their problems. These communities were demanding a problem-solving partnership of the university that would be of some benefit to them.

The EIP was conceived in the turbulence of these crosswinds of change. White and minority students, college faculty, and leaders of two Philadelphia black neighborhoods cooperated in designing the project. Haverford's Center for Nonviolent Conflict Resolution provided the framework for developing the project. The designers first asked questions. How can students best learn about urban society, its structure and dynamics, its social conflict and conflict management processes? Will students' direct, continuing involvement in what they study increase their motivation to learn, their sensitivity, their accuracy of observation, their critical sense? How can action and study best be combined to increase the students' "educability" (Heath, 1968) as well as their knowledge? These are intriguing but difficult questions indeed.

The EIP drew especially upon the contributions of three important educational and psychological theorists, John Dewey, Jean Piaget, and Carl Rogers. For Dewey, formal learning should be a liberalizing process, requiring continual interaction of the abstract with the concrete:

> The aim of education should be to secure a balanced interaction of the [concrete and abstract] types of mental attitude, having sufficient regard to the disposition of the individual not to hamper and cripple whatever powers are naturally strong in him. The narrowness of individuals of strong concrete bent needs to be liberalized. Every opportunity that occcurs within practical activities for developing curiosity and susceptibility to intellectual problems should be seized. Violence is not done to natural disposition; rather the latter is broadened. Otherwise, the concrete becomes narrowing and deadening. As regards the smaller number of those who have a taste for the abstract, purely intellectual topics, pains should be taken to multiply opportunities for the application of ideas, for translating symbolic truths in terms of everyday and social life. *Every human being has both capabilities, and every individual will be more effective and happier if both powers are developed in easy and close interaction with each other.* Otherwise the abstract becomes identical with the academic and pedantic [Dewey, 1933, p. 228, emphasis added].

A second influence in the conceptualization of EIP was the humanistic Quaker orientation of education at Haverford where the values of peacemaking, justice, and social responsibility have long shaped the academic program. Yet, Haverford's intellectual rigor was influential as well. Experiential learning, as we thought of it then, was not merely "learning by doing." It involved action certainly, but also depended heavily on reflection upon the action. The actor corrects the action with this reflective feedback. This interaction of theory and praxis produces the learning. At the intersection of the planes of action and reflection lies the secret of a student's learning how to observe accurately, analyze correctly, and make wise decisions to rectify a problem.

The objectives of the program, then, were twofold. It was intended to enhance the social science training of student participants but also to develop their urban problem-solving and conflict management skills. Educational enrichment for students and their involvement in remedial action in urban and suburban neighborhoods were the desired payoffs. Internship projects were developed in such neighborhoods. The urban projects were built around three problem areas of special concern to students and faculty: schools, housing, and closed institutions such as prisons and hospitals. Specific neighborhoods and institutions were selected where the interest of their leaders promised close cooperation. (See Fig. 12.1).

School-Community Assistants (SCAs). Through the Independent Urban Education Corporation in North Philadelphia, ten students served as teaching assistants each semester in the East Poplar neighborhood elementary schools. The SCA role was to combine service to both the school and the community. While some students did relate to their neighborhoods outside their school activities, the community dimension of the SCA role was inhibited by two factors. First, transient students were mistrusted by these neighborhoods, which were wary of hippies, drugs, and white saviors. In fact, the most notable interaction with the neighborhoods occurred when the SCAs offended the sensibilities of local parents—by smoking marijuana, for example. Such incidents involved considerable conflict and peacemaking activity and while they were painful for all concerned, they were heuristic in terms of conflict education.

Students were also too involved with their work in the schools and in working out problems in their living groups to have more than superficial involvement with the host communities. This was the case with students in all three urban projects. The academic and field work demands on them precluded strong ties with the neighborhoods although close relationships with individual neighbors were often established.

In the schools, SCA work included tutoring individual children, settling classroom and out-of-school disputes, small-group teaching, home-visiting and after-school recreational and instructional programs. Since the SCA bore little resemblance to the student teacher familiar to classroom teachers, the SCA-teacher relationship was difficult to define, though often quite successful. The SCA role was one of inherent tension. On the one hand, SCAs supported the existing educational system by assisting children and teachers within it. On the other, SCAs

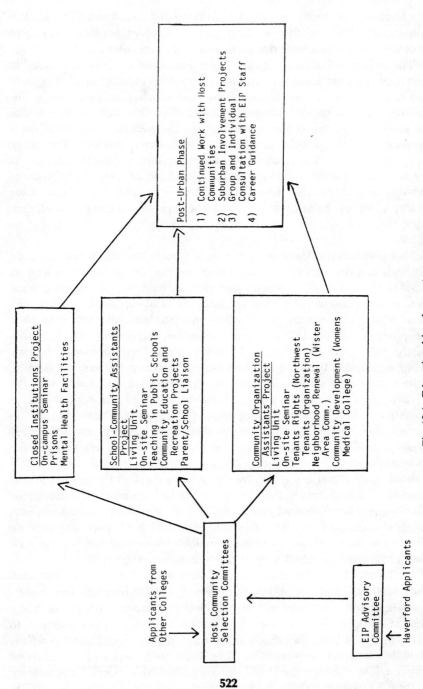

Fig. 12.1. Educational involvement program.

Applicants from Other Colleges

Host Community Selection Committees

EIP Advisory Committee

Haverford Applicants

Closed Institutions Project
On-campus Seminar
Prisons
Mental Health Facilities

School-Community Assistants Project
Living Unit
On-site Seminar
Teaching in Public Schools
Community Education and Recreation Projects
Parent/School Liaison

Community Organization Assistants Project
Living Unit
On-site Seminar
Tenants Rights (Northwest Tenants Organization)
Neighborhood Renewal (Wister Area Comm.)
Community Development (Womens Medical College)

Post-Urban Phase
1) Continued Work with Host Communities
2) Suburban Involvement Projects
3) Group and Individual Consultation with EIP Staff
4) Career Guidance

522

expected to introduce some creative change within that system. These conflicting self-images—the system supporter and the subversive change agent—caused considerable psychological tension for many of the SCAs. As they came to understand the demands made on educators, parents, and children, their rhetoric of outrage gave way to empathy with the victims of an educational system that was not working. The SCAs retained their critical sense but moved away from general condemnation toward focused criticism and experimentation with alternatives.

The SCAs' on-site academic seminar initially centered around topics we felt would help them understand their new environment: for example, race relations, conflict management, Afro-American history and culture, urban politics, and learning theory. The course was largely unsuccessful for it did not deal with what students observed daily in the schools and in their living groups. A "transplanted" academic course just did not meet the SCAs' immediate problem-solving needs and was therefore rejected. In the second year, the project developed a seminar that both faculty and SCAs felt did meet those needs. It studied the city and the immediate school neighborhood, the Philadelphia school system, educational opportunities for Philadelphia students, simple teaching techniques, and conflict management and problem-solving strategies for the classroom. SCAs suggested sessions appropriate for their needs and applied insights from their field work. Simulation and group problem solving supplemented the reading and discussion.

Community Organization Assistants (COAs). Community Organization Assistants worked in the Germantown section of Philadelphia with community action organizations. Their assignments involved organizing for tenants' rights, assisting neighborhood renewal programs, and intervening as neutral third parties in interracial conflict.

Unlike the SCAs who worked together in two schools, COAs had diverse work assignments and schedules. It was therefore more difficult to create for them a sense of unity in the living group and a common focus for their on-site seminar in community organization. COA field work included preparing and presenting claims against slumlords, organizing neighborhood food cooperatives and preschool breakfast programs, and organizing a youth recreation program in a racially tense neighborhood.

Closed Institutions Project. Aware of closed institutions as a locus of violence and despair in society, we established a total-care institutions unit in the final year of the program. Student interns worked in a medium security prison, schools for the deaf and blind, and a resocialization center for former mental patients. Since their assignments were scattered around metropolitan Philadelphia, these interns never formed a living unit and either lived with the other units or commuted from campus.

Closed institutions field work usually involved teaching, which ranged from instruction in philosophy and sociology for prison inmates to resocialization classes for mental patients reentering society. Student interns took a course on closed institutions at Haverford geared to their fieldwork.

The Suburban Program. The EIP staff expected many of the students returning from inner-city experiences to continue part-time involvement in surrounding suburbia. Provision was made, therefore, for relating their academic work to social change, and for using their knowledge and experience gained in the inner-city programs.

EIP staff organized the Suburban Coalition, linking change-oriented action groups in the area. The Coalition produced a student-edited monthly newspaper and college/community study groups working on health care delivery, the rights of students and the elderly, and racial harmony. The staff also found field work placements for social science and independent study students. Senior psychology majors, for example, worked with local high school teachers on an improved social science curriculum. Others did field work in mental hospitals and resocialization centers. Still others practiced conflict management in urban and suburban schools.

Evaluating the Program. A rough measure of the success of the Educational Involvement Program was made with (1) evaluations by persons with whom students worked in inner-city neighborhoods, (2) taped interviews with student participants before and after participation, and (3) other indicators such as participant involvement in the suburban program upon their return, the learning reflected in seminar papers, and responses on a final evaluation questionnaire. While such measures are admittedly inadequate and open to bias, they did give us some indication of the learning that did take place.

By all indicators, the participants had a rich educational experience. The EIP experience was not strictly speaking an academic one. To be sure, academic skills such as observation and analysis of social institutions, testing theory in praxis, and reflective study in seminars were important parts, but only parts of a total learning experience.

The participants gave the program high marks as an educational experience. Of the 67 who returned questionnaires, 55 (82 percent) judged it very positive and 11 (16 percent) as somewhat positive. The most prominent aspect of the learning seemed to be its active nature. The students were acting upon their immediate environments, getting feedback, and analyzing it under supervision.

The following aspects of the learning experience were mentioned more frequently by the students as being especially valuable:

1. *The opportunity for theory and reality testing.* The combinations of theory with practice, and of study with field work permitted the application of abstract concepts to real world experience. As one student put it, an "academic education can become extremely sterile if it is in an isolated environment where one is seldom forced in a practical way to make decisions and feel their consequences."

2. *Personal growth.* Most felt they had matured considerably through the experience. Autonomy in learning, empathy across race and class lines, self-knowledge, and the ability to be useful to someone else were all growth dimensions cited by returning participants.

3. *Group living.* New living groups were formed each semester. Normally these groups were characterized by racial and social diversity and were not created on the basis of mutual compatibility of members. The students had to learn to live together under severe space constraints. Some units were more successful than others in maintaining internal racial harmony and resolving personality conflicts. The presence of one or two "stabilizer members" was a dominant factor in a living unit's success, as were the degree of similarity in work and schedules, and the amount of staff time available for group conflict management. Many participants valued the semester for how it trained them in conflict management, cooperative living, and tolerance. Their living units forced them together and taught them how to handle tension, allocate space, and settle disputes both among themselves and with neighbors. "I was exposed to people from divergent backgrounds and the give-and-take in making the house run smoothly for all was instructive. When to be compulsive, when to let things ride—questions like that came up all the time."

4. *Understanding urban problems.* Participants expanded their awareness of racism, poverty, corruption, and other conditions of life for the urban poor. "[One gains] insight into the institutional process controlling the lives of people in the inner-city. Not only does one identify more closely with the oppressed ... one sees the day-by-day functioning of the agents of oppression."

5. *Preparation for postcollegiate life.* Skills development and field work related to an intended career were often mentioned as extremely valuable. Participants spoke of the connectedness of their on-site learning to the settings in which it would be used. Dewey's observations are

especially helpful here:

> One trouble is that the subject-matter in question was learned in isolation ... it was segregated when it was acquired and hence is so disconnected from the rest of experience that it is not available under the actual conditions of life. It is contrary to the laws of experience that learning of this kind, no matter how thoroughly engrained at the time, should give genuine preparation [1959, p. 48].

6. *Conflict education.* A valuable part of the students' training in EIP was in conflict analysis and conflict management. All of the field work communities and assignments were highly charged with conflict and tension—interpersonal, racial, interinstitutional. Most of the EIP participants had not experienced much overt conflict in their lives, yet they found themselves at the intersection point of several conflict planes (Fig. 12.2). The staff helped them learn to manage conflict both among their peers within the living units, and in their work settings. Important

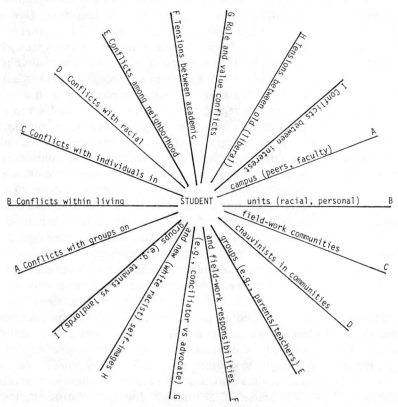

Fig. 12.2. EIP conflicts and tensions.

conflicts were discussed in the on-site seminars and over dinner or coffee. Strategies for resolving a specific dispute, and for managing more general conflict and tension, were often developed. Students learned different resolution techniques and when to use them. One participant observed:

> conflicts definitely existed in the house. And I was very aware of conflict just working on the community newsletter. I knew that somehow conflicting interests and groups within the community had to be reached in a way that would alienate the fewest people. Our ultimate goal was to get as many people involved (in the community project) as possible. Not only did I learn different ways of dealing with conflict, but the most profitable way at a given time. What might work in the community . . . simply wouldn't work in the [living unit].

Since violence and conflict are often closely related in urban neighborhoods, EIP students were forced to confront the problem of violence in our society more directly and personally than most had before. For most of them it was their first exposure to real physical insecurity. EIP staff urged prudent behavior such as travelling in groups after dark and keeping doors locked, and fortunately there was no serious incident in the three-year period. In fact, the neighborhoods were quite protective of the students. One white student who intervened to stop an interracial gang fight was beaten by the whites and rescued by the blacks. In another incident, an EIP student was shot at, then roughed up by the police who suspected him of drug dealing. Each case stimulated profound discussion by students and staff about the causes and conditions of the crises and how they might have been managed with minimal risk.

From this immersion in a setting where violence and aggression were more overt than in their normal lives, EIP students grew to understand the root causes of that societal violence. They also learned how to anticipate it and to develop creative responses to it. Middle-class students of diverse racial and ethnic origins experienced the different types of *behavioral* violence common to cities—police brutality, gang warfare and other street violence, intrafamilial violence. Such experience taught students to act with caution and foresight, not to panic. They also learned to understand the behavioral violence in relation to *structural* violence, the structures of poverty and exploitation that created the conditions for behavioral violence. The two types became for them interpenetrating and mutually reinforcing. Conflict education for EIP students included much learning in how to manage violence, aggression and crisis.

7. *Other learning dimensions.* Other aspects of the EIP learning experience that supported the conflict education included direct experience with racism, building cooperative personal relationships un-

der conditions of tension, exposure to ways of life radically different from one's own, growth in personal autonomy, and increased capacity for empathy across class and racial lines.

Returning EIP students appreciated this experiment in experiential education, more than they understood it. They were excited about it for the most part. For the large majority of them, intellectual and emotional growth needs unmet in the standard academic curriculum had been met in an integrated and meaningful way; their experience was like that described by Dewey:

> When the mind thoroughly appreciates anything, that object is experienced with heightened intensity of value. There is no inherent opposition between thought, knowledge, and appreciation. There is, however, a definite opposition between an idea of a fact grasped *merely* intellectually and the idea or fact which is *emotionally* colored because it is felt to be connected with the needs and satisfaction of the whole personality. In the latter case, it has immediate value; that is, it is *appreciated* [1933, p. 277].

EIP participants, in large part, were appreciative of the experience because they saw it to be of immediate value to them as whole persons, not merely as intellectual beings. Yet, Haverford EIP students appeared to resume their academic studies quite successfully upon their return to campus. There had been some concern among faculty that the EIP experience would ruin them as academic learners. Most (85 percent) of them subsequently increased their grade point averages by more than did their peers who had remained on campus. The EIP group also produced a number of honors graduates including a *Phi Beta Kappa* and a *magna cum laude* degree. EIP participants returned to campus with new needs and interest areas such as institutional change, poverty, racism, and urban politics. They realized that they needed intellectual discipline as well as practical skills to deal with such problems effectively. To use Heath's (1968) term, these students were more "educable" when they returned to campus than they were when they left.

The EIP impacted the host communities, but probably to a lesser degree than it did the student participants. The presence of the SCAs in neighborhood elementary schools not only provided additional teaching personnel but helped teachers and administrators conceive of new ways to use auxiliary personnel in the schools. Through their open classroom and other teaching experiments, SCAs generated interest in innovative curriculum.

The COA project strengthened community action in the Germantown section. It provided the support personnel for the Northwest Tenants

Organization where activities ranged from apartment house tenant organizing to researching housing legislation. Other COAs organized food cooperatives and neighborhood renewal projects, established a Spanish-language newspaper, and a breakfast program for school children.

Returned EIP participants developed social change projects in the Suburban Program, predominantly in citizen education about racism, war-peace issues, and movements for securing the rights of students, women, and the elderly. A major national organization for the rights of the elderly, the Gray Panthers, had its origins in the EIP Suburban Program. In these projects the concern was less for conflict resolution than for generating creative conflict and action programs through college/community collaboration. The Main Line Citizens Center for Peace, the Suburban Coalition, and the College Council for Community Involvement, all social action networks established by EIP staff and students, made that collaboration possible.

In retrospect, the EIP experiment made a substantial impact on its urban and suburban host communities in the form of organizations advancing the rights of minorities, but little lasting impact on the curriculum of participating colleges. Haverford College, after the program, seemed to pull back from a concern for *educational* excellence to a narrower emphasis on *academic* excellence. Since Haverford is consciously an academic college, one might have expected this. Though there are several high quality academic institutions that might have integrated such an experiment into the regular curriculum, one should probably not expect such experiments to continue. Experiments of this nature illustrate alternative approaches that may or may not be adopted in one form or another, then they end. I have briefly described the EIP in order to illustrate one possibility for formal conflict education at the university level.

Some peace and conflict studies programs have taken root to become permanent parts of a curriculum. Others, like Haverford's experiment, have not. Many lost favor and support as concern over the Vietnam War faded, though not all of these have folded. Several, like the Institute for Peace and Justice (St. Louis) and the Center for Conflict Resolution (Madison), voluntarily cut their ties with universities and now serve and are supported by their urban communities.

A number of these programs, though, have just disappeared—victims of budget cuts, departmental territoriality, or ineffective leadership. Learning about conflict and aggression management, then, has been only partially institutionalized. It is well established in the form of peace research and individual courses in universities but remains a fringe specialty and its students too often lack opportunity for practical experience. One could argue that peace and conflict education might lose its cutting edge were it to become established and "respectable." The risks posed by its remaining on the fringes of the educational system, though, seem much more serious to me. One recent development may soon shift conflict and peace education from the wings to at least left-of-center stage. A proposal to establish a national peace academy is being studied as of this writing.

The National Peace Academy

In amendments to the Elementary and Secondary Education Act of 1978 (PL 95–561), the United States Congress established the U.S. Commission on Proposals for the National Academy of Peace and Conflict Resolution. A $500,000 Congressional appropriation permitted the selection of a nine-member commission to study for one year the feasibility of establishing what would be the peacemaking counterpart of West Point and the other military service academies. It would be called, according to the enabling legislation, the National Academy of Peace and Conflict Resolution (NAPCORE). Senator Mark Hatfield, a cosponsor of the legislation, clearly expressed its intention:

> One important purpose for this establishment would be for the training of students in the arts of conflict resolution. For example, arbitration and negotiation are two peaceful methods of conflict resolution which could be researched and studied. The second purpose ... would be to train individuals in new methodology which will be extracted from the arts of negotiation, arbitration, conciliation and mediation [Paley, 1980].

After its study, the commission is to make recommendations to the president and to Congress. Should the recommendation be to establish the academy, supplementary recommendations will determine its structure, specific functions, and requirements. It would probably not resemble its military counterparts. It might be decentralized and located in several parts of the nation. It might have a modest permanent faculty and bring in visiting academic and professional faculty on a rotating basis. It might create an extension service such as those now serving agricultural and energy constituencies (Wehr, 1980).

The idea of formal federal involvement in peacemaking is as old as the nation. As early as 1783, George Washington expressed his hope that "Congress will recommend a proper Peace Establishment for the United States" (Paley, 1980). Over the next two centuries the concept of a formal peace institution surfaced time and again. A Peace Academy Commission missed creation by one vote in the House in 1976. In 1979, the commission was finally created. The likelihood now is that the academy will be established. If so, regardless of its character, the institution should give conflict resolution, as both a craft and a science, a substantial push forward. It should legitimize and encourage conflict and peace education and research at all levels of formal education. It should start quickly to provide us with trained persons whose very existence will stimulate the growth of a profession.

Graduate Peace and Conflict Research

While conflict learning is in the early stages of development in schools and undergraduate colleges, the knowledge base for that development has been expanding in graduate education for several decades.

At the graduate level, learning about conflict and aggression most often takes the form of research. The past two decades have seen explosive growth in conflict research. Transnational networks now link peace and conflict researchers around the globe: for example, the International Peace Research Association and its regional councils; the Peace Science Society (International); the Inter-University Seminar on Armed Forces and Society; and the Consortium on Peace Research, Education and Development. In addition, a number of national associations have developed, as have permanent sections on peace and conflict research within numerous professional societies. The American Sociological Association, the International Studies Association, and the Society for the Psychological Study of Social Issues all have active conflict research sections.

Under what conditions and by way of what institutions does conflict between nations lead to war? What methods can preclude destructive conflict or terminate it once it has begun? Early peace scholars such as Lewis Richardson, Quincy Wright, and Pitirim Sorokin were the first to research these questions systematically. Building on that early work, Kenneth Boulding, Anatol Rappaport, Herbert Kelman, and their counterparts in Europe created the pioneer journals and institutes during the 1950s and 1960s. Some important research was also being done during that period by James Coleman, Lewis Coser, Margaret Mead, and others into the nature of conflict within societies. Oddly enough, the societal and international conflict research groups remained relatively isolated from one another until the present decade.

There seems to be no identifiable mainstream of peace and conflict research. Competing paradigms, diverse ideologies, and discordant methodologies characterize the field. The dominant cleavage in recent years has separated those primarily concerned with behavioral violence, who see conflict as dysfunctional for peace, from those who concentrate on structural violence and inequality within and between nations, who emphasize the functional potential of conflict. This dissensus produced a schismatic break in 1969 from which the field has yet to recover (Eide, 1972).

Through the 1960s, peace research was primarily directed to the application of game theory to the arms race phenomenon, to the causes of great power hostility, to civil war and insurgent movements, and to intranational collective violence such as the urban riots that punctuated that period in the United States. Attention was focused on behavioral violence and East-West conflict.

By the mid-point of the decade, however, a growing number of conflict analysts in Europe were turning their attention to the structural bases for war and social violence. This was partially a response to American involvement in Indochina and to the Soviet invasion of Czechoslovakia, but it was also motivated by the deep roots of radical political theory in European universities. A broader concept of peace was emerging that called for the elimination of dependency relationships between rich nations and poor, of militarism, and of economic under-development. This new theoretical school encouraged a shift of conflict and peace research somewhat away from the East-West toward the North-South plane. Galtung's (1971) structural theory of imperialism is illustrative of this emerging school of radical peace research.

The behaviorists, on the other hand, continued their preoccupation with conditions for stable peace, with the nature of military institutions, with disarmament and international peacekeeping, and with the importance of the international system in the peace process. This last concern with the systemic properties of a world in transition has been a point of partial agreement for the two schools. They can agree on the centrality of the system for an understanding of conflict but they have widely disparate views of the nature of that system.

In the 1970s, a third group of researchers emerged that may yet provide a bridge between the behavioral violence researchers and those concerned with structural violence. This group looks at the changing nature of the global system, developments occurring across national boundaries that are creating a global as opposed to an international community. Research interests in this group range from transnational networks that facilitate global integration, to value shifts among national and international elites, to transnational social movements responding to arms proliferation, economic and social injustice, and environmental degradation.

Despite significant internal differences and disparities, the community of peace and conflict researchers has been a remarkably productive one. I will suggest some recent trends these scholars have developed as they look at the conflict process in its several dimensions: (1) its *origins*; (2)

the dynamics of conflict as strategic *interaction*; (3) how conflict parties *communicate* with and perceive one another; (4) how conflict is *waged*; and (5) how it can be better *regulated*. As we shall see, disparate assumptions about the origins of conflict lead scholars to quite different conclusions on how to manage that conflict.

Origins. The origins of conflict are a source of much controversy among conflict theorists. The tension between the conflict and the functionalist paradigms in sociological theory is a longstanding one. It issues from the question of whether conflict is inherent in or peripheral to the social order. Two decades ago, Dahrendorf (1959) produced a bridging theory that permits the use of both conflict theory and functionalism to explain the origins of social conflict. According to his theory, challenge groups seek access to authority and are not motivated by specific class interests. More recently, Gamson (1975) has suggested that such groups—the major initiators of conflict in society—become aware of inherent conflicts of interests and pursue their interests through rational action. Resistance against the Vietnam War, for example, was increasingly effective as movement leadership engaged in rational planning.

At the opposite end of the theoretical spectrum from the rational challenge group theory are the instinctual theories. The view of the ethologists and sociobiologists is that conflict originates in the fighting instinct (Wilson, 1978). This view seems to complement the Freudian theory of innate human aggressiveness. There is little doubt that humans have an inherent *capacity* for aggression, violence and conflict; whether they also have a *propensity* for such action remains a highly debatable question.

Causal theories range from such poorly defined concepts as national interest and balance of power to more concrete factors such as the influence of military institutions and miscommunication. Each conflict formation is, of course, best understood within a multicausal analytical framework. Nevertheless, the origins of a particular conflict may be better described by one theory rather than another. Dependency theory, with its emphasis on common interests of elites in center and periphery nations, might contribute more to an understanding of the origins of the Vietnam War than would, say, balance-of-power theories. A theory of leader misperception (White, 1970) may be more explanatory for that war than a Marxist theory of imperialist protection of resources and markets.

Approaches to conflict regulation are as diverse as the theories. Instinctualist theories look to conflict institutionalization and displacement of aggressive impulses into acceptable behavior such as sports.

Conflict functionalists such as Coser (1970), who view conflict as a normal social process, might encourage its institutionalization by way of a society's greater tolerance of challenge movements and better training of its members in conflict management. Structural functionalists, who consider conflict as a symptom of strain in social systems, would eliminate the conflict by fine tuning the dyssynchronous elements. Coercion theorists, who see conflict as inherent in grossly inequitable social structures, would prescribe struggle by the coerced to alter the structures and thus to eliminate the conflict.

Dynamics. A second attribute of conflict is its dynamism, in particular its interactive nature. Since conflict is a goal-oriented, interactive process, conflict parties base their strategies largely on each other's moves. An action-reaction dynamic is therefore common. It is this *reciprocal causation*, as Coleman (1957) has termed it, that sustains arms races and other types of spiralling escalation so resistant to conflict management. Reciprocal causation, however, is two-directional and has deescalatory as well as escalatory potential, as Osgood (1974) convincingly demonstrates.

In negotiation one sees, within limited parameters, the interactive nature of conflict in sharp relief. Bargaining occurs sometimes as formal negotiation, sometimes in tacit form. Our understanding of negotiation has been furthered through systematic analysis of the process itself, the roles individual negotiators play, and the larger negotiating context within which they operate (Druckman, 1973). More successful bargaining strategies might be developed by drawing on such research. Fisher (1970) suggests how negotiators can structure their strategies to encourage accommodation from the other side. Of particular interest to conflict research are those aspects of negotiation that interfere with successful negotiating, such as conflictual personal styles of negotiators, cultural differences between them, and poor communication.

Small groups experiments in negotiation have shown how the potential for cooperation found in most conflict relationships can be enhanced. The Bartos (1977) experiments lead to the conclusion that fairness is the most effective bargaining principle and that strict adherence to it facilitates settlement. Yet, the styles of negotiators and mediators may be a more significant determinant of success or failure of negotiation; where a negotiator opts out of the interactive process, it cannot work. Experiments by Alcock and Mansell (1977) showed some individuals predisposed to be noncooperative and inflexible in negotiations, and influenced little by the behavior of their opponents. While the style and stance of negotiators is important in determining bargaining outcomes, how negotiations are structured by a mediator may be as important as the give and take of negotiators. The Baumgartner, Buckley & Burns (1975) study showed the importance of "relational control" over the conflict parties by prior structuring of the interaction, and of the system of payoffs.

The interactive nature of the conflict relationship will carry it toward or away from resolution. More and better research is needed to produce methods for using the potential for resolution and regulation inherent in the conflict process.

Communication. Conflict researchers have examined the subjective elements in conflict, which are often extremely influential in determining outcomes. Parties to conflict often misperceive their opponent's intentions, miscalculate each other's strength, or make decisions from nonrational motives. Actors may initiate conflict, or continue it long after it has become dysfunctional for all parties, for reasons that have little to do with rational goal attainment. Reduction of the nonrational elements in conflict, through improved communication, could enlarge the potential of rationally based methods such as negotiation.

International conflict reduction through communication has been a prominent focus in peace research. Small groups researchers are particularly well represented here. Burton's (1969) "controlled communication" method was applied in controlled settings with representatives of warring states. Techniques were designed to break down stereotypes, to modify the totally subjective way in which disputants viewed the conflict situation, and to facilitate joint-costing by which conflict parties together assess the costs and benefits of continuing the conflict.

Doob (1970) and his associates have applied group process techniques, the "problem-solving workshop," to several international conflicts including a Kenya-Somalia dispute and the Northern Ireland conflict, but with mixed results. Cohen, Kelman, Miller & Smith (1977) have used similar small groups techniques on the Arab-Israeli conflict. Such research assumes that a part of any conflict formation is subjective—a part that can be reduced through issue clarification, tension reduction, image modification, and other small groups techniques. This emphasis on the subjective elements of a conflict characterizes the international conciliation program of the Quakers (Yarrow, 1978), who have intervened as a neutral third party in some of the most rancorous interstate conflicts.

Research has also been done on interpersonal and community conflict reduction. Frost and Wilmot (1978) have brought together much of the work on interpersonal peacemaking. Walton's (1969) research is seminal here, as is Gordon's (1975) work in family conflict management, which emphasizes modifying communication styles and patterns.

Waging Conflict. A growing amount of conflict research in recent years has concerned itself with the question of whether conflict can be waged less destructively. Violent conflict, particularly at the international level, occurs with increasing frequency as specialized military and intelligence institutions are created to engage in it. In recent years, mainstream scientists have begun to question directly whether modern military institutions and their policies are more likely to deter or to precipitate war. The validity of the "more is better" principle of military spending has recently been called into question by the Boston Study Group (Morrison & Walker, 1978). It concludes that current U.S. military spending policies decrease rather than increase American and global security. The group suggests that rather than continuing the present worst-case overkill strategy, the United States should fit weapons systems and personnel to limited functions and needs. The resulting effective, low-risk military force would increase deterrence capability and reduce the risk of war.

Military institutions do seem to develop an autonomous momentum. As Senghaas (1974) and Melman (1974) suggest, they may grow to operate independently of their counterparts in opposing nations, in an autistic fashion. As weapons systems become more complex and vulnerable to human error, technical malfunction, and terrorist attack, scholars are doing more analysis of military institutions, arms control and transfers, and militarization of civilian institutions.

European peace research has produced what one might call a "middle view" of the superpower arms race. The disarmament study group of the International Peace Research Association has analyzed that race particularly as it affects European security (IPRA, 1975). The Stockholm International Peace Research Institute (SIPRI) provides annual analyses of weapons proliferation and development of military technology around the world. SIPRI studies provide us with a chilling view of destructive means of waging conflict. Yet, with the more destructive systems such as nuclear weapons and chemical-biological agents, means become quite divorced from goals or ends. If these weapons are used, no goals can be attained and one must question whether such an exchange can any longer be defined as rational conflict.

At the same time that research on militarization has increased, so has inquiry into the development of nonviolent, nondestructive means of waging conflict. Such research includes social scientific studies of nonviolent direct action, sponsored by the National Institute for Mental Health (Walker, 1976), and feasibility studies of nonviolent national defense strategies funded by the Danish (Boserup and Mack, 1975) and Swedish (Roberts, 1972) governments. Bruyn and Rayman (1979) present a diverse group of case studies that suggest how nonviolent direct action works. Coover, Deacon, Esser, & Moore (1977) go further to examine the methods by which nonviolent actionists are trained, and Desai (1972) describes how this is accomplished in India. "Doing" conflict creatively is also the central theme of Frost and Wilmot's (1978) review.

There is, then, a substantial group of serious scholars and scholar-activists working at both ends of the conflict waging problem: toward a full understanding of how destructive conflict is carried on, and toward the development of methods of waging conflict without destructive consequences.

Regulation. While conflict parties can be trained to keep the conflict within bounds, conflict regulation is also done by third parties. Practitioners themselves have generated much of the research on third-party intervention. The interposition of peacekeeping forces in international and intercommunal conflicts has been carefully analyzed. Moskos (1976) has given us a scholarly view of the military peacekeeping process, while Rikhye, Harbottle & Egge (1974) provides a practitioner's perspective. Schonborn (1975) treats third-party peacekeeping as one aspect of the larger problem of crisis management, in which armed agents such as peacekeeping troops and domestic police forces are responsible for enforcing order. Schonborn's primary interest is in refining nonviolent and nonlethal responses to crisis situations. Forces of order are often violent because they have neither the training nor the technology to react otherwise. Their violent response to disorder tends to heighten tension and escalate the violence. Police behavior is changing, however, as police departments show new interest in training their people to respond to crises with minimal violence. New York City police, by way of example, have developed sophisticated programs in crisis response and intervention training (Bard, 1970).

As noted earlier, there has been a resurgence of researcher interest in international third-party mediation and conciliation (Young, 1972). Some of that research examines the complexities of behind-the-scenes inter-mediation at close range. Once again, much of this analysis is done not by scholars but by careful observers and practitioners such as Yarrow (1978), and Berman and Johnson (1977) who look at a number of successful unofficial and quasiofficial intermediation techniques. Intervention by nongovernmental agencies may lead us to new approaches once they are carefully studied.

Scholars have also studied the possibility of reducing and regulating conflict and aggression by more effective inculcation of the values of cooperative, nonaggressive modes of interaction. Boulding's (1974) work on children and nonviolence focuses on the normative contexts within which children are raised. Judson (1977) creates cooperative games and other methods for counteracting violence-promoting norms in the schools.

One international thrust at values reorientation is directed at university students and policy elites. Scholars from five continents, through conceptual research, have articulated several basic world order values: peacemaking, environmental balance, social and economic justice, equitable resource distribution (Mendlovitz, 1975). Their assumption is that just such a common set of supranational survival values is a prerequisite for cooperative relations between states. As one might expect, the authors' strategies for actualizing the values differ markedly.

In summary, a good deal of conflict research has been done but the link between research and practice remains a tenuous one. One serious weakness is the form in which the research is usually produced—in technical language and with no suggested policy applications. A second equally thorny problem concerns the nature of the tougher problems to which conflict resolution methods might be applied. There are usually high stakes involved, such as in international conflict, and conflict parties are generally reluctant to admit outsiders in, even to attempt to resolve the dispute. We need, then, to learn how better to utilize the research already available and to package it for more direct application in a greater range of conflict situations.

Supporting the peace and conflict research effort just described are a number of special collections of peace and conflict literature such as the Hoover Library at Stanford University, and the Peace Collections at Swarthmore and Haverford Colleges. There are as well the *Journal of Conflict Resolution*, the *Journal of Peace Research*, *Peace and Change*, and *Peace Research Abstracts*, all of which report current research in the field.

NON-FORMAL CONFLICT EDUCATION

Thus far, we have seen how learning to respond creatively to conflict and aggression has emerged in schools and universities over the past two decades. A similar development has occurred at a somewhat slower pace outside of formal education. This development has been particularly noteworthy in three arenas: the family, the community, and within complex organizations.

The home is an important environment for learning to manage conflict. Family relationships tend to become more conflictual as the stress of modern life pushes us both to require more from and to release more tension within those relationships. The alarming increase in family violence, child and wife abuse, and divorce can be only partially explained through more accurate reporting and heightened public awareness.

Some movement has been made in training family members in conflict and aggression management through family therapy, marital counselling, and a literature on family peacemaking (Blood, 1960; Gordon, 1975) and creative fighting (Bach & Wyden, 1968). Key concepts in both the literature and the techniques emerging from it include: (1) identifying behavior acceptable to all parties in conflict; (2) clarifying the power and goals of conflict parties; and (3) getting parties to develop strategies, tactics, and conflict styles that are compatible for purposes of reaching accommodation.

Conflict management and violence minimization are also being learned through formal training in professions in which crisis and conflict are what one might call occupational hazards. Police work would be the best example. Professionals regularly involved in intense conflict can now receive training in conflict management from organizations designed specifically for that purpose. Social workers, urban officials, school administrators, police in cities like New York learn through role playing, video replay, and simulation how to manage conflict and crisis (Nicolau, 1973). Other programs train for conflict and crisis management within complex governmental and corporate organizations (Blake & Mouton, 1970). There has even been a program developed for training international civil servants in different peacemaking skills (IPA 1971).

Urban communities are a third area in which conflict education has developed (Laue and Cormick, 1974). The Dispute Resolution Act recently passed by Congress and signed into law provides $40 million over a period of four years to state and local governments to establish community dispute settlement programs. One such program already operating, the Denver Conciliation Service, trains people for intervention in several types of conflict including landlord-tenant disagreements, child custody disputes, and commercial dispute resolution. In India, an organization known as the Shanti Sena has developed a unique program for training in community crisis intervention and dispute settlement (Desai, 1972). Thousands of people trained in the skills of village development, conflict resolution, and crisis management take up residence in villages and towns all over India. They become, in effect, resident community peacemakers who, in turn, train community members in conflict management.

Such training is designed generally to develop further personal conflict management skills that people may already have. Carpenter (1977) suggests a number of these skills such as verbal articulation, skills of objective observation, and empathetic listening that many already have and are essential for peacemaking, but that are not usually thought of in that way. Training permits individuals to refine and develop their potential, thereby expanding the range of responses they can make to conflictual and aggressive behavior.

CONCLUSION

Let me restate what I feel are the major requisites for the future growth and refinement of our society's capacity to manage conflict and aggression successfully.

First, there must develop an understanding of the dualistic nature of the problem. On the one hand conflict is natural in some measure, as is aggression. In reasonable amounts, these processes can be managed and kept within acceptable bounds. We can learn how to use conflictual and aggressive behavior effectively, where it is appropriate.

Conflict and aggression management must become institutionalized in American society both in formal education and in the various conflict sectors. Control of conflict and aggression now occurs within the web of social relationships unconsciously, for the most part. What I foresee is an expansion of conflict skills consciously learned and regularly practiced by people and institutions who need those skills. Such skills can be developed to a certain degree in our formal educational institutions. Training and research must go on there and curricula at all levels must be revised to include substantial treatment of the subject.

More must be done to train persons who work in such high-conflict settings as international relations, closed institutions, the deviance professions, the community, commerce and industry, and the family. Vested interests may resist the expansion of conflict management skills—the legal profession, for example, whose investment in the adversarial approach to conflict may make it hostile to methods of conflict regulation that do not require legal expertise. Yet even lawyers can enhance their skills through a reorientation toward more diverse conflict management strategies.

People with formal training in conflict regulation will increasingly need professional outlets for practicing their craft. Possibilities that come immediately to mind are the helping professions such as mental health and family therapists, positions in labor relations, police and others working constantly at crisis intervention, international civil servants, and community organization specialists.

Institutionalization of conflict management will involve both retraining professionals, creating new specialized roles within existing organizations, and forming new organizations expressly for dispute settlement.

Teaching large numbers of citizens how to manage conflict and aggression effectively is a response to the behavioral aspects of conflict and violence in society. There must, however, be a parallel awareness of the structural requisites for a peaceful society. Conflict management can handle the normal conflict and aggression but not the inordinate levels of conflict and social violence generated by inequitable social and economic structures. The more a society eliminates what I have earlier referred to as structural violence, the more manageable conflict and violence will become. A society must learn to manage its normal conflict and to eliminate the conditions that produce its aberrant conflict. The former will not work without the latter.

REFERENCES

Abrams, G. & Schmidt, F. *Peace is in our hands.* Philadelphia: Jane Addams Peace Association, 1974.

Alcock, J. & Mansell, D. Predisposition and behavior in a collective dilemma. *Journal of Conflict Resolution*, 1977, **21**, 443–457.

Bach, G. & Wyden, P. *The intimate enemy: How to fight fair in love and marriage.* New York: Avon, 1968.

Bard, M. Family intervention police teams as a community mental health resource. *Journal of Criminal Law*, 1970, **60**, 2–9.

Bartos, O. Simple model of negotiation. *Journal of Conflict Resolution*, 1977, **21**, 565–579.

Baumgartner, T., Buckley, W., & Burns, T. Relational control: The human structuring of cooperation and conflict. *Journal of Conflict Resolution*, 1975, **19**, 417–440.

Berman, M. & Johnson, J. (Eds.). *Unofficial diplomats.* New York: Columbia University Press, 1977.

Blake, R. & Mouton, J. The fifth achievement. *Journal of Applied Behavioral Science*, 1970, **6**, 413–426.

Blood, R. O., Jr. Resolving family conflicts. *Journal of Conflict Resolution*, 1960, **4**, 209–219.

Boserup, A. & Mack, A. *War without weapons.* New York: Schocken, 1975.

Boulding, E. The child and nonviolent social change. In L. Wulf (Ed.), *Handbook on peace education.* Frankfurt/Main: International Peace Research Association, 1974.

Bruyn, S. & Rayman, P. (Eds.). *Nonviolent action and social change.* New York: Irvington Publishers, 1979.

Burton, J. *Conflict and communication.* New York: Free Press, 1969.

Carpenter, S. *A repertoire of peacemaking skills.* Bethel College, North Newton, Kansas: Consortium on Peace Research, Education, and Development, 1977.

Cohen, S., Kelman, H., Miller, F., & Smith, B. Evolving intergroup techniques for conflict resolution: An Israeli-Palestinian pilot workshop. *Journal of Social Issues*, 1977, **33**, 165–189.

Coleman, J. *Community conflict.* New York: Free Press, 1957.

Coover, V., Deacon, E., Esser, C., & Moore, C. *Resource manual for a living revolution.* Philadelphia: New Society Press, 1977.

Coser, L. *Continuities in the study of social conflict.* New York: Free Press, 1970.

Dahrendorf, R. *Class and class conflict in industrial society.* Stanford, Calif.: Stanford University Press, 1959.

Dedring, J. *Recent advances in peace and conflict research.* Beverly Hills, Calif.: Sage, 1976.

Desai, N. *Towards a nonviolent revolution.* Varanasi, India: Sarva Seva Sangh Prakashan, 1972.

Dewey, J. *How we think: A restatement of the relation of reflective thinking to the educative process.* New York: Heath, 1933.

Dewey, J. *Experience and education.* New York: Macmillan, 1959.

Doob, L. *Resolving conflict in Africa: The Fermeda workshop.* New Haven: Yale University Press, 1970.

Druckman, D. *Human factors in international negotiations: Social psychological aspects of international conflict.* Beverly Hills, Calif.: Sage, 1973.

Eide, A. Dialogue and confrontation in Europe. *Journal of Conflict Resolution,* 1972, **16,** 511–530.

Fisher, R. *International conflict for beginners.* New York: Harper & Row, 1970.

Frost, J. & Wilmot, W. *Interpersonal conflict.* Dubuque, Iowa: William C. Brown Publishers, 1978.

Galtung, J. A structural theory of imperialism. *Journal of Peace Research,* 1971, **8,** 81–112.

Gordon, T. *Parent effectiveness training.* New York: New American Library, 1975.

Heath, D. *Growing up in college.* San Francisco: Jossey-Bass, 1968.

International Peace Academy. *International peace academy Helsinki project.* New York: International Peace Academy, 1971.

IPRA Disarmament Study Group. Between peace and war: The quest for disarmament. *Bulletin of Peace Proposals,* 1975, **3,** 262–280.

Judson, S. (Ed.). *Manual on nonviolence and children.* Philadelphia: Friends Peace Committee, 1977.

Laue, J. & Cormick, G. The ethics of social intervention: Community crisis intervention programs. St. Louis: Community Crisis Intervention Center, Washington University, 1974. Mimeo.

Mariani, J. Playing the games: Adult toys become fashionable. *Saturday Review,* 1979, December, 40–44.

Melman, S. *The permanent war economy.* New York: Simon & Schuster, 1974.

Mendlovitz, S. (Ed.). *On the creation of a just world order.* New York: Free Press, 1975.

Morrison, P. & Walker, P. A new strategy for military spending. *Scientific American,* 1978, October, 48–61.

Moskos, C., Jr. *Peace soldiers: The sociology of a United Nations force.* Chicago: University of Chicago Press, 1976.

Nesbitt, W. *Teaching about war and war prevention.* New York: Thomas Y. Crowell, 1972.

Nicolau, G. Training in community conflict resolution skills. New York: Institute for Mediation and Conflict Resolution, 1973. Mimeo.

Ohio Department of Education. *Dealing with aggressive behavior.* Columbus: ODE, 1971.

Osgood, C. GRIT for MFBR: A proposal for unfreezing force-level postures in Europe. Urbana-Champaign: Department of Psychology, University of Illinois, 1974, Mimeo.

Paley, R. Briefing report for members of the U.S. Commission on proposals for the National Academy of Peace and Conflict Resolution. Washington, D.C.: U.S. Commission on Proposals for the National Academy of Peace and Conflict Resolution, 1980. Mimeo.

Rikhye, I., Harbottle, M., & Egge, B. *The thin blue line.* New Haven: Yale University Press, 1974.

Roberts, A. *Total defence and civil resistance: Problems of Sweden's security policy.* Stockholm: Research Institute of Swedish National Defense, 1972.

Schonborn, K. *Dealing with violence.* Springfield, Ill.: Charles C. Thomas Publishers, 1975.

Senghaas, D. Armaments dynamics and disarmament. In P. Bredow (Ed.), *Economic and social aspects of disarmament.* Oslo: BPP Publications, 1974.

Stanford, B. *Peacemaking: A guide to conflict resolution.* New York: Bantam, 1976.

Walker, C. (Ed.). *Monograph series in nonviolent action.* Haverford, Pennsylvania: Nonviolent Action Research Project, Haverford College, 1976.

Walton, R. *Interpersonal peacemaking.* Reading, Mass.: Addison-Wesley, 1969.

Wehr, P. & DeHaan, R. Conflict education: A new direction in higher learning. In I. Charny (Ed.), *Strategies against violence: Design for nonviolent change.* Boulder, Colo.: Westview, 1978.

Wehr, P. *Conflict regulation.* Boulder, Colo.: Westview, 1979(a).

Wehr, P. Peace and conflict processes: A research overview. *Armed Forces and Society,* 1979, **5**, 467–486(b).

Wehr, P. Testimony prepared for the U.S. Commission on Proposals for the National Academy of Peace and Conflict Resolution. Boulder, Colo.: Institute of Behavioral Science, March 10, 1980.

Wehr, P. & Washburn, A. M. *Peace and world order systems.* Beverly Hills, California: Sage Publications, 1976.

White, R. K. *Nobody wanted war: Misperception in Vietnam and other wars.* New York: Doubleday Anchor, 1970.

Wilson, E. *On human nature.* Cambridge: Harvard University Press, 1978.

Yarrow, C. H. *Quaker experiences in international conciliation.* New Haven: Yale University Press, 1978.

Young, O. Intermediaries: Additional thoughts on third parties. *Journal of Conflict Resolution,* 1972, **16**, 48–53.

Subject Index

Author Index

Author Index

About the Authors

Arnold P. Goldstein is Professor of Psychology at Syracuse University. He received his doctorate in 1959 from Pennsylvania State University, and worked at the University of Pittsburgh and the Veteran's Administration Outpatient Research Laboratory (Washington, D.C.) before coming to Syracuse in 1963. His career-long interests have been in studying the effectiveness of psychotherapy and related small group intervention procedures, particularly with resistive or aggressive individuals. His publications include *Aggression in Global Perspectives*, *Aggress-Less*, *Hostage*, and *Police Crisis Intervention*.

Edward G. Carr is Assistant Professor of Psychology at the State University of New York at Stony Brook. He was awarded his Ph.D. in 1973 from the University of California at San Diego and has focused his research and clinical efforts in the field of behavior modification, with special emphasis on children. His publications include numerous journal articles and chapters examining the utility of behavior modification and related techniques, especially with autistic and retarded children.

William S. Davidson, II is Associate Professor of Psychology at Michigan State University. He earned his Ph.D. at the University of Illinois at Urbana-Champaign, where he has been research associate at the Community Psychology Action Center. Davidson has also been director of Kentfields Rehabilitation Program. He received the 1976 Watson-Wilson Consultation Research Award from the American Psychological Association's Division of Consulting Psychology. Davidson is coauthor of *Behavioral Approaches to Community Problems*, with M. Nietzel, R. Winett, and M. MacDonald, and of *Evaluation Strategies in Criminal Justice*, with J. R. Koch, R. G. Lewis, and M. D. Wresinski.

Paul Wehr is Associate Professor of Sociology and Director of Environmental Conciliation Project at the University of Colorado, Boulder. Wehr holds advanced degrees from the University of North Carolina and the University of Pennsylvania and taught at Haverford College before coming to Boulder. He was a founder and first Director of the Consortium on Peace Research, Education and Development. His current teaching and research focus on the problem areas of environmental conflict management, peace systems, and the use of appropriate technology in economically developed and developing nations. Wehr is currently working with federal, state, and local governments on resolving conflicts over energy and recreational facility siting, water planning, and conversion of military industries to nonmilitary production. His publications include *Peace and World Order Systems*, and *Conflict Regulation.*